totallyguitar
THE DEFINITIVE GUIDE

Jawbone

An imprint of the Outline Press Ltd

2a Union Court, 20–22 Union Road,

London SW4 6JP

www.jawbonepress.com

totallyguitar
THE DEFINITIVE GUIDE

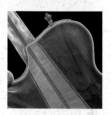

ISBN-13: 978-1-906002-12-1
ISBN-10: 1-906002-12-6

1 2 3 4 5 12 11 10 09 08

ART DIRECTOR Nigel Osborne
DESIGN Paul Cooper
EDITORIAL DIRECTOR Roger Cooper
EDITOR Paul Quinn
PRODUCTION Phil Richardson
PRINCIPAL PHOTOGRAPHY Miki Slingsby

Origination by Global Graphics (Czech Republic)
Printed by Colorprint Offset Ltd. (Hong Kong)

totallyguitar

THE DEFINITIVE GUIDE

Backbeat
Books

Introduction   **6**

CHAPTER ONE

Sound and   **8–41**
Construction
*Essential ingredients that
determine the sonic
characteristics and playing
feel of the world's most
popular guitars*

Classical   **10**
  *Smooth sounds from
  nylon strings*

Steel-String Flat-Tops   **14**
  *From bluegrass belters
  to rockin' rhythm*

Archtop Acoustics   **20**
  The big-bodied jazzers

Archtop Electrics   **24**
  *From big bands to the
  birth of rock'n'roll*

Solidbody Electrics   **26**
  *Real playing power
  and rock pyrotechnics*

Semi-Acoustics   **34**
  *Blues to bop – the
  do-it-all alternative*

Piezo-Magnetic   **40**
Hybrids
  Headfirst into the future

CHAPTER TWO

Amps and   **42-59**
Effects
*A look under the hood
of the gear that shapes
your sound*

Classic Tube Combos   **44**
  The simplicity of great tone

Tube Hotrods   **46**
  *Channel-switching
  gain monsters*

The Big Stacks   **48**
  Stadium rock powerhouses

Solid State   **50**
  Versatile workhorses

Modeling Amps   **52**
  Guitar goes digital

Classic Pedals   **54**
  Stomp box sonics

Racks and Multi-FX   **58**
  Sound-packed performers

CHAPTER THREE

Maintenance   **60–115**
*A guide to care, cleaning,
set-up, repair, and minor
customization of your guitar*

Stringing Up and   **62**
Tuning
  The first step to great tone

Set-Up   **70**
  *Check and adjust neck
  relief, nut height, playing
  action, string height,
  vibrato performance,
  intonation, and more*

Electrics   **91**
  *Soldering technique,
  pickup replacement,
  wiring mods and more*

Professional Repairs   **106**
  *A look at jobs best left
  to the pro techs*

Cleaning   **110**
  *Get your gear crud-free
  to keep it playing smoothly
  and sounding great*

Care and Storage   **114**
  *How to select the right
  case for the job, plus
  correct storage, and
  shipping procedures*

contents

CHAPTER FOUR
Play Guitar   116–295
Take a taste of the ten most popular guitar styles – to find new inspiration for your own playing, or an entirely new direction

Acoustic   122
From basic chords to advanced fingerstyle and alternative tunings

Rock and Pop   140
A comprehensive guide, from hard-hitting rhythm styles to lead proficiency

Blues   178
Shuffles, grooves, riffs and rhythms – and all the real deal soloing skills you need

Country   204
All the essential tools of twang for roots rock and hardcore country

Rock'n'Roll   220
The double-stop lead lines and boogie rhythms that started it all

Metal   228
Picking, legato, sweeping and tapping techniques for hard-rocking soloists

Latin   254
From mambo rhythms to Afro-Cuban melodies

African   260
Palm wine grooves and highlife tunes

Classical   266
An introduction to formal technique, to enrich any playing style

Jazz   282
Chord comping, bebop lines, and a full bag of improvisational tools

CHAPTER FIVE
Guitar Manufacturers 298-587
A unique illustrated directory with all the inside info on the great electric guitars and the stories of their development for 130 leading brands

Acoustic	**300**
Airline	**300**
Alamo	**300**
Alembic	**300**
Alvarez	**302**
Ampeg	**303**
Aria	**305**
Baldwin	**309**
Bartolini	**309**
B. C. Rich	**309**
Bigsby	**311**
Bond	**312**
Brian Moore	**313**
Burns	**313**
Carvin	**317**
Casio	**319**
Chandler	**319**
Charvel	**320**
Coral	**322**
Cort	**322**
Custom Kraft	**323**

Danelectro	324	G & L	387	Jackson	496
D'Angelico	329	Gibson	388	James Tyler	500
D'Aquisto	329	Gittler	441	John Birch	500
Dean	330	Godin	441	Kapa	500
De Armond	331	Godwin	442	Kawai	500
Domino	331	Gordon-Smith	443	Kay	501
Dwight	331	Goya	443	Kent	505
Eggle	332	Gretsch	444	Klein	506
Egmond	332	Grimshaw	462	Klira	507
Eko	333	Guild	463	Kramer	507
Electar	333	Guyatone	468	Krundaal	510
Electra	333	Hagstrom	469	La Baye	510
Electro	333	Hallmark	470	Magnatone	511
Epiphone	334	Hamer	470	Martin	512
ESP	345	Harmony	472	Maton	512
Fender	346	Harvey Thomas	475	Melobar	512
Fenton-Weil	384	Hayman	476	Messenger	513
Fernandes	384	Heartfield	476	Micro Frets	514
Framus	385	Heritage	476	Mighty Mite	515
Futurama	387	Hofner	477	Modulus Guitars	516
		Hondo	482	Mosrite	517
		Hopf	482	Music Man	519
		Hoyer	482	National	523
		Ibanez	483		

contents

Ovation   526
Parker   528
Peavey   529
Premier   531
PRS   532
Rickenbacker   550
Rick Turner   561
Robin   561
Roger   562
Roland   562
Samick   562
Schecter   563
S. D. Curlee   563
Shergold   563
Silvertone   564
Spector   564
Squier   564
Standel   566
Starfield   566
Steinberger   566
Stratosphere   567
Supro   568

Teisco   569
Teufel   570
Tokai   570
Tom Anderson   571
Travis Bean   572
Vaccaro   572
Valley Arts   572
Vega   573
Veillette-Citron   574
Veleno   574
Vigier   576
Vox   576
Wandre   578
Washburn   579
Watkins   581
Welson   582
Westone   582
Wurlitzer   582
Yamaha   583
Zemaitis   587

Glossary   **588**
*A detailed, comprehensive
and fully illustrated guide
to the language of guitar*

Index   **602**

Acknowledgments 608

"Unlike rosewood, maple accentuates the higher frequencies to produce a crisp, cutting sound. In the hands of a country star, the maple-bodied J-200 could double as a snare drum in the days when the Grand Ole Opry would not permit drums on stage."

"Gretsch, Guild and Harmony were among the many U.S. manufacturers who opted to champion the twin-cutaway cause, usually adding their own touches. Surprisingly, none initially perceived the benefit of adding a solid center block as Gibson did."

chapter 1

TOTALLY GUITAR
SOUND & CONSTRUCTION

Any good instrument is far more than the sum of its individual parts, but the design and materials used for each component – and the way they all come together – determine the sound and playability of your guitar. From the bright twang of a Tele to the warm wail of a Les Paul, this chapter tells how great guitars are built, and what factors shape their voices.

Excelling in moods that are mellow, mysterious, romantic and enchanting, yet able to exhibit startling aggression and impressive dynamic range in the hands of the right performer, the classical guitar manages simultaneously to be both the six-string world's highest achiever and its most undersung instrument. Whatever its generally accepted refinement, it is also often widely misunderstood by those who fail to probe the subtleties of its performance and construction – but is capable of an addictive allure for both player and listener.

Thanks to its obvious associations with classical music, we tend to think of the classical guitar as the somehow more noble and ancient member of the six-string family. In fact, although differently built and strung "guitars" were in existence since the end of the 15th century, the template for the classical guitar as we know it today goes back no further than that of the steel-strung flat-top, and is just a few generations senior to the modern archtop. Indeed, pioneering flat-top builder C.F. Martin was born a full 21 years before the father of the modern classical guitar, Antonio de Torres. By the 1850s both were making instruments which set molds for their type that are still referred to today.

As a musical instrument the guitar was traditionally a humble beast, even an outcast at times, more at home in the campsites and cornfields of the working classes than in the parlors and concert halls of the gentry. Its slow acceptance into the upper strata of the arts influenced its status as a late-bloomer among concert instruments, with far fewer virtuoso builders applying

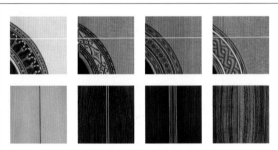

Among the most-prized woods used for soundboards today are (top, l-r): European spruce, Hokkaido spruce, and western red cedar (seen in a matt finish far right). For backs (bottom row): cypress, Brazilian rosewood (in both center photos) and Indian rosewood are highly valued.

A look inside this guitar from contemporary British luthier Paul Fischer reveals many of the most-used materials of the classical builder today: spruce top (here with "fan strutting"), rosewood back and sides, mahogany neck and ebony fingerboard.

their talents to the evolving six-string (then generally a four or five-string) than to violins or cellos – although there do exist two five-course guitars built by the great Antonio Stradivari of Cremona, Italy, and rare examples by other known master builders. From its earliest incarnations, however, the guitar proved its abilities both to express the emotions of players and win the hearts of listeners – whatever their social status. Louis XIV of France employed his own court guitarists, while Charles II of

1

American virtuoso Alice Artzt recorded her 1979 album of music by Tárrega (above left) on a guitar once thought to have been a Torres, but now considered to be from another maker. Andrés Segovia was an important endorser for builders from Ramírez III to German luthier Hermann Hauser; Brazilian duo Sergio and Eduardo Abreu also played Hausers.

A close friend of many famed classical and flamenco players of his time, luthier José Ramírez II was sent this postcard in 1921 by Paraguayan virtuoso and composer Agustín Barrios, and was also on good terms with Ramón Montoya and Miguel Llobet.

England was so enamored of the instrument he took it up both as player and patron. Yet among concert musicians the guitarist long remained an underdog – in part, it has widely been acknowledged, due to the primitive form of the instrument prior

to the 19th century. Yet, as with any means of expression that is passionately embraced, the enthusiasm of a growing rank of virtuoso musicians dragged the guitar from the peasantry to the performance stage, and inspired builders to design better and better instruments.

Prior to Torres, guitars were generally smaller, of shorter scale and had fewer frets than instruments we would recognise today. The Spanish luthier standardized the modern six-string by enlarging the body, increasing the scale length to the now-familiar 25½" (650mm), developing the internal "fan" bracing system that supports and strengthens the top, and refining the now-ubiquitous bridge/string anchor with its structurally integral but functionally separate saddle. Torres's approach proved so timeless that the raw materials which continue to comprise the majority of quality hand-built classical guitars today – spruce top, rosewood back and sides, cedar neck, ebony fingerboard (with some notable alterations in each case) – are little changed from

British virtuoso Nicola Hall played a Smallman on her debut release, above...

... Which she borrowed from John Williams, the best known classical guitarist today.

1. 1882 TORRES
Materials: *solid two-piece spruce top; solid three-piece Brazilian rosewood back and rosewood sides; cedar neck with rosewood fingerboard.*
Features: *rosewood bridge with then-revolutionary separate saddle.*
Historical note: *this rare Torres was discovered in South America in 1989.*

2. 1992 SMALLMAN
Materials: *solid western red cedar top; laminated Brazilian rosewood back and sides; mahogany neck with ebony fingerboard.*
Features: *this builder from New South Wales, Australia, uses unusually thin tops on his guitars, supported with a unique latticework-style balsa and carbon fiber bracing.*

3. 1994 GILBERT
Materials: *solid western red cedar top; solid Indian rosewood back and sides; mahogany neck with rosewood fingerboard.*
Features: *Gilbert's ebony bridge is of an unconventional design, using individual 'pin' saddles for each string rather than the more common one-piece saddle.*

4. 1956 RAMÎREZ II
Materials: *solid two-piece spruce top; solid Brazilian rosewood back and sides (note inset photos); mahogany neck with ebony fingerboard.*
Historical note: *son of famed Spanish builder José Ramírez I, José Ramírez II built his guitars in his adopted home of Buenos Aires. His son Ramírez III carried on the tradition.*

classical guitars

While X bracing is almost universal on steel-string flat-top acoustics (below left), classical builders generally select between a Torres- **inspired "fan-strut" system (bottom right) or a more modern technique of choice, such as Paul Fischer's "TAUT" latticework bracing system.**

the ingredients selected as best by Torres some 150 years ago.

With this template in mind, the primary constructional elements of the modern classical guitar include:

1. A top (known in the classical world as a "table") light enough and thin enough to resonate tonefully, but strong enough to withstand the string tension of a full-scale neck.

2. Back and sides strong enough for structural rigidity but, like the top, light enough to be musically responsive.

3. A neck made of wood strong enough to withstand string

tension but not so heavy as to impair the guitar's resonance.

4. A wide, flat fingerboard – often approaching or exceeding 2″ (51mm) at the nut, versus a standard 1¾″ for steel-string flat-tops – to aid fingering in the thumb-behind-neck playing position.

For many players today, the terms "classical guitar" and "nylon string guitar" are interchangeable but, while they both do bear the same types of strings, they can be greatly different instruments.

Built roughly along the lines of the proper classical guitar but without its refinement, the mere nylon-strung "folk" guitar is an instrument associated with the first lessons of the fledgling musician and pain-free playability for tender fingertips. Its tonality and build quality, however, are often indifferent at best. Ironically, cheap instruments aping the scale and dimensions of genuine classical models can turn off as many new players as they attract. Despite callus-friendly nylon strings, the wide neck and flat fingerboard of the design makes chording extremely difficult for unfamiliar hands, and the mellow tones that ultimately result may in no way resemble the bright, steely jangle of Bob Dylan or the bluesy wail of Stevie Ray Vaughan that first inspired the student to learn to play – before he or she was sold a "classical" guitar because it would be "easier to play."

Approached for what it is, however, the classical guitar yields some of the sweetest, subtlest tonalities in the instrument world. Whether plumbing classic compositions in the hands of John Williams, oozing mellow jazz melodies at the fingertips of Earl Klugh, or thrumming out pop-fusion arpeggios strapped around

Frédéric Zigante plays his 1987 Kohno on this recording of Giuliani's Le Rossiniane.

1

2

3

Even in the modern Alhambra factory in Muro de Alcoy, Spain, much of the more detailed work on classical guitars is still done by hand. Left, one craftsman shapes a headstock, while another makes final adjustments to the sides before gluing.

acoustic tone and playability. Whether it's being refreshed and renewed in the "TAUT" bracing system of English luthier Paul Fischer, the "double body" construction of Spaniard Manuel Contreras, or Australian Greg Smallman's ultra-thin tops and supporting balsawood and carbon fiber latticework bracing, the art of the classical guitar builder is a form which resolutely refuses to stagnate.

Meanwhile, other instruments offering affordable quality or revolutionary performance-aiding elements extend the feel and vibe of the nylon-stringed guitar through the jazz and pop worlds. An attainable excellence is championed, for example, in Japanese builder Kohno's distillation of master-grade luthiery into well-priced midrange guitars, while US giant Gibson's development of the easily amplified semi-solid thinline Chet Atkins models with piezo-pickup-loaded bridge saddles helps to further demolish the boundaries between musical genres.

Sting sideman Dominic Miller, its genre is a compelling and ever-expanding one.

Strongly associated even today with its native Spain – where the modern instrument was certainly established and refined under Torres, Jose Ramírez I, Manuel Ramírez and others – the form has been adapted and updated in workshops around the world, and continues to evolve as craftsmen seek the ultimate in

---

1. 1992 BERNABÉ
Materials: *solid European spruce top; solid European maple back and sides; mahogany neck with ebony fingerboard.*
Features: *back, sides and headstock facing of beautifully 'flamed' maple (less often seen in classical construction), with intricately detailed inlay work at soundhole rosette and delicate purfling.*

2. 1974 KOHNO
Materials: *solid Hokkaido spruce top; solid Brazilian rosewood back and sides; mahogany neck with ebony fingerboard.*
Features: *this high-end model from the Japanese builder (whose company also builds student-priced Sakurai guitars) features unusual dual ebony inlays at the back of the neck for strengthening purposes.*

3. 1990 GIBSON CHET ATKINS CEC
Materials: *semi-solid spruce-topped body with two 'tone chambers' for improved acoustic sound with low feedback; mahogany neck with ebony fingerboard.*
Features: *electro-acoustic bridge carries six under-saddle piezo pickups, each individually adjustable for volume; onboard preamp/EQ.*

4. 1934 ESTESO
Materials: *solid European spruce topped flamenco guitar; solid Spanish cypress back and sides; mahogany neck with ebony fingerboard.*
Features: *flamenco models such as this are generally more lightly constructed than their classical brethren; traditionally, they also feature wooden 'friction peg' tuners rather than geared machineheads.*

Virtuoso Pepe Romero (far left, above) plays a Rodriguez guitar on this 1970s recording.

5. 1976 RODRIGUEZ
Materials: *solid western red cedar top; solid Brazilian rosewood back and sides; mahogany neck with ebony fingerboard.*
Features: *as the inset photos demonstrate, this instrument features highly figured rosewood with distinctive stripes, which the builder supposedly salvaged from a church door.*

4

5

Manitas de Plata (left), whose name means "hands of silver," popularized flamenco guitar in the 1960s, while Paco de Lucia (center) revolutionized the art in the late '60s and '70s, taking it to an even wider audience. In the early '90s, pop-flamenco became a world craze at the hands of the Gipsy Kings (right).

The steel-string flat-top guitar can't scream with the intensity of an electric guitar, and it can't purr with the serenity of a nylon-string classical, but it can do everything in between – and otherwise offers plenty of voices unique to its breed.

Utter the word "guitar" and the flat-top acoustic is probably the instrument that comes to mind more than any other. It can lay down a steady rhythm, whether it's an easy strum on a country record such as The Eagles' *Lyin' Eyes* or the heavy strumming

that kicked off the rock'n'roll era on Elvis's *That's All Right*. It can sing out as a lead instrument on a melodic, finger-picked statement by James Taylor or a blazing, flat-picked run by Doc Watson. It can even serve up rhythm and melody at the same time. And all this versatility is accomplished by surprisingly few variations in design and materials.

Generally speaking, the bigger the body, the bigger the sound is going to be. Since the 1850s, when C.F. Martin developed the flat-top guitar that we know today, acoustic guitars have grown progressively larger as guitar-makers have tried to meet players' needs for louder instruments. Martin's largest size in 1854, designated by the numeral 0, was only 13" wide (measured across the widest part of the body). By 1916 Martin bodies had grown over two inches, to the 15⅝" D or dreadnought size (although it wouldn't appear with the Martin brand until 1932).

Gibson started small, too, with a 13" flat-top in 1926, but by 1938 the company was making a 17" Super Jumbo model. Other makers pushed on to the extreme, such as a 21" guitar made by the Larson Brothers of Chicago, but such behemoths went beyond the limits of practicality. Dreadnoughts and "jumbos" (Gibson's term for a 16" body) still dominate, although the advent of high-quality acoustic amplification has brought new popularity to the smaller, more comfortable sizes.

Martin and Gibson body shapes are the reference points for almost all steel-string flat-top bodies. Traditionally the most popular shape is the dreadnought, named after a British battleship that was the largest of its kind. A dreadnought guitar, such as a Martin D-18 or a Gibson J-45, is identifiable by its thick waist which makes it more box-like than other styles and contributes to a big, booming sound.

Gibson's jumbo body shape is identifiable by a circular lower bout. Although Gibson used the term jumbo as a size designation for any 16" guitar, most guitar people use it to describe the shape rather than the size. The shape is found on Gibsons ranging from the original 13" L-1 used by Robert Johnson to the 17" J-200 that is a badge of identification for many country stars.

Of the smaller body styles, Martin's 000, 15" wide with a pinched waist that gives it an hourglass look, has became one of

The exploded view of this steel-string flat-top displays the major constructional characteristics of the contemporary design. Note, in particular, the X bracing pattern underneath the thin spruce top, established as standard by Martin as long ago as 1850 and a major contributing factor to the breed's lively yet powerful sound.

The archaic-looking Martin & Coupa below, built in 1840, pre-dates the X-braced guitars Martin built just a decade later that would point the way forward for steel-string guitars. C.F. Martin had arrived in the United States just seven years prior to this. Far right, a Martin price list, probably circa 1870s.

the most popular, due in no small part to Eric Clapton's use of a 000-42 on his MTV *Unplugged* appearance in the mid 1990s. In Clapton's wake, Gibson's 1930s L-00 style (14" wide with a slightly more elongated look than the Martin 000) has also made a comeback.

Woods that are suitable for the back and sides of a guitar are referred to as tone woods, and with good reason. More than any other factor they shape the tone of the instrument.

When practically all guitars had gut strings, Brazilian rosewood was the preferred wood for back and sides. It delivered a warm, rich tone that suited the guitarists' repertoire of semi-classical music. The changeover to steel strings in the 1920s, along with the move to larger guitars, only accentuated the sonic qualities of rosewood. Martin's rosewood dreadnought D-28, for example, has a booming bass sound as its calling card, and it is still the favorite of bluegrass players. Due to Brazil's restriction on

exporting unsawn rosewood logs in 1969, the great majority of rosewood guitars are now Indian rosewood.

Gibson approached the steel-string flat-top from a different direction than the classical tradition of Martin. Gibson's earliest guitars had been carved-top models conceived as members of the mandolin family. Gibson started with walnut backs and sides but soon settled on maple (or in some cases birch as a cheaper substitute) as the ideal tone wood. Although the company would make flat-tops in the years prior to World War II out of rosewood and mahogany as well as maple, their top model, the J-200, emerged after the war with maple back and sides. Unlike rosewood, maple accentuates the higher frequencies to produce a crisp, cutting sound. In the hands of a country star, the maple-bodied J-200 could double as a snare drum in the days when the Grand Ole Opry would not permit drums on stage.

Mahogany stands in the middle of the spectrum, offering some

Edna Leeper clutches a Martin D-28 with The Oklahoma Sweethearts in 1941.

1. '24 DITSON DREADNOUGHT STYLE
Materials: *two-piece solid spruce top; solid mahogany back and sides; slot-head mahogany neck with unbound ebony fingerboard (12 frets to the body); ebony bridge.*
Historical note: *built by Martin for the Ditson music stores in Boston and New York, who first suggested the design as far back as 1916.*

2. '38 GIBSON J-200 SUPER JUMBO
Materials: *solid spruce top; solid rosewood back and sides; mahogany neck with bound ebony fingerboard.*
Features: *rosewood 'mustache' bridge; Grover Imperial tuners.*
Historical note: *post-WWII, Gibson's biggest flat-top featured maple back and sides rather than rosewood.*

3. '41 MARTIN D-28
Materials: *solid spruce top; solid rosewood back and sides; mahogany neck (14 frets to the body) with ebony fingerboard.*
Features: *ebony bridge; herringbone trim.*
Historical note: *herringbone inlay (purfling) featured on pre-1947 D-28s; post-1969 Martins used Indian rosewood after Brazil embargoed exportation of its own highly-figured variety.*

In the early days, Elvis Presley thranged out his own rhythms on a Martin D-18.

Richard Thompson put his 000-18 to more eclectic use, as on this early '70s album.

of the low-end "warmth" of rosewood without sacrificing the high-end "brilliance" of maple. Mahogany is also cheaper than rosewood or maple, giving mahogany-bodied guitars an extra economic attraction.

Many other woods have been used for guitar bodies, such as koa, ash, walnut and cocobola, and each adds its own subtle differences to sound and tone.

The soundboard of a good flat-top has different requirements from its back and sides. Spruce has the best combination of strength and flexibility – the qualities required by the vibrating top of a guitar. There is an art to finding the right combination, however. The more the top can vibrate, the louder the sound will be, but the top must be a certain thickness to withstand the pull of the strings, which is about 175 pounds on a standard steel-string flat-top. Unfortunately, a top that thick won't do much

vibrating, so guitar makers have little choice but to use braces under the top in order to strengthen it without dampening the vibrations, which in turn allows them to use thinner and more toneful wood in the soundboard.

Most steel-string makers use some variation of an X-pattern of bracing developed by C.F. Martin by 1850. Cheaper guitars have used simple cross braces, known as "ladder" bracing, and this – more than any other element of flat-top construction – can be the difference between a good sounding guitar and a dud.

Even before ecological concerns prompted the search for alternatives to wood, guitar-makers experimented with new materials. Wood laminates made from thin veneers, for example, are cheaper and stronger than solid pieces. However, all things being equal, laminated wood doesn't perform as well as solid wood. Predictably, the earliest examples – particularly those with a laminated top – were inferior. Ovation pioneered the use of fiberglass for the back and sides of a guitar, utilizing sensitive aeronautical vibration-measuring devices in an attempt to quantify "good sound" and replicate it with the new designs and materials. In recent years, manufacturers have redesigned bracing systems and construction techniques specifically for laminates and man-made materials, and the quality of these guitars has risen.

Most guitars have a neck made from the same wood as the back and sides, except for rosewood-body guitars, which usually have a mahogany neck. Virtually all makers reinforce the neck with a metal rod (truss rod) that can be adjusted to change its curvature. Fingerboards are typically rosewood or, on more expensive models, ebony. The traditional manner of fastening the neck to the body is with glue by way of a large dovetail joint, although many contemporary makers now use some form of a

The wood used for the back and sides of a flat-top has a significant impact on its voice, and wise players choose accordingly. Maple (above, left) is bright and precise; rosewood (second from left) is warm and rich with a pronounced low end; mahogany (third from left) retains fair low-end presence with good high-end sparkle; the lesser-seen koa (far right) offers brightness blended with decent warmth.

flat-top acoustics

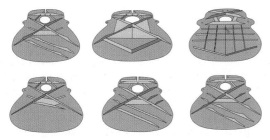

BRACING PATTERNS

The bracing pattern – that is, the configuration of struts glued to the underside of a guitar's top – plays an enormous part in shaping an instrument's tone. The six illustrations above come from C.F. Martin, and like them, most steel-string acoustic builders today use some derivation of the X-brace pattern. Variations (aside from extremes like the latticework system, top right) are found in the number of support struts and the precise position of the X in relation to the soundhole.

otherwise have.

In the early 1930s guitar-makers began offering musicians more playing room on the neck, putting 14 frets clear of the body rather than the 12 which is still the standard for classical guitars. However, a 14-fret neck requires either a smaller body length or different placement of the soundhole and bridge, and some musicians believe that the larger body of a 12-fret guitar (a Martin dreadnought 12-fret, for example) gives it a more desirable sound. Other players want even more accessibility in the higher registers of the neck, and they are willing to sacrifice or "cut away" part of the body to get it. Cutaway flat-tops began appearing shortly after World War II and have become more and more popular with advances in amplification.

The term "steel-string" covers a variety of string alloys and gauges. Different alloys – the metal content of the string wrappings – such as "80/20" (the ratio of copper to zinc) or "phosphor bronze" (a combination of copper, tin and phosphor), make for subtle differences in tone. Different gauges, however, make for great differences in performance. Heavier-gauge strings will be louder because they require more tension to reach

bolt-on neck. The critical factor regarding a guitar neck is rigidity. Although some woods are stronger than others, the reinforcing rod makes up for the difference. A neck that is not rigid enough will vibrate – not enough to make any noise, but enough to diminish the tone and sustaining quality that the guitar would

Martin body sizes form the most commonly used standards of flat-top size designation for many builders today. Shown below, left to right in ascending order of size, are the five most popular shapes.

1. '27 MARTIN 0-45
Materials: *solid spruce top and Brazilian rosewood back and sides on 13½"-wide body. Bound slot-head mahogany neck (12 frets to the body, 24⁹⁄₁₀" scale) with ebony fingerboard.*
Features: *ebony bridge; deluxe Style 45 abalone inlay.*

2. '38 MARTIN 00-21
Materials: *solid spruce top and Brazilian rosewood back and sides on 14½"-wide body. Unbound slot-head mahogany neck (12 frets to the body, 24⁹⁄₁₀" scale) with ebony fingerboard.*
Features: *ebony bridge; herringbone soundhole trim and back stripe.*

3. '36 MARTIN 000-28
Materials: *solid spruce top and Brazilian rosewood back and sides on 15"-wide body. Unbound mahogany neck (14 frets to the body, 24⁹⁄₁₀" scale) with ebony fingerboard.*
Features: *ebony bridge; snowflake fingerboard inlays.*

4. '33 MARTIN OM-45
Materials: *solid spruce top and Brazilian rosewood back and sides on 15"-wide body. Bound mahogany neck (14 frets to the body, larger 25⁵⁄₁₀" scale length) with bound ebony fingerboard.*
Features: *ebony bridge; deluxe Style 45 abalone inlay.*

5. '37 MARTIN D-18
Materials: *solid spruce top and solid mahogany back and sides on 15½"-wide body. Mahogany neck (14 frets to the body, larger 25⁵⁄₁₀" scale length) with unbound ebony fingerboard.*
Features: *rosewood bridge; rare sunburst finish on this example.*

Bryan Sutton applies a dread to some stunning flat-picking on this Ricky Skaggs release.

4

5

This 1990 Martin HD-28P is the 500,000th instrument built by C.F. Martin & Co and has been signed on the top by the entire workforce. At the time of printing – thanks to heavy production in the '90s – Martin is already closing in on its 800,000th instrument.

pitch (about 12 extra pounds) and exert more tension on the top of the guitar. The downside is that heavier strings make a guitar harder to play, especially if the added tension causes the neck to bow, raising the "action" or string height and adversely affecting intonation (although this can usually be compensated for by careful adjustment of the truss rod).

In the early 1900s, probably in response to the popularity of the mandolin (whose eight strings are arranged in pairs), the 12-string guitar appeared. Typically the four lower-pitched pairs are tuned in octaves and the higher two pairs are tuned in unison, which accentuates single-string-style picking and creates a powerful ensemble effect when the 12-string is strummed. However, the extra tension creates significant problems for the player, who has to develop extra hand-strength, as well as for the maker, who must strengthen the top bracing and the neck joint.

Guitar builders in the Martin factory display how hand-craftsmanship is still used in flat-top manufacture today – even by a company producing tens of thousands of guitars each year. Below, one for the road: the Martin Backpacker.

1. '90 TAKAMINE LTD-90
Materials: *solid bookmatched koa top with solid koa back and sides on cutaway dreadnought-shaped body; mahogany neck with bound ebony fingerboard.*
Features: *ebony bridge; gold-plated hardware; slotted diamond fingerboard inlays.*
Historical Note: *A specially designed Takamine 'Limited' series guitar made of different woods is offered every year.*

2. 1976 OVATION CUSTOM LEGEND
Materials: *solid spruce top with molded Lyrachord fiberglass bowl-back. Bound mahogany neck (14 frets to the body, 25.27" scale length) with ebony fingerboard.*
Electrics: *under-saddle piezo pickup and onboard preamp.*
Features: *abalone neck and binding inlays; deluxe rosette; 'pinless' rosewood bridge.*

3. 1987 MANSON SLIDESLAMMER
Materials: *two-piece solid spruce top; solid rosewood back and sides; mahogany neck (14 frets to the body) with unbound ebony fingerboard.*
Features: *Manson's 'Slideslammer' device to instantly raise nut for slide playing; acoustic B-string bender at bridge; ebony bridge; abalone inlay.*

4. 2000 TAYLOR PALLET GUITAR
Materials: *solid 'pallet-grade' oak for top, sides and neck. Ebony fingerboard and bridge.*
Features: *Abalone 'forklift' neck inlay; abalone rosette.*
Historical Note: *The first Pallet Guitar was made from scrap wood by Bob Taylor in 1995 to prove that it's the luthier's skill rather than the wood that determines a toneful guitar.*

5. '99 SANTA CRUZ MODEL D
Materials: *solid bookmatched spruce top with solid rosewood back and sides on a dreadnought-shaped design; mahogany neck (14 frets to the body, 25.34" scale length) with bound ebony fingerboard and ebony bridge.*
Features: *Schaller mini-tuner machineheads; mock tortoiseshell pickguard.*

6. '01 COLLINGS D-2H
Materials: *solid bookmatched spruce top with solid rosewood back and sides on a dreadnought-shaped design; mahogany neck (14 frets to the body, 25.5" scale length) with bound ebony fingerboard and ebony bridge.*
Features: *abalone snowflake position markers; herringbone purfling; mock tortoiseshell pickguard.*

1

2

3

flat-top acoustics

Although there have been virtuosos on the 12-string – from Leadbelly to Leo Kottke – it is still considered a specialty instrument rather than a mainstream flat-top model.

The quest for true-sounding amplification of acoustic guitars began in earnest in the 1970s with the development of piezo-electric pickups and various specialized microphones (some mounted directly onto the instrument, others fitted inside). Amplifiers and, by the late 1990s, digital processors designed specifically for steel-string flat-tops advanced the cause and at the same time undermined the traditional demands on the guitar itself for exceptional volume and tone. Today a guitar with virtually no unamplified volume at all such as the "solidbody acoustic" (a solidbody, amplified guitar meant to sound like an acoustic) can be more desirable to some players in a concert or recording setting than the finest traditional acoustic, thanks to the instrument's ease of amplification and lack of feedback.

As a result of advances in amplification, guitar-makers can now design instruments that would not have been practical in earlier years, with smaller or oddly-shaped bodies and even solid bodies. Although there will always be a demand for guitars with outstanding natural acoustic qualities, the range of instruments that can be categorized as steel-string flat-top guitars is today wider than ever.

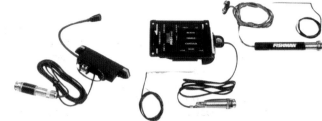

ACOUSTIC PICKUPS

The increasing popularity of using acoustic guitars in all forms of live performance has led to a boom in pickup development, and more makes and styles of acoustic pickups are available today than ever before. This selection from Fishman displays a good cross-section of the market, with something to cover most requirements.

The unit above-left is a blender-style system which includes the familiar soundhole-fitted magnetic pickup plus a miniature electret microphone on a small gooseneck to be positioned inside the guitar. Center is a Prefex Pro Blend system, which includes a piezo pickup strip, built-in mic, plus preamp unit with volume and EQ for onboard mounting. An even simpler system, the final unit consists of Fishman's under-saddle piezo strip plus a battery-powered preamp mounted in the end-pin jack housing, with no volume or EQ controls attached.

Steve Earle used a Santa Cruz Tim Rice model to belt out the rhythm on this bluegrass album.

4

5

6

The acoustic archtop guitar is still very much rooted in tradition, with its strong violin design influences, and has been enchanting musicians since its inception 100 years ago. Played to create some of the most advanced music today, as well as some of the most traditional, the acoustic archtop – in its highest form – represents the epitome of the luthier's art.

Funk & Wagner ought to define the acoustic archtop guitar as "the consummate fretted instrument." That would be a somewhat biased view, but the archtop guitar is certainly enjoying a renaissance in the marketplace, and the influence of particular makers on others is quite obvious. D'Angelico's earliest guitars were direct descendants of Gibson's groundbreaking L-5, yet the

very popular Gibson Johnny Smith model was designed after a D'Angelico. Epiphone also followed Gibson's lead, as did Gretsch and Guild.

Other individual makers, too, have had an influence – and have been influenced by others in turn: Albanus's blend of D'Angelico's designs and Stromberg's single diagonal tonebar (the latter perpetuated by Bill Barker); the evolution of the ebony/brass-hinged tailpiece through Albanus, then Phil Petillo, then Jimmy D'Aquisto; D'Aquisto's development of segmented sound openings as used by German maker Artur Lang some 25 years before, and so on. This ebb and flow of ideas is not always the result of friendly sharing, but it's the way that the builder's art progresses – an evolution equally indebted to the collaboration of the player, who is after all the builder's most reliable and consistent link to reality.

Through all of these contributions, the archtop guitar continues to evolve at a slow but steady and energized pace. It is still primarily a jazz instrument and, to date, has not been truly embraced by other genres.

The voice of the archtop is of course a direct result of the acoustical design and materials used. It should be balanced so that the high notes are as "fat" and clear as the mid-range, blending with a rich bass – not at all typical of its flat-top cousin.

For the laboriously carved arched top plate (often known as the "top" or "face" of the guitar), spruce is most preferred. Redwood, cedar, pine or any other conifer will function equally as well. Spruce is an industry standard. It is readily available, affordable and easily marketable. From that point of view, there's not much incentive to use alternative woods.

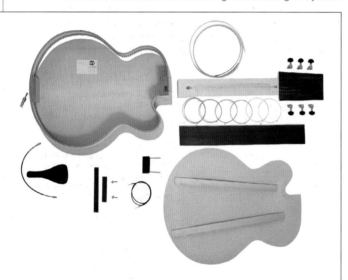

This disassembled jazz box reveals the key components of a carved-top acoustic archtop guitar. Note the parallel braces – making it a strong projector for rhythm playing – and the one-piece ebony tailpiece and two-piece bridge. Neck, back and sides are all of maple.

D'Angelico fan Johnny Smith captures the archtop's smooth tones for posterity.

Quarter-sawn, close and straight-grained stock is most desirable. Is there a difference in sound between close-grained and wide-grained spruce? Contrary to popular consensus, no – but close-grained cuts continue to get the nod.

The back plate (or simply, back) and matching ribs (sides) are traditionally made from flamed maple. Maple has two categories: soft and hard. The soft varieties are most desirable for carving the back, not necessarily because soft maple is easier to carve than hard, but because it's more acoustically responsive. It is one of many components which contribute to the rich, warm timbre of a well-made archtop guitar.

The wood used to make the neck can be either matching flamed maple or, by extreme aesthetic contrast, mahogany. Traditionalists will invariably prefer flamed maple. The hard American maples, with the obvious advantage of having stiffness and strength over and above that of the soft varieties, have long been the mainstay for neck construction. Ideally, the back, ribs and neck should have matching grain, flame and color.

Because of its many attributes, however, it's likely we will begin to see more use of mahogany. Unfortunately, mahogany has often been used for necks on less expensive guitars, while maple has enjoyed its regal status on the most expensive and prized instruments. Thus with mahogany comes a stigma rendering it a less desirable choice for necks – a "cheaper look." Interestingly, mahogany is far more stable than maple and lighter in weight, which, setting tradition aside, qualifies it as a better choice, especially on high priced instruments. Its lighter weight does certainly qualify its marriage to today's more lightly constructed modern bodies. Nevertheless, maple's beautiful flaming and luster helps to keep it the top choice for many builders and players alike.

Many great makers in the past have used what would be considered by today's standards to be inferior tone woods. Great notables, like Stradivari, Guarnieri, D'Angelico, Lloyd Loar and others have had great success using woods with irregular grain patterns, knots, and a variety of cosmetic blemishes.

---

1. '50 D'ANGELICO EXCEL
Materials: *solid carved spruce top on 17"-wide body with cutaway; maple back and sides; maple neck with ebony fingerboard.*
Features: *deluxe metal stairstep tailpiece; two-piece ebony bridge; abalone block fingerboard inlays; Grover Imperial tuners.*

2. '28 GIBSON L-5
Materials: *solid carved spruce top on 16"-wide non-cutaway body; maple back and sides; maple neck with ebony fingerboard.*
Features: *basic metal trapeze tailpiece; two-piece ebony bridge; dot fingerboard inlays; pearloid button tuners*
Historical note: *model conceived mainly by influential Gibson designer Lloyd Loar.*

3. '51 STROMBERG DELUXE CUTAWAY
Materials: *solid carved spruce top on 17¼"-wide body with cutaway; maple back and sides; maple neck with ebony fingerboard.*
Features: *deluxe engraved metal tailpiece; two-piece ebony bridge; abalone block fingerboard inlays; tulip-button tuners.*

4. '45 GRETSCH SYNCROMATIC
Materials: *solid carved spruce top on 18"-wide non-cutaway body; maple back and sides; maple neck with ebony fingerboard.*
Features: *metal stairstep tailpiece; two-piece stairstep ebony bridge; abalone 'hump-top' fingerboard inlays; 'cat's eye' f-holes; Grover Imperial tuners.*

Joe Pass – accompanying Ella Fitzgerald here – at one time played an Epiphone Emperor.

5. '54 EPIPHONE EMPEROR CUTAWAY
Materials: *solid carved spruce top on 18¼"-wide cutaway body; maple back and sides; maple neck with ebony fingerboard.*
Features: *metal 'Frequensator' tailpiece; two-piece ebony bridge; abalone 'V-top' fingerboard inlays; deluxe multiple binding.*

Freddie Green cooked up a swingin' rhythm on his Gretsch Syncromatic for Count Basie.

Grant Green offers another take on the Epiphone archtop's sonic splendor.

In addition to tone woods, there are many other components and design factors which affect the outcome, one of which is bracing. Of the many possible bracing configurations, the "X" brace is most desirable, fitted to a top plate with a thickness of slightly less than ¼" under the bridge, and tapering toward both f-holes to a final thickness of approximately ³⁄₃₂" in the recurve. Conversely, the parallel bracing pattern fitted to a thinner top plate is better suited for acoustic rhythm guitar.

If we keep in mind that a lighter instrument produces a more responsive sound, then it is relatively easy to understand that a smaller Schaller mini tuning machine with ebony buttons will certainly have an advantage over the massive and considerably heavier Grover Imperial tuners that appeared on many high-end vintage guitars.

The ebony tailpiece, lighter in weight and acoustically superior to its metal counterpart, is now widely accepted among individual makers as an integral component of the acoustic archtop guitar. Nevertheless, at the time of this writing, there are – strangely – no production guitars fitted with a solid ebony tailpiece. Smaller headstocks, although not as fashionable to some, are another means of reducing weight from the

BUILDING AN ARCHTOP

The creation of a high quality, hand-built archtop guitar is one of the finest expressions of the luthier's art, requiring levels of skill that can be traced back to the classic violin makers. In the photos below Robert Benedetto, the author of this chapter and one of the world's most respected makers of acoustic jazz guitars, takes us inside his workshop for a look at some of the major steps in the construction process.

While the building of any high-end guitar – whether a flat-top, classical or solidbody electric – undoubtedly requires great craftsmanship, the touch, eye and "ear" needed to carve a well-tuned arched top and back are arguably unparalleled in the guitar-building world. While such labor-intensive construction methods translate to high purchase prices for the player, they also yield some of the sweetest, subtlest tonalities in acoustic guitar music. The finished guitar above, with a top of rough-sawn construction-grade pine, was built to prove the importance of craftsmanship over wood selection.

1

2

The quest for tone starts here: using a palm plane to shape the rough top arch.

Applying thumb pressure to the top arch as part of the tuning process.

Gluing the side braces. These will help hold the top and back in place.

Robert Benedetto hand-shaping the fingerboard radius with a belt sander.

Fitting neck to body – the guitar is finally starting to come together.

Buffing the finished guitar: the result will be a resonant, high-gloss finish.

archtop acoustics

instrument. Likewise, eliminating inlays and bindings also results in a more acoustical outcome. The soundholes of an archtop guitar can be of traditional "f" design or any number of variations. For the best acoustical balance, the traditional f-hole locations are optimal. Several new bridge designs have appeared in recent years, but none are real improvements as the small, lightweight , traditionally-shaped two-piece adjustable type has yet to be improved upon.

The most popular neck width has evolved to 1¾" at the nut. Although with no advantage in sound or intonation, the 25" fingerboard scale now overshadows the older, more traditional, 25½". A round shaped neck has always been, and remains, the preferred "feel" for the jazz artist.

String selection is of course a matter of personal preference, although pure nickel roundwound gauges .012–.052 are today's most popular choice. The preferred finish – and still the industry standard – is nitro-cellulose lacquer. Tried and true options are of course oil varnish and spirit varnish, the latter of which can be French polished. All of these variations yield great results. The intended result for the maker is a clear, thin protective coating with enough elasticity to allow the wood to vibrate freely, yet hard enough to buff or rub to a high gloss. Most modern hard poly or epoxy finishes are not at all suitable and will only serve to impair an otherwise good guitar's sound.

Amplifying the acoustic archtop requires more thought and planning than simply fitting it with an "electric guitar" pickup. Generally, a suspended mini-humbucker is preferred. It should be engineered to produce a sound similar to that of the guitar's natural voice: well-balanced, fat, and warm. It should blend with – and enhance – the guitar's acoustic voice.

---

1. '55 MACCAFERRI G-40
Materials: *plastic top, back and sides on 13¼"-wide flat-cutaway body; bolt-on steel-reinforced plastic neck.*
Features: *rosewood bridge.*
Historical note: *builder Mario Maccaferri had earlier designed the flat-topped Selmer Maccaferri Jazz model guitar, as used by the legendary Django Reinhardt.*

2. '42 GIBSON SUPER 400
Materials: *solid carved spruce top on 18"-wide non-cutaway body; maple back and sides; maple neck with ebony fingerboard.*
Features: *deluxe metal tailpiece; two-piece ebony bridge.*
Historical note: *this example exhibits Gibson's post-'40 shift from X-bracing to parallel.*

Accomplished jazzer Jimmy Bruno is a long-time player of Benedetto archtops.

3. BENEDETTO LA CREMONA AZZURRA
Materials: *solid carved spruce top on 18"-wide body; solid maple back and sides; maple neck with ebony fingerboard.*
Features: *ebony bridge, tailpiece and pickguard; floral design upper and lower bout soundholes.*
Historical note: *this guitar is a feature piece of the famous Chinery Blue Guitar Collection.*

4. '92 D'AQUISTO SOLO
Materials: *solid carved spruce top on 17"-wide non-cutaway body; flamed solid maple back and sides (see inset photo); bound maple neck with ebony fingerboard.*
Features: *ebony bridge, Brazilian rosewood tailpiece; ebony pickguard; minimalistic segmented soundholes and modernistic slotted headstock (but with rear-loaded tuners).*

5. '96 FENDER D'AQUISTO CUSTOM ULTRA
Materials: *solid carved spruce top on 17¾"-wide body; solid maple back and sides; bound maple neck with ebony fingerboard.*
Features: *ebony bridge and tailpiece; abalone block inlays. (This model was also built for the Chinery Blue Guitar Collection, by Stephen Stern in the Fender Custom Shop.)*

Seemingly anathema today to anything pertaining to heavy music, the electrified archtop acoustic gave birth to rock'n'roll. Even before Fender's "plank" and Gibson's "canoe paddle" were invented, the acoustic-electric was bringing jazz, blues and country swing guitarists out of the shadows – and before the fledgling solidbodies were fully accepted, it was still on hand to usher in a whole new way of playing.

Occasionally rather muddy of tone, lacking in sustain, prone to howls of feedback, the "electric Spanish" guitar, as it was generally first known, was nevertheless nothing short of a miracle in its day, and built the bridge to modern guitar music as we now know it. In the hands of a player like Charlie Christian – known for taking up Gibson's first electric model, the ES-150, almost from

its arrival in 1936 – it gave the guitarist a means of competing with the horn player as a soloist… and finally being heard doing so. We have never looked back.

The first electrified archtop models were essentially standard acoustic archtops with slightly adapted lap steel pickups bolted on to them. They retained the full-sized body and elaborate hand-carved spruce top, even though when amplified at the back of an orchestra in a large, crowded dancehall the tonal subtleties of the luthier's art weren't likely to be appreciated. Early production electrics from big makers like Gibson and Epiphone were still fully hand-built, but were generally somewhat low-end models compared to their upscale archtop-acoustic brethren. The makers saw no particular problem with this right from the start, because they still saw the electric guitarist as a fringe market, and even something of a novelty.

---

1. '37 GIBSON ES-150
Materials: *solid carved spruce top, maple back and sides on 16¼"-wide non-cutaway hollow body; mahogany neck with rosewood fingerboard.*
Electrics: *one single-coil Charlie Christian (blade) pickup; single tone and volume controls.*
Features: *basic trapeze tailpiece; two-piece floating rosewood bridge.*

2. '41 EPIPHONE ZEPHYR
Materials: *solid carved maple top, maple back and sides on 16⅜"-wide non-cutaway hollow body; maple neck with rosewood fingerboard.*
Electrics: *one single-coil Master pickup and Mastervoicer control system.*
Features: *basic trapeze tailpiece; two-piece floating maple/ebony bridge.*

3. '69 GIBSON SUPER 400CN
Materials: *solid carved parallel-braced spruce top, maple back and sides on 18"-wide cutaway body; maple neck with triple-bound ebony fingerboard (25½." scale).*
Electrics: *floating DeArmond pickup; pickguard-mounted tone and volume controls.*
Features: *deluxe engraved tailpiece; split-block inlays.*

4. '53 GIBSON ES-175D
Materials: *laminated maple top, back and sides on 16¼"-wide cutaway hollow body; maple neck, bound rosewood fingerboard (24⅝" scale).*
Electrics: *dual P-90 pickups with individual volume and tone controls; three-way switch.*
Features: *trapeze-shape tailpiece; floating two-piece rosewood bridge.*

5. '58 KAY BARNEY KESSEL ARTIST
Materials: *pressed spruce top and laminated back and sides on 16"-wide cutaway hollow body; mahogany neck with rosewood fingerboard.*
Electrics: *dual single-coil pickups with individual tone and volume controls; three-way toggle switch.*
Features: *Melita bridge; Grover Imperial tuners.*

6. '58 GUILD STUART X-550
Materials: *carved solid spruce top; maple back and sides; maple neck with bound ebony fingerboard.*
Electrics: *dual single-coil pickups with individual tone and volume controls; three-way toggle switch.*
Features: *engraved lyre-shape tailpiece; floating two-piece ebony bridge; abalone inlays.*

The first electric guitar hero, Charlie Christian, still impresses with his virtuosity.

A young George Benson puts a Gibson Super 400 through its paces.

1

2

3

Gibson bosses gather round a gold-finish cousin of the company's ES-175, their first archtop with a laminated top. On its debut in 1949 the ES-175 had a P-90 pickup, developed just years before. Never as highly lauded as the humbucker, Gibson's single-coil P-90 is nevertheless the oldest pickup design still in popular use today. Known for a hot, raw sound with gritty highs and aggressive mids, if first appeared on Gibson acoustic-electrics in 1946, and in 1952 graduated – in its "soapbar" guise – to the new solidbody Les Paul model.

Robert Benedetto in the previous chapter, and as still preferred by many traditional jazz guitarists today.)

The burgeoning awareness that the electric guitar was indeed a breed apart, with different requirements and capabilities alike, led naturally to the notion that acoustic-electrics could be designed to accentuate their electric qualities – while making welcome cost savings through compromises in the acoustic department. Why go to the trouble and expense of hand-carving a spruce or maple top when you couldn't tell it from plywood after the body-mounted magnetic pickup and tube amp had dealt with the tone? In 1949 Gibson introduced its first electric with a pressed, laminated top in the form of the ES-175, which has since proved good enough for the likes of Joe Pass, Jim Hall, Pat Metheny and many others.

Of course, the cheaper production techniques were not widely publicized at the time. But as well as these savings at the factory, the use of laminated woods also gave the guitars a brighter, snappier edge than their predecessors, which suited amplification even better for many purposes. A number of rival manufacturers followed suit with laminated construction and it quickly became the standard for acoustic-electric archtops.

Still thought of first and foremost as a jazz box, and a rare breed in the rock arena – despite the efforts of noisemongers like Ted Nugent and Billy Duffy, or prog whiz Steve Howe – it behoves us to remember what a revolution-in-the-making the acoustic-electric was half a century ago or more in the hands of Scotty Moore, Chuck Berry, or T-Bone Walker.

Even top-of-the-line electric models like Gibson's ES-300 or Epiphone's Zephyr lacked such niceties as bound f-holes, deluxe trim and upgraded hardware found on the acoustic-only L-5 and Emperor that were their respective contemporaries. Of course, as players of these and other high-end models decided they wanted to be heard too, Gibson Super 400s, Gretsch Syncromatics and even D'Angelicos soon appeared with retro-fit pickups mounted to them. (At first these were generally of the less intrusive, "floating" neck- or pickguard-mounted variety, as described by

Jim Hall is a long-standing proponent of the 'plywood' topped Gibson ES-175..

4

5

6

It's difficult to conceive of rock without the solidbody electric guitar, even though the instrument was developed before that radical musical genre even existed. Plenty of early rock'n'roll was played on big-bodied archtops with pickups mounted on top (as discussed in the previous chapter), but their limitations were always clear. For real power with volume and attack, enough brightness to cut through the clutter, and a sound free from the severe restraints of feedback, solidbodys proved the only way forward.

They were scorned, jeered at, derided and generally shown little respect by the traditional guitar-playing masses of the day. But the introduction of early solidbody designs in the '30s and '40s and the arrival of the first mass-produced solidbody electric in 1950, the Fender Broadcaster, nevertheless represented a revolution in the making. The sound and the look and the sheer volume of popular music would never be the same again.

As with all of his early successes in the manufacture of electric instruments and amplification, Leo Fender arrived at the first mass-production solidbody guitar by a combination of careful R&D, clever artist liaison, and happy accident. A mere stylized rendering of the existing guitar, the Broadcaster (which by mid-1951 and forever after was known as the Telecaster) took the concept of the instrument back to the drawing board, preserving little more than its six strings, scale length and standardized tuning.

The essentially acoustic "electrics" by Gibson, Epiphone, Gretsch and others were great instruments but had inherent limitations that were still making it difficult for guitarists to step front-of-stage and seriously compete as soloists. The relatively dark, often muddy sound of these guitars could get lost amid the brass sections of large western swing orchestras and smaller jazz combos alike, and they were prone to howls of feedback when turned up loud enough to be heard in larger halls.

Leo Fender's Telecaster had improved pickups, a treble-enhancing, sustain-encouraging and highly adjustable bridge design, and resonant through-body stringing in a solid ash body. It combated all the limitations of the acoustic-electric and gave guitarists the chance to be heard on a grand scale. (Similar models followed from most of Fender's major competitors.) Furthermore, the rugged construction and the screw-off, screw-on repairability of nearly every part on the Telecaster made it a workhorse able to withstand the knocks of the road and be easily serviced when the need arose. Coupled with that, the instrument's slim, fast neck and easy action introduced exciting new levels of playability.

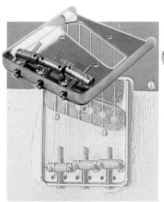

What could be simpler? As this view of a disassembled Tele-style guitar shows, the ingredients of a standard bolt-on solidbody instrument require significantly less craftsmanship and sheer workshop sweat to whip into shape than, for example, a hand-carved archtop or quality flat-top acoustic. The results, nevertheless, have fueled rock history.

Any guitar's bridge contributes to its sound, but the original Telecaster unit has a character all its own. Brass bar saddles on early models add bite and sustain, while the steel pickup-mounting plate gives zing and twang to the tone. Of course the three-saddle design limits intonation accuracy, too, so many later bridges were upgraded to six saddles for full adjustability. Some purists argue, however, that the original with three brass or steel saddles yields the truest Tele tone.

Albert Lee set the frets afire for Head Hands & Feet on, first, a Fender Tele, then a Music Man.

1   2

solidbodies

WOOD SHED

The wood(s) used to make a guitar's body play a major part in the instrument's sound: 1. swamp ash offers solid lows and sparkling highs, with somewhat scooped, open mids; 2. alder produces a thicker midrange, with firm lows and enough high-end articulation to cut through; 3. mahogany tends toward a dense and warm tonality, combining gutsy lows and powerful mids; 4. basswood produces even, balanced frequency response with a full midrange; 5. the "classic combination" – mahogany body with maple top – offers dense, powerful mids with good definition and balanced high and low response.

Originally devised to save labor and make repairs or replacement simpler, the bolt-on-neck guitar (the neck is in fact screwed on in most cases) has a tonality all its own. It offers a bright, edgy, cutting tone (the classic "twang"), a woody resonance, and decent natural sustain (particularly from through-body designs), as well as a good tuning stability.

Not only did the new era in guitar construction help make the guitar the star in dozens of popular country and swing bands, it saw the electric guitar virtually taking the job of an entire orchestra, ushering in guitar groups (typically two guitars, a bass and drums) that would change the face of popular music forever and pave the way for rock'n'roll. More than merely a point of evolution in the look and feel of the instrument, however, the solidbody electric triggered a giant leap in the sound and power of the guitar-based band. There was little point developing large, high-powered amplifiers when guitars would only squeal with feedback after a certain volume was reached. With the solidbody, suddenly the sky was the limit in amp design – and in the volume wars the guitar was the new victor.

Since those early days countless other brands have followed the form of Fender's production-line original, and it has proved – with a number of variations – to be one of the most successful templates for the solidbody electric guitar.

1. '53 FENDER TELECASTER
Materials: *solid swamp ash body; bolt-on one-piece maple neck/fingerboard; 25½" scale.* **Electrics:** *dual single-coil pickups; single volume and tone control; three-way switch (originally selecting neck p'up with bassy sound, neck p'up with tone control; bridge p'up).* **Features:** *through-body stringing; brass saddles.*

A rosewood-neck early '60s Tele provides Steve Cropper's signature tone with the MGs.

2. '63 FENDER CUSTOM TELECASTER
Materials: *solid bound ash body; bolt-on maple neck with rosewood fingerboard.* **Electrics:** *dual single-coil pickups; single volume and tone control; three-way switch (switch selections as on '53 Tele description, left).* **Features:** *through-body stringing; threaded steel saddles; three-ply pickguard.*

3. '77 MUSIC MAN STINGRAY I
Materials: *solid two-piece alder body; bolt-on maple neck and integral 22-fret maple fingerboard.* **Electrics:** *dual humbucking pickups; bass, treble and volume controls; four-way rotary switch and active preamp switch.* **Features:** *through-strung non-vibrato 'hardtail' bridge.*

4. '94 ERNIE BALL/MUSIC MAN ALBERT LEE
Materials: *solid ash body; bolt-on maple neck with maple fingerboard cut from same timber.* **Electrics:** *three single-coil DiMarzio pickups; single volume and tone control; five-way switch.* **Features:** *through-body stringing; six-saddle bridge; four/two headstock layout.*

A lifetime Tele man, Roy Buchanan shows what Leo's creation can do.

The designs of many the single-coil pickups in use today – in basic technical terms – are largely unchanged from those seen at the dawn of amplification, but there are many variations on the theme. The classic Tele bridge pickup is biting, snappy and punchy, while its neck-position partner is mellower and more rounded in tone. Vintage Strat units tend toward the thin and edgy, with piercing highs. Now seen on plenty of bolt-neck guitars too, the Gibson-style humbucker is characteristically fat, warm and powerful.

Telecaster bridge pickup

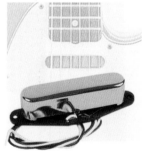

Tele neck pickup (covered)

Strat pickup (uncovered)

Gibson-style humbucker

3

4

Gibson's Les Paul managed to do most everything that Fender's Telecaster could do, if somewhat differently (see following pages). So Fender needed a new trick to bring the spotlight back in their direction. In 1954, with the launch of the Stratocaster, they found it. While the Tele set the prototype for bolt-neck solidbody electrics, the Strat took the format right out of this world, introducing the most-played and most-copied electric guitar design of all time.

Aside from its radical shape, if the Strat had been fitted with Tele pickups and hardware it would have sounded and performed much like a Tele. But two major areas of design development significantly altered the instrument's sound and playability.

The first innovation came in the Strat's electronics. Ostensibly much like the single-coil units on the Telecaster, new pickups were developed by Fender for the Stratocaster. They were brighter, with sharper highs (though often somewhat less powerful than the Tele

bridge unit) in an era when cutting through a muddy bandstand "mix" in order to be heard was a key priority. Also, the three-pickup switching with dual tone controls offered a broad range of voices.

Second, there was an even more radical advance: the Strat's fully-adjustable self-contained "tremolo" tailpiece. This allowed more down-bend than any previously available production unit, in an age when heavier string gauges made left-hand bends more difficult, and offered reasonable tuning stability when set up correctly. Even when not in use it changed the guitar's core tonality, shifting the path of string routing and tapping off some of the acoustic resonance through a bridge block and the unit's associated springs.

The Strat vibrato – now taken for granted – ushered in a whole new range of playing styles, from the new hard-twang country styles, through the sproingy, heavily vibrato'd surf instrumentals of

---

1. '56 FENDER STRATOCASTER
Materials: *solid ash body in two tone sunburst; bolt-on maple neck with integral 21-fret maple fingerboard; 25½" scale.*
Electrics: *three single-coil pickups; tone controls for neck and middle p'up; master volume; three-way switch.*
Features: *vibrato tailpiece with internal rear-mounted springs single ply white pickguard.*

No single player displayed the Strat's capabilities better than Jimi Hendrix.

2. '61 BURNS BISON
Materials: *solid alder body; one-piece un-bound bolt-on maple neck and rosewood fingerboard.*
Electrics: *four single-coil 'Super Sonic' pickups; four-way selector; mode switch; volume control.*
Features: *Burns vibrato.*
Historical note: *Britain's answer to the Strat in its rare four-pickup incarnation.*

3. '89 IBANEZ RADIUS 540R
Materials: *solid alder body; one-piece un-bound bolt-on maple neck and rosewood fingerboard.*
Electrics: *single F1 humbucking pickup in the bridge position plus two C1 single coils; single volume and tone, five-way selector.*
Features: *Ibanez-made locking vibrato tailpiece.*

4. '97 JACKSON STEALTH TH2
Materials: *solid ash body; glued-in maple neck with unbound 22-fret rosewood fingerboard.*
Electrics: *two Jackson humbucking pickups plus center-position single coil; master vol and tone; five-way selector.*
Features: *two-post Jackson vibrato bridge.*

5. '89 G&L COMANCHE
Materials: *solid swamp ash body; bolt-on maple neck with unbound 22-fret rosewood fingerboard.*
Electrics: *three G&L single-coil-style hum-rejecting 'Z-coil' pickups; five-position selector plus mini toggle switch for neck+bridge or all three p'ups.*
Features: *G&L 'dual fulcrum' vibrato bridge; GraphTech string tree.*

Blueser Stevie Ray Vaughan squeezed hot, wiry tones from his beloved Stratocasters.

An Ibanez 'superstrat' proves the weapon of choice for Joe Satriani's virtuoso shred-rock.

1   2   3

solidbodies: bolt-on neck

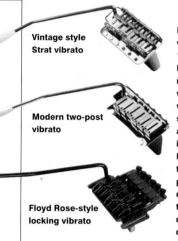

Vintage style Strat vibrato

Modern two-post vibrato

Floyd Rose-style locking vibrato

In developing the ingenious vibrato tailpiece for the 1954 Stratocaster, Leo Fender listened to musicians' requests, and worked to build what they wanted. The result was a self-contained unit with full adjustability and impressive down-bend. Improvements on the theme have included two-post knife-edged fulcrum designs for improved tuning stability, and locking units for serious rock divebombing action.

Just another solidbody? On the contrary, Danelectro's famous minimalistic look appears solid outside, but the body hides a lot of airspace between the hardboard front and back and central solid wood core. Like this reissue U-3, most are characterized by a bright, thin tonality with ringing highs and somewhat limited sustain.

the early '60s, to Hendrix's wild divebombing and air-raid effects. Taken to new levels in subsequent decades by the likes of Eddie Van Halen and Jeff Beck, it has proved one of rock's most expressive tools.

In purely visual terms, the Stratocaster has become a design icon honored and loved even by non-guitar players, and has a surprisingly timeless appeal. More than just a radical stylistic coup, however, the Strat's body contouring made it a more comfortable, even intimate instrument to play. The upper back contour made it easier to tuck in under the ribcage for long sets, while the chamfer at the top of the lower bout braced the player's right forearm without cutting into it as a Les Paul or Tele's square edges did.

As familiar as we are today with the Strat's look, sound and feel, any consideration of the inherent "rightness" of all its ingredients reminds us once again of what a great leap forward Leo Fender's second solidbody represented at the time.

The Strat has been the subject of countless upgrades and modifications, most of which have evolved into production models available off-the-shelf, including single and dual-humbucker models, locking nut and vibrato, deluxe wiring and switching layouts and other "superstrat" configurations. It remains the most emulated basic template for the solidbody electric some 50 years after its arrival – and, in most cases, without straying radically from its original form.

NECK WOODS & FRETS

Not as influential on a guitar's overall tone as its body wood, the neck wood can nevertheless add its own special flavor to the brew. (Below, L-to-R: maple; rosewood; mahogany.)

1. A solid maple neck (with maple fingerboard) lends tightness and definition to both the low and high end, bringing notes into sharp focus.

2. In the maple neck/rosewood fingerboard combination, the rosewood lends some roundness and looseness which can be perceived as a louder bottom end and more "sizzling" highs.

3. A mahogany neck with rosewood fingerboard – the classic Gibson combination – is characteristically full and warm, with a balanced response. An ebony fingerboard, the other most common variable (and usually found on a mahogany neck in solidbodies), adds note definition and clarity – and makes for an extremely hard-wearing option.

Fret widths also affect the guitar's feel and – some say – tone. High, narrow frets (below left) offer good chording and accurate noting; wider frets (center) are more bend-friendly. Some players believe wide, low frets (right) also allow more neck resonance into the sound, though it's much debated.

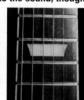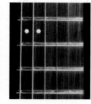

4

5

solidbodies: superstrats

Distinguished not only by their glued-in or bolt-on neck/body join, the differing neck angle between traditional Fender-style and Gibson-style guitars gives them very different playing feels. Note how the Les Paul's neck leaves the body at a much steeper pitch than the near-parallel Strat neck.

Strap on a Les Paul today and one thing comes instantly to mind – and fingers: rock. It's incredible to think, then, that when the model arrived in 1952 there was no such music. Gibson's premier solidbody was a response to the growing success of the Telecaster. But, mindful of their reputation and eager to tap a market with more traditional players still put off by Fender's bolt-together radicalism, Gibson wasn't about to offer their own slab-styled canoe paddle.

Instead, Gibson applied its skill with carved archtop "jazz" guitars to a maple cap atop a solid mahogany body, sticking with their time-tested set neck construction, and attaching a pair of the P-90 pickups already in use on hollowbody f-hole models in the late-'40s. In this way, Gibson arrived at the "other electric" – the archetype for the solidbody with glued-in neck. Perceived as more classy, with a big nod toward tradition but with all the

power needed to pump out the new music, the Les Paul has evolved in many directions, but remains the third significant electric-guitar blueprint. Several elements define its character.

Perhaps most important is the Les Paul's body construction. The chunky mahogany slab lends sustain and a generally warm, rounded resonance to the tone, given a degree of brightness and "cut" by the maple top. Tonally, the glued-in neck aids sustain and sonic depth somewhat, and can introduce a certain darkness to the overall sound. As for playability, Gibson's neck pitch, or angle to the body, which is significantly steeper than that of Fender's, brings the neck more within reach of the left

1. GIBSON LES PAUL STANDARD
Materials: *solid mahogany body with two-piece carved maple top; glued-in mahogany neck with bound 22-fret rosewood fingerboard; 24¾" scale length.*
Electrics: *dual humbucking pickups with individual vol and tone controls; 3-way switch.*
Features: *stop tailpiece and Tune-o-matic bridge.*

2. '58 GIBSON LES PAUL JUNIOR
Materials: *double cutaway solid mahogany body; glued-in mahogany neck with unbound rosewood fingerboard; 24¾" scale length.*
Electrics: *one P-90 single-coil pickup; single vol and tone control; 3-way toggle switch.*
Features: *wrapover 'stop' tailpiece/bridge; Kluson tuners; yellow 'TV' finish.*

Who said 'fat tone?' The LP that sealed it for the Les Paul and British blues-rock.

3. '59 GIBSON FLYING V
Materials: *solid korina body; glued-in korina neck with unbound rosewood fingerboard.*
Electrics: *dual 'Patent Applied For' (PAF) humbucking pickups; individual volume and master tone controls; 3-way toggle switch.*
Features: *through-body stringing via 'V' tailpiece; Tune-o-matic bridge; Kluson tuners.*

4. '59 GIBSON LES PAUL SPECIAL
Materials: *double cutaway solid mahogany body; glued-in mahogany neck with unbound rosewood fingerboard; 24¾" scale length.*
Electrics: *dual P-90 single-coil pickups; individual volume and tone controls; 3-way switch.*
Features: *wrapover 'stop' tailpiece/bridge. Plastic-button Kluson tuners.*

5. '97 PRS ARTIST III
Materials: *solid mahogany body with bookmatched quilted maple top; one-piece mahogany neck with rosewood fingerboard; PRS's regular 25" scale length.*
Electrics: *dual humbucking pickups; five-way rotary switch; master tone and volume.*
Features: *PRS wrapover bridge; abalone-bound neck and headstock.*

BRIDGE WORK
The bridge and tailpiece used on a set-neck solidbody have a lot to say in determining its sound. The simple one-piece Gibson-style wrapover unit – the original hardware for this type of guitar if you exclude the ill-conceived "wrap-under" trapeze tailpiece of the first Les Pauls – has long been admired by tonehounds for its stability and solid, resonant string anchoring, but has clear limitations for intonation adjustment. PRS's update of the type was designed for improved intonation. The classic stop tailpiece/Tune-o-matic combination offers solidity with precise intonation adjustment. If wobbles are desired, a Bigsby fits the bill – though tone can suffer due to lost string tension over the bridge.

Wrapover bridge/tailpiece.

PRS wrapover bridge.

Tune-o-matic bridge.

Bigsby with Tune-o-matic.

solidbodies: set-neck

hand, which some players find more comfortable. The slightly shorter 24 3/4" scale, meanwhile, also makes it somewhat slinkier and more bend-friendly than Fender's 25 1/2" scale length. However, the glued-in neck construction makes repairs and major adjustments difficult and often costly.

As for electronics, a Les Paul fitted with P-90 pickups is biting and edgy, with gritty highs and punchy mids. With humbuckers, it's generally a smooth, warm, powerful and sustaining guitar. Either way, output is hotter than standard Fender-type single-coil pickups, driving tube amps into distortion more quickly.

Other post-Les Paul Gibson-style solidbodies such as the Les Paul Special and Junior, Flying V, Explorer and SG, along with roughly similar designs from other makers, leaned more toward slab body construction, cut from a single type of wood and without the Les Paul's elaborate carved maple top. While the voice of some of these guitars is determined by body and neck woods, the set-neck join which they share with the Les Paul still lends them a round, warm and full-throated tonality, particularly when partnered with humbuckers.

Today, myriad combinations of bolt-on and set-neck designs provide tonal performance and playability that range between the two camps. PRS offers some roughly Gibson-like designs with bolt-on necks; big rock-axe companies like Jackson or Ibanez build superstrat-style models with set-necks, hot humbuckers and double-locking vibratos. With the borders demolished, it's no longer simply a matter of choosing between Fender and Gibson.

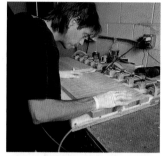

Gluing together bookmatched maple tops at the PRS factory.

Before the neck is fretted, the 10" fingerboard radius is applied.

Pre-cut frets are hand-installed and pushed into the radiused fretboard.

Finally, PRS "robots" buff the finished body to a high sheen.

One respected latter-day builder, Paul Reed Smith, manages to come close to doing most of the sonic and stylistic tricks previously ascribed to one side or the other of the set-neck/bolt-neck divide. A single PRS guitar can run the gamut from Les Paul-like warmth and power to Strat-like cut and twang – while excelling at a range of voices in between. A look inside the PRS factory, above, reveals the cohabitation of computer-aided assembly techniques and tried-and-tested hand craftsmanship. In addition, PRS were among the first production builders to extend the use of dramatic natural wood figure – in flamed, quilted and tiger-striped maple tops particularly – combined with striking translucent finishes, as illustrated below.

3

4

5

solidbodies: through-neck

According to the prophecies of makers such as Ibanez, Yamaha, Alembic, Carvin and a number of others in the late '70s and early '80s, the through-neck guitar was the way of the future. They preached about added constructional stability, increased resonance and sustain, and an all-around improved instrument. The through-neck guitar was being touted as the new top of the line, the crème de la crème, the ultimate evolution of the solidbody electric guitar.

So what happened? Not a lot. Just as through-neck designs existed well before the 1970s, they continue to be built today, but they've always been at the fringe of constructional techniques. Three things seem to account for this. First, the manufacturing complexities required of some designs didn't justify any

"improvements" gained over set-neck guitars – improvements that are, arguably, negligible anyway. Second, according to some builders and players, the apparent advantage of a central body core and neck carved from the same piece (or laminated pieces) of wood only proved detrimental to tone. And third? Well, these old bolt-on and set-neck guitars that were lying around all sounded pretty good already. Why go to the trouble of redesigning the wheel?

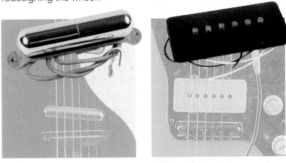

Danelectro's lipsick tube.   **Fender's Jazzmaster pickup.**

Fender Strat and Tele-style single coils and Gibson-style humbuckers may have set the templates for the majority of pickup derivations found today, but a number of quirkier units have made their mark on music history, and found fans in particular genres. Danelectro's bright, wiry lipstick pickup and Fender's punchy, rounded Jazzmaster unit have both been favorites of the new wave, indie and alternative camps.

Slide supremo Johnny Winter gets it on with a 'reverse-body' Gibson Firebird.

1

Thin and toppy? Pah! Pete Townshend let his Ricky go wild with The Who.

2

3

Used as a marketing tool around 1978, a "through-neck" hailed the ultimate in tone and sustain. In reality, many players noticed no quantifiable improvement in resonance, power or general sound over glued-in or even bolt-on necks. Interestingly, many classic makes and models of solid or semi-acoustic electrics that employed through-neck construction in the late '50s and early '60s, notably a number of Rickenbackers and Gibson's first "reverse body" Firebirds, usually did so without calling much attention to the fact.

There's little doubt, though, that the integral neck/body core design lends great structural stability to a well-built guitar, and the mere fact of the effort required to build a quality instrument using this technique generally signals that extra craftsmanship has gone in elsewhere, too. And the strength of such a neck makes it easier to design a guitar with deep cutaways and excellent upper-fret accessibility since it's no longer necessary to leave enough solid body wood free from the upper and lower cutaway to secure a sturdy neck join.

In any case, the major through-neck designs offered from the 1970s onward tended to be high-end models, and generally powerful, weighty, humbucker-loaded guitars aimed at the rock or fusion player. Yamaha's SG-2000, first introduced in 1976 and reissued recently (though always available in Japan), was the first Japanese guitar to gain wide acceptance among Western pros, with an important early endorsement from Carlos Santana.

Even before this, Alembic – best known for deluxe active-electronics basses – were building some of the most expensive production solidbodies then available, all with through-neck designs, exotic woods and elaborate active electronics. These designs further inspired more affordable models from Ibanez, Carvin and others… until the way forward was found by looking backward to "retro" fashions.

---

1. '65 GIBSON FIREBIRD V
Materials: *solid mahogany through-neck/body core with mahogany body 'wings' in original 'reverse body' style; bound rosewood fingerboard.*
Electrics: *dual covered mini humbucking pickups; individual volume and tone controls; three-way toggle switch.*
Features: *vibrato, Tune-o-matic bridge; banjo tuners.*

2. '61 RICKENBACKER 460
Materials: *bound maple body with maple through-neck and rosewood fingerboard.*
Electrics: *dual single-coil 'toaster-top' pickups; individual volume and tone controls; three-way lever switch; Rick-O-Sound (stereo) blender control.*
Features: *shark fin position markers.*

3. '59 RICKENBACKER 360
Materials: *semi-solid maple body with maple/mahogany laminated through-neck and rosewood fingerboard.*
Electrics: *dual single-coil 'toaster-top' pickups; individual volume and tone controls; three-way lever switch.*
Features: *'cooker' control knobs; two-tier gold plastic pickguard.*

4. '78 ALEMBIC SERIES I
Materials: *carved solid body of exotic hardwoods including walnut and others; laminated 'sandwich' through-neck of maple and walnut, with 24-fret unbound rosewood fingerboard.*
Electrics: *low impedance single-coil pickups with rotary selector and low-Z XLR out.*
Features: *brass nut & saddles.*

5. '84 YAMAHA SG-2000S
Materials: *bound solid mahogany body with carved maple top; bound laminated maple/mahogany through-neck with ebony fingerboard.*
Electrics: *dual humbucking pickups; individual vol and tone controls with push/push coil taps; three-way switch.*
Features: *brass sustain block mounted under bridge.*

6. '78 IBANEZ MUSICIAN MC500
Materials: *solid walnut/maple/walnut body with maple/mahogany laminated through-neck and ebony fingerboard.*
Electrics: *dual humbucking pickups; active on-board preamp and coil-split switching.*
Features: *brass bridge and tailpiece; abalone vine inlays.*

Carlos made that note sustain for days on his SG-2000 with early-'80s era Santana.

4   5   6

Are you seeking the power and versatility of a solidbody electric but with some of the vibe of an archtop jazzer – or just desperate for a little weight reduction? Step this way. The dictionary defines the prefix "semi" as meaning half or partially, hence its use in descriptive terms such as semi-detached and semi-precious. When applied to the electric guitar it is generally associated with the words "acoustic" or "solid," and in each case the description refers to the method of construction involved. However, the two terms do actually overlap to some extent and on some instruments the distinction is sufficiently blurred so that either definition can be correct.

The designation "semi-acoustic" relates to an instrument that usually employs the same or similar frontal dimensions as those of a full-size acoustic-electric – although proportions may be more compact – but with significantly slimmer body depth. The amount of air within can vary considerably; some guitars described as "semis" (incorrectly, technically speaking) are completely hollow, while others incorporate differing quantities of internal timber, ranging from small reinforcing blocks to full-length or full-width solid sections.

Those electrics that contain an appreciable amount of wood rather than open space may also be described as "semi-solid," which is where the duplication of terminology arises. On a strictly solid guitar, the body mass has a major effect on tonal properties

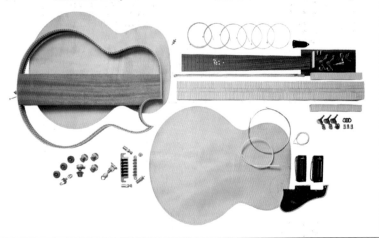

Most players know what is meant by the term "semi," though they may be coming at it from opposite directions. This photo of the constituent parts of a semi-acoustic electric reveals the solid mahogany block between the arched top and back of an otherwise hollow body.

1

Looking, from the front, every bit a full-bodied jazzer like the Super 400CES or L-5CES, Gibson's Byrdland was among a trio of "thinline" electrics launched in 1955 which reduced the standard body depth of approximately 3½" to nearer 2". Still a hollowbody instrument – as were its new thinline cousins the ES-225T and ES-350T – it showed the early evolution of Gibson's thinking toward semi-acoustic lines with a bid to improve playing comfort and reduce feedback while still retaining some of the feel and look of a traditional archtop.

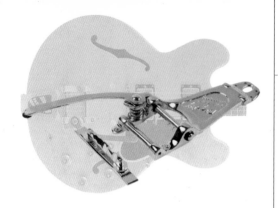

BIGSBY VIBRATO

Though it has made an appearance on most styles of electric guitar over the years, the Bigsby is the vibrato tailpiece of choice for the semi-acoustic. A rather crude device mechanically – causing tuning instabilities unless set up well and allowing pitch bends of only a semitone or so – it nevertheless has a distinctive sound loved by many players.

and sustain, while the inherent natural sound of a full-depth acoustic-electric exerts a great influence on the character of its amplified output.

In keeping with its name, the semi (whether considered acoustic or solid) represents something of a halfway house between the two. The idea is that the resonance created in the hollow chambers of the body audibly contributes to the overall amplified performance. Even playing a semi "unplugged" should reveal a louder acoustic response than that derived from a solid six-string, although it's still appreciably less than the volume produced by a deep-bodied, all-hollow equivalent. But this will of course only be of minimal importance when it comes to practical performance, because an amplifier will naturally negate any such discrepancies in volume.

Warranting much greater consideration are the overtones generated, because these can have a discernible effect on the

1. '57 GIBSON BYRDLAND
Materials: *thinline hollow body with laminated spruce top and maple back and sides; maple neck with ebony fingerboard.*
Electrics: *dual single-coil 'alnico' pickups, with individual volume and tone controls; three-way toggle switch.*
Features: *trapeze tailpiece and floating Tune-o-matic bridge.*

Chet's fluid style perfectly spotlights the semi's warm yet articulate tone.

2. '55 GRETSCH CHET ATKINS
Materials: *hollow body with laminated maple top, back and sides; maple neck with bound rosewood fingerboard.*
Electrics: *dual single-coil DeArmond pickups with individual volume and tone controls, master tone, master volume and three-way selector.*
Features: *fixed Bigsby vibrato.*

3. '59 GIBSON ES-335TN
Materials: *semi-hollow body of laminated maple with mahogany center block; mahogany neck with bound rosewood fingerboard.*
Electrics: *dual 'PAF' humbuckers, with individual volume and tone controls; three-way toggle switch.*
Features: *Bigsby vibrato and Tune-o-matic bridge.*

An ES-335 (among others) proved to have power aplenty for Cream-era Clapton.

4. '61 HOFNER VERITHIN
Materials: *hollow body of laminated spruce and other woods; laminated maple neck with bound rosewood fingerboard.*
Electrics: *dual single-coil pickups with master vol and tone controls and 'Solo' switch.*
Features: *Bigsby vibrato and floating Bigsby bridge.*

Former Suede guitarist Bernard Butler used an ES-335 for his fiery indie riffs.

end results – although it must be said that the differences so derived are more marked with some guitars than others. The aim is that these qualities should enhance rather than impede the sound, but exactly how such benefits are perceived and employed is really down to the individual player. In general, the semi-acoustic's extra resonance imparts a degree of sweetness and often mellowness to the sound, but with the low end staying well defined and treble content relatively unimpaired.

In recent years the semi-solid concept has become considerably more popular, with most company catalogues now offering at least one obviously more airy alternative. But to most players, the word "semi" conjures up images of big but slim electrics, epitomised by the creations bearing the Gibson brandname. This company was the first to offer the convenience of thinner-bodied archtop-electrics, beginning with the Byrdland

in 1955. The absence of much body depth made the instrument much more manageable, while still retaining the friendly familiarity of conventional cosmetics, and this policy was soon extended to include slender equivalents of existing instruments, including the ES-350T ("T" for "thinline"), while the ES-225T was an even slimmer six-string. All employed single-cutaway styling, but in its size the 225 model paved the way for an innovative design approach.

In 1958 the company debuted the ES-335TD, featuring a body with novel twin cutaways and an internal solid centre block. Gibson correctly reasoned that the latter restricted the body's resonant properties, in turn reducing the risk of inducing the feedback cycle often apparent when using acoustic-electric instruments (thick or thin) in close proximity to an amplifier. The end result was certainly less prone to the horrible howl. It was still

---

1. '62 EPIPHONE SHERATON
Materials: *semi-hollow body of laminated maple; mahogany neck with bound rosewood fingerboard.*
Electrics: *dual 'New York' mini-humbucker pickups, with individual volume and tone controls; three-way toggle switch.*
Features: *'Frequensator' tailpiece, Tune-o-matic bridge.*

2. '61 GIBSON ES-330
Materials: *hollow body of laminated maple; mahogany neck with bound rosewood fingerboard (note 16th fret neck/body join).*
Electrics: *dual single-coil P90 pickups; individual volume and tone controls; three-way toggle switch.*
Features: *trapeze tailpiece, Tune-o-matic bridge, plastic-button Kluson tuners.*

3. '64 RICKENBACKER 360/12 12-STRING
Materials: *carved and routed semi-hollow maple body; laminated mahogany and maple through-neck with bound maple fingerboard.*
Electrics: *dual single-coil 'toaster-top' pickups with individual vol and tone, three-way switch and blend control.*
Features: *two-tier pickguard, semi-slotted headstock.*

4. '90 RICKENBACKER 381V69
Materials: *carved and routed maple body, laminated mahogany-maple through-neck with bound rosewood fingerboard.*
Electrics: *dual single-coil 'toaster-top' pickups with individual vol and tone, three-way switch and blend control.*
Features: *'R' tailpiece, 'German carve' body.*

5. '77 FENDER TELECASTER THINLINE
Materials: *routed semi-solid ash body; bolt-on maple neck and fingerboard.*
Electrics: *dual humbucking pickups; master volume and tone controls; three-way lever switch.*
Features: *through-body stringing; fully-adjustable six-saddle bridge; 'bullet' truss rod adjuster.*

6. '98 PRS HOLLOWBODY II
Materials: *carved and routed mahogany body with bookmatched carved flame-maple top; glued-in mahogany neck with bound rosewood fingerboard.*
Electrics: *dual humbucking pickups; master vol and tone controls; three-way toggle.*
Features: *PRS wrapover bridge; locking tuners.*

Eight miles high, 12-strings, and one Roger McGuinn – and classic Ricky jangle is born.

FIFTH DIMENSION
THE BYRDS

1   2   3

semi-acoustics

not as safe as a full solid body, but it was at least a significant improvement. Almost at once Gibson exploited this advantage, adding the more deluxe ES-355TD and ES-345TD to make up a line of slimline semi-acoustics.

Also introduced at this time was the similarly styled but fully hollow ES-330TD, while sister brand Epiphone boasted respective equivalents in the form of the Riviera, Sheraton and Casino. The popularity enjoyed by Gibson's twin-cutaway quartet soon prompted most competitors to revise their ranges. The slimline treatment had already been adopted by a great many makers worldwide, and the company would now exert even greater influence on styling.

Gretsch, Guild and Harmony were among the many US manufacturers who opted to champion the twin-cutaway cause to a greater or lesser degree, usually adding their own touches to the overall outline. Surprisingly, none initially perceived the benefit of employing a solid centre block as Gibson did, although for a while Gretsch removed f-holes on some semis in an attempt

Modern mechanization means PRS hollowbody archtops are built somewhat differently than those of more traditional makers. After the solid body section has been "scooped out" by a computer-guided router its rough-cut top is glued in place (top right). The rough arch is then carved into the top by one router (near right), then finished by another – and the final result is now beginning to take shape as a PRS guitar.

4

5

6

to curtail feedback. Gibson's twin-cutaway concept was taken up by numerous contemporaries in many countries, with virtually all the European makers offering their own interpretations.

Again the constructional aspects were ignored in favor of retaining an all-hollow interior, but this position would change over the next two decades as the practical performance advantages became clear. The Japanese were quick to copy both cosmetics and construction methods for their more upmarket repros of the Gibson originals. The same principles were adopted when some of the makers in that part of the world decided to employ more original thinking, and the better examples of semis bearing brand names such as Aria, Ibanez and Yamaha certainly put Gibson's groundbreaking work to good use.

More recently there has been a less slavish adherence to the long-established twin-cutaway styling, with PRS in particular breaking with tradition – at least visually – by applying tried and tested semi-acoustic construction principles to the brand's own ideas on design.

Regardless of price, most semi-acoustics employ laminated wood for the body front and back as this lends itself to the manufacturing methods involved. This contradicts the choice made for solids, where the use of plywood indicates penny-pinching production. Internal differences affect the choice of certain hardware components, and in many instances the bridge and tailpiece in particular can provide clues as to how much

wood actually lurks within a semi. A floating bridge points to an all-hollow interior offering no purchase for body-mounted supports, and the same often applies to a trapeze-type tailpiece or vibrato unit secured to the side of the guitar. Instruments that incorporate some sort of center block tend to employ it to provide adequate anchorage where necessary, allowing the use of well-secured hardware such as bridge pillars and tailpiece.

A semi-solid can yield some of the same sonic seasoning as a semi-acoustic, although another prime purpose behind introducing some air into the construction is to reduce the guitar's physical weight. Ever since its inception, the solidbody electric has endured criticism concerning weight, levelled by players and also many makers. With this in mind, numerous competitors to Fender and Gibson's original designs have sought to offset the inevitable increase in ounces.

There's a limit to how light wood will go and still be a practical

Jeff Beck strapped on the requisite Duo Jet for his Cliff Gallup tribute, Crazy Legs.

1

2

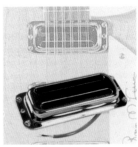

Rickenbacker 'button top' single-coil pickup.

Rickbenbacker 'toaster top' single-coil pickup.

Gibson's legendary single-coil P-90 pickup.

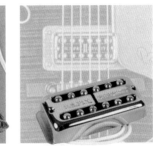

Gretsch Filter'Tron humbucking pickup.

Seymour Duncan mini-humbucker replacement.

DiMarzio's super-hot Super Distortion humbucker.

Like their solidbody cousins, semi-acoustic electrics carry a dizzying number of different pickup types, and these variations in design play a major part in the different voices heard from each model of guitar. Lower-powered single-coil units like the classic Rickenbacker pickups exhibit pronounced high-end response with plenty of sparkle, while Gibson's meatier P-90 single-coil packs more midrange punch. Humbucking designs do anything from solid twang (Filter'Tron) to bright-with-bite (mini-humbucker) to full-on rock (DiMarzio Super Distortion).

semi-acoustics

proposition for guitar building, so the obvious solution is to incorporate some space inside the body. It's surprising how many makers have adopted this approach over the years, and with the absence of any soundholes to confirm the presence of cavities within, such semis successfully masquerade as straightforward solids, often helped by marketing that does little to alter this impression. Early so-called "solids" from famous US names such as Gretsch, Guild, Harmony, Kay and Rickenbacker employed degrees of hollow construction in an effort to shed pounds and make their creations more appealing, weight-wise, than those from Fender or Gibson, but of course these changes also altered tone and sustain.

Other major names flaunted the routing of a little wood from an otherwise solid body – Fender's Tele Thinline being perhaps the most notable – as a variation on a tested theme, appealing to players seeking only a small step toward an airier semi.

They may look much alike at a glance, but Gibson's ES-330 and ES-335/345/355 are very different. Aside from the pickup differences, the ES-330 (far left) has a truly hollow body, with a 16th-fret neck joint. The ES-345 beside it has a central core of solid wood and neck joint at the 20th fret.

Generally, the semi suits a player who wants to hear a little more of the unplugged tone of the instrument in their amplified sound. Sure, this can sometimes introduce unwanted problems – feedback, occasional muddiness – but many guitarists are willing to overlook or overcome any drawbacks in return for the alternative aural texture of a good semi.

1. '58 GRETSCH DUO JET
Materials: *semi-solid routed mahogany body with laminated pressed arched top; glued-in mahogany neck with bound 22-fret rosewood fingerboard.*
Electrics: *dual Filter'Tron humbucking pickups, with individual tone switches and vol controls plus master vol.*
Features: *Melita Synchro-Sonic bridge.*

2. HARMONY STRATOTONE JUPITER H-90
Materials: *semi-solid body with spruce top; bolt-on maple neck and 20-fret rosewood fingerboard.*
Electrics: *dual single-coil pickups; selector switch; individual volume and tone controls plus master volume.*
Features: *floating two-piece rosewood bridge.*

The man whose name defined the beat, with a Jet Firebird in pre-rectangular-body days.

3. '00 GUILD BLUES 90
Materials: *semi-solid chambered mahogany body with carved solid maple top; glued-in mahogany neck with 22-fret rosewood fingerboard.*
Electrics: *dual single-coil P-90 style pickups; 3-way selector switch; individual volume and tone controls.*
Features: *Grover tuners; Tune-o-matic bridge with stop tailpiece.*

4. '79 HAMER SUNBURST
Materials: *semi-solid chambered mahogany body with carved solid maple top; glued-in mahogany neck with 22-fret rosewood fingerboard.*
Electrics: *dual humbucking pickups; 3-way selector switch; individual volume and master tone controls.*
Features: *strings-through-body bridge design; Grover tuners.*

5, '00 BRIAN MOORE M/C1
Materials: *semi-hollow composite body with solid 'tone' block and solid bookmatched quilted maple top; glued-in maple neck with 24-fret ebony fingerboard.*
Electrics: *Seymour Duncan pickups: one humbucker and two single-coil size Hot Rails.*
Features: *Wilkinson vibrato; elaborate abalone neck inlay.*

Nine hundred and ninety-nine players out of a thousand might feel that the electric guitar has evolved about as far as necessary – or possible. But there is always that one dissenter who's looking to get something more from the instrument. It's this kind of musician who inspires designers to search for the un-tapped tone, to forge new combinations of voices, to coin a radical feature or a fresh new feel – with one ear always cocked toward the musical horizon.

Guitars generically dubbed "hybrid" usually combine two or more means of sound reproduction for entirely new blends of tone and playability. This is more than just giving new shapes to the old familiar formulae – as did, say, Steinberger with the headless design or Floyd Rose with the locking vibrato. Typically, the new aural melange appears in the form of traditional magnetic and acoustic-like piezo pickups mounted on the same guitar; as an otherwise trad electric carrying MIDI/synth access; or simply in the form of an instrument with the look and feel of a solidbody

Despite his guitars' versatile pickup systems and slinky playability, Ken Parker has sometimes been taken to task for the modern, even "synthetic" outer appearance of some of his instruments. This advertisement (far right) was an effort to prove once and for all that there really is timber inside a Parker guitar. In 1996 Parker introduced the wood-bodied NiteFly (near right) aimed at more traditional tastes.

piezo-magnetic hybrids

1

2

Toto leadmeister Steve Lukather was an early convert to the Music Man vibe.

3

but delivering feedback-free amplified-acoustic performance. Many also use this futuristic sonic template as a springboard for nouveau looks and radically re-thought features. The result is an ever-expanding array of makes and models which, in fairness, can hardly be categorized.

"I hate the term hybrid," says Ken Parker, co-founder with electronics expert Larry Fishman of Parker Guitars. "I build the best electric guitar I know how to make." Yet despite the objections of the man behind probably the best-known and defining example of the breed, it's a term the general public can latch on to. There's little doubt, however, that other visionaries in the industry share Parker's simple defining goal: "The point of the guitar is to make a guitar sound better."

By allowing the player to combine acoustic and more traditional electric sounds – all treated through the effects and amplification set-up of his or her choice – the piezo/magnetic hybrid offers near-endless nuances of color between the previously isolated primary voices of the guitar. Additionally, it offers an instant leap between the two sounds, an enormous boon for any live performer who previously had to deal with the major hassle of squeezing a dramatic electric lead break into the middle of an otherwise mellow acoustic ballad, for example.

Add synthesizer access to the brew and the sky's the limit sonically, though even with the improved tracking and pitch detection of newer units, the guitar synth remains an under-used musical tool.

Whatever the hardware, the new breed is earning a growing list of name users, from former Red Hot Chili Peppers and Jane's Addiction guitarist Dave Navarro to David Bowie sideman Reeves Gabrels. It's a future just beginning to reveal itself.

---

1. '99 TOM ANDERSON HOLLOW DROP TOP
Materials: *semi-solid 'tone chambered' basswood body with quilted maple top; bolt-on maple neck with 22-fret rosewood fingerboard.*
Electrics: *humbucking and dual single-coil Anderson pickups; individual series/parallel switching; piezo-saddle LR Baggs X-Bridge vibrato with volume control and switch.*

2. '00 MUSIC MAN AXIS SUPER SPORT
Materials: *solid mahogany body with two-piece maple top; bolt-on maple neck with maple fingerboard.*
Electrics: *dual DiMarzio humbucking pickups with five-way switch, volume and tone; Fishman piezo-saddle vibrato bridge with volume, mode switch, and rear-pocket trim-pots for treble, bass and trim.*

3. '97 PARKER FLY ARTIST
Materials: *solid spruce body, top and neck with composite glass/carbon fiber/epoxy strengthening 'exoskeleton' and fingerboard; glued on frets.*
Electrics: *dual magnetic humbucking pickups with three-way selector switch; piezo-loaded 'flat-spring' vibrato bridge with controls for blended or individual use.*

Reeves Gabrels uses his Parker to smash sonic boundaries with Tin Machine.

4. '94 HAMER DUO TONE
Materials: *semi-solid mahogany body with maple top; glued-in mahogany neck with rosewood fingerboard.*
Electrics: *dual humbucking pickups with master vol and tone; piezo-pickup-loaded acoustic-style bridge saddle; controls for blended or separate use.*
Features: *mini soundholes.*

5. '98 GODIN LG-XT
Materials: *solid silver-leaf maple body with carved maple top; bolt-on mahogany neck with ebony fingerboard.*
Electrics: *dual Seymour Duncan magnetic humbucking pickups with five-way switch, volume and tone controls; piezo-loaded LR Baggs vibrato X-Bridge with separate graphic EQ; 13-pin synth output with associated controls.*

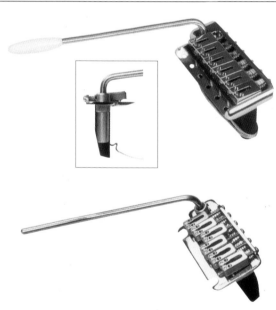

BRIDGE POWER

More than just a factory option these days, the proliferation of retro-fit piezo-saddle bridges means that many guitars with Strat-style vibratos can be converted to "hybrid" operation with relative ease. So far, two models are clear leaders in the field: the Fishman Power Bridge (top) is designed for a six-screw vintage Strat vibrato-type mounting (though other models are available), while the L.R. Baggs X-Bridge vibrato fits more contemporary two-post designs.

4

5

"However gorgeous your '51 Nocaster, '56 Gretsch 6120 or PRS Single-Cut may be to play, you've never heard it at its best until you have floored it through an equally rarified amp, vintage or contemporary. While we're not all fortunate enough to be able to choose from the world's finest amps, however, the good news is that achieving great sounds can be relatively simple, and needn't be overly expensive."

"Imagine Jimi Hendrix without fuzz, The Edge without delay, Scotty Moore or Dick Dale without reverb. Without effects, these players' trademark sounds would be hugely different."

chapter 2

TOTALLY GUITAR
AMPS & EFFECTS

Most players know that their amps and effects play a huge part in the sound chain, but have had little chance to look under the hood of these crucial sonic ingredients to learn what makes them tick. In this chapter, we lift the lid on the ways in which circuit types, tube variations, speaker designs, construction techniques and more can shape your tone.

Players gush and enthuse endlessly about guitars, but relatively little attention is paid to amplification. An amp sits behind you, you switch it on, plug in, play, and the sound comes out. What's to think about? Ah, but there's the key: *the sound comes out!* The amp has the final say in what you and your audience hear of your playing, and adds the final twists that determine "your tone."

TUBE TASTING

In any tube amp, the tubes (valves) themselves are where the real work is done – where your guitar signal is married to high voltage electricity to create amplified sound. It's the way in which tubes distort that, historically, has for many players made them preferable to solid-state, or transistor, systems. Transistors distort too, but without a lot of extra engineering the result tends to be harsh and relatively unmusical. Tubes, on the other hand, make a more gradual transition into distortion, during which the guitar signal gains what our ears perceive as added dimension and a compression-like smoothness. Even "clean" tube amp sounds have an element of distortion, which adds richness and texture to the tone. Different tubes have different characteristics: 6L6 – bright, tight, big-Fender sound; EL34 – the Marshall favorite, with crunchy mids and juicy overdrive; EL84 – the sweet and ringing "baby Brit;" 6V6 – the Jr. Fender-type, creamy and easily distorted. Others include preamp tubes (the 12AX7 is easily the most common) and rectifiers like the GZ34 or 5Y3 that convert AC electricity to DC.

Still unclear about the significance your amp plays in the overall sonic picture? Try this imaginary test: side by side in your mind's ear, plug a Korean-built Squier Stratocaster into a Matchless D/C-30 combo, and plug a Fender Custom Shop Strat into a Squier practise combo. Now play each rig a while. Which sounds better? No competition. That hand-built Matchless can induce spasms of tonal ecstasy, even with a competent but underwhelming budget guitar. Yes, it's an unfair contest – but it's not over yet. Reverse the set-ups and play again. Sure, the D/C-30 is even more heavenly with the Custom Shop Strat injected. But here's the rub: rank all four combinations in order of best to worst. Bet you the hand-built, all-tube amp comes out number one and number two, right?

A foregone conclusion, perhaps, but a good amp – one that's well-built for its price, suited to your style of music, and kept in good working order – plays a major role in taking you closer to aural paradise, however fine, vintage or custom-built your electric guitar. Similarly, however gorgeous your '51 Nocaster, '56 Gretsch 6120, or 2000 PRS Singlecut may be to play, you've never heard it at its best until you have floored it through an equally rarified amp, vintage or contemporary. While we're not all fortunate enough to be able to choose from the world's finest amps, however, the good news is that achieving great sounds can be relatively simple, and needn't be overly expensive.

Your first glance under the hood of many modern tube amps can be a little daunting, but as with cars today a lot of the tangle inside has nothing to do with getting you (or your basic guitar sound) from A to B. Channel-switching circuitry, effects-loop routing and other added features all jumble the picture. But from input to tone-shaping circuit to tubes to output, there needn't be a whole lot of excess science to get in the way.

Consider, for example, the early '50s tweed Fender Deluxe pictured here. Countless rock'n'roll hits were played through such an amp and bluesmen have pushed them into sweet, creamy overdrive, while raw rockers crank them up for excesses

'53 FENDER DELUXE
Specifications: *two channel class A/B all-tube combo; 15W output; cathode biased; single 12" speaker.*
Controls: *individual volume for each channel, shared tone.*
Features: *fully hand-wired circuit (model 5C3); one 12AY7, one 12AX7, two 6V6s and one 5Y3 rectifier; Jensen P12R alnico-magnet speaker (note replacement speaker on this example); open-backed 'wide panel' fingerjointed solid pine cabinet.*

'96 PEAVEY CLASSIC 30
Specifications: *footswitchable two channel class A all-tube combo; 30W output; single 12" speaker.*
Controls: *Ch1: volume; Ch2: gain and master volume, shared: bass, middle, treble, reverb.*
Features: *circuit on printed board (PCB); three 12AX7 preamp tubes, four EL84s, solid state rectification; Peavey Blue Marvel speaker; top-mounted controls; open-backed plywood cab covered in repro tweed.*

After giving birth to rock'n'roll, the tweed Fender Deluxe helped launch the signature "grunge" sound when Neil Young injected his Bigsby-equipped '50s Les Paul for *Rust Never Sleeps*.

of distortion and hot, edgy lead tones. Neil Young, for example, is a fan of later-'50s tweed Deluxes, while Ted Nugent recorded with early '60s examples.

A closer look inside shows that there isn't a whole lot to this classic design – and the electronic magic behind most great vintage tube amps is equally simple. In the case of this "tweed" Fender, the only things to come between the guitar's signal at the input and the output transformer and speaker – the team that puts the sound we hear into the air – are a couple of resistors, four signal capacitors, a volume and tone control, and the preamp and output tubes themselves. Everything else contained within the amp's chassis has to do with shaping and filtering the high voltages and getting them to the tubes in the right condition to induce as little unwanted noise as possible.

While this Deluxe only produces 15 watts, bigger tube amps follow the same design principles, adding just a few more components for tone-shaping with larger (and sometimes more) tubes for more power. Still, countless guitar greats have recorded legendary solos on cranked Deluxes and similarly diminutive models (including ultra-tiny 3W '50s Champs), and record-buying fans never suspecting they were hearing anything less than a quartet of 100-watters through a wall of Marshall 4x12" cabs.

Of course, many factors influence great sound, and there's as much variety in amp design and component choice as there is in the world of guitar building. Makers today follow a wide range of topologies to suit players' needs: lower gain preamps coupled with tight, powerful output sections for big clean sounds with plenty of headroom; medium-gain preamps with vintage-style output designs that are easily pushed into crunchy, chunky distortion; multiple high-gain cascading preamp stages coupled with a firm but responsive output stage and master volume, for scorching leads and singing, near-infinite sustain.

At the heart of it all, however, lies a technology not much more complicated than that which produced great-sounding little combos like our tweed Deluxe some 50 years ago.

MARSHALL ARTS

In the early '60s, London music shop owner Jim Marshall saw an opportunity to build his own version of the Fender amps popular with British guitarists, but almost prohibitively expensive to acquire. Using a late '50s tweed Fender Bassman as a template (with initially only a few changes to account for more-easily available British components) he and colleagues Ken Bran and Dudley Craven gave birth to a rock legend. Following a handful of early prototypes the first proper production models arrived in 1963 (pictured above is a "sandwich front" '63 MKII JTM45). Other than the slight variables in components, which originally included the use of great Mullard preamp valves and GEC KT66 output valves, the main sonic distinction from their American-made inspiration was the speaker cabinet – a closed-back unit carrying four low-powered 12" Celestions rather than the four 10" Jensens in the Bassman's open-backed cab. This, as much as the amplifier itself, played a major part in the birth of the "British sound." As Marshall designs evolved they grew further and further from their Fender-inspired roots, though closed-back 4x12" speaker cabs remain a trademark.

'95 MATCHLESS T/C-30
Specifications: *two-channel class A all-tube combo; no negative feedback; cathode biased; 30W output; dual 10" speakers.*
Controls: *Ch1: volume, bass, treble; Ch2: volume, tone; shared: cut, master.*
Features: *all hand-wired circuit; one EF86 and three 12AX7 preamp tubes, four EL84s, one GZ34 rectifier; Celestion G10L-35 ceramic magnet speakers; half-power switch; individual effects loops; speaker phase switch.*

'99 CARVIN BELAIR 212
Specifications: *footswitchable two-channel class A/B all-tube combo; 50W output; dual 12" speakers.*
Controls: *Ch1: volume, bass, middle, treble; Ch2: gain, volume, bass, middle, treble; shared: reverb.*
Features: *printed circuit board (PCB); five 12AX7 preamp tubes, four EL84 power tubes, solid state rectification; two proprietary speakers; open-backed plywood cabinet and speaker baffle covered in reproduction tweed.*

'00 VOX AC30TBX REISSUE
Specifications: *three-channel class A all-tube combo; no negative feedback; cathode biased; 30W output; dual 12" speakers.*
Controls: *volume for each channel (vib-trem, normal, brilliant); shared EQ (treble, bass and cut); speed and vib-trem switch.*
Features: *PCB; top-mounted controls; five 12AX7 preamp tubes, four EL84s, one GZ34 rectifier; Celestion Alnico Blue speakers; open-backed plywood cab.*

'01 FENDER '65 SUPER REVERB REISSUE
Specifications: *two-channel class A/B all-tube combo; fixed bias; 45W output; four 10" speakers.*
Controls: *Normal ch: bright switch, volume, treble, bass; vibrato ch: bright switch, volume, treble, middle, bass, reverb, speed and intensity.*
Features: *PCB; four 12AX7s, two 12AT7s, two 6L6s, one 5AR4 rectifier tube; Jensen P10R alnico magnet speakers; tube reverb and vibrato.*

Belting out its gritty chime with anything from a Rickenbacker to a Gretsch at the input, a Vox AC30 has stood behind The Beatles, Tom Petty, and many, many more. On the other side of the tracks, Fender's Super Reverb is a classic blueser, favored by the likes of Buddy Guy and Stevie Ray Vaughan.

Like just about any field of technology, the amp world has always had its hot-rodders. Ever since tube amps were first commercially available, players and engineers alike have tinkered with and modified stock units to get more gain, better tone, more distortion, less distortion… whatever it takes to achieve that illusive sonic nirvana that rings in guitarists' heads.

For years most hot-rodding went on as after-market modification. Eager engineers took in standard amp models and adapted circuits and specs to convert them to fire-breathing superbeasts. Inevitably, however, a whole new breed was born –

As with taking your guitar on the road, it's important to give your amp the right protection if and when it is subjected to the rigors of touring. Flightcases are available in many standard sizes or custom-built to fit any combo or stack, and offer the best protection from the truck to the stage and back again.

a genre of small-run, often hand-built and sometimes custom-order "boutique" amps that sought to rise above the perfectly respectable but perhaps rather tame offerings of such mass manufacturers as Marshall and Fender.

In the late '60s and early '70s San Francisco amp tech Randall Smith started converting modest little 12W Fender Princeton amps into high-gain, 60W rock monsters for players on the scene who wanted a little more than most production amps of the day could offer. Smith's "cascading gain" circuit fed multiple tube preamp stages one into the other to create a hotter front end than any amp commercially available. The results were extreme overdrive sounds and ringing sustain of the sort only previously attained by maxing out a large power amp. An early conversion

THE FENDER YEARS
Leo Fender's amps were far from the first on the market, but their rugged build, workmanlike simplicity and impressive sound, combined with Fender's knack for discerning and fulfilling the needs of musicians, ensured that they were some of the best available from the very start. Compare Fender amps from as early as 1948 – when their construction quality really began to come into its own – with just about any other production model of the time and the superiority is clear. It's also obvious at a glance both inside and out why modern amps echo these early Fender designs more than they do those of any other 55-year-old combo. When you get it right first try, there's not a lot of room to evolve.

Remember: for Fender, the amp came first. While the K&F company and, later, Fender built a number of electric lap steel guitars in the '40s, the early amps were clearly a cut above their stringed partners. Check out the Fender catalog from 1949, for example, and familiar combo models like the Pro, Super (above), Deluxe, Princeton and Champion are already available, still 12 months before the first production solidbody electric guitar (Fender's first "standard" guitar of any type) was listed for sale.

While makers like Supro, Gibson, National, Premier, Rickenbacker, Gretsch and Ampeg brought us a great amp or two – some before Fender even existed – Leo's successive series of amps have arguably launched more classic models than any other brand.

'00 MESA RECT-O-VERB
Specifications: *footswitchable two-channel class A/B all-tube combo; 100W output; dual 12" speakers.*
Controls: *separate gain, master, bass, mid, treble, reverb and presence controls and voicing switch for each channel; dual shared output controls.*
Features: *PCB; five 12AX7 preamp tubes, four EL34s or 6L6s (with switchable bias), two 5AR4 rectifiers; Celestion Vintage 30 speakers; half-open-backed plywood cabinet.*

'01 VHT PITTBULL FIFTY/CL
Specifications: *footswitchable two-channel all-tube combo with switchable class A/class A/B; 50W output; 2x12".*
Controls: *Ch1: gain, volume, treble, middle, bass; Ch2: volume, treble, middle, bass; boost, shift and bright pushbuttons for each; shared: reverb, graphic EQ.*
Features: *PCB; four 12AX7 and one EF86 preamp tubes, two EL34s or 6L6s (with switchable bias), 5AR4 rectifier; Eminence speakers; plywood cabinet.*

In addition to revealing more controls than the front panels of many standard amps, a rear view of the Mesa R-O-V displays those dual rectifier tubes.

hotrod combos

hotrod combos

job tested by Carlos Santana elicited the comment, "Man, that little amp really boogies!" The rest is history.

As used Princetons got harder to find, Smith started building his own amps from scratch, selling by direct order right from the workshop. In just a few years, Mesa/Boogie became one of the most heavily pro-endorsed lines in the rock world. Progressing through the famous Mark I to Mark IV lines of mostly 1x12" 60W and 100W combos and heads to the Dual and Triple Rectifier arena-blasters of today, Mesa/Boogie remains the first and prime culmination of an amp fanatic's quest for more. Now manufactured in the sort of mass volume that lifts it out of the boutique category – using printed circuit boards for consistency and expediency – Mesa/Boogie nevertheless remains at the front of a line of custom-style production builders.

Plenty of other designers have chased the mega-gain dream, and many have become well-known mass-manufactured makers in their own right, even if elevated prices sometimes mean ordinary players rarely get their hands on these amps. Today, fellow Californians like Soldano, VHT, Rivera (run by former Fender designer Paul Rivera) and Budda all offer imposing tube amps with more fire and fury than any rock guitar hero of the early '70s could have imagined. Then there's the creamy, lush drive tones of George Dumble's high-end creations, which were around before Mesa/Boogie but have remained ultra-rare thanks to high costs and low production numbers.

Not all the visionaries are pursuing the ultimate overdrive. Matchless, Bad Cat, Dr Z, Trainwreck, and the many vintage Fender repro guys (THD, Victoria, Kendrick and Clark among them) have crafted their appreciation of simpler vintage designs by Vox, Marshall and Fender into lushly toneful and often stunningly over-engineered homages to the classics. As ever, such quality comes at a price (though many of the tweed Fender-style reproductions are impressively good value), but these builders' work genuinely approaches high art in the amp field.

Not surprisingly, all of the big boys now do their own hotrods. Peavey's Van Halen signature amp is the 5150; Carvin's Steve Vai

MAN VS. MACHINE
Arguments continue to rage about the virtues of hand-wired circuits (as in this vintage Vox AC15, above right) versus more affordable printed circuit board (PCB) construction. Many connoisseurs insist a hand-wired amp will sound better every time, but the difference might be beyond the average guitarist's ability to discern – and, in fairness, could also be down to variations in components and specs. There's no doubt whatsoever that many of the very best guitar amps built today are assembled by hand and individually tuned by artisans at the top of their trade; so it goes with most any craft. Many excellent amplifiers are also built using PCBs, however, which offer greater consistency of performance and better affordability than hand-building could ever hope to achieve.

signature is the Legacy model; Marshall has its Triple Super Lead series; and Fender the flexible, high-gain Prosonic model. All are recent incarnations of these major makers' adaptations of modifications which independent custom builders first applied to some of Fender and Marshall's own basic designs.

Echoing a similar what-goes-around-comes-around philosophy but from a different tack, in the late '80s and early '90s many major manufacturers eventually spotted the popularity so many classic, non-master-volume models had attained – along with the success of the boutique reproduction builders – and released their own "vintage reissue" models. Along came amps such as a more vintage-correct Vox AC30 TBX, Marshall's JTM45 and Bluesbreaker combo, and Fender's tweed '59 Bassman, '65 Twin Reverb, '65 Deluxe Reverb and '65 Super Reverb. They all display that the big corporations are again catching up to players' desires... eventually.

'01 SOLDANO LUCKY 13
Specifications: *footswitchable two-channel class A/B all-tube combo; fixed bias; 50W output; dual 12" speakers.*
Controls: *Ch1: bright switch, volume, bass, middle, treble, reverb; Ch2: gain, bass, middle, treble, reverb, volume; shared: presence.*
Features: *PCB; six 12AX7 preamp tubes, two 6L6s; solid-state rectification; front-mounted Eminence Legend speakers; open-backed plywood cabinet and baffle.*

'99 MARSHALL JCM2000 TSL602
Specifications: *footswitchable three-channel all-tube class A/B combo; 60W output; dual 12" speakers.*
Controls: *Ch1: volume, treble, middle, bass; Chs2/3: shared treble, middle, bass with independent gain and volume; shared presence, master and reverb; effects loop mix control.*
Features: *PCB; four 12AX7s and two EL34s; solid-state rectification; Celestion speakers.*

'01 RIVERA QUIANA
Specifications: *footswitchable two-channel all-tube class A/B combo; fixed bias; 55W output; dual 12" speakers.*
Controls: *dual channels with individual gain, bass, middle, treble, volume and footswitchable boost; shared reverb, presence and focus (resonance).*
Features: *PCB; five 12AX7 preamp tubes, two 6L6s; solid state rectification; vintage/modern (high/low power) switching; Celestion Vintage 30 speakers; plywood cabinet.*

CLASSIC SPEAKERS
A: Celestion Alnico Blue. *The British speaker giant's reissue of their 15W alnico-magnet 'Blue Bulldog' which appeared in classic Vox amps.*
B: Celestion G12H-30. *Reissue of the 'heavy magnet' ceramic driver that powered classic '70s 4x12" cabs.*
C: Jensen P12R. *Reissue of the alnico-magnet Jensen 12" as featured in countless '50s Fenders and Gibsons.*
D: JBL D-120F. *Vintage driver known for piercing highs, fat mids, tight lows.*

Eric Clapton helped put Soldano on the map when he used an SLO-100 for his appearance on the TV show *Saturday Night Live*.

While non-American six-strings barely figure in the early history of the electric guitar, rockers from the other side of the pond were getting one thing right from the very start. British amps rival any in the world for quality, power and sound – and for heavy rock in particular, the Brits set the standards for others to follow.

Removing the otherwise closed back from this contemporary Marshall 4x12" cabinet reveals the four reissue Celestion "Greenbacks" that give it plenty of bottom-end oomph, with juicy, crunchy mids.

The "Brit sound" remains a rock byword, defined by sweetly compressed and saturated drive tones with punchy, often crunchy mids and gut-slugging lows. Although Fender had introduced its radical new piggyback rigs (an amp head atop a separate speaker cabinet) in 1960, before any other large-production manufacturer, we still credit British builders with inventing the "stack" – the high-powered arena-rock head with one or two large speaker cabs, classically 4x12"s. If one setup defines this so-called British sound it's probably a late-'60s 100W Marshall "plexi" Super Lead head and closed-back, slant-front

cab with four 12" Celestion Greenback speakers. But there are many more variations in classic English amplification than any single catchphrase can sum up.

For many players Britain's greatest success – and tone heaven – is contained in one short word: Vox. Organ manufacturer Tom Jennings entered rock'n'roll history in 1956 when he employed designer Dick Denney to mastermind the company's first combo aimed at guitarists, the AC15. Vox lays claim to being the first manufacturer to design an amp circuit from the ground up with electric guitar specifically in mind. Others had been marketed for guitar for years, adapted from such general applications of amplification as broadcasting, PA, and radio, or developed from early lap-steel amps.

As the rock'n'roll craze escalated in Great Britain and bands performed in bigger and bigger venues, Jennings heeded the call for more volume and put Denny on the case again. In 1959 the resulting combo hit stages across the UK – and soon the world – in the form of the AC30 (pictured in reissue form on p45). Undoubtedly one of the finest amps of all time, it used four archetypically British-sounding EL84 output tubes in a class A circuit to pump about 30 Watts through a pair of alnico-magnet Celestion G12 speakers. Today's reissues again follow much the same formula.

If 30W doesn't sound like a lot of power, a quick blast through a good AC30 will show you how much volume these amps can put out. Even so, the quest for more power continued, and when Jim Marshall adapted Fender's Bassman circuit for his JTM45 in the early '60s (see *Marshall Arts*, p45) he addressed the demand

'01 MARSHALL JCM2000 TSL100
Specifications: *footswitchable three-channel all-tube class A/B head; fixed bias; 100W output.*
Controls: *individual gain, volume, bass, middle and treble controls for each channel; individual reverb, presence, FX mix and mid-boost for clean (shared by crunch and lead).*
Features: *PCB; four 12AX7s and four EL34s; solid-state rectification.*

'82 HIWATT LEAD 100 HEAD
Specifications: *footswitchable two-channel all-tube class A/B head; fixed bias; 100W output.*
Controls: *Ch1: volume, treble, bass; Ch2: gain, volume, middle, treble, bass; shared and master volume.*
Features: *hand-wired circuit on tag strips; four 12AX7 preamp tubes and four EL34 power tubes; solid-state rectification.*

From the "crank it and play" non-master-volume simplicity of their '60s JTM45 (main photo, far left) to three-channel rock wonders like the TSL100 (left), Marshall has evolved by keeping with contemporary hotrods.

for volume and projection head-on. If the popular big-amp speaker formats of two 12s, four 10s or a 15 alone or in pairs still didn't cut it with the day's generally lower-power drivers, why not just keep going? For one, because it makes an unwieldy rig for the average gigging musician without a roadie.

But Marshall's monster 4x12" enclosures with closed backs for improved damping of low powered speakers and tighter lows all round helped usher in a new era in rock firepower. Like to crank your 100-watter to the max? Stick two cabs under it. Got an arena date on the tour? Daisy-chain four full stacks for 400W of music power through 32 12" speakers. From the late '60s the stack was king, a genuine necessity on the big stage until vast improvements in PA systems arrived in the mid '70s. But the "wall of Marshalls" remains the hallmark of a real rock guitar hero.

Not that a "Marshall" has to be a Marshall, in a manner of speaking. The huge-sounding, crunch-of-doom Hiwatt Custom 100s that Pete Townshend made famous, the robust Sound City heads, the funky Orange amps (particularly the 120 Overdrive) of the early '70s, and the big Laneys adopted by Black Sabbath's Tony Iommi and other metal players all belted their own version of the British sound from stages around the world. US makers like Ampeg, Randall, Acoustic, Sunn, Music Man and indeed Fender offered up their own popular mega-watt rigs to the stadium rockers through the '70s and '80s. Meanwhile, most big names and specialists alike offered solid-state alternatives, too.

Like other formats, the stack has evolved considerably, and today many examples couple all the high-gain and channel-switching features of the hotrod combo with ever-more-efficient output sections. Super-deluxe models like Mesa's three-channel,

SPEAKER CABINETS

Even the design of a speaker cabinet and the type of drivers it contains will affect the sound your amp produces. Open-backed cabinets accentuate the higher frequencies, with a wider, more "surround-sound" type of dispersion. Closed-backed cabs keep the low end tight and full, with more directional sound projection. Of course, the more speakers a cab carries, the more air it will move and the greater the perceived volume – although the power output from the amp remains the same however many speakers it is driving, with each unit dividing the wattage equally. Speaker size also influences tone. Those 10s have a faster response with super-articulate highs, but still good low-end reproduction when used in multiple numbers, while 12s typically have a wider, more open low-end and full-throated midrange.

150W Triple Rectifier Solo Head are flagships of the field, while major names like Peavey, Marshall and Carvin have similarly put some of their best engineering into high-powered, pro-standard stacks with creative tone-shaping options and instant footswitchability. And even if you don't really need a full stack to get your music across… hey, it still looks great up on stage.

'80s ORANGE OVERDRIVE SERIES TWO HEAD	**'66 VOX SUPER BEATLE HEAD & 4x12" CAB WITH HORNS**	**'01 MESA TRIPLE RECTIFIER SOLO HEAD & 4x12" CAB**	**'00 CARVIN STEVE VAI LEGACY HEAD & 4x12" CAB**
Specifications: *single-channel all-tube class A/B head; fixed bias; 120W output.*	**Specifications:** *three-channel solid state head with footswitchable effects; 120W output.*	**Specifications:** *footswitchable three-channel class A/B all-tube head; 150W output; four 12" speakers.*	**Specifications:** *footswitchable two-channel all-tube class A/B head; fixed bias; 100W output; four 12" speakers.*
Controls: *single channel with volume, bass, treble, presence, contour and master volume.*	**Controls:** *Ch1: volume, treble, bass; Ch2: volume, treble, bass; Ch3: volume and tone; shared: fuzz, MRB (wah-like mid frequency shift) and reverb.*	**Controls:** *separate gain, master, bass, mid, treble, reverb and presence controls and voicing switch for each channel; dual shared output controls.*	**Controls:** *Ch1: volume, treble, mid, bass, presence; Ch2: gain, volume, treble, mid, bass, presence; shared master and reverb.*
Features: *hand-wired circuit on tag strips; four 12AX7 preamp tubes and four EL34 power tubes; solid-state rectification; characteristic orange vinyl covering.*	**Features:** *field effect transistors (FET) on PCB circuit construction; cabinet contains four 12" Vox Bulldog speakers plus two high-frequency horns.*	**Features:** *PCB; five 12AX7 preamp tubes, six EL34s or 6L6s (with switchable bias), three 5AR4 rectifiers. Cab has four Celestion Vintage 30s.*	**Features:** *PCB; five 12AX7s and four EL34s or 6L6s (with switchable bias); solid-state rectification; Celestion speakers in closed-back plywood cab.*

London-based Orange captured an appropriately groovy vibe to launch its amp range at the end of the '60s, and perpetuated it through some lean times to make a comeback in recent years – still as bright as ever.

Around back: six output tubes, three rectifiers… *plus* preamp!

Heavy rockers – including Metallica's Kirk Hammett and James Hetfield – have made the big Mesa/Boogies the byword in rock power. The similarly high-gain Carvin Legacy was developed to shredder Steve Vai's specifications.

A lot of space in this chapter has already been devoted to extolling the virtues of tubes. But good solid-state amps definitely have their fans and their applications, and a player on a tight budget can certainly get a lot more bells and whistles on a new amp by going transistorized. While the components required to build any tube amp are relatively costly by mass-marketing standards, transistors designed to perform similar functions can be had for pennies – and the savings in basic circuitry construction often translate into an abundance of bonus features for the same retail price: clean/overdrive channel switching, reverb and maybe some other onboard effects, headphone outs, recording DIs and more.

Even more importantly, the sound quality of more affordable solid-state amps has improved dramatically over the years, with some models – to many ears – running hard-fought A/B comparison tests against the tube amps they still generally seek to emulate. A breed that was largely received as tonally deadweight upon its first widespread introduction to the market in the mid '60s has evolved into a viable playing option, to the credit of R&D teams everywhere.

There were some notable solid-state amps right from the start, and of course some maverick engineers throughout the history of this variety have put time, effort and expense into designing great transistor-based models which are simply excellent guitar amps in their own right, regardless of cost. Models by Standel, Kustom, Polytone, Pignose and – a little later – Roland, Award-Session and Randall have all had their big-name followers.

In recent years even some of the legendary names in tube amps have made great leaps in solid-state development. The models in Marshall's AVT line do carry a lone preamp tube – placing them in a genre generally referred to as "hybrid" – but are for all intents and purposes 90 per cent solid state – and fierce sounding rock amps they are. Fender's Dyna-Touch series

of all-solid-state models is a world away tonally speaking from their efforts of decades past, and even the popular, workmanlike Peavey Bandit has evolved considerably.

It's also important to note that there are certain styles of music to which solid state amps are even considered by some to be better suited, where the low-end tightness and/or cleanness at – often – the massive volume required would be difficult to achieve from all but the most expensive and meticulously over-engineered tube amps.

Odd bedfellows perhaps, but thrash metal axemen and jazz players often choose solid state: the former because of the massive bottom end, fast response, tight punch and lack of spongy "squash" in big tranny amps by makers such as Randall; the latter mainly because of the successful way in which a couple of great models like the Polytone Brute and Roland Jazz Chorus addressed jazzmen's tonal needs right from the start.

The '90s saw a proliferation of hybrid amps carrying a single preamp tube, occasionally a pair, in a bid to bring "real tube tone" – as the advertising team frequently phrases it – to players on a low to medium budget. It's worth being aware that in some amps these tubes are fully functional components, but in others they're mainly there as a marketing tool to lure less-informed buyers who've been told they simply must have a tube amp. In any case, one lonely 12AX7 can't perform all the preamp functions in an amp of this format, so at best such preamps are still 50 to 75 per cent solid-state. At the most cynical end of the genre, "hybrid" amps are functionally solid-state and the tube is just injected with enough voltage to make it glow.

It's also worth noting that many tube freaks argue vehemently that the bulk of any great tone is generated in the output stage, not the preamp. Unsurprisingly, however, adding a single tube to an otherwise solid state preamp and power amp is a lot cheaper than linking a solid-state preamp to an all-tube output stage.

'00 MARSHALL VALVESTATE 2000 AVT50
Specifications: *footswitchable two-channel 'hybrid' combo; 50W output; single 12" speaker.*
Controls: *Ch1: gain, volume, bass, treble; Ch2: gain, volume, bass, middle, treble; shared: reverb depth.*
Features: *transistorized PCB construction with single 12AX7 tube in the preamp, all solid state power amp; CD input; headphone output; closed-back cab with Celestion speaker.*

'01 ROLAND JC-120 JAZZ CHORUS
Specifications: *footswitchable two-channel solid-state combo; 120W stereo output (60W per side); two 12" speakers.*
Controls: *Ch1: volume, treble, middle, bass, bright switch; Ch2: volume, treble, middle, bass, bright switch, distortion, reverb, vibrato speed and depth, chorus/vibrato switch.*
Features: *all-solid-state circuit on PCB; 'riveted' cabinet edge.*

A favorite of jazzers, the Roland JC-120 also helped define the punk-pop sound at the hands of Bob Mould (Hüsker Dü, Sugar, solo artist), who cranked his Strat through two of the big, clean 120-watters paired with two Rivera-era Fender Concerts.

solid state

SOLID ROCK

Solid-state amplifiers use transistors rather than tubes to amplify a sound source. Almost every other type of amplifier in the home today – hi-fi, television, clock radio, active PC monitor speakers – uses transistors in roughly the same way. In its raw form, this technology doesn't flatter the electric guitar. In early transistor amps, engineers virtually replaced tubes with discreet solid state components in circuits that, broadly speaking, weren't radically different in their function from the tube-loaded designs. Advertisements touted "better reliability" and "no tubes to replace." The amps worked, certainly, but players with a taste for tonal subtleties quickly gave them the cold shoulder. To be fair, though, some of these early solid-state models built with particular attention to detail are great-sounding amps in their own right, have occasionally been favored by major players, and have provided the voice for a good few classic guitar recordings over the years.

With the tube guitar amp's lasting appeal widely confirmed, many big builders continued to pursue solid state lines not so much because they were more reliable, but because they were considerably cheaper to build.

As with everything in consumer electronics, however, the transistors used in guitar amps have become vastly better, smaller and cheaper over the past 30 years. They can now pack a multiplicity of functions into a single integrated circuit chip to do the work achieved by a Super Beatle-sized head cabinetful of FET electronics in the '60s. The size and affordability, as well as the skill of the engineers, means builders can squeeze in circuitry to shape and filter the signal to more closely mimic the sound of a tube amp.

The fact that solid-state amps don't require costly (and heavy) output transformers and can run off less-extreme high voltages than tube amps also makes them cheaper and simpler to build, and easier to keep within an appealingly budget-minded price range.

Though the tube amp was and is king with the majority of guitar heroes, plenty of major names have played through solid state models down the years – both vintage and modern. This 70W 1966 Vox Conqueror, for example, was believed to have been a temporary choice of The Beatles around the time of the recording sessions for the *Sgt Pepper* LP.

Interestingly, in building some of the first widely available hybrid amps in the mid-'70s, Music Man did just that. Deciding that the output tubes were crucial to the feel, sound and response of a good guitar amp, while a tranny preamp could do the job perfectly well, they reversed the current trend, resulting in a line which drew endorsements from the likes of Eric Clapton and Steve Miller.

When you go shopping for an amp, the best advice is to seek out the model that sounds best to you and carries the features you desire for the amount of cash you have to spend. Ultimately, let your ears decide – and if an all-solid-state amp sounds perfectly good, don't be swayed to spend a little more for a "hybrid" carrying a lonely 12AX7 simply because someone's told you there ain't no mojo without a glowing glass bottle under the hood. And putting the word "tube" or "valve" in the model name without using the real thing anywhere in the circuit does not a tube amp make.

'79 PIGNOSE
Specifications: *solid-state practise and recording amp; 3W output (5W peak); single 5" speaker. Powered by six AA 'pen light' batteries or dedicated AC/DC adaptor.*
Controls: *volume with integral on/off switch; single input.*
Features: *brown vinyl covered cabinet is hinged for battery replacement.*

'01 PEAVEY BANDIT II
Specifications: *footswitchable two-channel solid-state combo; 80W output into 8Ω (100W into 4Ω); single 12" speaker.*
Controls: *Ch1: volume, low, mid, high, modern/vintage voicing switch; Ch2: pre-gain, low, mid, high, post-gain, high-gain/modern/vintage voicing switch; shared: reverb, presence, dynamics.*
Features: *all solid-state circuit on PCB; Peavey Sheffield speaker.*

'00 FENDER DELUXE 90
Specifications: *footswitchable two-channel solid-state combo; 90W output; single 12" speaker.*
Controls: *Ch1: volume, treble, mid, bass; Ch2: drive, volume, more drive switch, treble, mid, bass; shared: reverb.*
Features: *Dyna-Touch Series solid-state circuit on PCB; open-backed plywood cabinet and ply baffle; Celestion G12T-100 speaker.*

'02 RANDALL DIMEBAG DARRELL WARHEAD STACK
Specifications: *footswitchable two-channel high-gain solid-state head; 300W stereo output; four 12" and two 15" speakers.*
Controls: *individual three-band active EQ, gain and volume controls; shared 9-band graphic EQ and 14 presets for 16 digital effects.*
Features: *closed-backed speaker cabinets with Celestion Greenbacks (top cab) and 15" Jaguars (bottom cab).*

The ability to get 'good'n dirty' at low volumes has made the wee 3W Pignose a recording favorite since the '70s.

Sometimes solid-state is the only way to go for the huge-and-tight bottom end that thrash-metal players demand – as Pantera's Dimebag Darrell proves in spades with his Randall Warhead stacks, right.

modeling amps

AMPS DU JOUR

The heart of any digital amp is its model "menu," the list of emulations of classic amplifiers which it is able to conjure up. Whoever the manufacturer – Johnson, Crate, Peavey, Fender, or Line 6 (who make the Flextone II shown in close-up below) – the legends ringed around the amp selection control are often thinly veiled codenames denoting great vintage or modern tubesters, and aren't usually too tricky to figure out. For example, "Small Tweed" or "Studio Tweed" usually denotes a '50s Fender Champ or Deluxe, while "Big Tweed" or "Blues Tweed" invariably means a Bassman. Others include:

"Brit Class A" = Vox AC30
"Modern Class A" or "Boutique Class A" = Matchless D/C-30
"Brit blues" = Marshall JTM45 Bluesbreaker
"Recto" or "Rectified" = Mesa Dual Rectifier
"Modern High Gain" = Soldano SLO

STUDIO SMARTS

A good workman selects the right tool for the job. Where guitar amplifiers are concerned, performing live and recording in the studio can be very different jobs indeed. It can be a risky venture to purchase a particular make of amplifier primarily because you like the sound of a certain famous guitarist and have been told it's the amp he uses. Are you blown away by Jimmy Page's sound on *Led Zeppelin II* and looking to acquire just the right mega-stack after seeing him wail away in front of a wall of 4x12s on *The Song Remains The Same*? Think again: legend has it Mr Page recorded most of the first two Zep albums through a diminutive Supro combo (using his '58 Tele, as it happens, not a Les Paul). Busily rigging up high-gain heads in search of an enormous grunge sound? You'll be interested to know that Kurt Cobain recorded most of Nirvana's *Nevermind* album on a 22W Mesa/Boogie Studio 22 and a 30W Vox AC30.

The thing to remember is that most amps sound their best when set to within a very narrow "sweet spot," which usually occurs at or past halfway up on the volume control. Try that with a 100W Marshall Plexi in most studios today and it's just too loud for the room – or the mikes – to handle. Set your Fender Pro Junior to 8, however, with the right mike placed in just the right place in front of its 10" speaker, and the tone on tape might be as huge as you'd hoped for from your half-stack, without deafening the engineer into the bargain.

Big amps played at lower volumes often sound dull, flat and lifeless. Crank them up until they sound good, then trap them inside a too-small room, or record them using poor technique or a mike that can't handle the sound pressure levels, and you might get ragged, harsh results. Your precious 100-watter ends up a blur in the mix, or it swamps the other instruments fighting for a place in the frequency spectrum.

A growing number of artists are finding a use for digital modelers in the studio, too, using DI products such as Line 6's POD. Where to some ears digital amps may still sound a little "cold" in the real world, once placed in the track – which more often than not, after all, is digital anyway – many amp emulations provide another solution to the trick of miking and recording a large, raging amp in a small studio space.

Born out of more hours in the R&D lab than any guitar tool which has come before, the modeling amp is neither tube (though some employ one or two) nor solid-state as we have commonly come to know it. This is a third breed. Rather than being engineered to present a sound of its own, it has been designed to mimic many of the best-loved tube amps of all time. This, then, is the paradox at the heart of the digital amp movement: a truly computer-age product claiming to be the way forward, but only acceptable to its own marketplace so long as it successfully emulates the technologically-archaic designs which have gone before.

Pioneered by the likes of Line 6 and Johnson, later taken up – and given further acceptability – by Fender, Peavey, Crate and others, modeling amps are mainly based on the same sorts of digital signal processing that allows a multi-FX unit to mimic a spring reverb and a tape echo, or a keyboard to hop between a Hammond B-3 organ and a Rhodes piano at the push of a button. By digitally mapping the parameters of a great tube amp's sound and performance, designers of the better modeling amps have gone to great lengths to program in not only the basic tones of the classics, but to emulate things like their playing feel, response to pick attack, and EQ quirks.

Though it generally looks like a modern but traditional guitar combo, a digital amp's very format approaches signal reproduction in an entirely different way, right down to the choice of speaker. Rather than being the final link in the tone-coloration chain as in many tube or tranny amps, the speaker functions in a context more akin to a speaker in the hi-fi world. It is there to accurately project the full sound of the amp itself, which in most cases already includes the appropriate speaker emulation to suit the amp model selected.

There's no doubt that digital amps can sound pretty incredible. Most experienced reviewers continue to agree that even the best few sounds in any make's emulation menu still don't quite capture the nuances of the real thing. But digital amp designers are pushing the envelope all the time and certainly many players would have trouble distinguishing the model from its inspiration in

---

'02 LINE 6 VETTA
Specifications: *footswitchable multi-channel digital modeling combo; 100W output (optional mono/stereo); dual 12" speakers.*
Controls: *too numerous to mention: includes full array of buttons and controls for programming and preset selection.*
Features: *45 amp models; 28 cab models; 64 factory and 64 user presets; numerous onboard 'stomp' and digital effects; DI facilities.*

'01 CRATE DXJ112
Specifications: *footswitchable multi-channel digital modeling combo; 60W output (mono cab, stereo headphone and line out); single 12" speaker.*
Controls: *master output, amp selector, gain, bass, mid, treble, channel level, effects selector, effect adjust, reverb level and depth, plus keypad.*
Features: *16 amp models; 8 digital effects; DI facilities; headphone out; footswitchable presets; MIDI sync; Eminence speaker.*

Line 6's broad palette of tones has already lured a diverse following, from country picker Pete Anderson to rocker Art Alexakis of Everclear.

a number of cases, a verdict upheld by the ever-growing lists of pro endorsements for digital modeling amplifiers.

Even more impressive for the average buyer than the virtue of any individual emulation is the sheer number of amp tones which most digital makes now offer. While players happy with just a few variations on the one good sound or professionals who can afford a large collection of vintage amps are still likely to turn to the real thing, the modeling amp presents an incredible sonic playground to the average Joe who couldn't hope to ever own a '62 Vox AC30, a '68 Marshall Plexi, a '59 Fender Bassman, an '83 Mesa/Boogie MkIIC, and a Matchless D/C-30... or to get them all into the trunk of his Ford.

And there's that paradox again. By including amps like the above and many others on its emulation menu (the true identities of which are often thinly disguised on the control panel rotary selector – see *Amps Du Jour*) the new breed continues time and again to re-confirm just how much we love the old. But so it goes with much in the guitar world. The basic tonal templates for rock, blues and country were laid some 50 years ago, and we as players don't often want sounds that are new and original, but yearn for sounds that take us somewhere close to the heroes that have gone before. The point is, of course, that most guitarists simply don't want their new Digitone Space-O-Matic to sound like a Digitone Space-O-Matic. They want it to sound like a '65 Twin Reverb, a '68 Plexi, a '57 tweed Deluxe and a Soldano SLO – all within the same song, at the tap of a footswitch.

The resurgence in acoustic gigs has brought us another new breed of amplifier. In the early days of large-venue acoustic performance it took a skilled live sound engineer to mike up a guitar in a way that would keep it sounding natural but powerful, while still minimizing feedback. As soundhole and under-saddle piezo pickups improved, life for the small-club troubadour became easier, and it was often enough just to inject the guitar straight into the PA or – preferably through a dedicated acoustic preamp – into a standard guitar amp. Neither tended to render particularly pleasing sonic results (generally sounding rather dead and muted on one hand, or tinny and lacking any punch on the other) but they were an easier option than miking-up for the novice soundman.

The unplugged music revolution of the early '90s changed the scene dramatically: if so many players wanted to perform acoustically, they might as well sound acoustic. A new amp market had been clearly defined, and the manufacturers eagerly hopped to it.

In crude terms, acoustic guitar combos lean more toward hi-fi design than they do toward the traditional electron-tube-based electric guitar amp. Firstly, on the electronics side, they seek to reproduce as realistically as possible the natural sound of the acoustic guitar plugged into them, rather than coloring, warming and distorting the signal as most guitar amps do. Secondly, on the speaker side, the drivers – rather than adding their own further coloration – aim to transfer the signal with accuracy and high fidelity into the moving air which the human ear perceives as sound (much as with the modeling amps discussed earlier).

This approach has somewhat more in common with bass amp design than it does with building amplifiers for six-string electrics. Unsurprisingly, great bass amp builders like Trace Elliot, SWR, Ashdown and others have introduced some impressive models for acoustic, with deserved success. Creative features like dual active and low-impedance channels, XLR inputs, mid notches and feedback filters have set new standards of tone shaping for acoustics, and secured a lasting place for the genre in the player's arsenal.

Many big manufacturers have made forays into the field, with some worthy offerings from most. The achievements of Marshall's AS50R and AS100D and Fender's Acoustasonic line prove neither was content to merely re-badge a tranny practise amp – as some ultra-budget models from occasional B-list makers have certainly done. On one hand, the acoustic amp now seems yet another piece of kit the cash-strapped player feels pressured to buy; on the other, if an acoustic is your main tool of choice, you'll want and need an amp that does it justice.

'01 FENDER CYBER-TWIN
Specifications: *footswitchable multi-channel digital modeling combo with tube preamp; 130W output (optional mono/stereo); dual 12" speakers.*
Controls: *trim, gain, volume, treble, middle, bass, presence, reverb, master; pushbuttons for programming; rotary model selector.*
Features: *35 amp models; 85 factory and 85 user presets; 28 effects types; DI facilities; stereo headphone outs; motorized main amp controls.*

'98 TRACE ACOUSTIC TA200S
Specifications: *three-channel solid-state acoustic combo; 200W output; eight 5" speakers.*
Controls: *individual gain and EQ for each channel (piezo/low-level, active/high-level, balanced XLR); shared: master volume, shape and notch; controls for 16-bit digital effects and reverb (footswitchable).*
Features: *balanced DI; phantom power for XLR mike input; link/line out; effects send and returns.*

'99 ASHDOWN RADIATOR 2
Specifications: *two-channel hybrid tube/solid-state acoustic combo; 120W output; 8" speaker and dual tweeters.*
Controls: *Ch1: phase switch, input level, seven-band EQ (on rotaries and sliders), mid feedback, reverb; Ch2: phase switch, input level, tube drive, seven-band EQ, low feedback, reverb; shared: reverb type, output level.*
Features: *XLR, piezo and active inputs; XSL DI out; solid cherry hardwood cabinet.*

'99 SWR STRAWBERRY BLONDE
Specifications: *single-channel solid-state acoustic combo; 80W output; single 10" speaker and piezo tweeter.*
Controls: *gain, master volume, aural enhancer, bass, midrange, treble, effects blend, reverb.*
Features: *balanced XLR out; spring reverb; parallel effects loop; strawberry red control panel; blonde Tolex-covered cabinet.*

Ever since the magnetic pickup was first mounted on a guitar, electronics designers have sought ways to enhance, augment and affect the signal from the source. The very first "effects" were often integrated into the amplifier itself, although the Rocco Company, owned by Epiphone, manufactured stand-alone units in the 1930s. Guitar effects pedals as we know them, however, really date from the early '60s.

Two very popular effects – reverb and tremolo – were included within many amps' electronics from the 1950s. Compared to modern IC-chip-loaded units these and other early effects employed relatively bulky circuitry and often mechanical devices and even moving parts to enable them to manipulate the sound of an electric guitar or other amplified instrument. The Leslie rotating speaker cabinet (originally built for use with the Hammond organ) was an early attempt at a chorus effect – and sonically very successful, if extremely cumbersome – while the first echo units employed moving loops of recording tape. They were complicated, but sounded quite fantastic. Great guitarists throughout the ages have utilised these tools with stunning effect. Imagine Jimi Hendrix without fuzz, The Edge without delay, Scotty Moore or Dick Dale without reverb. Without effects, these players' trademark sounds would be hugely different.

A lot of early experiments with effects can be traced back to Les Paul himself who, innovator that he was, created some of the sounds we take for granted today. He built a delay unit, for example, by linking a pair of tape recorders together and recording the signal from the guitar back and forth between the machines to achieve a repeating echo effect.

Guitar pedals perform a vast array of sonic functions; this chapter will outline many of the most popular, along with some quirky options. The possibilities that can be created by using and combining effects are almost endless. Although pedals can be broadly cast into the categories defined here, the fact that each manufacturer uses different components means that few units sound identical. So an Ibanez and, say, an MXR phaser certainly do sound different, with their own quirks and tonal characteristics.

DISTORTION PEDALS
1. *Maestro FuzzTone,* **2.** *Colorsound Tonebender,* **3.** *Electro-Harmonix Big Muff Pi,* **4.** *Ibanez Overdrive,* **5.** *Ibanez TS808 Tube Screamer,* **6.** *Ibanez TS9 Tube Screamer. Opposite page: Dallas/Arbiter Fuzz Face and Boss OD-1.*

COMPRESSORS
1. *MXR Dynacomp,* **2.** *Ross Compressor,* **3.** *Marshall ED-1 Edward The Compressor.*

CHORUSES
1. *Boss CE-1 Chorus Ensemble,* **2.** *Boss CE-2 Chorus. Following page: Uni-Vibe.*

PHASERS
1. *Early issue Electro-Harmonix Small Stone and (***2.***) later issue Electro-Harmonix Small Stone,* **3.** *MXR Phase 45, Phase 90 (***4***) and Phase 100 (***5***).*

FLANGERS
1. *Electro-Harmonix Electric Mistress,* **2.** *Electro-Harmonix Deluxe Electric Mistress,* **3.** *Ibanez FL-305 Flanger,* **4.** *MXR Flanger,* **5.** *Ibanez FL-301 DX Flanger,* **6.** *Ibanez FL-303 Flanger.*

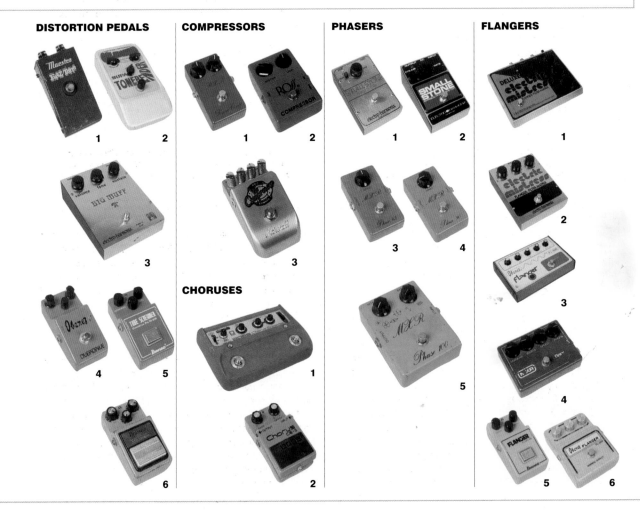

DISTORTION PEDALS

1 2
3
4 5
6

COMPRESSORS

1 2
3

CHORUSES

1
2

PHASERS

1 2
3 4
5

FLANGERS

1
2
3
4
5 6

classic pedals

The way the guitar's signal can be "effected" can be divided roughly into five categories.

BOOST AND DISTORTION EFFECTS

These overdrive your amp through use of a boosting circuit, or add fuzz or distortion to the sound, without affecting pitch. In the beginning guitarists turned their amps up full to get tube distortion. When it became apparent this wasn't enough – or required oppressively loud volume levels – creative engineers developed fuzz and distortion pedals, and the guitar world was never the same again. There have probably been more fuzz and distortion pedals produced than all other pedals combined.

The Maestro Fuzztone, manufactured by Gibson, was arguably the first commercially produced fuzz guitar pedal, although the Sola Sound Tonebender Fuzz was also introduced at around this time. The Fuzztone is reportedly the unit Keith Richards used to create the guitar sound for the famous riff on The Stones' 'Satisfaction'. The example pictured opposite is also interesting in having a Gibson "Patent Applied For" sticker on its base. These, of course, are more usually found on Gibson's first humbucking pickups. The Fuzztone has two controls, one for Volume and one for Attack. The Attack control varies the amount of distortion while Volume controls the volume level of the pedal when it is activated. This unit creates a harsh, rambling fuzz.

The Tonebender was the brainchild of Larry and Joe Macari. It was initially produced under their Sola Sound banner until the company was renamed Colorsound. This early, no-holds-barred fuzz was much loved by Jeff Beck. This famous unit, with the orange "fuzz flash," has three controls: a Volume control, a Bass/Treble control to adjust the tone, and a Fuzz control to set the amount of distortion required.

Electro-Harmonix's Big Muff was first made in the late '60s. It went through four cosmetic facelifts. The third version is the most commonly seen and it's the one that has been reissued, too. It features the classic metal E-H case with three controls – Volume, Tone and Sustain – all of which have drastic ranges. Volume, of course, sets the required boost when activated, Tone does pretty much what it says, and the Sustain control determines the amount of distortion (which also, indeed, influences the sustain of the note). A compression control was added to the cocktail for the late '70s mains powered version. All Big Muffs create an enormous wall of dense fuzz; no subtle overdrive here.

Ibanez, the Japanese company better known for its electric guitars, started offering guitar pedals in the early '70s. Their units were actually produced by the Maxon company. The first overdrive unit they made was simply called Ibanez Overdrive, and came in an orange case with script lettering. It has three controls: Distortion, Volume and Tone. Most fuzz pedals have similar variations on these basic controls. This pedal evolved – through about three incarnations – into the legendary TS-808 Tubescreamer Overdrive Pro, much admired by Stevie Ray Vaughan and many others. The TS-808 produces a very natural sounding and smooth overdrive supposedly recreating the tone of tube distortion. The essential component to this circuit is the RC4558 chip, which many believe is crucial to the pedal's sound. The 808 was succeeded by the highly regarded TS-9, which replaced it in the early '80s – and has since been seen on thousands of stages worldwide. It has also now been reissued.

The Dallas/Arbiter Fuzz Face was introduced in the mid '60s and was distinctive thanks to its round "smiley face" design. With two controls for Fuzz and Volume, the circuit is pure simplicity.

ROLAND SPACE ECHO
For years regarded as one of the finest-sounding delay units available, Roland's classic tape-loop-based Space Echo still sounds great by any standards, and has become a highly desirable vintage unit. This version adds chorus and reverb to the brew.

Fuzz Faces most commonly came in red, blue or silver-grey, although there are other colors, including black. Constantly reissued by an ever-changing host of manufacturers, including Jim Dunlop, the originals from the '60s are most sought after on account of their components. Many argue that circuits containing "top hat" style NKT275 germanium transistors sound the best. The Fuzz Face is a true fuzz rather than distortion pedal, creating thick fuzz tones that compress and break up more as the Fuzz control is turned up. Jimi Hendrix is a well documented early user of the Fuzz Face, though at times he played through a Big Muff and a number of custom-built Roger Mayer pedals as well.

The first series of small-case Boss pedals from Japan included

Something old, something new(ish): the Dallas/Arbiter Fuzz Face is a true '60s original, while Boss's OD-1 is more typical of latterday pedals – but both offer some serious drive tones.

the Boss OD-1 overdrive, a great little distortion unit, favored by Pete Townshend. The OD-1 has just two controls. One for volume, in this case labelled Level, and one for the amount of distortion, which Boss labelled Overdrive. Some of the newer Boss distortion and fuzz units, such as the popular DS-1, offer unbeatable value for money. The DS-1 features three controls: Level sets the overall volume, Tone adjusts just that, and Distortion sets the severity of the overdriven sound. The Boss line is now manufactured in Taiwan.

COMPRESSION EFFECTS

These units amplify any signal detected above a given level to add sustain and "squash" to the sound. Relatively basic compressor pedals work by performing a simplified function akin to the more complex and expensive studio units, maintaining a constant level of volume by boosting quiet passages and "limiting" loud ones. A compressor is commonly used to give sustain and definition to jangly arpeggiated chordal parts or to soften and "warm up" lead lines, and is one of the classic ingredients in many Nashville session guitarists' bag of tricks. Compression is also the effect that gave Byrds guitarist Roger

McGuinn's 12-string playing its trademark chime and ring. Without it, McGuinn has said, his Rickenbacker sounded relatively dull and sustainless.

One of the all-time classics, the MXR Dynacomp, has been around for years and has two controls: Output for overall volume, and Sensitivity for the amount of effect. It can also be useful as a straight booster for solos if Output is put on full with Sensitivity kept low.

Many players and pedal collectors regard the Ross Compressor from the early '80s as an improvement on the Dynacomp, though this gray box can be even harder to find. It too has two controls, this time labelled Sustain (for the amount of compression) and Level. Beloved for its rich, warm tone, it is one of the key stompboxes on the pedalboard of Trey Anastasio, guitarist with Vermont-based alt-rockers Phish.

Often misunderstood and generally underappreciated, compressors have been manufactured by most big pedal makers at one time or another. For functional low-budget squash, Marshall recently issued the very acceptable sounding and cleverly named Edward The Compressor. It carries more functions than most of its breed, with four controls to govern Emphasis, Volume, Attack and Compression.

MODULATION EFFECTS

Taking many forms, modulation alters all or part of the pitch of the original sound to create spacial effects such as chorus, flanging, phasing and octave-below effects. In the early days,

chorus was closely related to vibrato (which, correctly speaking, is the sound created when a note is modulated upward and downward, as opposed to tremolo, merely a rhythmic fluctuation in the volume of a signal). Accordingly, many units performed both effects, or something in between. The massive rotating speaker cabinets – such as those built by Leslie – were an early means to create a chorus effect, and Uni-Vox's legendary Uni-Vibe unit of the '60s was largely an effort to produce the sound of a rotating speaker in a smaller, more portable box. It has a Chorus/Vibrato switch to select the desired function, along with controls for Volume and Intensity, and a footpedal to control the rate. A Uni-Vibe is responsible for the hypnotic swoosh on Jimi Hendrix's 'Machine Gun' and 'Star Spangled Banner,' and it can also be heard on much of Robin Trower's work.

Modern choruses are more efficient, high-tech affairs but achieve their results in much the same way, by splitting off a portion of the signal, modulating its pitch slightly in relation to the original, and blending it back to create a multi-voiced sound. Flangers, on the other hand, sweep a modulated portion of the signal up and down against the original at a (usually) variable rate to create a familiar swooshing, spacey effect.

Phase pedals appeared slightly before modern-style choruses and flangers and simulate the sound of tape phase, where two tape machines are run very slightly out of sync. Early versions were made by Ibanez, Jen and Maestro.

Boss started making pedals in the late '70s. Their first units were offered in a large metal case before the more familiar small

---

DELAYS
1. *Boss DM-2,* 2. *Boss DD-5,* 3. *Electro-Harmonix Deluxe Memory Man. Previous page: Roland Space Echo. Following page: Line 6 DL4 Delay Modeler.*

TREMOLOS
1. *Selmer Tremolo,* 2. *Boss PN-2 Tremolo/Pan,* 3. *Nobels TR-X Tremolo.*

WAH-WAH PEDALS
1. *Vox Wah,* 2. *Colorsound Wah-Wah,* 2.. *Jen Cry Baby.*

ENVELOPE FILTERS
1. *Electro-Harmonix Queen Triggered Wah,* 2. *Musitronics Mu-Tron III,* 3. *Ibanez AF201 Auto Filter,* 4. *Electro-Harmonix Dr. Q,* 5. *MXR Envelope Follower.*

OCTAVE DIVIDERS
1. *MXR Blue Box,* 2. *Boss OC-2 Octivider.*

WEIRDOS
Shinei Siren/Hurricane.

DELAYS

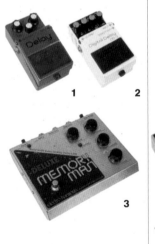

1 2

3

WAH-WAH PEDALS

TREMOLOS

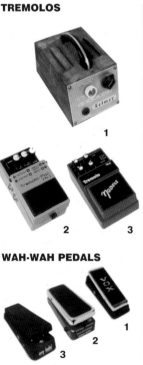

1

2 3

ENVELOPE FILTERS

1

2 3

4 5

OCTAVE DIVIDERS

1 2

SIREN/ HURRICANE

size pedal case was introduced. The Boss line is vast and the pedals are consistently popular, having been around for over 20 years with little change, although some of the early pedals have now been deleted. From the first "large case" line, the CE-1 Chorus/Vibrato is regarded as a classic – liked by artists ranging from Lenny Kravitz to Pantera's Dimebag Darrell – and it can be heard on a large array of '80s recordings. It features mono or stereo outputs with a Level control and an Intensity control for the amount of effect. A footswitch enables the player to change the unit between chorus and vibrato modes. Vibrato uses a Depth and Rate control. The large-case line was deleted in favor of the "small case" models in the early '80s.

As the '80s progressed the range of Boss pedals available grew extensively. The CE-1 chorus was replaced by the CE-2, which is available to this day and is a very decent sounding unit. Simple to use, it carries two controls: Rate and Depth.

The Electro-Harmonix Electric Mistress is described on its case as being a "Filter/Flanger Matrix," and it sounds like no other pedal. It has three knobs: a Rate control determines the speed of the flanging, Range governs the amount of oscillation, and Color sets the amount of effect. First offered in the early '70s in a battery powered unit, it evolved a few years later into an AC-powered version and has now been reissued. In short, it offers flanging and other great modulation effects. Essential! The Boss BF-2 has been another mainstay in the flanging world for many years. This little purple pedal is inexpensive and sounds good.

Ibanez made a host of flangers from the early '70s onward, including the large FL-305 and FL-303, and the FL-301 from the same series as the famous TS-808 overdrive. These were followed by the Ibanez FL-9, which is still an inexpensive bargain on the used market. Four controls determine Speed, Width and Regen ("regeneration," which controls the depth and sweep) and Delay Time which controls how quickly the flanging begins.

MXR's acclaimed mains-powered gray flanger also has four controls, three of which bear the same description as the FL9. The exception is the "delay time," which MXR labelled "Manual." You can hear this unit on much of John McGeoch's playing with Magazine and Siouxsie And The Banshees.

Electro-Harmonix introduced the famous Small Stone in the early '70s. It boasts a unique Color switch, which adds more depth to the effect, as well as a Speed control, which adjusts the speed of the phasing.

When MXR introduced its line of pedals in the early '70s their three phasers – the 45, 90 and 100 – were instant hits. The most popular was probably the Phase 90, which was used extensively by Mick Jones of The Clash, as you can hear prominently on 'Lost In The Supermarket' on the album *London Calling*. The Phase 90 only has one control – to adjust the speed of the phase. Many phasers have a depth control too. Boss, Dod, Danelectro and many other modern makers manufacture excellent phase pedals.

Octave dividers add one or two octaves below the note struck by the guitarist. The MXR Bluebox was one of the first. It featured a Blend control to adjust the amount of dry and effect signal. This pedal was sometimes used by Jimmy Page.

Another very useful Boss pedal is the OC-2 Octivider, which adds two lower octaves if required, with separate blend controls for each. This brown unit has been around for over 20 years. Of the three knobs, the one in the center controls the Blend between normal and effect signal. The other two are labelled Oct 1 and

A classic '60s Uni-Vox Uni-Vibe, the pedal loved by Jimi Hendrix and Robin Trower. (There is also a foot control, not shown here.)

Oct 2 and control the amount of the first or second octave sounded below the source signal.

A true oddball in the pedal world is the Siren/Hurricane pedal manufactured in the '70s by the Shinei Company of Japan. The unit adds white noise (surf), pink noise (hurricane) or, by clicking the switch on the side, a police siren! This pedal was used for the siren effect on The Sweet's '70s UK hit 'Blockbuster.'

TIME-BASED EFFECTS

Units in this category repeat or recreate the original signal without altering its tone or pitch (unless they mix in chorus or flanging), and come in different forms, including delay, tremolo and reverb. Delay is one of the most widely used guitar effects. The pedal or unit repeats the source signal generated by the guitar. The speed of the delay (delay time) and number of repeats (feedback) can usually be controlled by the unit.

The first delay units used moving tape, recording and playing back the signal between different tape heads. The further away the head which recorded the original signal from the one which played it back, the longer the gap between the direct and repeated sound. Delay times are usually measured in thousandths of a second or "milliseconds." Typically, analog pedals produce delay times up to a maximum of about 500 milliseconds, whereas digital and rack mounted units can produce repeats of up to two seconds or more. But beware: digital pedals eat batteries, so a mains adaptor is useful here.

The Watkins Copicat was one of the first tape units available and was widely used in the '60s, in Britain particularly. Good working units, particularly the early tube models, are still great sounding delays. As the tape motor can be turned off, they also make excellent tube preamps. Maestro's Echo-Plex is a similarly desirable American-built tube-driven delay unit that is getting extremely difficult to find.

Roland introduced its famous Space Echo line in the '70s, and at the time these gave what seemed a very modern twist to the echo unit. The final version, the RE-501, added chorus and reverb. There are six delay modes, each accessing a different tape head, as well as Delay-Time and Feedback controls. It also has controls for Bass and Treble along with pushbuttons to access chorus, echo and "Sound on Sound," a control that adds further delays to the actual repeat signal. Any combination can be used at once.

Boss introduced delay pedals with the rest of its line. The early analog pedals, such as the DM-2 and DM-3, were succeeded by digital versions like the DD-3 and DD-5. The DM-2 features three controls: Repeat for the time between the source and delay signal, Intensity for the amount of effect, and Echo for the number of repeats or feedback. The digital DD-3 offers much longer delay times. The four controls each determine Level of effect, Feedback, Delay Time and Hold – which sets the unit's starting point at 50, 200 or 800 milliseconds.

MXR, Ibanez and Electro-Harmonix all made analogue delay units. The E-H Memory Man has been extensively used by The Edge of U2 (you can clearly hear the effect's analog "dirtiness" on the track 'I Will Follow,' among others). This pedal, which has now been reissued, has three controls: Blend for the ratio between the direct and effect signal, Feedback, and Delay to set the delay time.

Tremolo is a long standing guitar favorite. In effect it cuts the guitar signal in and out at a consistent speed, as if you were turning the volume control on the guitar up and down. It is often built into amplifiers. Many Beatles recordings feature the tremolo built into Vox amps. Tremolo pedals have been made by most of the major manufacturers, including Colorsound, Electro-Harmonix and Dallas-Arbiter, who made the Trem Face to match their famous Fuzz Face distortion.

Distinct from tremolo – although the term is sometimes used as a misnomer for tremolo – vibrato achieves a similar bouncing, volume-cut effect, but in its truest sense does also alter a portion of the pitch of the original signal in the process. A more complex effect to achieve electronically, vibrato is less often seen in stand-alone units (though Matchless once made an intricate tube-powered pedal, and others have offered variations) and is rarer than tremolo as an on-board amp effect. It was included on a few early-'60s Fenders, '50s Magnatones and the early Vox AC30s. Gibson offered the now-rare GAV1 vibrato unit in the '50s, designed as an "add-on" between guitar and amp, and Selmer made a tube powered stand-alone unit in the '60s. Simple to operate, each had controls for depth and speed.

The now-deleted Boss PN2 Tremolo/Pan pedal can be used as a straight tremolo unit or as a stereo pan box, panning the signal between the left and right channels in a stereo field. This requires two amps, of course. It has a Rate (speed) control, a Depth control (for the severity of the effect) and a Mode control. Four modes can be accessed, two each for tremolo and panning – each with a differing waveform. It has been succeeded by Boss's TR2 pedal which lacks the panning facility.

Tremolo has come back into vogue in recent years, and newer pedal versions of the effect are beginning to surface, from Voodoo Lab's deluxe and lush-sounding Tremolo, to Nobels' affordable but extremely functional option. The latter features four controls – Depth, Speed, Tone and Level – plus a four-way switch to set the "hardness" and wave shape of the tremolo.

EQ-BASED EFFECTS

This category of effect alters the frequencies of the signal's tonal range, and includes EQs and wah-wahs – the latter among the most widely used of all guitar effects pedals. Many players are happy to go on stage with no pedals at all except a wah-wah.

In widespread use since the mid '60s, wah-wahs contain a potentiometer which governs what is essentially a tone circuit within the pedal that is altered by a foot control. The further forward the foot control is depressed the more treble is produced. A similar effect can be achieved by turning the tone pot on the guitar itself, but obviously a greater versatility is achieved by leaving the guitarist with both hands free, and the active circuit of the wah pedal generally has a broader frequency

range, used in combination with coloration and boost in some models of wah-wah.

The visually appealing Vox Wah was made by the Italian company Jen, and was electronically identical to their own Cry Baby Super. Hendrix, of course, was famous for using one (for a classic example listen to the intro to 'Voodoo Chile'). The tonal sweep isn't as broad as that of, say, a Colorsound Wah of the same period, but the narrower range makes the effect somewhat more controlable for the guitarist.

Colorsound produced their Wah in the early '70s. It had a very

Digital technology has brought us affordable processors which perform a dizzying number of functions and are often designed into a format which combines floorboard switching options, too. Zoom's GFX-4 (1) is styled to capture nostalgia for older pedals but offers six simultaneous effects out of a possible 44, as well as 60 user and 60 factory presets, plus amp and cab simulation. Boss's relatively upscale GT-3 (2) does much of the same and more, with unusual pickup simulation, acoustic-electric preamp, impressive routing facilities, and nearly 350 user and preset patches.

At the forefront of digital technology in today's guitar world, "modeling" units are blurring the lines between effects processors and amp emulators – and most of the frontrunners pack in plenty of both. Johnson's J-Station (3) is a handy desktop unit for home recording, while Line 6's POD Pro (below) expands upon the features of their own similarly styled desktop POD, but improves the routing and connecting facilities for studio use.

multi-fx units

large sweep which resulted in a trademark sound. Colorsound also produced a Fuzz/Wah which combined fuzz into the wah pedal by clicking a second rocker switch.

The Dunlop Cry Baby reissue is a great wah pedal; robust and functional. It's not a true reissue in that some of the components differ from the original Jen version, but it captures much of the same sound and is good value for the money.

Envelope filters or followers are basically automatic wah-wahs, but the tonal change and sweep are triggered automatically by how hard the string is hit: the harder you pick, the more it "wahs." They were extremely popular with funk guitarists and bassists in the late '70s and early '80s, and have come and gone from fashion ever since.

The Boss T/Wah was a big hit in the '80s. It is a sensitive unit, with three controls: knobs for Sensitivity and Peak determine the amount of effect and the range of the sweep respectively, while a Drive switch presets the sweep range. It has been succeeded by the Boss Auto-Wah.

Many consider the Musitronics Mu-Tron III to be one of the best sounding envelope filters ever. It boasts three knobs, one each for Mode, Peak and Gain, with three switch controls: one to turn the unit on and off; the other two for Drive and Range. It offers a huge range of possibilities and is often used by bass players – think Bootsy Collins. Ibanez offered its first auto wah in the AF-201. It had three switches: two for Mode and one for Range, combined with two slider controls for Sensitivity and Peak. This pedal was succeeded by the AF-9 unit.

Electro-Harmonix manufactured the Dr. Q envelope follower along with a deluxe version, The Zipper. The Dr. Q has a slider switch which augmented the bass response and a "Q" knob to control the range of the effect. The Zipper has a switch for a high or low range, marked 1 and 2, a Range control for the range of the sweep and a "Q" control for sensitivity – the speed at which the high peak is reached.

MXR originally made their Envelope Follower, now reissued, in the late '70s. The company named the range and sensitivity controls Threshold and Attack respectively.

One of the rarer Electro-Harmonix pedals is the '70s Queen Triggered Wah. This unit can be used as a conventional wah-wah – and a very good sounding one too – or as an envelope follower/auto wah. The unique aspect of this pedal when used as an auto-wah is that the position of the pedal determines the tonal range accessed. So if the pedal is fully upright the tonal range is in the lower registers; fully depressed, the effect is in the higher registers. The sensitivity, or amount, of auto wah or "Q" is determined by a control on the side. It's an impressive box.

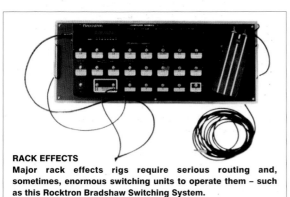

RACK EFFECTS
Major rack effects rigs require serious routing and, sometimes, enormous switching units to operate them – such as this Rocktron Bradshaw Switching System.

Capitalizing on the popularity of vintage delay pedals, Line 6 has employed its amp modeling experience to produce a series of floor units which model a broad range of classic stompboxes. The DL4 Delay Modeler emulates 15 delay units, from the Space Echo to the Memory Man, and adds a 14-second loop sampler.

MULTI-FX UNITS

Pedals doing all of the above jobs – and sometimes combining two or three sounds – have provided the portable answer to altering the guitar's straight sound since the early '60s, with a resurgent popularity again in recent years. But digital technology has signaled a major revolution in what this or that box of tricks can do for you. Studios and large concert stages have long seen the use of powerful, sophisticated rack units, at first usually dedicated to doing one job well (reverb, delay, chorus), and then capable of complex multi-functions.

But the cost of digital components has decreased while their processing capabilities have dramatically increased. It's this particular combination of changes that has put a vast array of previously complex effects in the hands of everyday musicians – whether they are hardworking sidemen, amateur guitarists, or dedicated hobbyists.

The largest portion of this new market in relatively affordable digital effects comes in the form of multi-FX pedals, or "floorboards." These combine the processing power of rack units but do away with the need to string separate patch-triggering footswitches across the stage or practise room floor. They do this by incorporating their own stomp switches and expression pedals. Such units are designed to sit on the floor in the usual front-line pedal position for easy and instant access.

Most of the prominent music electronics manufacturers offer multi-FX units – names like Boss, Zoom, Digitech, Korg and others – often in a range of prices broad enough to suit any budget. Even basic and astoundingly affordable models like Zoom's GFX707 offer capabilities that would have sounded impossible 10 (and certainly 20) years ago: nine effects simultaneously, multiple user and factory patches, even a built-in drum machine. The power of some of the more heavy-duty units truly boggles the mind.

While different makers do have their own sound and character to some extent – one excelling at reverbs, for example, while another does great vintage-style chorus – the nature of digital technology does homogenize the business. Price and the number and combinations available of effects, therefore, often decide what you might buy as much or more so than the inherent sound qualities of different makes and models.

Many guitarists still prefer the sound created by older-style analog units, too, which they argue are warmer and more natural in tone. Plenty of records which contain classic guitar effects were made before digital technology was invented, so there's certainly a valid argument in the claim that the old analog boxes sounded pretty good already. But there is a trade-off. Analog effects are noisy, and linking a number of such units together can produce unacceptable hiss or "white noise" – and of course you would need to string together nearly all of the stompboxes pictured on the preceding pages to get the sonic options of, say, a single Boss GT-3 processor. For quantity, digital technology is unrivaled – but for quality, the jury is still out.

"Learning to change your strings efficiently is the first stage of guitar maintenance, and it can be surprising how many people who've been playing for years still put on a fresh set in a manner that may impede their ability to stay in tune and sound their best."

"Setting intonation is one of the main goals of any set-up. Without getting this crucial step right, your guitar will never quite sound in-tune, nor will the resonance and harmonic content of its natural voice ring true."

60

TOTALLY GUITAR
MAINTENANCE

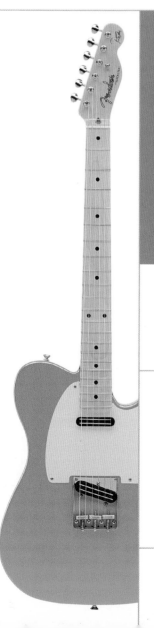

In order to play your best, you need a guitar that is optimized for peak performance. By doing the work yourself, you can both save money and keep your instrument in the best possible shape for your own style and sound. This chapter shows you how to string up correctly, adjust all factors crucial to "action" and feel, change pickups, perform wiring mods, and much more.

STRINGING UP

Chances are you're constantly aware, if only subconsciously, of the effects that the feel and freshness of your strings are having on your playing and sound. Even so, it's all too easy to overlook this vital first link in the chain – the component which most directly connects you to the music you're making. The type of strings you use, their condition, and the stability of their attachment and contact with all points of the guitar will all affect both tuning and tone. When all of the above are at their optimum, there's that much less to get in the way of your playing. Appropriately, then, we'll begin by looking at options for correct string loading and ways of maximizing their condition and effect on tuning stability.

STRING TYPES

You've probably given a lot of thought to the type and style of guitar you want and struggled to find the money to buy it. But have you ever given a thought to the strings you're going to use, or how frequently you should change them? Let's face it, the type of strings you use on your guitar and their general condition will form the starting point of good guitar tone.

The variety of string choices available can be dizzying, though you need to keep in mind that the majority of brands are produced by just a few string manufacturers. In fact, you should try to choose the strings you use based on their consistency and their availability as well as their "feel" and tone.

The most common type of strings for electric guitar are "nickel"

If your strings are poorly attached there's little chance of good tuning stability, and your tone will probably suffer too. Even plenty of experienced players load their strings in ways that fail to optimize their performance, but it's easy to learn a stable and efficient technique for stringing-up – either a basic wind or more advanced locking technique.

roundwounds. What that means is that the wound strings – typically the three low strings – have nickel-plated steel windings (wraps) around a steel core. The unwound strings – typically the top three – are "plain" high carbon steel. A small metal "ball" is wound onto each string at one end; this is the "ball-end" that secures the string into the anchor point at the bridge. You'll need to cut this off before you can use a string for a Floyd Rose vibrato (see the discussion of vibrato adjustmnent that follows). Some special strings do come already without ball-ends for this purpose.

You will also see "stainless steel" strings. D'Addario introduced this type back in the mid-'70s, and they now use "400-series magnetic stainless steel" instead of nickel-plated steel wraps. D'Addario use this material on their flatwound Chromes (where a flat-section outer winding is used). They also use it for their Half Round strings (where the oversized stainless steel winding is partially ground down to offer some of the smoothness of flatwound strings) which offer reduced finger-noise and less fret wear, but without abandoning all of the brightness of roundwounds.

Stainless steel strings typically sound a little brighter initially, but become duller more quickly than nickel. Nickel-plated strings usually sound slightly more mellow, but tend to die less quickly. Custom string pioneer Ernie Ball has recently re-introduced their original pure nickel wrap strings, which offer an even warmer tone than the nickel-plated variety.

Do bear in mind that these are generalizations, and that you're advised to experiment with different strings. However, when you do experiment, it's more useful to compare the different winding types of the same brand and the same gauge, to keep the variables at a minimum.

STRING LOADING I: BASIC

Learning to change your strings efficiently is the first stage of guitar maintenance, and it can be surprising how many people who've been playing for years still put on a fresh set in a manner that may impede the strings ability to stay in tune and sound their best. There are many ways to attach the strings to the tuners. You need to establish your own working practice, one that secures the strings efficiently and suits your own guitar and the style you play in. Here's a basic method:

1 Lay your guitar on your worktop in front of you with the headstock to your left (supported if it's back-angled) or whichever way is most comfortable. Unless you need to clean your fingerboard, or do any other maintenance or modification, always replace your strings one at a time, which helps to keep neck tension fairly regular and to hold any "floating" bridge or tailpiece parts in place. Use a string winder to quickly slacken the string and remove it from the tuner's string-post – start with the low E-string.

2 Remember that the plain end of the string was probably cut to length with wire cutters and will be extremely sharp, so watch your fingers, eyes and guitar finish. Remove the old string from the bridge and discard it. Set the tuner so that the hole in its string-post (diagram a, following page) is parallel to the nut. Thread the new string through the tailpiece or bridge and carefully pull it down to the tuner's string-post. Place the string against the inside edge of the post and pull it tightly, as pictured on the left.

3 Now wind the string around the string-post counter-clockwise for one full turn (diagram b), keeping the tension on, and thread it through the string-post hole (diagram c). This will add another turn above the first.

4 Pull the string out of the other side of the string-post hole and pull it as tight as you can (pictured right). Bend the loose end of the string at a right angle and slightly downwards immediately at the point it emerges from the string-post hole. Tune up to pitch. Repeat this procedure for the A-string and D-string. If you have a six-a-side headstock, use the same technique for all strings; if you have a three-a-side headstock the procedure is the same except it becomes a mirror image for the second set of three tuners, which are mounted on the opposite side of the headstock.

5 Now wind on your plain strings. Whereas you have ended up with just a couple of turns around the string post on the wound strings, the plain strings need a few more turns. Wrap the string neatly around the string post three or four times before poking the loose end through the post hole. Stretch your strings (a process described in depth later in this section), tune the strings up to pitch, and then check that your intonation is accurate and reset it if necessary.

6 Finally, clip the loose end of the string a few millimetres away from the post for a tidy finish. Some players like to curl the loose string in a circle, which is fine – but never leave the loose ends hanging because they can be dangerous.

a   b   c

For correct basic string loading, wrap the wound strings once around the tuner post before threading through the hole and tuning up to pitch, as illustrated above. Plain strings require three or four turns before being poked through the post hole. Done right, this yields tidy, firm results – as pictured left.

STRING LOADING: GOLDEN RULES

Don't wind the string around the post from the speaking length side. Some people place the un-cut string in the post hole and then wrap the slack, by hand, around the post. This is not advised as it may well distort the windings on the wound strings.

Never cut a wound string without first making a right-angled bend. This is recommended by most string makers and will prevent the winds (wraps) from distorting or unwinding.

Never have any overlapping winds around the post. Keep things neat and tidy and always wind the string in a downward direction under the string-post hole.

Never leave any slack in the string as it winds around the string-post. This could cause future tuning problems.

Never leave excess string hanging from the end of the tuners. Either cut the strings close to the post or wind the free length into an interlocking circle.

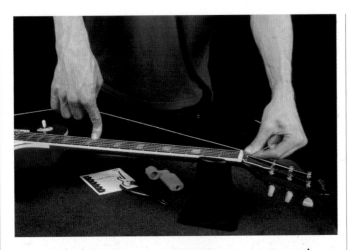

a   b   c

Slightly more involved than basic string loading but potentially very effective – and favored by many players – this locking wrap provides a high degree of tuning stability thanks to minimal string slippage around the tuner post.

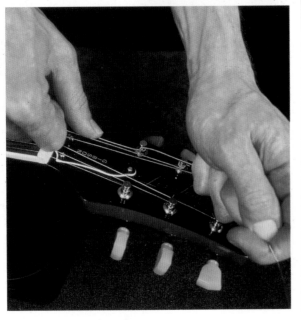

STRING LOADING II: LOCKING

Many players and repairmen prefer to lock the string around the tuner's string post for additional security and tuning stability, and it makes sense to do this if you have a vibrato (without a locking nut or locking tuners). This method requires a little more dexterity and, because of the lock, it may not be quite as quick to remove the strings – something to consider if you break a string on-stage and you haven't got your own guitar tech. However, practise makes perfect.

1 Start off exactly the same as the basic method but this time turn the tuner's string post so that the hole is approximately 60 degrees to the nut. With your left hand, pull the string to the inside edge of the string post but hold it with your right hand to create some slack length (top left). Holding the string firm at the tuner with your left hand, move your right hand down the string to the tuner, and grip the string. (Alternatively you could poke the string through the string post first and then estimate your slack, but you must be very careful not to bend the string in the wrong place.)

2 Poke the loose end through the string-post hole from the centre of the headstock outwards (see diagram a, left). Pull the loose end through the hole but don't lose the grip on your right hand because that's still creating the slack. Bend the loose end clockwise around the post (diagram b) and under the point where the string is entering the post (diagram c). Hold the string momentarily with the first finger of your right hand, then grab the loose end again with your left hand and pull it tightly as you bend it upwards and over the string (lower photo).

3 Hold the string in place with your right-hand thumb and tighten the tuner so that the "speaking length" of the string clamps the loose end tightly (the speaking length is the portion that goes from the tuner, over the nut, and on to the bridge). Then, with your string winder in your left hand, carefully wind on the slack, making neat turns below the first turn. If you've estimated your slack correctly you should get approximately two to three turns around the post. Again, if your guitar has a three-a-side headstock, the procedure on the treble strings is a mirror

ALTERNATE LOCKS

Follow the locking procedure described above to the point that you start winding on the slack. Instead of your first wind going under the locked string try one over and the remaining turns under. For extra security try two over and the remainder under. Whatever locking method you use, be flexible. If your tuner has a short string-post, it will not be practical to use a double locking method, especially with heavy gauge strings (see String Loading: Golden Rules on the previous page).

Locking Tuners take the guess-work out of string loading. Sperzel's Trim-Loks, for example, require that you simply thread the string through the post hole, pull it tight, tighten the lock on the back of the tuner housing and tune up. One thing to remember with any locking tuners is that you must always fully slacken the string before undoing the lock – don't undo the lock with the string tuned to pitch.

image. Having attached, tuned, and stretched all your strings, and if necessary re-set your intonation, make a final downward bend where the loose end of each string emerges from the post, and clip off the string as close as you can to the post.

STRING LOADING III: SLOT-HEAD TUNERS

Vintage Fenders and the numerous modern re-issues often use split-post vintage-style tuners (often called Safeti-Post tuners) as originally supplied by Kluson from the early '50s until the mid-'60s. While you can attach your string in any of the ways already shown – the slot is just like an open-topped post hole – they were originally designed so that the loose end is placed down the hole in the centre of the post. This is a very neat and tidy way of string loading and you never have any protruding and sharp string ends. Remember: replace the strings one at a time. If your guitar has a vibrato and you need to remove all the strings at once, place the vibrato's backplate, or a stack of business cards, under the back edge of the vibrato *before* you remove the strings to keep the balance between springs and string tension approximately correct.

1 Lay the guitar in front of you, remove the old string' set the tuner slot so it's parallel with the nut and load the new string through the bridge. Pull it tight against the inside of the tuner post. You need to allow approximately the distance of two machineheads (2"/50mm) for winding on (*see Headstock Angles*, below) so if you're fitting the low E, make a right-angled bend in the string at a point coinciding with the D-string tuner. Cut the string to length approximately ½"/10mm beyond that right-angled bend, as pictured above.

2 Poke the loose end down as far as it will go, into the central hole in the tuner's string post, and bend it down to the bottom of the slot (near right photo). Hold it in place with your right-hand thumb while – with your string winder in your left hand – you tighten the tuner, making sure that the slack string is neatly wound down the post.

HEADSTOCK ANGLES

The type of headstock you have affects the ways in which you need to load your strings. The reason is that the angle at which the string "breaks" from the nut to the tuners plays a part in the tone of your guitar and its tuning stability. If the string angle is too shallow the string can rattle in the nut slot, causing a loss of tone and at worst a sitar-like buzz. On guitars with a standard back-angled headstock (without a locking nut) you need to aim for around two to four neat string turns around the tuner post. Clearly this depends on the gauge of the string and the height of the string-post hole above the tuner bushing (the washer-like or nut-like fitting around the post which sits against the face of the headstock and into the post hole). For example, a heavy gauge low E string on a short tuner post will require fewer turns than a lighter gauge E on a longer post.

On Fender-style, straight headstocks you need to be a little more clever, especially when you only have one string tree on the top two strings. On the low E string aim for two turns (too many here will create too steep an angle which main impair tuning stability, especially if you have a vibrato). On the A string aim for two to three turns; the D string needs around four turns. The G string is the most problematic and you need as many turns as you can down the post almost to the tuner bushing itself. This will

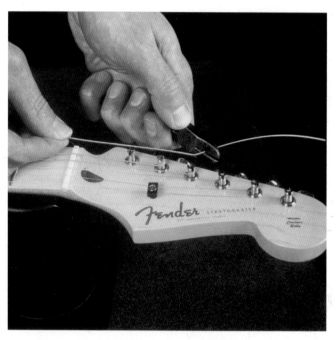

After allowing a distance of about two string posts from the post you're winding onto, make a right-angle bend in the string and cut its remainder, leaving enough length after the bend to poke down into the hole at the center of the slot in the tuner post.

One of the oldest types of tuners found on solidbody electric guitars, primarily because of their use on early Fender models from the '50s to the mid-'60s, Kluson (and similar styled) split-post machine heads are a deceptively clever design. They offer an integral solution to stray, finger-jabbing string ends, while also providing a degree of string-anchoring stability beyond that of a basic wrap.

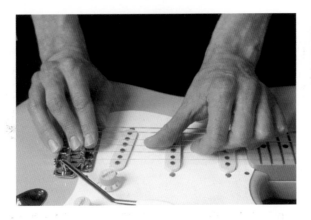

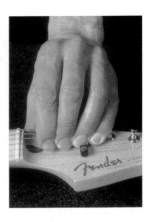

Correctly stretching new strings is vital to getting them settled and able to hold their tuning. After pulling each string firmly away from the body to seat it, grip and squeeze between thumb and fingers.

Do this for the length of each string to ensure it is evenly stretched in.

And don't forget to stretch behind the nut, where further tuning problems can occur.

create the maximum behind-the-nut string angle. The top two B and E strings, because they pass under the string tree, need only four or so turns. Obviously the more turns you require, the more slack you need to gauge or the longer the length the string must be before you cut it off. It takes some experience to gauge these different numbers of turns, especially with slot-head tuners, but after a few careful re-stringings you'll get the hang of it.

Some locking tuners help the problem, especially on Fender-style headstocks as they have "staggered-height" posts to help you achieve the correct behind-the-nut string angle. Gotoh have recently introduced their HAP locking tuners which allow you to precisely set the height of each individual tuner post.

STRING STRETCHING

Without getting too scientific, a string has three stages in its life-cycle. When you first put on new strings they are extremely elastic and sound very bright and "fresh." Until they settle, however, they won't stay in tune. Once stretched and played in, they're in their optimum state. How long they stay like this depends upon how much and how aggressively you play and how much you sweat. The combination of playing, your sweat and the dirt that will accumulate on the strings will lead to the strings becoming "dead," losing their tonal brightness and physical elasticity, making them much more prone to breakage – especially at friction points at the tuners and saddles. You can prolong the life of the strings by wiping them after every playing session with a cloth or a string cleaner, but you can't alter the physical decay due to playing wear. Any new strings must be stretched. Players have different techniques for this though the aim is the same: to ensure they settle and therefore stay in tune.

1 First, hold the string over the pickups and lightly pull them away from the guitar one at a time. This will relieve any hitching at the tuners, nut and bridge, as pictured above left.

2 Next, lay the guitar in front of you and grip and squeeze each string with your left-hand thumb and fingers, moving along the entire length of the string. Bend each string a few times behind the nut and, if relevant, behind the bridge. We find holding the string over the bridge saddle with your right-hand thumb stops any unnecessary friction wear which could lead – especially on the lighter strings – to premature breakage. Stretch

each string one at a time, constantly re-checking your tuning: when the string no longer de-tunes after some pretty heavy bending, the string is stretched.

String-stretching is a balancing act between getting your new strings to settle in-tune, but not over-stretching them so much that the winds around the core distort and impair your tone.

STRING GAUGES

String gauge (the diameter of the string) is measured in inches. The most commonly used set runs (top E to bottom E) from .009" to .042" – nine thousandths of an inch to forty-two thousandths of an inch – and is usually referred to as a "set of nines." "Tens" typically go from .010" to .046". The thinnest readily available set is "eights" (.008" to .038"), while "elevens" typically run from .011" to .049". Then there are many "hybrid" sets where, for example, the top three of a set of "nines" are combined with the bottom three of the heavier "tens." All this makes for a bewildering choice – as evidenced in the string gauge chart, below – but remember: if everything else remains the same, the thinner the gauge the easier the strings are to fret and bend, but the lighter the tone will be – and vice versa. So while a set of "elevens" may well give you the meatiest tone, they will be a lot harder to fret and bend compared to "nines." Deciding what's right for you will probably mostly come down to feel: whether you opt to work a

Chart of Popular String Gauges

"LIGHT": .009, .011, .016, .024w, .032w, .042w

"REGULAR": .010, .013, .017, 026w, .036w, .046w

"POWER" (med.): .011, .014, .018, .028w, .038w, .048w

"HYBRID" (light top/regular bottoms): .009, .011, .016, 026w, .036w, .046w

Most electric guitar string sets today are made up of gauges selected from a range that runs anywhere from .008" (the high-E on "super light" sets) to around .048". The chart above shows the individual string gauges for four of the more common complete sets. (w = wound)

little harder for the extra power a set of "tens" can give you, or go for the easy bendability of a set of "eights," you're the boss.

TYPES OF TUNERS

On most modern electric guitars, except some of the cheapest, you should find a pretty decent set of tuners (machineheads). Most are pre-lubricated, fully-enclosed units based on the original Grover/Schaller design. These have a high gear ratio, which means you have to turn the button more to get one rotation of the string post, giving finer adjustment. They also have a small tension-adjustment screw at the end of the button.

On some electrics you'll find tuners modeled on the older Kluson design (Kluson-brand tuners have recently made a return to the market, and are proving popular with players looking to replicate an accurate vintage look, though they are now manufactured by a different company than the US-made originals). Japanese reissue Fenders, for example, use this type with a "split" string post and non-adjustable metal buttons. Certain Epiphones use a similar tuner but with a vintage-like green-tinged plastic "tulip" button or a keystone-shaped button, and a standard string post. Despite their vintage look, most have a higher gear ratio than the originals.

A new breed of locking tuners began to appear in the 1980s which "lock" the string onto the string post by clamping it into place in its hole or slot, usually by means of a tension-adjusted internal peg. Specifically designed for guitars with non-locking vibratos, they bring an end to all that fiddly winding of the string-end around the string-post. Installing strings on these is very easy and you can be confident of eliminating any potential movement that can cause string slippage and, therefore, return-to-pitch problems. They are a fine upgrade for any guitar, with or without vibrato, as they make re-stringing very quick and should aid overall tuning stability. The US-made Sperzel heads lead the way, though locking tuners are also available from makers such as Schaller (as used by Fender and Ernie Ball/Music Man), Gotoh, Grover and LSR. There are even some units available which outwardly replicate the look of vintage-style tuners.

TUNER ADJUSTMENT

Little alteration is necessary with most modern tension-adjustable tuners. When you change strings, check that the fixing nut on the face of the headstock is tight. If it's loose you'll need to tighten it with a conventional wrench or socket wrench of the correct size. Never use pliers, or you risk both damaging the edges of the nut and severely scratching the finish on your headstock.

The small screw at the end of the tuner button affects the feel of the machinehead. Technically it doesn't reduce what is called "backlash" or "slippage," the free play of the tuner between clockwise and anti/counter-clockwise rotation. Tightening the screw (pictured right) will create a firmer feel. Don't over-tighten, or tighten it so far that you can't easily move the button. Your aim here is to get an even feel (tight or slack, whatever you like) on all the tuners.

PRS use their own design of Schaller-made locking tuners, without the white nylon washer between the button and the housing, leaving just the bent metal washer in place. PRS tighten their tuners for a positive (some would say stiff) action, based on their belief that the firmer the tuner the more stable the tuning.

Finally, it's worth underlining that tuning problems caused by the nut or by the string tree – or simply by bad string attachment – will not be cured by the tuner, whatever its type.

Schaller: fully enclosed, tension adjustable.

Gotoh Magnum Lock: tension adjustable, locking.

Economy type: non-adjustable.

Kluson-style "vintage" reproduction: non-adjustable.

Sperzel Trimp-Lok: tension-adjustable, locking.

As shown here (above and left), a wide range of tuner types are available today as stock and retro-fit equipment. While budget guitars may still come with generic types like that pictured above left, most midrange instruments are now fitted with enclosed, adjustable tuners like the Schaller (top left) or similar, while locking units are commonly found on high-end electrics – and are now popular after-market upgrades, too.

Most decent tuners today come with a screw set into the end of the button. Not a means of correcting "slippage" as such, it is provided to let the player adjust the feel of the unit for a firm or easy action, according to personal preference.

The same basic principles of loading strings securely and stretching them prior to tuning up as applied to electric guitars will help acoustics hold their pitch longer and more accurately. There are, however, several variations to acoustic guitar bridge and headstock designs – including the classical types – which occasionally require a different approach to string loading.

Most flat-top acoustics have their strings fixed at the bridge by means of push-in bridge pins. Always use the correct tool to remove them.

Slot headstocks can be trickier to string up than the standard variety, though the winding procedure is much the same.

TUNING TIPS

An accurate, low-cost electric tuner makes getting your guitar in tune a breeze, and is almost a must for setting intonation (described later in this chapter). As such, it's a worthwhile investment for any guitarist. If you haven't got an electronic tuner to hand, however, you'll need some kind of reference – a keyboard, pitch pipe or tuning fork.

Tune the low E string first, plucking an open string or 12th-fret harmonic, and always tune *up* to pitch from a *flat* note. If the string is already sharp, drop it down below the correct pitch then bring it back up. Carry on from here using the standard "relative tuning" method (fifth fret to open string, fourth fret on G to open B), though be aware that this can introduce inaccuracies to your tuning. Once you feel you're "in tune," play some unison and octave pairs in other positions, then try some low-position open chords to check the "sweetness" of your tuning, and adjust as necessary. These last steps are worthwhile even when you have tuned using an electronic tuner, to ensure your guitar *sounds* good rather than just being "in tune" according to the machine.

ACOUSTIC VARIATIONS

In practise, the majority of acoustic guitars are strung up and tuned just like any electric guitar, but there are several variations worth mentioning. One factor that is different on almost all, however, is the bridge design: most standard steel-string flat-top acoustics use bridge pins to hold the strings in place behind the bridge saddle.

The tapered pins – themselves made of ebony, rosewood, bone, plastic or other synthetic material – fit into holes drilled through the bridge and the face of the guitar, to hold the string's ball ends in place in a slot in the bridge block mounted inside the guitar (for more detail, see the *Acoustic Bridges* section on page 81). Bridge pins should not need to be pushed so firmly into their holes that they are difficult to remove. If they don't come loose after a tug with the fingertips, however, use the slotted handle of your string winder, which is designed specifically for this purpose. Never use pliers or the head of a screwdriver, which may damage the pins – or worse, the bridge or the face of your guitar.

Some other acoustic guitars have different designs for string anchoring at the bridge end – classical guitars especially – which either will be delt with here, or are so obvious as to require little instruction.

STRINGING UP SLOT-HEAD ACOUSTICS

Correctly stringing a guitar makes all the difference to its tuning stability. We have covered conventional electric and acoustic guitars, but there are other styles of instrument which deserve mentioning. Certain vintage style steel strung instruments, such as those based on the early Martin and Washburn designs, as well as most resonator guitars from makers like National and Dobro, have "slot head" side mounted machine heads in a fashion similar to classical guitars. These are much trickier to string up than conventionally mounted machine heads. However, there is a simple method which will make the job easier.

In essence it's the stringing sequence that will prevent you from tying knots in your fingers. Starting with the two E strings, pass the strings through the holes in the metal machine head posts, pulling them through so that only a small amount of string slack is evident over the fingerboard. Now pass the string through the slots between the E and A string posts for the bottom E string, and the E and the B string posts for the top E string. Now loop the string around behind the string where it entered the post originally, so that when you turn the machine heads the string clamps onto itself in a simple locking manoeuvre. Cut off the excess string and tune to pitch.

Now repeat this procedure for the A and B strings, but passing them this time through the slots between the A and D string (for the A string itself) and the B and G string (for the B string itself). Finally repeat the procedure for the D and G strings, passing the strings through the slots between their relative posts and the top of the slots. You can use the same method to re-string a classical guitar. The benefits of this self-locking technique are that the strings reach concert pitch quicker and stay in tune longer – which is normally a problem for classical guitars especially.

CLASSICAL GUITARS

When stringing up a classical guitar you must tie the strings to the bridge first. To do this, pass the string through the hole behind the saddle and pull it through until you have approximately 6cm – 8 cm (2"– 3") of string visible. Now pass the string over the top of the bridge and loop it under the tail end of the string where it passes through the hole. This will create a loop where the string passes over the bridge. Take the remaining few centimetres and pass it two or three times through the loop so that when you pull on the main length of the string it tightens the loops into place.

The strings used for classical guitars are generally made from nylon, or in the case of the lower strings, a multi-fibre nylon core with a metal wrap – usually brass, bronze or a silver alloy. Classical guitar strings are not normally rated by their thickness but by their tension. Beginners often use low tension strings whereas proficient players use medium or high tension strings for a firmer tone. The action height on a classical guitar is also set much higher than a steel strung guitar because the vibration pattern is much greater, and the strings need extra clearance to avoid buzzes against the frets.

STRING TYPES

The range of string gauges for steel strung acoustic guitars is enormous. Before the advent of amplification many acoustic guitars were fitted with heavy gauge strings to aid projection of tone and volume. The tops of these instruments were often more heavily braced than they are today. Typically, a heavy gauge set of strings may range from .013" for the top E to .062" for the bottom E.

Most manufacturers today recommend medium or medium light gauges. Medium gauge strings typically range from .012" – .056", whereas medium light gauge strings normally range from .011" – .052" from the top E to the bottom E. Light gauge or ultra light gauge strings are available nowadays for acoustic instruments with typical gauges of .010" – .047".

Of course the gauges quoted here are typical and not necessarily those represented by any specific manufacturer. Most companies have websites now so you should be able to get the details of a particular set of strings and the range of gauges before you purchase. If you like bending your strings for "bluesy" style playing then we suggest you use light or ultra light gauges. You may sacrifice a small amount of volume and tone but string bending will be easier. For fingerpickers and folk guitarists either light or medium light gauges would be the most suitable. If you want the most projection and volume then you should fit medium gauge strings. Unless the manufacturer of your particular instrument states otherwise, heavy gauges should be avoided due to the possibility of damage occurring because of the tension applied to the modern, lightly braced tops.

Acoustic guitar strings are made from various bronze alloys, with plain metal used for the B and E strings. Some manufacturers even plate the strings with real gold in an effort to increase the life of the string. This works fairly well if you're not string bending, or strumming fiercely, but if you do thrash your guitar metal fatigue will do its damage irrespective of the type or quality of plating.

Other string manufacturers, such as Elixir, coat their steel strings with a Teflon-like substance to keep dirt and moisture from entering the windings, thus improving string life. Some players find these types tend to sound a touch duller and more "played in" from the start, but they have found many fans, too, and all indications are that the technique does increase use able string life.feel (tight or slack, whatever you like) on all the tuners.

The technique for winding strings onto sideways-mounted tuners in slot-headstock guitars is similar to that used with standard tuners. A simple locking method will suffice, but follow a different sequence, and be aware your perspective is rotated by 90 degrees.

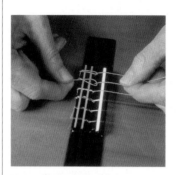

Nylon classical guitar strings need to be "tied" to the bridge for a secure hold before being wound onto the tuners.

The process involves making a loop of the string-end behind the bridge, and winding this under the speaking length to lock it firmly in place.

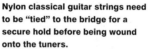

The same basic self-locking method of stringing up steel-string slot-head acoustics can be used for classical guitars. This simple locking technique is especially useful with nylon strings, which tend to have a longer stretching-in period and therefore can remain "unsettled" for longer periods before holding concert pitch consistently when wound on using less stable techniques.

NECK AND ACTION ADJUSTMENTS

Many perfectly competent guitarists limit their dealings with action and string height to occasionally raising or lowering bridge saddles, scared off from touching a truss rod by legends of warped necks or fractured headstocks. But by following instructions carefully, and using the correct tools, there is a lot you can do yourself to fine-tune the playability of your guitar without ever putting your neck at risk.

TRUSS ROD ADJUSTMENT

When you buy a new guitar you'll usually find included an owners' manual and a truss rod adjustment key, and the manual will provide some basic info on making any necessary adjustments yourself. Conversely, most repairers generally discourage their customers from attempting any truss rod adjustment, which is usually good advice but can leave the beginner understandably confused. So what's the mystery?

Paradoxically, truss rod adjustment can be both simple and

Measuring neck relief is relatively simple, and you can do it with feeler gauges, an accurate steel ruler, or even a plectrum of a known thickness. For all measurements, hold the guitar in playing position (as below) and place a capo at the first fret to free up your left hand. Fret the G string at the 14th fret.

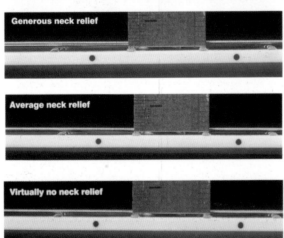

Generous neck relief

Average neck relief

Virtually no neck relief

complex at the same time. On the simple side, a minor adjustment to either straighten a neck with too much concave bow (achieved by tightening the rod) or to relieve a convex bow (by slackening the rod) is possibly all that's needed to make some dramatic improvements and can easily save you a trip to your repairman. On the complex side, adjusting the rod will simultaneously alter other aspects of the set-up such as overall action, the string height at the nut, intonation, and so on. Furthermore, the actual effect any rod adjustment has on the neck will vary between instruments according to the type of rod and the different woods used for the neck's construction. Even on two identical models, the rods can have differing effects. It also sometimes occurs (even with new guitars) that fully slackening the rod won't have the desired effect and other measures are necessary, but with new instruments that's what the warranty is for. Also, don't forget that necks are subject to movement caused by changes of temperature and humidity, so be prepared to tweak the rod when necessary.

CHECKING RELIEF

For any guitar to play with a low, buzz-free action, a slight amount of concave forward bow is necessary due to the elliptical shape of a string's vibration. The small amount of gap (concave bow) in the neck is called "relief," which is usually (but not always) necessary for a buzz-free action. This concave bow, in really, occurs between the first fret and approximately where the heel of the neck starts – typically between the 14th and the 16th fret depending on the guitar. Relief is measured at the mid-point: the 7th-8th fret.

With your guitar in playing position, fret the low E string at the first fret with you left hand and the 14th fret with your right hand. Now look at the seventh/eighth fret. There should be a small gap between the fret and the fretted string. That's the relief.

The amount of relief varies according to string gauge, action height and how hard you actually play. For example, if you use light gauge strings with a low action and a light touch, you'll probably need less relief and a virtually straight neck.

Before you make any adjustments you need to measure the relief and evaluate the neck's condition...

MEASURING NECK RELIEF

Just playing your guitar (normally thorough an amp) can give you a good indication of how much relief you need. If, for example, you're getting fret buzz on most strings when you play on the lower frets it could mean you don't have enough relief. If the lower frets sound fine but as you move up the neck you're getting more buzz it may mean you've got too much relief. Note, however, that this latter scenario could also mean that there's a more serious problem that the truss-rod can't cure. Part of any guitar neck is held firmly in the body. The main, unsupported length is pulled slightly forward by the string tension; the resulting concave bow can be corrected by the truss-rod. However, if there's a fault in the neck itself (maybe the truss-rod is too short, or the timber too weak) the neck can bend at this fulcrum point creating an "up-tilt" which can't be corrected by the truss-rod.

If you don't realise this and continue to tighten the rod, you may create an S-shape bend, where the main playing area has a convex bow (because you over-tightened the truss-rod) and the final part of the neck still tilts up because the neck itself is at fault.

This Washburn D-61 dreadnought's truss rod adjustment is very easily accessed through the soundhole, with strings slackened slightly and the correct allen key applied.

ACOUSTIC NECKS/ADJUSTMENTS

There are many variations in acoustic truss-rod adjustment facilities, though most follow similar procedures to those used on electrics. The through-soundhole approach used for Martins and others (such as the Washburn above) is similar to that used for vintage-style Fender solidbodies, with truss-rod adjustment accessed at the body end of the neck. Others, including Gibsons, are accessed under a plastic cover on the headstock behind the nut.

With these types and others, however, be aware that acoustics may be more sensitive to any adjustment which alters string tension as this has greater structural implications on the glued bridge and the thin wooden top of the guitar, which is much more vulnerable to distortion caused by the strings' pull than a solidbody electric guitar. For this reason, it is all the more important to slacken strings slightly when making any truss-rod adjustment on an acoustic, and to make all adjustments only by small fractions of a turn at a time, letting the guitar rest, then bringing strings back in tune, and carefully gauging the changes before proceeding further.

1 Place a capo at the first fret. Press the G string down at the 14th fret. Look out for a small gap of about. 0.25mm (.010") between the top of the seventh-to-ninth fret and the underside of the string. You can measure this gap with feeler gauges, even a steel ruler (or use a light guage plectrum, approximately 0.5mm thick, as a rough guide).

Headstock-end truss-rod adjustment is simple: just remove the coverplate (if one exists) to access the adjustment nut and proceed according to instructions.

2 Move the capo to the seventh or eighth fret, and with your right hand fret the last fret. Now measure the gap over the 14th fret (as described above). If this second gap is a lot more than the first relief measurement, it could mean that your neck is at fault. In this case do not attempt to tighten the rod; take your guitar to a pro.

ADJUSTING THE TRUSS ROD

Once you've followed the steps to evaluate the relief you can adjust the truss-rod if necessary. *Always* follow the manufacturer's recommendations and use the supplied truss rod key or allen wrench. Before you touch the truss-rod read, *If In Doubt... Don't* (following page). For guitars with nut-end adjustment the basic procedure is relatively simple. If you need less relief, tighten the truss-rod adjusting nut (turn it clockwise). Obviously you may need to remove the coverplate behind the nut. If you have too little relief, slacken the adjusting nut (turn it counter-clockwise).

Vintage Fender-style guitars have the rod adjustment at the body, end which is a little more involved...

1 Having evaluated the relief, slacken the strings and place a capo at the first fret. Turn the guitar over and undo – but don't fully remove – the neck screws. Slip the neck upwards so you can see the cross-head truss-rod adjusting nut.

2 Make your adjustment as above, re-tighten the neck screws, remove the capo and tune up. Check the relief again and if you need to make further adjustments repeat the above steps.

Note that when tightening the truss rod it is advisable to slightly slacken the string tension. Because the metal strings are in contact with the metal frets you must always expect a certain degree of fret buzz, magnified by how hard you hit the string. With electric guitars, always listen for fret buzz through an amp. Minor un-amplified buzz that occurs when you play "acoustically" on an electric but which can't be heard through the amp doesn't necessarily indicate a real problem.

Vintage Fender-style body-end truss-rod adjustment can be somewhat more involved, often requiring loosening the neck to access the adjustment nut.

set-up: bolt-on necks

A neck is a precious thing, so it's not surprising that even many pro players won't attempt truss-rod adjustments. But if you feel inclined to try any small adjustments in accordance with the manufacturers' manual, here are some tips.

Always use the correct tool for the job.
Never force the adjuster if it feels very tight.
Make any adjustment in very small degrees at a time and monitor progress. Usually the correct adjustment is achieved within about a quarter turn in the appropriate direction. Avoid making adjustments greater than this.
Leave some time for the neck to settle between adjustments
If you have any doubts, take the guitar back to the shop or a qualified repairer.

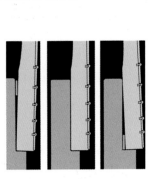

The angle of a guitar's neck relative to its body face is called "neck pitch." Short of major surgery, a set-neck guitar's neck pitch – as with that of the Les Paul pictured near-right, which has quite a steep pitch – is set during the manufacturing process, but there's a lot you can do to fine-tune the neck pitch of a bolt-on guitar. The exaggerated drawings above show three types of bolt-on neck pitch: fingerboard parallel to body face without a shim (center), increased neck pitch with shim placed deep into the neck pocket (right), and an upward tilt created by placing a shim at the front edge of the pocket (left) – the latter a rare scenario.

ADJUSTING A BOLT-ON NECK

In theory, the face of a bolt-on neck will be parallel to the face of the body. In practice the neck often tilts back slightly (this back angle is called the "neck pitch") so that the correct action height can be set. With its carved top, the neck of a Les Paul – or similarly designed guitar – leaves the body at quite an acute angle, which many players find much more comfortable to hold and play.

It's important to understand the relationship between the bridge height and the neck pitch. On a bolt-on Stratocaster, for example, the individually adjustable saddles – especially the pressed steel-type of a vintage tremolo bridge – have a limited range of height adjustment. You may find that even with the saddles as low as they can go the action is still too high. By slightly increasing the neck pitch the action can be made lower. Viewed from the side of the guitar, the tip of the heel (that "lip" of wood at the underside of the body which supports the end of the neck) acts as the fulcrum point. Think of a see-saw: behind that point the neck drops, in front of that point the neck rises.

Imagine the reverse situation: that even with the saddles adjusted to their full height, the action is too low, so you need to reduce the neck pitch – possibly even creating an upward tilt. The saddles-at-lowest/action-too-high scenario is the most common, whereas the saddles-at-highest/action-too-low scenario, where you need to reduce the neck pitch, is actually quite rare.

Fender's American Standard series guitars have a four-screw neck-to-body fixing plus a micro-tilt adjustment which makes neck pitch adjustment easy. For bolt-on necks without this micro-tilt adjustment – the majority – you'll need to add a neck shim: a small piece of thin hard material (ideally wood veneer, hard plastic sheet or hard cardboard – cigarette packets or business cards will work in an emergency). Here's what you do...

1 If the guitar is fitted with a vibrato, place a stack of business cards or the vibrato backplate under the back of the vibrato bridge. This keeps your vibrato close to its correct in-tune setting, and makes it quicker and easier to get back to correct string tension after adjustments have been made.

2 Slacken strings, place a capo at the first fret. Remove the vibrato arm if one is fitted and lay the guitar on a flat surface, face down.

3 Using a correctly sized cross-head screwdriver remove the four neck screws. Turn the body and neck over and place the neck to one side.

4 Cut a shim with scissors to the appropriate size and place it between the end of the neck pocket and the two screws furthest into the body. A couple of small dots of PVA glue (any basic wood glue – alternately use double sided adhesive tape) will hold the shim in place, but don't use so much that's it's difficult to remove the shim for further adjustment at another time.

5 Re-assemble guitar. Put some tension back on the strings and reset saddles. If everything seems OK carefully reset the action (as described in the *String Height* and *Vibrato Adjustment* sections which follow from page 78). If the shim is too low or too high don't worry – remove the neck, take out the shim and try again.

set-up: bolt-on necks

TECH'S TIP: NECK ACHE

It's pretty rare that a misaligned bolt-on neck cannot be corrected, even if you have to take it to a pro. A set-neck guitar, however, is a different matter. But, as top London repairman Charlie Chandler points out, "It's pretty rare these days that set-neck guitars with alignment problems get through quality control – if they can't set them up properly they don't leave the factory." If you're unlucky enough to have problems, unless it is a valuable instrument, re-setting the neck is probably not worth the time and trouble.

"The majority of less-expensive guitars have a thick polyester finish," continues Chandler, "so even if a neck reset is undertaken it will always be evident that it's been repaired. Unlike older cellulose finishes, where we have numerous techniques to disguise the repair, with polyester it's virtually impossible to hide."

Sometimes the bridge and tailpiece can be repositioned, however, especially on a Gibson-style guitar with a Tune-o-matic bridge and stud tailpiece. This may also mean that the pickups have to be slightly moved, yet these methods are a more cost-effective answer than a total neck reset.

So, while the problem is rare, it's worth checking on a new purchase that the neck is aligned correctly. You can visually check (or take a 6" ruler with you) that the outer strings sit approximately equidistant from the fingerboard edges at the 12th fret. Remember, the distances should be the same – or, if anything, a greater distance on the treble side (as previously discussed) is preferable.

A set-neck may also be glued in at the wrong neck pitch. If the angle is too flat you might not be able to get the bridge low enough for your required action, and vice versa. Again, this can be a serious problem and, as Chandler says, "if you're thinking of buying a set-neck guitar ask the store to set it up to your requirements. If they can't or won't... don't buy it.'

DESIGN STRENGTH
While their glued-in nature gives the impression of being universally "stronger" than bolt-on necks, not all set-neck guitars are created equal. For example, a Gibson Les Paul (above left), has much more wood to adhere to on the bass side of the guitar's body than a Gibson SG (above right) with its deep cutaways on either side of the neck. Before the SG design was modified in other ways in the late-'60s, neck breaks were a significant problem for these models.

On vibrato-fitted guitars, begin by placing the vibrato backplate (spring cover) or a stack of business cards under the back edge of the bridge to maintain your bridge angle for easy re-tuning.

Place a capo at the first fret to keep strings clamped in the correct position at the nut end.

Remove the neck screws – *always* using the correct size screwdriver – and set the neck aside.

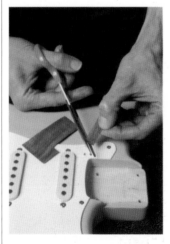 

Cut a shim to the appropriate size – wood veneer or other hard material is preferable for this.

To increase neck pitch, place the shim between the end of the neck pocket and the inside screw holes.

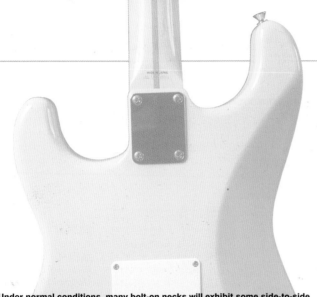

Under normal conditions, many bolt-on necks will exhibit some side-to-side movement, which can usually be corrected. You may be able to simply manhandle your neck into better alignment, then tighten slightly.

To accurately assess alignment, measure the clearance between low and high E and fretboard edge.

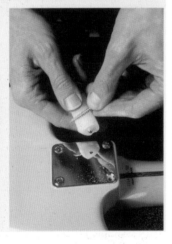

If re-alignment requires heavy tightening of the neck screws, apply some candlewax first to ease the job.

MORE BOLT-ON NECK ADJUSTMENTS

Unless a bolt-on neck is really well fitted, the chances are it may move sideways if it's roughly handled or knocked. This movement is usually pretty subtle, but the first check you want to make is to see if your neck moves.

Hold the guitar in a seated playing position and push down quite roughly on the neck. Did you feel it move, did it creak? Don't worry. If it did move, yank in the opposite direction and it should move back again. What you've established is the likelihood that your guitar neck will move in the future – that's not ideal. But the cure can be simple.

Firstly, measure the distance from the outer strings, at the 12th fret, to the edge of the fingerboard. The distance should be the same. If anything a greater distance on the treble side facilitates hammer-on and pull-off techniques and stops you slipping off the board.

Manhandle the neck until you achieve the right position. Lay the guitar face down on your work surface and tighten (don't over-tighten) the neck screws. Sometimes this is all you need to cure any movement. Now see if you can move the neck under reasonable pressure. If you can't, you've solved the problem: most bolt-ons just need a little tightening from time to time.

If the neck still moves, remove it and check the condition of the neck pocket and bottom of the neck. Are there any loose wood shavings? Are the surfaces rough? The flatter the surfaces, the more neck-to-body contact and the more stable the joint will be (also, the better your tone). We're not advising trying to smooth the neck pocket – take it to a pro – but one thing that may help is to apply some dry lubricant (candle wax is ideal) to the neck screws and re-assemble the guitar. This simple tip may allow slightly more pressure to be applied without damaging the screw heads and thus cure any movement.

Removing a bolt-on neck may seem dramatic on your first attempt but so long as you use the correct tools, lubricate the screws and don't over-tighten them you'll be okay. Never force a screw. If it doesn't want to move, *leave it* – and seek pro advice.

CHECKING NUT HEIGHT

Our main concern with the top nut is to ensure that it is cut to the "correct" height and has friction-free string slots. Altering or replacing a nut is definitely a pro's job, and nut replacement is usually necessary when you have your guitar re-fretted.

Most new production guitars have nuts that are cut a little too high. This may make it harder to press the strings down and fret them (and might cause intonation problems), but it is simpler for a repairer to lower your nut height than to increase it. To check your top nut height, first fret each string between the second and third frets (pictured opposite). Ideally there should be a very small gap above the first fret and the bottom of each string. Even if it is almost touching, don't worry – the open, unfretted string may still vibrate cleanly. If the open string buzzes, then it probably means that the nut slot is too low – but check both your neck relief and string action height.

To check if the string groove in the nut is impeding the return-to-pitch of the string, pick an open string and bend it by pushing down on the string behind the nut. Can you hear any clicks? This will indicate a tight string groove in the nut. Does the string come back into tune? Re-tune and try again. So long as your strings are properly stretched, a behind-the-nut up-bend of around a semitone should come back in tune. Again, getting the string grooves perfectly smooth is a tricky job. If you've got problems,

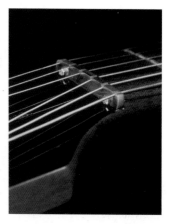

A little pencil lead (graphite) still makes a simple and effective lubricant for curing minor string-hitching problems. To check nut height, fret each string between second and third fret (above). The string should be touching or *just* above the first fret...

... Then, if the nut's string groove is impeding string-movement on bends etc, rub a soft pencil lead in the groove, and return the string.

Once nut grooves have worn too low, replacement is the only option, though Gordon-Smith's adjustable nut (above) offers a longer lifespan.

lift the string out of the groove, rub a soft pencil lead (graphite) into the groove (as pictured above, center), and return the string. Try those bends again. The graphite lubrication may have helped, but won't necessarily cure the problem.

The ever-resourceful British maker Gordon-Smith uses a height-adjustable brass nut (far right). It's a neat idea. If over a long period the nut slots become worn you can loosen the nut with the two screws, place a thin shim under the nut to raise it, and if necessary re-cut the slots. Of course, if you just want to raise your string height – for slide or bottleneck playing – it's very easy: just use a thicker shim.

FINGERBOARD FUNDAMENTALS

The fingerboard holds the frets and provides the playing surface of the instrument. Obvious, really. But, as ever, the role of the fingerboard is more complex and worthy of some examination. Made from a hard-wearing hardwood – typically rosewood or ebony – the fingerboard is usually unfinished. Only if a light-colored wood such as maple is used will a finish be applied, to protect it from getting dirty.

Some makers such as Music Man use a light oil finish on both the maple neck and fingerboard, and this does get dirty. Some players like it; others (including store owners) often don't. Back in the 1970s Fender used a very thick finish on their maple fingerboards, and this may be why people think that maple and rosewood 'boards feel different.

With the modern choice of typically higher-gauge fretwire, the fingerboard material really makes little difference to its playing feel. Tonally, however, the fingerboard will have an effect. Maple is perceived to have a bright and twangy tone, contrasted by the warmer tone of the softer rosewood. Ebony is the hardest and smoothest wood used for the job, and creates a bright sound with a lot of definition. But, as ever, the "sound" of wood is a highly subjective area.

FINGERBOARD RADIUS

Much more important to the player than the wood from which the fingerboard is cut is its slight radius (camber, or curving from side to side). Combined with the size of the frets and the overall set-up, this is what contributes most to different fingerboard

feels. Radius is measured by considering the fingerboard as a wedge from a cylinder of a certain radius.

Fender originally used a small 7¼" (184mm) radius, although US/Mexican-made Fenders now uniformly use a flatter 9½" (241mm) radius. Gibson went for a flatter 12" (305mm) radius, PRS uses an "in between" 10" (254mm), and Parker uses a "conical" radius increasing from nut to top fret, from approximately 10" to 12" (254mm–305mm) so that the board is flatter in its upper reaches. Modern rock guitars typically use a flatter radius of anything from 14" (356mm) upwards.

So why all the options? Fender's vintage radius feels great for comfortable chording, but with a low action, high-fret bends can lead to "choking" (the bent string colliding against a higher fret, thereby killing off your note). The only way to stop this is to raise the action or flatten the fingerboard radius, hence Fender's current 9½" (241mm) radius. But fashions constantly change.

TECH'S TIP: NEW NUTS FOR OLD

Hugh Manson, a UK repairman and custom-builder for the likes of former Led Zeppelin bassist John Paul Jones, says the main reason to replace a top nut is because it's too low, either from the abrasive action of the strings, or when a re-fret sets the new frets higher than the old ones.

Another problem occurs when players increase the gauge of strings they use. "Never try to force a heavier-gauge string into an old nut slot that was cut for a lighter gauge," advises Manson. "At worst, you may crack the nut, or suffer from tuning problems as the new string sticks in the old slot."

A repairman will use special tools to cut and/or widen the slots. When it comes to nut replacement, some guitars are problematic. "The ones I hate are those 1970s Fenders where the thick polyester finish is sprayed over the nut. Getting the old nut out is difficult" says Manson.

The same can apply to many Gibson guitars where the nut sits at the end of the fingerboard but is partially recessed into the neck wood and then sprayed over. Many modern guitars, including those of PRS for example, have the nut fixed after finishing, so nut replacement is relatively easy. "A nut has a finite life," concludes Manson. "It must be solidly fixed, but removable in the future when replacement becomes necessary."

set-up: fingerboards

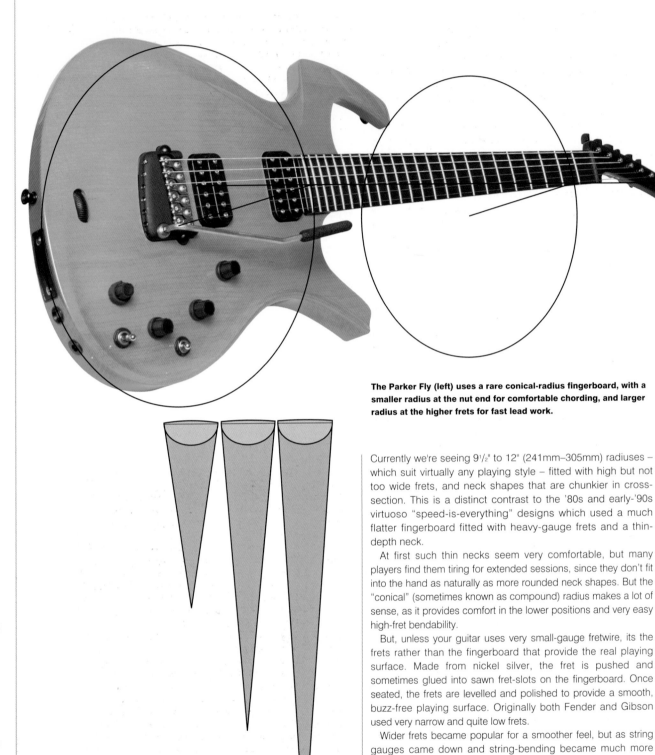

The Parker Fly (left) uses a rare conical-radius fingerboard, with a smaller radius at the nut end for comfortable chording, and larger radius at the higher frets for fast lead work.

Most production electric guitars use a fingerboard radius that is constant throughout the length of the guitar. Vintage Fenders (and reissues) use a very rounded-feeling 7¹/₄" (184mm) radius, above left; Gibsons use a flatter 12" (305mm), center; while Floyd-Rose equipped guitars use an extremely flat 16" (406mm), right.

Currently we're seeing 9¹/₂" to 12" (241mm–305mm) radiuses – which suit virtually any playing style – fitted with high but not too wide frets, and neck shapes that are chunkier in cross-section. This is a distinct contrast to the '80s and early-'90s virtuoso "speed-is-everything" designs which used a much flatter fingerboard fitted with heavy-gauge frets and a thin-depth neck.

At first such thin necks seem very comfortable, but many players find them tiring for extended sessions, since they don't fit into the hand as naturally as more rounded neck shapes. But the "conical" (sometimes known as compound) radius makes a lot of sense, as it provides comfort in the lower positions and very easy high-fret bendability.

But, unless your guitar uses very small-gauge fretwire, its the frets rather than the fingerboard that provide the real playing surface. Made from nickel silver, the fret is pushed and sometimes glued into sawn fret-slots on the fingerboard. Once seated, the frets are levelled and polished to provide a smooth, buzz-free playing surface. Originally both Fender and Gibson used very narrow and quite low frets.

Wider frets became popular for a smoother feel, but as string gauges came down and string-bending became much more popular, makers and players realised that higher frets made strings easier to bend. Wide and low frets were popular for their smooth feel, but if the top of the fret (the "crown") is too flat you can get intonation problems. Likewise, if the fret is very high you have to be very precise about how you fret each note, as it's easy to sharpen notes by applying uneven finger pressure, especially within a tricky chord.

CHECKING FOR FRET BUZZ

Fret buzz can be caused by too-low string height, too much or too little neck relief – as already discussed – or isolated individual height problems (where, for example, one fret has popped out of its fingerboard slot). Always test for fret buzz through your amp. Bear in mind that minor buzzing due to hard playing and the proximity of metal-to-metal (string against fret) is unavoidable. Nonetheless, play every string at every fret and if you hear a deadening clonk at, for example, the 12th fret, it could mean either that this fret is too low or that the next fret (the 13th in this example) is too high. Note the problems, and have a pro check your guitar.

WHAT IS ACTION?

For many players the "action" of a guitar is the height of the strings above the frets, typically measured from the top of the 12th fret to the underside of the outer two strings: the low E (bass) and the high E (treble). But if only it were that simple. In fact "action" is a general term used to describe the combination of the entire playing "feel" of the guitar. You'll hear comments like "this guitar has a really low action", or "the action's really high on this one" and the reasons are not just to do with the physical distance of the strings from the frets. Neck condition is crucial: the neck's straightness and relief, the fingerboard radius in relation to the bridge's saddle radius, and the nut and even fret height all contribute to the player's perception – that's you! – of action.

For example, as we discussed earlier, the relief of the neck, when you think about it, will alter the string height. More relief (concave bow) places the frets further from the strings, and vice versa. Big, high frets often give the impression of a higher action simply because the fret's top, or playing surface, is further from the fingerboard face. Of course, without having your guitar re-fretted you can't do anything about this yourself, but what you can do – having adjusted the neck is – set a string height that's most suitable for you.

Many players simply strive for the lowest possible action "without buzzes". As we've already discussed, that may never be achievable and is not always the "best" set-up. The best set-up is simply the one that suits you and your playing style, your guitar, and the frequency at which you practise and play. If you're too busy to play for more than a short while every other day or so, a medium to high action will probably feel a little hard on your fingers. But if you practise every day you could cope well with a higher action, and you might prefer the tone this affords.

There is of course a fundamental that we've purposely left until last: your strings. We've already discussed the effect of string gauge on the neck itself and the feel of the strings in relation to your guitar's scale length. But those aspects aside, a heavier gauge will simply feel harder to play (initially at least). Likewise the higher the string height of your guitar the tougher the guitar feels to fret and bend. Certainly, the additional mass of the heavier gauge should give you a bigger sound, and a higher action should mean a cleaner, less buzzy tone, but it's going to require more physical effort and practise. A guitar with a low string height and light gauge strings will feel fine for bedroom practice; but on-stage – with all that adrenaline pumping through you and the natural tendency to play harder in front of an audience – a heavier gauge and possibly higher action might be more suitable. So changing your string gauge is a lot more complex than just re-stringing your guitar.

Fretwire is available today in a wide variety of sizes, though most is still identifiable in simple terms by the era from which it originates or a maker by whom it is commonly used. The illustrations below show the cross-sections of three types of wire, inset against photos of the actual frets on different types of guitars. Fender's "vintage" fretwire (below left) is of a relatively small gauge, while Gibson traditionally uses fretwire of a larger cross-section (center). The Jackson fingerboard (right) carries an even larger wire, usually called "jumbo", which has become popular on guitars favored by some rock and metal players.

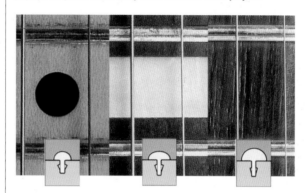

TECH'S TIP: FRETFULNESS

Fret wear, unless extreme, rarely requires a total re-fret; usually the repairer can level the frets and then re-shape them (also called "crowning" or "dressing") to a smooth, dome-like section. Of course, as experienced repairer Tim Shaw (Manager, Product Development of Acoustics – both for Fender and Guild – at Guild's Custom Shop) points out, "The more times frets are re-crowned the flatter they get. In extreme cases they become so flat that your intonation goes down the tubes and your only option is a re-fret.

"But one of the main reasons for a re-fret is when you get a twisted neck that can't be straightened by the truss rod. Similarly, guitars with a small fingerboard radius, which can lead to string choking, are another candidate. On occasions the radius in the upper fret areas can be increased (by careful levelling and re-dressing) but in other cases the old frets must be removed and the 'board re-radiused. Then there are players – especially those who like a high fret – who will prefer a re-fret rather then re-crowning. Of course, you may simply want to change to a different gauge of fretwire.

"The hardest – and therefore the most expensive – are guitars with bound fingerboards. Finished maple fingerboards are problematic too, especially those old '70s Fenders with a really thick finish. You have to re-fret and re-finish the 'board. Rickenbacker often combine binding with a finish; they require a lot of work."

Conversely an unbound, unfinished rosewood board is probably the most straightforward. "Yeah," agrees Shaw, "an old '56 Gibson Les Paul Junior… the necks are really stiff and if you can't re-fret one of those you're in trouble."

set-up: string height

CHART OF 12th FRET STRING HEIGHTS

String Heights	12th fret treble	12th fret bass
LOW	3/64" (1.2mm)	1/16" (1.6mm)
MEDIUM	1/16" (1.6mm)	5/64" (2.0mm)
HIGH	5/64" (2.0mm)	3/32" (2.4mm)
SLIDE	3/32" (2.4mm)	9/64" (3.6mm)

The measurements listed above are merely approximate guides and will depend on string gauge, neck condition and nut height.

You can easily check your string heights using a ruler with fine gradations. Measurements are traditionally taken at the 12th fret, from the top of the fret to the underside of the outer strings.

STRING HEIGHT

Assuming that your neck is pretty much correctly adjusted and your nut isn't too high or too low, you can proceed to setting the string height.

Using a steel ruler with fine gradations for tight measurements, measure the string height at the 12th fret – from the top of the fret to the underside of the string – of the outer strings (as pictured, center left). A basic guide would be approximately 1/16" (1.6mm) on the treble side (high E), 5/64" (2.0mm) on the bass-side (low E). (See chart, left.) What about the other strings? They should gradually curve from the low E to high E heights, creating a radius that will follow that of the fingerboard. That'll give you – with all the previous considerations taken into account – a slightly high, but hopefully clean, buzz-free playing guitar: This is a good starting point from which to fine-tune to your own taste.

To adjust the string height you need to raise or lower the bridge or the individual saddles. If you have a new guitar, the chances are you'll have an owners' manual. *Always read this thoroughly!* The most specialist tool you'll need is the correctly sized Allen key, for the height adjustable saddles and tremolo pivot posts.

TUNE-O-MATIC

The Tune-o-matic type bridge, as fitted by Gibson and Epiphone, for example, has overall height adjustment either via two thumb wheels or a slot-head screw. The radius created by the bridge is not adjustable except by notching the saddles, a job for a pro.

To lower the action, turn the wheels or slot screw clockwise (the pitch of the strings will drop slightly); to raise the action, you must slacken the strings to achieve any upward movement, then turn the bridge's set screw or thumbwheel counter-clockwise. Tune back to pitch and re-measure.

Once you've achieved the correct string height, check the stud tailpiece – the strings should run from the back of the Tune-o-matic saddles to the tailpiece *without* touching the back edge of the bridge. You may need to raise the stud tailpiece, but keep the angle as steep as possible. The adjustment of this tailpiece is the same as for the one-piece wrapover bridge (as described on the opposite page).

The radius of a Gibson-style Tune-o-matic brige is fixed, but usually allows for a fairly wide range of string-height adjustment. Simply turn the set screws or thumbwheels at either end clockwise to lower the action. To raise it, slacken strings slightly to allow movement, then turn screws or thumbwheels counter-clockwise to raise the bridge. Some units are too tight for easy thumbwheel movement, so you'll need to apply the correct-sized screwdriver anyway, as pictured left. After adjustment, set the stud tailpiece for the correct break angle over the bridge saddles (above left).

ONE-PIECE WRAPOVER

Gibson's one piece wrapover bridge/tailpiece (or any of the variants) has two large slot-head studs which adjust the string height. (Again, like the Tune-o-matic, the radius of the bridge is preset.) It's doubtful you'll have a big enough screwdriver – don't use one with a blade width that's smaller than the stud slot, because you'll damage the stud. Instead…

Slacken off the string tension and you may find you can simply move the studs by hand or with the aid of a stiff (or a couple) of plectrums – some find a small coin ideal – placed in the slot. A tip passed on by the late Sid Poole, a top UK luthier, is to slacken off the string tension and place a piece of paper towel over the slot and insert the curved end of your 6" steel ruler, as pictured right. The edges of these rules can be very sharp – you may also want to wrap a piece of paper towel around the rule. Make a turn on the bass stud then the same on the treble stud, tune up and re-measure you string height. Take your time otherwise you'll damage those stud slots. *Always remember to slacken your strings before adjusting these studs!*

OTHER SIX-SADDLE TYPES

Bridges with six saddles usually have height adjustment for each string. For non-trem, six-saddle Tele or Strat bridges, for example, the adjustment is the same as for the Stratocaster tremolo bridge (below). Three-saddle Tele bridges don't give as much precise height control as a six-saddle bridge. But by setting the height screw next to each string – thereby angling the paired bridge saddles – you can achieve the necessary radius.

If you have a bolt-on guitar and for any reason you don't have enough or have too little saddle adjustment to achieve your desired action, you will probably need to shim your neck slightly, as discussed in previous pages.

VIBRATO BRIDGES

The Floyd Rose-style vibrato is quite a complex piece of hardware, but thankfully setting string height is dead easy. There are two height adjustable pivot posts; because the saddles are preset in terms of height – and therefore radius – these are the main way to adjust the string height (pictured near-right). Usually a Floyd Rose has a flat-ish saddle radius of about 16" (406mm). If your fingerboard radius is smaller you'll have to put up with the outer strings being slightly higher than the inner ones to avoid fret rattle, so here measure your action height firstly from the G and D strings, not the outer E strings. (Tip: You can alter the height of a Floyd Rose's saddle with very thin shim steel – try your local hardware store. Simply cut small pieces to fit under the saddles, therefore rasing the height and creating a small radius.)

A Strat – especially with tremolo – is more complex, as there are six saddles, individually adjustable for height. Having set the outer two strings for height, use the steel rule to measure the inner four, and, gradually increase the height from the treble to the bass strings. As we've said, if you have a vintage spec Fender guitar with its small (7¼") fingerboard radius, you may encounter upper-fret choking. So once the string height is set try some upper-fret bends. If the string chokes on a higher fret, raise the saddle further.

You might find that using a radius gauge (pictured right as available from Stewart-MacDonald, or you can make one yourself) is a more convenient way to match the radius of the saddles to the radius of the fingerboard once the outer two string heights have been set. Current Fender USA/Mexican guitars have

In theory, the Gibson-style wrapover bridge/tailpiece is simple to adjust – but you're unlikely to have a big enough screwdriver handy. After slackening the strings, place a paper towel over the stud slots and then insert your steel ruler to make the adjustment.

The Floyd-Rose style vibrato, as on this Jackson, allows for overall height adjustment only.

A Strat's six individually-adjustable saddles allow for precise string-height and radius setting.

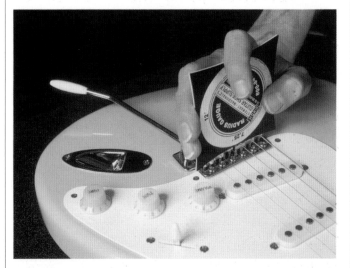

A radius gauge, as pictured above (this one from leading guitar-tools supplier Stewart-MacDonald) provides a quick-fire means of setting your bridge to accurately reflect your fingerboard radius.

Unlike the six screws of the vintage Strat-style vibrato, the Wilkinson VS100 uses two pivot posts as its fulcrum points. These also serve as a straightforward means of overall height adjustment...

To adjust string height on the Wilkinson VS100, first slacken off the saddle lock-down screw, then set the outer saddles flat against the bridge plate and adjust the overall height accordingly, raising or lowering the pivot posts...

...while fingerboard radius is matched by raising or lowering the six individually-adjustable saddles. When introduced, the Wilkinson VS100 – seen in detail at the top of the page – represented one of the more significant advancements in non-locking vibrato tailpieces.

a 9½" fingerboard radius; Japanese Strat reissues (and some older spec USA models) still have a smaller 7¼" radius.

Using a radius gauge is a fine starting point, but no adjustments are written in stone. Once you've set the saddle radius you might, for example, want to slightly reduce the height of the centre strings, but you must retain a gentle curve.

Alternatively, with any multi-saddle bridge you can set the action totally by "feel". Simply lower each string until you get continuous buzzing on most frets, then raise it until most of the buzzes disappear.

Wilkinson's VS100 bridge has adjustment both for pivot-post height and individual saddle height. The pivot posts are for height adjustment and the individual saddles are to match the fingerboard radius. *Before making any height or intonation adjustments on a Wilkinson tremolo, slacken off the saddle lock-down screw.* The outer saddles should be flat on the tremolo base-plate. Adjust these accordingly, then turn the pivot posts clockwise, lowering the vibrato until the outer strings just touch the last fret on the fingerboard. You can then alter the heights of the other saddles to just touch that last fret, thereby perfectly matching the fingerboard radius of your guitar. Now raise the pivot posts until you achieve the correct action height. This works with an American Standard Strat vibrato too, only the outer saddles should sit approx ³⁄₃₂" (2.4mm) from the face of the baseplate. As with the saddle adjustments, always slacken off string tension before you raise these pivot posts.

VINTAGE-STYLE STRAT VIBRATOS

The vintage-style Strat vibrato pivots on its six front-mounted screws and does not float above the body like a Floyd Rose or Wilkinson vibrato. Therefore the back of this Strat vibrato usually tips up to create up-bend. But you can, for example, have the vibrato set flat on the body so you only have down-bend, with the advantage that if you break one string the others won't be pulled out of tune by the springs. Another option is to make the guitar into a totally non-vibrato instrument by setting the vibrato hard down on the body and leaving the arm in the case.

Achieving different set-ups is relatively easy. Basically, the strings' tension is counteracted by the tension on the two (or more) springs in the vibrato cavity in the rear of the body. Remove the vibrato backplate and you'll see that the springs are hooked at one end onto the vibrato's sustain block and at the other onto the spring "claw". This claw is held to the body with two cross-head screws. The number of springs (and their combined tension) plus the distance of the spring claw from the neck-facing end of the spring cavity will affect the position of the vibrato.

The number and type of springs you fit will affect not only the overall tension but also the feel of the vibrato. Three springs with .010" gauge strings on a Strat is pretty standard. Drop down to two springs and the vibrato feels lighter and its return-to-pitch can be less stable. With lighter .009" gauge strings and two springs it usually feels very smooth, but the firmer feel of three springs is often preferred. Heavier-gauge strings need more springs, and if you want to defeat the action of the vibrato so it sits flat and tight on the body, put all five in. Remember, the "correct" setting of the vibrato is always a balance between strings and springs.

It's worth pointing out that, because of this string-to-spring balance, a Strat vibrato (or indeed any vibrato based on this principle) has limitations. If you bend one string, the rest go flat (try it). You have to bend the string further to achieve the same degree of pitch change as you would on an equivalent fixed-bridge guitar. Country-style bends become tricky too. You might bend one string upwards while fretting and voicing another string… and the un-bent string will go flat. Products like the Fender/Hipshot Trem-setter and WD's Tremolo Stabiliser aim to reduce this problem, but they are not easy to set up and you'll need a pro's help. If this type of bending is important to your style you might want to consider a fixed-bridge guitar, or set the Strat vibrato flat on the body so it doesn't move. Keep in mind that if you don't use a vibrato in your playing, keeping one on your guitar – and dealing with the inherent tuning and set-up difficulties – is almost certainly more trouble than it's worth.

Different springs vary in tension. Combine this with how you like your vibrato to feel and there really are no set rules. So long as the set-up works for you and stays pretty much in tune, then that's the right one.

Typically, however, a vintage Strat vibrato is set so that there is a gap of approximately ⁵⁄₆₄"–⅛" (2mm-3mm) between the back of the bridge and the face of the guitar. This should give an up-bend of approximately one semitone on the top E-string and around a tone on the low E-string, assuming that .009"–.042" gauge strings are fitted.

VINTAGE-STYLE STRAT VIBRATO SET-UP

Assess your existing set-up. Measure the height of the tip-up angle – if there is one – at the back of the bridge. Remove the backplate cover and check the springs. For a lighter feel, use two springs set from the sustain block's outer holes to the spring claw's two inner hooks. For a firmer feel, use one more spring from the block's central hole to the claw's central hook. Move the springs one at a time if necessary; lift off the springs at the block first, then hook them onto the claw and reposition the other end into the block.

The length of the spring cavity differs between Strat models, and of course springs (and strings) vary in tension, so there is no one set position for the spring claw. However, to give you an idea of how it moves, we measured a Fender reissue Strat fitted with a set of .009"–.042" gauge strings. The spring claw with three springs measured approximately ⅝" (16mm) from the neck-facing edge of the back cavity to the neck-facing edge of the claw, and when fitted with two springs measured about ⅜" (9mm-10mm). If you're using .010"s you're better off with three springs – we set the claw ½"–⁹⁄₁₆" (13mm-14mm) from the cavity edge. Make sure the claw is parallel to the neck-facing edge of the cavity.

Yet another of Leo Fender's surprisingly dead-on innovations, the vintage-style Stratocaster tremolo is still a favorite nearly half a decade after its introduction. While cumbersome and difficult to set-up in some ways, it provides a wide range of smooth down-bend, and is highly adjustable for string height and radius.

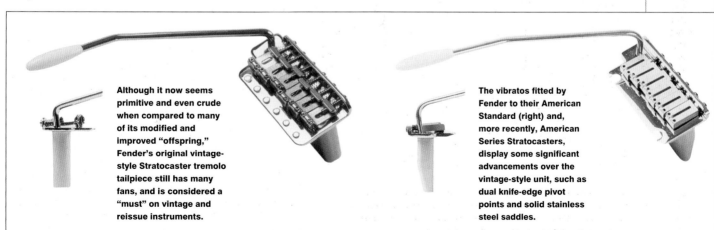

Although it now seems primitive and even crude when compared to many of its modified and improved "offspring," Fender's original vintage-style Stratocaster tremolo tailpiece still has many fans, and is considered a "must" on vintage and reissue instruments.

The vibratos fitted by Fender to their American Standard (right) and, more recently, American Series Stratocasters, display some significant advancements over the vintage-style unit, such as dual knife-edge pivot points and solid stainless steel saddles.

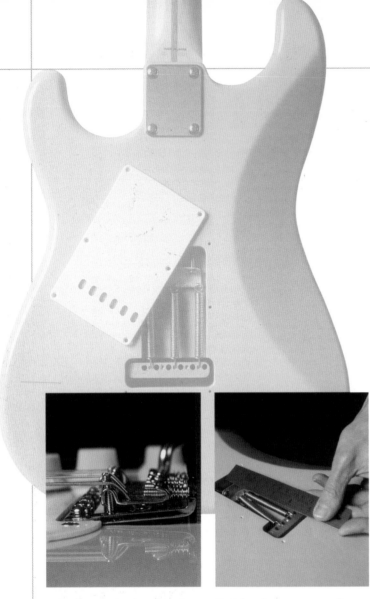

Tune to pitch. Measure the height of the tip-up angle and adjust both the spring-claw screws. If you need more tip-up angle undo (turn anti/counter-clockwise) the two claw screws. Start with two full turns per screw and keep the spring claw parallel with the cavity. Tune the guitar back to pitch and re-measure the up-tilt. If you've gone too far, tighten both screws; on the other hand, if you need more tip-up, loosen the screws. After every small adjustment it's important to re-tune to pitch and then re-measure the up-tilt. When you've got about ³⁄₃₂" (2.5mm) of tip-up angle, check the amount of up-bend. You should find, with the vibrato pulled all the way up, that you have about a one-semitone up-bend on the top E-string, that the low E-string will easily rise by two or maybe even three semitones, and that you can achieve around a tone up-bend on your G-string. You can precisely tune this up-bend by adjusting the spring claw screws.

Now check the position of the six pivot screws at the front of the bridge. Undo the center four screws a couple of full turns so they sit slightly above the vibrato. Hold the vibrato flat down on the body with the vibrato arm, and screw the two outer screws down (not overtight) onto the bridgeplate. Release the vibrato arm and unscrew the outer screws until they just clear the top of the plate after the vibrato has rested in its angled position. If you've already set your action (string height), then all you need to do is just re-check it. You're now ready to set your intonation and maximise tuning stability.

To begin assessing the set-up of your vintage-style Strat vibrato, measure the height of the tip-up angle of the bridge plate.

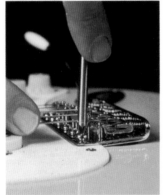

Next, for reference, measure the distance of the front of the spring claw from the front of the spring cavity.

After adding or removing springs to account for preferences of feel and spring/string tension, re-tune to pitch, re-check height of tip-up angle, and adjust the spring claw as necessary to correct any changes.

Once you have adjusted the springs and re-set your tip-up angle, you are ready to adjust the pivot screws – as described in detail in the text. Done carefully, this work should maximize your vibrato's action and stability.

TECH'S TIP: BLOCK PARTY

A tip handed on from British luthier Phil Norsworthy (and used by Fender, as reported by Dan Erlewine in the *Guitar Player Repair Guide*) is to use a small, wedge-shaped wooden block, approximately 2" long by 1" (50mm by 25mm) wide with a depth that tapers from around ½" to ⅓" (12mm to 9mm). You place it in the rear trem cavity between the back of the trem's sustain block and the cavity. Because of the block's taper, this allows you to set the precise tip-up angle. Norsworthy recommends a generous ⅛" (3mm), the Fender Custom Shop, ³⁄₃₂" (2.4mm). With the block in place, slacken-off the spring tension so the string tension holds the block. Now you can make your string height, radius and intonation adjustments without the trem moving. Once set, tighten the spring claw. Keep it parallel and, when tight enough, the block just drops out, leaving you with the trem perfectly set and in tune. This time-saving block can also be used – because of the taper – on numerous other floating or vintage style trems.

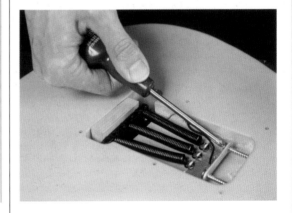

SETTING UP TWO-SCREW FLOATING VIBRATOS

Floating vibratos like the Floyd Rose, Wilkinson and modern American Standard vibratos work on the same principle as the vintage versions – the string tension is balanced by the spring tension. But they all use a more efficient pivot point in the form of two height adjustable posts, and they "float" parallel to the face of the guitar. Note that the American Standard vibrato can float parallel or be set like a vintage, though you will probably need to adjust the neck pitch to alter the set-up.

Setting these vibratos to the correct position is identical to the vintage, and only instead of measuring the tip-up height at just the back of the bridge, you should measure the distance of the underside of the bridge to the face of the body at the front of the bridge, then at the back of the bridge. For optimum performance, these two measurements should be the same.

The distance from the front of the bridge to the body directly affects action height; adjust the spring tension to match the distance of the back of the bridge to that of the front.

ACOUSTIC BRIDGES

Acoustic guitar bridges play a dual role, anchoring the strings and transmitting string vibration through to the top. The size, height and position of the bridge depends upon the instrument's scale length, neck angle and string spacing. On steel strung guitars the bridges are usually made of either rosewood or ebony, or lesser woods that are "ebonised," which means that they are painted black to hide the material's true nature.

Bridge saddles use many materials, some man made, some natural. Popular materials include hard plastics, synthetic bone and natural materials such as animal bone and ivory. The saddle slots are angled to allow for intonation. On some instruments there are two saddles, one for the E-A-D-G strings and another for the B and E strings, placed at different angles for correct intonation of the top B and E strings.

On most steel strung acoustic guitar bridges the strings are held in place with bridge pins which go through the bridge and into the body. The strings are then held securely between the shaft of the pin and the bridge plate (a piece of wood which re-enforces the underside of the bridge). Another method of securing the strings has small holes drilled behind the saddle through to the rear end of the bridge. The strings are passed through the back of the bridge towards and over the saddle. A small brass strip with holes to accommodate the strings is often placed at the back of the bridge for reinforcement. Obviously this style of bridge doesn't require bridge pins and has been a popular feature on budget instruments over the years. The design is good that it makes for easy and quick restringing but it is difficult to shave the bridge height down if the guitar develops a high action (due to the top pulling up) at some in the future.

Classical bridges are simpler in construction and feature a straight saddle with no apparent compensation for intonation. They are generally made of either rosewood or ebony but, like steel string bridges, poorer quality materials are often used which are again "ebonised." The strings are tied to the back of the bridge after being passed through small holes behind the saddle. Expensive models generally feature bone saddles but on cheaper instruments plastic is the material of choice.

Adjusting string height on most acoustics involves precise sanding down of some of the underside of the saddle to reduce its height – a job best left to a professional, as one slip can necessitate replacing the entire saddle.

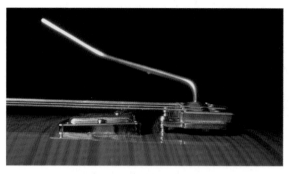

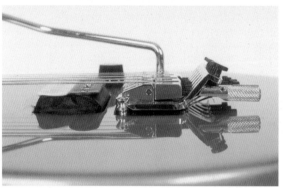

Though very different in other ways, the non-locking Wilkinson vibrato (top) and locking Floyd-Rose vibrato (above) – and others designed like them – both use two adjustable posts as efficient pivot points. These posts are adjustable for action height, while adjusting spring tension ensures they "float" parallel to the body.

Most acoustic guitar bridges have no means of simple string-height adjustment. Normally, as on the dreadnought above, the strings' ball ends are held secure by bridge pins, with the strings passing over a one-piece bone or synthetic saddle set into a slot in the bridge. Sanding down the underside of the saddle is the only means of adjusting its height. As any slip ups – or simply going too far – will necessitate replacing the entire saddle, however, this is a job best left to an experienced professional.

Resonator guitars, such as the National Resophonic Delphi above, have a bridge design unique to their function – but again, it's a tricky unit to work on, with no easy facility for string-height adjustment. Loading strings into the National's old-fashioned style tailpiece is simpler than with most standard acoustics. But because the bridge saddle is integral with the guitar's resonator cone, its height can't easily be altered by the player. Lowering the action requires deepening the string slots – again, a job for a pro.

INTONATION

Setting intonation is one of the main goals of any set-up. Without getting this crucial step right, your guitar will never quite sound in-tune, nor will the resonance and harmonic content of its natural voice ring true. Put simply, correct intonation lets your guitar sound its best. But fear not – this is a job well within the capabilities of most players.

ADJUSTING INTONATION

We discussed the reason for intonation adjustments earlier in the *Neck Relief* section. The making and checking of any such adjustments is crucial. Also, whenever you change string gauge (or indeed brand) you must re-check your intonation.

Fine-tuning the intonation, especially with individually adjustable saddles, is fairly straightforward – but you'll need an electronic tuner. The bridge or vibrato, string height, truss-rod

Intonation adjustment of Gibson-style Tune-o-matic bridges is usually made with a flat-head screwdriver, often from the front side of the bridge. Always slacken string tension before making any adjustment.

Fender's Stratocaster-style tremolo tailpiece – and many others – use a Phillips head screwdriver for intonation adjustment. The job is best done with new strings fitted, and pickup heights not set too close to the strings.

and nut height should be properly set up before you set the intonation, and ideally the frets should be in good condition. Here is the basic procedure for setting the intonation on all guitars, except those fitted with a nut lock, for which see the technique for Floyd Rose-style vibratos overleaf.

1 Tune strings to pitch and sound the 12th fret harmonic of the first string. Now, compare this with the note produced by fretting the same string at the 12th fret.

2 If the fretted note is sharp compared to the harmonic, the string length must be increased by moving the saddle away from the neck.

3 If the fretted note is flat the saddle must be moved forward, towards the neck, shortening the string length. You can remember this by the simple phrase: "Fret, Flat, Forward." This should help you recall that if the fretted note is flat, move the string saddle forward towards the neck. Just remember the three Fs: Fret, Flat, Forward.

Repeat this procedure on all strings, until the harmonic and the fretted notes are the same.

INTONATION AND BRIDGE TYPES

The intonation adjustments just described are usually made with a Phillips (cross-head) screwdriver or with an allen key. But note that Gibson's Tune-o-matic bridge (pictured left) – and the various versions thereof – is a notable exception that is typically adjusted for intonation using its slot-head screws.

Bear in mind, once again, that you must slacken the string tension before you start to move an individual saddle away from the bridge, especially on Fender-style Strat and Tele bridges (*photo below*), although this also applies to the various brands and varieties of one-piece combination bridge/tailpieces.

Always have new strings fitted, and don't have the pickups too close to the strings, especially the neck pickup, as the magnetic pull will interfere with string vibration and distort the pitch.

On bridges such as the one-piece wrapover type (see photo at bottom-right of opposite page) that have overall intonation adjustment, you use the small grub screws that protrude from the back of the bridge to set the overall intonation. Here you need only check the outer strings; the angled position of the bridge itself allows a basic compensation for the rest. You may find that setting the bass-side intonation using the D-string, rather than the low E-string, sounds more accurate.

Similarly, on a three-saddle Telecaster bridge you can only set the intonation per pair of strings. If you start by intonating the first paired saddle to the top E-string, the theoretical result is that the fretted B-string will sound sharp at the 12th fret compared to its harmonic there. If you find the B-string too sharp when you come to play chords in high-fret positions, then move the saddle backwards a little. This will bring the B-string more in tune, but make the top E-string slightly flat.

On the middle G-string/D-string saddle, if you use the D-string to set the intonation, the G-string will probably end up sharp. Again, you can always move the saddle backwards a little to improve this string, but this will in turn make the D-string slightly flat.

These compromise settings are inevitable and will be magnified by all the factors that affect intonation such as string gauge and action height. (Also see *Tele Tuning Hell opposite*.)

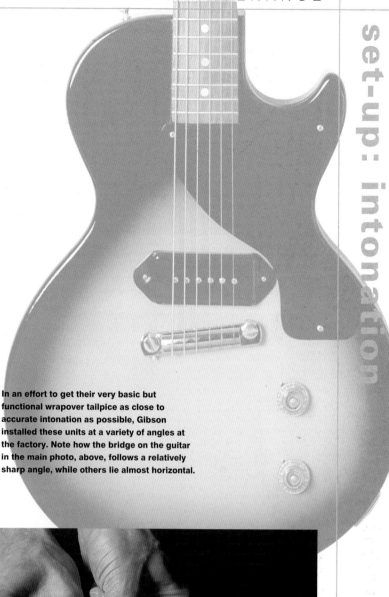

TELE TUNING HELL

The Hellecasters' Jerry Donahue is very particular when it comes to setting-up his guitars. Over the years he's evolved a very neat method that not only solves the problems of a three-saddle Telecaster bridge but also, Donahue believes, makes any guitar with a six-saddle bridge play more in tune. So, here's how Jerry sets his three-saddle Teles.

Tune all open strings as normal. But set the center saddle so that the G-string, fretted at the 12th fret, is marginally sharp of its harmonic (which is in tune). The D-string, fretted at the 12th, is therefore marinally flat of the harmonic.

Now, via the machinehead, adjust the G-string so you get that fretted note in tune, effectively flattening the G-string. Use your ears as a guide. A root position E major chord should sound in tune to your ear with the G# (first fret G string) being slightly flat, but not so much that a root positon E minor chord sounds out.

Donahue finds that the top strings are usually fairly in tune, but sets the B-string, fretted at the 12th, very slightly sharp of the harmonic; the top E-string fretted at the 12th and its harmonic should be spot on.

On the low E and A-string saddle Jerry sets the A in tune – fretted at the 12th and the harmonic. Again, he finds the difference here is usually minimal – and he regularly flattens the low E very slightly anyway.

In an effort to get their very basic but functional wrapover tailpice as close to accurate intonation as possible, Gibson installed these units at a variety of angles at the factory. Note how the bridge on the guitar in the main photo, above, follows a relatively sharp angle, while others lie almost horizontal.

Close enough for rock'n'roll? Setting intonation on some earlier electric guitar designs like the Les Paul Junior and Fender Telecaster (right and below) is often a matter of maximizing inherent flaws.

Setting the intonation on the rather primitive three-saddle Telecaster bridge inevitably involves making a few compromises. As you're forced to alter the string lengths in pairs, adjustment here usually means choosing between which of each set of strings to leave a little sharp or flat in relation to its partner.

One of the crudest of all bridge designs for setting intonation, the Gibson-style wrapover unit only allows for adjustment via grub screws at either end of the bar. The angle at which the bridge is installed, however, (and the raised ridge on some types) often helps you get surprisingly close intonation.

set-up: intonation

Any adjustment of a Floyd Rose-style vibrato starts with loosening the bolts on the locking nut, to free the strings at the headstock end.

Undoing the saddle locks leaves you free to make adjustments. Always use the correct tool here to avoid stripping small screw heads.

Set the intonation in small steps – again using the correct size Allen key – by moving the saddle either forward or backward only about

¾₄" (1.0mm) at a time. Then lock down the saddle, re-tune, and check intonation again. If still off, adjust further as necessary.

A Saddle Singers insert can help prevent saddle wear and cure many string seating problems, improving tone at the same time.

Often misunderstood, the Floyd Rose string retaining bar is there to ensure that strings sit flat over the surface of the nut lock.

INTONATION OF FLOYD ROSE-STYLE VIBRATOS

Setting intonation on a guitar with a double-locking Floyd Rose-style vibrato is complex and it's best to get the job done professionally. If you want to try it yourself, here's what to do.

1 Unlock the three locking bolts at the locking nut. Compare the 12th fret harmonic with the note at the 12th fret.

2 Remember: if the fretted note is flat, compared to the harmonic, the string length is too long, so the saddle needs to be moved closer to the neck; conversely, if the fretted note is sharp, the string length is too short, so the saddle needs to be moved further away from the neck.

3 Slacken off the individual string tension and visualise the position of the saddle. Undo the saddle lock with the correct Allen key while holding the saddle-locking bolt with your spare hand. Only undo the saddle-locking screw enough to move the saddle either slightly forward or slightly backward as required, and no more than about ¾₄" (1mm) in the appropriate direction.

4 Having made your adjustment, lock down the saddle-locking bolt and re-tune the string. Re-check the intonation, if it is not correct, make further adjustments as described earlier.

5 When you've completed this for each string, re-check your tuning (see *Vibrato Tuning,* opposite), and don't forget to re-clamp the nut lock.

FLOYD ROSE TIPS

The Floyd Rose and other double-locking varieties may be less fashionable than they once were, but for wide-travel, in-tune bending and serious divebombing, they take some beating. As we've discussed, setting intonation is complex and can be time-consuming, as can re-stringing, but the overall set-up is pretty straightforward.

STRING LOADING

When you're fitting strings on a Floyd Rose vibrato bridge, don't over-tighten the saddle locks. You'll get a feel for the "correct" tightness after a while, and if serious problems occur you should be able to track down replacement saddles from the instrument's manufacturer.

Make sure you always carry in your case or gigbag a good quality pair of wire cutters (and spare strings!) so that prior to loading in the saddle you can cut off the ball-end on the wound strings, at least ¾" (19mm) from the ball-end. Alternatively (and some players do this anyway) load the string (ball-end still attached) through the tuner and then load the plain end into the saddle. This method is used by some players who suffer string breakages at the saddle. You can unwind some of the spare string that has wrapped around the tuner post, and in this way you'll give yourself enough extra length to re-fit the old string into the saddle.

Speaking of string breakage, a UK company markets neat Saddle Singers inserts for Floyd Rose-type vibratos, and they're recommended. These prevent saddle wear – which can lead to premature string breakage – and cure string seating problems, benefiting tone. They're easy to fit when you're changing strings – the photo (far left) shows one in position at a saddle and with the string ready to load.

Whenever you're replacing one or all of your strings, remember to "center" the fine-tuners to their mid-way position so that there is plenty of fine-tuning adjustment left in either direction after you've tightened the nut lock.

STRING RETAINING BAR

An often misunderstood feature of the Floyd Rose system is the string-retainer bar situated behind the nut lock. Because the surface of the nut lock is slightly curved, it's important that the string lays flat over the curve, otherwise you will find that when the nut lock is tightened the strings go noticeably sharp.

Visually check that, once threaded under the retainer bar, the strings sit flat over the nut lock. If they don't, then screw down the string-retainer's screws. Now, if any of these screws should feel tight as you screw down, don't force them. Instead, you should first try removing them and applying a little candle wax to the threads for lubrication.

VIBRATO TUNING

Tuning any vibrato can be problematic for the simple reason that as you sharpen one string (increasing the tension) the rest will go slightly flat. A good procedure for any floating (or even vintage) vibrato, especially a Floyd Rose, is to tune from the low E-string first. When that's in tune, go to the A-string. With that one tuned go back to the low E-string, then the A-string again. Only then go to the D-string. With that tuned, return and re-check the previous strings, and carry on using this repetitive back-and-forth procedure.

As with any vibrato it's advisable – even if you're replacing all your strings – to change them one at a time. If you do want to remove all the strings, place a vibrato backplate and/or some stiff card between the back of the vibrato and the face of the guitar to stop the springs pulling the vibrato back. Otherwise the vibrato can come off its pivot points. This is not only inconvenient but can lead to unnecessary wear at these important places.

Finally, having made all your adjustments on the Floyd Rose, you should always remember to tighten the nut locks.

TUNERS AND STRING-STRETCHING

Having set up your vibrato as described you should note once again how careful you must be not to overwind the string around the tuner's string post. Untidy wraps here will be a major problem. Likewise, no vibrato, not even a Floyd Rose, will return to correct pitch unless you've extensively stretched your strings (see *Strings* earlier in the chapter).

On a Strat, for example, not only should you stretch the full length of the string between the saddle and the nut, but you should also make sure you bend the strings behind the nut. This should show up any other problems caused by the string trees and the nut itself.

If you have tension-adjustable tuners fitted, tighten the screws at the end of the button so the action of the tuner feels tight but not too stiff.

STRING TREES

On a Strat, for example, you'll have one or two string trees of varying design. Not only can the tree itself cause the string to hitch up, but if the tree(s) sit(s) too low on the headstock then the behind-the-nut angle will be too steep and, even with the best cut nut slot, the string may hitch in the nut. Graph Tech make excellent friction-reducing string trees which are inexpensive.

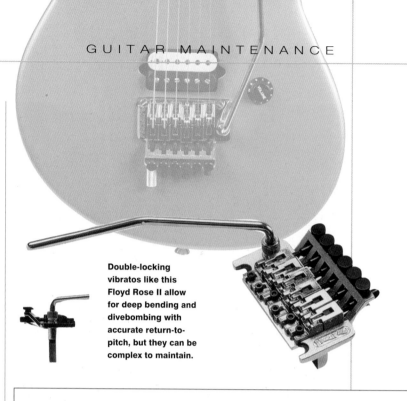

Double-locking vibratos like this Floyd Rose II allow for deep bending and divebombing with accurate return-to-pitch, but they can be complex to maintain.

KEEPING YOUR VIBRATO IN TUNE

Don't consider any vibrato bridge in isolation. The problem of the vibrato returning all the strings to pitch after use is invariably down to a combination of factors. It's not always the vibrato bridge or tailpiece that is the main culprit; more often it's the points beyond the bridge. The nut, string trees and tuners – and the way you attach your strings – create the major problem, which is friction. The Floyd Rose vibrato system, by locking the strings at the nut and saddle, not only eliminated any friction points but also the effect of the "dead" string length (that is the portion of the string behind the nut and behind the saddle – within, for example, the sustain block of a Strat vibrato).

A simple device, the string tree plays a crucial role in many guitars' tonal integrity and tuning stability – and some vintage designs can be a headache when they misbehave.

Friction-reducing string trees – like those built by Graph Tech, shown above – can go a long way toward reducing hang ups and improving your ability to stay in tune.

To prevent string breakage at the saddle, the late Stevie Ray Vaughan's guitar tech slipped wire insulation

over the wrapped portion of his strings to protect this often-delicate contact point.

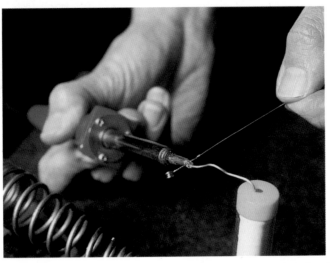

If your strings have a tendency to come unwrapped with extreme vibrato use – inducing tuning

troubles with slippage at the ball-end – "tinning" them with solder may help keep them intact longer.

Frustrated by a loose-swinging or ill-positioned Strat vibrato arm? Fitting a small spring in the screw-in vibrato arm hole helps to increase the tension on the screw threads and hold it more firmly in place.

They are moulded to include a spacer, giving plenty of height (and therefore a shallow behind-the-nut string angle).

Should the string angle be *too* shallow – you'll hear a slight buzzing and consequent loss of tone on the open strings if this is the case – you can simply rub the string tree over a piece of medium abrasive paper laid on a flat surface in order to reduce its height. You may be able to remove the G-string/D-string tree altogether, but adding a couple more winds on the string post when you attach the G-string to the tuner will increase the back-angle and, if this job is done neatly, it shouldn't create any slippage problems.

The best solution for problems with tuners and string trees is to replace your tuners with locking types such as those made by Sperzel, Gotoh and Schaller. The Sperzel Trim-Lok tuner, for example, comes with three different post heights so that the behind-the-nut string angle is nicely graduated – and you shouldn't need string trees at all. Tuner replacement is best left to a pro. While it's also a pro job to sort out a nut, you can apply some useful lubricant (soft pencil lead) in the nut slots and under the strings where they pass over the nut.

VINTAGE STRAT VIBRATO TIPS

The vintage-style Strat vibrato has caused many problems and provoked much debate over the years. The pivot points of most modern vibratos of this type have been improved. For example, the underside of the bridgeplate holes are usually countersunk for a better, more knife-edge-like pivot against the six screws.

Lubrication of these points has little lasting effect and should be unnecessary. However, check for noticeable wear on the screws and bridgeplate; if necessary, replace any worn parts.

The vintage-type Strat vibrato has additional friction points both at the saddle and at the point where the string passes over the baseplate on its way to the saddle. Wear on the pressed-steel saddles can cause friction points – especially on the low wound strings – but with a small needle-file and abrasive paper you can smooth these if necessary. Alternatively, if you retrofit friction-reducing saddles these can help with tuning problems and avoid premature string breakages.

STEVIE RAY'S INSULATION WIRE

A tip passed on from Stevie Ray Vaughan's former guitar tech is to slip over plastic wire insulation (as pictured top-left) at the point where the string bends over the block, to prevent breakage. You can easily try this yourself.

SOLDER WRAP

Tinning (soldering) the wrap at the ball-end of your plain strings is easy to do and will prevent the wrap coming undone with extreme vibrato use.

SPRING THING

Nothing to do with tuning stability but worth considering here is the fact that some players find the screw-in vibrato arms used by Fender (and many others) really annoying: the arms either swing loosely, or tighten up in totally the wrong position.

On the Fender American Standard Stratocaster, Fender's simple cure is to fit a small spring in the vibrato arm's hole which keeps the arm in the right position. Available as Fender spares for a few pennies each, these springs (pictured left) will fit virtually any screw-in vibrato arm hole so long as the hole doesn't go right through the block. Also, keep the arm in the vibrato

permanently – just swing it to its lowest position before putting the guitar in its case.

BIGSBY TIPS

One of the many designs that re-appeared in the retro-influenced 1990s and remains popular today is the Bigsby vibrato. Originally fitted from the 1950s on Gibsons, Gretsches and even Fender Teles, for example, the Bigsby is a rather archaic pitch-bending device that adds as much to the visual appeal of your guitar as it does to your bag of sonic techniques.

The design is simple, yet the large tailpiece to which the strings anchor overshadows the fact that the travel is minimal – around a semitone up or down. Guitars equipped with Bigsbys are notorious for poor pitch stability, although usually it's not so much the actual tailpiece that's at fault as the nut and bridge.

Many modern guitars fitted with Bigsbys – such as Epiphone's Les Pauls and Washburn's "P" series solidbodies – come with Tune-o-matic-style bridges, as well as large back-angled headstocks where the strings splay out considerably, creating a steep angle over the nut and therefore more chance of strings hitching in their slots. Tune-o-matic bridges can be retrofitted with Graph Tech friction-reducing saddles, or you can fit a new roller bridge as made by ABM, for example.

The nut must be carefully cut: again, a friction-reducing material is ideal. But both jobs are for a pro. However, you might cure minor problems by careful string-loading at the tuners, extensive string-stretching, and lubrication of the nut and saddles. Ultimately, don't forget that the Bigsby is intended for light use. Treat it with respect!

The Bigsby vibrato is a favorite for vintage-style wobbles, but is a notorious source of tuning troubles.

BILL'S BIGSBYS

Changing strings on a Bigsby vibrato can be a fiddly, frustrating job. Bill Puplett, one of the UK's leading repairmen, has these tips.

"You'll find that pre-bending the ends of the new strings to match the diameter of the string-retaining roller-bar helps, especially with the Bigsby models B5, B7 and B12 that feature a secondary hold-down roller-bar. Use any cylindrical object which has a similar diameter to the retaining bar, for example a pen or piece of dowel. Hold the ball-end flat against the object and firmly wrap the end of the string about one full turn (as pictured near-right), then release it. This will produce a hook-shaped curve at the end of the string.

"Pass this end under the hold-down bar from the bridge side before attaching the ball-end to the retainer pin (pictured far right). Make sure the string is properly attached to the tuner's string-post and tune up so the string has just a bit of tension – don't tune to pitch at this stage. Repeat the bending and installation for the other strings, and then check the string alignment from the retainer bar through to the bridge. Aim to get the strings evenly spaced and running in as straight a line as possible, and make any repositioning adjustments before tuning to pitch. It helps to apply some thorough sharpened and flatened vibrato with the arm, to help the new strings settle.

"When the strings are tuned to pitch, the vibrato arm should come to rest approximately one inch (25mm) clear of the pickguard or face of the guitar. You can adjust this by adding or removing the fiber disc spacers at the base of the spring housing."

Pre-bending the ball-ends of new strings before fitting them to your Bigsby vibrato can make this job a lot easier, and improve tuning and string stability too. Any similar-diameter pen or dowell will work.

Slip the hook-like end of the bent string under the roller-bar string retainer and hook the ball-end on the small retainer pin. This technique also helps to keep the ball-end from popping off the pin as you tune up.

The vintage three-saddle Telecaster bridge (top, right) has a lot of fans, despite its limitations. For those who get annoyed with the oldie's quirks, retro-fit six-saddle alternatives offer more accurate intonation adjustment.

DEALING WITH SADDLE WEAR

As we've already pointed out, your bridge saddles are very important for tone, sustain, intonation and string longevity. The quality of bridge saddles is often overlooked by manufacturers working in the lower price areas because they need to keep down costs, and consequently the materials used often don't maximize a budget guitar's performance. Combine that with general wear-and-tear and you have a situation that's far from ideal.

Graph Tech's line of replacement String Saver saddles can provide an easy retrofit answer. They are made of a friction-reducing plastic and should cure any string-hitching problems. They can also maximize string life, and should improve your tone a bit too as compared to budget saddles.

Graph Tech also make a synthetic ivory material called Tusq used for some electric guitar saddles, though mostly for acoustics. These will give a slightly different tone, increasing acoustic resonance and "zing".

Graph Tech's saddles come in a variety of sizes for a variety of guitars, so consult your local store to find the right ones (and remember to take along your guitar). You can easily fit them yourself, and the right time to do this is when you're changing your strings. We fitted them to a Strat, as follows.

1 On Strats and Teles (and other similar guitars) fit one saddle at a time. Remove the first string and unscrew the intonation screw and spring, as pictured left.

2 Fit the new saddle and match its position and height approximately in relation to the other saddles. Fit your new string and adjust the height and intonation. Do this individually for all the saddles. Then check the string height. Last, check and if necessary adjust the intonation.

Tune-o-matic saddle replacements are also produced by Graph Tech but not all types are available, and the bridge's saddle screws don't always match the thread of the new saddles (unlike the Strat and Tele types which come with their own new screws). It's really important to get the right ones for your bridge, so replacement here is a little more tricky. Also, the tops of the saddles may need to be notched to achieve the correct string spacing. Consult your store and/or repairman.

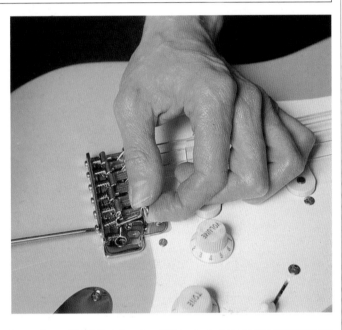

Some players find their guitars benefit from the tuning stability and improved resistance to string breakage that Graph Tech saddles may bring, and it's a job you can usually do yourself...

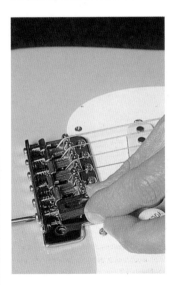

Simply remove old saddles and replace one at a time with new units, matching approximate settings and string heights as you go. When finished, fine-tune your intonation (above).

90

ELECTRICS

These are the mysterious "ghost in the machine" to many players, but there's no reason you should shy away from doing basic electrics repairs and modifications yourself – and even undertaking some more elaborate jobs with practise and experience. Just as learning to set up and intonate your own guitar will optimize its acoustic performance, doing your own electrics adjustments, repairs, wiring mods and pickup replacements is a great way to fine-tune your tone.

ELECTRIC MAINTENANCE

There is a big distinction between the acoustic and electric "sides" of your guitar. The acoustic side of the instrument includes all the factors covered so far: the neck, the truss-rod and the hardware, and how each part is adjusted. Now that we've taken care of the acoustic side, we can move to the maintenance and adjustment of the electric side – as well as looking later at retrofit pickups and wiring modifications.

PICKUP HEIGHT

There are a couple of adjustments to pickups that can improve and balance the guitar's output. Both single-coils and humbuckers have overall height adjustment. The closer the pickup is to the strings, the more output you'll get, and vice-versa.

If the pickup is too close to the strings, however, problems can occur with the magnetic pull of the pickup or, in the worst case, the strings can actually collide with the pickup, stopping them dead. Here's what you do.

1 Fret the outer strings (one at a time) at the top fret (21st, 22nd or 24th). Measure the distance from the top of the pickup to the underside of the string. There is no precise distance at which this should be set. It depends on the pickup itself and, just as importantly, how you want to hear the sound balance between the two or three pickups. A rough guide for full-size humbuckers is to go for a gap of around 3⁄32" (2.5mm) on the treble and bass sides of the neck and bridge pickups.

2 Plug in your guitar and check the output balance of the pickups. If the neck humbucker dominates then screw it down further into the guitar body, away from the strings. Some pickup makers such as Seymour Duncan offer "calibrated" sets of pickups. Because there is more string movement the further you move from the bridge, the strings' output will be greater over the neck pickup than over the bridge pickup. This can be compensated for by altering the pickup's output. So as a guide, Duncan recommends setting a calibrated set of Duncan humbuckers at 1⁄16" (1.6mm) on the treble side and 1⁄8" (3.2mm) on the bass-side (top of pickup to underside of string).

3 For single-coils you can go for a similar distance of 3⁄32" (2.5mm) on the treble side and slightly more, around 1⁄8" to 9⁄64" (3 to 3.5mm), on the bass side. With a Strat (again, unless you're using a calibrated pickup set) you may want to screw further down into the guitar the neck pickup and, to a lesser extent, the middle pickup. Be prepared to sacrifice output by lowering the pickup – especially on the bass side of the neck pickup – to avoid the magnetic string-pull that can distort the strings' vibrational pattern and create a double-note effect which can impair tone and hinder accurate tuning.

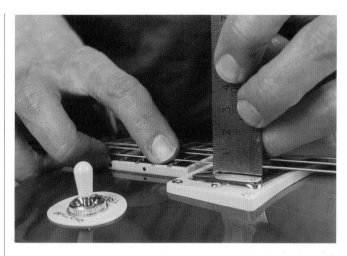
Setting a pickup's height is an important means of adjusting and balancing its output, but your range here will be limited by string clearance and the possible damping effects of magnet on string.

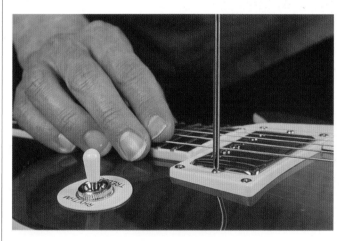
A rough guide for setting humbuckers is to aim for a gap of 3⁄32" (2.5mm) at the treble and bass polepieces, but there's no hard and fast rule – and some calibrated sets require different settings.

The magnetic polepieces in Strat neck-position single-coils can cause string-pull, resulting in dead notes and ghost tones. You might need to sacrifice some output and set these a little low.

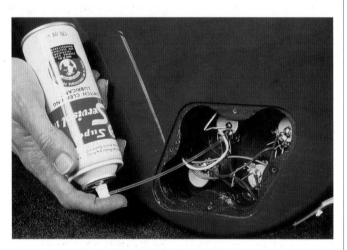

Not so much intended as a means of overall height adjustment, individually-adjustable polepieces can be set to follow a guitar's bridge and string radius, and balance individual string output.

Servisol – or another suitable electrical cleaner/lubricant – can be a great quick-fix for scratchy pots and switches. If this stuff doesn't cure the problem, replacement is usually the only option.

To clean and lubricate a gritty, crackling pot, aim the spray through the intended hole in the pot casing.

To correct scratchy switches, spray the contact/friction points of the lever mechanism.

POLEPIECE HEIGHT

Most humbuckers (and some single-coils) have one or two rows of adjustable polepieces. Once you've set the pickup's overall height you can adjust these to compensate for both the radius of the fingerboard and the strings, as well as their differing volumes caused by varying diameters and whether they're wound or plain types. Start off with the polepieces virtually flush with the top of the pickup.

Play your guitar amplified, preferably with a relatively clean amp tone, and compare the string outputs up and down the neck – and, obviously, one pickup at a time. You may find that the wound D-string is a little quiet compared to the A, so with the appropriate tool – usually either a flat-blade screwdriver or hexagonal Allen key – you can raise the polepiece slightly. Note that you should avoid raising the top E polepiece too far as you could easily catch the string on it, with nasty results. Instead, use that string as your reference and reduce the height, if necessary, on the polepieces for the B and G-strings.

CLEANING POTS AND SWITCHES

Even brand new guitars can suffer from scratchy-sounding pots and selector switches (especially the Fender-style lever switch). Plug your guitar into your amp and continually rotate or activate the scratchy pot or switch. Does the scratching become reduced? If it does, all you need is an aerosol can of pot-and-switch cleaner such as Servisol.

Expose the controls of your guitar and spray the cleaner into the small hole at the front of the pot or into the lever switch. Again, plug in your guitar and quickly rotate the pot or move the switch. You may need a couple of goes at this before the scratchiness is gone. If the pot still sounds scratchy or clicks, replacement is advised. On some guitars you may need to remove the control knobs and the pot itself to clean it, so next we'll show you how to do this.

STAGGERED POLEPIECES
Vintage Fender Strat (and some Tele) pickups have staggered polepieces to compensate for differing string-output levels – though these were originally designed with a wound G-string in mind.

ADJUSTABLE POLEPIECES
Gibson's groundbreaking PAF humbucker allowed for a greater degree of player-adjustability from the start, with one row of threaded polepieces which can be set with a flat-blade screwdriver.

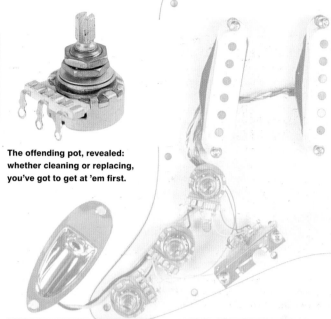

REMOVING KNOBS AND ACCESSING POTS

Disassembling your guitar's electronics is often straightforward, but a few tips can help make the job easier – and avoid costly breakages or mistakes.

To remove a knob, first inspect it to see if there is a grub-screw holding it to the pot. If there is, undo it with an Allen key or screwdriver. Most guitars have push-on knobs, so try lifting the knob by hand.

If the knob is too tight to move by hand, proceed as follows and with care. On Les Paul-style guitars, a tip passed on by UK maker Phil Norsworthy is to wrap a cloth tightly around the knob and gently pull it upwards while gripping the knob with your finger. If it still won't budge, seek pro advice. Do not try to lever it with a screwdriver as it's easy to crack the knob or, worse, to damage the front of your guitar.

On Strat-style guitars the less brittle plastic knobs do not crack so easily – but usually they sit lower on the guitar so you can't get a cloth around them. Here you can protect the pickguard with an old plastic credit card and, using a small flat-blade screwdriver, carefully and gently lever upwards. (Don't turn the screwdriver: this will mark the bottom edge of the knob.) The key here is to slowly rotate the knob as you lever upwards. Once you've moved the knob up a little, wrap the cloth around it; you should now be able to pull it off.

With the knob removed, undo the pot's fixing washer with the correct-size wrench (box spanner). The pot can then be moved, without unsoldering, to allow enough space to clean it. Be careful not to disturb the wiring.

Sometimes pots work loose and rotate, but re-securing the control is easy. Remove the control knob as described and tighten the fixing nut with a box wrench, holding the pot itself firmly in place to stop it rotating. Box and socket wrenches are also very handy for tightening the fixing nuts of the output socket (jack) and the tuners – a job for which you should never consider using pliers.

Lever switches are easily removed and/or secured using the two fixing screws at either end of the switch.

A Gibson-style toggle switch has a ribbed circular nut to secure it onto the guitar. This is tricky to tighten and/or loosen as there is no "correct" commonly-available tool for the job. (Stewart-MacDonald's Guitar Shop Supply offers an appropriate Toggle Switch Wrench, but it's a specialist repairer's tool and perhaps not worth purchasing to use only once every few years.) The late British luthier Sid Poole explained his approach to seemingly basic but rather tricky little job.

"Before I got the Toggle Switch Wrench I dreaded this job. It's all too easy to damage either the nut itself, the plastic rhythm/lead ring, or the guitar's finish. So I suggest that you protect the rhythm/lead ring with masking tape, and then use a pair of pliers held very carefully upright to slowly move the nut. You'll probably need to stop the switch rotating by holding it with a pair of needle-nosed (snipe-nosed) pliers from the rear of the guitar, obviously with the coverplate removed. It's a tricky job." For further protection you can wrap some masking tape around the tips of the pliers. Never attempt to over-tighten this nut. Above all, this apparently simple operation could damage your guitar, and so it really is a job for a pro if you find it isn't successfully accomplished using the above tips.

Unless any component needs replacing, your existing electrics should now be in top condition. It's only at this point that you should consider whether you need a new pickup or maybe want to alter your guitar's wiring.

The offending pot, revealed: whether cleaning or replacing, you've got to get at 'em first.

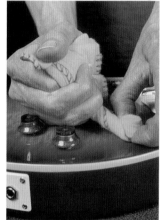

Wrapping a soft cloth tightly around a Les Paul style knob can often help you ease it off the pot shaft.

For tight Strat knobs, slip a flat-blade screwdriver underneath and gently ease it upwards.

The correct sized box wrench is the safest and easiest means of removing a pot retaining nut.

Specialist tools are available for other tricky jobs, but might not be worth buying for occasional use.

electrics: servicing

ELECTRICS HEALTH CHECK

Check pickup heights are approximately correct.

Check that each pickup and the selector switch is working.

Check each volume and tone control – plus any coil-splits – are working and whether any sounds "scratchy."

Check that the switches, pots and output socket are firmly mounted.

Precisely set pickup/polepiece heights.

Clean pots and switches if needed.

If necessary, remove control knobs and tighten pot fixing nuts and output jack socket nut.

REPLACEMENT ALTERNATIVES

The replacement pickup you choose depends on how you want to alter your sound, and there are hundreds of alternatives to select from today. The list below provides a starting point by suggesting a range of popular retrofit options to achieve different sounds in the bridge position (the most common mod), and presumes your current guitar has stock pickups.

	SOUND	REPLACEMENT PICKUP
TELECASTER		
	vintage	SD Antiquity Tele, JM
	hot vintage	SD Vintage Lead Stack, DiM,
		RioGr Muy Grande
	noise-free	DiM Virtual Vintage
	ultra-hot	SD Hot Rails, Quarter Pounder
STRATOCASTER		
	vintage	SD Antiquity Strat, JM
	hot vintage	DiM FS-1,
		RioGr Halfbreed or Stelly
	noise-free	DiM Virtual Vintage
	ultra-hot	SD Hot Rails or Hot Stack
LES PAUL/SG STANDARD		
	vintage	SD Antiquity
	hot vintage	SD Pearly Gates,
		RioGr BBQ Bucker
	ultra-hot	DiM Super Distortion,
		EMG 81 or EMG 60
LES PAUL/SG SPECIAL/JUNIOR		
	vintage	SD Antiquity
	hot vintage	SD, DiM, etc
		RioGr Bluesbar
	noise-free	DiM Virtual Vintage

SD = Seymour Duncan

DiM = DiMarzio

EMG = EMG

JM = J.M. Rolph

RioGr = Rio Grande

RETROFITTING

If you're happy with the feel, style and overall playability of your guitar but would like a slightly different amplified tone – hotter, brighter or more vintage-like – pickup replacement is often the answer, and it's a job you can probably do yourself.

REASONS TO RETROFIT

There are four primary reasons for considering pickup replacement. First, your pickup may simply have stopped working. Uncovered pickups such as open-coiled humbuckers and Telecaster bridge pickups are susceptible to moisture penetration (beer, sweat, tears, etc) which can lead to corrosion of the delicate pickup coil windings and shorting of the pickup. One answer is to have the pickup rewound, a service that should be considerably cheaper than investing in a new unit.

Second, and a more common occurrence on new and old guitars alike, is that your pickup(s) may squeal, or be "microphonic." These problems have a variety of causes depending on the type of guitar. Covered humbuckers – currently making quite a comeback – can squeal at high volumes. Often this is because the pickup has not been fully wax-saturated (potted); be aware, however, that original-style PAF humbuckers are like this by design. Another reason is that the cover or pickup mounting may vibrate and cause microphonic feedback. Invariably the problem is magnified when you're using a high-gain, high-volume set-up. The options are to get your pickup properly potted and maybe take specialist advice on the pickup mounting, or to fit a new pickup.

The third reason for considering pickup replacement is to do with the original design. Fender Strat and Tele pickups and Gibson's P90 are single-coil types, so they are susceptible to both low-cycle mains hum, and higher-pitched hum and interference from fluorescent and stage lights and computer monitors. If the hum bothers you (or your band), the cure is to replace the offending pickup(s) with humbucking replacements, now available to retrofit most single-coil-size routings.

Finally, and perhaps most commonly of all, you might feel that your pickup is a weak link in your sound chain and you simply fancy a tonal change. Kent Armstrong reckons this is the main reason. Similarly, a technical adviser for EMG says: "It's probably the least expensive and most direct way to change your tone. Most people get pretty comfortable with their guitar, so it's the quickest way to upgrade it." Seymour Duncan concurs that players often look for a tone from their guitar that is not always provided by its stock pickups. "That's obvious," Duncan admits, "but many players are searching for a dream. They want to play and sound like their idol or someone they aspire to. Changing pickups helps further that dream."

PICKUP CONSIDERATIONS

Before we look at what a pickup can do, you need equally to be aware of what it can't do. As we've already discussed, an electric guitar can still be considered as an "acoustic." The combination of the guitar's design, materials, hardware, strings and set-up all contribute to that "acoustic" tone. The pickup then takes that inherent sound and sends it off to your amplifier. While no one is denying that the pickup forms a major part of your sound chain – and of course most pickup makers figure it's *the* major part – it should not affect the acoustic performance of the guitar. Ideally the pickup should take the "information" – the strings' vibration –

and ferry it as effectively as possible to your amplifier. So before you start pointing a finger at your pickups, make sure you've followed the instructions so far to adjust your guitar to its best potential. That includes fitting new strings – and always using a good-quality guitar cord (lead).

CHOOSING A PICKUP

For most of us, choosing a new pickup is always a risk. The only way to know if the new pickup is exactly what you need is to buy it, fit it and sound-test it through your own set-up. So to minimize the possibility of a mistaken purchase, do some homework.

First you need to establish what it is that you don't like about your existing tone – assuming of course that you're happy with your amp, FX and guitar. "That's the key," says Seymour Duncan. "Figure out why the existing pickup isn't happening for you. Does the bridge pickup in your Strat sound too thin? You have to identify the problem. Then you have to work out what you need: better harmonics, chunkier power chords? Think about your guitar and amp. What is the body and neck wood? Do you use a clean tone or melt-down metal? Then you can ask a dealer or repairman a specific question. 'I want a better sound from my Strat,' is too vague, but, 'I want to beef up the bridge pickup on my alder-body maple-neck Strat which I use through a Fender Princeton amp to play blues,' is what we need."

"Ideally you should test before you buy," says Kent Armstrong. "But that's the problem: you can't try everything. Talk to other players who have played them, and get some advice."

Both Seymour Duncan and DiMarzio provide tone charts in their product catalogues, comparing output (high or low) and bass, midrange and treble tone. A high-output pickup will drive a tube amp into overdrive more easily than a lower-powered pickup. The down-side is that you can often lose dynamics: there will be less distinction between light and heavily picked notes and the sound will be more compressed. You should be familiar with bass, midrange and treble from your hi-fi, but the electric guitar is really all about midrange. A classic Les Paul tone, for example, has a strong lower midrange helping to create its notorious thickness, but with enough upper midrange bite to cut through. But a classic Strat pickup will have less pronounced midrange, resulting in a "flatter," more acoustic tone. It'll also have plenty of upper-mids and highs for its classic sparkle.

Artist endorsements can help your choice too. All the big three companies – Seymour Duncan, DiMarzio and EMG – list in their catalogues many players and the set-ups they use, and this will at least give you some idea of the stylistic application of a certain pickup. "There are too many brands out there," says EMG, "and you can't hear them all. We'd suggest looking at your favourite players, finding out what they play and then taking a listen." For example, if you're after a vintage tone from your Les Paul you shouldn't buy a DiMarzio Evolution humbucker designed for Steve Vai, but go for their more classic-sounding PAF model. "As far as we're concerned," says EMG, "if an artist uses our pickups, it's their choice and they found them."

But in the end you're going to have to buy a pickup and live with it. If it's not 100 per cent right for you, at least by following the company's various comparative tone/output information it will be easier to fine-tune your future choice. These charts would tell you, for example, that if you'd purchased a DiMarzio Super Distortion humbucker but found it too aggressive sounding, then a DiMarzio PAF with its close approximation of the original Gibson PAF might be a better choice.

STACKED "SINGLE-COIL" HUMBUCKERS

Looking for hum-free performance in a single-coil-sized package with fairly authentic sound? Some manufacturers achieve this by stacking two coils rather than placing them side-by-side, as with the Seymour Duncan pictured right.

VINTAGE SINGLE-COILS

Not all pickup swaps are in a quest to achieve more power: a large number of players are looking to replicate the tones of the '50s and '60s, and pickups with vintage-correct alnico magnets and precise-spec windings fit the bill.

HOT "SINGLE-COIL" HUMBUCKERS

Fitting a hot single-coil-sized humbucker in the bridge position is one of the most common mods for rock-playing Strat owners, and the Seymour Duncan Hot Rails is a popular choice. With over-wound side-by-side coils and dual blade polepieces, it greatly increases power and sustain compared to standard single-coils, and requires no major alteration of your guitar.

On any Strat or similarly constructed guitar, start by removing the pickguard to get at the electrics.

Trace the wires of the pickup you're replacing and unsolder them from the five-way switch.

Unscrew the old pickup from the pickguard, setting any mounting hardware carefully aside...

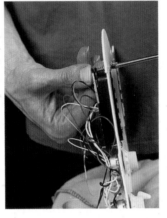

And load in the new unit, using the screws supplied (its mounting holes may differ from your old pickup).

Before re-assembling your guitar, it's important to test that the new pickup and the rest of your electronics are functioning correctly. If all is well, bolt it back together – and give your mod a good playing-in.

REPLACING A SINGLE-COIL PICKUP

Many current Fender Strats are perfect guitars for electrics modification. Under the pickguard there's a large oblong pickup cavity rather than the three separate pickup routs (plus channel) found on a vintage-spec Strat. The oblong rout means that fitting humbuckers is easy, and new pickguards are readily available as spares so you don't have to cut up your original one. The fact that you can remove the neck with the strings still on also makes life easier: the pickguard is accessible, and you can quickly re-assemble the guitar to try it out.

1 Remove the neck (as described in detail in previous sections) and put it aside; unscrew the pickguard and set the screws safely aside – a jar or old film can is useful to keep these safe while you work. Carefully turn over the pickguard and rest it securely on the covered guitar body. Trace the wires from the pickup that you're replacing: one should be already soldered to the five-way switch, the other to the back of a volume pot. Sketch the circuit so you can find your connections again once you have removed the original components, then unsolder the relevant wires by heating the joints and pulling the wires free.

2 Unscrew the old pickup, taking care to keep the springs and the rubber tubing that goes over the fixing-screw between the pickup and the pickguard.

3 Load in the new pickup using the supplied screws and the old springs or rubber tubing. Strip and tin the ends of the pickup wires, but at this stage don't cut them to length. When you've sound-tested your new pickup and are sure that's the one you want, then you can go back into the guitar and tidy up your wiring.

Solder the new pickup wires in place but don't, at this stage, worry about a mechanical fixing – such as hooking the wire through the pot tag – as there's a 50/50 chance that your new single-coil will be out-of-phase with your existing pickup (see *Phased And Confused* on page 97). Before you re-assemble your guitar, plug it into your amp (keep the volume low) and lightly rub (don't tap) the tip of a screwdriver on the pickup polepieces. You'll hear a sound through your amp if the new pickup is working. Then check that the selector switch and the volume and tone controls are all working correctly. Re-assemble your guitar.

4 Test out your new pickup (or any wiring mods) thoroughly before you finally decide it's right. When you've given it the thumbs-up, open up your guitar and tidily cut, re-strip and re-solder the connections, using mechanical joints if possible.

REPLACING A HUMBUCKER

Working on a set-neck Les Paul-style guitar is less easy than a bolt-on. Also, we're showing the bridge pickup; if you're replacing the neck humbucker on a solid-topped Les Paul-type guitar you'll have to remove the bridge pickup too so you can thread the neck pickup's hook-up wire through the bridge pickup's cavity into the rear control cavity.

1 Before you start, make sure the existing pickup heights are about right. Measure and note down the distance from the top of the mounting ring to the top of the humbucker(s) you're replacing.

Remove your strings (or alternatively put a capo at the first fret, slacken off the strings, and remove the tailpiece and bridge). Remove the rear control cavity's backplate. Unsolder the live pickup wire from the correct control, and unsolder the ground (earth) wire from the back of the pot. (It may not be clear which pickup wire goes where. Don't worry, just partially remove the pickup as described in the next step and gently pull on its hook-up wire, and trace which pot it's soldered to by observing which wire moves at the other end. Put two of the mounting-ring screws back, then unsolder the relevant wires.)

2 Turn the guitar over and remove the pickup by unscrewing the four cross-head screws that hold the pickup mounting ring. Carefully pull the pickup, still held in its mounting ring, away from the guitar.

Unscrew the two pickup height-adjustment screws carefully. Make sure you don't lose the two long springs as new ones are not always supplied. Before you mount the new pickup, check to see if the old height-adjustment screws fit the threaded lugs on the new pickup. Don't force them – just use your fingers to see if they'll turn in the thread. If they do, then go ahead and use them. If not, use the screws supplied.

3 Mount the new pickup in the old mounting ring. This is actually quite a tricky job. Insert one screw at a time through the ring, place the spring over the screw, and grip the pickup and mounting ring so that the end of the screw is held over the thread on the pickup's mounting lug. With a small cross-head or slot-head screwdriver (depending on the screw type) carefully turn the screw so that it bites into the pickup's thread. Don't force it – you might damage the thread.

The new height adjustment screws will probably be too long and you'll need a pair of heavy duty cutters to trim them to length. But first screw the pickup down into the ring to match the distance you measured originally. Replace the pickup in the guitar. Does it sit flush on the body, or are those screws stopping it? If necessary, cut them to length with heavy-duty cutters about 1/16" or so (a few millimeters) past the back face of the mounting lugs.

4 Carefully thread the hook-up wire through the hole that connects the pickup cavity to the rear control cavity (below right), wrapping masking tape around any loose wires so they don't bunch up and catch in the hole. Replace the pickup into the guitar, securing it with just two of the mounting-ring screws at diagonally opposite corners.

At this stage don't cut the pickup wire to length. Strip, tin and re-solder the live wire to the relevant volume control and the earth wire to the back of the pot. If the pickups have four-conductor wiring, make sure you follow the supplied wiring diagram and join the remaining two conductors (for series linkage) as described later in this section.

5 Rub the tip of a screwdriver on the pickup polepieces to check that the new pickup is working and check that all the controls function (as described opposite in *Replacing A Single-coil Pickup*). Fit a set of new strings and tune your guitar to pitch. Set the height of the new pickup. Refit the remaining mounting-ring screws and refit the control cavity backplate. Only after fully sound-testing your guitar should you cut the pickup wires to correct length and re-solder the hot connection using a mechanical joint.

HUMBUCKER VARIATIONS
There are almost as many replacement options for humbuckers as there are for single-coils, and models available perform jobs nearly as diverse as there are styles of music. Seekers of vintage tones generally opt for PAF-style pickups like the Seymour Duncan TB-'59, top, while Joe Barden's dual blade models suit players who appreciate high-end tone without concern for vintage cosmetics. Even more contemporary in design (though they've been with us for years), EMG's active pickups do everything from sweet blues to power metal.

Unsolder the pickup's live and ground wires from the correct control or switch point.

Remove the four screws that hold the mounting ring in place, and lift out pickup and ring.

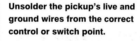

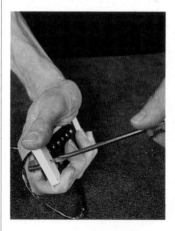

Mounting a new pickup in an old mounting ring can be a surprisingly tricky job – so proceed with care.

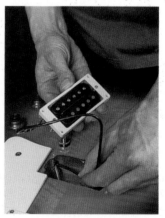

Next, carefully thread the wire through the hole connecting the pickup cavity and control cavity.

The grounding plate underneath a Tele bridge pickup is a unique part of its design – and must be connected.

The standard-style Tele's controls are easy to get at – merely unscrew the control panel and flip it.

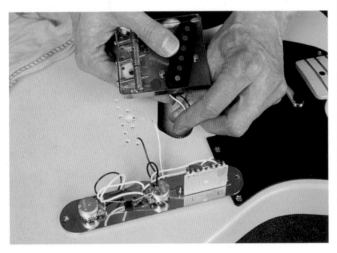

After unsoldering the pickup wires, remove the entire bridge unit before proceeding to swap pickups. This

bridge design is a major part of a Telecaster's distinctive tone – but makes pickup replacement tricky.

Mount the new pickup in the bridge's baseplate before making any solder connections.

Make your solder connections, then re-mount the bridge unit, string up, and give 'er a play.

REPLACING A TELE BRIDGE PICKUP

Unlike any other electric, the Telecaster and its derivatives has a bridge pickup that is mounted within the bridge's baseplate. It's held with three screws, and under the pickup is a grounding plate. The combination of these design features contributes to the Tele's unique tone – but can also add to microphonic squeal, especially if the pickup's windings are not properly wax-potted and if there's any movement of the pickup and/or the bridgeplate.

In order to replace a Tele bridge pickup, first remove the strings. You have little choice with this, because to access the bridge pickup you'll have to remove the bridge itself. Measure the height of the pickup from the face of the bridgeplate, on both treble and bass sides. Make a note of these dimensions.

1 Unscrew the control plate and sketch the wiring layout. Unsolder the pickup's hook-up wires. As with the humbucker replacement, if you're unsure which wires are which, then remove the bridge's baseplate by undoing the four mounting screws and gently pull on the two hook-up wires to trace one to the three-way lever switch and one to the back of a pot.

2 With the hook-up wires unsoldered, remove the bridge's baseplate and the pickup, undoing the four baseplate screws first if you haven't already. Replace the control plate and place the guitar to one side.

3 Remove the pickup from the bridge's baseplate and mount the new pickup. Some players and makers insist on replacing the pickup's mounting springs with small pieces of plastic or rubber tubing to reduce microphonics. Others stick with the springs. Either way, the key is to make sure that springs or tubing are very tight and firm, and that once the pickup is mounted there's virtually no movement within the baseplate. Set the pickup to the original position. Strip and carefully tin the hook-up wires.

4 Undo the control plate and thread the hook-up wires into the control cavity. Solder them to the correct positions: the live wire goes to the three-way lever switch, the ground (earth) wire to the back of a pot. Place both the control plate and the bridgeplate in position and scratch-test the pickup to check that it's working. Replace all the screws and re-string the guitar. Tune up, and then set the pickup height – then play-test thoroughly.

WIRING MODIFICATIONS

Now that we've covered all the basic aspects relating to your electronics, you can use this *Wiring Modifications* section should you need to replace any components or you want to upgrade and modify your guitar.

REPLACING COMPONENTS

For any component replacement there are some basic rules…

Sketch out your guitar's existing circuitry *before* you start!
Unsolder the component.
Remove old component and re-install new part.
Re-solder new component and scratch-test before re-assembling guitar.

Note that semi-solid guitars like Gibson's ES-335 are popular again but are among the trickiest guitars to work on as far as electronics are concerned. The problem is that these guitars have no backplate. To service the parts or replace the pickups you must remove the pots and switches through the f-holes. For this reason we suggest you take your semi to a professional.

VOLUME AND TONE POTS

To replace these, in most cases a standard split-shaft (splined-shaft) pot of the required value and taper will be fine (as discussed earlier in this section). Before you install the new pot, however, check that the control knob actually fits onto the new pot's shaft. The slotted split shaft can be widened *slightly* by carefully opening it up at the tip with a flat-blade screwdriver, or narrowed by slightly compressing the split with a pair of pliers. *Be warned*: the tips of these shafts are surprisingly fragile.

The tools and techniques for un-mounting a pot are the same as those previously shown for cleaning; here, of course, we completely unsolder the old component and load in the new one in its place.

OUTPUT JACK (SOCKET)

The majority of electric guitars use a mono output jack (socket). The exceptions generally are those with on-board active electronics, where the second "stereo" hot connection serves to make the 9V battery connection when plugged in. A mono output

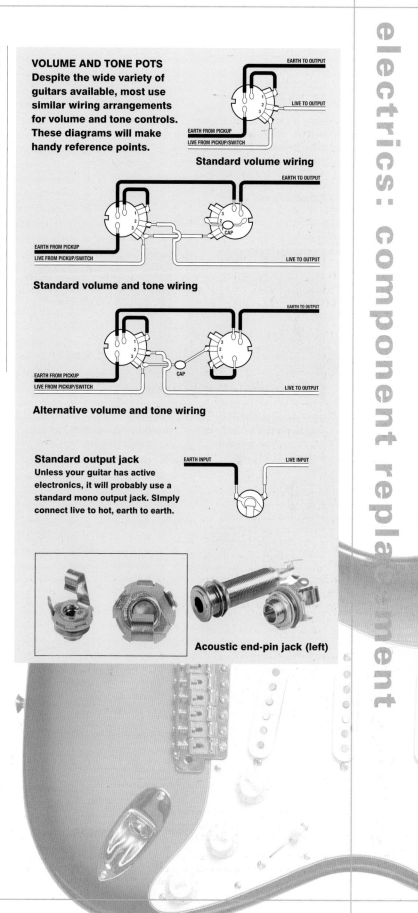

VOLUME AND TONE POTS
Despite the wide variety of guitars available, most use similar wiring arrangements for volume and tone controls. These diagrams will make handy reference points.

Standard volume wiring

Standard volume and tone wiring

Alternative volume and tone wiring

Standard output jack
Unless your guitar has active electronics, it will probably use a standard mono output jack. Simply connect live to hot, earth to earth.

Acoustic end-pin jack (left)

PHASED AND CONFUSED

When two pickups – humbuckers or single-coils – are combined (positions 2 and 4 on a Strat, the middle positions on a Les Paul or Telecaster) they'll be either in-phase or out-of-phase. If they're out-of-phase (caused primarily by reversed magnet polarity) the resulting mixed sound will be thin (bass light) and "strangled" or overly nasal sounding. Now, you may like this sound especially for high-gain grungy tones or reggae/funk/country clean tones but you may not. (Note that the standard 2 and 4 positions on a Strat, sometimes referred to as "out-of-phase" positions, aren't actually wired out of phase: the thinner, funkier tone of these "notched" bridge-plus-middle or neck-plus-middle settings simply results from the natural frequency cancellations of two closely-positioned pickups selected together in parallel.)

For genuine out-of-phase problems, standard single-coils are easy to cure – simply swap the live and earth connections of one pickup where they connect to the pickup switch. Humbuckers with just one live wire and earth are more difficult because the earth wire – unlike a standard single-coil – is connected to the metal baseplate and the cover (if fitted). Swapping these two around will result in hum. Telecasters can be especially problematic because the earth wire of the bridge pickup is connected to its own grounding plate and the neck pickup's earth wire connects to its metal cover. The most simple solution is swap the connections for the neck pickup but you must rewire the neck pickup's cover to the 'new' earth output, a job for a pro or specialist pickup repairer.

If you're mixing brands of pickups always make sure the humbucker has 3- or preferably 4-conductor and separate earth wires (see *Replacing a Humbucker*) – this way any phase problems for standard pickup linkages can be easily identified and solved.

FIVE-POSITION LEVER SWITCH

The top diagram here shows the standard wiring for a US five-position lever switch. The lower diagram demonstrates how Fender wire their lever switches – and this is typically the reverse of the first method. Either way will work.

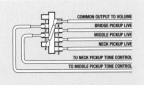

COMMON OUTPUT TO VOLUME
BRIDGE PICKUP LIVE
MIDDLE PICKUP LIVE
NECK PICKUP LIVE
TO NECK PICKUP TONE CONTROL
TO MIDDLE PICKUP TONE CONTROL

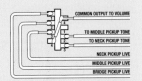

COMMON OUTPUT TO VOLUME
TO MIDDLE PICKUP TONE
TO NECK PICKUP TONE
NECK PICKUP LIVE
MIDDLE PICKUP LIVE
BRIDGE PICKUP LIVE

By viewing the contacts in a toggle switch as you move the lever, you can determine correct connections.

Each side of a three or five-position lever switch carries three input/output tags and one common tag.

PICKUP SELECTORS

The five-position Strat-type switch (top right) and three-position variety (center right) are virtually identical in construction, although the former is notched for dual-contact positions between the input/output tags. The type of switch typically used in Gibsons and other similarly-built guitars (below right) looks radically different to the Fender unit, but performs the same job as any three-position Tele switch: selecting bridge pickup, neck pickup, or both together.

THREE-POSITION TOGGLE SWITCH

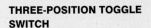
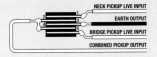

NECK PICKUP LIVE INPUT
EARTH OUTPUT
BRIDGE PICKUP LIVE INPUT
COMBINED PICKUP OUTPUT

jack simply has one connection for the hot output and another for the ground output. Take care to replace the jack (socket) with one of a similar size, especially on Stratocaster-style guitars where it sits under the separate "dished" mounting plate, or a standard Telecaster where it's mounted in a body rout without much room to spare. Generally, a standard "chassis" type jack is recommended in these situations.

PICKUP SELECTOR SWITCHES

Most Fender-style guitars and many, many others use either a three-position lever switch (for two-pickup guitars) or a five-position lever switch (for three-pickup guitars) to select the pickups. The other industry standard switch is the three-position toggle or leaf switch used on Gibson-style guitars, primarily with two pickups.

THREE AND FIVE-POSITION LEVER SWITCHES

You'll encounter a number of different types within two basic categories: "open" and "closed." A standard US-made open type is preferred, and is featured here. Measure the distance between the centers of the two mounting holes, which can differ, to check that your new switch will fit.

For three or five-position switches, the mechanics are the same. It's a "two-pole" switch – it has two circuits that are switched simultaneously. We refer to these poles or circuits as "sides," simply because of the physical construction of the switch. On each side there are four connection tags: three input/output tags and one common tag.

If your replacement switch doesn't come with a wiring diagram, you can visually check the switch.

1 Hold the switch upside down in front of you with the non-spring side facing you and the selection lever all the way to the right. When the switch is wired in, this position (position one) will select the Stratocaster's bridge pickup.

2 Below the row of connection tags you'll see that the large square lug is in contact with one of those four connection tags. Sketch out the switch and mark this tag as number one. Move the lever to the furthest position to the left (position five) and make a note of which connection tag the square lug is now in contact with, and mark this as number three; this is where you connect the neck pickup.

Mark the tag between these two as number two; this will be your middle pickup connection. (Remember, originally a Strat had a three-way switch – you couldn't combine the pickups. The five-way switch simply joins connection tags one and two and connection tags two and three to create the famous mixed-pickup Strat sounds.)

3 The fourth connection is the common connection. Mark this as number four.

4 Return the lever all the way to the right. Now turn the switch so the spring side is facing you and mark on your sketch which connection the square lug is now in contact with. Mark this as number one. Do the same for all the switch positions as above and mark them, finally marking the common connection. Now, when the switch is in position on the pickguard you can follow your sketch to determine precisely which wires go to which connection tags.

THREE-POSITION TOGGLE SWITCH

Like the three and five-position lever switches, the three-position toggle or leaf-style switch comes in a number of styles and sizes. (Again, not least because you can see which connection tag does what, go for an "open" type as opposed to the square "closed" type.) Typically, a longer switch is used in a Les Paul and a shorter type in a thinner-bodied guitar like an SG. The switch has two input connections (for each pickup) and two output connections, which must be joined on the switch to provide the common output. A fifth connection – usually in the center of the switch – connects to ground (earth). Again, you can visually check which contact does what, as follows.

1 Hold the switch upright so that the toggle moves from left to right with the outer (or both sets) of connection tags facing you.

2 Place the toggle to the left (the up position, which on a Les Paul selects the neck pickup) and you will see that the right pair of contacts are opened, so you wire the neck pickup to the outer connection tag of the left pair, and the bridge pickup to the outer tag of the right pair. With the toggle in the center position you'll see that both pairs of contacts are joined – that's how you get both pickups on together.

BASIC WIRING MODIFICATIONS

If your pickups and controls are working properly, you can use the following simple wiring mods – referring to the diagrams shown on the right and the following page – to alter the way in which the controls affect your pickup's output.

TREBLE BLEED NETWORK

This is a simple modification that can be applied to any volume control. By placing a small capacitor (typically .001µF) between the input (connection tag one) and output (tag two) of the pot, as you turn down the volume control you'll retain the high end of your tone. When wiring in the capacitor you're advised to use a heat-sink (crocodile clip) as you solder each leg.

Some companies prefer the effect of an additional resistor wired (in parallel with the capacitor) between the same two tags. The reason is that you may find the capacitor alone makes the sound too thin with the volume control reduced. "The additional resistor tends to restore the lower (bass) end when the control is turned down," reckons DiMarzio's Steve Blucher. The normal value for this resistor is 150kΩ, but Blucher thinks this allows too much bass resistance. "The bigger the resistor's value, the less you're limiting bass. I don't use anything below 300kΩ."

TONE-CONTROL CAPACITORS

Another subtle change you can make involves experimenting with a range of capacitor values in your tone control(s). In this circuit the capacitor shunts off the treble frequencies to ground (earth), in other words the opposite of the treble bleed network. Standard values are .047µF, .02µF and .01µF (all values measured in microfarads, sometimes written as "mf"). Remember, the value of the capacitor determines the frequency point above which the treble roll-off takes place. The smaller the capacitor's value, the higher the frequency point and the less effect the capacitor will have in terms of cutting the treble as the control is wound down.

So, if you find your tone control sounds too dark – and it uses a .047µF capacitor – try a .02µF or a .01µF. Conversely, if it doesn't sound dark enough and you're using a .02µF or .01µF, try a

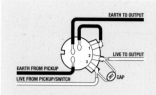

Treble-bleed network

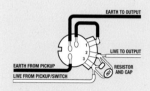

Treble-bleed with resistor

WIRING MODIFICATIONS
Without risking major damage to your guitar or altering it in any irreversible way (especially important for instruments with any collectable value), there are a number of small changes you can make which may open up new tonal horizons that you prefer to the stock wiring. Use these diagrams for reference, and proceed with care and caution. If you haven't yet developed soldering skills through experience, first read the *Soldering Techniques* section which follows these wiring mods on pages 102/103.

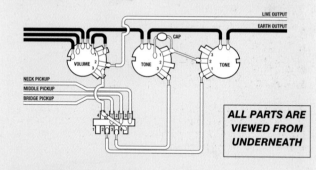

ALL PARTS ARE VIEWED FROM UNDERNEATH

Standard Strat-style wiring

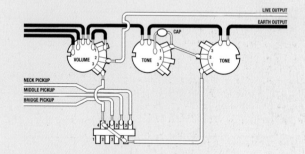

Strat-style wiring with 2nd tone as master tone

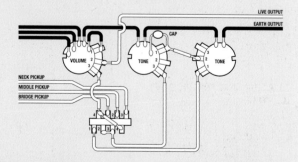

Strat-style wiring with 1st tone for neck and middle pickup, 2nd tone for bridge

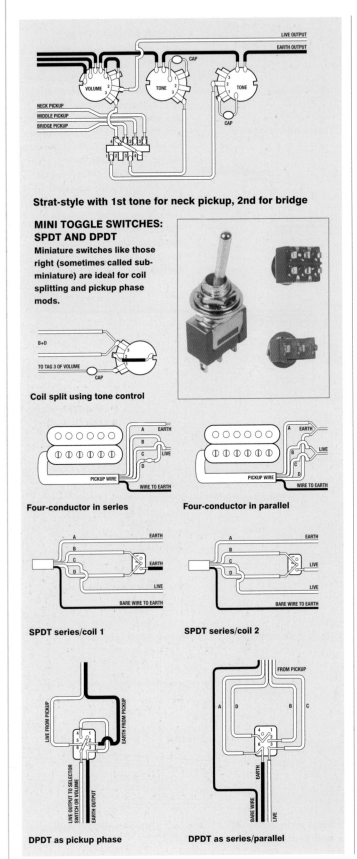

Strat-style with 1st tone for neck pickup, 2nd for bridge

MINI TOGGLE SWITCHES: SPDT AND DPDT

Miniature switches like those right (sometimes called sub-miniature) are ideal for coil splitting and pickup phase mods.

Coil split using tone control

Four-conductor in series

Four-conductor in parallel

SPDT series/coil 1

SPDT series/coil 2

DPDT as pickup phase

DPDT as series/parallel

.047µF. On a guitar with two tone controls, like a Les Paul or Strat, you can use different values to fine-tune the tone controls to individual pickups.

STRAT TONE CONTROLS

Typically a Strat is wired so that the first tone control (the center of the three controls) affects the neck pickup, and the second tone control (furthest from the bridge pickup) works on the middle pickup; there is no tone control for the bridge pickup. Some players like to change this, and it's easy to do. The late Rory Gallagher, for example, wired his Strat so that only the second control functioned, but as a master tone control for all three pickups (refer to diagrams, previous page).

Alternatively, you could use the first tone control for both the neck and middle pickups and the second tone control for the bridge pickup. Another popular option is to use the first tone control for the neck pickup and the second tone control for the bridge pickup, leaving the middle pickup without a tone control. This gives tone control for the often-used soloing pickups (neck and bridge) while the "rhythm" settings (the Strat's combined pickup tones) benefit from the full treble of the middle pickup. Try this with different tone capacitor values.

PICKUP SWITCHES

Fitting a new full-sized humbucking pickup to your guitar, so long as the pickup has four hot conductors and a separate ground, opens up a host of switching options. We've shown the standard wiring for a four-conductor humbucker in series operation (left) and parallel operation. Please note that the four conductors are labelled a, b, c, and d, which relate to the *Mister Conductor* chart, opposite. There are, however, numerous ways to switch between these standard wirings – and also to add more sounds – simply by installing an additional switch (or two).

MINI TOGGLE SWITCH MODS

Adding a two-position (on/on) single pole, double throw (SPDT) or double pole, double throw (DPDT), or three-position (on/on/on) DPDT mini switch to your guitar can open up a range of possibilities, some of which are illustrated in the diagrams, left.

An SPDT can be used to coil-split a humbucker from its standard series humbucking mode to either one of the humbucker's single coils. You can achieve a similar effect using the spare lug on a tone control.

An on/on DPDT switch is like two SPDT switches ganged together. To coil-split two humbuckers simultaneously, use either of the SPDT diagrams but assign one to one side for the neck pickup and the other to the other side for the bridge pickup. But this switch also has many other uses. For example, it can be used to switch the phase relationship between two pickups (see diagram bottom-left), or to switch between the way the humbucker is wired, either in series (standard) or in parallel, that will produce a brighter tonal characteristic with a lower output that is noise-cancelling.

An on/on/on DPDT can be used to offer series, single-coil and parallel wiring of one humbucker (as in the diagram near-left), offering three sound variations from a single pickup, all achieved with one switch.

If you want to avoid altering your guitar in any way (for example the drilling through a pickguard required to mount a mini switch) a "pull/push" pot with a DPDT switch mounted on its housing can do any of the jobs assigned here to a standard on/on DPDT.

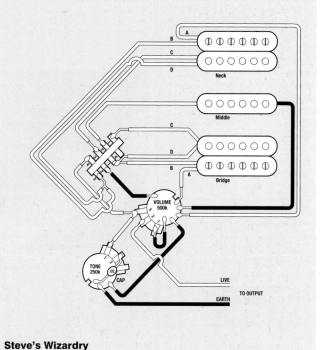

MISTER CONDUCTOR

Virtually all of the major-brand retrofit pickups come with four-conductor (plus ground) hook-up wire. If you're swapping brands and/or plan to add some wiring options this format is recommended. The four conductors come from each end – the start and finish of the two wound coils, I & II. We've included a color code comparison chart of the three major brands to help you. However, all pickups should come with clear instructions – follow those first and use our chart as reference.

		DiMarzio	Duncan	WD/Sky
COIL I	start (a)	green	green	green
	finish (b)	white	red	white
COIL II	start (c)	red	black	red
	finish (d)	black	white	black

(Note: The uncovered wire is always wired to ground.)

Series humbucker: conductor a) goes to ground; b) and d) are joined; c) is hot. Note that if pickup is out-of-phase, reverse the position of conductors a) and c).

Parallel humbucking: a) and d) joined to ground; b) and c) joined to hot.

Coil I (screw polepieces) single-coil: a) ground; b) hot. Note that if the pickup is out-of-phase, reverse the position of conductors a) and b).

Coil II (slug polepieces) single-coil: c) hot d) ground. Note that if the pickup is out-of-phase, reverse the position of conductors c) and d).

HOT-ROD MODS

Here's a couple of our favorite hot-rod wiring mods, both of which are simple and effective.

THE MAGNIFICENT SEVEN

By changing the volume or one of the tone controls on a Strat (or similar) to a pull/push switched pot (or by adding a separate on/on DPDT mini-toggle) you can, with the pull/push switch pulled up and the neck pickup selected on the five-way switch, add the bridge pickup to the neck pickup for a Tele-like mix (in parallel). Also, if you select the neck-and-middle mix on the five-way switch, by pulling the pull/push up you add the bridge pickup for all three pickups on. This expands the Strat's five pickup selections to a magnificent seven.

STEVE'S WIZARDRY

Designed for Steve Vai in 1986 by DiMarzio's Steve Blucher, this wiring is found on numerous Ibanez guitars that have a humbucker at neck and bridge plus a single-coil in the middle position. Because the set-up uses a master volume and master tone on one side of a standard five-way lever switch, the other side can be used to automatically coil-split the neck and bridge humbuckers.

Blucher's wiring gives us: position one, neck humbucker; position two, bridge-facing single-coil of the neck humbucker plus middle single-coil; position three, middle single-coil; position four, neck-facing single-coil of the bridge humbucker plus middle single-coil; position five, bridge humbucker.

With a reverse-wound middle pickup of opposite polarity to the outer-facing single coils of each humbucker, all positions except number three – middle pickup alone – are hum-cancelling. Note that because this circuit was designed for DiMarzio pickups, to achieve the correct noise-cancelling and phase relationship with other models you may need to reverse one humbucker in its mounting ring.

MOD SQUAD

These hot-rod mods take matters a few steps further than the basics of the previous page. Achieve seven sounds from a standard Strat by adding a pull/push pot, or try Steve Vai's wiring mod.

ALL PARTS ARE VIEWED FROM UNDERNEATH

The Magnificent Seven

Steve's Wizardry

Before soldering any insulated wires, you'll need to strip them with the correct wire-stripper.

To make a bare wire easier to solder, first "tin" it by flowing a coating of solder over the strands.

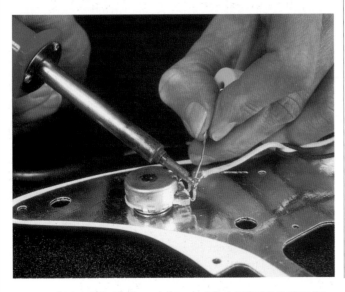

For good electrical connections, heat the joint first then place the solder to it and let it flow. Like anything, good technique takes practice, but you'll develop a feel for it over time.

The small hook made in the stripped wire end, seen in this close-up photograph, represents a "mechanical" connnection in the joint, to help hold it more strongly than solder alone. Make such connections only after you are sure the modification or repair is correct.

SOLDERING TECHNIQUES

Soldering is a process used to join electrical components and wires securely. If you want to fit your own pickup and maybe try some wiring mods, you'll have to learn how to solder. Fear not: it's much easier than learning to read music.

You'll need a small-tipped soldering iron, and it's worth buying a stand for it too. Small irons (25 watts) are fine for small connections but a more powerful iron (40 watts) is necessary for heavier jobs such as when you want to solder ground (earth) wires to the backs of control pots.

First you need to have your iron in good working order. If it's a new iron you'll need to tin the copper tip. If it hasn't been used for a while, clean the tip with fine to medium abrasive paper. Heat up the iron and place your solder (use a 60/40 rosin-core type) on the tip. Let the solder flow over the tip, then wipe off any excess with a damp – not wet – rag or sponge. Keeping your tip conditioned in this way is essential for good soldering. Periodically wipe the tip with a damp cloth. Some soldering-iron stands have a small sponge that can be dampened and used to wipe the iron tip. When your tip becomes blackened with use, re-clean it occasionally and re-tin it as previously described. Good preparation is the key to good soldering.

Having disassembled your guitar so you can access the relevant parts to be soldered, always cover the surface of your guitar with a cloth to stop splatters of solder marking the finish. Make sure you're clear on exactly what you are wiring where. Draw out the existing circuit before your start work, and then draw your modifications. That way you can always return the guitar to "stock." Clearly label these sketches and keep them for future reference.

Most wires you'll be soldering have plastic or cloth insulation. Strip off about ⅛" to ³⁄₁₆" (3mm to 5mm) with proper wire-strippers. If the core wire is multi-strand, twist it so it becomes solid. To "tin" the wire, apply heat from the iron to the bare end of the wire then touch the bare end with your solder, which should flow over the

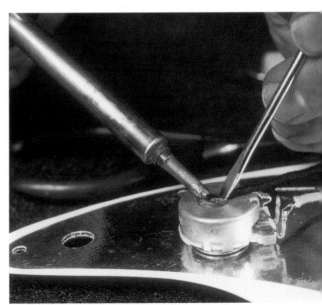

When soldering to the back of a pot, use a small flat-blade screwdriver to hold the wire firmly in place while you wait for the dome of solder to cool sufficiently to form its own solid joint.

exposed metal. You don't want too much solder. If a large blob transfers itself to the tip of the wire, re-heat and wipe off excess with a damp cloth. A helpful addition to your soldering kit is a desoldering pump, or "solder sucker." Its spring-loaded piston is held over a fluid solder joint; when released it sucks away any excess solder. It's handy for working on mini-toggle switches.

Wherever you can, make a "mechanical" joint before you solder the wire to the component. For example, pass the tinned wired halfway through a lug on a pot and bend it back on itself with a small pair of needlenose pliers. This will help secure the wire prior to soldering.

Place the iron on the joint. Leave for a few seconds to heat. You'll get a feel for this, depending on exactly what you're soldering and how powerful the iron is you're using. Then place the solder on the joint and let it flow. Remove the solder, then the iron, and let the joint cool. Don't blow on it. When it's cool, just tug on the wire to make sure the joint is secure. It should look shiny and chrome-like. A grey and dull appearance is a sure sign of a "dry" joint, where the solder hasn't flowed – and neither will the electrical signal. You'll need to resolder the connection.

Securing wires to the back of the pots is always difficult. First, prepare the pot. Rough the soldering surface with medium abrasive paper or score with the edge of a blade-tip screwdriver, wipe off any debris (with a cloth, not your greasy finger) and tin the back of the pot, creating a small dome of solder. Lay your tinned wire in place, hold it, and heat it with the tip of your iron. Apply solder. When the solder has flowed, place the tip of a small screwdriver or probe on the wire, to keep it in place while the solder cools, and remove the iron.

Wire insulation can melt if subjected to excessive heat, while small components like capacitors can be damaged. So when soldering a capacitor, for example, use a crocodile clip as an absorbing "heat sink" by placing it on the relevant "leg" between the component and the joint. Don't forget the most important rule: soldering practice makes perfect.

SOLDER-FREE SOLUTIONS
If the idea of soldering frightens you, don't worry. Many stores will wire up your new pickup for you free of charge (or for a minimal fee). Also, some companies – a good example would be EMG – offer pre-wired pickguards that have new pickups and controls already mounted and wired, requiring just a couple of connections to get them up and running in your own guitar.

Before purchasing any new replacement pickup, check carefully what the manufacturer's and/or guitar store's returns policy is. Some will let you swap a pickup you have tried out but found unsatisfactory for your needs, as long as you haven't trimmed the unit's wires in the process of making your connections.

Plastic wire insulation and smaller capacitors can melt when exposed to the high temperatures of a directly-applied soldering iron. You can use a crocodile clip as a makeshift heatsink that will disperse any excess heat.

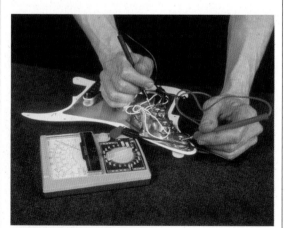

MARVELOUS MULTI-METER
Not an essential tool for a basic home guitar workshop, a good multi-meter can nevertheless be extremely handy at times. With settings for reading AC/DC voltages, capacitance and resistance – and many other features – they're good for checking the validity of suspect solder joints, for reading the DC resistance of pickups and for determining whether a pickup short or other malfunction has occured.

LEAVE IT TO THE PROS!

With a little care, and attention paid to the advice given in the rest of this chapter, there are plenty of things you can do yourself to maximize the playability of your guitar. Even so, many jobs remain that should be consigned to a professional – unless of course you are extremely experienced in such work, or are testing your hand on a guitar of little or no value. In addition to the jobs covered here and on the following four pages, other pro jobs might include:

• Repairing body cracks in acoustics, or headstock breaks in acoustics and electrics.
• Finding and fixing loose top braces.
• Routing jobs to install Floyd Rose vibratos, humbuckers, etc.
• Re-wiring semi-acoustic guitars.
• Fret removal and replacement.
• Tuner replacement where headstock drilling is required.
• Unsticking tight or frozen truss rods.
• Refinishing work on valuable instruments.

A veteran guitar tech who has tackled countless repair, maintenance and modification jobs for notable pros and local amateurs alike, Charlie Chandler (below) runs the workshop at the much-respected Chandler Guitars store in Kew, London, with a staff of five skilled repairmen.

PROFESSIONAL MAINTENANCE

There are some maintenance jobs you might consider but that are best not approached by the player. Many require the skill and experience of a trained pro, and taking them on yourself – and messing them up – can result in repairs along with the replacement of major components that end up being far more costly than the original job would have been. A quick look at some of these procedures, however, will show you how a pro might approach the job, and help you understand what is required if you ever need to take your guitar into the shop for similar work. Respected London-based guitar tech Charlie Chandler takes us through four of the most called-for jobs in his workshop.

FITTING AN ACOUSTIC PICKUP

Fitting a pickup to an acoustic guitar may seem a simple enough job, but it requires a pro's touch. It's been an extremely popular modification in recent years, with the "unplugged revolution" sending countless guitarists back into the coffee houses and acoustic club. The necessary precision of connecting pickup and preamp wiring, and the delicate nature of working on acoustics in general means mistakes can be costly to put right. Fitting an end-pin jack may require drilling to widen the hole accordingly – a bad job for an amateur to get wrong – and internal electronics can be difficult to access and connect. Also, if an under-saddle piezo pickup is to be installed as part of the job, as with the Fishman blender-style unit featured here, this usually means

precise measuring and sanding-down of the bridge saddle, along with the other mounting requirements. The good news is that all of this is straightforward work for a trained repairman, and shouldn't cost an arm and a leg to get done.

"Getting the end-pin jack hole right in the first place is one of the hardest things," says Charlie Chandler. "Usually you have to enlarge it. We tend to use a reamer, then countersink it. Once the hole is correctly positioned, most end-pin jacks are easier to fit than they used to be, because you can adjust them and tighten them outside the guitar."

Before setting the jack in place, however, Chandler says it's important to make all soldering connections, and to get the cable lengths correct. "You don't want yards of spare cable rattling around inside the guitar; fortunately, these days most systems come with cable restraints to help you get this right." Once all the connections have been made, Chandler inserts a screwdriver in the end-pin hole to help guide the jack into position, then holds it firmly while tightening it into place.

Mounting the soundhole pickup can seem a simple enough job, but even this has its tricks and fine points.

"With most of them, the positioning is ordained by the soundhole itself," says Charlie. "With the Fishman pickup, which is currently our most popular one – and also with the Sunrise pickup – there's a jaw that will butt up to the narrowest points on the inside dimension of the soundhole. This usually works fine, but the problems you can have are that sometimes a pickguard comes up to the edge of the soundhole on one side, or there's a reinforcing ring underneath the rim of the soundhole. In either case it can prevent the jaws closing evenly. Ideally, you want the mounting jaws to close as evenly and as flush to the guitar's top and underside as possible." In such cases, rather than cut into the pickguard or reinforcing ring, the only solution is to tighten the mounting jaws enough to hold the pickup firmly in place in whichever position minimizes the unevenness of the closure.

Most factory-ready electro-acoustic guitars purchased new today come with rim-mounted preamps already installed. According to Chandler, however, customers who these days are having pickup systems mounted in formerly acoustic-only instruments rarely request the major work of adding a rim-mounted preamp where no hole already exists for one.

"That would be a whole different thing, because you get involved with cutting out a portion of the side of the guitar and then reinforcing it. There are very few people now who have a guitar they will entertain putting something like that on. If they want that style of guitar, they'll go out and buy one. They are so readily available that the cost of converting a guitar not originally built in that way is almost prohibitive."

The popular alternative for after-market fitting is the straight-out system such as the Fishman unit pictured – for use with an external preamp – or a system with a small preamp housed in the end-pin jack.

The key, then, to getting satisfactory work of this type done begins even before the tech sets hands on your guitar. Seek the advice of repairmen and dealers, of friends who have had the work done already, and of pros whose sound you admire, to determine which pickup system is right for you and how invasive the "surgery" required to install it will be. Most techs will hesitate to drill or cut into an especially valuable or vintage acoustic unless the owner convinces them he or she is aware of the consequences and still wants the job done, so be sure you know what permanent changes may result before the work is underway.

Soldering above or in proximity to the face of the guitar can be a real danger to the instrument's finish. A piece of heat-resistant cloth is used for protection while making this wiring connection to the end-pin jack.

A screwdriver placed through the slightly-widened end-pin hole helps to locate the jack held inside the guitar with the other hand and to slide it into place for mounting – which can be a fiddly job otherwise.

The end-pin jack is held firmly in place while the fixing nut is tightened with the correct wrench.

Finally, the magnetic pickup is mounted and adjusted to sit tight and flush in the soundhole.

Chandler uses a calliper to measure the height of the saddle above the face of the bridge.

Measuring the overall height of the saddle determines how much material has to be removed.

Finishing the sanding-down with wet and dry paper laid in a flat bed made from a length of aluminum.

Feeding the piezo pickup cable into the pre-drilled hole in the bridge's saddle slot.

ACOUSTIC SADDLE ADJUSTMENT

Want lower action on your acoustic? Usually the only satisfactory solution is to reduce the saddle height by the required amount. Similarly, if the installation of a new pickup system includes fitting an under-saddle piezo strip, the saddle height might need to be reduced to account for the thickness of the piezo pickup and restore the guitar to its original playing action.

In our sample procedure pictured to the left, Charlie Chandler performs both jobs for a customer: a piezo strip is being fitted as part of the "blender" pickup system installed on the previous page, and a reduction in string height has also been requested.

"The first thing to do," says Chandler, "with the guitar still strung up, is to measure the height from the saddle top to the face of the bridge. Do that at three different points and use it to cross-check how much you are taking off the bottom of the saddle." Next, Chandler removes the strings, takes the saddle out of the bridge's saddle slot, measures its height outside the guitar, and marks it to remove the required amount of material.

"You can take most of it off with a belt sander," he explains. "Then you need to get a very flat bed – we use a piece of aluminum here in the workshop – and put wet and dry paper on it and sand the saddle until it's perfectly flat to the correct depth."

Even with a perfectly flat sanding bed to finish the saddle, however, the job can throw up a few obstacles. "For example, quite often acoustics belly-up slightly around the bridge, and if you've got a bridge that's slightly arched but a saddle that has been sanded perfectly flat, it won't sit flush in its slot. There are a number of things you can do here. For one, companies like Fishman recommend using man-made saddles because they're uniform, whereas anything organic – like bone – may have different hardnesses in different parts of the saddle. Another one is that companies have made saddles, like Fishman's Clear Tone, with slots cut on the underside between the string positions so that it's almost 'sprung' and can curve to the shape of the guitar top's arch."

Other points to look out for? "You need to satisfy yourself that the saddle slot is clean and flat, so the saddle will sit flush inside it. Most guitars now come with a hole pre-drilled at the end of the saddle slot for the piezo pickup lead, or if they don't pre-drill it then indent it, so that part of the job is usually done for you."

From there you insert the strip, make the wiring connection to the system, replace the saddle, string up and tune and, finally, check that the new action is satisfactory. After a saddle has been lowered, slight truss-rod adjustment may be required too.

To level the frets on this '53 Fender Esquire, our tech first reduces their height with a diamond file.

A special slotted guard protects the fingerboard from scratches and gouges while individual frets are polished up.

FRET LEVELING AND DRESSING

Most any fret work is a job for a pro. The owner of this vintage '53 Fender Esquire (brlow, opposite) has asked Chandler to level and reshape its upper frets, where uneven crowns were starting to mean the guitar wouldn't note accurately up above the 12th fret. Taking on a job like this without knowing exactly what you're doing risks major damage to frets and fingerboard, perhaps necessitating an entire re-fret – or more, if you slip up badly.

The work itself is fairly straightforward for an experienced repairman, and shouldn't be an especially costly procedure to have done, certainly much less than re-fretting the whole neck.

"The first thing I do in any job like this is tape off the guitar body and pickguard surrounding the neck join to protect them from any slips with the files. Then I start by taking the frets down to even heights with a diamond file," Chandler explains. "Next, I use a fret file to reshape them to get the roundness back into the crowns, and use another fret file to round off the ends. Finally, I cover the fingerboard with a little slotted guard to protect it – letting only one fret show through at a time – and polish each individual fret to get out any marks left by the files."

Often, "professional" guitar maintenance is as much about having the correct, specialized tools handy as it is about experience and skill. With this fret work, using the wrong type of file can damage frets badly, while one slip without protection can put an ugly gouge into a precious fingerboard.

CUTTING NUT SLOTS

Before a repairman even begins to cut a new nut or adjust an old one, he will ensure that the truss rod is correctly adjusted and the desired action has been set at the bridge. "If you've got a new nut on there to start with," explains Chandler, "you put a capo on at the first fret to take the nut right out of the equation."

To begin, Chandler needs to decide how deep the nut slots need to be cut – which is determined by fretting each string at the third fret and looking at the gap of the string over the first fret.

"The amount of clearance you leave here depends upon the playing style of the guitar owner. If he plays hard, you're going to have to leave more clearance than if he plays soft or you'll get some buzz against the frets. If he plays real fast legato style then you get it as low as you can. If he really digs in, or plays a bit of slide too, leave it a little higher. But again, if he's picky about his intonation you need to get it as low as you can."

Experienced techs will generally know the gap they need by sight, but as a rough rule Chandler says he doesn't want a gap of less than ten thousandths of an inch (0.010") – the width of an average high-E string. "Take it below that and you can expect problems. Allow that gap and, as long as you don't play real hard, you'll probably be all right."

Although all good repairmen will have a set of fret files made to correct sizes for each popular string gauge, there's more to the cutting than simply picking up the right tool and hacking away. "You've got to cut the slot so that the witness point of the string – where the nut surface first meets each string – is at the start of the scale length. Otherwise it'll never play in tune."

Also crucial is to provide enough support on either side of the slot so the string won't pop out when bending and vibrato are applied, but not such a tight fit that it sticks and impedes tuning. "If you look at a PRS, they tend to cut slightly V'd grooves that come down to the right size at the bottom, so it doesn't move side to side." To finish the job, Chandler usually applies dry graphite powder to the slot to keep it well lubricated.

With this Firebird correctly set up and action adjusted at the bridge, the nut slot height is checked by fretting each string at the third fret, then measuring its clearance over the first fret.

Files specially sized to each popular string gauge are essential tools of the trade.

Chandler uses a finger to guide the file and protect the fingerboard while smoothing a newly cut slot.

A well-cut nut slot should support the string on both sides, but without pinching it too tightly. Even so, a touch of lubricant – such as liquid Teflon or graphite powder, as used here – helps make for trouble-free tuning.

cleaning and polishing

CLEANING PROCEDURES

Keeping your guitar clean not only helps it look better, but can improve the life of its finish, strings, hardware and even the electronics. Grime, sweat, grease, dust, moisture, beer, blood, tears – they all contribute to eroding and corroding the various parts of your instrument, and it's fair to say a proper regular cleaning can even help your guitar sound better, by keeping all components in top working order. As with every aspect of guitar maintenance, however, there are a series of dos and don'ts, and by following a few pointers you can maximize your cleaning efforts. Your guitar will thank you for it – and you'll feel better too.

If your finish gets shabby enough to require more serious attention than a regular rub-down and an occasional rub-polish, buffing cream could do the trick. Remove the strings, apply a little cream to a soft cloth, and work in small circles – using plenty of elbow grease.

Most rosewood or ebony fingerboards can be kept clean with a basic, regular rub-down. Using a soft cloth, with strings pushed aside – and always with the back of the neck well supported – wipe gently but firmly, paying particular attention to the grime that can collect at the edges of frets.

CLEANING "PLASTIC" FINISHES

The majority of modern electric guitars are finished with a high-gloss "plastic" finish like polyester or polyurethane. Some major brands still use nitro-cellulose based finishes (Gibson, for example) though due to a combination of factors, not least air-pollution regulations and drying time, cellulose finishes are rarely used, apart from occasional high-end "custom shop" guitars.

These finishes are applied from a spray gun and are then flattened and polished up to a mirror-like gloss on a high speed buffing wheel. It's a time-consuming process requiring numerous coats of finish, and for many production instruments actually forms a major part of the manufacturing time. Apart from looking good, the finish protects the guitar from dirt and grease which, once it gets into the wood-grain, is hard to remove. It also seals the wood from moisture penetration which can cause numerous problems related to the timber's stability.

Most manufacturers simply suggest you polish up your guitar body and other finished wood parts like the back of the neck with a "guitar polish", usually wax-based, and with or without silicone. The problem with products containing silicone is that it makes any future re-finishing and/or repairs even more difficult. So if you do use a guitar polish, make sure it's silicone-free.

The best way to clean your guitar is with a dry, lint-free cloth or duster *immediately* after playing. This will remove all the sweat and grease before it has time to solidify and form a harder-to-remove residue. Stubborn build-ups can be removed with a *barely* damp cloth. Never, never use a wet cloth. Always rub the guitar immediately after with a totally dry and clean cloth to keep any residual moisture from penetrating.

If your guitar is looking a little shabby and dirty then your best bet is to apply to the instrument a *mild* proprietary finish restorer, a fine burnishing cream. Don't use car products. They're too coarse. Mirror Glaze Plastic Polish or Manson's Finish Restorer are ideal. Here's how you go about it.

1 Remove the strings and apply a little buffing cream to a dry, soft cloth and work on the guitar's surface in small, circular areas. The buffing cream will do its job, removing dirt, grease and small scratches.

2 Keep rubbing on the same small area until it achieves a high sheen, then move to an adjacent area, apply some more cream and, of course, liberal amounts of elbow grease.

3 Finally, polish the guitar all over the finish with a new, and dry, soft cloth without any buffing cream.

CLEANING OIL FINISHES

These have had a light oil applied directly to the wood, and enjoy a varying reputation among guitar builders, repairers and store owners. Although there is credibility to the belief that the thinner the body finish the better the tone, a thin oil finish is very susceptible to dirt and moisture penetration. Apart from any tone considerations, many players simply like the look and feel, especially on a neck, of the natural wood.

An oil finish requires very regular maintenance – and even then an oil-finished maple neck and fingerboard will inevitably look dirty very quickly. First, you must always wipe an oil finish after playing. You may notice, especially if you sweat a lot, that the back of the neck begins to feel "furry" where the sweat has caused the grain to rise. You can flatten it with wire wool or preferably a very fine abrasive paper, and then apply a little furniture wax on a soft cloth. Occasionally you may need to re-oil the wood, for which some makers recommend lemon oil while others promote a tung-based oil like Behlen Master Tung Oil Finish. Certainly you can achieve a very good-feeling neck with this regular maintenance program, but even if you're extremely careful an oil finish will rarely give you the protection of a proper finish that seals the guitar's wood parts. Consequently, some manufacturers now use a very light matt finish to simulate the look of an oil finish, and this requires less maintenance and offers better moisture protection.

CLEANING YOUR FINGERBOARD

The majority of fingerboards are unfinished rosewood or ebony. Most maple fingerboards have a finish much like the body and can be cleaned in the same fashion. Be careful, however, with old, fragile and cracked finishes where bare wood is showing; you won't get these clean, and if the discoloration really bothers you then you should consult a professional, who may suggest some preventive repairs.

For bare rosewood and ebony fingerboards you need an *occasional* application of a lemon oil-based fingerboard cleaner. Several companies offer such a fingerboard cleaner which has a lemon-oil base.

Make sure you always use a preparation intended for fingerboard cleaning. Remove the strings and apply a small amount of lemon oil to a soft cloth or paper towel and rub it into the fingerboard. (It's worth noting that some makers discourage the use of lemon oil or indeed any oil-based preparation for fear that it could have a softening effect on the fingerboard. Used sparingly and occasionally, however, it's unlikely to do any damage.) Leave the oil to penetrate for a few minutes then rub it off with a clean cloth or paper towel which should remove most of the grime and leave the board looking brand new.

Grime can build up right next to the fret, so work some lemon oil into these areas by dabbing a drop on a cloth wrapped around your fingernail (a plectrum will work if your nails are too short or too valuable).

Stephen Delft's Boogie Juice is a fingerboard cleaner with a felt tip that makes it ideal to remove hard-to-access fingerboard grime. Always use lemon oil sparingly and occasionally; again, your best line of defence against fingerboard grime is to rub down the strings and fingerboard after every playing session with a dry, soft cloth.

CLEANING STRINGS

There are various string cleaning and lubrication products available. Washburn Guitar Juice String Cleaner or Manson's String Cleaner or similar work well to remove gunk from strings. Apply a little directly to the strings then wrap a piece of soft cloth or paper towel around and under each string and move it quickly up and down the entire length. (Any residue that goes onto the fingerboard itself can be cleaned off in the same fashion and actually helps to remove fingerboard grime.) Fast Fret is another string preparation that many swear by. It won't make you play faster (only practice does that) but a little application on the plain strings helps to keep the strings in good condition. Avoid any "lubricating" string preparations with an oil base, especially on the wound strings. These can actually attract dirt in between the wrap wires and so you'll find those strings go dead more quickly.

Far less regularly, an application of lemon-oil-based fingerboard cleaner will help get your rosewood or ebony fingerboard into top condition, and keep the wood from drying out. Remove the strings, apply a small amount of oil to a soft cloth, and rub it in...

... Leave the oil to penetrate for a few minutes, then rub off thoroughly with a clean, soft cloth. To get at the grime along fret edges, dab a drop of oil on a piece of cloth wrapped around your fingernail, or around a plectrum if your nails are too short, and work at the fret edges.

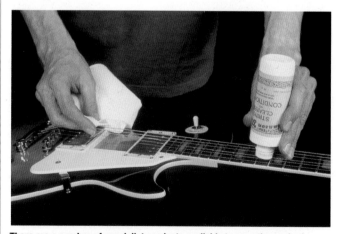

There are a number of specialist products available to ease the work of cleaning, some with clever twists to the usual formula. Stephen Delft's Boogie Juice (above) has a felt-tipped applicator to help you get at the muck that can clog your fingerboard's grain and fret edges.

111

HARDWARE AND PARTS

The metal parts on your guitar typically have a nickel, chrome, or gold plating. Sweat (or any moisture) is the major enemy, and again that post-playing soft-cloth rubdown is your best defence. Saddles often become caked with grime and can corrode – or in some cases rust – after years of playing and non-maintenance.

Remove the strings, then the saddles, but be very careful with the small screws for intonation and height adjustment. If these are tight they may have corroded, so remove the whole bridge assembly and, away from your guitar, spray on some penerating oil like WD-40 (never spray oil anywhere near your guitar).

Give the penetrating oil some time to do its job and then carefully try (without excessive force) to turn the problem screw again. If it's still tight, leave the part to soak over-night. Still stuck fast? Well then you may have to consider replacement, or professional help. For mildly corroded saddles, a good rub with WD-40 will not only clean off any debris but stop, for the short-term, any further corrosion.

 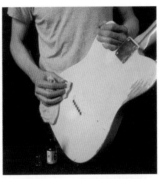

If your guitar requires an occasional deeper cleaning than the casual after-play wipe-down, remove the pickguard or other hardware that might be in the way...

... Then you can apply appropriate buffing cream – and plenty of elbow grease – to help dig out years of accumulated grime from the wood grain and the hardware edges.

As described on the previous page, an *occasional* application of lemon oil to a rosewood or ebony fingerboard (perhaps not more than every couple of years or so) will help restore its rich luster and keep it from drying out. Equally as important as the correct application procedure is that you ensure all excess oil is wiped from the fingerboard with a dry cloth, and that none gets into other components of the guitar.

If your guitar's plating has become dulled, or if the metal part is unplated brass or aluminum, a brand-name metal polish will restore most of the sheen. Even the mild buffing cream works very well too. Black hardware was popular a few years back. In some cases this amounted to little more than thin black paint which wears off very quickly. Proper black-coloured plating or black chroming should have the same lifespan as standard plating methods and should be cleaned accordingly.

Plated pickup covers should just be cleaned with a dry cloth; you really don't want any "wet" polishing compound getting into the pickup. But for a little extra cleaning power, take a cloth you've used to apply metal polish elsewhere and use that on your pickup covers, without applying any more polish to either the cover or the cloth.

Plastic pickguards, knobs and pickup covers can be simply wiped down with a dry cloth or cleaned and polished, if necessary, with the fine buffing cream. You don't want to get any cream in the pickup or control components, however, so remove the plastic pickup covers from the pickups and remove any other components from the pickguard before you clean it. Uncovered pickups should be cleaned with just a dry cloth (or one that's slightly dampened – but never dripping – if the grime is stubborn. Make sure you rub any slight moisture away immediately with another dry cloth.

YOUR WORKING ENVIRONMENT

It's well worth considering your working environment before you attempt even the most basic adjustment techniques described in this book. A comfortable, efficient workspace makes it less likely you'll rush the job and screw something up, and you'll also enjoy your work more. To get started, all you need is a firm table or work-surface in an uncluttered, well-lit area.

Always protect the table with a blanket, a thick towel or newspapers, or a non-slip rubber mat. A neck support is very useful; in fact, any solid block protected with cloth will suffice.

Keep tools away from your main working area and somewhere accessible where you can pick them up one at a time as you need them. Wherever possible, protect the finish of your guitar with a cloth or duster, especially when soldering. Get in the habit of keeping old cotton t-shirts for this purpose and to use as cleaning rags, rather than throwing them out. Always put screws and other tiny parts in a small container so that they don't get lost or damage your guitar.

A quiet, calm environment really is essential so that you can concentrate. Distractions like young children and family pets should be removed.

Wear safety glasses when soldering and snipping wires or strings, and never leave tools or string-ends just hanging around. Remember that they are potentially dangerous.

Always double-check that you've switched off and unplugged your soldering iron, and leave plenty of time for it to cool down before your pack it away.

TOOLS AND MATERIALS

Most of the tools you'll need will be available from a good hardware and/or electrical store.

Your basic equipment certainly must include an accurate steel ruler (and ideally a set of feeler gauges) for all kinds of measurements. Screwdrivers are essential too, especially Phillips head (cross-head) drivers, and you'll need a small, medium and large size to fit, for example, pickguard and intonation screws (small), and neck and spring-claw screws (medium/large). A small and medium-sized flat-blade screwdriver will serve most other applications. Remember: always use the right tool for the job; don't be tempted to undo or tighten a cross-head screw with a flat-blade screwdriver. There are exceptions. A medium-sized flat-blade screwdriver can be used to adjust the cross-head truss rod adjustment nut on vintage-style Fenders, for example.

A small collection of Allen keys (also known as hex keys) is also essential. Most new guitars come with the correct size Allen keys for truss-rod and bridge. You should always keep these in a safe and accessible place.

American-made hardware invariably uses Imperial-size Allen keys; European and Far Eastern-made parts (from Japan and Korea, for example) invariably use metric sizes. To adjust the saddle heights on a Japanese-made reissue Strat, for example, you'll need a 1.5mm Allen key; to adjust the same on a US-made American Series Strat you'll need a slightly smaller .050" or marginally smaller ⁹⁄₆₄" key.

Imperial-size keys of .050", ¹⁄₁₆", ⁵⁄₆₄", ³⁄₃₂", ⁵⁄₃₂" and metric-size keys of 1.5mm, 2.5mm, 3mm and 3.5mm will get regular use on most types of bridges and vibratos. Truss-rod adjustments are made with either a larger Allen key, around the ³⁄₁₆" to 7mm sizes, or a supplied socket-head nut wrench typically either ¼" or ⁵⁄₁₆".

Other basics like needlenose pliers, wire snippers and wire strippers are also likely to come in handy, along with the soldering iron and related accessories mentioned earlier in the *Soldering Techniques* section.

> For many home guitar toolboxes, it's enough to have a steel ruler, a selection of Allen keys, a couple each of flat and Phillips-head screwdrivers, needlenose pliers, wire snips and a string winder. If you plan to do more involved work or a great variety of repairs and modifications, then keeping a few extra tools to hand will make these jobs easier and generally more successful.

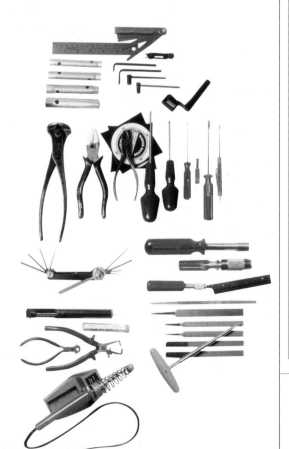

Where would we be without it? Stuck, probably. A quick squirt of WD-40, the mechanic and guitar tech's friend, will usually help loosen corroded adjustable components...

... While a little of the same on a soft cloth is great to clean grime from metal parts – though ensure you protect pickups and other electronics from any stray spray.

Heavy rust usually requires more drastic measures, but for deep-down grime on metal hardware, wrap a cloth soaked in WD-40 around a fingertip (as shown above) and dig in. This generally removes most of the surface crud and helps prevent further corrosion from setting in for a while. If a plated part has become dulled, on the other hand – or you want to clean unplated brass or aluminum – a name brand metal polish will usually help restore much of its sheen. Rub on, allow to dry as per instructions, then buff vigorously as below.

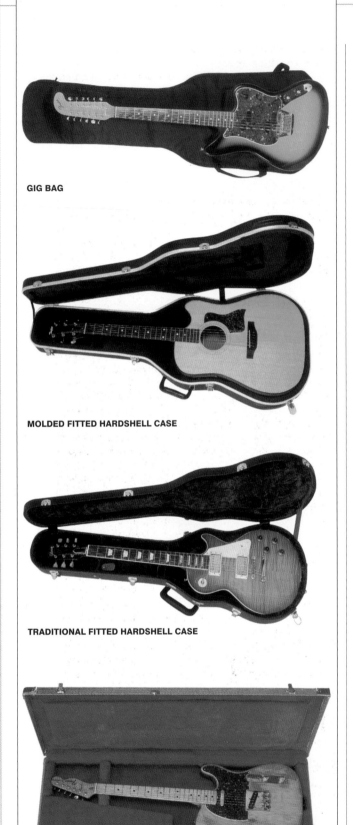

GIG BAG

MOLDED FITTED HARDSHELL CASE

TRADITIONAL FITTED HARDSHELL CASE

RECTANGULAR HARDSHELL CASE

FULL FLIGHT CASE
**If you want to offer your guitar total ATA-approved protection,
the padded armor of a full flight case is the only way to go.**

It's a false economy to rely on a cheap or flimsy case to protect your beloved guitar. This is especially true for acoustic instruments, where their fragility makes them particularly vulnerable when traveling. Gig bags come in all shapes, sizes and prices. If you're not intending to travel far and the weather conditions are not too hot (or too cold), a padded gig bag will suffice – so long as you don't throw it in the back of a truck.

The next best form of protection for your guitar is a hardshell case. These come in either rectangular form, or are shaped to fit your particular instrument. They are made from either plastic or plywood. The ply versions are covered in tough Tolex-style material. These cases are best suited for medium/light duty and offer reasonable protection from the elements and the knocks and scrapes encountered when travelling. Ironically some high-end versions can be as expensive as a heavy duty flightcase. You might like to ponder the fact that most new high-quality instruments come supplied complete with a hardshell case.

For medium to heavy use a light flightcase is a good choice. These are generally like a tougher version of a hardshell case and are molded from a heavy duty plastic such as ABS. The inside is also moulded to fit the particular guitar it's made for and lined with a soft fabric for protection. These are suitable to fly in the hold of an aircraft with certain electrics, such as Strats or Teles, but not more delicate electric or acoustic instruments.

For ultimate protection you should opt for a proper "full" flightcase. These are of seriously heavy-duty construction and made from high grade ply faced with tough metal or plastic sheet, with aluminum extrusions on all edges. They are normally rectangular in shape and have large metal corners and heavy duty latches. On the inside of the case is a thick foam panel which is cut out to receive the guitar. If you manage to get that gig with an international touring band a case like this is essential. Makers such as Anvil, probably the biggest name for this type of case, offer lines which meet ATA specs (Air Transportation Association). Such ATA-approved cases are the only types that some airlines will accept as adequate protection for a guitar stowed in the luggage hold of an aircraft.

The only drawback with flightcases – other than their price, generally considerably higher than standard hardshell cases – is their weight, although new, lighter materials are being tried in an attempt to improve the weight/strength ratio. If you're carrying your own guitar to and from the gig, propped carefully in the trunk or back seat of your car, a full flightcase probably isn't necessary – or worth the backache.

SHIPPING GUITARS

If for any reason you need to send your guitar by carrier for repair or some other reason, then you must make sure that it is adequately packed prior to shipping. Most people think that the case alone is sufficient ... but it's not! We have seen many damaged cases over the years which have suffered in the hands of shipping companies.

The ideal method of packaging is to place the guitar securely in its case, with the strings de-tuned, and then place the case in a large cardboard box. To prevent the guitar rattling around in the box, roll up sheets of newspaper to act as padding to fill the space around the case. Then tape the lid of the box securely with proper parcel tape and not ordinary cellophane tape.

Label the box clearly on both sides with the destination address and also your address as the sender. Make sure your address is smaller than the destination address and use the words "to" and "from" to ensure that you don't get your guitar returned straight back to you.

LONG-TERM STORAGE FOR YOUR INSTRUMENT

Should you wish to store your guitar for any length of time it's wise to take the following suggestions into consideration. First, de-tune all strings by one tone so as to prevent any possibility of the neck pulling forward should there be some fluctuation in temperature. Second, make sure the instrument is cleaned and polished. Then place it in its case with a small bag of silica-gel to absorb any moisture generated by fluctuations in humidity. Finally, place the case in the largest plastic bag you can find (a large trash bag will suffice) and store it in a cool, dry place out of direct sunlight and away from sources of heat or moisture.

The following places are not suitable for storing a guitar long term: your garage, attic, kitchen, bathroom, cellar, garden shed or anywhere there may be changes in temperature or humidity. Suitable storage locations are closets under the stairs (as long as they are not damp), a dry closet in your living room or bedroom, or under your bed.

EFFECTS OF ATMOSPHERIC CONDITIONS

Two of the main enemies when you try to maintain a healthy acoustic guitar are extremes of temperature and humidity. A sudden change in temperature can cause lacquer checking (fine cracks on the finish surface) and, in extreme cases, cracks in the guitar itself. To avoid this, as far as is possible always transport an acoustic guitar in a hard case, or at the very least in a padded electric-guitar type gig-bag.

If the guitar has been transported in extremely cold conditions (below freezing point), allow the instrument to rest in its case for an hour or so before opening. If this is not possible for any reason, open the case lid for a few seconds then close it for a minute or so. Repeat this operation several times until the instrument has acclimatized.

Keeping a guitar at a constant humidity can be even more difficult. If an instrument gets too dry the timber will crack or split and the action height may increase. Conversely, if it gets too

damp the tone may not be so clear or resonant and action may also be adversely affected.

Specialist acoustic dealers often stock devices for the guitar's case to help maintain the correct humidity for your instrument. Even electric guitars can be affected by humidity – too much and the hardware may tarnish and the neck may warp. Too little and the fingerboard may dry out and split. To avoid such damage it helps to keep your guitar in its case whenever possible.

IMPORTING AND EXPORTING INSTRUMENTS

If you wish to take your guitar abroad, or you want to import or export a new instrument, there are certain things that you should be aware of to avoid problems with the authorities at home or in the country of destination. First, if you wish to take an instrument owned by you to a foreign country, then you would be wise to obtain a "carnet." This is a document which is generally obtained from the port of embarkation, or alternatively from your local Customs office in advance. A carnet allows you to temporarily export your guitar without having to pay duty and local taxes at the destination country, although a small refundable bond may be payable upon entry. Professional touring bands obtain carnets for their entire road rig.

If you are a UK resident traveling within the EC, then it's wise to carry proof of ownership. Something as simple as a purchase receipt will suffice. If this is not possible for some reason then it may still be a good idea to obtain a carnet. Carrying proof of ownership is also sensible for American musicians traveling regularly around the US, even if not actually crossing foreign borders.

If you buy a guitar in a foreign country and it exceeds the current allowance for free importation into your country of residence of goods bought abroad, you must declare it at Customs upon entry with proof of purchase. You will be liable for import duty and local sales tax (or VAT in the UK) at current rates. Don't be tempted to lie about the purchase price, or obtain a false purchase receipt, as Customs departments can easily determine the purchase price of most new and secondhand instruments. They have access to current dealer-price lists and have experts on hand to provide a realistic value for collectable secondhand guitars. The penalties for this type of fraud can include confiscation and a heavy fine.

It is important to remember that levels of taxation as well as local rules and regulations change often, so it's wise to consult the Customs authorities in both relevant countries before you travel.

If you buy a guitar on the internet from overseas you will have to arrange for it to be shipped by a company that specialises in exportation and who will arrange all the necessary paperwork and will then bill you for the relevant amounts due for duty and import tax. This is often all taken care of by the seller, especially if they are a dealer who often sells online to overseas customers.

115

"Instrumental guitar groups were everywhere in the early '60s, until the triple-voice-double-guitar songs of The Beatles and countless followers pushed them aside. Mid-'60s bands like the Stones, The Kinks, The Who, The Animals and The Yardbirds made the electric guitar riff more of a feature. The electric 12-string, bigger amps, distortion boxes and wah-wah pedals all increased the sonic palette. By the late '60s blues-rock and heavy rock were pushing into the mainstream."

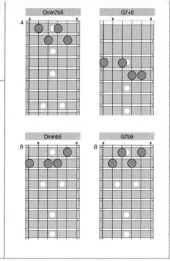

Dmin7b5   G7+5

Dminb5   G7b9

chapter 4

TOTALLY GUITAR
PLAYING STYLES

Music today has pushed beyond conventional boundaries of easy categorization. Whatever your main playing style, broadening your chops in other directions will help you to be a better all-around guitarist, and could open up entirely new avenues for further exploration. This chapter offers detailed primers in ten of the most important guitar styles.

polydor

More than ever before, the modern guitarist needs to be able to adapt to a number of playing styles in order to be considered a comprehensive musician. Most players will still specialise to some extent in one type of music or another, but the degree of cross-fertilisation between genres today is considerable – and as a guitarist you stand to benefit enormously from the inspiration offered by previously unfamiliar forms. Jazz can influence blues, classical can influence metal, Latin can influence pop, country can influence jazz... and on it goes, in a near-infinite variety of combinations.

This section will give you a grounding in ten of the most popular forms of guitar playing today, with the dual aim of improving your skills in your favourite style and also broadening your awareness of an eclectic mix of fascinating and useful genres. None of them is pitched at the absolute beginner (although *Acoustic* does start with more basic lessons than the others), but each offers a range of exercises suited to everyone from novice to advanced player – even the most skilled pro should be able to take away a few new licks from a chapter or two. Nor does any of them attempt to be the final word on a particular style (though a few, such as *Pop-Rock*, *Blues* and *Metal* are comprehensive primers), but each provides enough new chops to give your playing a serious freshening-up. Should you get hooked on any of the new techniques – which is a distinct possibility – you'll at least be well prepared for more intensive pursuit of the style elsewhere.

THE *PLAYING* AUTHORS

Acoustic, Blues and ***Rock-Pop*** by Rikky Rooksby
Rikky is a UK-based teacher, songwriter, and author of nearly 30 books on playing, including *How To Write Songs On Guitar*, *Inside Classic Rock Tracks*, and *Riffs*.

Country by Lee Hodgson
Lee is a UK-based country session guitarist and performer, a contributor to numerous guitar publications, a tutor at the London Guitar Institute, and author of the book *Hot Country*.

Rock'n'Roll by Max Milligan
Max is a performing and recording guitarist, songwriter, and journalist of more than 20 years experience, as well as a tutor at the London Guitar Institute, specialising in R&B and Soul.

Metal by Martin Goulding
Martin is a London-based session guitarist and live performer, and a tutor at the London Guitar Institute, specialising in Rock and Metal styles of the post-Van Halen era.

Latin by Nestor Garcia
Nestor, based in Spain, has published several articles on playing Latin guitar, taught at Goldsmith's College, London, and performed with Björk, Tumbaito, and the Afro Cuban Allstars.

African by Kari Bannerman
Kari is a renowned Ghanaian guitarist who has played with Hugh Masekela, Peter Green, Osibisa and his own band Boombaya, and led workshops at Goldsmith's College, London.

Classical by David Braid
David is a London-based classical guitar tutor, performer, writer and composer, magazine contributor, and author of *How To Play Classical Guitar*.

Jazz by Carl Filipiak
Carl is a Baltimore-based jazz guitar tutor, a recording artist with six albums released on Geometric Records, and presenter of the tutorial video *Use What You Got*.

CHORD BOXES

A chord box is simply a diagram representing a portion of the guitar neck, with strings running vertically, so that the line on the far left side represents the low E- string. The thick horizontal bar at the top of the box represents the nut in diagrams depicted in the first position, while the thinner horizontal bars represent frets, with position markers (dots) given to help you find your way. For chords higher up the neck, a number alongside the box provides a fret number for positioning.

The Xs and Os across the top of the box indicate which strings should be played open (O), and which muted (X).

GUIDE TO NOTATION SYMBOLS

If you're not familiar with the symbols used in standard music notation and tablature (TAB), this page and the following two will provide an introduction to most of what you will encounter. As the range of musical symbols is vast, this primer won't necessarily be exhaustive, but it will provide enough to get you through the *Playing* chapters. You'll find further guidance to any new symbols or instructions encountered – particularly in more advanced notation – within the explanatory text accompanying the exercises themselves. All exercises, other than those of pure rhythm notation, will be represented in both standard notation and TAB; be aware that while some symbols are common to both, others are used only on one or the other. While many exercises will include suggested chords for accompaniment below the bottom TAB line, chord boxes will not always be given, unless the chords themselves are the point of study, or the author feels some guidance to unfamiliar chords will be particularly helpful. Note also, as in the Sample Exercise below, that indications of rhythm will be given only in the stave (the standard notation), through the use of traditional note values. For example, the first bar's notation line offers quarter, eighth and 16th-notes, while the TAB indicates finger positions only.

READING TABLATURE

A complete course in reading music in standard notation would take more space than is available here (though the *Classical* section does offer an excellent lesson in this which will at least get you started). But tablature – or TAB for short – is easily explained.

TAB is essentially a method of showing finger placements that correspond to the notes shown on the stave of music directly above it. If you're new to TAB, the key points to note are that it uses no traditional "notes" as such but carries numbers in their place, is made up of six horizontal lines instead of five, and carries no clef or key signature. Each of the six horizontal lines represents a string on the guitar – beginning with the lowest line representing the low E-string. To help you remember which way is up, these string-note values are written alongside the TAB lines (see right top). For exercises in "alternate" tunings, the altered string-note values will be given instead, as in the exercise in DADGAD tuning (right below). Numbers on the lines indicate the fret at which to play that string, while a zero (0) indicates an open string is to be played.

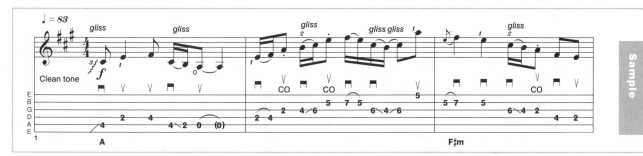

The majority of notation symbols are used to instruct you in the nuances of finger movement required to play a piece with the correct "feel." The dots on the stave – or string/fret number combinations on the TAB – tell you which notes to sound, but without the symbols it would be nearly impossible to determine the subtleties of playing technique that make a particular style of riff recognisable.

Bends

String bends are indicated by a starting note to be played before the bend occurs, and a small "arch" symbol linking it to a second note (sometimes in parentheses), which is the note achieved at the peak of the bend (or, in TAB, to the fret number which equates to that note, even though the bending finger stays at the same fret).

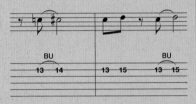

"BU" instructs you to "bend up." Bend releases are signified in the reverse, "BD" telling you to "bend down" (below-left).

When the pre-bend note is not to be sounded but merely provides a starting fret position to bend from, it will be in parentheses, with "PB" for "pre-bend" (below-right). "LD" means "let down."

You will also see an upside-down arch below notes where the symbol would otherwise clash with an un-bent note on a higher string (below-left). Where an up-bend is intended as more of an inflection, without a concluding note a full tone higher, you will see the initials "BSS" for "bend semitone sharp" (below-right).

Fingering

Some exercises offer fingering guidance in the form of arabic numerals alongside the notes in the stave, which tell you which finger to use for fretting that note, where 1=index. (If a riff is repeated, these fingerings will generally be given for the first example to avoid cluttering the stave.)

In the *Classical* chapter, where the traditional fingerstyle technique is used, the right-hand fingerings will also be indicated with a special code, but a thorough guide to this is offered in the chapter itself.

Gliss

Gliss is short for "glissando," the term used in classical music to indicate a steady slide between notes. In more contemporary forms the technique is often referred to as a "slide" or "finger slide," but still indicated as a gliss in the notation. A gliss can go either up and down (below right).

With a gliss from one note to another, an arch symbol – similar to that used to indicate a bend – appears in the stave, with an arch or adjoining line in the TAB. The technique involves simply playing the first note, then sliding across the required number of frets to reach the second note.

A gliss symbol placed before or after a single note (below) tells you to slide to or from an unspecified pitch, but to land on the note given.

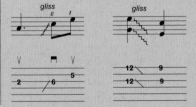

Hammer-ons and Pull-offs

Notes generated by hammering-on or pulling-off a string at a particular fret are indicated with a linking arch and the absence of a picking symbol. Other runs are generated with a picked note to start, with those following hammered or pulled.

Interpreting which is required is based on the direction of the musical line. Ascending notes are hammered, and descending notes are pulled off. This applies whether a phrase is totally hammer/pull generated (below-left) or is launched with a pick stroke (below-right).

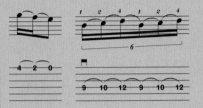

Two-handed Tapping

Found particularly in the *Metal* chapter, two-handed tapping combines right-hand taps with hammer-ons and pull-offs from the left hand. The right-hand taps are indicated in the stave with a downward arrow pointing to the tapped note, and in the TAB with a circle around the fret position at which the string is to be tapped.

Notes which come after the right-hand tap follow the rules for hammer-ons and pull-offs, with ascending notes hammered and descending notes pulled.

When a key note is to be generated by a left-hand tap, however, this will occasionally be indicated, with a symbol like an inverted upward arch – as with every third note in the example below.

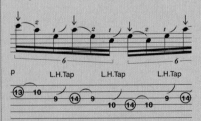

reading notation

Harmonics

Natural harmonics – those achieved by damping a string directly over the 12th, fifth or seventh fret for example – are indicated by a diamond-shaped note in the stave accompanied by a "Nat harms" direction and a broken line extending the length of the harmonics' duration. The same is indicated in the TAB by the letters "Nh" followed by a broken line (below).

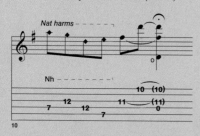

Artificial harmonics – those performed by fretting a note and damping the same string 12 frets higher – are indicated in the stave with the fretted note in parentheses and the damped (harmonic) note in the shape of a diamond, an octave higher and accompanied by the letter "T" followed by the fret number (example below). In the TAB, this is indicated with a number given for the fretted note followed by the damped note an octave higher given in parentheses, along with the "Ah" symbol.

Picking Symbols

Pick strokes are indicated with two types of symbols:

⎯⎯ = downstroke

⎯⎯ = upstroke

They are not universally given in all exercises, but are generally included where picking direction is critical to the feel of the piece.

Rake

A rake – where the pick is dragged smoothly across the strings, hitting each string individually but in swift succession – is indicated by a wavy vertical line concluded with an arrow pointing in the direction in which the pick should flow (usually from low note/string to high in these chapters). This is generally accompanied by the word "rake" between the stave and TAB line.

Rhythm Patterns

Lines representing pure rhythm patterns without tonal note values occur in a couple of different forms, and generally appear in the *Latin* and *African* chapters, where non-melodic rhythm patterns played by drums and/or percussion are crucial to the genre. These may be represented as one-line "staves" with beat values given per instrument…

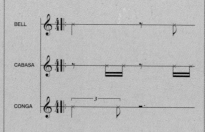

…or as normal five-line staves with atonal beat values given, or ordinary notes falling all on the same space, indicating a lack of tonal value.

The correct interpretation of each will be explained within the relevant individual chapters themselves.

Triplets

Whatever the rhythmic value of the individual notes (which, of course, is always the same for each note of a three-note grouping), triplets are indicated by the number "3" and linking brackets above or below the appropriate notes in the stave.

Similarly, sextuplets (which occur in astonishing numbers in the *Metal* chapter) are indicated by the number "6" and linking brackets above or below the appropriate notes in the stave.

As for septuplets and "fivetuplets" (quintuplets) – yes, they exist – the same applies.

Vibrato

Generally encountered as "finger vibrato" in these chapters, vibrato is represented by a wavy horizontal line above the stave, accompanied by the abbreviation "vib".

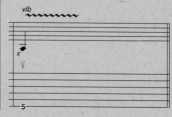

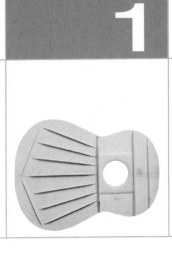

1

PLAYING
ACOUSTIC

COLUMBIA

The acoustic guitar is one of the most common instruments right across the whole spectrum of popular music. Whether it's country, traditional folk, blues, soul, pop, indie, rock'n'roll, rockabilly, protest, or rock, the acoustic guitar is there, somehow, even if it's not up front in the mix. The acoustic ethos even led to the launching of the MTV *Unplugged* shows, where performers put aside their electric instruments and renewed their music (and sometimes their careers) by dipping their feet in the "pure" spring of acoustic performance. In turn, that series helped to spawn an acoustic rebirth, and the "unplugged" ethos continues to be popular. ● RIKKY ROOKSBY

Whether it's a classical model or steel-strung "folk," for many players the acoustic guitar is where they begin. Generations of would-be rockers have heard their parents say they should start on an acoustic before thinking about an electric. Is there any sense in this beyond a parent's understandable desire to protect their ears and their wallet from too much guitar-induced stress?

Much of what is learned on an acoustic guitar can be transferred to an electric and vice versa. Despite their different appearances, both types of guitar are tuned the same and have the same configurations of notes laid out on the fingerboard. If you know how to play an Am or D7 or F#m9 chord or an E major or D pentatonic minor scale on an acoustic, you can play it on an electric, and vice versa.

Working first with an acoustic can build more strength into the hands. An inexpensive acoustic guitar is more likely to be harder to play – by virtue of its heavier gauge strings and higher action (the height of the strings from the fretboard) – than an equivalent lightly-strung electric, and therefore isn't necessarily a preferable instrument for a beginner. This is why it is important to get an acoustic properly set-up, to have its action checked, so the initial phase of learning isn't needlessly made more difficult.

You'll also find that lead guitar solos with plenty of string-bending cannot be played effectively on an acoustic. So if you're sure that's the direction you want to go then start on electric. Young women in particular with smaller hands, who tend to get saddled (no guitar pun intended!) with nylon-strung "Spanish" guitars with no regard to the type of music they want to play, should certainly consider an electric. This is because they often are put off playing guitar by the physical struggle involved in forming unfamiliar chords around a wide, flat neck. An electric can reduce this struggle with its generally slimmer, more comfortable neck. Just because you play an electric doesn't mean you have to make a racket with it: strummed unplugged, there's still plenty of volume to hear yourself for practise, and more and more good headphone amplifiers are available on today's market, often with built-in effects.

Acoustic guitar has always been popular because it is a relatively portable instrument,

and doesn't need electricity or an amp in order to function. It is ideal for accompanying yourself singing songs, and many people only desire to learn enough to take them to this point. To do this the technical requirements are straightforward: first, learn chord shapes; second, practise changing chord shapes until you can do so fast enough to keep up with a song; third, learn to strum evenly.

The chief hurdle in learning chords is getting to grips with the "barre" chord – the chord in which several notes are held down with one finger. The barre is often first encountered with the F or B chords. Moving these a little further up the neck can assist, where string tension is not as great as it is right by the nut.

A further refinement of accompanying yourself on guitar is to be able to finger-pick the chords instead of strumming them. This is especially useful in slower, quieter material. Initially such finger patterns will be in a simple rhythm. Later, they can be syncopated and incorporate an "alternating thumb" in the bass part. This is where the thumb moves between the bass strings while the fingers strike the higher ones, creating a tapestry of sound. Further refinements come with the ability to add little melodic phrases and riffs into the accompaniment without wholly abandoning the supporting harmony.

Beyond this lies the realm of guitar instrumental music in all its diversity, whether in the classical repertoire or the "folk baroque" of players like Davy Graham, Bert Jansch, John Renbourn, Gordon Giltrap, Pierre Bensusan, Leo Kottke, John Fahey, Stefan Grossman, Michael Hedges and many others. It is in this arena that players have looked for new sounds from the instrument.

Most obviously this has come from altered tunings, where the standard EADGBE is changed by one or more strings being tuned to a different note.

In this section we will look at basic rhythm and finger-picking techniques, chords, how to use a capo, and finish with a quick look at the types of altered tunings that are so rewarding on the acoustic guitar – covering, in the process, a range of exercises appropriate to beginners, intermediates, and even some more advance players less experienced with these styles.

MAJOR AND MINOR CHORDS

It makes sense to start with some chords, so here are the shapes for the most-used major and minor chords. Notice that in comparison to the majors, the minors sound sad. The emotional contrast of "bright" major with "sad" minor is crucial to the vast bulk of Western music.

As you tackle the shapes check that each string that should be sounding *is* sounding. When the fingers are in the right place play each string individually. If notes do not sound the usual causes are: a finger on the metal fret, a finger too far away from the metal fret, not pressing hard enough, or a fretting finger touching and therefore muting an adjacent string.

A special word must be said about the shapes for B, Bm, F and F#m. These involve playing a barre, but you can use the version without the full barre for now, until your fingers get used to the required positions. With B and Bm the bass note on the 5th string is therefore optional.

SEVENTHS

The next most common group of chords is the sevenths. Here are two types formed by adding a single note to the major chord. Don't worry if you can't play the B7 and F7 barre chords initially. The B7 barre version will give you a different A7 if you take off the barre and move the fingers two frets toward the nut. The little finger with F7 is optional.

The major seventh chord has a richer sound than the first type. Again, leave the Bmaj7 and Emaj7 if you find them difficult. The F#maj7 has the advantage of being a movable chord that doesn't have a barre. Make sure that all the strings that should be sounding are, otherwise you may miss the seventh!

USING A CAPO

In order to make playing in difficult keys easier, guitarists use a device known as a "capo." This may look like a medieval instrument of torture but, as a guitarist, it's one of your best

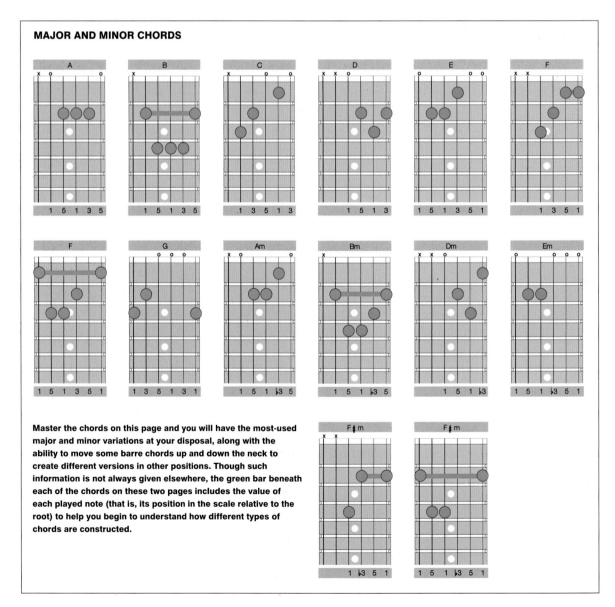

MAJOR AND MINOR CHORDS

Master the chords on this page and you will have the most-used major and minor variations at your disposal, along with the ability to move some barre chords up and down the neck to create different versions in other positions. Though such information is not always given elsewhere, the green bar beneath each of the chords on these two pages includes the value of each played note (that is, its position in the scale relative to the root) to help you begin to understand how different types of chords are constructed.

basic chords

friends! It acts as a first finger substitute holding a barre, or can be alternatively thought of as a movable nut. If a key would normally mean lots of barre chords (and an aching hand) the capo will allow you to turn most of the barre chords into open string shapes.

Here's an example: you need to play a song that was recorded in Ab major and uses Ab, Bbm, Cm, Db, Eb and Fm – all barre chords. If you put the capo at the first fret each chord can be played with the shape of the chord a semitone below it.

Actual pitch:	Ab	Bbm	Cm	Db	Eb	Fm
Capo I shapes:	G	Am	Bm	C	D	Em

Much easier, and it sounds better too! And that's not the only way we could do it…

Actual pitch:	Ab	Bbm	Cm	Db	Eb	Fm
Capo IV shapes:	E	F#m	G#m	A	B	C#m

Or, for an extreme contrast…

Actual pitch:	Ab	Bbm	Cm	Db	Eb	Fm
Capo VIII shapes:	C	Dm	Em	F	G	Am

You will notice that as the capo goes up the neck the timbre of the guitar will change. This is something that songwriters use deliberately. They also use a capo to shift a chord sequence up or down a key to better suit their voice, which saves learning a new set of chords. Lastly, if you play guitar with a friend, using a capo high on one of the guitars can create a resonant sound with the two guitars playing the same chords high and low:

Actual pitch: Guitar 1	G	Am	Bm	C	D	Em	F
open chords Guitar 2	G	Am	Bm	C	D	Em	F
capo VII shapes	C	Dm	Em	F	G	Am	Bb

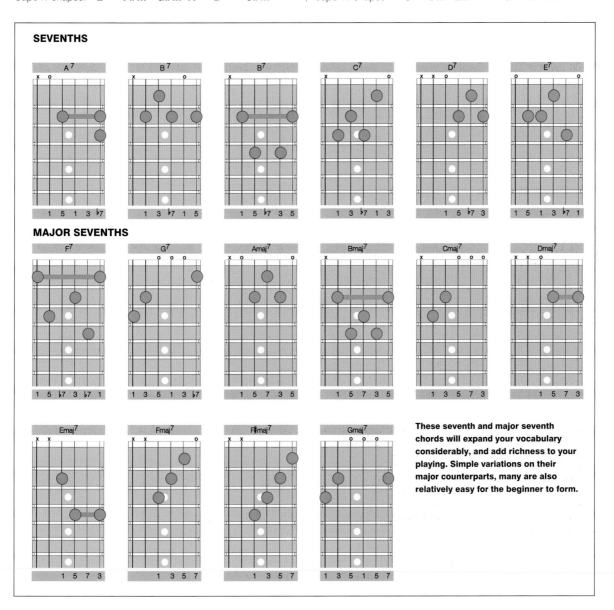

SEVENTHS

MAJOR SEVENTHS

These seventh and major seventh chords will expand your vocabulary considerably, and add richness to your playing. Simple variations on their major counterparts, many are also relatively easy for the beginner to form.

British acoustic ace John Renbourn melds ragtime, blues, folk and medieval music into his own brew. From his formative work at the center of the mid-'60s London folk scene to his contemporary recordings, Renbourn's playing always impresses.

MINOR 7, SUSPENDED 4, SUSPENDED 2 CHORDS

By merely moving beyond the basic major chords – where appropriate – to other shapes that aren't much more difficult to play, simple songs can take on added tension and atmosphere. Here are three other types of chord that are often found in songs, and can be useful mood builders. The minor sevenths are the minor version of the A7, B7 and so on previously shown. The Bm7 will yield an alternative Am7 if you take off the barre and move the fingers two frets down toward the nut. The little finger with F#m7 is optional.

The suspended fourth chords are often used to inject drama into song accompaniment because of their tension. In the case of Asus4, Dsus4 and Esus4 all that is required is to add a note to a simple major chord shape. The Asus2 and Dsus2 are popular because the reverse happens: you just lift a finger off a string that would usually be fretted for A or D. The sus2 is not as tense and has an open, "hollow" sound.

A MISCELLANY OF EFFECTIVE ACOUSTIC CHORDS

Here are 16 chords that sound great on an acoustic guitar. Some are created by either lifting a finger off a note with a common barre shape (Bmadd4, F#m7add11, Fmaj7add11) or moving a chord shape up (D6/9, Amaj7), or are unique "voicings" – like the C which has a 12-string resonance because within it there are two Gs and two Es at the same pitch.

Also included are two first inversion chords – G/B and D/F# – which often feature in acoustic songs. First inversion simply means that the root note is not the lowest in the chord, the "third" above it is played instead – the note that is two tones higher than the root in a major chord. Try these out and learn the ones you like for your own playing.

EFFECTIVE ACOUSTIC CHORDS

American fingersylist Leo Kottke, above, is a seminal instrumentalist and one of the true "godfathers" of the acoustic scene over the past thirty years. Running from folk, to jazz, to bluegrass, to blues, his work is consistently inspiring.

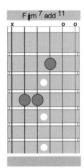 F#m7 add 11

 D 6/9

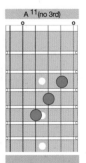 A 11(no 3rd)

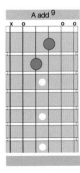 A add 9

advanced chords

MINOR 7 AND SUSPENDED CHORDS

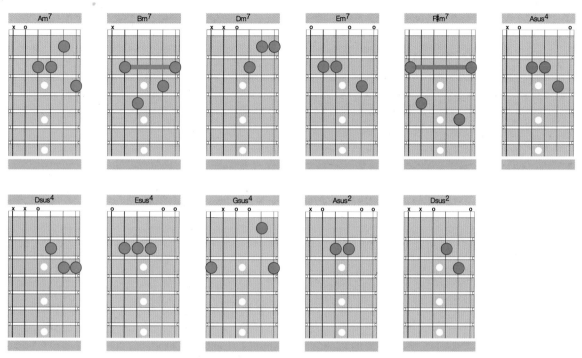

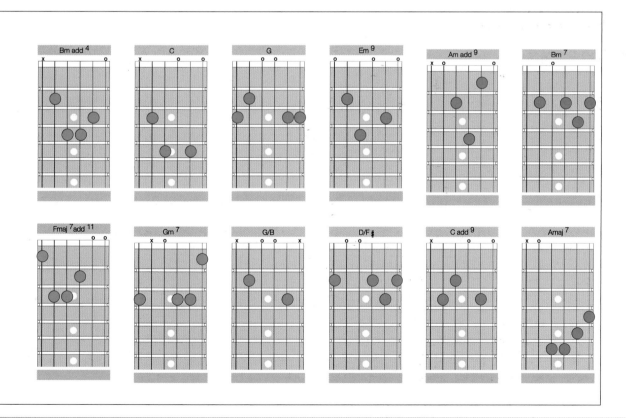

STRUMMING PATTERNS

Now you have plenty of chords to play with! So let's turn our attention to the hand that hits the strings. Although it is possible to strum with your thumb or the upperside of your fingers, the best tone for straight-on rhythm playing is produced by using a pick, or plectrum. These small pieces of plastic are held between thumb and forefinger (don't use your second finger because you might want to pluck a string with it at the same time as holding the pick). The thumb crosses the finger at approximately a right angle. Most of the pick should be gripped – there doesn't need to be much showing to hit the strings. Picks come in various shapes and thicknesses. For acoustic strumming a thin one is easiest to begin with and might give the best tone for jangly but not-too aggressive rhythm playing. Thick picks put up more resistance against the strings and take a little more effort, while also inducing a little more volume. The strumming action is mostly from the forearm as it hangs off the top of the guitar but the hand sometimes contributes a little for emphasis.

The essence of good strumming can be summarized as follows: evenness of tone, avoiding bass strings that are not meant to be hit, the ability to strum up and down with equal facility, controlling the volume, and keeping steady time. It also means knowing when and how to leave out strums.

Exercise 1 gets us started. Hold down an E major chord. Tap your foot, count to yourself, or set a metronome going at a medium tempo (around 80 to 90bpm). This exercise is in 4/4, which means four beats to each bar. Strum downwards every

other beat, then on each beat, then twice on each beat (8ths or quavers), then four times on each beat (16ths or semi-quavers). Depending on how fast or slow you're going you may find that strumming twice and four times to a beat is too difficult just going downwards. The answer is to strum down and up, alternating.

Exercise 2 gives nine strumming patterns. The first is a strum in straight 8ths. Notice how with each example some strums are taken away; the chord is allowed to ring. The rule is: the faster the tempo the longer a gap you can leave. With IV there is the introduction of a "tie." This is the line joining the 5th quaver to the 4th. A tie means you strike the first of the joined pair but not the second. Instead, the first lasts for the length of time of both notes. In any song you could use any one or a mixture of strumming patterns. Your choice will depend on mood, tempo and "groove."

One way to make your strumming more interesting is to pick some of the bass notes of the chords individually and then hit the chord, as in **exercise 3**. This style is known as pick'n'strum. The bass note is usually the root note of the chord. Here is a well-known chord sequence that lends itself to this approach.

In **exercise 4** the bass notes are not all root notes, though the technique is the same. Introductions to songs and links between choruses and verses sometimes feature a phrase played in single notes, with chords in between, as in **exercise 5**. A song like *Wish You Were Here* by Pink Floyd or the intro to Led Zeppelin's *Over The Hills And Far Away* are examples of this popular approach to pick'n'strum.

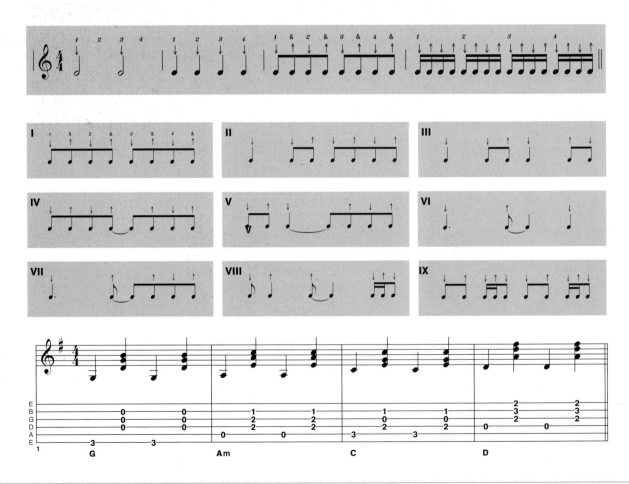

strumming patterns

Look no further for acoustic inspiration: 12-string specialist Leo Kottke, DADGAD wizard Pierre Bensusan, and eclectic stylist Michael Hedges offer different techniques with equal virtuosity (albums, left, from left to right respectively).

Far from being limited to the extremes of the campfire sing along, the folky, or the blindingly nimble fingerstyle soloist, the acoustic guitar is found somewhere in the mix in a lot of straight-on rock'n'roll too – as Rolling Stone Keith Richards demonstrates, right.

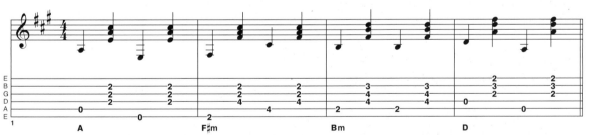

Exercise 4

Exercise 5

More than just an easy-strummin' singer/songwriter, Bob Dylan is a gifted – if underrated – musician in his own right. Check out his early work in particular, such as 1963's *The Freewheelin' Bob Dylan* (above left), for a quick education in compelling fingerstyle accompaniment with simple, effective fills. At the other end of the spectrum, Led Zeppelin's Jimmy Page (below) is best known for his bombastic electric work, but he knew a thing or two about how to use an acoustic guitar in a rock context, and even pushed beyond the genre with Eastern scales and complex open tunings. Examples of both are plentiful on Zep's *Houses Of The Holy* (above right).

BASIC FINGERPICKING PATTERNS

Exercise 6 shows 14 different finger-picking patterns. Notice how the thumb looks after the bass notes. In each case the notes of the chord are sounding but in a different manner to the simultaneous effect of strumming. Fingerstyle playing generates its own rhythm, too. You can easily adapt the patterns for 6/8 to 3/4. Most of the examples use a C chord, a five-string chord with its root on the 5th string. You can find variations of these patterns for chords with their root notes on the fourth or sixth strings. Obviously the more strings in a chord the more patterns you could devise to play them.

Let's continue by trying some slightly more complex fingerpicking exercises. Examples XI-XIV take a bit more work before you can do them unconsciously because of their syncopated rhythm. Remember to work out the thumb pattern first and then fit the other notes to it. Example XIV is a two-bar blues pattern in swung rhythm – each beat divides into the feel of three rather than two.

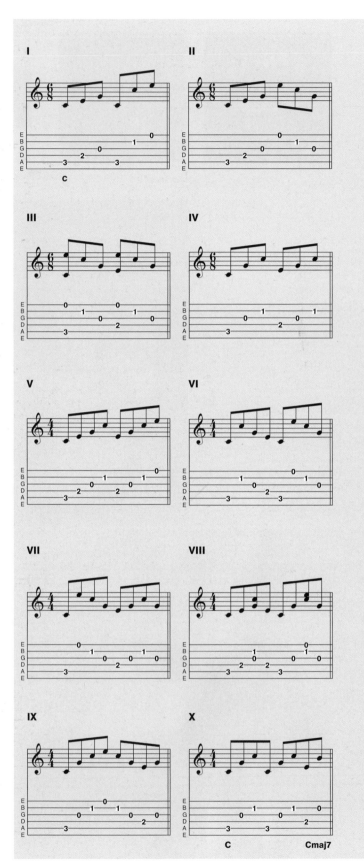

basic fingerpicking

XI

XII

XIII

XIV

The fleet-fingered Adrian Legg, above, rivals the best acoustic artists as a pure technician, but his creative use of effects, amplification, and adventurous string-bending take him well beyond the usual sonic realm of the instrument.

Exercise 7 is a simple ascending fingerpick applied to a popular chord progression with a descending bass-line. The 6/8 time signature means two beats in a bar, each dividing into three: 123, 456. Take it slowly at first, then build speed and play ad-infinitum until you get the hang of it. It will feel repetitive, certainly, but this is the sort of exercise that really builds your fingerpicking skills.

Exercise 8 also starts on Am but in the later bars move up the neck. Notice the way the open B string is used. Initially the notes are in ascending order, but from bar 3 that pattern is broken up and the pitch order is less predictable.

In exercise 9 a simple ascending finger-pick is applied to a chord sequence in which a number of inversions are used to join up root position chords. This is common in folk playing. D/F# and C/E are first inversions; the note after the forward slash sign (/) is the lowest in pitch. The Bm7/F# and Am/E are second inversion chords in which the "fifth" of the chord (the note 3 half-tones from the root) is at the bottom.

Exercise 10 also uses some common inversions but the direction of picking is reversed. Notice also that two notes are sounded together for each group of quavers in bars 1-3. Like 3/4, 6/8 time lends itself to up-and-down patterns like this one. Exercise 11 is another common progression with a descending bass line. Exercise 12 is a syncopated piece with an alternating thumb playing the bass notes (marked "T"). The progression is similar to Ex.7. Let the notes ring for as long as possible.

advanced fingerpicking

Exercise 7

Exercise 8

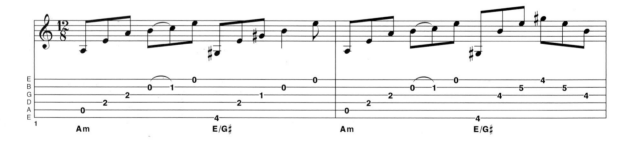

132

Open tunings have helped a number of great artists find their instrumental voices, from Richie Havens's rootsy, eclectic, world-music-inflected arrangements to the unique jazz-cum-folk of Joni Mitchell (seen in concert, opposite page). Haven's album *The End Of The Beginning* and Mitchell's *Clouds* (both pictured above) are fine examples of what each does best.

ALTERED TUNINGS

Standard tuning – EADGBE – is a wonderful compromise that allows a guitarist to work in many keys, despite its bias toward E minor. Many acoustic guitarists, however, have searched for new tones by altering this tuning. Some players stumble on altered tunings by default – no-one showed them how to tune the guitar properly so they simply used their ear and tuned the strings to an open chord (Richie Havens and Joni Mitchell spring to mind). Others chased new tunings consciously to emulate the droning effects of non-Western instruments such as the sitar, or to make it easier to keep a bass going and improvise a melody.

An altered tuning can create beautiful new chords and stimulate your creativity. These new musical territories come at a

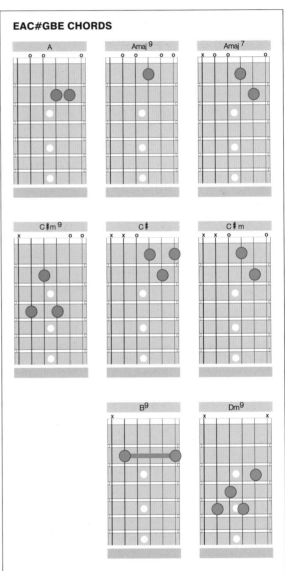

EAC#GBE CHORDS

These chords provide a quick guide to some easy shapes in the tuning of EAC#GBE, which itself makes a simple introduction to altered tunings, having only one string – the D – changed from standard tuning.

A self-styled guitarist of vast creative capacity, Richie Havens stumbled on his own open tunings as a natural means of producing the tones he sought to express, and thus forged an uncategorizable style of his own that remains distinctive today.

price, however. First, there is the tuning in and out of them, with the attendant risk of broken strings and iffy intonation. Second, if you find some beautiful chords you had better write them down. Remembering chord shapes in ten different tunings is okay if you play the pieces regularly, but once they slip from the mind it can be a frustrating job trying to recall what they were!

SINGLE STRING ALTERATION

The simplest way to begin playing around with new tunings is simply to change one string. For this book I've invented a tuning in which the D string is detuned by a semitone to C#, giving us E A C# G B E. To do this, fret C# on the 5th string at the 4th fret and lower the open D until the two are in tune (to get back to standard reverse the process). This implies an A dominant ninth chord. I've supplied eight chord shapes and two short exercises you can play in this tuning.

Exercise 13 is a riff with a bluesy swing rhythm but some unusual chords. Try to keep the bass note steady and fit the higher parts around it. **Exercise 14** is simple upward picking. The idea is to play it slowly and let the strings ring so you can hear the unorthodox chord tones caused by the altered tuning. If these give you some new ideas, you can make up your own.

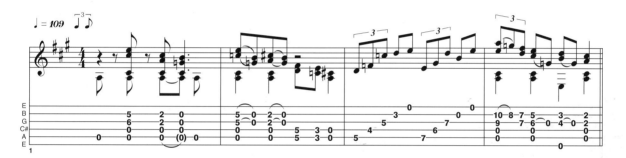

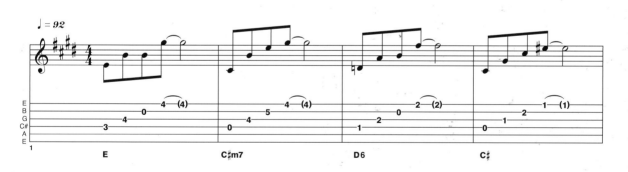

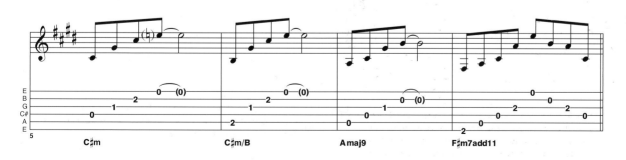

One of the original smashers of musical barriers on acoustic guitar, Davy Graham (near right) melds baroque, blues, jazz and folk into a style entirely his own. John Fahey (center) is another virtuoso forefather of solo acoustic performance, while Gordon Giltrap remains at the center of an underappreciated scene.

DROPPED D

The most famous single-string alteration is known, somewhat confusingly, as "dropped D." More accurately, the bottom E is "dropped" – that is, tuned down a tone to D. This tuning is popular with rock players because the bottom three strings make a power-chord and the low D is good for launching heavy riffs. Folk players like it because it provides an octave open string D with the fourth string for an alternating thumb technique. The fretting hand is thus free to move wherever it wants on the neck. This tuning produces much deeper sounding six-string D and Dm chords.

In **exercise 15** the fourth and sixth open strings are played by the thumb. Above these, a series of thirds and fourths move up and down. This is one way of creating an accompaniment for a voice.

The thumb only alternates on the beat in the 12/8 piece in **exercise 16**. Above, the fingers fret a single-note melody with some decorative hammer-ons and pull-offs. Again, get your thumb working right first, then fit the melody to the steady pulse of the bass notes, not the other way around.

Exercise 15

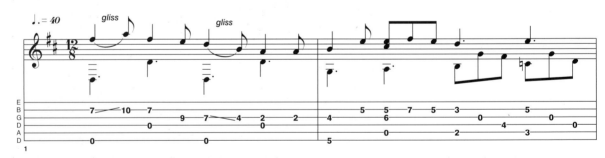

Exercise 16

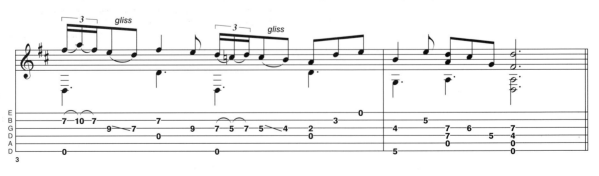

dropped D tuning

OPEN G MAJOR

After the single-string alteration we have the open tuning proper, where the strings are tuned to make a simple major or minor chord. This means that each of the six strings will be tuned to one of three chord tones. The most popular open tuning is open G (which is also one of the most popular tunings for five-string banjo). The notes of a G chord are G B D. Standard tuning already has those three notes on strings 4, 3 and 2, so the tuning is created by lowering strings 6, 5 and 1 down until they come to the nearest of those three notes. The distance is measured in semitones.

E	A	D	G	B	E
-2	-2	–	–	–	-2
D	G	D	G	B	D

The immediate practical effect of this tuning is that a barre placed across the top five strings at any fret will create a root position major chord. The three chords needed for a 12-bar progression and many other songs will be found on the open strings, at the fifth and seventh frets, with the twelfth fret giving an octave higher. Strong harmonics are also available at frets 5, 7, and 12 by laying a finger across the strings right over the metal fret but not pushing them against the fretboard. Strike the strings and gently pull the finger away and you will hear the ghostly, bell-like tones of harmonics.

Open G makes a very full sound if strummed. If a barre is held down various notes can be added by the other fingers. The first three chord boxes below indicate how this is done. The tuning is also used to provide drone notes as octaves or sixths or thirds are moved up the neck. Try holding down the 2nd fret on the 1st and 4th strings (an octave) and move this up and down as you strum all the strings.

Open tunings also lend themselves to slide playing. Keith Richards has made extensive use of open G with many Rolling Stones classics like *Brown Sugar* and *Start Me Up*. You can also use a capo with an open tuning if you wish to change its key. Open G with a capo at the third fret becomes open Bb major.

OPEN G CHORDS

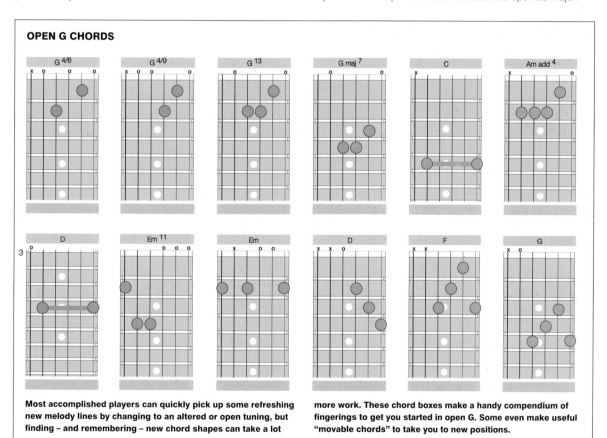

Most accomplished players can quickly pick up some refreshing new melody lines by changing to an altered or open tuning, but finding – and remembering – new chord shapes can take a lot more work. These chord boxes make a handy compendium of fingerings to get you started in open G. Some even make useful "movable chords" to take you to new positions.

137

DADGAD

Altered tunings need not make a simple major or minor open chord. "DADGAD" is one of the most popular examples of a more complex tuning. It has misleadingly been called a "modal" tuning. In fact, it's a Dsus4 chord. DADGAD was introduced into the world of folk guitar in the early 1960s by Davey Graham, a key figure in the English folk scene. It has been used by many players since, including Pierre Bensusan, for whom it is now "standard tuning," and in a rock context by Jimmy Page who used it for the mighty Led Zep epic *Kashmir*.

Here are some DADGAD chord boxes for you to strum or finger-pick.

To conclude, **exercise 17** is a composition entitled *Postcard To Denys*, a fun piece with lots of bends and decorative hammer-on/pull-off figures typical of the style known as "folk baroque." It should be played with a slightly sloppy touch. In keeping with its humorous spirit the intro alludes to *Purple Haze*.

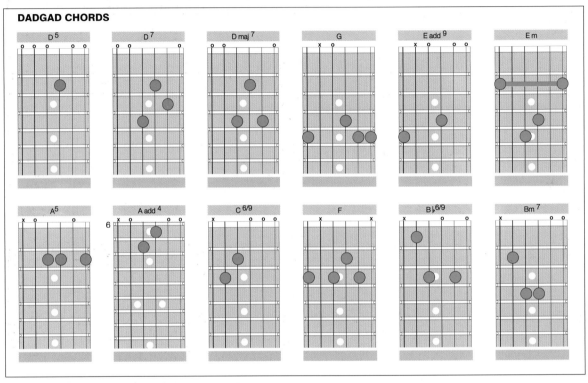

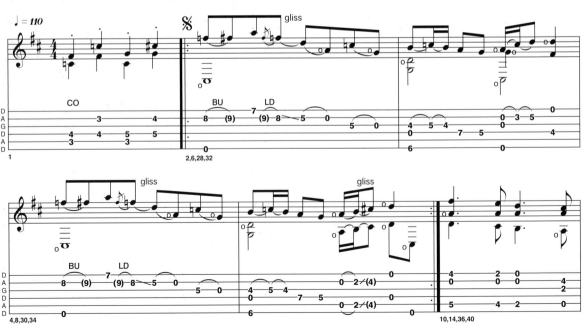

DADGAD tuning

Exercise 17

139

PLAYING
ROCK — POP

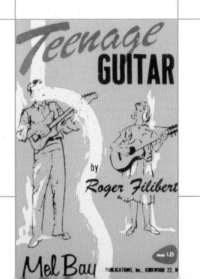

There is no rigid boundary between pop and rock music – and this chapter will deal with playing a range of musical forms broadly classifiable as falling within or between the two, from the late 1950s to the present; in short, the bulk of the most popular music played and enjoyed today. ● **RIKKY ROOKSBY**

By "pop" we generally mean a lighter, less aggressive type of song, more suited to being chart material, possibly with more conservative lyrics, and with less reliance on the blues element that was carried to rock by '50s rock'n'roll. There are also production differences, of course. Rock guitar tends to make more use of distortion. Hard rock styles like heavy metal and the advanced lead techniques that go with it (all covered later in the book) are beyond the scope of this overview. Despite the development of many sub-genres within rock and pop the guitar basics remain quite stable. Eddie Cochran and Kurt Cobain might have had 30 years of rock between them, but from a guitar playing perspective they are still recognisably connected.

It was in the mainstream rock'n'roll of the '50s rockers like Elvis Presley, Chuck Berry, Buddy Holly, and Eddie Cochran that a new instrument, the electric guitar, came to fame. Befitting of this cultural revolution, a new music ensemble was created around the new instrument: two electric guitars, electric bass and drums. This quartet was easy to form among your friends, and the combination of amps and hard-hit drums gave it a strong and dynamic presence. The two guitars could punch out a thick, resonant harmony, underpinned by the bass (up to 16 strings sounding together). In this format, one guitar could play a solo or melody and be supported by the other's chords – thus the roles of rhythm and lead guitar were born.

Players like Duane Eddy, The Ventures, Hank Marvin and Vic Flick (who played the James Bond theme) recorded many guitar-led, echo-haunted instrumentals. Instrumental guitar groups were everywhere in the early '60s, until the triple-voice-double-guitar songs of the Beatles and countless followers pushed them aside.

Mid-'60s bands like the Stones, The Kinks, The Who, The Animals and The Yardbirds made the electric guitar riff more of a feature. The electric 12-string, bigger a m p s , d i s t o r t i o n boxes and w a h - w a h pedals all increased the sonic palette. By the late '60s blues-rock and heavy rock were pushing into the mainstream,

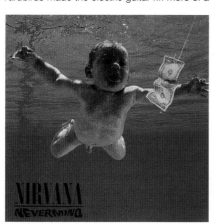

their groups invariably built around the first generation of guitar heroes who paraded their virtuosity in long, often improvised solos: Hendrix, Clapton, Page, Beck, Kossoff, Iommi, Blackmore, West, Garcia, Santana, and many others. Since then glam rock, late-'70s punk, early-'80s new wave, '80s rock, indie, grunge, alternative rock, Brit-pop and nu-metal have all recycled riffs and ideas and sometimes taken advantage of the stunning expansion of guitar-related technology. The digital revolution has meant the availability of an increasing range of amp tones, many simulated from earlier decades, and the electric guitar has linked up with the wonderful world of MIDI. The electro-acoustic has also been improved to enable an acoustic guitar sound in an amplified quartet.

The relatively limited harmony used in many rock and pop songs means that you can play most styles with quite a small number of chord shapes. When learning chords, first learn the open string shapes. These are easiest to finger and create a resonant, satisfying tone. The most common chords used in songs are A, C, D, E, F, G; Am, Bm, Dm, Em, F#m; A7, B7, C7, D7, E7, G7; Amaj7, Cmaj7, Dmaj7, Fmaj7, Gmaj7; Am7, Dm7, Em7; Asus4, Dsus4, Esus4, Gsus4; Asus2, Dsus2; Cadd9 – all of which, and more, can be found in the *Acoustic* section.

One essential task will be to master the barre chord. A barre chord involves holding more than one string down with a single finger, usually the first. Your aim should be to have two shapes for each type of chord, one with the root note on the 6th string, and the other with the root on the 5th. This will give two options for any required barre chord in any key, including all the sharps and flats. The four most important are derived from open string A, E, Am and Em shapes. At the first fret, turned into barre chords, these become Bb, F, Bbm and Fm. In the exercises that

follow we'll look at many of the key techniques and ideas used in rock and pop since the early '60s. The pages that follow include sub-sections on Rhythm Playing, Riffs, T r i a d s , Intervals, Fifths, Scales and Lead.

THE EXERCISES

A tempo indication in "beats per minute" (BPM) is given for each exercise. With a metronome or drum machine you can hear how fast it should be played. Chord indications are given below the stave. These do not necessarily apply to the notes of the exercise. They may be implied chords or chords for a backing. To hear the full tone-colour of these exercises get a friend to play the chords for you, or record them on tape and then play along.

RHYTHM

Let's begin with an easy-to-play rock figure that has been around since the '50s and almost defines the word "boogie." It's important to master this playing feel for all sorts of music you might want to tackle. For **exercise 1**, play to a steady rhythm, at first with downstrokes of the pick. Later try alternate down/up picking for a somewhat different rhythmic feel. (The "shuffle" variation of this figure can be found in the *Blues* section). This popular rhythm has powered great rock playing from Chuck Berry to Oasis (whose lead guitarist and songwriter, Noel Gallagher, is pictured right).

Exercise 2 is a variation where the note on the fretted string goes a further semi-tone up. Notice also the change from E to A

Exercise 1

Exercise 2

rhythm

comes on the last off-beat of bar 1. This syncopation – with its distinctive "pull" across the bar-line, is typical of rock. Remember to try to get each pair of notes the same volume.

Exercise 3 shows a subtle yet distinctive third variation on this theme, where two notes are introduced that temporarily eclipse the root note in each bar. Syncopation is once again present on the last off-beat.

It is also possible to use this rhythm figure in a new way by turning it into a set of single notes instead of striking two notes at a time, as in **exercise 4**. Watch out for the transition in bar 4 from hitting the 6th string to hitting the 4th string.

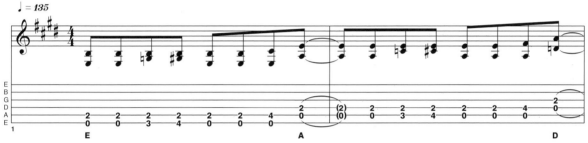

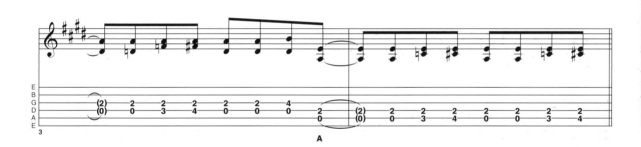

Exercise 3

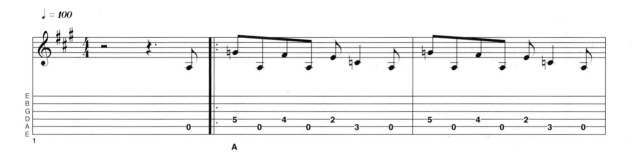

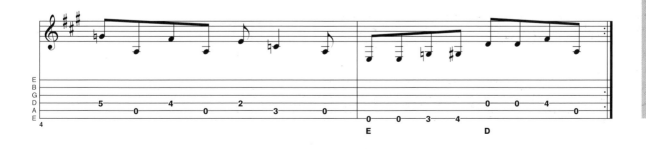

Exercise 4

Exercises 1-4 work well in the key of A major. But what if we want to play this rhythm figure in other keys? The answer is to convert it into a fretted figure with no open strings. Don't worry if you find this a bit of a stretch at first. Drop your thumb well behind the neck. That will help your fretting hand open out. **Exercise 5** shows the boogie figure following a common chord progression (chords I, IV and V in B major).

Exercise 6 displays the same idea in E major starting on the 5th string. Starting on either the 5th or the 6th strings enables you to play it in any major key, and to pitch it higher or lower. Songs like Status Quo's *Paper Plane*, Queen's *Now I'm Here* and Super

Furry Animals' *Rings Around The World* feature this.

To help you memorize the pattern that governs the I-IV-V changes, **exercise 7** isolates the root notes. Bars 1-2 give the pattern for starting on the 6th string; bars 3-4 for starting on the 5th. **Exercise 8** shows how original effects can be had with this rhythm figure by moving between less related root notes. Chord VI in E major should be C#m, not C#, and there is no A# in the key of E, which is what the boogie figure demands. You can hear this change in T.Rex's *Mambo Sun* from the album *Electric Warrior* (1971). A further innovation is to flatten the expected note, as in bar 4.

Exercise 5

Exercise 6

rhythm

144

rhythm

♩ = 105

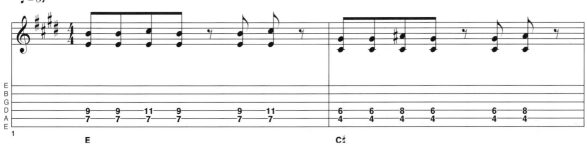

G   C   D   G   C   D

♩ = 87

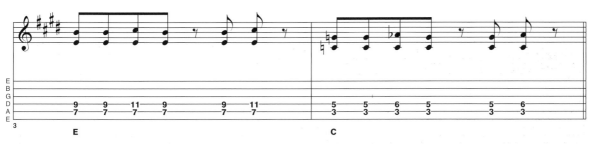

E   C♯

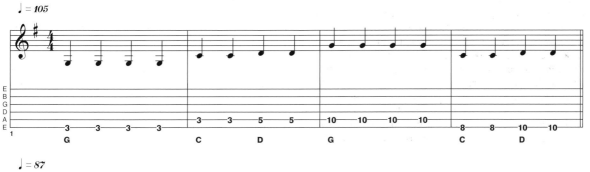

E   C

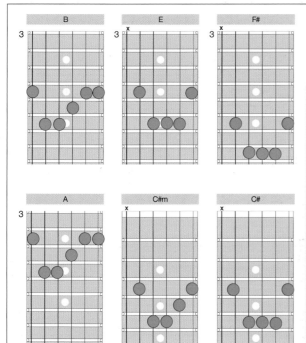

T.Rex's Marc Bolan was a major proponent of the basic boogie rhythm, and applied it to many pop-rock classics. Learning your barre chords – such as those in the diagrams shown left – will help you transpose these useful rhythmic figures to any key.

A related version of the rhythm figure we have been playing occurs on the higher strings and is based on a major triad held by the first finger. Play **exercise 9** to try it in C major.

Exercise 10 is a variation related to Ex.2 where the finger goes up one additional fret. The note you added to each chord in Ex.9 is known as the sixth of the chord. If we add the fourth as well as the sixth we get the rock rhythm figure displayed in **exercise 11**. Bars 1-2 lack a root note. This is suggested in bars 3-4. It is possible but awkward: the little finger must hold down the root and damp the 5th string. In **exercise 12** a related figure adds the fourth and the ninth to the basic triad. Notice the A chord in bar 2 has a powerful sound because the root note is

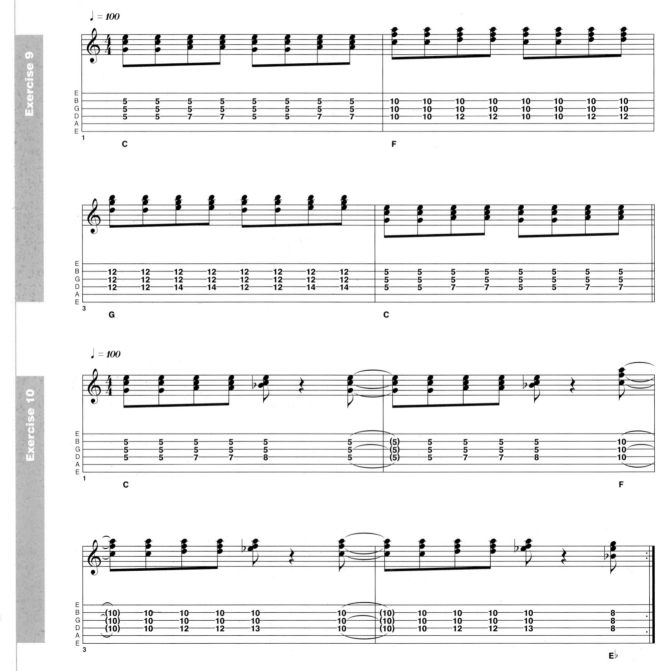

Exercise 9

Exercise 10

rhythm

146

merely the open 5th string. This figure on A is very popular for this reason. Exercises 9-12 will remind you of the Rolling Stones, the Faces, and the Black Crowes – good-time rock'n'roll. They are standard tuning versions of figures that occur in open tunings (the *Acoustic* section deals further with open G).

Apart from the A chord in the last example, the other open-string chord that yields excellent results with these 4/6, 4/9 shapes is G. In **exercise 13** bar 1 adds just the sixth, bar 2 the sixth and fourth, bar 3 the ninth and fourth, and bar 4 shows a common pull-off fill making good use of the open strings. Listen to *John, I'm Only Dancing* by David Bowie, or *If It Makes You Happy* by Sheryl Crow (playing live, left; album opposite page).

Exercise 14

Exercise 15

power chords

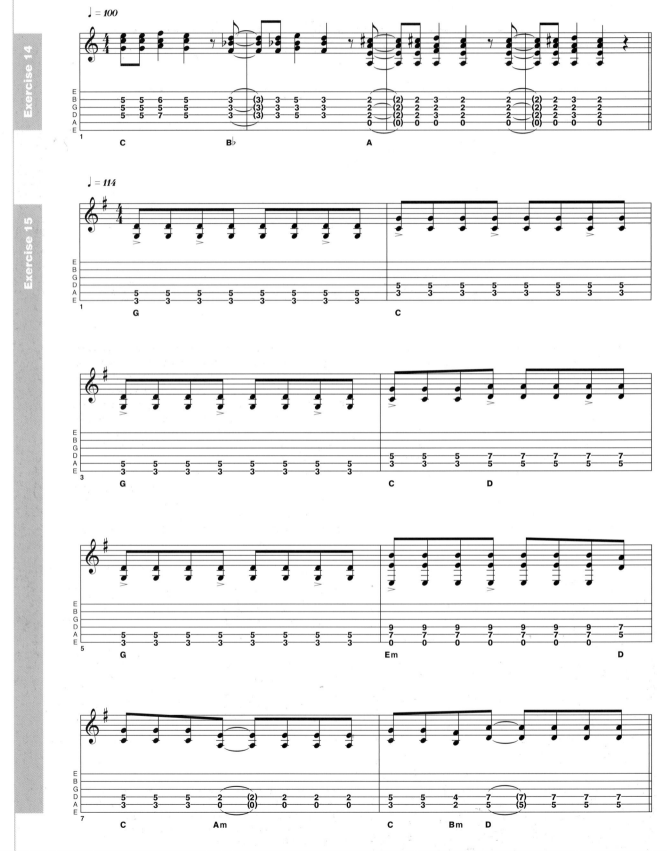

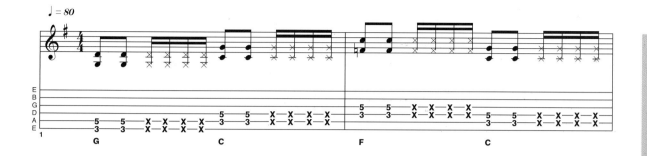

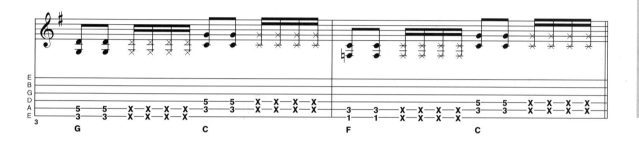

Exercise 14 shows how new effects can be had by giving these shapes a less predictable twist. Bar 2 has an E where we would expect an Eb, and bar 3 has an F where we would expect F#. This is now less Keith Richards and more Jimmy Page.

RHYTHM FIFTHS

In many of the above exercises the interval of a perfect fifth (3½ tones) from E-B, A-E, D-A, dominates. The perfect fifth is crucial to rock guitar. It has a bare, tough, assertive sound and tolerates any amount of distortion. You may already know it under the name commonly used by rock guitarists, the "power chord," and it is essential to master for comprehensive rock playing. The concept will be covered in more detail and with further exercises in the *Metal* section, but the style applies equally to both rock and heavy metal, and it's worth addressing here too.

Strum this sequence in **exercise 15** with open-string chords. Then play it as fifths, as written out. Notice the difference. Even with a clean tone the fifths toughen up the progression if a second guitar plays full chords. Played at various speeds, with or without damping (to give more "thud"), rhythm fifths are a surprisingly diverse tool which occur in rock, metal, punk, new wave and grunge – heard in the music of everyone from Soundgarden to Devo. If you play any form of rock, you'll find a use for them sooner or later.

In **example 16** damp all the strings on beats 2 and 4. If you use your little finger to fret the higher of the two notes in each pair it will lie flat enough to stop most of the strings sounding when needed. To damp the lower note just let the string come off the fingerboard but keep your first finger on it. Notice the F5 occurs in bar 4 an octave lower than in bar 2.

Devo couldn't have made their quirky, jerky bizarro-punk without the help of the muted power chord (and the occasional open G, as demonstrated left in a rare moment *sans* flowerpot hat). For full-blast rock examples of the breed, look no further than Soundgarden's Seattle grunge-metal.

Fifths can be found in the same shape on all string pairs except 3 and 2. **Exercise 17** shows how U2's guitarist The Edge (pictured with vocalist Bono, right) might use a high 5th with an open G string, which is characteristic of his guitar playing and a significant factor of his band's sound in general.

Exercise 18 gives us a fifth with an open G string inside it. As you move the fifth the open G forms different relationships with the other notes, with a moody effect.

Fifths on 4 and 3 can be moved up and down in the key of E or E minor to combine with the top two open strings. Notice the

Green Day guitarist Billie Joe Armstrong offers plenty of great examples of how to use chunky, tight fifths and fourths to power compelling punk-pop tunes.

resonance in bar 1 of **exercise 19** where there are two Bs at the same pitch. As you move the fifths try to let the open strings ring for as long as possible.

Fifths also combine well with sixths. A sixth is produced when you move either the first finger down a fret or the little finger up a fret, as in **exercise 20**. This is an idea frequently explored by Paul Kossoff, the late guitarist of Free.

If you invert a fifth you get a fourth: A-E (a fifth) becomes E-A (a fourth). Fourths combine well with fifths. In **exercise 21** fourths appear in bar 4, but watch out for the way open bass strings add extra interest; this could be Eddie Cochran, Mick Ronson or Green Day – you choose!

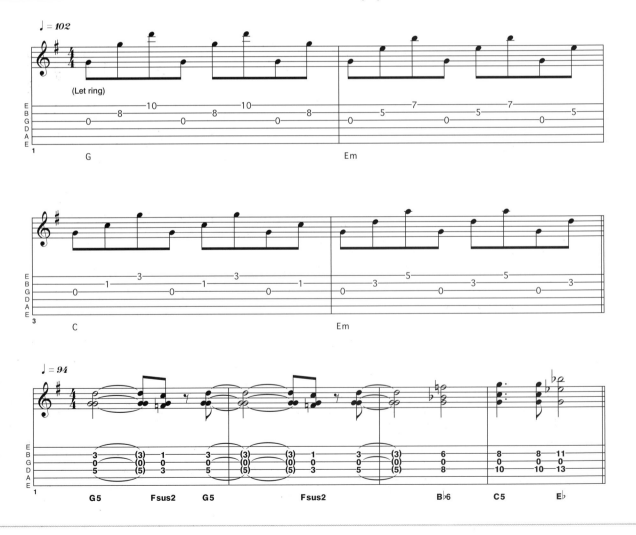

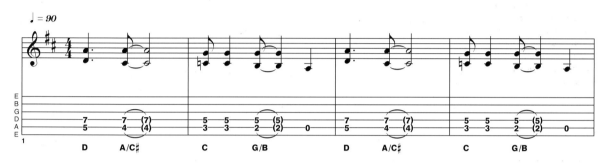

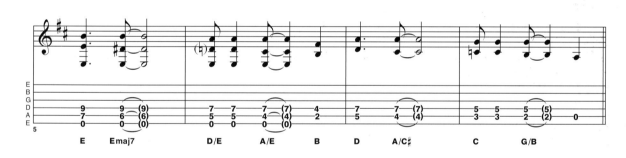

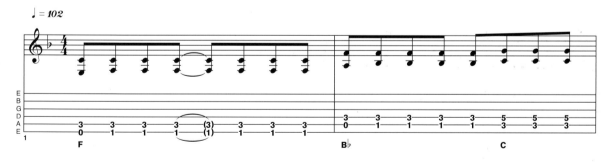

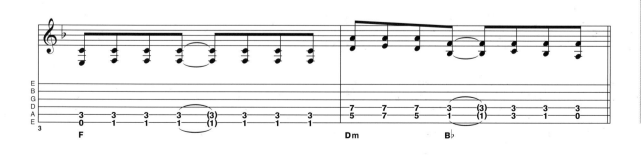

power chords

| Aadd9 | Ebadd9 | Dmaj7 |
| Gm/D | Cmin/D | D9no3rd |

The chord block diagrams above offer an added visual approach to some of the concepts explained on this page. Though the chords in these exercises are written out in the notation of each individual example, it might help some readers to try them in this familiar form before exploring the exercises fully.

If you take a fifth and "copy" its shape onto the next string an add9 figure is the result. The chords in **exercise 22** are excellent stretching practice and spice up a sequence of fifths. They are associated with Andy Summers, who used them on Police hits like *Message In A Bottle*. Another fine example of such usage is the song *Palace Of Dreams* by Dubh Chapter.

TRIADS

Though much guitar-playing uses full chords with 4, 5, or 6 strings played at a time, guitarists should not forget the humble triad. It only takes three notes to make a major or minor chord. This builds directly on the fifths we have just been working on, adding just one extra note to the chord – but it's a crucial addition, changing the mood of the chord dramatically between major and minor. Triads are easy to play and lend themselves to rhythm parts, fills, riffs and (as we will see later) even lead solos. (In the *Jazz* section, you will further see how the use of triads can allow any intermediate guitarist to play convincing jazz-style rhythm parts without immediately needing to learn complicated chord forms.)

The fretted notes of an ordinary D chord make a D triad. In **exercise 23** that shape is moved up the neck in a chordal riff. The open D string remains throughout, an example of a "pedal" note (a note which remains unchanged while chords or melody lines change around it). The major triads form different relationships with that D. Watch out for the open top string at the end of bars 1 and 2. This is a simple but effective approach used by Pete Townshend in many Who songs.

There are three major triad shapes on the top three strings. **Exercise 24** shows them over a D pedal. Compare this progression with strumming D, C and G in full chords. You can hear similar effects in Focus's *Sylvia* (intro) and Wishbone Ash's *Blowin' Free*.

There are also three minor triad shapes on the top three strings. In **exercise 25**, notice how the D string modifies their sound quite considerably at certain points, turning the F#m triad of bar 1 into a Dmaj7 chord in bar 2.

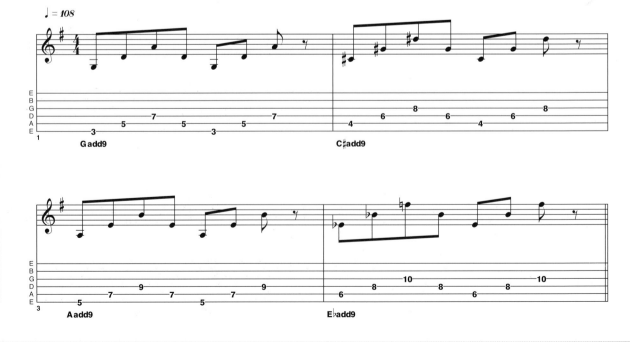

Exercise 26 uses major and minor triad shapes as they occur on strings 2, 3, and 4. This time the pedal note is A. This could be played clean or with a little distortion. Mark Knopfler of Dire Straits is a guitarist whose idiosyncratic picking technique led him to use triads for songs like *Sultans Of Swing* and *Lady Writer*, as in **exercise 27**. It was easy for him to choose triads because he was plucking the strings with his thumb, index and middle finger only. This time there is no pedal note.

FOUR-NOTE CHORDS

Sometimes it's not necessary to include the lower strings. With a strong bass line it can be sufficient for the guitar to play chords on the top four strings only. The Spin Doctors' *Two Princes* is a fine example. A well-known pop and soul recording trick is to put a "stab" guitar chord on beats 2 and 4, as in **exercise 28**. A bright, clean tone is used and the chord is immediately followed by a rest. This chord will often sit with the snare drum. Listen to many '60s soul records, especially from Motown, where the high stab guitar was often played by Joe Messina on a Telecaster.

One of the tricks of professional song-arranging is to know when you don't need to change chord but can let the bass guitar do the work. The G-Gsus4 change stays the same throughout bars 1-3 in **exercise 29**, yet the chords written above change. To hear the effect either get someone to play the root notes of G,

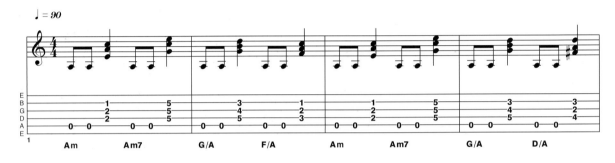

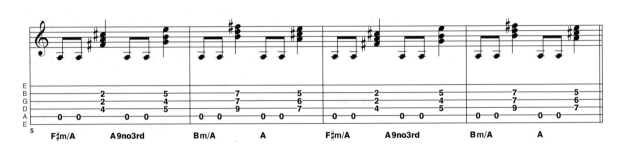

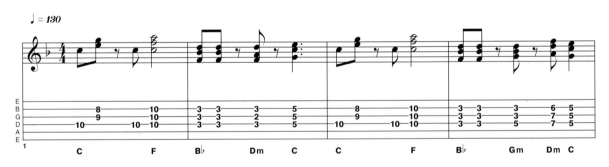

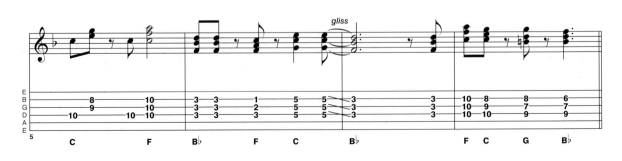

Exercise 26

Exercise 27

stab chords

154

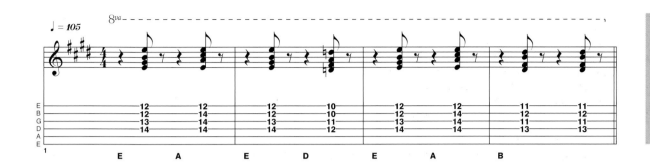

Exercise 28

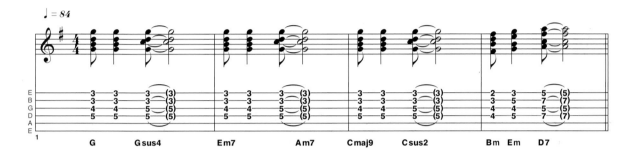

Exercise 29

Em, Am and C, or play those chords on guitar or keyboard while you play the written part. The changing root notes change the harmonic value of the written G-Gsus4 change even though it stays the same – so it sounds different in each bar.

RIFFS

A riff is a memorable phrase of between one and four bars. In rock it often focuses much of the energy of the song, and is generally repeated as a central "hook" of the guitar part. Riffs occur in almost all guitar music from '50s rock'n'roll to contemporary nu-metal, and in other genres like reggae, soul, blues and folk; they're the building blocks of countless pop and rock guitar parts. Riffs are quick to write and learn, and great fun to play – and chances are you know a few good ones already. Prepare for some head banging!

Many riffs are derived from the same scales used for rock and blues lead. Bars 1 and 2 of **exercise 30** ascend E pentatonic minor. "Pentatonic" means five notes – in this case, E G A B D. Bars 3 and 4 provide the riff itself, using the lower notes of this scale.

Exercise 30

Exercise 31

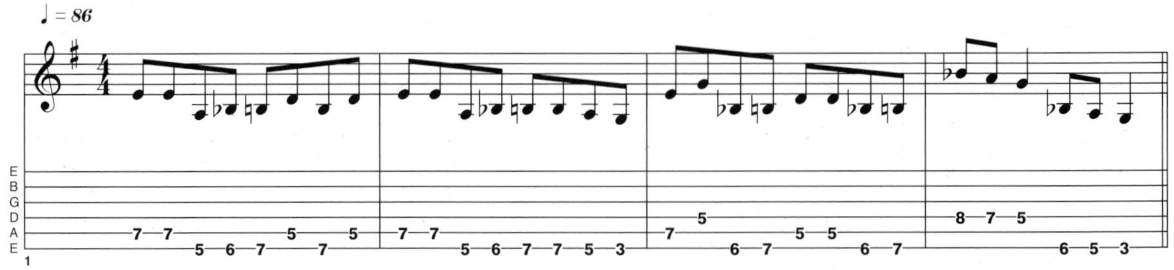

Exercise 32

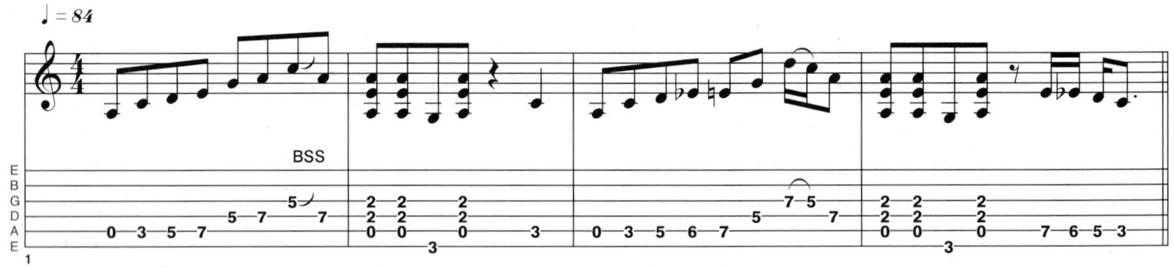

Exercise 33

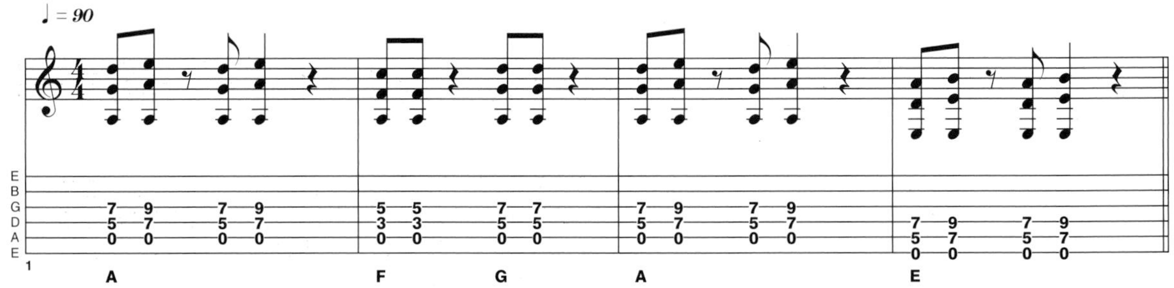

Exercise 34

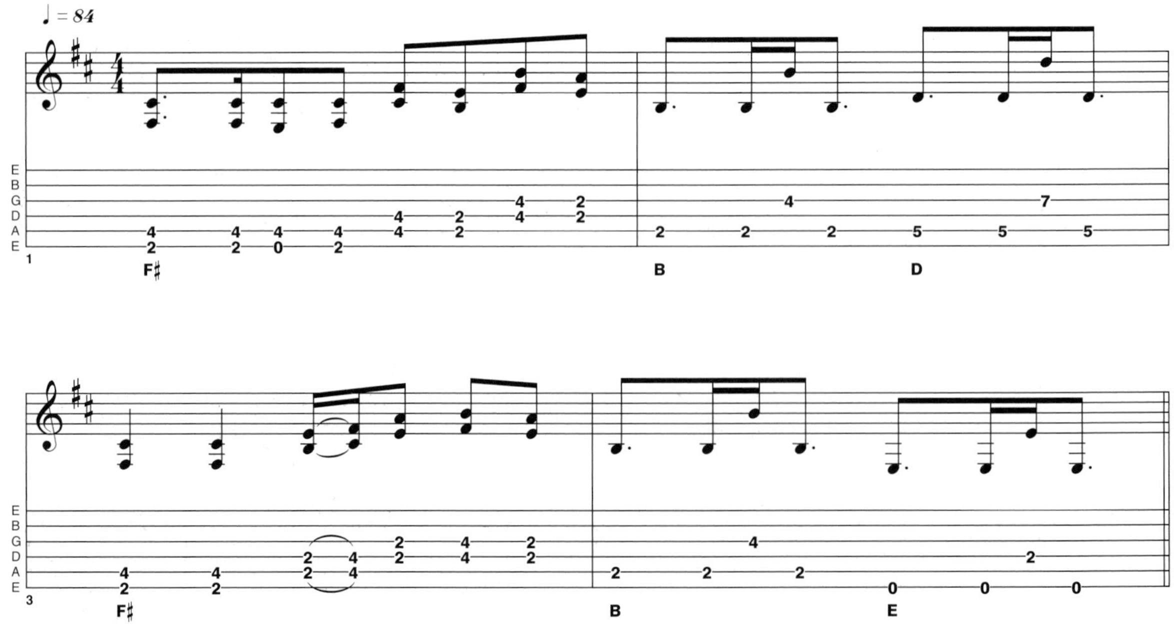

By adding one note to the previous pentatonic scale – Bb – we get the E blues scale, as utilized in **exercise 31**. This extra note is called a flattened 5th and is important for its dissonance: it sounds mean! This note allows a riff with creeping semi-tone movement.

E/E minor are popular keys for the guitar because the strings are naturally biased toward E. However, a pentatonic scale can be played from any note. Since the second lowest open string is A, A pentatonic minor (A C D E G) is also popular. **Exercise 32** is a riff on that scale. Watch out for the powerful A5 chord in bars 2 and 4, and the b5 (Eb) that appears in bars 3 and 4.

Fifths are popular for riffs. In **exercise 33** the fifths are strengthened by the open A and E strings. You can hear this in rock bands like Thin Lizzy and Iron Maiden.

Exercise 34 is a riff that uses fifths, fourths (the pairs of notes here with the same fret number) and octaves (bars 2 and 4). The riff sequence in **exercise 35** uses fourths. Fourths have their own flavor; they're less stable than fifths because the root note is no longer the lower of the two. Ritchie Blackmore used fourths for riffs on many Deep Purple and Rainbow tracks.

Transferred to the top two strings, as in **exercise 36**, fourths become less heavy rock and more new wave. Their slightly "oriental" colour was exploited by Television on their masterpiece *Marquee Moon*, and on the intro to Wings' *Band On The Run*.

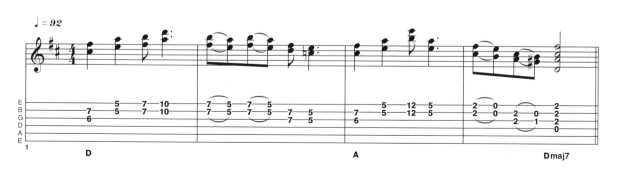

riffs

Exercise 37

Exercise 38

Exercise 39

Bands like Led Zeppelin have forged memorable rock songs from riffs built on octaves, not unlike those in **exercise 37**. These types of riff are especially effective when the guitar and bass are together on the riff. Octave riffs can also make a good accompaniment during a verse structure, as in **exercise 38**. Bars 1-4 feature a basic figure of an octave that falls to the b7 and then the 5th. In bars 5-8 a variation introduces the b5 note previously featured. Here, it's the C# in bars 5 and 6.

Riffs can use single notes over a pedal note, as in **exercise 39**. The pedal note is supplied by an open string. Here over D is a scale known as the "mixolydian mode." You can read more about this mode in the Scales section. It differs from the D major scale (D E F# G A B C#) merely in having the 7th note flattened to C. This effect is featured on The Cult's *She Sells Sanctuary*

and R.E.M.'s *Green Grow The Rushes*.

Exercise 40 is a similar pedal riff, this time using A and having two notes at a time above it. Rock music favors the sus4 chord because of its tension (great for building drama) and its neutrality. Like fifths and fourths, the suspended fourth chord, explored in **exercise 41**, is neither major nor minor. This riff takes a triadic form and moves it down through small changes. Sus4 chords feature strongly in the Who's *Pinball Wizard*, T.Rex's *Cadillac*, Argent's *Hold Your Head Up*, and John Lennon's *Happy Xmas (War Is Over)*.

The bends in **exercise 42** – two strings bent together – were established in rock guitar by Chuck Berry and have been used by many other players ever since. They are very effective at faster tempos, as in Motorhead's *Ace Of Spades*.

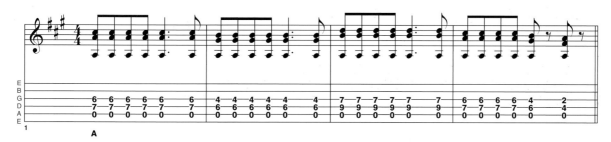

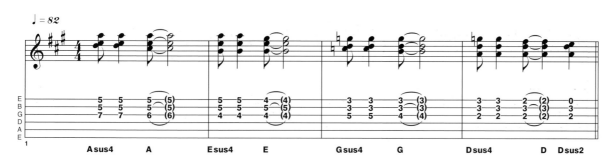

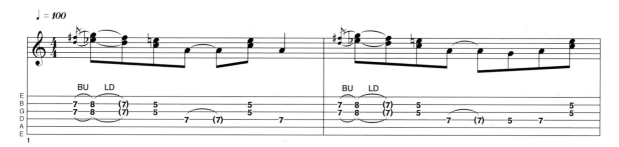

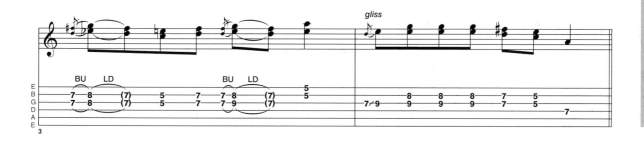

159

No look at riffs would be complete without the 1-3-5-6 figure, so called after the notes of the scale and explored here in **exercise 43**, which is closely related to the rock'n'roll rhythm parts you played in exercises 1-4.

Exercise 44 is a slightly decorated version. You can hear something similar on Roy Orbison's *Pretty Woman*, though in that song the riff stays on E.

The term "chromatic" refers to the use of extra notes that do not belong to the key, as employed in **exercise 45**. Chromatic riffs have an element of surprise about them. They can sound "jazzy" – as in Pink Floyd's *Money* or toward the end of Hendrix's *Hey Joe* – or sinister, as in Led Zep's *Dazed And Confused*. Look for a fingering that will make use of all your fretting fingers.

USING INTERVALS

Already we've played exercises that use significant intervals. In a major scale the intervals are major second (C-D), major third (C-E), perfect fourth (C-F), perfect fifth (C-G), major sixth (C-A), major seventh (C-B) and perfect octave (C-C). We have seen how fourths and fifths are used in rhythms and riffs. Seconds and sevenths can be discounted because they are not harmonious enough for consecutive playing, so let's move on to octaves.

One use of octaves is to thicken a melody or melodic phrase, as Hendrix did in *Third Stone From The Sun*. For **exercise 46** use a pick and your middle finger, or damp any strings in between and just use a pick. Octaves lend themselves to sliding up or down.

1-3-5-6 figures

Exercise 43

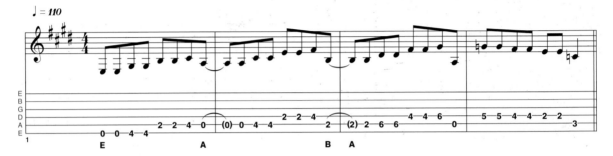

Exercise 44

Exercise 45

Exercise 46

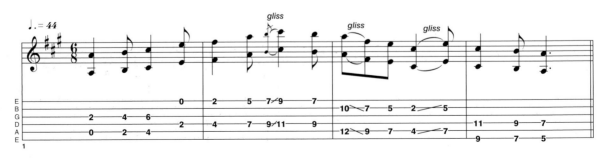

octave riffs

Jimi Hendrix remains a comprehensive single source of inspiration in a wide range of playing styles and techniques. From his jazzy use of chromatic notes to his deft approach to octave riffs, he is still a guitarist very much worth tapping into.

Exercise 47 gives you a chance to practise a 16th-note strum of "damped" octaves. Mute all four of the other strings with your fretting hand, then strum up and down in groups of four with the first of each group accented. When you get comfortable with this you can try cutting out some of the fretted 16ths. By muting more of them in the bar you can generate funk rhythms. There is a hint of this in the last bar.

Here's more muting practice for octave riffs in **exercise 48** – but listen for the altered intervals in the last bar.

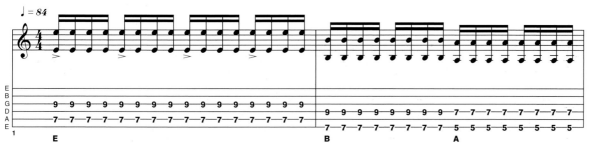

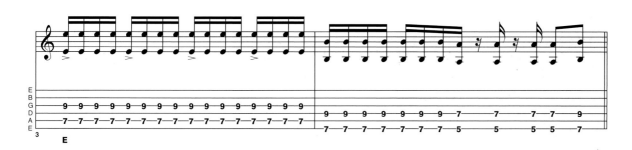

Octaves are crucial to the sound of a 12-string guitar. But what if you don't own a 12-string? Well, **exercise 49** shows a way of generating a 12-string effect on a six-string. It requires some nimble finger-work in both hands but it's a valuable technique, and a great skill builder in itself. Use a pick and a finger and let strings ring as long as you can.

THIRDS AND SIXTHS

The only useful intervals we haven't touched on yet are thirds and sixths. Both have major and minor forms. A major third is 2 tones (C-E); a minor third is 1½ (C-Eb). A major sixth is 4½ (C-A); a minor sixth is 4 (C-Ab).

Exercise 50 shows a sequence of thirds in D major on the top two strings. All the notes on the top string should be fingered with the 1st finger; those underneath are either the 2nd or the 3rd. The 1st finger acts as a guide when you shift position. The key note for the sequence is on the 2nd string at the starting position. If you want to transpose this to another major key simply locate the new key note on the 2nd string and play the same sequence from there.

Exercise 51 is the equivalent sequence in A major on the 2nd and 3rd strings. The guide finger is the 2nd which plays all the notes on the lower string; the 2nd string notes are either 1st or 2nd finger. If this were played from the 7th fret you would have

the same notes as Ex.50.

Thirds have a sweetening effect, and can be used for guitar fills and lead solos. Van Morrison's *Brown-Eyed Girl* and The Smiths' *This Charming Man* use them. They can be played either simultaneously or one after the other, as **exercise 52** shows.

Remember: the harmonic value of notes depends on the underlying harmony. Change the harmony and you effectively change the notes even if they stay still. **Exercise 53** has a two-bar phrase in 3rds. Each time the chord changes it will sound different. Try continuing this riff through another four bars – two bars each against the underlying chords F and G – to hear this effect even further.

Exercise 54 is a sequence of sixths in G major on the 1st and 3rd strings. All the notes on the 3rd string should be fingered with the 2nd finger; those above are either the 1st or the 3rd. The key note for the sequence is on the 1st string at the starting position. To transpose this to another major key simply find the new key note on the 1st string and play the same sequence from there.

Exercise 55 is the equivalent sequence in D major on the 2nd and 4th strings. The guide finger is the 2nd which plays all the notes on the lower string; the 2nd string notes are either 1st or 3rd finger. If this were played from the 8th fret you would have the same notes as Ex.54.

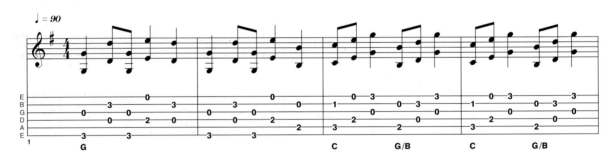

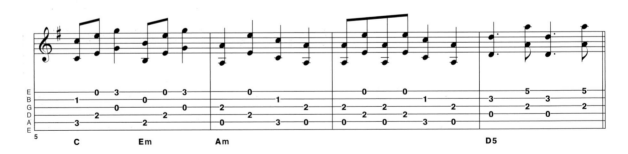

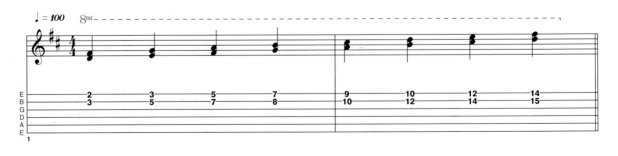

thirds

Exercise 49

Exercise 50

Exercise 51

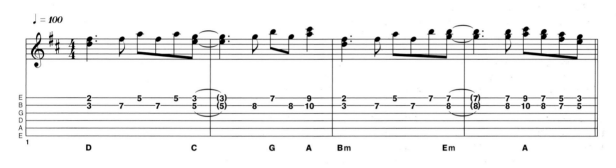

Exercise 52

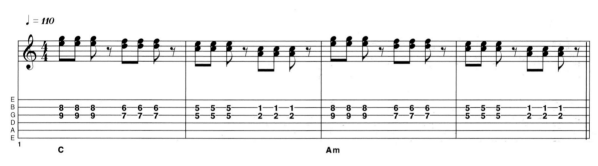

Exercise 53

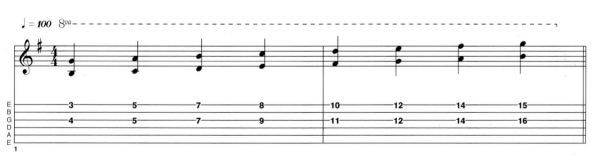

Exercise 54

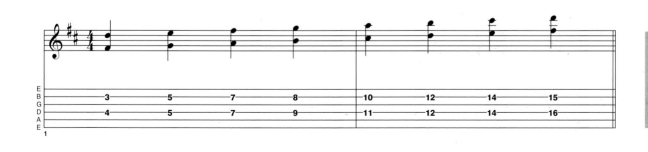

Exercise 55

Sixths are also used for fills and lead solos, though they don't sound as sweet as thirds. Soul guitarist Steve Cropper is renowned for his use of sixths on many '60s recordings like *Soul Man* and *Dock Of The Bay*. In **exercise 56** the addition of a couple of chromatic sixths emulate Cropper's slinky feel. This is yet another technique that can be simple to master, but has an extremely effective, melodic feel with a little extra bluesy groove to it too – and is usually yields positive results when employed tastefully.

Sometimes in a riff sixths make a refreshing change from fifths or fourths. In **exercise 57** the D G F D change could have been done with either – but here it is in sixths, combined with a D pentatonic minor single-note phrase.

Exercise 58 gives us a look at some thirds combined with an open G string.

Clever choice of key makes it possible to put the open B string in the middle of a run of sixths in **exercise 59**. Taking B as the key note, it is only necessary to find a run of sixths in B major. Andy Summers used a similar technique in E minor in The Police's *Bring On The Night*, where sixths in E minor straddle the open G string (the middle note of an E minor chord).

Learn each of these approaches to sixths, then see if you can make up a few in these keys and others. Use them to spice up your riffs and tunes where appropriate.

THE "JANGLE" STYLE

The last two exercises are reminiscent of a popular style which has become known as "jangle." It is associated with the 12-string sound of The Byrds' Roger McGuinn, Peter Buck's playing with R.E.M. in the '80s, Johnny Marr's work with The Smiths, and many "indie" bands of the '90s. The La's *There She Goes* is a superb example.

Jangle defines a clean, shimmery, ringing guitar texture, sometimes aided by sustaining effects like compression, chorus, echo and reverb. It also involves a certain approach to chord shapes and picking.

Jangle guitar requires open strings to ring out between changes, while chords are turned into arpeggios, the strings picked one at a time, as typified by **exercise 60**. The shapes can be simple but the end result pleasing to the ear and extremely effective in the right context.

In the early playing of Peter Buck there is often a quick picking of the chord to give drive and motion to otherwise fairly simple progressions, and that's the way to approach **exercise 61**. Make good use of up and down pick strokes as you weave among the strings. Notice in bar 3 the "harp" effect of having three notes each a tone apart all sounding at once. Hear Buck's jangle in songs such as *Radio Free Europe* from the album *Murmur* and *Good Advices* from *Fables Of The Reconstruction*.

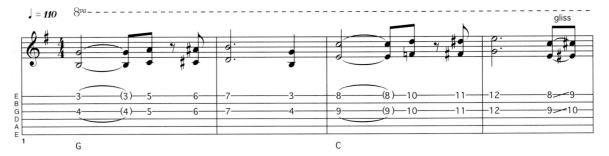

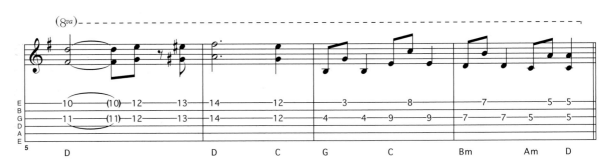

sixths

Exercise 56

Exercise 57

jangle

Exercise 58

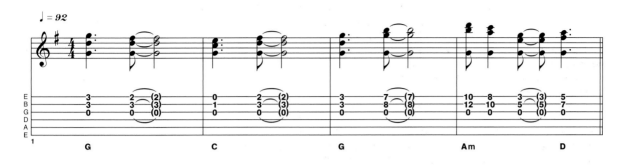

Exercise 59

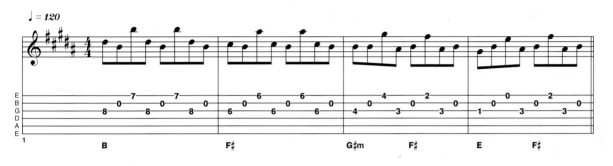

Exercise 60

Exercise 61

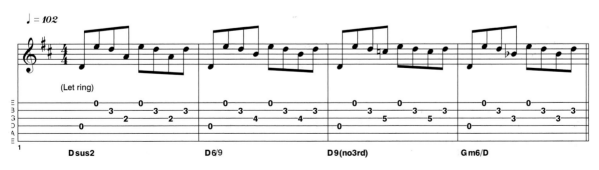

165

Exercise 62 demonstrates another of those "weaving" picking patterns, with a harp effect in bar 4. Notice the introduction of the open E into the D chord in bars 1 and 2, and the hollow ring of the Asus2 in bar 7. Take care that all the notes in bar 6 ring as long as they can for the full effect.

In **exercise 63** chord shapes are devised away from first position so that open strings can combine with higher fretted notes. Play this with distortion and hear why such arpeggio effects need a clean tone!

ARPEGGIOS

The jangle style plays the notes of a chord one after the other to generate an "arpeggio." Arpeggios are found elsewhere in rock and pop guitar. They are crucial in songs such as Cream's *Badge*, The Beatles' *Here Comes The Sun* and *I Want You*, Bebop Deluxe's *Maid In Heaven* and The Jam's *When You're Young*.

The figures in **exercise 64** exploit the slightly murky tone of low thirds on the guitar. Bryan Adams's *Run To You* and Nirvana's *Come As You Are* do likewise. In **exercise 65** most of the arpeggios are based on a triad, but watch for the C#m7 in bar 7. In **exercise 66** a common sequence moving from C down to G is transformed by the use of arpeggios. This might make a suitable conclusion to a chorus or a whole song.

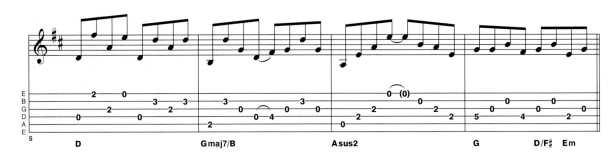

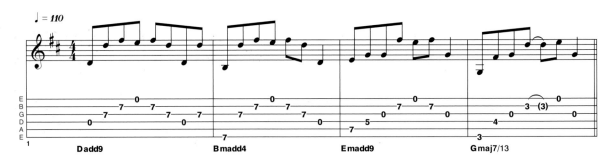

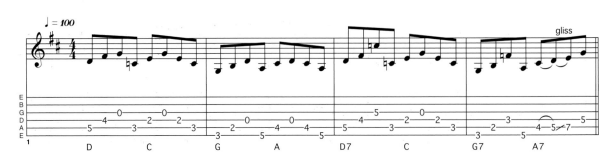

jangle

Exercise 62

Exercise 63

Exercise 64

Arpeggios figure into the guitar parts of songs by everyone from Bryan Adams (left) to The Beatles, Bebop Deluxe to The Jam. More than just a basic 'folky' technique for strumming slower tunes, they run the gamut from sweet and poppy to dark and moody.
Investigate *Here Comes The Sun* for the former, and *Run To You* or *Come As You Are* for the latter.

Exercise 63 features some accompanying chords which might outwardly appear rather complex, but are really fairly simple to play thanks to the use of open strings to double up tones within them for a ringing, jangly feel. The diagrams shown right give a quick visual reference to three of these which you might find useful elsewhere in your playing.

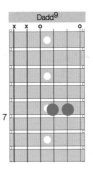

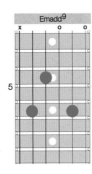

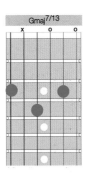

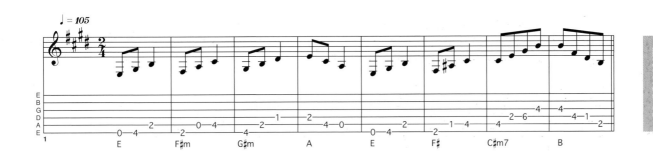

Arpeggios can also be included in a guitar solo. Many of the lead solos in Dire Straits' *Brothers In Arms* begin with a rising arpeggio. The triad in bar 4 of **exercise 67** is played with a "rake": the notes are not struck altogether but fractionally one after the other, either by pushing the pick through the strings, or "rolling" the notes with the pick and two fingers.

LEAD GUITAR

Playing lead guitar competently is a matter of learning a small number of scales and scale patterns, mastering the art of bending and fretting-hand techniques like vibrato, hammering-on, pulling-off, and slides; and gradually finding out which notes work over any given chord sequence.

BENDS

Each bar in **exercise 68** features one of the four commonest bends as measured by ascent in pitch. (Players do occasionally bend further than 1½ tones – but string breakage is always a risk!) In each bar you first play the target note by fretting it; then you bend the previous note up. This "primes" your ear each time so you can listen for when you're in tune. The exception is the final quarter-tone bend which is actually a fraction lower than the C# you play on the 1st beat. In Ex.68 the bends are all done with

the 3rd finger, with the 1st and 2nd on the same string behind it. This means you can push with all three. Try also having your thumb on the top edge of the neck to get more grip.

Welcome to the unison bend. There are some marvellous unison bends toward the end of *Stairway To Heaven*. The higher note (1st finger) stays still. The lower note (3rd finger, 2nd supporting) is bent up until its pitch is the same as the higher. In **exercise 69** the fingers are closer together when you move down a string in bars 2 and 4. **Exercise 70** is a group of ascending unison bends in action. Play them right and the higher they go the more they take on a wailing, vocal quality.

Exercise 71 displays the "pre-bend." This is so-called because you bend the string up before you strike it, then lower it. The listener gets used to hearing notes in a solo bent up, but does not expect to hear a note drop in this manner. The catch is that you have to guess how far to bend to get the starting note.

Exercise 72 contains two essential bend ideas that will give you full-on rock or a country twang depending how you use them. Bend with the 3rd finger as you hit the two notes together. The higher note is held down by the little finger. Notice the note F (6th fret, 2nd string) in bar 2. That note, two frets back from the bend, tells you which chord this phrase fits over. The equivalent is the 5th fret C in bar 3 for the lower bend.

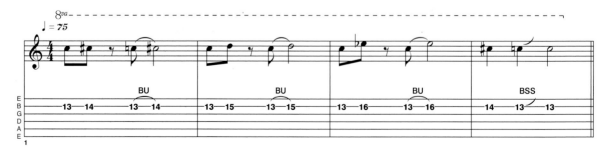

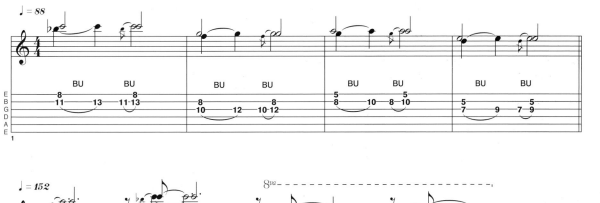

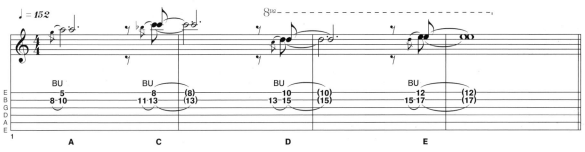

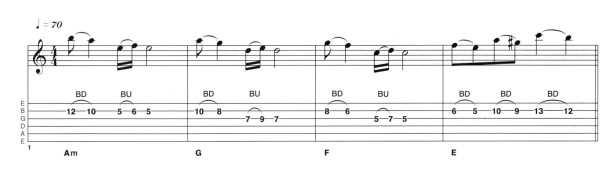

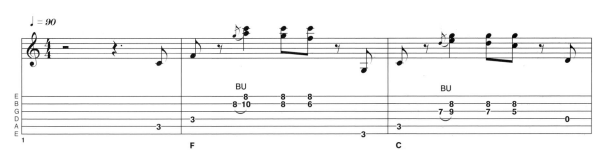

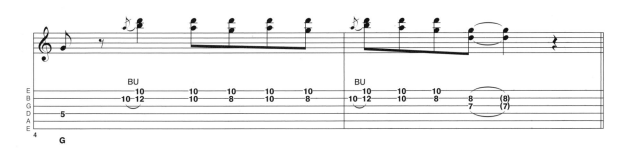

Exercise 73 combines the two individual figures of Ex.72 into one to give a single bend with two notes above it that will generate either a major or a minor chord depending on how far you push the bend. Hold the top two notes down with a little finger barre, and bend with the 3rd finger with 1st and 2nd supporting behind it. You can also play this progression hitting all the notes at once for a slightly different feel. The note on the top string is your root note. Select the root note for the chord you want on the top string, then bend 1/2 or 1 tone to produce the minor or major chord on that note.

It is possible to push a bend up a semitone at a time in order to get a sequence of notes, as in **exercise 74**. The B in bar 2 is pushed up first to C, then C#, then D, after which the E is supplied by the 12th fret on the top string. In bar 3 the idea is used in reverse. The bent E is dropped first a semitone from F# to F and then down to E. You'll see that a similar technique occurs again in bar 5.

Exercise 75 is an A pentatonic minor scale pattern that starts on the 6th string and moves through three octaves to reach A at the 17th fret on the top E.

Part of the same scale can be re-fingered as a two-octave pattern starting on the 5th string, as **exercise 76** demonstrates. This exercise uses triplets – a group of three quavers played on the beat.

Mark Knopfler, above, uses two fingers and thumb to execute his fluid, dexterous lead style – with cascades aplenty.

THE "CASCADE"

In order to make a scale pattern last longer when playing quickly, guitarists sometimes use a technique which we can dub the "cascade." The idea is to play down a few notes and then go back up one or two less. **Exercise 77** is a triplet cascade down the A pentatonic minor scale. You'll notice right away how the cascade helps to give the impression that you're not just running down a scale, but playing a more considered lead line.

Exercise 78 is an 8th note cascade down the same scale. In bar 2 the b5 (Eb) is added to make the A blues scale. Bar 3 is the same cascade idea starting one string lower than bar 1. In bar 4 the same b5 occurs but this time it is bent rather than fretted. Notice the difference in tone.

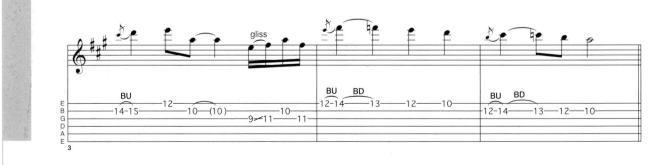

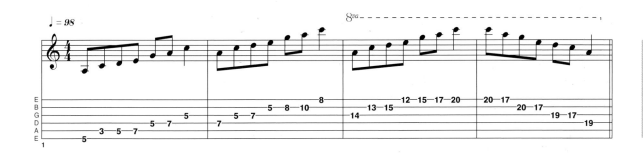

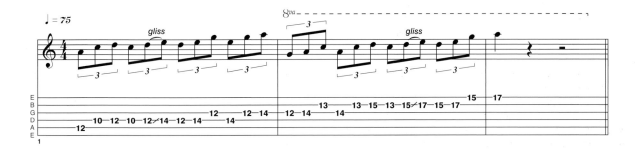

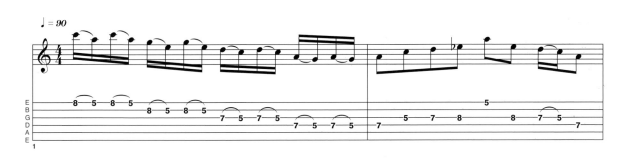

171

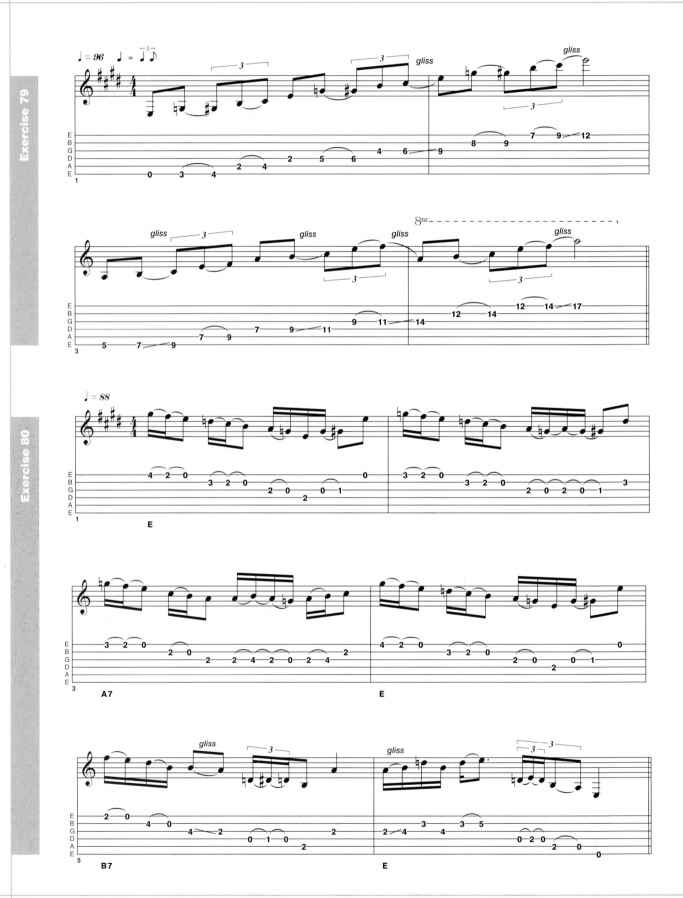

Exercise 79 is a three-octave E blues scale based on the E pentatonic major (E F# G# B C#) but with the addition of a b3, in this case G. This scale has an upbeat feel and is found in lead guitar solos that derive from '50s rock'n'roll.

Apart from string-bending, another decoration used by lead players is the hammer-on/pull-off, seen here in **exercise 80**, where notes are created by the fretting hand. This is based on a six-bar blues pattern. The scale is E Mixolydian (E F# G# A B C D) but with the b3 G also appearing.

REPEAT LICKS

Like the cascade, the repeat lick is a way of getting more from a small group of notes. The idea is to make a short phrase and repeat it for several bars. The one in **exercise 81** uses several that are based on a triad. Mark Knopfler used this idea very effectively at the close of *Sultans Of Swing*. In the right place, as in his energetic solo, these can sound more dynamic and driving than merely repetitive.

The E pentatonic lick in **exercise 82** is possibly the most famous of them all. Keep your 1st finger fretting the top two strings at the 12th fret throughout. Bend the 3rd string with your 2nd finger; do the 15-12 pull-off with your 3rd. Notice that the phrase will sound different with a C chord behind it contrasted with the E.

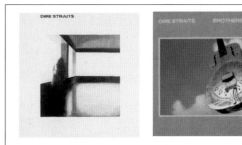

Mark Knopfler's lead work, especially in the early days of Dire Straits, makes an excellent example of how simple ideas and the careful use of repetition can sound effective and compelling when played with drive, energy and attitude.

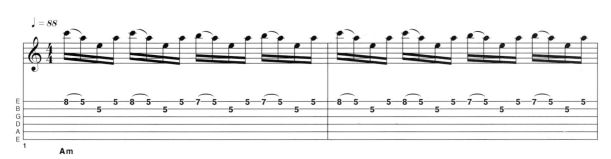

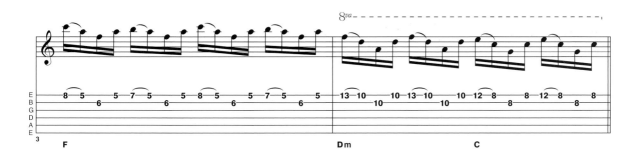

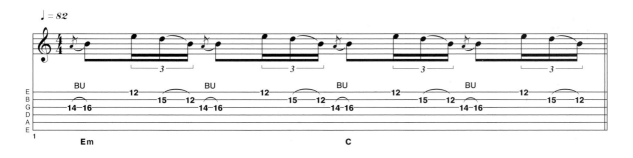

Exercise 83 is a five-note repeat lick that is based on A dorian (A B C D E F# G). Notice the shift up a minor 3rd – a favorite trick of Jimmy Page.

Once you've mastered Ex.83, try squeezing one more note onto the beat to get six – *voila*, **exercise 84**!

THE MODES

The pentatonic patterns are the most used by rock guitarists. A brief look at the group of scales known as the modes, however, will suggest some extra "color." Whether you can use these in a solo will partly depend on the chords over which you're playing.

The Aeolian mode, **exercise 85**, is also known as the natural minor scale. In A it would be A B C D E F G. Listen for the expressive sadness of the 2nd and 6th of this scale (B and F).

Contrast Ex.85 with the non-modal harmonic minor scale in **exercise 86**, where the 7th note is raised a semitone. Rock guitarists sometimes exploit the last four notes of this scale – E F G# A – to get an "Eastern" sound. The Dorian mode, **exercise 87**, can be thought of as the natural minor with a sharpened 6th: A B C D E F# G. It is favored by Santana in much of his lead playing. **Exercise 88** shows the Phrygian mode, which can be thought of as a natural minor with a b2: A Bb C D E F G. Many players consider it to have a Spanish sound.

The Aeolian, Dorian and Phrygian are all minor modes. There are three major modes. The Ionian is our major scale (in G: G A B C D E F# G). The Mixolydian is a major scale with a b7: G A B C D E F G. This is very common in pop and rock. **Exercise 89** shows it in various positions to fit the chord progression.

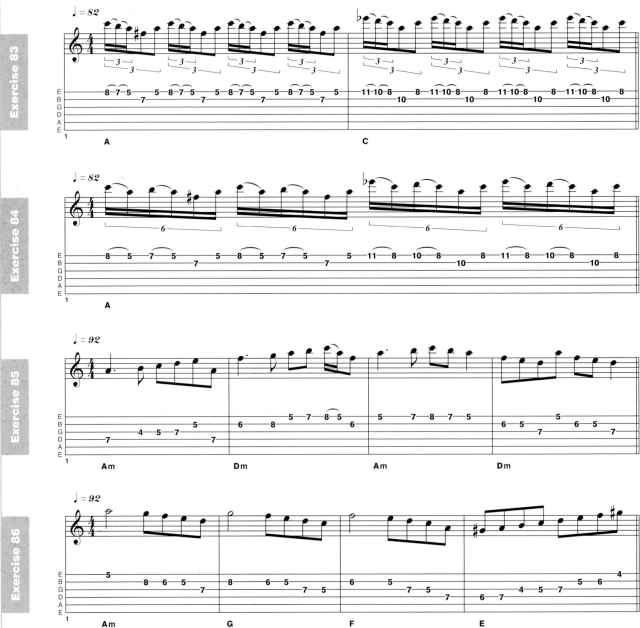

modes

Exercise 83
Exercise 84
Exercise 85
Exercise 86

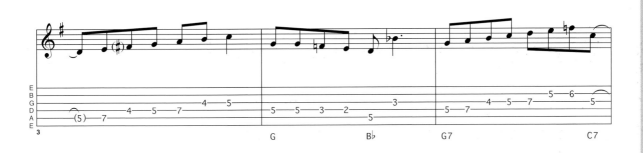

175

More than just a rock legend, Jimmy Page is also a great blender of styles, particularly in his classic work with Led Zeppelin. A great British blues-rocker, his playing also incorporates Eastern scales, traditional folk influences, and hard rock dynamics with seamless, fluid results. In addition to his guitar skills, Page's vast experience as a session musician before joining Zep meant he was also a deft arranger and producer right from the early years of the band.

The Lydian mode, **exercise 90**, is the major scale with a raised 4th: G A B C# D E F# G. The raised 4th gives this mode an edgy, unsettling quality.

To finish, try these two exercises chock-full of well-used bends. First, **exercise 91** is based around the 10th fret and lends itself to playing in D and A. Listen for the bluesy sound of the half bends; then **exercise 92** gives you some classic bends on 12th and 15th fret pentatonic shapes.

When you are working out a solo always check the chords over which you're playing. If the progression is in a single key with no odd chords a single scale will usually work all the way through. Any unusual chords may need an additional scale or perhaps just the adjustment of one note.

Exercise 90

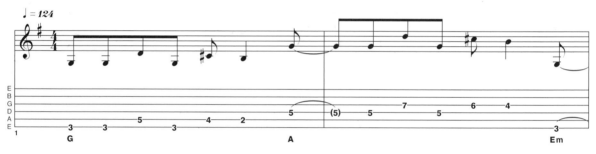

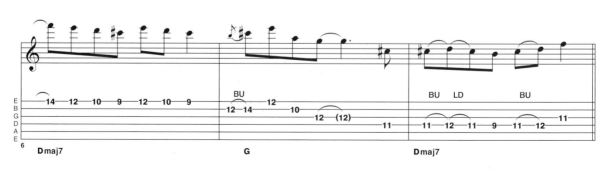

modes

You could do a lot worse than immerse yourself in Led Zeppelin for fine examples of great rock guitar playing, songwriting, arrangement and so on. *Led Zeppelin III*, released in 1970, contains such gems as *Immigrant Song*, *Gallows Pole* and *Braun-Y-Aur Stomp*, while the 1975 double album *Physical Graffiti* offers *Houses Of The Holy*, *Kashmir*, *Black Country Woman* and others.

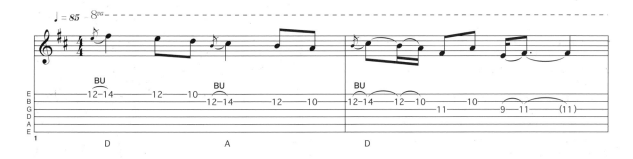

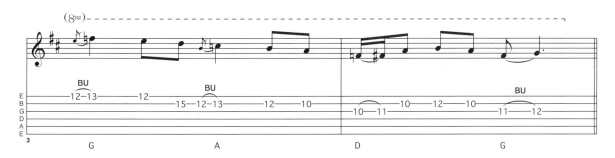

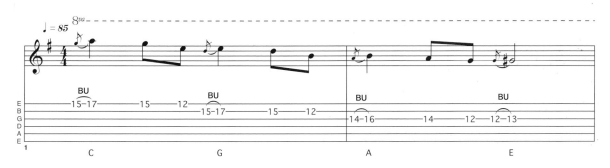

177

3

PLAYING
THE BLUES

Blues music in its various forms has influenced many strands of popular music and guitar playing since the 1950s. The blues originated as an acoustic folk music through which African Americans expressed the misfortunes of a disenfranchised people, as well as perennial human themes of frustration, love, sex and loss. Perhaps the ultimate voice for this style was Robert Johnson in the 1930s, though other early blues giants include Elmore James, T-Bone Walker, Son House, and Charley Patton. ● RIKKY ROOKSBY

The migration of many African-Americans from the rural south to cities further to the north eventually led to the development of an electric, urban-based blues, most famously in Chicago. During the '50s and early '60s performers such as Muddy Waters, Willie Dixon, Albert King, Buddy Guy, B.B. King, Albert Collins, Otis Rush, Hubert Sumlin, and John Lee Hooker, made their mark with blues played on an electric guitar.

Their sound and songs were emulated in the early to mid-'60s by a younger generation of singers and guitarists attracted to the earthy directness of blues, finding in it a raw energy and authenticity of experience which much pop and rock music lacked. This was especially true in the U.K., where a blues boom occurred. Artists such as the Rolling Stones, Eric Clapton, John Mayall, the Animals, the Yardbirds, Peter Green's Fleetwood Mac, Cream, and Free all either covered blues songs or wrote music in the same vein. In the U.S. a similar phenomenon brought forward talents such as Mike Bloomfield and Johnny Winter. It was highly significant that the most high-profile rock guitarist of the '60s, Jimi Hendrix, played some blues and wrote several classic blues-rock tracks, such as *Red House, Voodoo Chile* and *Hear My Train A-Comin'*.

Despite charges of plagiarism and their music being only a pale imitation of the real thing, it is now evident that the white musicians' interest in blues boosted the record sales and concert-drawing power of the older generation of bluesmen, enabling the latter to enjoy career success and longevity beyond their former expectations. For example, whatever critics think about the way Led Zeppelin played the blues on their 1969 debut album, there can be no doubt that that album (and others like it) acted as a door into the blues for a vast number of listeners. The effects of this new interest panned out through the '70s and '80s, with the result that the blues has taken its place in the broader range of commercial music styles, its legacy carried on by newer talents such as Stevie Ray Vaughan, Walter Trout, Jeff Healey, Robert Cray, Robben Ford and Bonnie Raitt.

Even if it is not your intention to play blues exclusively you will find that many of the ideas in this section can be used in rock and other genres. If you are just beginning to learn lead guitar the 12-bar blues format is a good place to start. This is because the blues style is comparatively "forgiving" once you know a few basic scales and how to use them. Simplicity and feeling are the hallmarks of much blues music, and you don't have to be a virtuoso to express yourself well as a blues guitarist.

At the heart of blues music is a form and a harmony that are easily grasped. Most blues is based on the 12-bar structure. Within those 12 bars there are three chords – chords I, IV and V of whatever key you are in. If the key is E major (the most common blues key on guitar) the chords are E, A and B. To get the distinctive blues sound these chords are often found in the extended form known in theory as "dominant sevenths": E7, A7 and B7. In standard harmony, the dominant seventh is a chord that can only occur naturally on the fifth (the dominant) note of the scale. So in E major that would be B7. Strictly speaking the chords E7 and A7 are not properly part of E major at all. This breaking of the rules, however, by allowing these three chords to be played in the same key, is part of what makes blues sound the way it does.

Most blues lead guitar is based on the pentatonic scale in major and minor forms. The clash between the pentatonic minor scale and the harmony based on the key's major scale creates the blues sound. Blues lead guitar is exceptionally repetitious. In the course of an average-length solo many players will play the same ideas many times over. This is another reason why this is a relatively easy lead style to grasp.

In this section we will begin by looking at rhythm playing and chords aspects of blues guitar, and then progress to the scales and licks that feature in a lot of blues playing to help you begin to improvise. Remember that whatever key the examples occur in, where there are no open strings you will be able to transpose phrases and licks into different keys simply by moving them up or down the fretboard.

RHYTHM

We'll begin with a single-note blues idea. **Exercise 1** has the distinctive "swinging" rhythm so often heard in blues. In 4/4 time each beat can be divided into two 8th notes, or four 16th notes, and so on. The 4/4 bar of 8th notes – counted as "one-and two-and three-and four-and" – is common in rock. In blues it is more usual to divide the beat into three 8th notes. Two 8th notes are thus played as if the first was a 1/4 note and the second an 8th note, giving the rhythm "one-and-uh two-and-uh three-and-uh four-and-uh;" the middle note of each three-note set is silent – it's there for rhythmic feel. There is a time signature – 12/8 – which

expresses this. But for ease of notation reading we will use 4/4 for most of these examples and add the direction to treat the rhythm as a "shuffle", displayed as ♫ = ♩♪

This example is in A major, whose scale is A B C# D E F# G#. In bar 1 you will see a C. This b3 note is a "blue" note. It clashes with the underlying harmony based on the major scale. In bar 5 there is an F which is the b3 of the D major chord and in bar 9 there is G, which is the b3 of an E major chord. Listen for the "tough" quality of these notes. This type of single-note progression will sound good if it is doubled by bass guitar. Just add a drumbeat and away you go: instant blues power trio!

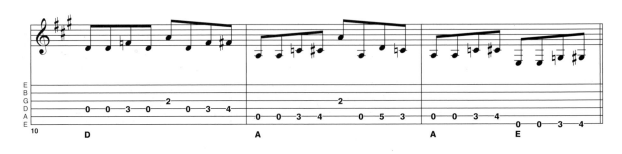

Exercise 1

blues rhythms

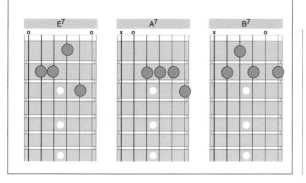

Exercise 2 is another single-note 12-bar, this time in E. Watch out for the syncopation across bars 1-2 and 3-4, 5-6, 7-8, and 10-11. Like Ex.1 this sounds good when doubled with a bass guitar. If you want to solo over either let the bass continue playing the notated progression.

Chord symbols are given in the exercise merely as guides to what you would be playing over. To get an early taste of chordal blues rhythm you can try playing through the exercise not with the straight chord forms below, but using the dominant sevenths as discussed in the introduction – basic examples of which are given left.

blues rhythms

Exercise 2

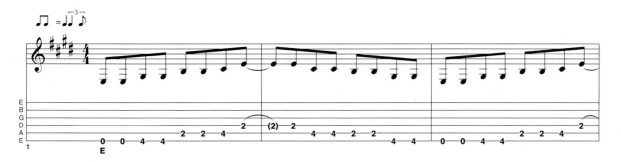

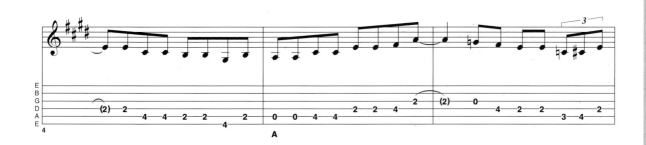

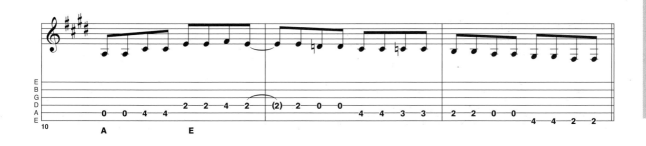

181

THE SHUFFLE

Here's the easy-to-play rhythm figure that you will find at the start of the Rock section too. The difference here in **exercise 3** is the shuffle rhythm. Watch out for the variation in bar 5, another in bar 6, and a third in bar 12. Also notice that in bar 10 the music does not return to D as it did in Ex.1. Staying on E for two bars is a perfectly valid alternative at this point in a 12-bar.

We need to be able to play this shuffle figure in any key, so **exercise 4** converts this 6-bar blues into a fretted figure with no open strings. If you find this a bit of a stretch drop your thumb well behind the neck. This will help your fretting hand open out. Ex.4 shows the "boogie" figure starting with the root note on the 5th string.

Exercise 5 shows the same idea in G major, over eight bars, starting on the 6th string. Starting on either the 5th or the 6th string enables you to play it in any major key, and to pitch it higher or lower. Notice the G figure in the final bars is an octave above the G figure at the start. Once you've got these down you'll be equipped to transpose this essential blues rhythm into any key required.

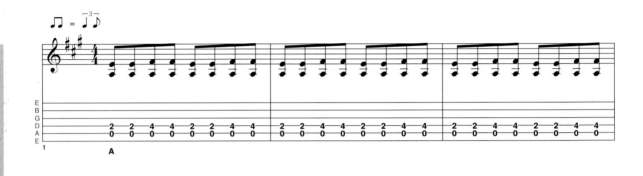

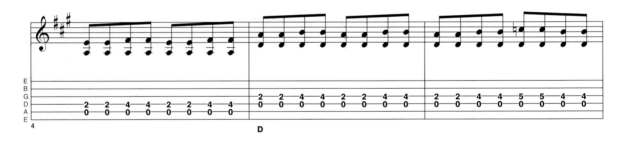

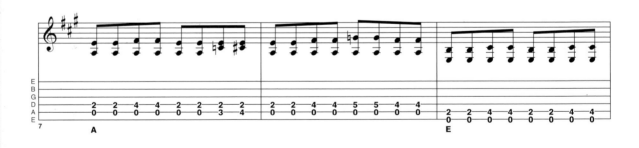

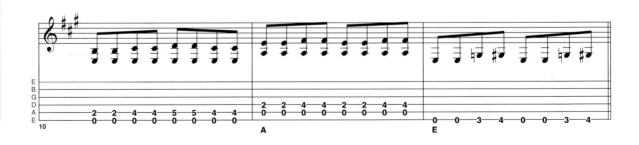

blues shuffle

Exercise 3

blues shuffle

Exercise 4

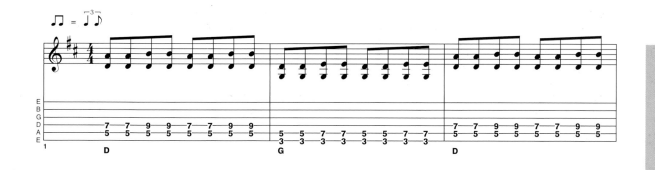

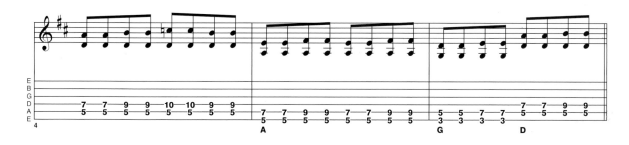

Exercise 5

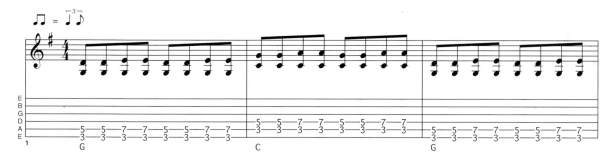

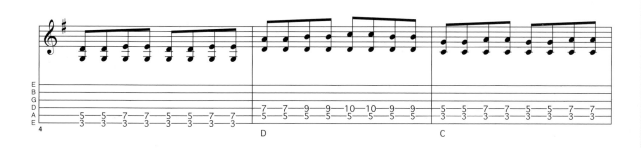

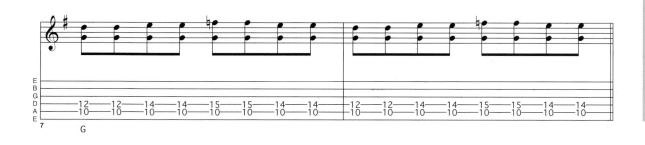

Muddy Waters, left, exhibits better than anyone the great vibe of southern blues played with an electrified Chicago-style energy.

THE IV-bIII-I CHANGE

In blues, movement between the first note of the scale and the b3 is very common. It occurs in vocal lines, in single-note riffs, in lead solos, and in chords. Muddy Waters, for example, features it heavily in songs like *Mannish Boy*, and Hendrix songs like *Voodoo Chile* and *Hear My Train A-Comin'* likewise.

Exercise 6 takes us through a set of variations on the E-A-G change, where G is the b3 blues note or chord. In bar 1 it occurs as single notes, in bar 2 as thirds, in bar 3 thirds with a different termination (in bar 4), in bar 4 as fifths, in bar 5 as triads, and in bar 6 as four-note chords. Each one has a different effect. You can combine these in any way you like during a blues number using the I-IV-bIII change.

We have already discussed a couple of times how the dominant seventh chord is central to blues. Before moving on, let's reinforce that further with another short exercise on its variations. In **exercise 7** D7 is D F# A C. In bar 1 F# and C are played together. By moving them down one fret we get part of G7 and by moving them up one fret part of A7!

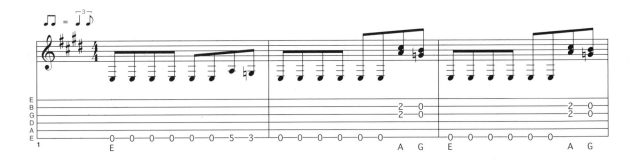

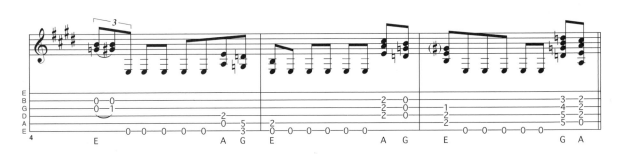

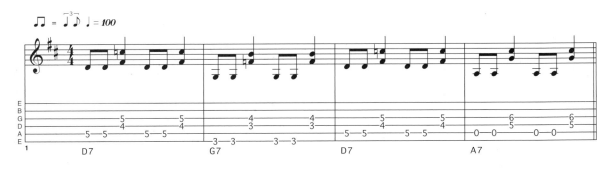

184

TURNAROUNDS

In many blues tunes a musical phrase signals that the 12-bar is reaching its end and is about to start again. It's a short phrase, often going down by steps, sometimes going up. This is the "turnaround." Turnarounds are mainly used in rhythm parts but if you are quick-witted enough you can put them into a lead solo at the end of each 12-bar. Here are eight typical turnarounds, seven in E and one in A.

Imagine that you have already played 10 bars of a 12-bar sequence. Each of these examples represent bars 11-12. When playing turnaround figures use alternate picking: strike the lower note of a triplet with a down-stroke and the upper note with an upstroke. In **exercise 8** the note moves down the 3rd string alone. **Exercise 9** displays a third moving down the 2nd and 3rd strings.

Exercise 10 is an equally effective turnaround, and is much like Ex.8 but with an ascending movement. **Exercise 11** is also like Ex.8 except notes are coming down in sixths on the 1st and 3rd strings. At this point, you should begin to see the subtle variation with which this seemingly simple figure can be played.

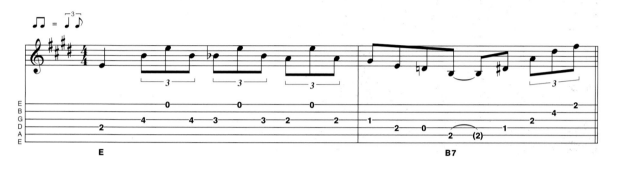

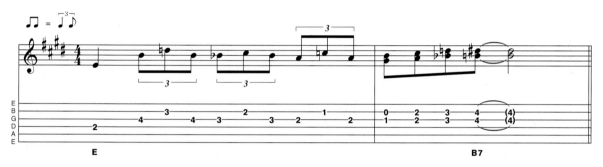

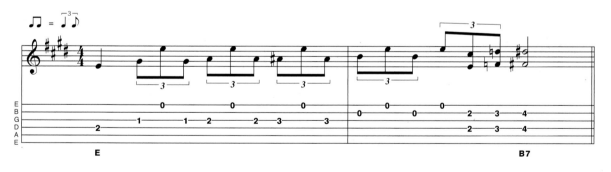

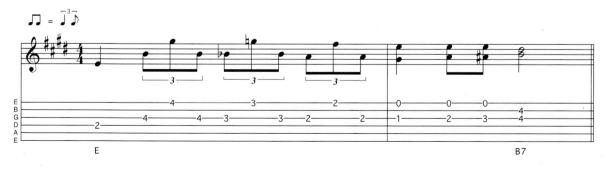

Exercise 12 continues our exploration of turnarounds with a pattern higher up the neck, which takes advantage of the open top E string.

Here are two patterns in descending sixths, one high, one low, grouped together in **exercise 13**. Use one or the other and then move to the expected B chord in the last bar. The example in **exercise 14**, moving upwards, is in the key of A major.

Turnarounds can also be made of a fast single-note run. **Exercise 15** is a typical one, with pull-offs, going down the E pentatonic minor scale in first position. It is similar to those heard throughout Stevie Ray Vaughan's *Rude Mood*, and is getting you into some fancier playing of this generally simple form. Check out more of Vaughan's playing for further examples of hot-rodded turnarounds.

blues turnarounds

Exercise 12

Exercise 13

Exercise 14

Exercise 15

BLUES LEAD GUITAR SCALES

Playing blues lead guitar competently is a matter of learning a small number of scales and scale patterns; mastering the art of bending and fretting-hand techniques like vibrato, hammering-on, pulling-off, and slides; and gradually finding out which notes sound stronger over any given 12-bar sequence.

THE PENTATONIC MINOR

This is the most important scale for blues (and rock). The pentatonic minor on E is E G A B D. Compare this with E major: E F# G# A B C# D#. Three notes – E A and B – are the same. Two – F# and C# – have been omitted, and two – G and D – are a semi-tone lower. When the pentatonic minor is played over a 12-bar in E major the ear picks up the G and D "blue" notes but

accepts this clash as the blues sound. Here are two open string patterns for this scale. The second has a small extension to it. Instead of playing the open B string, the same note is found at the fourth fret. This establishes the hand in third position. The pattern that follows for the last six notes of the bar is very important to blues.

THE E BLUES SCALE

The next two scale patterns repeat the previous two but add an extra note: Bb. Although this is not on the pentatonic minor, it is another blues note – the b5. This results in what is known as the blues scale. In a solo this b5 can be approached either by fretting it or by bending a note up to it; the effect is slightly different with each approach.

E pentatonic minor

E pentatonic minor with extension

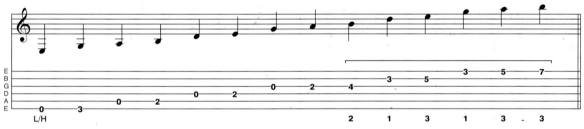

E blues scale

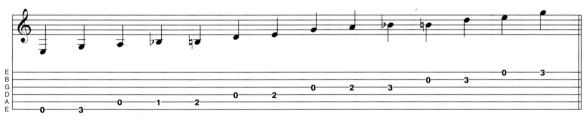

E blues scale with extension

Exercise 16 puts some of what we just learned into action, using the scale notes in first position. Notice that the open strings of the guitar – E A D G B E – have all the notes for E pentatonic minor. This is one reason why E is the most popular key for blues music on guitar. Each bar starts with a bass note. Let this ring throughout the bar, as it will give a "context" for the lead notes. Notice that bar 7 has the added flat note Bb, which you will begin to find familiar as another typical blues element.

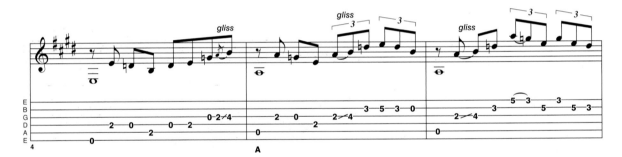

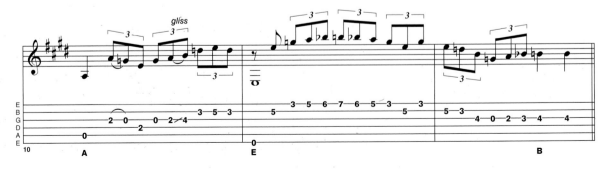

Exercise 16

blues lead scales

blues lead scales

Albert Collins, left, squeezes icepick-sharp licks from his Tele.

THE PENTATONIC MAJOR

There is also a pentatonic scale drawn directly from the major scale. E pentatonic major is E F# G# B C#. Compare this with E major: E F# G# A B C# D#. Two notes – A and D# – have been omitted, but otherwise the scales use the same notes. When the pentatonic major is played over a 12-bar in E major there are no clashing "blue" notes; the notes fit harmoniously with the chords. An important part of playing good blues lead is contrasting the pentatonic's minor and major forms to add greater interest to your solos. Here are two open string patterns for this scale. The second has a slight extension to it. Instead of playing the open B string, the same note is found at the fourth fret. This establishes the hand in third position.

THE E MAJOR BLUES SCALE

The third of these scale patterns adds an extra note: G. This is the b3 note we have already encountered. This results in what is known as the E major blues scale.

Blues scales

E pentatonic major

E pentatonic major with extension

E major blues scale with extension

There are countless derivatives and descendents of the blues – and many are worth checking out – but going straight to the source will provide inspiration every time. From left to right: Buddy Guy's *Feels Like Rain*, John Lee Hooker's *Mister Lucky*, and Albert King's *Born Under A Bad Sign*.

To further practise these scales, **exercise 17** is a 12-bar solo in E that uses the pentatonic major and major blues scales. The b3 is easy to see in the music because of the "natural" accidental added to G. Sometimes this G is fretted; sometimes, as in bar 10, it is reached with a bend. This break employs a "call-and-answer" technique, whereby the first five notes of bars 1-3, 5 and 6 make a phrase that is "answered" by whatever follows.

RULE OF THUMB FOR USING THE PENTATONICS

1. In a minor key 12-bar you can play the pentatonic minor but not the major. Note that the pentatonic minor will not sound as bluesy as it does in a major key because the notes are no longer flattened versions of notes on the key scale. Compare E natural minor – E F# G A B C D – with E pentatonic minor – E G A B D. All the latter's notes are in the former.

2. In a major key 12-bar you can play the pentatonic minor *and* the major. However, if the piece you are soloing over uses any of the three minor chords of the major key (in E = F#m G#m C#m) the pentatonic minor will clash with them in an undesirable manner. The easiest solution is to use the pentatonic major

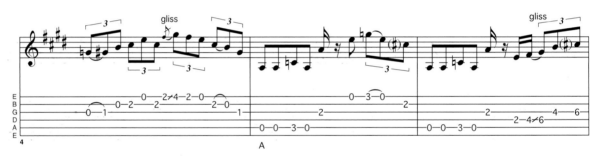

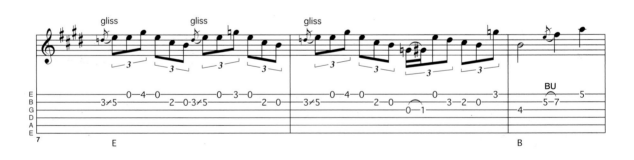

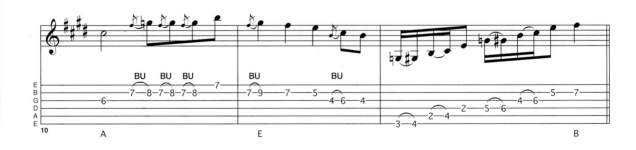

blues pentatonics

Exercise 17

wherever those minor chords occur.

3. Any pentatonic minor scale pattern moved down three frets will automatically "convert" to a pentatonic major on the same root note. Remember this and you will find it very easy to switch scales in a solo.

THE "EXTENSION" BOX

Let's just concentrate for a moment on the pattern found at the top of the previous set of scales. It is good discipline to restrict yourself to playing a 12-bar solo using only these five notes and nothing else, as in **exercise 18**. It will make you think more carefully about the way each note sounds against the harmony. By this method you get an appreciation of "chord-tones." (A similar approach to basic soloing will be taken in the *Jazz* chapter.) These are the notes on the scale that belong to each of the three chords in the 12-bar. Whenever you strike one of these over a chord to which it belongs, that note seems a strong fit. Notice in particular here in bars 1-4 the stress placed on E, the timing of the run that leads up to an A in bar 5 just as the chord changes to A, and in bar 9 the emphasised B.

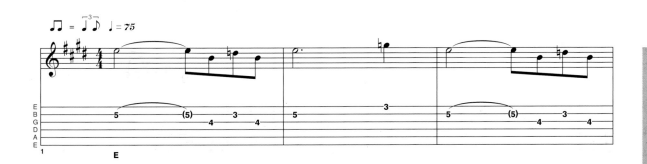

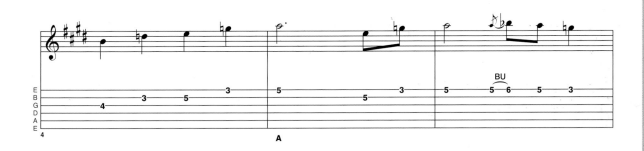

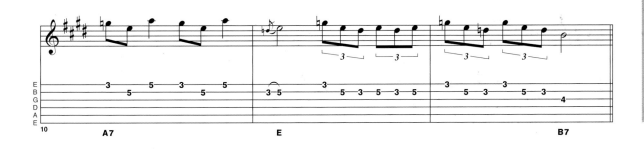

191

Exercise 19 presents the same extension box but with a few notes added – either by fretting or by bending – that lie within the box. We are still working with a small area of the fretboard to get the maximum musical possibilities out of it. This solo is full of blue notes.

Another important rule to remember is that every pentatonic minor scale shares its notes with the pentatonic major of the note a minor third above it (1½ tones). Thus E G A B D is the same notes as G pentatonic major: G A B D E. This means that over the chords of G, C and D we can put the extension box to a

Like Muddy Waters, Otis Rush (playing live and on record, opposite page) was born in Mississippi but moved to Chicago as a young man, where he became an authentic proponent of northern-style electric blues. A lefty, Rush plays his guitars "reverse-strung" – that is, strung as for a right-hander but flipped upside-down.

different harmonic use, as **exercise 20** shows. Notice the solo moves the patterns up for the C and D chords. (Also note here melodic elements which the pentatonic major blues shares with country guitar styles – from which it is mainly differentiated by the radically different rhythmic feel.)

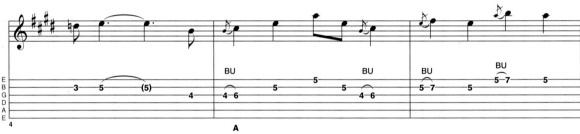

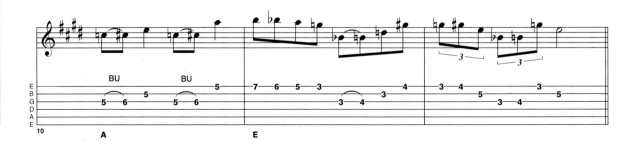

blues extension boxes

♩♩ = ♩³♪   ♩ = 88

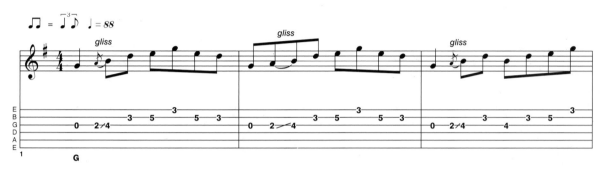

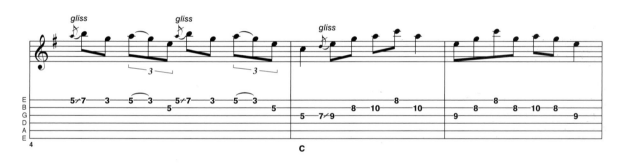

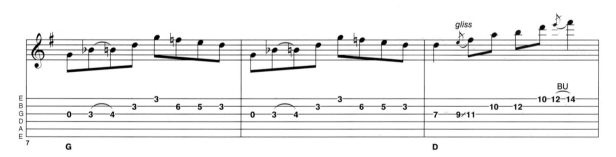

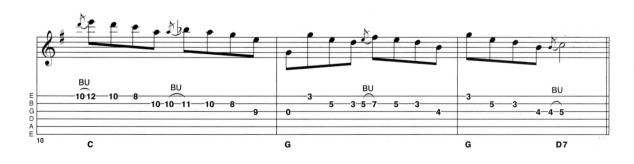

193

B.B. King's style has remained distinctive over a 50-year career.

Exercise 21 shows you how the pentatonic minor and major scales in G can be put in a sequence of answering phrases.
Exercise 22 is another "chord-tone" example, this time in G. The starting position is the extension box that lies at the top of a pentatonic minor scale that would start at the third fret – the scale pattern for which is given first. A variant has been added to this scale: instead of moving to D at the 7th fret, the D is played at the 3rd on the B string. This is the most common pentatonic pattern. With no open strings it is movable and gives the pentatonic minor of any key from G upwards. Move this up 12 frets to create a pentatonic minor one octave higher; or start it on the second note for a pentatonic major from that note. Here the second note is Bb, so starting there gives Bb pentatonic major.

blues pentatonic scales

Exercise 21

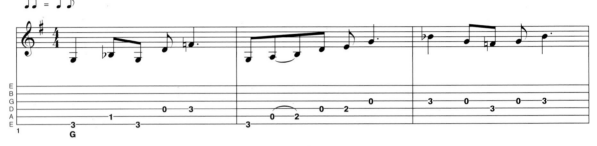

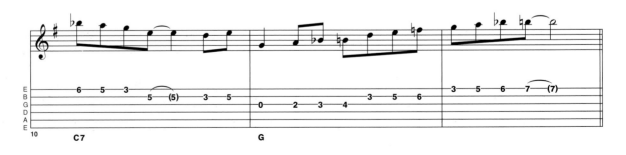

blues chord changes

Robert Cray, left, helped to revive mainstream electric blues in the mid-'80s with his blend of hot, stinging guitar lines and vocal performances that incorporated elements of soul and R&B with the traditional blues that lay at their core. Cray's skill as a songwriter has also helped to lift his recorded work well beyond that of the run-of-the-mill blueser, and he's an artist worth seeking out and studying on many fronts.

WHEN CHORDS CHANGE: BARS 2, 5 AND 9

Your lead playing will sound more confident if you are able to reflect in your choice of notes the moments in the 12-bar when there is a chord change. The first of these will be the change from chord I to chord IV in bar 5, or bar 2 if it is a "quick-change" blues. The five examples in **exercise 23** show how to navigate the I-IV change (here the change is from A to D).

A similar moment occurs in most 12-bars at bar 9 where chord V appears. In the key of A this is an E chord. Many players find that continuing to solo over the pentatonic minor at this point does not sound as effective as elsewhere in the 12-bar. **Exercise 24** shows eight ways of making the transition. Play bar 1 in each case, followed by any one of the E bars.

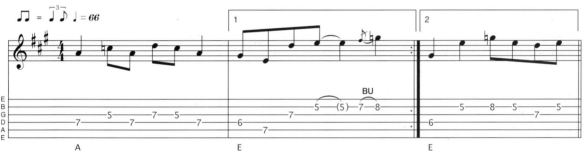

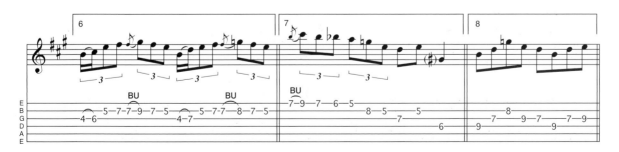

INTERVALS AND QUARTER BENDS

String bending is a significant part of blues lead playing. The usual bends are up a half or a whole tone, though some players go higher. It is important to be able to accurately bend either a semitone or tone because in practice this can mean the difference between playing a C against an A chord (the b3) or a C# (the normal third in A). Remember the golden rule of bending: always support the finger that is bending by putting the other fingers down, where possible, on the same string and pushing with two or three. Bends are almost never done with the fourth finger. **Exercise 25** is good for practising your bends. Play the fretted note first, then try to bend to the same pitch. Use your third finger to do the bend, with fingers one and two behind it on the same string. Pushing with all three gives more control. Be careful with the two-tone bend – strings can break!

Blues guitar also employs a bend actually smaller than a semitone: the quarter-tone bend. It amounts to little more than a "smudging" of pitch but it can be effective. Try it on the thirds that crop up throughout **exercise 26**. Another example of some typical blues double-stops is shown in **exercise 27**. They are mostly thirds, but there are sixths in bar 4.

MINOR KEY BLUES

Blues music is also found in the minor key. The first of two minor blues examples, **exercise 28** is in an elongated form and 6/8 time, where there are two beats in each bar and each beat divides into three. Notice that the half bend in bar 1 becomes a full bend in bar 5. Although some of the phrases are pentatonic minor (A C D E G), there are also bars like 8 where the A natural minor scale (A B C D E F G) is used.

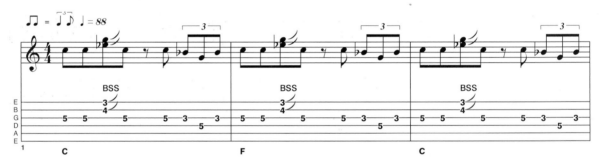

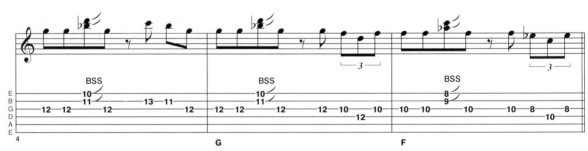

blues bends

Exercise 25

Exercise 26

Exercise 27

minor key blues

Exercise 28

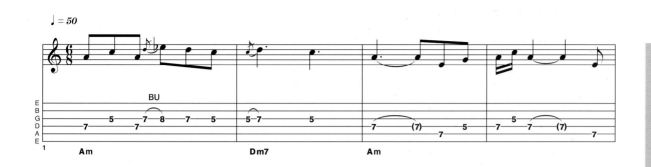

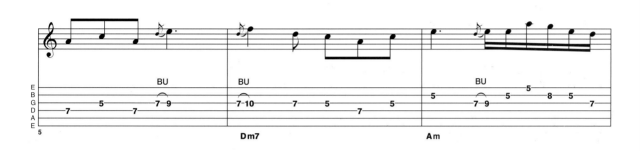

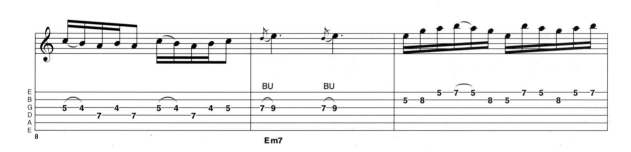

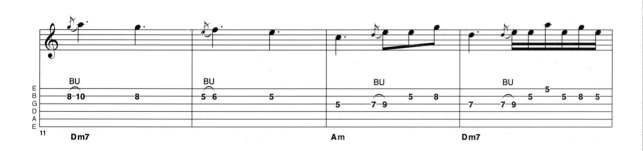

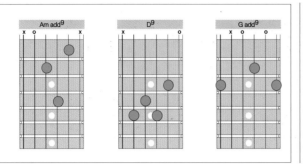

Exercise 29 is an example of a minor key blues progression that has more advanced harmony. For the first four bars you play chord tones that give the full flavour of the chords. Bars 5-8 repeat the progression but shift to a lead solo. As with the previous exercise, both the pentatonic and the natural minor scales are used. The chords backing this example are somewhat more complex than we have seen so far, so some suggestions are given, left.

MORE BLUES RHYTHM

A traditional rhythm, **exercise 30** is in the style of an acoustic blues and is best played with fingers or fingers and a pick.

minor key blues

Exercise 29

200

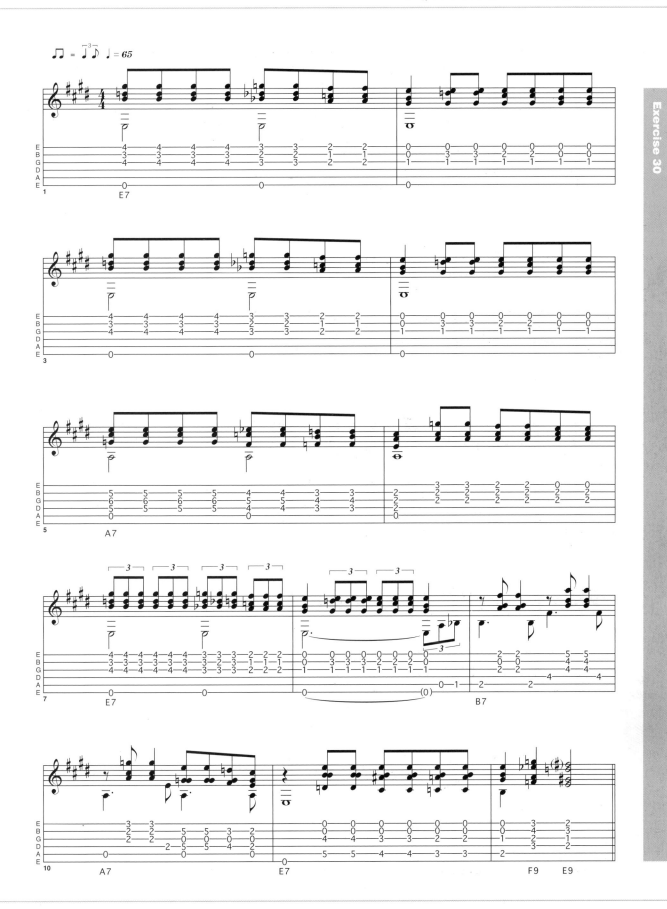

More appropriate as an electric blues, **exercise 31** is a funky blues style with rhythm chord and single note fills. Many of the chord shapes require you to damp the 5th string with your fretting hand thumb. It's a different sort of rhythmic feel than we have yet encountered: now that you've developed a good blues vocabulary, record a few bars to practise soloing over it.

CHORD BOXES

Here are a number of movable chord types that are useful in blues playing. Learn them in different positions relative to the root note (the I) given and, when you play a 12-bar, try occasionally substituting these for the straight majors you would otherwise play.

When playing with a band or a bass guitar it is not always necessary to play full chords. The **dominant 7** triads are useful for this purpose and for putting into solos for a rhythmic effect. Notice that some of them are missing a root note, which will often be played by the bassist anyway.

The **diminished 7** chord is an oddity – because any of its notes can be treated as the root! The **minor 7b5** is a colorful variation on the usual minor 7. The b5 is the same note you would be playing on the blues scale for that key.

The **7#9** (now popularly known as the "Hendrix chord") gives real edge; the **7b9** is more gloomy and resigned.

Ninths and **thirteenths** become increasingly difficult to finger on the guitar so they are often found in incomplete forms. They will substitute for the dominant 7.

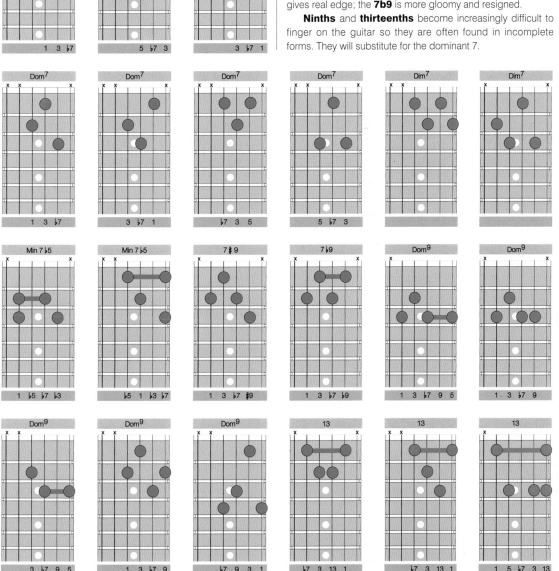

4

PLAYING
COUNTRY

Nashville, Tennessee, is one of the world's most respected centers of excellence when it comes to making records, and country music today has come along way from its roots as a form that was disparagingly called "hillbilly" by its detractors. The teams of session players who work in the studios of "Music City" are second to none and the guitarists, especially, are considered by discerning fans and fellow musicians alike to be among the hottest pickers on the planet. Yet most good country guitar still contains a healthy dose of rootsy twang, and the current genre – for the player – combines feel, attitude and vibe with technical demands that can rival those of the highest forms of guitar music. ● LEE HODGSON

Country lead guitar playing has its roots in Hawaiian (steel) guitar music, which co-existed alongside equally influential early blues and, to an extent perhaps, jazz (the incredible Belgian Gypsy guitarist Django Reinhardt's work throughout the late '30s and early '40s was clearly an influence on players as diverse as Chet Atkins, Les Paul and one of today's hottest guitarists, ex-Desert Rose Band member and current Hellecaster, John Jorgenson). But back to the lap steel guitar for a moment... It's significant that the instrument had legs fitted and ultimately pedals too – evolving into the pedal steel guitar – and, come the late '60s, its intriguing, passion-filled sounds would be mimicked by guitar virtuoso Clarence White and countless followers, bringing and essential new element of string bending into country guitar. Meanwhile, Chet Atkins and/or Jerry Reed (who both favoured a thumbpick, by the way) undoubtedly influenced modern day guitarists such as Steuart Smith and Brent Mason, whilst James Burton – who worked with, amongst others, Ricky Nelson, Elvis Presley, Merle Haggard and Emmylou Harris – was, along with country-jazzer Jimmy Bryant, a big influence on the phenomenal Albert Lee.

The development of country rhythm guitar, on the other hand, can be traced back to '20s hillbilly music and, in particular, the acoustic guitar playing of Maybelle Carter, whose thumb-plucked bass lines and to-and-fro finger strumming style was somewhat akin to the frailing of banjo players – which, interestingly, would be adopted in essence some forty or so years later by Beatle Paul McCartney (witness his technique on *Blackbird*). Consider too, if you will, the blues players of Maybelle Carter's era, such as the legendary Robert Johnson, Charley Patton and Blind Lemon Jefferson, and you might well ask yourself the question: where does rhythm

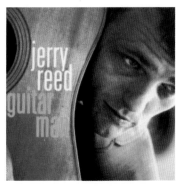

guitar end and lead guitar begin? Whatever, country guitar progressed when Kentucky guitarists, Mose Rager and Ike Everly pioneered that alternating bass and melody style, which Merle Travis continued and popularised so much in the '50s that a trademark style was born: Travis Picking. And, of course, in the '60s and beyond, the technique would be taken to unimagined heights by Chet Atkins (a name that keeps popping up!).

Finally, it's important to realise that the rock sounds of the '70s and the pop sounds of the '60s through the '90s have jointly impacted on modern country music. Meanwhile, pure country is alive and well.

This chapter aims to demystify the idiosyncrasies of country guitar playing by looking at the various approaches to both lead and rhythm guitar. Regarding solo and fill ideas, you'll be shown various classic and modern examples in the styles of some of the greats, including James Burton, Albert Lee, Jerry Donahue, Brent Mason and Dann Huff. And rhythm guitar-wise, you'll be guided through some relatively easy strumming in classic country style – including bluegrass and ballads – before tackling the alternating-bass style of Merle Travis, as well as the amazing finger style techniques of Chet Atkins and Jerry Reed.

Material-wise, after beginning with a few useful scale patterns (which will include the major pentatonic scale and the complete major scale – brief theory lesson on the mixolydian mode included!), you'll progress through practical exercises which introduce double stops (thirds and sixths) and essential vocabulary in the form of licks and runs. Plus, there are some tasty chords to learn along the way. And to improve your playing ability there are various technical exercises involving hybrid picking patterns, cross-picking, finger style/fingerpicking and so-called chicken pickin'.

lead scales

COUNTRY LEAD SCALES

The A scale pentatonic pattern outlined in **diagram 1** on the opposite page might look familiar. Indeed, the five "shape boxes" (as labeled alongside the fingerboard diagram) are essentially similar, if not identical, to what rock and blues guitarists may know as minor pentatonic scale patterns. Briefly, the root note for the "minor thing" would be a minor third – three frets – below that of the "major thing." Put another way, our A major pentatonic scale here has the same notes as F#m pentatonic. Country tunes, however, often work in the major side of things, so emphasise and resolve on the brown root notes.

After learning the five individual patterns you should ultimately try to see things in terms of the whole area of the fingerboard. Accordingly, practise weaving back and forth and across, through the complete pattern – which is essentially how Albert Lee works (many of his lines are based on major pentatonic scale patterns).

Next, against a slow, repeating A-D-A-D chord progression, practise shifting licks between the scale pattern boxes. Hint: D and A are a 4th (five semitones) apart so in order to match D major, simply shift any of the material seen here up five frets (or down seven frets). Hey, even professionals often negotiate chord changes by merely regurgitating a pre-learned lick, phrase or pattern elsewhere on the fingerboard. Hey – if it works, use it!

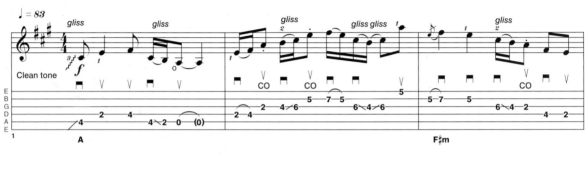

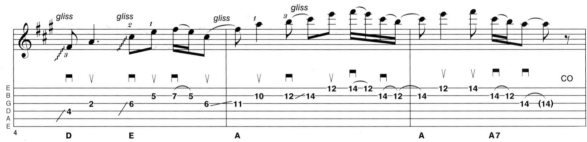

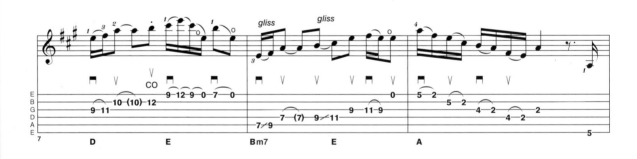

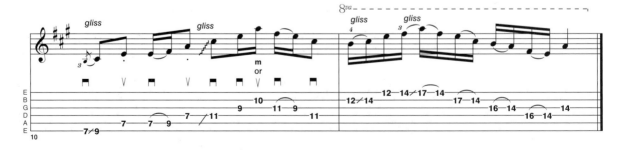

206

DIAGRAM 1: THE A MAJOR PENTATONIC SCALE

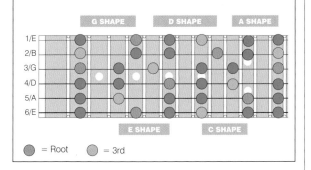

G SHAPE		D SHAPE		A SHAPE

1/E
2/B
3/G
4/D
5/A
6/E

E SHAPE		C SHAPE

● = Root   ○ = 3rd

Notes in the A major pentatonic scale

A	B	C♯	E	F♯
1	2	3	5	6

MAJOR PENTATONIC SCALE LICKS AND RUNS

You might wish to learn the individual licks in **exercise 1** at your leisure before seeing how the various fragments all fit together. Realise that only the notes of the A major Pentatonic scale are used throughout, despite there being chord changes. Analysis will reveal, for example, that what is the sixth of A is also the third of D. Remember though, country players often match the scale to the chord, e.g. A major pentatonic scale for A, D major pentatonic scale for D, and maybe E mixolydian mode for E – more on which later!

Picking-wise, you check out the picking suggestions shown in between the notation and TAB – it's pretty much strict alternate picking throughout, but notice that sometimes the up/off beat is a down stroke (in accordance with 1/16th note picking) while occasionally it's an up stroke, which feels natural for 1/8th note grooves. Also observe the liberal use of slides plus a few hammer ons and pull offs, which serve to keep it all flowing.

Exercise 2 introduces some basic stringbending licks. Note the following moves performed as bends: 2nd-3rd scale step (B-C#), 3rd-4th (C#-D), 5th-6th (E-F#) and 7th-Octave (G#-A) – which all relates to the I chord (A), although the notes' function may alter once the accompaniment changes e.g. C#-D becomes 6th-b7th when played against E. Observe the suggested fingerings, too.

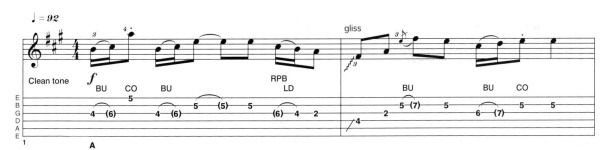

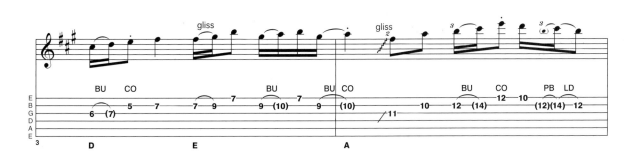

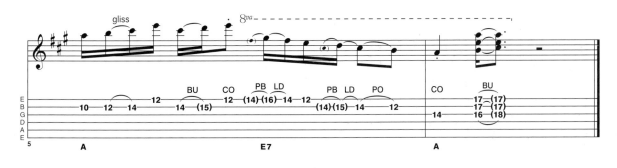

Exercise 2a will help develop your advanced bending skills. Fingerings are important here, so follow the suggestions given.

From the '50s on the sound of the pedal-steel guitar became ever more predominant in country music, so much so that standard 6-string guitarists were hankering to emulate it, but were struggling with the heavy string gauges in use at the time. It was teenage whiz James Burton who sparked a guitar-playing revolution when he fitted some light gauge banjo strings to his old red Fender Telecaster; soon easy string bending was within every guitarist's grasp.

In the '60s, Clarence White took things further when he and fellow Byrds bandmate, drummer Gene Parsons, had the insight to develop a retrofit system which "bends" (pulls, actually) the second or B string – usually on a Tele – up by a tone via a system of springs and levers activated by tugging on the strap button: *voila*, the Parsons-White "B-bender."

By the early '70s, The Eagles were featuring pseudo-pedal steel licks too, courtesy of the same B-bender, on tracks like *Peaceful, Easy Feeling*, while even Jimmy Page joined in the fun with future rock legends Led Zeppelin. It was perhaps Arlen Roth who, in the '80s especially, harnessed that raw, edgy Tele sound and style and brought it to the attention of more players. More recently, the legendary James Burton has offered praise to the undisputed stringbending king nowadays, Jerry Donahue.

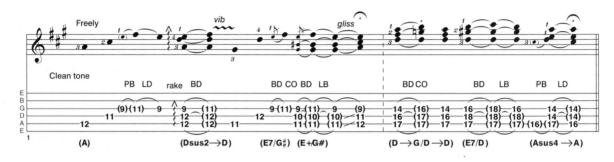

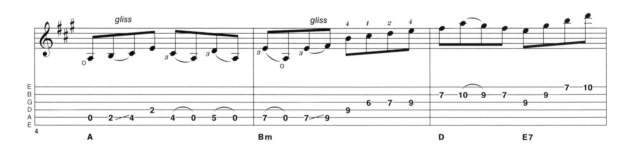

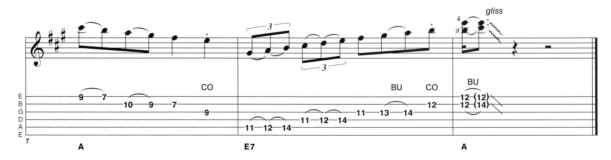

Exercise 2b

Exercise 3

string bending

DIAGRAM 2: THE A MAJOR SCALE

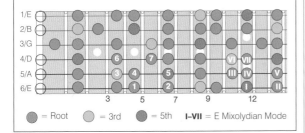

● = Root   ○ = 3rd   ● = 5th   **I–VII** = E Mixolydian Mode

THE A MAJOR SCALE

There may seem to be a lot of dots on **diagram 2** above – and there are, because it offers the full A major scale, from open strings at the nut right up to the 14th fret.

Examine at the area of the fingerboard where the scale steps are shown as arabic numbers (1-7), which correspond to the seven degrees of the major scale and hence, chords built from those degrees (I, II, III, IV, V, VI, and VII). This is the basis of the so-called "Nashville Numbers System." So, in the key of A major you might expect to find some or all of the following chords: A (I), Bm (IIm), C#m (IIIm), D (IV), E (V), F#m(VI), while the VII chord, which is rarely heard in country music, would be diminished. Some or all of these chords may appear as seventh extensions: Imaj7, IIm7, IIIm7, IVmaj7, Vdom7, VIm7 (... and VIIm7b5 aka "half diminished"). See if you can pick out some shapes of chords from within the overall scale pattern – they're all there!

Now take a look at the "Dominant Chord Tones" box (above-right). The line below the first portion of the scale highlights the relationship between the "one" (root), third and fifth of the scale as the dominant chord tones. As you will have learned elsewhere

The Dominant Chord Tones Plus Extension										
				1	2	3	4	5	6	b7
A	B	C	D	E	F#	G#	A	B	C#	D
1	2	3	4	5	6	7	8	9	10	11

(the *Jazz*, *Blues* and *Metal* chapters in particular highlight this), there's more within each major scale than simply that scale itself.

While the A major scale runs from A to A (and so-on from octave to octave right up the neck) on the neck diagram and as outlined in the explanatory box, we can also construct other modes by playing the notes of A major but starting from different degrees of the scale. One mode that is occasionally useful in country playing is E Mixolydian, found by playing from E to E in the A major scale (highlighted by the roman numerals in Diag.1). E Mixolydian provides a useful alternative for soloing over the V – that is, the E chord – of songs in A major. **Exercise 3** offers some A major licks and phrases to further test your new skills.

String-bender's central: The Byrds with Clarence White (left) and sometime-Hellecaster Jerry Donahue... with a few Teles.

CHORD VOCABULARY

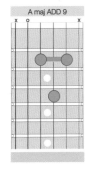
A maj ADD 9

A maj ADD 9

D sus 2

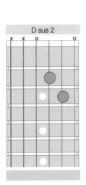
D sus 2

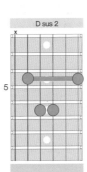
Bm7

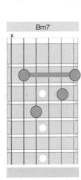
Bm7

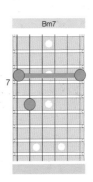

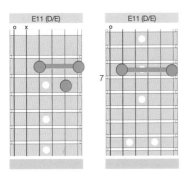
E11 (D/E)

E11 (D/E)

These chords would most likely be heard in a song in the key of A major, e.g. Aadd9 equals the I chord ("one"), Dsus2 is the IV, Bm7 is the IIm ("minor two"), E11 is the V11. Try playing them in various orders: I, IV, II, V; IV, II, V, I; II, V, I, IV... Keep rearranging them, sometimes omitting one or two chords, until you discover a progression that you like – hey, you're a composer!

LICKS IN THIRDS AND SIXTHS

In addition to single-note soloing and some complex bending, a great deal of country lead playing is executed in double-stops, two notes played together. This is done primarily in scales made up of pairs of thirds or pairs of sixths ascending and descending the major scale – that is, one note ascending from root to octave, paired by a second ascending the same scale, but starting from a third or a sixth away. The sound of this is likely to be instantly familiar to you: thirds have a slightly south-of-the-border flavor to them, while sixths ring of classic twang. Both are essential to your mastery of country lead playing.

The neck diagrams on the opposite page give you these scales in thirds and sixths respectively, all in the A major scale. Before moving on to Ex.4 below, spend some time with these diagrams, playing them up and down the neck on all suggested string groupings (five groups of adjacent strings for thirds, four groups of next-but-one pairs for sixths). It takes some practise to memorize them on all string pairings (and, beyond that, in all keys), but familiarize yourself with a couple different groupings before moving on, and you'll soon get the feel for them and learn to recognize their sound.

You should constantly monitor what sounds "resolved" and what doesn't; try to remember – in physical and sonic terms – the juxtaposition of where you are at any given point relative to either the "home base" for the root note or secondary points of resolution, as well as the "homes" for the third and fifth chords of your scale. As for memorizing the physical aspects of these scales, you'll soon note there are only three "shapes" for your fingers to make as you move up and down the neck: "straight" (both strings fingered at the same fret), "diagonal" (the lower string fingered a fret higher), and "stretch" (lower string fingered two frets higher). Simpler still, some pairings require only two shapes. In time, both sound and feel should become intuitive.

Exercise 4 lays out an extended run in thirds, keeping the double-stops to the highest two pairs of strings, with single-note licks linking them. Follow the recommended bends and glisses (slides) to start with, and use the chord accompaniment to check how the lead runs sound against the changes. Be aware of the two-string pre-bend toward the end of bar 2, and notice the brief yet effective use of pull-offs to the open high E string in bar 7.

Like all exercises in this chapter, this sequence merely represents one particular permutation and the possibilities are almost endless! It might be a good idea, therefore, to noodle around further for a while, stretch out the raw material that this exercise and the neck diagrams provide, and take the opportunity to develop your improvising skills.

210

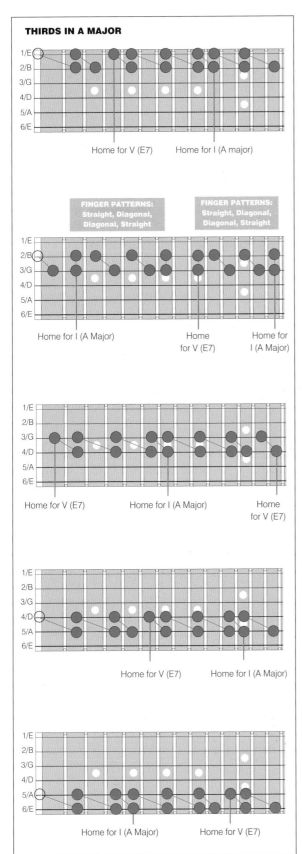

THIRDS IN A MAJOR

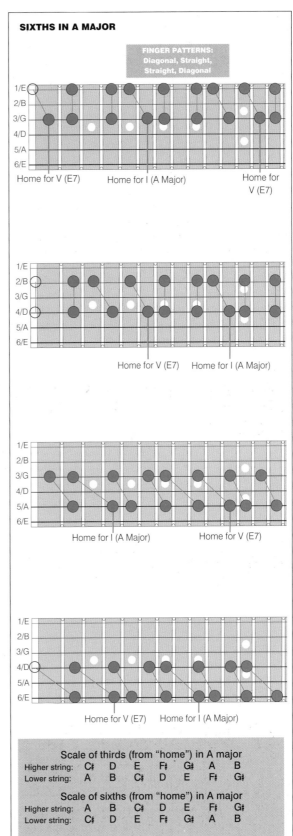

SIXTHS IN A MAJOR

Taking us into a full-length run in sixths, **exercise 5** comprises chords that are not all from the key of A major. There are three non-diatonic chords – A7 (I7), Dm (IVm) and B7 (II7) – along with the more unusual Dmadd9, A/C# and E7/G# (the diagrams for the latter three are given opposite to help ease the way). See if you can find ways of matching these chords using the sixths shapes already outlined. Incidentally, you might find of particular interest the fact that all this A stuff sounds great for E7 (V7), too; as you play bars 9 through 12 you'll be playing Mixolydian sixths, whether you know it or not!

Note that although two of the chords shown opposite appear to be "slash chords," they are in fact just first inversions (that is, the third is in the bass). A true slash chord would be a triad over a note that isn't a chord tone, such as a Bb/E (as used for the dramatic penultimate chord in Garth Brooks' live version of *Friends In Low Places* – play such a chord only if you can afford to bribe the jazz police!).

Once you've got the hang of Ex.5 as written, try improvising to the same chord changes using sixths in A major in different positions taken from the neck diagrams on the previous page. Your ear should guide you toward certain sounds and away from others. You'll hit some sticking points with the non-diatonic chords mentioned above, but try it out and see how you do.

George Strait, above, offers pure country while banging out rhythm on the frontman's weapon of choice: the acoustic guitar.

Exercise 5

sixths

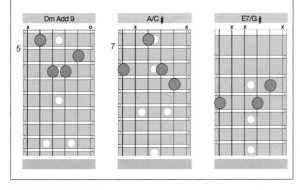

Brooks & Dunn (above-left) lean decidedly toward the pop-rock side of Nashville country, while Dann Huff's playing covers everything from crunchy rhythm to lightening-fast twangy riffs, much of which is heard in his work on Clint Black's *No Time To Kill*.

RHYTHM GUITAR

Turning our attention to rhythm guitar for a change, let's begin with the classic bluegrass-style strumming pattern in **exercise 6** (preferably played on an acoustic guitar). You could strum the full chord, but here it's a "bass-chord, bass-chord" approach. Observe the occasional fills – which shouldn't be overdone.

Exercise 7 ditches the pick for a while; try fingerpicking throughout the piece, being aware of the few "anticipated" moments where all or some of the upcoming chord appears early, adding momentum – which is effectively syncopation.

Steel String Acoustic Guitar

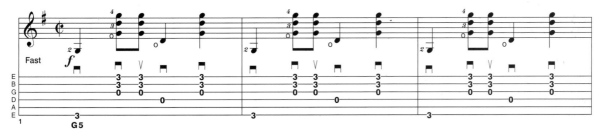

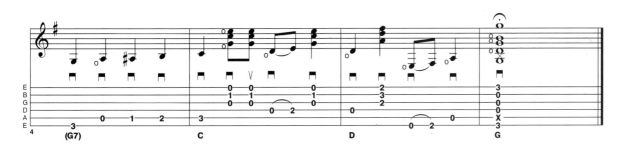

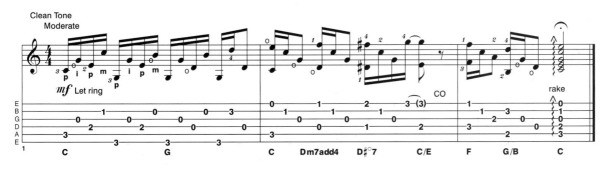

213

For **exercise 8** use a pick again, and aim to cleanly articulate the notes of the chords. It's a slow ballad that will give you some cross-picking practise. This isn't quite arpeggiating *per se*. Notice the sophisticated sounds which are on offer. The "rakes" aren't rock-style sweeping like you encounter in the *Metal* chapter; rather, they're controlled glide strokes (most often in a downward direction). Top session guitarist Dann Huff would probably add vibrato to certain chords (especially sus 2 types).

Speaking of Dann Huff, he would probably dial up a mildly dirty tone on his amp and chug away on something like **exercise 9**, which takes us to the key of D major. If you think the rakes are too gratuitous, stab at the chords more accurately. Ah, there's a real slash chord in bar 4: G/A, which is a "chord synonym" of

A11 – they're similar or identical sounds but spelled differently. (Note: the root note often tends to be perceived as being the bass note, as shown to the right of the slash.)

SOLOING

It's about time we put all the lessons into practise in the form of a complete solo, for which **exercise 10** should do nicely. Try to acknowledge the following ingredients: the A major pentatonic or A major scale (be especially on the lookout for E Mixolydian sounds over E7), stringbending, thirds and sixths, while checking out a little "chicken picking" plus the odd pinched harmonic. If you're unfamiliar with the latter, skip ahead a page for some clues. Otherwise, see how you get along with it for now.

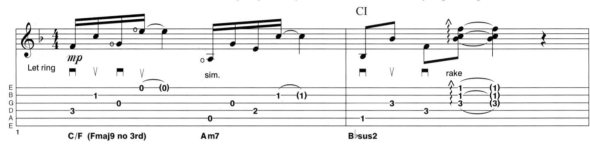

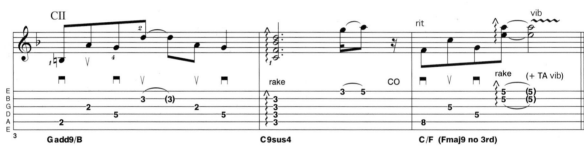

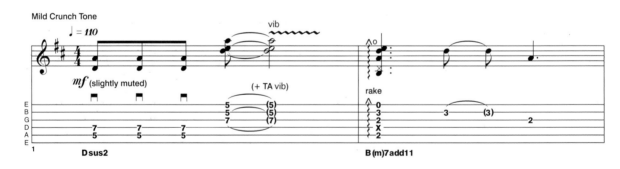

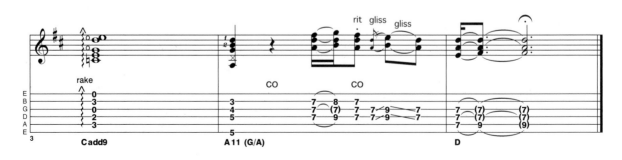

Exercise 8

Exercise 9

rhythm

214

CHICKEN PICKING AND PINCHED HARMONICS

"Chicken picking" derives its name from the sounds produced when you pluck percussively with your index finger ("popping" the string, some would call it) whilst damping quite a lot as you go. Furthermore, digging in aggressively and with just the tip of the plectrum should yield a so-called "pinched harmonic." Technically speaking, the flesh at the side of your thumb or the edge of a fingertip makes contact with the string fractionally after the pick strikes, and in doing so a harmonic is produced. Chicken picking and pinched harmonics may appear individually or one after the other, but they're often combined – and together or individually they provide another texture of country playing. The wild Telecaster squeals of Roy Buchanan (left) are a prime example of the style, and no doubt influenced many guitarists, including Jeff Beck, Danny Gatton and Arlen Roth.

Exercise 11 gets us into "Travis picking." Merle Travis was highly influential in the '50s – he even influenced Chet Atkins. Incredibly, he used a thumbpick plus index finger only! (Most thumbpickers, including Chet Atkins, Steuart Smith, Brent Mason, and Jerry Donahue, use at least the middle finger and commonly the third finger as well for plucking duties.)

If this style is totally new to you then take it slowly – and don't think about this kind of playing too much, just develop your motor skills while keeping that alternating bass pattern steady. Speaking of which, the bass notes should be palm damped (muted) for an authentic sound; just lean gently but firmly on the wound strings near the bridge/saddles. It can take some work to get into the swing of Travis picking, but once you've got it it's an effective and impressive tool, and can sound great in the right circumstances.

It's also important to get to grips with closed positions for your Travis picking – that is, barre chords. **Exercise 12** is in the key of E major but starts on the V chord of E, B7. Check out the rest

picking styles

Exercise 11

Exercise 12

216

of the chord shapes carefully because the fingerings and voicings may be unfamiliar to you, or at least unexpected. It should get your thumb and fingers working well together after a couple passes.

Exercise 13 introduces "hybrid picking," which involves using a pick plus fingers to grab chords or articulate patterns cleanly and relatively easily. Travis picking is itself a form of hybrid picking. Interestingly, Albert Lee and Danny Gatton have both featured the use of their pinky whilst plucking, which is very uncommon (see the explanation of right-hand finger use for Ex.11, too).

Turning our attention to the fretting fingerings, these may be atypical as well. It's a good idea to take it slower than suggested at first, and break down the individual sections to work out any tougher licks before linking them all together. Once you've got it all together you'll be into some pretty accomplished country guitar playing.

This workout should remind you of several great pickers: Chet, Albert, Danny Gatton, Brent Mason and maybe a hint of Dann Huff at the very end. Good luck – and remember: if you don't pick it, it won't get better!

From the frenetic picking of Roy Buchanan to the classy, refined fingerstyle of Chet Atkins, there's a lot to soak up in your quest to become a well-rounded country player – and all of it makes great listening.

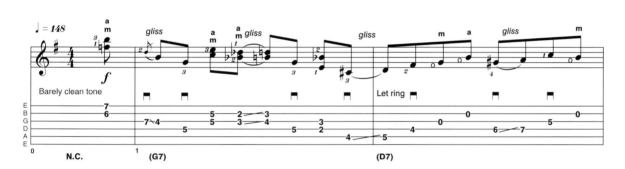

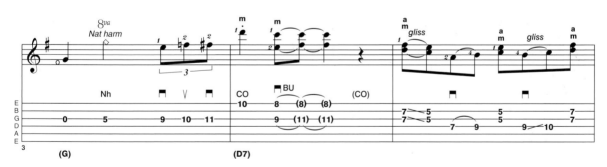

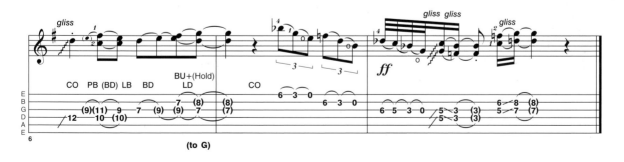

217

Exercise 14

advanced soloing

One of the most revered guitarists of all time, Chet Atkins (above) has long been respected by musicians of all genres. A performer of superlative taste and technique, his work is an abiding influence on country players.

Exercise 14 is entitled *Chetude*, and is a piece by the author respectfully dedicated to Chet Atkins. Chet always acknowledged the influence of the incredible Lenny Breau, especially when it comes to what Chet used to call "false" harmonics. Technically speaking, an artificial harmonic is the result of fretting a note – so it's not "natural," as is a harmonic produced by damping a string lightly over the twelfth, fifth or seventh frets, for example.

Here's how you play artificial harmonics: fret a note, then touch your index finger gently onto the point an octave (twelve frets) beyond it, and pluck it using your thumb(pick) (many people, including the author, just use a flat pick) whilst possibly also plucking a normally fretted/plucked string – which is typically two or three strings away – using your third finger. This gentle damping of a note an octave away from where it is fretted will produce a soft harmonic, through the same process that gives you open-string harmonics at the twelfth fret. The designations "T" and "Ah" in Ex.14 tell you where to perform these – with a number in parentheses telling you where to damp the string.

One of Chet's friends and collaborators, Tommy Emmanuel, can perform this technique at lightning speed, and it's amazing to hear! There's quite a lot of technically challenging stuff on offer here, so practise slowly and carefully, then work up to speed.

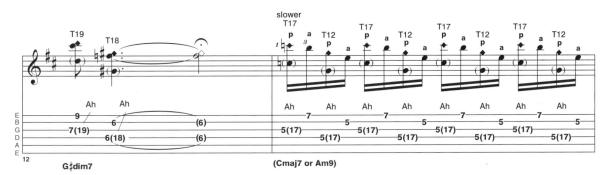

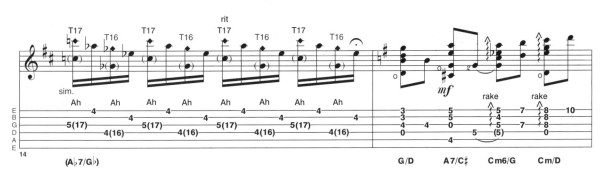

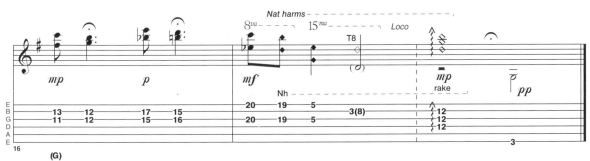

219

PLAYING
ROCK 'N' ROLL

THE CAPITOL TOWER,
HOLLYWOOD

Like a glorious laboratory accident, in the 1950s musical styles fused to form some of the greatest popular music of the 20th century. Rock'n'roll was an amalgam of country swing, big band jive and short crafted songs played with the energy of the Blues and R&B, and the early stars of rock'n'roll came from both country music and rhythm and blues. Though it was played in various related forms before it had a name, the style emerged as a recognisable genre around 1954; the term "Rock and Roll" was said to have come from the U.S. disc jockey Alan Freed, who risked his career to broadcast the music to the youth of America, though the term can also be heard in the sexual innuendoes of some early blues lyrics. ● **MAX MILLIGAN**

Rock'n'roll was enjoyed by both black and white audiences and gained popularity and notoriety as a rather aggressive form of music, disliked by parents and loved by the kids. It was the ultimate symbol of youthful rebellion, the sound of a new "teenage" generation, the embodiment of a cultural revolution in music and fashion. From the opening bars of *Hound Dog* by Elvis Presley or *Rock Around The Clock* by Bill Haley and His Comets, you can't fail to hear the energy captured from a unique period of American musical history.

We have already covered rock'n'roll guitar playing to some extent in the comprehensive *Rock And Pop* section, but as this '50s genre continues to be played today as a style unto itself, it's worth another brief but concentrated look. For many guitarists this style of playing is something from a long-gone era, but the legacy of this revolutionary age can be heard in popular music today. For those who remember the excitement of those early recordings the songs of that time have become the classics of the golden era. As with all forms of music, just knowing the chords and scales is not the whole story. To recreate the sound and feel of rock'n'roll it's important to listen to some of the-all time great players in action and check out their trademark sounds. You are what you listen to… and practice. Rock'n'roll is another musical language and we need to travel to that country to hear its cadence.

One name in particular stands out as the godfather of rock and roll guitar, Chuck Berry. Brandishing all the right ingredients – a Gibson ES-350T, slick suits, the duck walk, and stories of teenage love and hot cars – he almost single-handedly wrote the book on rock'n'roll guitar.

Born October 18th, 1926 in a cottage at 2520 Goode Avenue in St Louis, Missouri, Chuck Berry rose through the dance halls and bars to become one of the most prolific songwriters and innovators of rock'n'roll guitar, his driving double-stop lead intros being a particularly recognisable trademark. After years of being "ripped off" in publishing deals he studied the business and became his own boss. Berry's essential

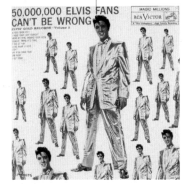

listening includes *Maybellene, Johnny B. Goode, Roll Over Beethoven, Memphis, Sweet Little Sixteen* and *No Particular Place To Go*.

Having started out playing country music, Eddie Cochran ventured into rock'n'roll in 1956. In the next three years he was to record some of the great rock'n'roll classics – playing a Gretsch 6120 with a Gibson single coil P90 in the neck position. Listen particularly to *Sittin' In The Balcony* for its cool tape echo frenzy and tasty solo, the groovy thirds riff in *Jeenie, Jeenie*, and the sheer energy of *Somethin' Else, Summertime Blues* and *C'mon Everybody*. Cochran died far too young in an automobile accident in Chippenham, England, in 1960.

Buddy Holly was another great rock'n'roller to move over to the new music after early adventures in country and western, and the string of hits achieved in his tragically short career made him one of the most important influences in popular music. He was also the first major star to brandish the hotrod styling of the beautiful Fender Stratocaster. For many guitar players the world over it became the must-have instrument. Between 1957 and his death in a plane crash in 1959 (which also took stars Ritchie Valens and The Big Bopper) Holly racked up chart hits with *That'll Be The Day, Not Fade Away, Peggy Sue* and many more classic singles.

Worth singling out for his frenetic energy, melodic soloing and sheer speed, Cliff Gallup is another of rock'n'roll's truly great guitarists. After joining Gene Vincent's Blue Caps in 1956 Gallup contributed stunning lead work to songs such as *Be-Bop-A-Lula, Blue Jean Bop, Race With The Devil, Crazy Legs* and many others. Check him out. Other must-hears include Duane Eddy, Bo Diddley, Bill Haley and His Comets, and of course Elvis Presley guitarist Scotty Moore.

The chord forms used in rock'n'roll are not as complex in their harmony as those a jazz musician would use but some voicings have crept in from that genre. The main thing to remember when tackling the exercises is to create the vibe of this raw exciting music.

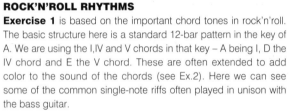

ROCK'N'ROLL RHYTHMS

Exercise 1 is based on the important chord tones in rock'n'roll. The basic structure here is a standard 12-bar pattern in the key of A. We are using the I,IV and V chords in that key – A being I, D the IV chord and E the V chord. These are often extended to add color to the sound of the chords (see Ex.2). Here we can see some of the common single-note riffs often played in unison with the bass guitar.

Looking at the A7 pattern we can see that we are playing the following chord tones: the root (A), major 3rd (C#), 5th (E), 6th (F#) and b7 (G). These patterns are then transposed to any key required.

The target speeds here for your metronome would be between 140 and 160 bpm (one quarter note per click). Adding slapback delay really brings the sound alive and is the staple diet of the rockabilly sound. The delay should be set to repeat once at about 75 per cent of the volume of the original note at a delay setting of about 100 milliseconds. If you have a tape echo handy, great – otherwise any delay will give you the right feel.

Exercise 2 offers some favorite chord voicings for rhythm sections, again in a 12 bar format in A. You will notice that the top four strings are being used to add the bright, bouncy vibe to the sound. Bars one and two could be repeated at bars three and four to give 4 bars of A7 but the A6 is a cool sound too, so mix and match.

This is played with a fast shuffle feel in the style of Bill Haley's *Rock Around The Clock*. You'll notice already how simple these parts can be, but it's the energy, "attitude" and attention to rhythm that will give them an authentic feel. Play it like you mean it and get that rhythm down, and you can't go far wrong.

Rock'n'roll rhythm guitar often borrows from the blues shuffle. In **exercise 3** each chord has its own pattern in the 12-bar sequence; the second fret notes would normally be played by finger 1, the index, and the 4th fret notes by finger 3. (Further related ideas along these lines are found in the *Blues* chapter.)

We also have the barre chord position shown so that we can later play in any key. For instance, finger 1 would play the barre chord position at the 5th fret on the E string for the A chord, finger 2 would play the A string 7th fret and finger 4 the 9th fret note. Okay, now we've got the rhythm section working well and playing tight – so let's move on to put the icing on the cake with some licks and fills.

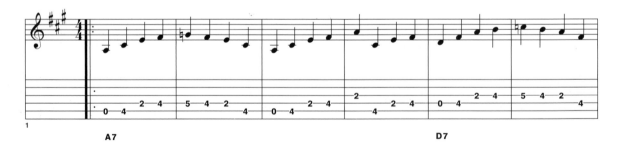

A7   D7

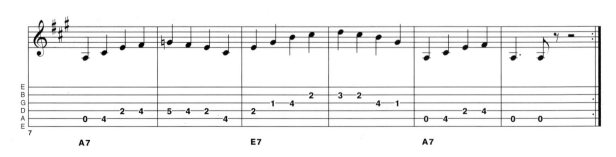

A7   E7   A7

rhythm

rhythm

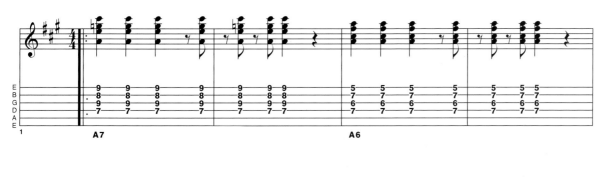

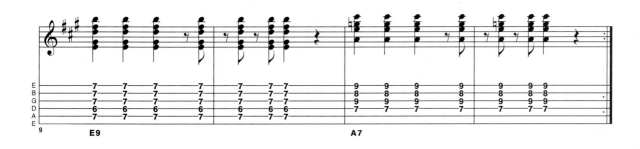

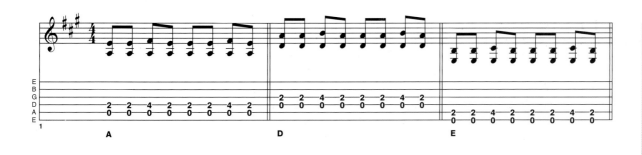

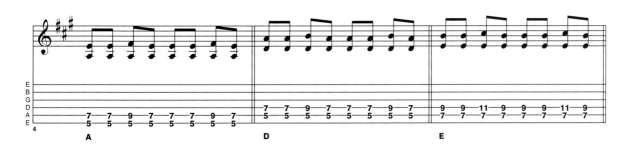

One of the most common sounds in rock'n'roll is the ear-ripping double stop. Although these sounds can be polished and honed for various styles of music the vibe needs to be raw to create the right effect. The first two bars of **exercise 4** is a movable pattern that can follow the I,IV,V sequences in the progression, for instance on the D (IV) chord play the line at the 10th position. The remainder of the lick should be played with a separate finger for each double stop. Remember the vibe. Check out Chuck Berry – including his classic intro to *Johnny B. Goode* – for a trademark approach to this style that defined the genre.

Exercise 5 features the technique common in Berry's playing of bending the double stop a semi-tone, or the pitch of one fret. The second bar works best starting with a release bend. That means the strings are bent on beat one then released on the off beat so the the double-stop sounds like it has fallen out the sky. Play these licks quite hard to give them an authentic, aggressive edge. These were considered raw, rebellious sounds in the '50s, and that's the way we want to approach them today.

For **exercise 6**, hold that pinky finger on the top E and don't let it bend on the first double stop. Use finger 3 assisted by the second finger to squeeze that B string up a semi-tone then descend the line using one finger for each double stop. The final slide fill to finish this lick should be played by fingers 1 and 2. Keep these nice and short – staccato. This line can be moved to the IV and V chord positions to give a full 12-bar solo: i.e. 10th

fret for D chord, 12th fret for the E.

There were many techniques from country music that influenced rock'n'roll guitar players. Merle Travis and Chet Atkins' picking styles were incorporated in many classic tracks. The line in **exercise 7** is played in the fifth position for our A7 chord, using the plectrum or thumb pick for the bass notes. Check Scotty Moore's work on the early Elvis Presley recordings. This type of lick would then be moved to the 10th position for the D7 chord but here we have an option of playing a similar style lick at the same fret. This line should be practised straight, and alternatively with swinging jazz eighths.

Many '50s guitarists were eager to build their chops and play jazz style lines. The solo in *Rock Around The Clock* features a lot of swing phrasing just like a sax break; it's a great example of the crossover playing often heard at the time. The solo in **exercise 8** follows an arpeggiated motif around the chord structure. All the eighth notes are swung, but try to nail those quarter notes right on the beat. When we reach the IV chord D, a Cliff Gallup style triplet pull-off run is played, giving the tonality of the D mixolydian scale, but it can also be played over the A chord. We return to A7 with a Chet Atkins style double-stop line. For the V chord the E augmented arpeggio gives a nice twist to the bluesy run before a Texas Playboy-style ending. Slide that final double stop away if you want, or even try an octave higher. This solo would fit nicely over a *Shake, Rattle And Roll* type of groove.

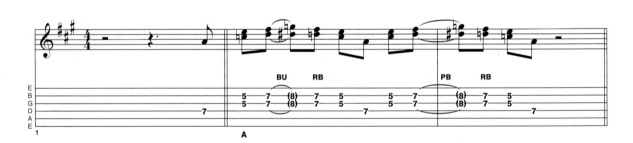

Exercise 7

Exercise 8

The augmented chord features in several classic rock'n'roll intros, such as Chuck Berry's *School Days* and *No Particular Place To Go*. In **exercise 9** the introduction is played with rapid-fire triplets and in this example the E+ (E augmented) would be used for a song in A. Two voicing options have been shown, one toward the middle of the fretboard and another high up.

The choked bend is a feature of many rock and roll solos. In **exercise 10** the bend on the 7th fret G string is played by finger 3 supported by finger 2. The double stop on the top two strings are played by finger 1. The bend should be choked as it reaches the pitch of the whole tone bend.

Exercise 11 is a great idea for a bouncy intro or can be incorporated in a solo. Check out the playing on The Beachboys' *Surfin U.S.A.*

Now let's try a couple of stock endings for your rock'n'roll tunes. In **exercise 12** the first one is a swinging scale run descending the major scale then finishing off with the A major arpeggio and an A13 chord. These runs would normally start on bar 11 of the twelve bar sequence. **Exercise 13** is another useful variation on the theme; just make sure the quarter notes on the first bar are not rushed and finish off with the swinging eighth notes and an A6 chord. This would then return to the tonic

Exercise 9

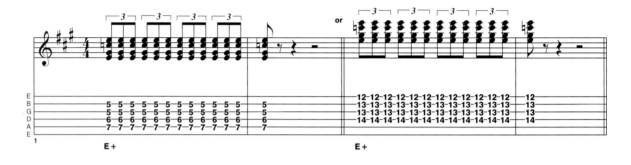

Exercise 10

Exercise 11

Exercise 12

rock'n'roll lead

or I chord A.

The final example, **exercise 14**, fuses some classic riffs and rhythms together and also features some triad licks that work really well over the dominant chords used in rock'n'roll. For example, an A7 chord is the V (five) chord in the key of D. The three major chords in this key are D, G and A. We can make up licks using the notes of these chords. The favorites are to use the IV and V chord tones, so over A7 the notes of A and G triads sound really cool.

The solo starts with a line usually played in unison with the bass; start with finger 2 to get on the right track then spread the fingers for bar two: finger 1 at the 5th fret E string and finger 2 at

the 7th fret A string to create the A5 tonality. Fingers 3 and 4 play the run on the E string then it's power chord boogie. From now on it's triad licks, except for the little arpeggio run on bar 8. This uses a tri-tone substitution idea. Any dominant chord like A7 can be substituted by its flattened fifth, i.e. Eb7.

To really get the lead ideas covered in this section down right, try recording some of the rhythm parts given toward the front over a number of bars (you don't even need any fancy multitrack – any tape recorder will do) and try out your newly-learned intros, riffs and solos over the top. Then transpose the parts into different keys to broaden your vocabulary, and even try making up some new riffs and leadlines of your own. Have fun.

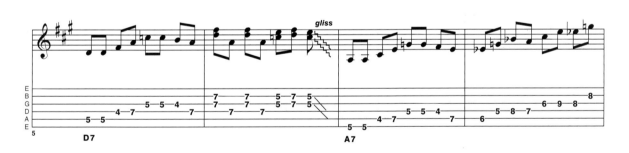

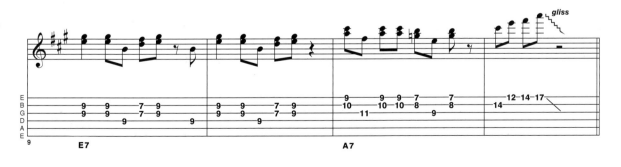

227

PLAYING
M E T A L

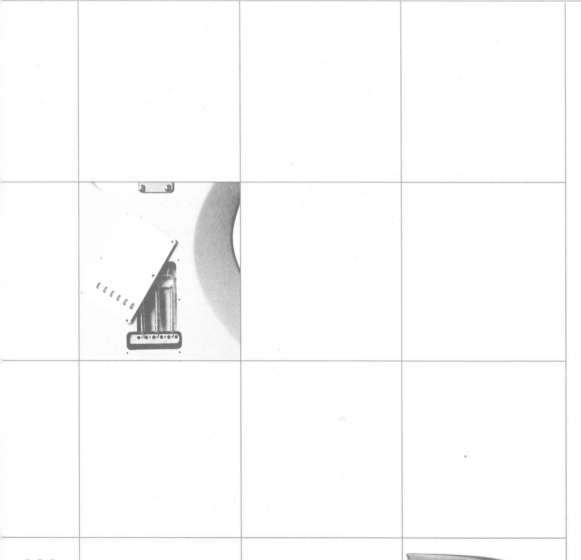

The psychedelic era of the late '60s, fuelled by the power trios such as Cream and the Jimi Hendrix Experience, crossed into a heavier age with the onset of the '70s. Hard rock and heavy metal styles were emerging, founded on energy and innovation. Led Zeppelin and The Who gave rise to Black Sabbath and Deep Purple, who would go on to influence the direction of modern heavy music. Blues licks and distorted riffs became a trademark of the genre. ● MARTIN GOULDING

By the late '70s, the nuances of rock and metal guitar playing were evolving into a more modern sound. With the wheels already set rolling by players such as Tony Iommi, Ritchie Blackmore, Uli Jon Roth and Michael Schenker, it was Dutchman Eddie Van Halen who would revolutionize the way modern electric guitar is played. Right from the arrival of his band's debut album *Van Halen* in 1978, it was clear he was an innovator who would influence a generation of guitar players.

With more interest in the exciting new styles, players were drawn to legato techniques and sought to extend their improvisation over the entire neck. Another contributing factor to the modern sound was the fact that the instrument itself was suggesting a new approach. With players modifying their necks, the advance of locking tremolo systems, a preference for light gauge strings, low actions and hotter pick ups the machine was advancing as rapidly as the person who played it. Meanwhile, advances in amplifier technology saw increased levels of gain which inspired a more vocal approach thanks to the drive and sustain now attainable.

These new characteristics were used to their maximum potential by mid-'80s Van Halen-influenced virtuosos Steve Vai and Joe Satriani, who launched full investigations into every possible nuance of the style, and highlighted the results with a series of guitar instrumental albums, which remain as "must-haves" for any serious student.

Swedish maestro Yngwie Malmsteen also made a massive impact when he released his instrumental debut *Rising Force* in 1984 as he blended his love for classical music into a heavy metal format, and influenced a legion of neo-classical players.

There was innovation on the band front, too. From the legacy of Black Sabbath came Metallica, Megadeth, Anthrax and Slayer, pioneers of the thrash metal movement which gained momentum throughout the decade. The later part of the '80s saw bands like Queensrÿche and Savatage introducing a more compositional approach, and as the '80s turned to the '90s there came more and more diversity. On one hand progressive metal was taking off, influenced by the legendary Rush, while Dream Theater was to provide a massive impact on intelligent rock playing. On another, the growing intricacies of death

metal and black metal – as played by bands such as Death, Sepultura, Emperor and Mayhem – showcased the most intense and certainly the most technical rhythm playing you can find. Grunge, a punk/metal hybrid, was also in full swing with bands like Pearl Jam, Soundgarden and Nirvana, as was the technological sound of industrial metal from bands like Ministry and Nine Inch Nails.

Today the rock/metal scene and its exponents are not so much moving forwards or backwards, but outwards in every possible direction. The world's most proficient masters of the genre – players like Greg Howe and Tony MacAlpine – are continually pushing their playing to the edge of the instrument's capabilities with their fusion-metal hybridization, as is top UK virtuoso Shaun Baxter, with his unique bebop-metal style. Likewise, Rage Against the Machine guitarist Tom Morello could be described as a "virtuoso of sound" who is pushing the guitar in yet another direction. Korn have blended west coast hip-hop with death riffs and framed them in a commercial accessibility. And with bands like Deftones and Slipknot also on the scene, we – as conscientious listeners – still find ourselves very much in a rock/metal dominated musical age.

In the following pages, I will introduce you to the four main areas of modern rock and metal technique: picking, legato, sweeping and tapping. There will also feature heavy rock rhythm techniques, an introduction to rock and metal playing through some traditional blues-based ideas, and we will cover some popular soloing scales and modes – with a section at the end on combining your techniques. All of these will be divided into sub-sections with specific numbered exercises relating to each.

Practise using a heavy, distorted sound as this will serve to highlight the effectiveness of your muting technique as well as providing an appropriate tone for these styles.

All of the exercises should be played with a metronome to keep your timing tight, and attempted very slowly at first. Speed is the result of perfected technique and is something which will happen with consistent practice sessions over time. Stay focused. Set short-term and long-term goals with your playing and always believe that you have the capability to succeed, whatever it is you are doing.

ROCK AND METAL RHYTHM PLAYING

Let's start by looking at some ideas used in the rock/metal rhythm style. Due to the heavy nature of the preferred tone, you'll find the big barre chords used in the pop styles sound muddy. By whittling down the intervals to the root and fifth we are left with a much more focused sound and an easier shape to move around. These diads are known as "power chords" and form the basis of many rock riffs. Play each of the individual rhythm exercises as constantly-repeating bars to build up stamina and drive in your rhythm work.

The first bar, **exercise 1**, shows the basic power chord shape voiced root and 5th on the sixth, fifth and fourth string. Make sure

you mute all other strings with the left hand index. **Exercise 2** shows the power chord voiced fifth and root. **Exercise 3** will develop the palm mute technique. The positioning of the palm mute should be back where the strings come out of the bridge. When done correctly, the result should be heavy and percussive. Use down strokes and set the right hand in lead playing position.

Exercise 4 shows a moving harmony over a static bass. Get your attack and rhythm right, and this is a simple yet ominous riff. **Exercise 5** reverses this for a moving bass over a static harmony, while **exercise 6** sees some variation on our basic power chord. Used by players such as George Lynch, raising and lowering the fifth can be an effective way of creating tension.

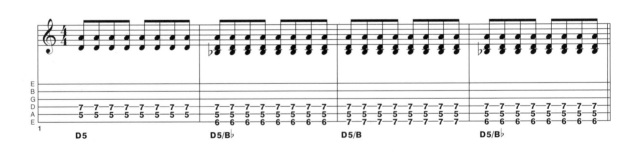

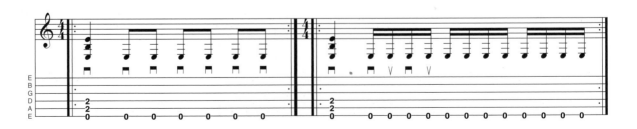

Exercises 7 to **10** are geared towards developing speed and stamina. When executing the bass rhythm, use the left hand to mute the remaining strings. Make sure you pick at the back near the bridge. You should use the palm mute technique on the bass and let the chord sustain for its duration and no more. These techniques should be executed with your right hand positioned similar to the lead playing position: rest your forearm on the front of the guitar and pivot from the wrist. Build the speed slowly and over time, trying to keep the arm relaxed. These exercises are in the style of the thrash metal movement of the mid '80s, led by bands like Metallica, Megadeth, Anthrax and Slayer. **Exercise 11** is a combination of some of the ideas that have come before.

The use of single-line ideas is very common in the rock/metal style. **Exercise 12** is an idea in the style of Randy Rhoads. Keep it as all down strokes and make sure that there is clear note separation. **Exercise 13** is a triplet-based idea in the style of Michael Schenker. Use alternate picking throughout, hitting every other note on the up and down stroke.

Single line riffing at its extreme can merge the boundaries of rhythm and lead playing, especially in the heavier, more progressive metal styles. I would recommend listening to *Awake* by Dream Theater and *The Politics of Ecstasy* by Seattle-based progressive metal band Nevermore.

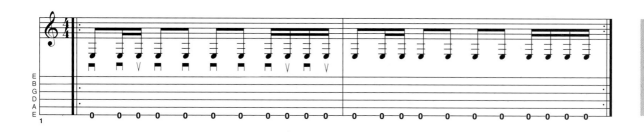

Exercises 9-10

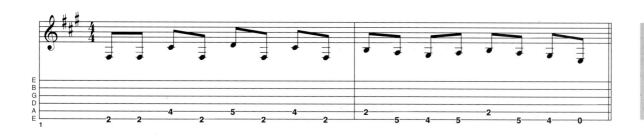

Exercise 11

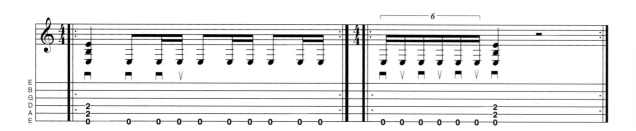

Exercise 12

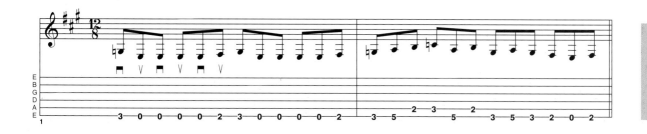

Exercise 13

rhythm techniques

Exercises 14

Exercise 15

Exercise 16-19

Exercises 20

Exercises 21

232

Exercises **14** and **15** are examples of the ways triads are used. By superimposing different triads over a static bass, you can come up with more sophisticated harmonies. Ex.14 is in the style of Edward Van Halen, Ex.15 John Petrucci. These triads will sound relative to the tonal centre of E, therefore the notes of the B minor triad, viewed from E, would make an E major 9 chord. Try working out what the G and D triads would be from an E root.

Next are some variations on the basic power chord. **Exercise 16** shows three versions of power chords voiced with the fifth on bass – a darker sound associated more with doom and death metal styles. Try these repeatedly, and transpose to different positions. The next couple will really start to stretch the reach of your pinkie! **Exercise 17** is a stacked power chord for a fuller sound, widely used by Swedish progressive death metal band, Meshuggah. **Exercise 18** is the add 9 power chord, also commonly used in progressive metal styles.

Exercise 19 is the flat 5 diad, which has a more demonic quality, while **exercise 20** is a modern sounding groove incorporating a stacked flat 5 diad in the style of Korn.

For **exercise 21**, drop your low E a whole tone down to D. The exercise uses the octave technique as a riff idea. Be careful with the muting, especially between the octave. This is in the style of the Deftones, and also serves as an introduction to dropped D tuning, which is popular among heavier bands.

TRADITIONAL ROOTS

The pentatonic scale is a fundamental template for hard rock and heavy metal improvisation. Digest **diagrams 1–5** until you are comfortable with the A minor pentatonic scale and its blues variation in all five positions – a skill essential to master in order to then "weld on" other concepts (many readers will already be familiar with the pentatonic scale from lessons in *Rock & Pop*, *Blues* and other genres, but refreshing your knowledge with these diagrams will help prepare you for exercises that follow).

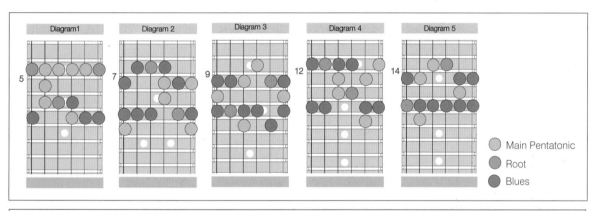

| Diagram 1 | Diagram 2 | Diagram 3 | Diagram 4 | Diagram 5 |

○ Main Pentatonic
○ Root
○ Blues

Edward Van Halen (left) forever changed the way rock lead guitar would be played with the fluid solo work and astounding two-handed tapping heard right from his band's eponymous debut album released in 1978. Ozzy Osbourne's *Blizzard Of Ozz* album (above-left) carries some stunning guitar work from the late – though perpetually influential – Randy Rhoads, including the instantly familiar riff on the hit track *Crazy Train*. From the other side of the metal tracks, John Petrucci's eclectic-progressive virtuosity, as heard with his band Dream Theater, proves equally inspirational.

German metal maestro Michael Schenker (left) remains a seminal force in heavy rock guitar. His instrumental power is heard to great effect on the solo album *Adventures Of The Imagination* (above-left), along with any of his work with UFO. An equally powerful, dynamic player on all fronts, George Lynch shines on Dokken's *Tooth And Nail* (above-right).

Exercises 22 through **28** are some traditional blues licks in first position A minor pentatonic. Since the '50s, these licks have stood the test of time and still form the basis of the rock and metal sounds.

Exercises 29 through **32** are double stop riffs, with Ex.30 and Ex.31 going on to incorporate the 6th to add colour. Ex.32 shows the short step from rock'n'roll to heavy rock, with a riff in the style of early rock pioneer Michael Schenker. Notice that the flat 5 gives it a bluesy slant. With Ex.31 we are also back into bending. Before taking this on, digest these pointers on executing the bend:

1. The thumb should be situated over the 6th fret, forming a pivot point with the index finger.

2. The actual bend comes from a rotation of the wrist, so keep the fingers rigid.

3. You should notice the thumb squeezing towards the second finger with each bend.

4. When bending with the third finger, also use the second finger for support.

In order to eliminate string noise, make sure that the left hand index finger always mutes the string above and all strings below the note being played. With the right hand, use the heel as a pivot point to rest on any idle bass strings. As with all exercises move from the wrist and keep the arm relaxed.

Exercises 33 through **36** are a batch of "hammer on" and "pull off" techniques. With their legato tone they make excellent rapid-fire licks, and have been a characteristic of the post-Van Halen rock players like George Lynch and Randy Rhoads. Again, play each repeatedly to build up speed and stamina. Ex.35 and Ex.36 use the bluesy flat 5. Strive to make the notes equal in volume by pulling downwards and away from the string. With the hammer on, try to be as powerful and accurate as possible.

traditional licks

Exercises 22-25

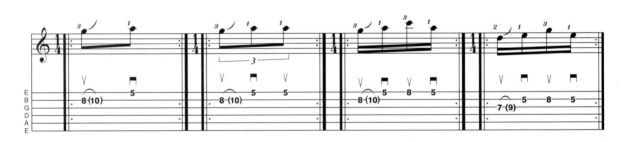

Exercises 26-29

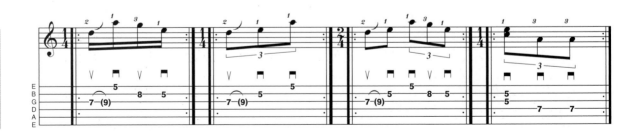

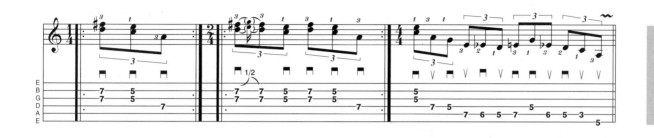

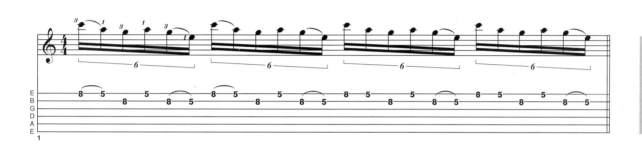

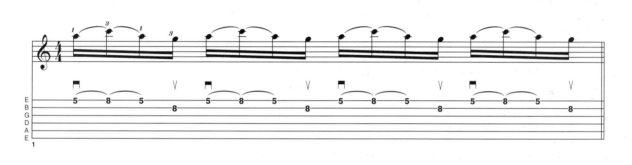

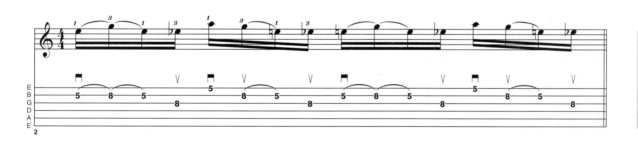

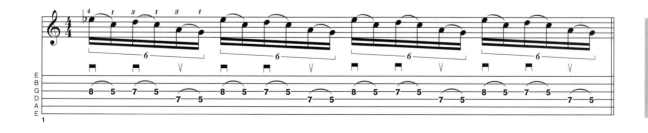

Exercise 37 is a run in the style of Zakk Wylde. It provides a great example of taking a motif and moving it up the neck horizontally using five positions. Try this approach to any other static licks you may know.

The series of ideas in **exercises 38** through **41** expands the range to cover two pentatonic positions. Rooted in the style of Steve Vai, they demonstrate how players were starting to stretch out technically. When attempting these exercises, try to avoid any jerky movements. Keep your thumb at the back of the neck and stretch out your fingers to reach for the notes. Even for many experienced players, this will be a serious workout for that little finger! Remember to practise these ideas slowly and with a metronome. Once the techniques have been mastered slowly, gradually start to increase the tempo.

Slides (as in finger slides up or down th neck, *not* bottleneck slides) are an essential element of metal technique as they help you navigate through positions and free up the neck. **Exercise 42** demonstrates how you can cover three octaves by using a 3rd finger slide. Notice that the move starts in fifth position, travels through first and second, and ends in third. **Exercise 43** shows a sliding technique which can be useful in moving horizontally. Once you've mastered it, try to apply this technique throughout the five positions. Also experiment on different string groupings and in different keys.

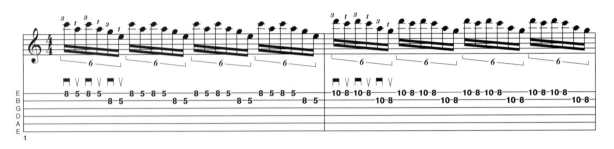

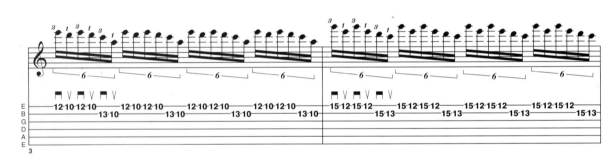

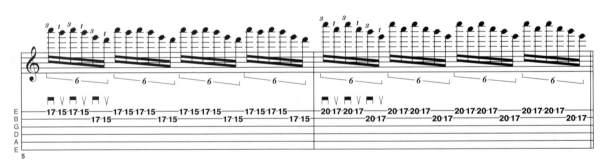

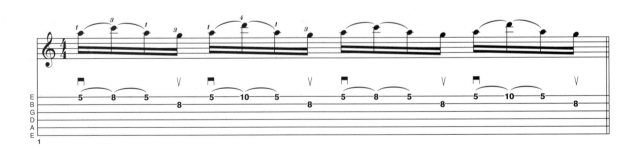

slides

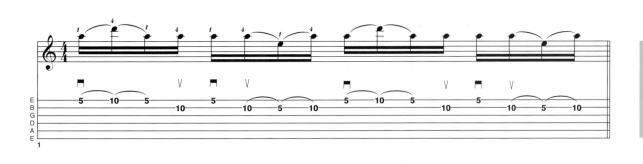

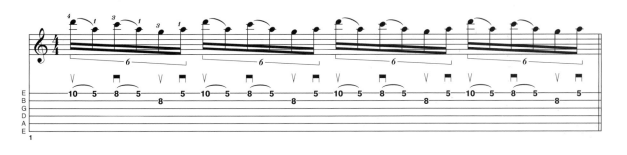

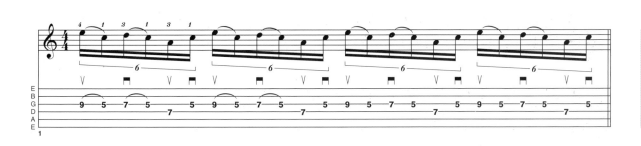

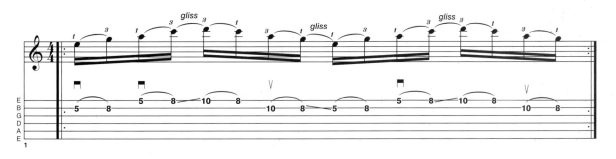

237

PICKING TECHNIQUE

One of the most fundamental techniques in the heavy rock style is the picking technique. Initially inspired by players outside the genre such as Al Di Meola and Steve Morse, it is widely used to add tension to solos and provide a more aggressive feel. Pushing things further, the integration of fast picking, blues phrasing and a strong melodic angle towards classical music gave birth to the neo-classical style consolidated by Yngwie Malmsteen. The following exercises will tighten synchronization between both hands and serve as examples of linear playing.

Before digging in, however, check out the *Scale Overview* below, which serves as a primer for what follows. **Exercise 44** uses A Aeolian to ascend the high E string. The exercise moves up the neck in beats by each consecutive note and then works back to create a cycle. **Exercises 45** and **46** are fragments to be practised statically at first and then applied to the framework shown in Ex. 46. **Exercise 47** is a picking piece in the style of Yngwie Malmsteen. Always tap your foot on the beat and accent the downstroke. With the right hand, move from the wrist and mute by resting on the bass strings.

DIAGRAM 1:
A AEOLIAN MODE

⬤ = Root

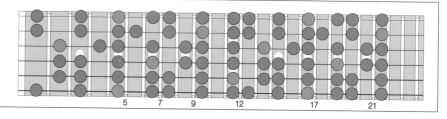

SCALE OVERVIEW

Diagram 1 (above) is a neck diagram showing the A Aeolian mode. A Aeolian is the sixth mode in the key of C major and is a commonly used sound in rock and metal improvisation. Looking at the notes of C major from the perspective of A yields the intervallic formula **R 2 b3 4 5 b6 b7**. **Diagrams 2** through **6** show the traditional scale shapes. Notice that within each shape can be found the minor pentatonic template, thus it may be more helpful to view the Aeolian mode as a pentatonic scale with the addition of the 9th (shown in green) and the b6 (shown in gray).

This is one of the minor modes within the scale. To construct the Dorian mode, which is built on the second degree of the scale, simply raise the b6 to a 6. To construct the Phrygian mode, built on the 3rd degree, simply flatten the 9.

Nowadays it is common to see two shapes "welded" together to form a three-note-per-string scale shape, which lends itself to fast execution. To help you with the *Picking Technique* exercises above and following, I have combined the fifth and first traditional positions in **diagram 7**. For the *Legato* study which follows from page 239, **diagram 8** combines shapes two and three.

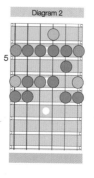
Diagram 2

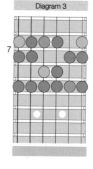
Diagram 3

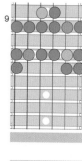
Diagram 4

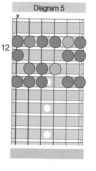
Diagram 5

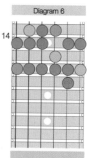
Diagram 6

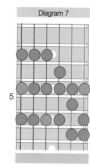
Diagram 7

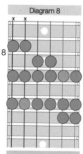
Diagram 8

⬤ = Root
⬤ = 9th
⬤ = b6

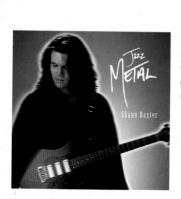

Lesser-known but highly respected British metal guitarist Shaun Baxter virtually invented the "jazz metal" genre with his 1994 album of the same name, left.

a aeolian mode

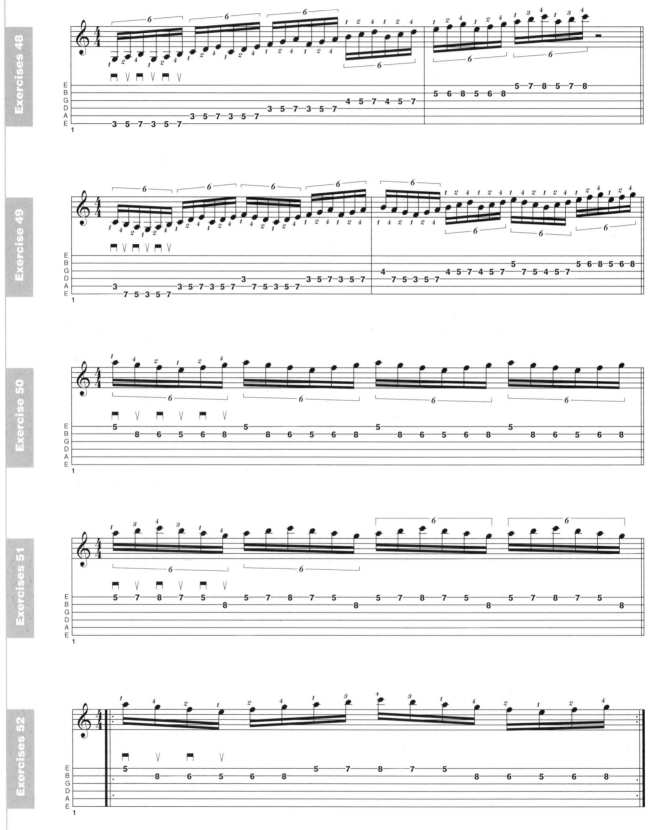

picking

Exercises 48

Exercise 49

Exercise 50

Exercises 51

Exercises 52

Exercises 48 and **49** are a couple of ideas that run vertically up the scale using our three-note-per-string scale. You should also work out the descending ideas by simply reversing the notes, and practice them both ways. To make the runs sound more aggressive, try palm muting the bass strings for a chunkier sound. Once you have established control in this position, start exploring all the others. Use your technique to learn the neck.

Exercises 50 through **52** are excellent technique builders in the style of Paul Gilbert (Racer X). Practise them slowly, try to keep your fingers close to the strings on all the exercises, and realise that speed is a result of good technique, which itself is a result of focus and patience. Build the tempo up slowly over time, and always use a metronome to chart your progress. One of the best pickers at the moment is John Petrucci from U.S. progressive metal act Dream Theater, and he's definitely worth a listen for his excellent execution of these techniques. Check him out on their albums *Images And Words* and *Awake*.

LEGATO TECHNIQUE

The next major technical area to focus on is legato playing. Smooth and fluid sounding, it serves as a contrast to the more aggressive picking style. As picking came into metal from the jazz-rock virtuosos of the '70s, likewise players such as Edward Van Halen were being influenced by the legato-dominated style of fusion maestro Alan Holdsworth, a player who has influenced the direction of many rock and metal soloists.

One of the most outstanding players of the '80s and '90s is Joe Satriani, whose fluid, lyrical style has won him success with the non-playing audience as well as respect among the top players in the world. Note that when playing legato styles, a smooth high-gain amp setting with plenty of sustain and natural compression is often helpful in getting the sound and feel right.

Exercise 53 through **56** are fragments in A Aeolian. Follow the rule that the first note on a string is picked and all subsequent notes on the same string are hammered or pulled.

Highly respected by players and non-players alike, Joe Satriani remains at the top of the tree of legato-style metal virtuosi. Having come to prominence in the '80s and '90s, he is still a major influence on budding rock guitarists.

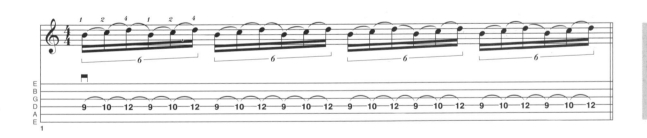

Exercises 53

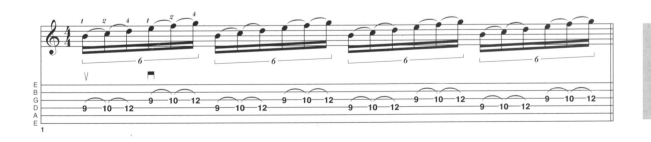

Exercise 54

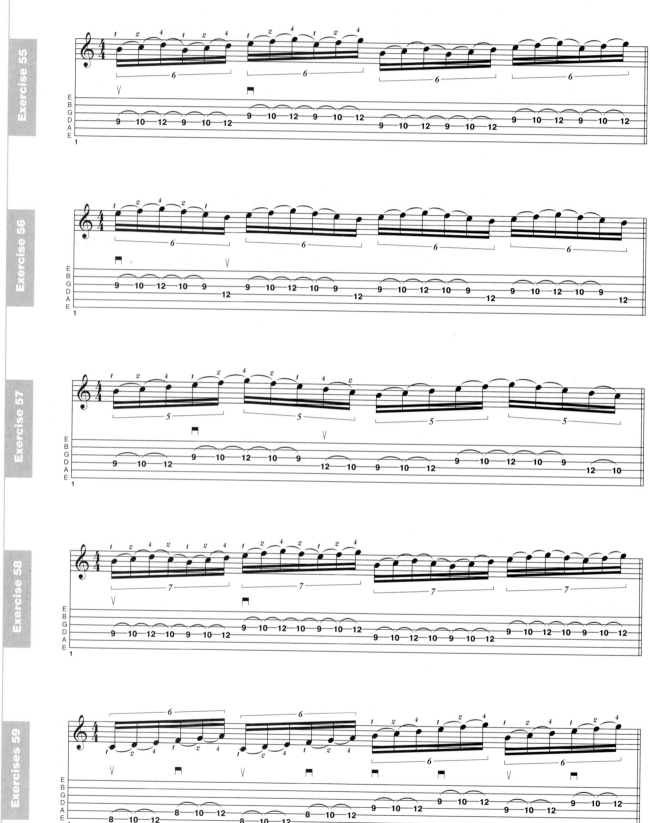

Long the dynamic duo of flamboyant shred, Steve Vai and Joe Satriani are both "must hears" for any student of metal guitar. Satriani's *Surfing With The Alien* (far left) and Vai's *Passion And Warfare* remain absolute classics of the genre.

Exercises 57 and **58** are two more fragments in A Aeolian. Through practise you will develop speed, stamina and accuracy which will also benefit your picking technique. Watch the timing as the fingers will try to go down like a reflex action. Control them by practising slowly, and keep the index finger down unless changing string.

Now let's try crossing the neck some. **Exercises 59** and **60** are simply fragments connected together, but they work as smooth runs once you begin to build up speed and fluidity over

time. Try expanding this idea with other fragments from Exs.57–62 to get yourself moving between different positions on the neck.

Exercises 61 and **62** demonstrate sliding ideas that will help you traverse the neck even more swiftly. Once you have mastered these, try applying the ideas to other string sets and start to learn the surrounding positions. It is a good idea to use the pentatonic scale as a pointer to where you are in relationship to the chord, so you don't get lost when meandering around the scale.

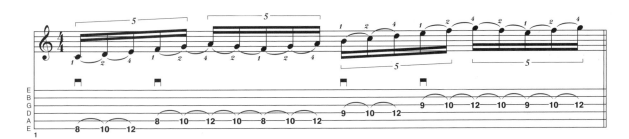

Exercises 60

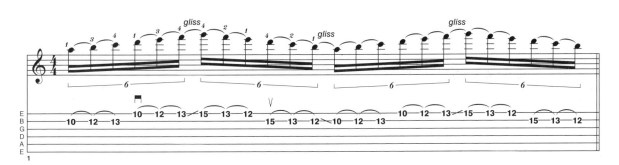

Exercises 61

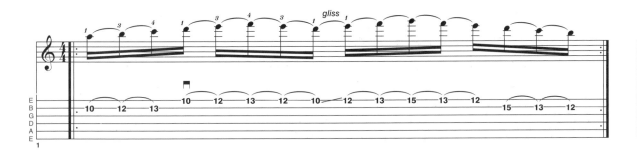

Exercise 62

243

Sweedish maestro Yngwie Malmsteen is the long-time supremo of neo-classical metal playing. His technique makes great use of impressive arpeggio-based runs which traverse the neck with astounding agility.

Exercise 63 is an example of Satriani's method for rolling around the scale using slides to create greater range. Try extending this idea all the way through the scale.

Exercise 64 is an octave block. The first six notes are then repeated in the next two octaves. This is a great way to expand the basic scale shape to create a longer line. Technically they are more straightforward as the shape of the first six notes is exactly the same in the second and third octaves. When you get to the top, try running back down again. **Exercise 65** shows how you can arrange two fragments symmetrically and then move the combination up the three octave pathway. Remember: these ideas are also excellent picking patterns. Again, try to keep an eye on your muting technique and keep your fingers as close to the strings as possible.

ARPEGGIO TECHNIQUE

Although earlier heavy metal players like Ritchie Blackmore used arpeggio-based ideas, it wasn't until the post-Van Halen era that arpeggio-oriented playing gained a major foothold in metal. This was a fast melodic style, heavily influenced by classical virtuosi like Paganini and Bach. It was a perfect complement to the scale-based ideas, and allowed great distance to be covered on the neck. Try these exercises in the style of Yngwie Malmsteen.

Exercise 66 is an E minor arpeggio idea on one string. Try to stabilise the hand with the thumb at the back of the neck and stretch out the fingers. The index hammer on will need to be as powerful and accurate as possible. **Exercises 67** and **68** are minor and diminished arpeggios respectively. Notice the diminished chord sets up tension which resolves to the minor.

Along with **exercise 69**, which serves as an example over three strings, these three lines employ the use of sweep picking, a technique allowing fast execution of one-note-per-string ideas. With these exercises, it is crucial that the notes do not ring into each other, so lift off when the note has been played. Follow the picking directions and allow the pick to "fall" on to the next string wherever indicated.

further slides

Exercises 63

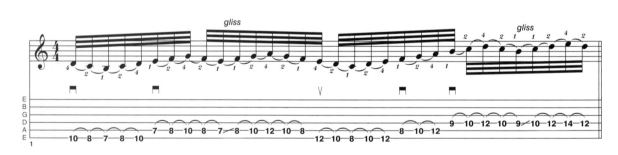

Exercises 64

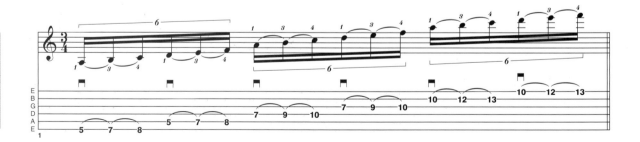

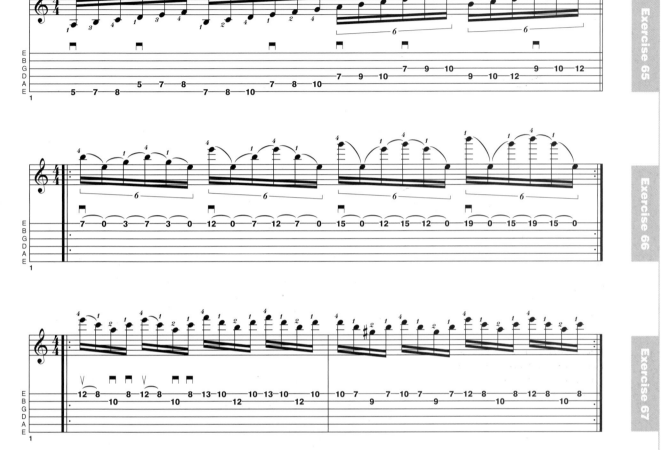

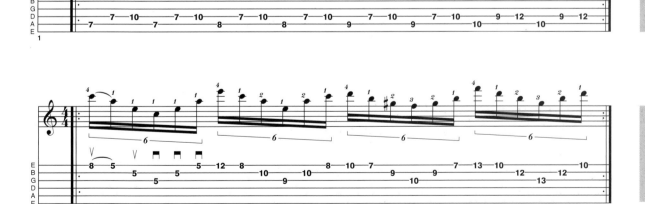

Exercise 70 is an arpeggio exercise based on a typical minor progression. Concentrate on clean execution, the pick dropping to the next note in one smooth glide. This has a different feel to articulating individual strokes. On the way up, drag the pick through the strings. Keep your hand relaxed, and don't hold the pick too tight: it should be flush to the string and slightly sympathetic to the direction in which you are moving.

Exercises 71 and **72** are A minor shapes commonly played in rock and metal. Play them repeatedly until your picking is clean and rhythmic, and the notes well defined. Ex.72 has a mini barre with the third finger on the 14th fret. Make sure you roll over the string to ensure note separation.

Exercise 73 is the colourful A minor add 9 arpeggio.
Exercise 74 is an A minor to G sharp diminished string skipping exercise. This was seen as an alternative way of playing arpeggios by players such as Paul Gilbert and Nuno Bettencourt. As the shapes are different they can provide ideas that would be difficult to sweep, so learning both techniques will inspire a different vocabulary of ideas. Make sure you mute the string above as you hit the note and keep your right hand pivoting on the bass strings to mute.

Exercise 75 is a sequenced run. Keep the down strokes even and accent the upstrokes on beats three and four to stabilise your timing.

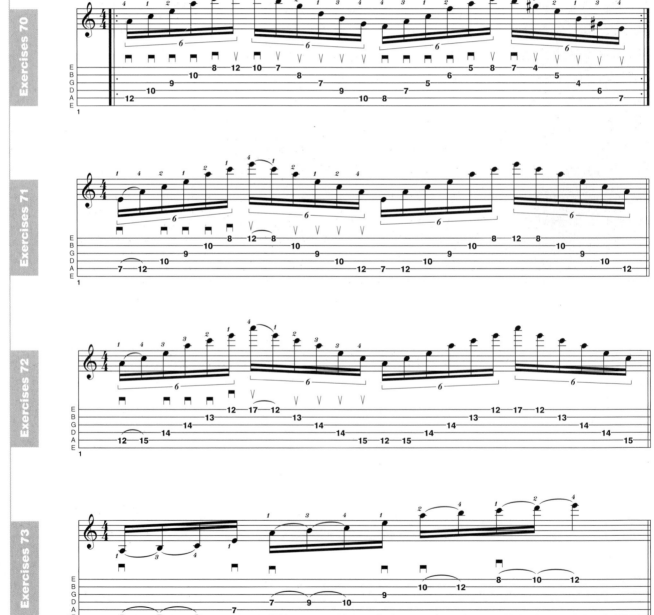

arpeggios

As with the work of many guitarists "let loose" from the confines of their usual band, Nuno Bettencourt's *Schizophonic* strives to exhibit the full – and rather eclectic – range of his skill.

Nuno Bettencourt, left, is a player respected for his great technical ability – including stunning alternative arpeggio technique – who has also crossed over to mainstream success with his band Extreme.

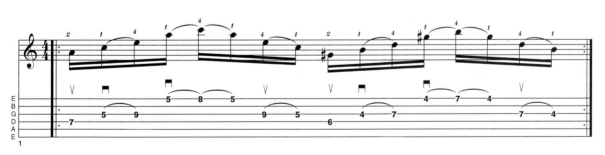

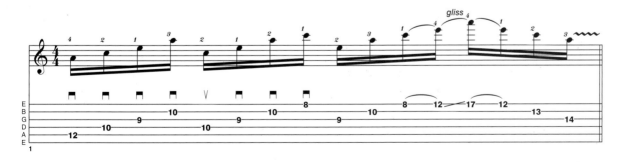

Paul Gilbert of Racer X is a gifted all-rounder, with plenty of lessons to teach the metal student – from speed picking to blinding arpeggios.

TWO-HANDED TAPPING

The last of the four main categories of rock and metal technique used to generate notes is "two-handed tapping." This was introduced by revolutionary guitarist Edward Van Halen on his band's debut album in 1978. Fairly straightforward after initial practise, it's an accessible way of playing very fast licks.

Exercises 76 through **78** are in the style of E.V.H. and feature A minor arpeggios. Although E.V.H. used his right hand index finger to execute the tap, I strongly advise you to learn this technique using your second right hand finger and hold your pick

normally in order to seamlessly integrate tapping into the other components of your style. When tapping, rest the heel of your hand on the unplayed strings and tap from the wrist. Make the tap powerful and accurate – do not dab at the string. Also ensure all pull offs are of a down and outwards direction.

Exercise 79 is in the style E.V.H.'s guitar extravaganza, *Eruption*. Play each segment a number of times, then try to link the fragments up bit by bit until you memorize the exercise. Once memorized, you can develop your speed. **Exercise 80** is a method used by E.V.H. to cross strings. The tap (indicated by the arrow) leads the way on to the next string. Elements similar to this are employed in his solo on Michael Jackson's hit *Beat It*.

Tapping gives players the technical facility to play lines at incredible speed; it has brought the guitar as an instrument in line with keyboard virtuosi, and many players use its almost un-guitaristic sound to broaden their style. The next six exercises are in the style of instrumental virtuoso Greg Howe. **Exercise 81** is a pentatonic sequence that enables an execution that would be impossible for the left hand alone. **Exercise 82** is the technique applied to an A minor arpeggio. Isolate the taps and you will recognise that the left hand is simply playing one shape and the taps are outlining the next position. (Hammer the left hand where indicated by the symbol.)

two-handed tapping

Exercise 76

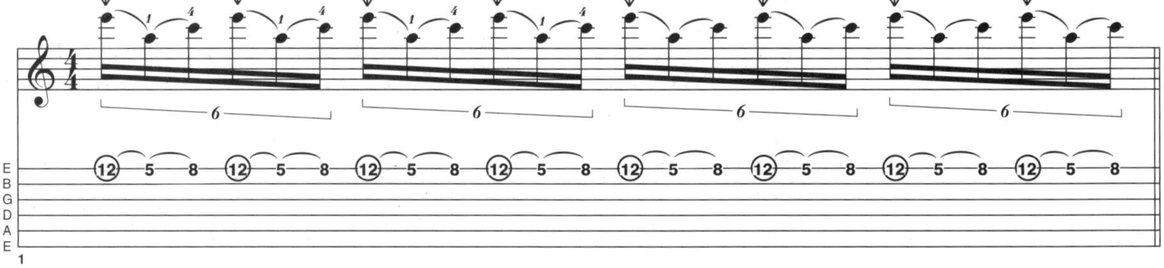

Exercise 77

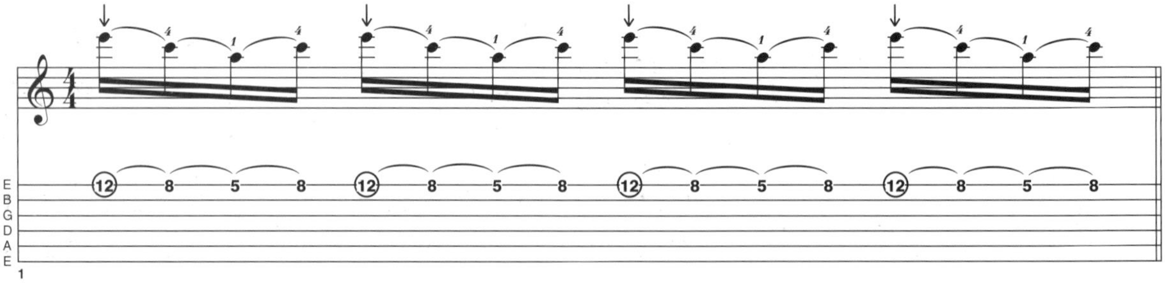

Exercises 78

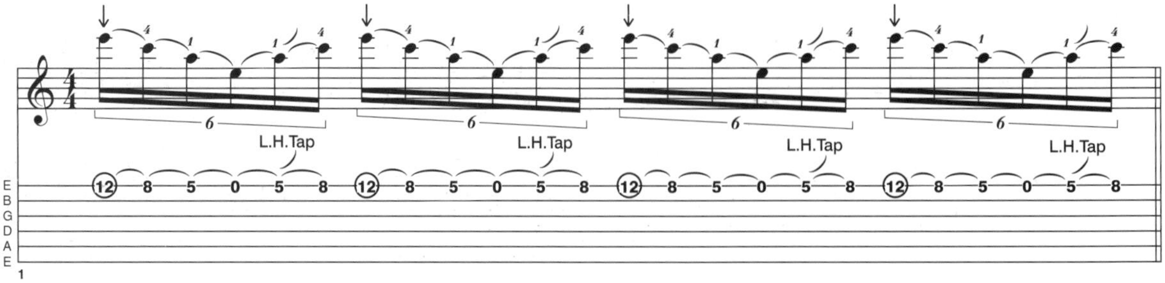

Continuing in the style of Greg Howe, **exercise 83** is a scalar sequence. Practise slowly and concentrate on the timing. **Exercise 84** is a two-handed approach to a blues scale fragment; **exercise 85** is an adaptation from conventional playing whereby the tap replaces the note normally played by the left hand pinkie, and **exercise 86** is a Cmaj7 arpeggio which uses a tap and slide. Try applying these last three ideas to the next two octaves to create fast lines over the whole neck.

COMBINING TECHNIQUES

Our final section looks at some of the ways you can combine the components of your technique to create musical concepts. In order to flow, you'll need to find "exit points" to lead you from one technique to another. This will help prevent you from getting caught up in a shape.

Exercises 87 and **88** are a rapid-fire pentatonic lick and a development adding the 9, respectively. This is a simple way to hotrod blues licks. Notice the "exit" point being the 8th fret bend. As this is a very popular blues-lick-oriented bend, you should have no problem in following up from here with some other related ideas.

Exercise 89 is a legato run up to its exit bend; **exercise 90** displays alternate picking; and **exercise 91** is a legato lick with a blues phrase providing us with another useful "exit" point.

two-handed tapping

Exercise 83
Exercise 84
Exercises 85
Exercises 86

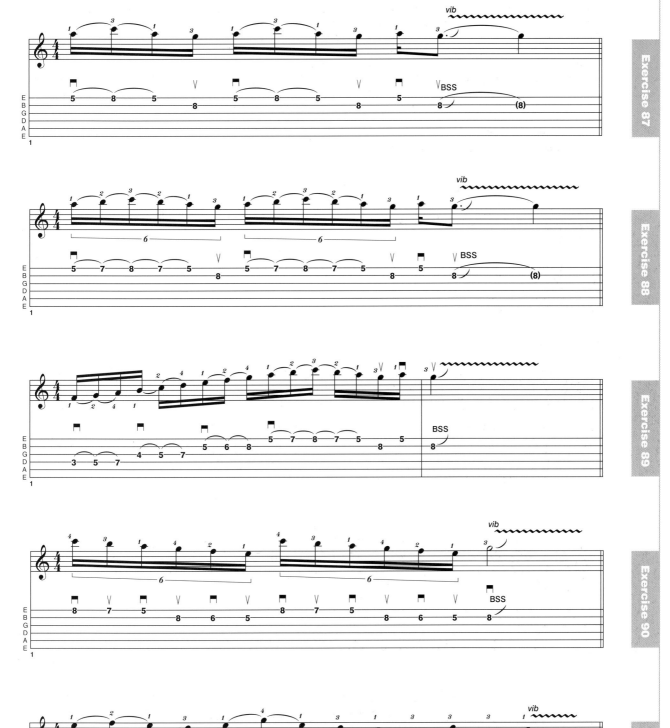

Exercise 87

Exercise 88

Exercise 89

Exercise 90

Exercise 91

combining techniques

Exercises 92

Exercise 93

Exercise 94

Exercise 95

Exercise 96

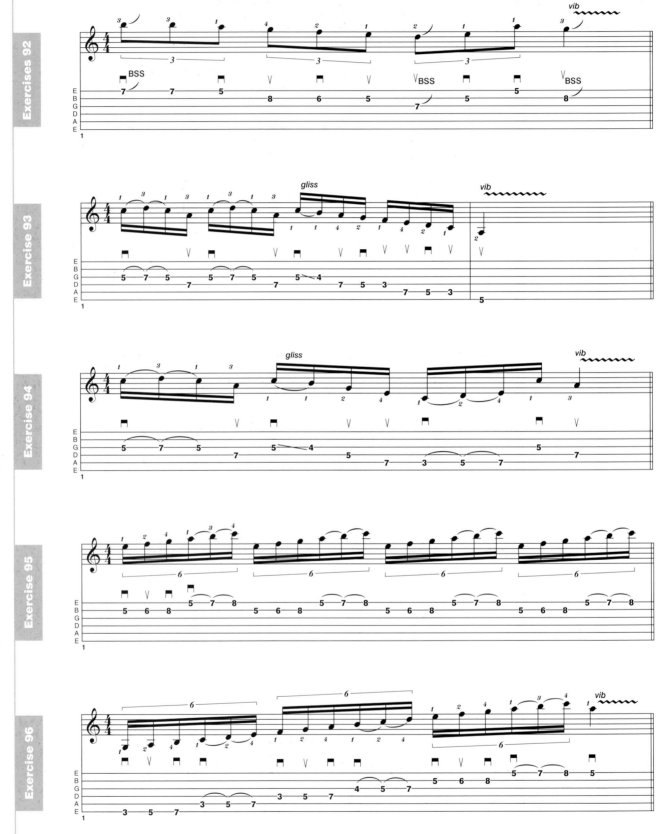

combining techniques

Exercise 92 is a triplet lick combining A Aeolian and pentatonic ideas. Be careful with the intonation on the semitone bend. **Exercise 93** is a riff that uses a slide to make the transition from blues phrase to scalar run, while **exercise 94** is a similar idea, but uses an arpeggio fragment. Both examples exit on the root note. **Exercise 95** demonstrates the combination of picking and legato, which gives a different sound to using one or the other exclusively. Make sure you practice slowly first as the changeover can often throw off the timing. **Exercise 96** is an extension of this idea.

Now let's combine an arpeggio and a scale fragment in **exercise 97**. Follow the picking directions and check your muting technique. **Exercise 98** ascends a two octave arpeggio into a legato-based run, exiting on a slide.

Exercise 99 is an arpeggio lick which is extended by a right hand tap. The descending form is executed with a series of left hand hammers before ending with a scalar idea. Finally, **Exercise 100** has an extended legato run climaxing with a tap before descending. Again, concentrate on timing and accuracy.

All of the "exit" points should be played with wide vibrato. On the top two strings, push upwards and on the remaining four, pull downwards. Like the bending technique, the motion comes from the rotation of the wrist, not the fingers. Concentrate on returning to pitch as you vibrato, and tail off by sliding down the neck.

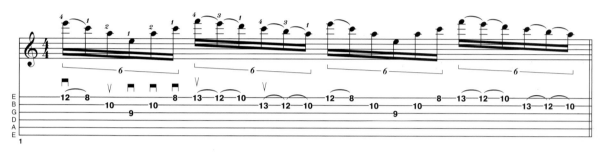

Exercise 97

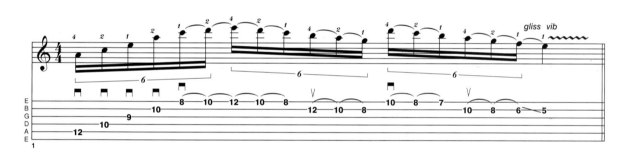

Exercise 98

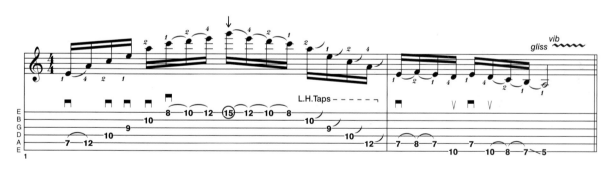

Exercise 99

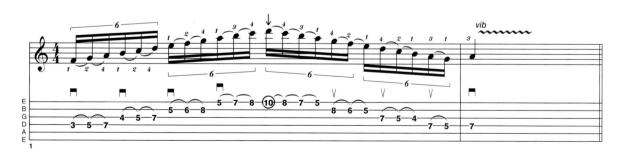

Exercise 100

7

PLAYING
LATIN

Latin music has long had a following at the pop and rock fringes, and has occasionally found its way to superstardom in the hands of a Carlos Santana, for example. The recent proliferation of Latin rhythms in pop and dance hits, however – along with the close focus on Latin styles in Ry Cooder's popular and influential *Buena Vista Social Club* – has breathed new life into the genre, and turned new listeners on to the infectious rhythms and melodies of this compelling music. ● NESTOR GARCIA

To avoid some common misconceptions and misuses of this style of music, let's start by learning the original patterns so you can identify the source of these traditional tunes; then you can transform them, if you like, into something more original or blend them into whatever other styles you play.

We're going to look at some basic riffs from the Afro-Cuban tradition: son montuno, mambo and cha-cha-cha. These are three of the most common styles in a *descarga* – a Latin jam session – and we're going to examine some of the basic ingredients to help you cook up some hot salsa. This music is all about rhythm, but even a whole heap of rhythm is useless without feel. Latin music is designed to make you move your hips, so if they're stationary you haven't quite got it yet!

The guitar, like the piano, is used as a percussion instrument; think drums, cowbells, anything. The way to take control of the groove is to use repetitive patterns, just like a percussionist would. In this context, most of the guitar patterns are based on piano and Cuban *tres* patterns.

Rhythm patterns are centered around the *clave*. A clave is one of a pair of short wooden sticks used as a percussion instrument in Latin music. They usually play the clave rhythm, which is considered to be the centerpoint of Afro-Cuban music. Sometimes they are referred to as 3:2 or 2:3 This merely refers to the amount of rhythmic hits in the bar. The 3:2 has three in the first bar, and two in the second. In a tune, all the other instruments will play rhythms that are related to this basic rhythm.

Exercise 1 is the two basic types of clave: Son clave and Rumba clave. Away from your guitar and in any possible situation, tap a clave rhythm with your right hand while keeping time, in quarter notes, with your left hand. Then reverse hands. (I've written the son clave in 2:3 as this is the most common form used for cha-cha-cha and mambo, though you find them in 3:2 as well – just reverse the bars.) In 2:3 clave the guitar starts on a downbeat; the upbeats are in the 3 side of the clave.

Exercise 2 is the pattern played by the timbale player on the side of the timbales, here transposed with a 2:3 Son clave. It is called *cáscara*. Use this as a warm up exercise, playing it purely as a rhythm pattern, and then try to use it in the scale in **exercise 3** and play it with your own scales and arpeggios, just to get the idea firmly seated in your body.

Exercise 4 is a line based on the pattern played by the *tres cubano*, an acoustic guitar with three pairs of strings, tuned G, C and E, outlining a second inversion C major triad. Sometimes you can find it in D. This is used primarily to play *son montuno*, the oldest form of what we today know as salsa. This line is played in the 2:3 son clave. All the salsa and mambo patterns are based on *son montuno* patterns.

Hundreds of tunes and styles are based on the I-IV-V chord progression. Faster, slower, in major or a minor flavor… Three

chords, three inversions and twelve keys equals 108 possible varieties of finger entertainment for a Sunday morning, and you can transpose the line in **exercise 5** over many variations of them. Then add some of these rhythms and you are done. What about a bit of tapping at the same time? Perhaps a 2:3 son clave? Sunday afternoon is starting to look busy too? It's easy to change into a minor feel, if you ignore the trickier fingering. Just take the thirds of the I and IV chords and flatten them, taking them from major thirds to minor thirds, as in **exercise 6**. Try transposing the major riff from Ex.5 to other keys, then transpose it into the minor as has been done here for you. If you also slow the tempo down to something around 70-100 bpm, it becomes a *guajira* tempo. Pronounced "gwa-hear-ah," this is a traditional music of the peasants of Cuba, usually accompanied by *tres cubano*.

Exercise 7 is another typical chord progression, similar to those found in the *Buena Vista Social Club* (check out this CD for some pure Afro-Cuban grooves). It outlines the I-V-V-1 in A minor key in 2:3 clave. Transpose it to different keys.

Exercise 8 is a *montuno* line. This is one of the most common patterns found in salsa and Latin jazz. You may find you'll get a better feel if you follow the pulse in "cut-time." It outlines a Dm7 type of vamp but you can use it also over Dm7-G9 progression.

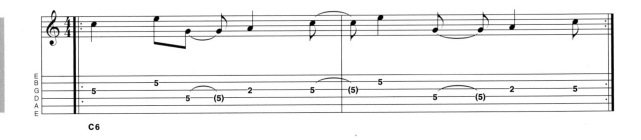

latin

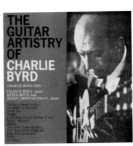

From trad Latin to salsa-spiced jazz. Influential Brazilian guitarist Baden Powell shaped the form of the bossa nova (far left), while Charlie Byrd adapts such textures for his *The Guitar Artistry Of...* album (center). Saxophonist Bud Shank and guitarist Laurindo Almeida travel south of the border for *Brazilliance*.

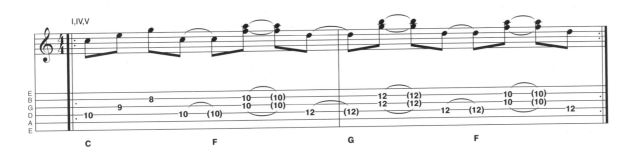

Exercise 5

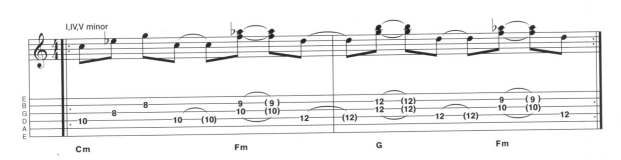

Exercise 6

Exercise 7

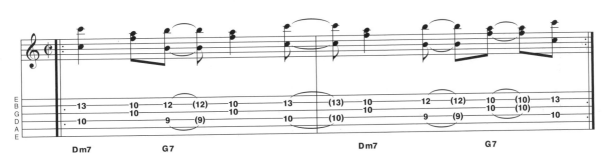

Exercise 8

257

Exercise 9 is a typical *son montuno* line in 2:3 clave. Notice that the downbeat of the montuno falls on the "two-side" of the clave (the bar with two notes in it), and the syncopated bar of the *montuno* falls on the "three side" of the clave. How you use the clave direction depends on whether the melody of the tune is in either direction (2:3 or 3:2). For the moment just try to get this line together. Concentrate on tempo and the ability to hold it for a long time. Record the clave and then play the line over it.

Exercise 10 is a pattern in the 3:2 clave. This is a very basic pattern to describe the concept of playing with the clave, but remember that there are many variations to this pattern. It is just a starting point. It maintains the same chord progression as the previous example in 2:3 and begins with an eight-note rest.

The basic rhythm for the cha-cha-cha is found in **exercise 11**. We all know this pattern from the organ riff in Santana's version of *Oye Como Va*. Try to play this line while tapping the 2:3 son clave with your foot. Concentrate on the note lengths, don't rush!

Exercise 12 is going to add some variation to the cha-cha-cha. It would originally have been played on a piano, and this has been adapted for guitar. It is important to have some co-ordination between thumb and fingers here, so don't worry if it takes a bit of time to get going. Remember, this is only a

variation, so don't overdo it unless you want a really busy feel. Hold it tight.

Playing during a percussion solo, like congas or timbale, requires lots of concentration and good sense of rhythm. Close your eyes if necessary to improve your concentration and be relaxed at the same time. **Exercise 13** is a common *montuno* line, often used over a percussion solo. This is just another exercise to reinforce your rhythm. This time it outlines a C7 mambo in 2:3 clave (remember?). Transpose it. You would use the same pattern over, for example, D7 to C7, for two bars each. Try taking it through the A blues progression.

Exercise 14 is the sort of thing you might find in a Mongo Santamaria tune. It's just two triads with a nicely syncopated rhythm. If you're playing this over a conga solo, be prepared to play this groove, and only this groove, for five to ten minutes, and maybe even longer. You think it sounds easy, but you'll need to really focus on your playing, because the soloist will be playing patterns and fills that will throw you off in no time.

Exercise 15 and **16** are examples of lines used in mambo and cha-cha-cha. Take note of the use of octaves, with fingers 1 and 4 of your left hand, and double stops. Start playing them slowly (90 bpm cut time) up to 120 bpm. The first example can be played over Am7- D7 or over just a D7. Hips starting to move?

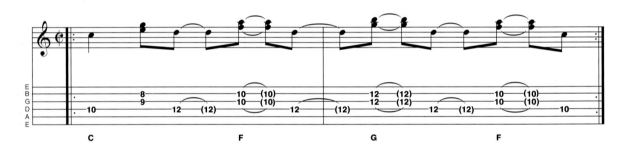

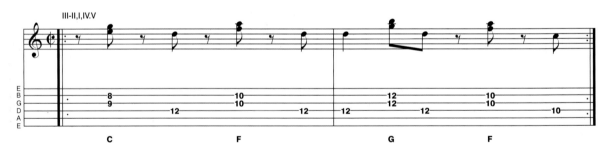

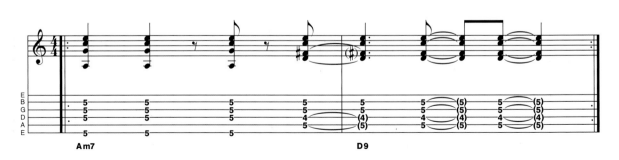

salsa

Exercise 12

Am7   D9

Exercise 13

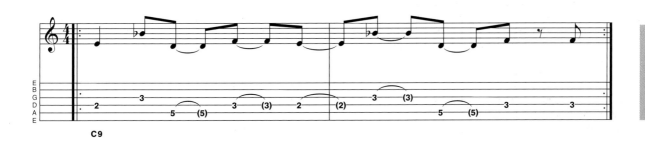

C9

Exercise 14

Exercise 15

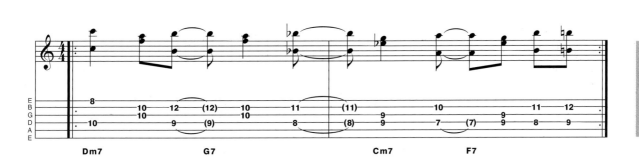

Dm7   G7   Cm7   F7

Exercise 16

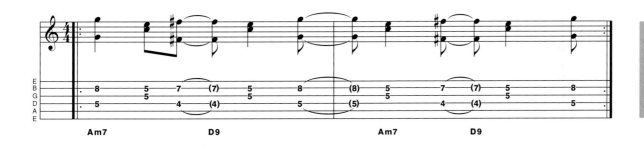

Am7   D9   Am7   D9

8

PLAYING
AFRICAN

Infectiously rhythmic, explosively joyous, delightfully melodic – African guitar is a style that works its way quickly into your blood, and stays there for good. It's as much fun to play as it is irresistible to listen to, and the fundamentals aren't particularly difficult to tackle with a little practise and special attention to the rhythmic essentials. Once mastered, it can be pursued as a style unto itself, or blended into countless other genres of music to give your usual playing some extra life and sparkle. ● **KARI BANNERMAN**

It is hardly surprising that the list of stars influenced yearly by their collaborations with African musicians is growing. Take Ry Cooder's work with Ali Farka Toure, Taj Mahal and Fouday Musa, or Paul Simon's work with Ladysmith Black Mambazo. Africa possesses the largest menu of both traditional and urban grooves in the world, a potential source of inspiration for anyone needing to resuscitate their depleting creative energy.

In this brief look at African guitar styles we're going to explore two "Palm Wine" guitar grooves: the *Sikyi* (pronounced see-chi), and the *Amponsah* (arm-pawn-sa), then move on to explore the broader "highlife" style of music. There was a time when no palm wine drinking session was complete without acoustic guitar music; hence the label. It is a characteristically happy sounding music, a music of celebration. It's influences can also be heard on albums like Jean-Luc Ponty's *Tchokola*, Koo Nimo's *Osabarifa*, and Peter Gabriel's *Passion*.

Highlife is a generic name for various types of dance music from west Africa. Essentially, though, it is the music created when west African musicians used the instruments provided by

their colonial bosses to play indigenous music, instead of the European waltzes, foxtrots and other expatriate music.

Amponsah-style guitar – created by the itinerant seamen of Liberia – is central to highlife music. Even the intricate guitar melodies that characterise the Congolese "*soukous*" style of African popular music contain at least one guitarist playing Amponsah groups – as does Paul Simon on his *Rhythm Of The Saints* album. Other fine examples of these sounds on Eric Agyeman/Ab Crentsil/T Frimpong's *Classic Highlife* and Bessa's *Bessa Live*.

Be aware that much of this style of playing has been adapted for guitar down the years, and would originally have been played on a more traditional stringed instrument, such as a kora. The kora is a traditional Senegambian instrument which resembles a balalaika in shape, using a large gourd as a body. It does, however, have considerably more strings, which are played in a harp-like fashion, without fretting them at all. Some of the exercises to following will contain suggestions for approximating this sound and feel on the guitar.

SIKYI RHYTHMS

The heartbeat of Sikyi and most African music is to be found in the drum section. For practical reasons, we will use a drum machine to recreate that feel.

Exercise 1 is a simple, three-part rhythm you can set up to accompany yourself with. Otherwise, if you don't have a drum machine, you could play the bell rhythm with a coin on an empty bottle, as is done in west Africa. Once you have programmed it in (a cabasa is a shaker, incidentally) try to feel the rhythm so that

you hear the pattern of the bell, and not the four-beat pulse of the time signature. It's a pattern that is similar to the "chop" rhythm of reggae but without the first beat of the eighth-note.

Rhythmical independence is crucial to all African music. Some forms have no time signature at all, being made up of a polyrhythmic structure whereby, for example, signatures of 2/4, 4/4 and 6/8 will coexist in a staggered bar system. This makes them completely unintelligible to the uninitiated. In any case, it's a music you have to develop a *feel* for to play right.

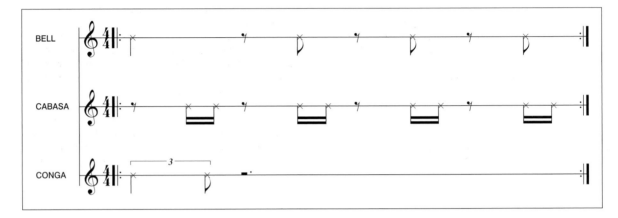

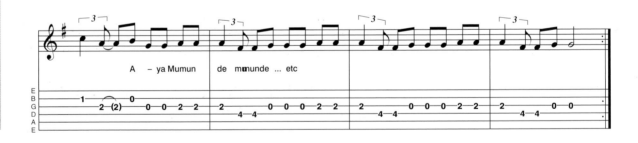

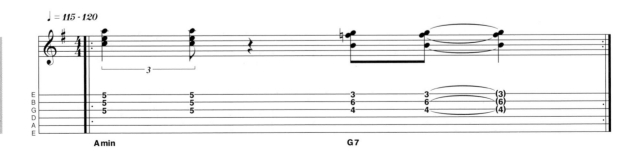

african rhythm

Exercise 1

Exercise 2

Exercise 3

262

TRADITIONAL TUNES

The most direct translation that I can manage of the folk tune *Mumunde* that we're going to look at now (pronounced "Mom-moo-dey") is "Happy Magical Dwarf." **Exercise 2** gives us the melody, the chorus repeating three times from bar four onwards. Play it with a happy feeling and record it, along with the drum pattern you have programmed, four or five times. We'll use this as the backing to practise our other exercises to. Listen to it over and over again until you really feel it.

Exercise 3 is a simple rhythmic strum. Even though it is based on two chords, the note and inversion choice is important to retain the flavor of Sikyi. Play the A minor with a crisp and tight plectrum action, and the G7 a little looser. If you're using a 4-track, record this onto your tape as well.

You may find that when you play exercise 4, you will start to feel the African vibe coming through, what Osibisa used to call "criss-cross rhythms that explode with happiness." Practise it with your ever-expanding backing track. Whether you are playing this with a plectrum or fingerstyle, practise it until there's a flow, or dance, to your right-hand action. Left-hand fingerings are suggestions only (t: thumb, i: index, m: middle), so check them out and then make up your mind.

Play the groove in **exercise 5** smoothly and in time to the backing tape and you will be merrily adopted by every Ghanian family in town, for you are now playing Sikyi music. If you add a "head" with a slur starting on the fourth beat of the intro, and a pulled-off tail on the next fourth beat, you will be playing the style as an Ashanti would really play it. We are using the mixolydian mode here, as the F is being kept natural, and this can be used as a tool for soloing.

Try playing Ex.5 an octave higher than written to get an ethnic Kora feel. use your index finger as a capo at the 12th fret – or even try it in open position on a Nashville-tuned guitar (a standard six-string guitar strung with the high-octave strings from a 12-string, or similar gauges).

Exercise 6 is a typical Palm Wine guitar solo intro, which you could join up to Ex.5 (as the start Ex.5 and end of Ex.6 imply). The phrase is in thirds from 12th position and moves down to third position. This downward movement is characteristic of most African melodies (see Ex.1). Note also how breaking away from the diad on the fourth beat adds more character to the line you're playing. The line also echoes the cyclical, non-resolving nature of Sikyi, which is typical of the vast majority of African music forms. Use your whammy bar to slide into the notes to get a Sunny Ade "Juju" feel. Again, a happy feel is vital before you can join it up with Ex.5.

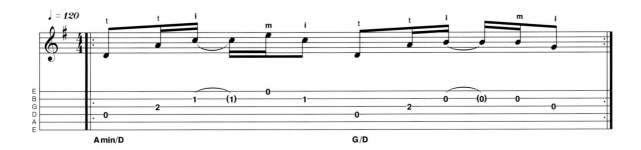

HIGHLIFE RHYTHMS

Our basic rhythm for this style is found in **exercise 7**. It cannot be overemphasized just how crucial rhythm is to this kind of music, so make sure you get it under your skin: dance to it. Make sure the tempo is comfortable; anything from 100bpm to 120bpm will be fine.

Exercise 8 is the melody from the song *Yaa Amponsah*, which is the story about a young, newly married bride. As before, record the melody and rhythm track to play along to.

Exercise 9 is a typical Amponsah guitar groove. Practise it with your rhythm section slowly at first, gradually building up the tempo until you can reach 120bpm comfortably. Essentially, it is a fingerstyle or two-fingers-and-plectrum groove, because some of the voicings are unplayable with a plectrum alone. In Africa, because of the dominant influence of the kora and the *nyatiti* (another lute-style instrument), the right-hand two-finger picking style is predominant, but use whatever is comfortable.

The chord symbols are just a guide; to get the flavor use my exact inversions. Numerous variations of this progression have spawned a thousand songs all over west Africa and beyond – just ask Brian Eno or Mick Fleetwood. It is related to calypso and I know that it plays a crucial part in the ongoing cross-fertalization of grooves between Africa, Europe and the Caribbean.

HIGHLIFE JAZZ

Exercise 10 is a rhythm lick using the 7sus and 7 chords. Here we are moving into the area of highlife big bands and highlife jazz. Try the more complex chords written underneath as a jazzier variation. This is more big band highlife, as it utilizes these crossover chords. The essence of Amponsah is retained in the melody lines, the rhythm and the bassline. Use a right hand semi-muted, snappy plectrum style to make the rhythms come alive. When you have mastered it, practise it alternately with Ex.3.

Exercise 11 is a typical Amponsah phrase used by local guitarists – the sound of the diminished chord is very reminiscent of the tonality of several indigenous harmonies and that's why it's used. This exercise is really quite simple. Start with the diminished triad and just move the shape down the fretboard, retaining the fingering until you hit the F6 chord and C. The following phrases are sixth diads, much as you'd find at the beginning of *Soul Man* by Sam and Dave.

Finally, **exercise 12** gives you an impression an Amponsah bassline. Note the syncopation and polyrhythms against the guitar. Practise until you really feel it, when you don't need to think of the notes, the bars, or the phrases. This is called the "*adakamu*" style, as it is traditionally adapted from the phrasing of the square box bass drum, and adakamu means "box."

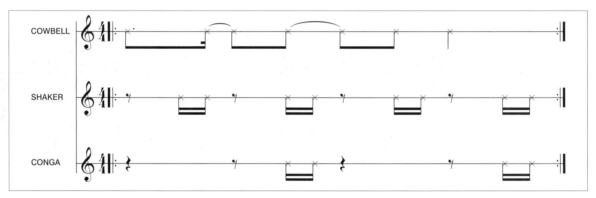

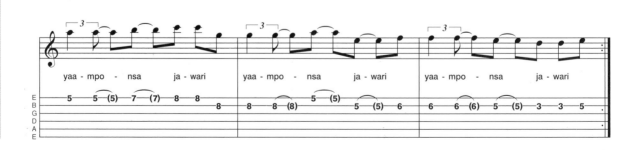

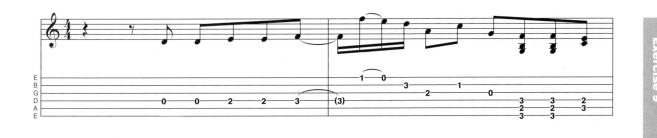

Exercise 9

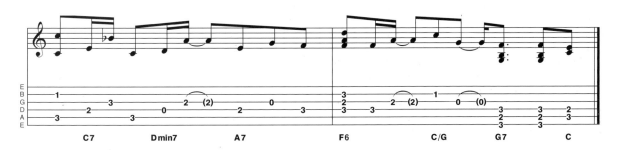

Exercise 10

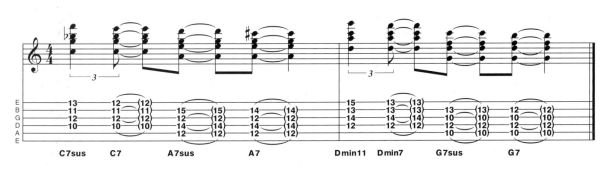

Exercise 11

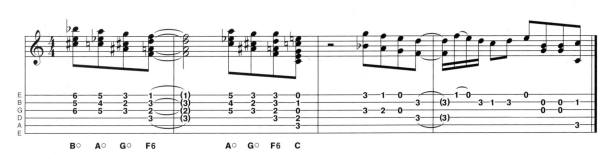

Exercise 12

9

PLAYING
CLASSICAL

Like the study of any classical instrument, the serious pursuit of proficiency in classical guitar is a major discipline. That said, any competent guitarist willing to put in some time and effort can learn enough of the basics of classical guitar technique, sound and style to add an exciting new element to his or her repertoire. As genre distinctions fall further by the wayside in contemporary guitar-based music, achieving a basic grasp of classical technique can add diversity to your own style, and perhaps turn you on to a whole new direction in your playing. ● DAVID BRAID

The 10 exercises in this section are designed to give an overview of classical guitar technique and types of music played in this style. Most of the pieces are specially composed studies, each highlighting particular playing techniques and/or musical devices. Before getting into the exercises, however, it's important for us to take a quick look at classical playing technique.

PLAYING POSITION

The classical playing position stems directly from the practicality of keeping the instrument steady while being free to play. The position not only allows the player to move easily around the fingerboard with the left hand, but also enables them to make sudden right hand position changes, for example, from an arpeggio to a chord strum. The left leg should be raised by the use of a small foot stool which raises the guitar neck so all parts of the fingerboard can be reached easily. Without using the hands at all the guitar is held in four places:

1. Resting on the left thigh
2. Leaning against the right inner thigh
3. Underneath the right forearm (before the elbow)
4. The back leaning on the left side of the chest.

POINTS TO NOTE

1. The force of gravity ensures the right hand falls naturally into place over the sound hole
2. The shoulders and arms should be completely relaxed
3. The guitar neck should be angled sufficiently so that the left hand is quite close to the eye. As most music is played from memory, the left hand is guided by looking at the frets you are about to go to. (The hand follows the eye, not vice-versa.)
4. Both thumbs should be in a natural, straight position and all fingers should be curved in (on both hands).

BASIC TECHNIQUE

One of the fundamental aspects of classical guitar music is counterpoint: two or more lines played simultaneously. It is because of this musical requirement that the independence and collaboration of fingers and thumb in the right hand is so essential. Although other styles of guitar playing use right hand finger style, the demands of accuracy and speed in the classical repertoire have given rise to special exercises designed to bring these points to great refinement. It can take some work to get to this point, but it will pay dividends in your performance ability.

ARPEGGIO TECHNIQUE

The photo above is from the player's point of view. Points to notice are, 1: that you are positioned over the middle of the instrument; 2: the right-hand (RH) thumb is straight and well in front of the fingers; 3: the left-hand (LH) thumb is approximately opposite the second finger and well behind the neck.

It is important that the RH does note move between individual strokes of the fingers and thumb, both because one's spatial relation to the string can be lost and also because time (one of the most important aspects of music) is lost moving the hand back to a position where the string can be reached.

ARPEGGIOS

The basis of the right hand technique is the arpeggio. This is shown below in four stages. In classical guitar notation the fingers on both hands are given special letters and numbers (numbers for the left and letters for the right in order to make a clear distinction between them).

The right hand fingers and their notation symbols are: Thumb: **p**; Index: **i**; Middle: **m**; Ring: **a**. The little finger is not used. The left hand fingers are numbered 1–4 from the index to the little finger.

HALF-ARPEGGIO

The half-arpeggio is when strings four (or five or six) to one are played with the thumb and three fingers of the right hand, with a particular finger assigned to each string. Before playing it is important to prepare the fingers on the strings (as in the photo top-left) in order to ensure the correct angle of playing stroke. As you can also see in this photograph, the thumb is far in front of the fingers in order for both to move freely without colliding with each other. This is especially important, as to make a strong tone it is essential that the fingers and thumb follow through after playing the string.

Of the five individual photos seen left, the top-left photograph shows the same stage of preparation from the front. Note the slight angle in the wrist, which produces enough height for the fingers to move into the hand. The remaining photos show the progression of movement of the thumb and three fingers as they play strings four to one.

Note that the fingers which are yet to play remain on the string until it is their turn to move. This is necessary to ensure that no time is lost looking for the string. Ideally the exercise should be repeated a number of times in succession without a break between each cycle. When playing in this way it is important not to replace the fingers on the strings for preparation each time until the moment they are required to play the string again, as it would stop the previous notes from sounding, resulting in an unpleasant sudden break in the sustained note.

FULL-ARPEGGIO

The full-arpeggio is an extension of the half-arpeggio where two extra notes are played, making it a cycle of six instead of four. This is done by playing the second string (with **m**) and then the third string (with **i**) again immediately after the **a** finger has played the first string.

LEARNING NOTATION

Musical notation is written on a grid of five horizontal lines called a "stave" (or staff). Each line and each space on the stave represents a note of a different pitch, named after the first seven letters of the alphabet: A, B, C, D, E, F, G. After this the notes start repeating in a higher or lower "octave" – so-called because there are eight main steps from one note to its equivalent note, above or below.

The symbol at the beginning of the stave is called a clef. There are several types of clef, but this one, a treble clef, is really the only one you will come across as a guitarist (other clefs, such as the bass clef, show different parts of the musical range).

The notes on the lines of the treble clef stave are, from the bottom: E, G, B, D, F (it may help you remember this order if you make up a mnemonic using these letters – a common one is *Every Good Boy Deserves Fun*). The notes in the spaces, going

The six CDs shown here cover a wide range of styles within the guitar repertoire, ranging from the concerts of Vivaldi to the virtuosity of Paganini (top-left, who also played the guitar as well as the violin), and the original recordings of Llobet (the main mentor of Segovia). Also included here is the exotic composer and guitarist Barrios, who played on a steel strung guitar to avoid the rotting of the gut strings in the South American climate (nylon was not available then). Barrios was half native American and would sometimes come on stage wearing traditional clothes and full head-dress.

up, are: F, A, C, E (as illustrated on the sample stave below). When notes are used that go outside the range of the stave, either above or below, short lines called "ledger lines" – long enough for just one note – are added to extend the stave.

Most music is divided into bars, as shown in the second diagram above, by vertical "barlines" which group the music into equal sections to make it easier to read. Although the bars divide the music evenly according to the time signature they are not to be heard as such – you must not pause or stop at each barline. A double barline indicates the end of the piece of music.

The notes themselves can last different lengths of time, as indicated by symbols called "note values" (illustrated below). A whole note is called a *semibreve*, a half note is called a *minim*, a quarter note is called a *crotchet*, an eighth note is called a *quaver*, and a sixteenth note is called a *semiquaver*.

TIME SIGNATURES

The type and amount of note values in each bar is indicated at the beginning of the music by the "time signature." This consists of two small numbers arranged vertically. The top digit indicates the number of beats per bar and the lower number indicates the value of each, which is represented by its fraction of a semibreve (whole note). So, for example, the crotchet (quarter note) is indicated by the lower number 4; the minim (half note) is

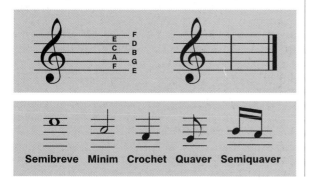

Semibreve Minim Crochet Quaver Semiquaver

indicated by a 2; and the semiquaver (sixteenth note) is indicated by a 16.

The most frequently used time signature is 4 4 – four crotchets in a bar – often called "common time," and therefore sometimes indicated by just a capital C at the start of the passage instead of the two fours. Other frequently used time signatures are 2/4 and 3/4 and 6/8. The latter has the note value of a quaver and divides the bar into two halves of 3/8.

GUITAR NOTATION

As well as the standard musical notation, there are some additional signs specific to written guitar music:

A number from 1–4, written above or under a note on the stave, indicates which left-hand finger is to be used to hold down that note on the fingerboard. (If the number 0 appears, the open string is to be played.)

A number in a circle indicates which string is to be played.

Roman numerals (I, II, III, IV, V etc) indicate the fret position at which to hold down the notes.

The letters p, i, m and a (as already mentioned in the introduction) above or below the stave refer to the right-hand fingering.

To ease the way for non-music readers, all exercises will also be represented in TAB, but you can use this chapter to brush up on your music-reading skills – which will be essential for any further pursuit of classical guitar study.

ACCIDENTALS

On the following pages, our first two exercises deal with two main points: accidentals (sharps in exercise 1 and flats in exercise 2) and music in two parts. Accidentals are sharp, flat or natural signs placed in the music next to particular notes in order to raise or lower them by a semitone (one fret on the guitar). The note affected remains sharpened or flattened until the next bar line or until it is returned to its original pitch by a natural sign. The lower part in both exercises is played with p and the top part with alternating i and m.

In **exercise 1**, Note the marking *f* at the start: this stands for "forte" – strong/loud. The piece gradually drops in volume to *p* "piano" – soft/quiet – in bar five. These symbols are called "dynamics" and are indications to alter the volume of the piece. In bars seven and eight the piece picks up in volume again to *mf* – "mezzo forte" (medium loud).

The word "rit" is short for "ritardo" which means to hold back, or slow down. This is to be done throughout the section indicated by the dotted line. The curved line between the two Ds in bar eight is a "tie." The tie tells us that the second of these notes is not to be played, but that the first-played note is merely sustained through this beat.

The tie should not to be confused with a "slur," which is between two notes of different pitch and means that the second one is only played with the left hand (by executing a pull off or hammer on).

Exercise 2 is another piece in 2/4 with further accidentals to keep an eye out for. Also, notice that the notes in bar eight have two stems, going up and down. This is because both parts have the exact same notes at this point, playing in unison, even though they are still considered two parts.

The G in bar nine should be left to ring on so it makes a passing harmony with the E-flat which you will play at the start of the next bar.

The great Andrés Segovia, who throughout the twentieth century single-handedly raised the status of the guitar from a humble salon instrument to a full classical instrument capable of high art music.

accidentals

Exercise 1

270

accidentals

British guitarist Julian Bream is in many ways an heir to Segovia, even though he is self-taught and developed independently. His exciting, fiery playing and devotion to authenticity of repertoire quickly established him as the leading guitarist of the second half of the twentieth century.

Exercise 2

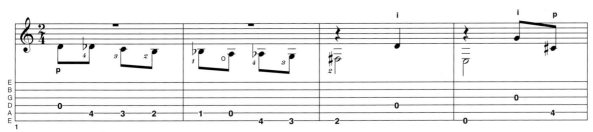

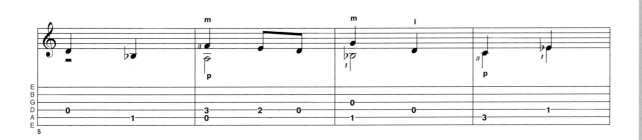

271

Exercise 3 is the theme from *The Surprise Symphony* by Joseph Haydn (1732-1809). This piece has a "key signature" of A. This is a set of sharps or flats written at the start of the music which indicates that those particular notes are to be raised or lowered by a semitone throughout the entire work (unless canceled out by a natural accidental). The key signature indicates a "key," which is a hierarchy of chords based around one main chord called the "tonic triad." The sharps and flats always appear in the same order so that it is not necessary to actually check which line or space the sharp or flat sign appears on. The order of Sharps is: F#,C#,G#,D#,A#,E#,B#. A simple way of remembering this order is by using the mnemonic: *Father*

Charles Goes Down And Eats Breakfast. The order of flats is simply the reverse: Bb,Eb,Ab,Db,Gb,Cb,Fb. In exercise 3 there are three sharps: F#,C#,G#.

There is a loud chord right at the end of the piece which in the original version for orchestra was put in by the composer to stop the audience talking during the performance. The word "*sempre*" before the dynamic marking of *pp* means "always" so the entire piece is to be played at *pp: pianissimo* (very quiet) until a different dynamic is encountered. This happens at the final chord which is marked *sfz*. This stands for "*sforzando*," meaning forced – an indication to accent the chord heavily and suddenly (strummed very quickly across with p).

dynamics

Exercise 3

dynamics

This piece in **exercise 4** is based entirely on the half-arpeggio technique discussed in the introduction. These change direction now and then, for example in bar four and from the section marked *p* (piano).

There is an *f* (forte) marking right at the start, and the piece returns to this dynamic three bars from the end. Note, however, the hairpin marking before the *f*. This means that the music gets gradually louder during this section. The indication "rall" on the third to last bar means "rallentando" which means to slow down. This is to be done gradually during section marked by the dotted line. Getting such dynamics right – or indeed wrong – makes an enormous difference in the feel of a classical piece.

One of many female guitarists who rose to prominence in the third generation following Segovia, Sharon Isbin has also collaborated with jazz guitarist Larry Coryell.

Exercise 4

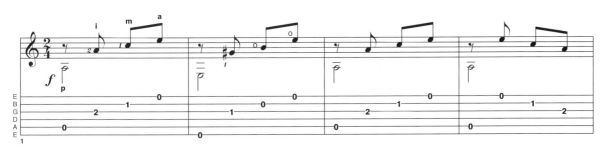

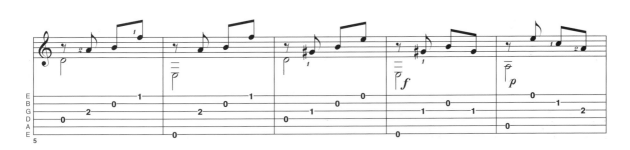

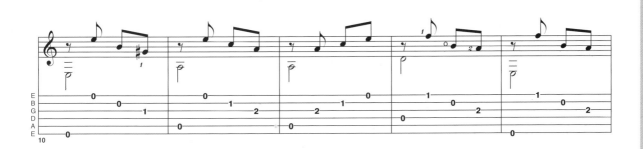

273

Exercise 5 brings in four new points. The first is playing in higher positions. When playing at first position the first finger plays all the notes at the first fret, the second at the second fret and so on. When playing at a different position the first finger determines which number that position is called. For instance, if playing in second position, the first finger now plays the notes at the second fret, the second finger those at the third and so on. This piece is played entirely in the second position.

The second technique is the half-barre. This is when the first finger is used to hold down three or four strings simultaneously.

This is done by holding it straight across the strings just behind, and in line with, the fret. The notation for this is as written above the first note: a fraction 1/2 followed by a capital C and a Roman numeral indicating the position at which the half-barre is to be held, in this case second position.

The third point in this piece is the dotted note. This is simply a way of increasing the length of a note by half. So when, for instance, a minim is dotted, it is worth three crochets instead of the usual two. This is done in the lower part in bar one, two and later in the piece.

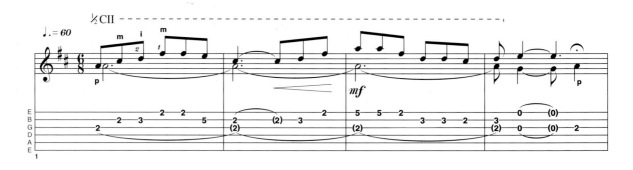

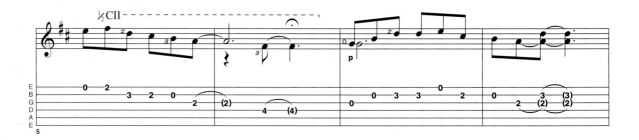

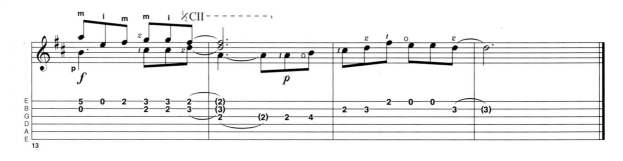

Exercise 5

higher positions

The fourth point in this piece is the metronome marking. This is an exact way of determining the speed or "tempo" of a piece. It is written as a note equaling a number, which means that that particular number of the written note value should occur in one minute. In this piece there are 60 dotted crochets per minute. The work begins *mp* (*mezzo piano* – medium quiet). There are two sharps in the key signature, F# and C#, making it the key of D (when the key is not specified as either major or minor, it is always major).

Exercise 6 is arpeggio-based, as was exercise 4, but this time the full-arpeggio is used, with the added difference that the a finger plays together with p at the start of most bars. The "3" and the square bracket above the first three notes indicates a "triplet," which is a type of "irrational rhythm." This means that there are three notes in the time of two. In this case three quavers (in the time of one crochet – ordinarily two quavers). The triplet is used continuously throughout the piece but is only written in at the start in order not to clutter up the score.

This piece makes use of the full-barre, which is similar to the half-barre except that it covers all six strings. This is used at the third position throughout lines one and three.

Regarded by many as one of the truly great living guitarists, David Russell's astounding technical ability has allowed him total musical freedom to transcribe and perform such major works as Handel's harpsichord pieces.

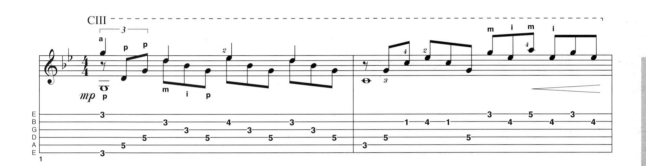

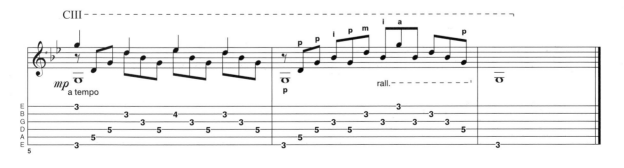

275

The high esteem in which Andrés Segovia continues to be held still reverberates through the classical guitar world, as indicated by this tribute album from Christopher Parkening. The CD bottom-left, on the other hand, Eliot Fisk's *Rochberg: Caprice Variations*, shows a contemporary musician's devotion to the music of his time, a necessary predisposition for guitarists due to the limited amount of works dedicated to the guitar in the past.

Exercise 7 uses an irrational rhythm, this time a sextuplet, with six semiquavers in the time of the usual four (in one crochet). Additionally, there is a tune in the top part indicated by the stems going upwards. This use of melody with an arpeggio is very idiomatic for the guitar. Ideally, this top part is played using a right hand technique called "apoyando" or "rest stroke." This is achieved by the finger coming to rest on the adjacent (lower) string after the string is played. This makes for a particularly strong and warm tone. Due to its opposing movement, the thumb, however, comes to rest on the next higher string. Apoyando is usually used for a part with little accompaniment. Combining it in an arpeggio, as here, requires careful practice.

At the last bar there is the marking *D.C. al X*. This means that you are to return to the beginning ("Da Capo," meaning from the start) and stop when you reach the first symbol (at the end of line two) then jump from there and play the as-yet unplayed last bar. This piece has a key signature of one sharp (F#) which indicates the key of E minor. Note also the accidentals of B-flat and D# in bars two and five.

Exercise 8 uses "slurs," known as "*ligado*" on the classical guitar. Ligado going up, as in bar one, is played by hammering the left hand finger onto the string so that it sounds and produces the note found at the fret where the finger lands. It is

Exercise 7

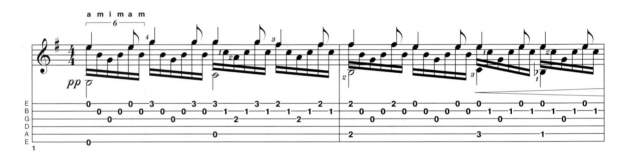

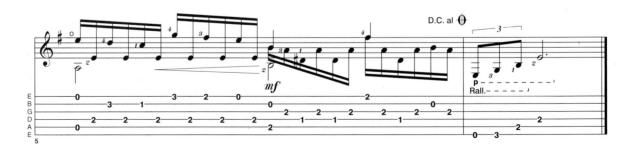

apoyando

ligado

important for the hammer-on finger to hit the string on the beat, rather than anticipate the note and push it ahead of the beat. In bar five there is an example of ligado going down. This is done by removing the finger quickly (downwards) so that the note beneath (either an open string, or one held by another finger as in this piece) is sounded. This is more difficult than slurring up as the left hand finger must pluck the string slightly as it comes off to produce some movement in the string.

Several types of ligado can be produced, ranging from a smooth connection between notes to a percussive attack. Ligado

going up is varied by the speed of the finger landing on the string. The sound of slurring down depends on how much sideways movement (in relation to the string) is applied. A very smooth type is produced by very little plucking (sideways movement) with the finger, but with more of a quick lifting up of the finger off the string.

Also in this exercise there are several changes of position. These are marked throughout the score by Roman numerals. Notes: "Con brio" means "with life;" "Acc" is short for "accelerando," which means to speed up throughout the section.

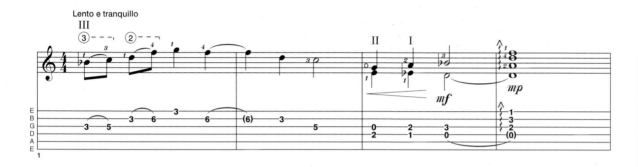

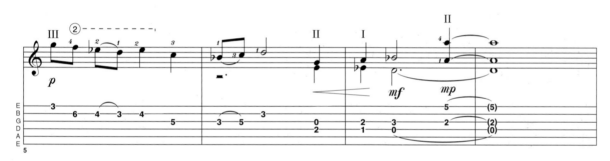

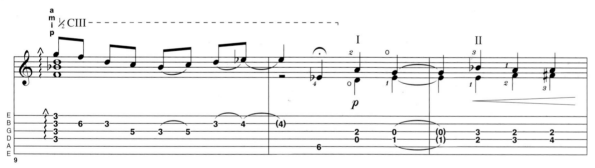

Kazuhito Yamashita, an extremely gifted player – though one who sometimes appears to be vying with Eliot Fisk for the title of "world's fastest guitarist" – is a great artists and interpreter of the main repertoire and much new music. Seemingly more lighthearted but no less serious in its pursuit of the art, Leo and Ichiro's CD Penny Lane (below left) takes a stroll through the Lennon and McCartney composition by way of framing classical guitar in a pop context.

Exercise 9 has a key signature of three sharps, making the key of A. In the major keys, the key note can be easily found from the amount of sharps as it is always one semitone higher than the last one. For example, in this piece there are three sharps: F#, C#, G#, (*Father Charles Goes...*), so the key note is A, a semitone above G#. Triplets are used throughout this piece (again, only marked at the start to keep the score clear).

There are also repeated sections such as bars three and four which appear later as bars seven and eight. Repetition is a device found in most styles of music as it helps to re-establish important compositional themes and also has the added bonus that, because of the new context in which the repeat appears, it sounds slightly different due to its new function, being altered somewhat by what is going on around it at that point.

In bars five and six there are two notes playing together in the top part. These are to be played with i and m and must sound exactly together. The best way to achieve this is to actually keep the fingers together while playing as if they were one large finger. The marking "*Molto Rall*" in the last bar means to slow down considerably, i.e. rather quickly. *Molto* means "much" or "a lot," and can be annexed to various words in music such as "*molto accelerando*" – speed up a lot.

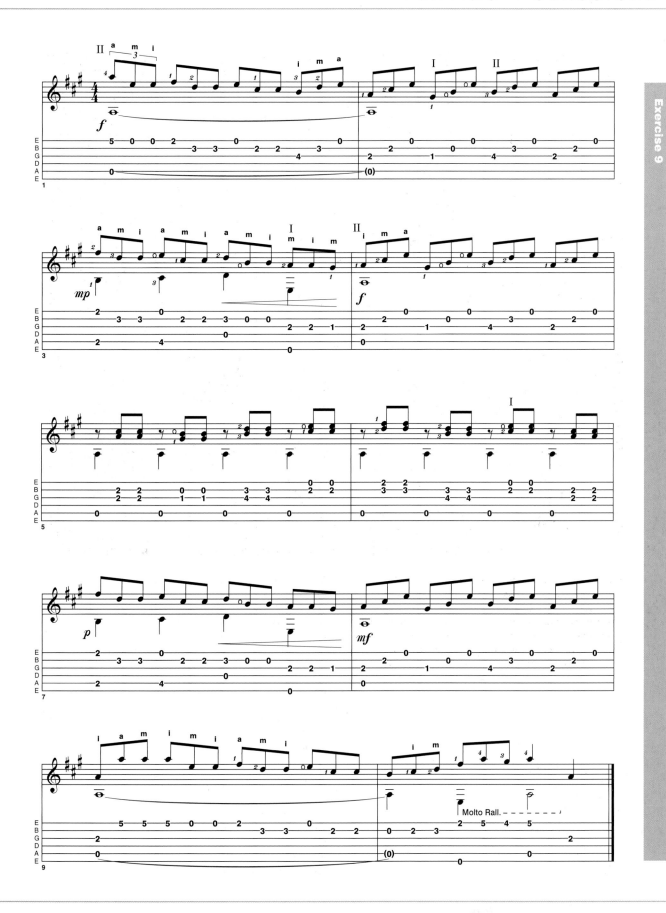

Cuban guitarist Manuel Barrueco, two whose albums are pictured far left, is considered by many to be the "players' favorite." His is a balanced approach somewhat akin to the pianist Dinu Lipatti's school, where the composition itself takes precedence over the performer. Near left: a moment of deep concentration from Sharon Isbin in concert.

There is a metronome marking at the start of this piece in **exercise 10** which indicates 72 crochets to the minute. This is rather quick, and is designed to give the piece a lively character. The word "*Allegro*" means quick and imparts a particular brisk quality required by the composer with the more exact tempo given by the metronome marking.

There are two new types of dynamic marking in this piece: "*cresc*," short for *crescendo* – meaning to get louder, as many players may already know – and "*dim*," short for "*diminuendo*," meaning the reverse, to get quieter. These are gradual indications and are to be realised throughout the passage marked by the dotted line.

This piece is written in the Baroque style and is highly linear or "contrapuntal," that is, it makes much use of the play between two lines (known as counterpoint, as discussed in the introduction). A device particular to this style is "imitation." This is done by the lines copying one another, as in a canon or round, so the piece gives the impression of chasing itself. Imitation can be clearly seen between bars one and three where the initial figure on C is repeated on the lower pitch of E. Imitation is used later in the piece between bars 14 and 15, where the tune starting on the low G (bar 14, marked *ff*) is repeated exactly at the end of the next bar, but an octave higher.

Note that the first bar has only one crochet beat in it. This is called an "*anacrusis*" or "up beat" and is used to give an animated start to the music.

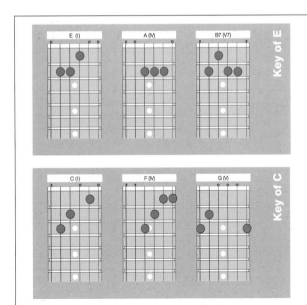

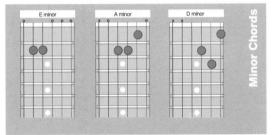

Though exercises in this chapter apply techniques for single-line playing primarily – if occasionally in two parts – a look at some basic chords on the classical guitar (namely the I, IV and V in two popular keys and some basic minor chords) is also worth a brief detour. The width of the classical guitar neck and the flatness of its fingerboard can actually make it a more difficult instrument to chord than many other types of guitar, and full barre chords are not easily achieved by the beginner.

baroque style

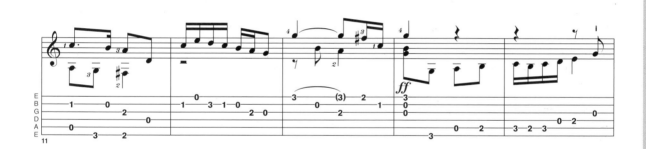

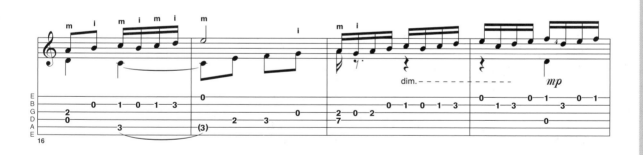

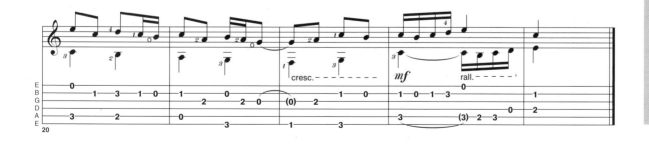

PLAYING JAZZ

From the early days of jazz to the present, guitarists have constantly challenged the limitations of their instrument – not only with their sound but also with their technique. Charlie Christian, the father of electric jazz guitar, and Pat Metheny, one of today's modern jazz innovators, both play jazz on an electric guitar but the difference in their sound and approach is quite apparent. ● CARL FILIPIAK

They each have a distinct tone, technique, and uniqueness to their soloing, yet both are parallel players in the evolution of jazz guitar. From Charlie to Pat – and everything in between and beyond – there's a world of great guitar styles to learn and enjoy.

Let's take a quick look at a few things that shaped Charlie Christian's sound and ideas. Using a hollowbody guitar plugged into an amp, his swing-influenced lines were amazingly fluid, executed by his technique of using all down strokes. Pat Metheny's sound incorporates a variety of guitars, stereo amplification and effects to create his ambient signature sound. His post-bop lines are played amazingly fluidly by the heavy use of left hand hammer ons and pull offs. You can see how a change in any of those four parameters – guitar, amplification, technique and style – can create such a diverse sound.

A look at how the guitar evolved from Charlie Christian to Pat Metheny will help us get started. Charlie Christian made a tremendous impact on jazz guitar in the late 1930s, and some of his greatest work can be heard on recordings with Benny Goodman. Christian joined Goodman's band in 1939 and died just a few years later in March of 1942. Let's examine some things that shaped the aural landscape of guitar during his era.

Electricity+Amplifier+Guitar=MUCH LOUDER!

With more volume than the acoustic guitar and banjo, the new wave of electric guitarists could now compete with the horn sections. Feel the power! This monumental change now elevated the guitarist's position from an accompanist in the band to one of the soloists. It wasn't long before the sounds of amplified guitars were heard on more and more recordings and not just in jazz. The electric guitar became a defining sound of rock'n'roll and the blues. Many jazz guitarists were influenced by these sounds and by the mid to late '60s would be part of the new movement to be known as jazz-fusion. More about this a little later.

Wes Montgomery came into prominence in the late 1960s and many consider him to be the father of modern jazz guitar. Wes was a modern bop player who displayed a sophisticated melodic and harmonic sense. The keys to his style were the use of his thumb, which produced a very warm sound, and his ability to play octaves faster than most guitarists could play single lines. At that time this made him instantly recognizable and created a new standard in modern jazz guitar.

Also carrying on in the tradition of Wes were two incredible guitarists, George Benson and Pat Martino. Both had amazing technique and used a pick for most of their

single note lines. These two virtuosos became the new standard and elevated the sound of jazz guitar once again. Just check out their solos on George Benson's *Cookbook* CD and Pat Martino's *Footprints* and you'll see what I mean.

Electricity+Louder Amp+Guitar+Effects=Jimi Hendrix

What's Jimi Hendrix got to do with Jazz? A Lot! He influenced the sound of jazz guitarists that were entering the next movement, which was called fusion. Jazz was now beginning to borrow heavily from the sounds of rock music. Using a solid body guitar, massive amplification and effects in an innovative way, Hendrix created sounds that fit in perfectly with the new direction of jazz. These concepts would be incorporated in a jazz context by guitarist John McLaughlin. Using a solid body guitar with increased sustain was a radical departure from the sound of an archtop guitar and a relatively small amp. Considered the first fusion record, Miles Davis's album *Bitches Brew* was a landmark recording during this era, and featured John McLaughlin turning up the volume.

With the increased volume the guitar entered the realm of the wind instrument. Unlimited sustain meant one could now play lines by using hammer ons and pull offs alone. That sort of sound was developed and perfected by Allan Holdsworth, who uses legato technique with an overdriven and compressed tone that sounds remarkably "horn like" in nature. It's what jazz guitarists have wanted to do all along!

Jim Hall, an incredible guitarist, has probably influenced and changed the sound of contemporary jazz guitar more than anyone else. A jazz player with some serious history, he was one of the early guitarists to employ hammer ons and pull offs to achieve a more fluid sound. This was quite a departure from the more percussive technique of picking every note. He helped inspire the next generation of great players that includes Mick Goodrick, Pat Metheny, John Scofield, Mike Stern, Bill Frisell and John Abercrombie. Jim Hall is the bridge that connects the traditional elements of jazz and points them to the future. It now becomes easier to hear how contemporary guitarists fit into all this, their unique styles arising from the infinite possibilities of combining jazz with the elements of rock and beyond. Contemporary guitar is capable of incredible sounds and has come a long way musically since the early days of Charlie Christian. No longer on the sidelines, guitarists are now much more harmonically advanced, technically proficient and have a much higher profile in the jazz world than ever before. I can't wait to hear where it takes us to next.

SEVEN BASIC SOUNDS

Now that we've seen the direction jazz guitar is headed, let's take a look at some of the things we have to learn in order to get there. Knowing how to recognize the seven basic sounds in all keys is very important. They are the major, minor, dominant, diminished, minor 7 flat 5, augmented and suspended sounds.

The first three (major, minor and dominant) sounds are especially important. Use the sixth and the fifth string to locate the nearest root, match the appropriate sound and you will be able to play just about any chord progression (we'll get to them soon). For now, try these examples in the keys of G (sixth string root) and C (fifth string root), then see if you can transpose them elsewhere.

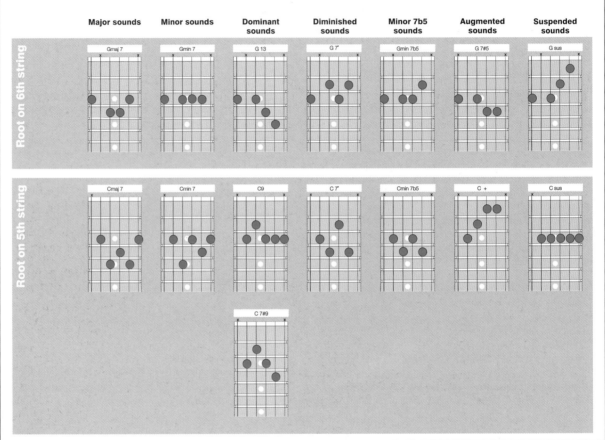

TWO NOTE DIADS

Don't be deceived by the simplicity of these two note diads. In many musical settings they sound great! They are the guide tones of chords, which are the 3rds and 7ths and imply the quality of the chord (major, minor or dominant). They work great played alongside a bass player who fills in the root of the chord.

Even before Charlie Christian took the amplified guitar to new heights, Eddie Lang was on the scene as the first real jazz guitar virtuoso. In his short career (his tragic, premature death was caused by a poorly performed tonsillectomy), Lang performed with early jazz greats such as Bix Beiderbecke, Frankie Trumbauer, Paul Whiteman, King Oliver, Red Nichols and Bing Crosby.

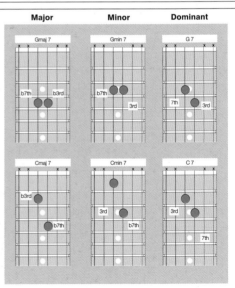

basic chords and diads

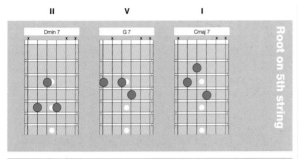

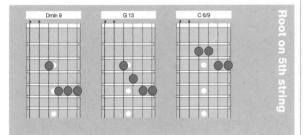

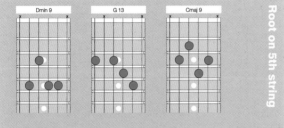

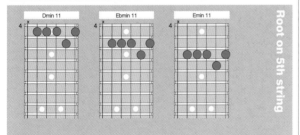

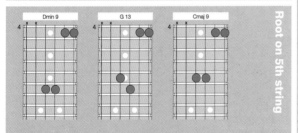

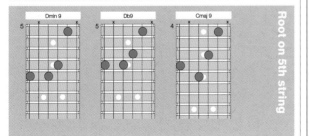

2–5–1 PROGRESSIONS

The 2–5–1 is one of the most widely used sequences in jazz. When you take a C major scale and build chords in thirds on each note of that scale, the seven chords will be:

C major 7,
D minor 7,
E minor 7,
F major 7,
G7,
A minor 7,
B minor 7 flat 5.

The 2nd chord is D Minor 7, the chord that starts on the fifth degree of the scale is G7 and the "one" chord is C Major 7. A 2–5–1 in the key of C is: D Minor 7, G7, and C Major 7. Here is a page of assorted 2–5–1 patterns. I would suggest starting out by mastering the first two examples, then proceed to each of the remaining progressions.

Charlie Christian is the original star of electric jazz guitar, and was enormously influential in the early days of the instrument. Some of his best work was recorded with the Benny Goodman orchestra from 1939 to 1942.

progressions

MINOR 2–5–1 PROGRESSIONS

The 2–5–1 in a minor key is a minor 7 flat 5 chord, followed by a dominant 7 flat 9 chord, then a minor 7 or minor 9 chord. In C minor the sequence would be Dmin7b5, G7, and Cmin7. The first two examples are extremely useful but try all of them for different settings (which we will explore later).

UPPER VOICINGS

Master this page and you will see how you can move chords around and resolve to the next sound with great voice leading. Practise by transposing to different keys and work out some 2–5–1 sequences. Resolve to the nearest form when the sounds change from minor to dominant to major.

Root on 5th 6th string

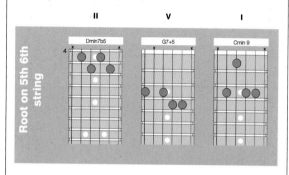

Root on 5th 6th string

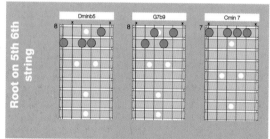

Upper 4 strings no roots

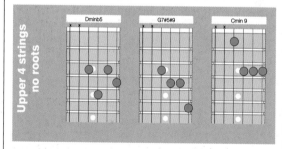

Upper 4 strings no roots

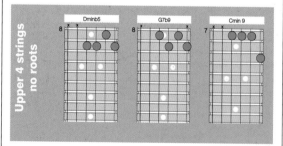

Major sounds   **Minor sounds**   **Dominant sounds**

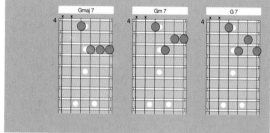

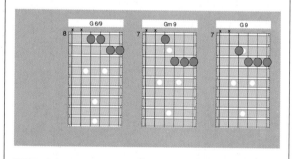

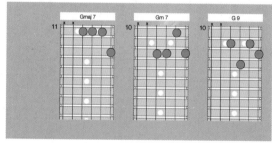

chord progressions

1–6–2–5 PROGRESSIONS

This is another pattern of equal importance. A quick look at the seven chords in the key of C (diatonic harmony) shows that the chord that occupies the sixth scale degree is an A minor 7th chord. A 1–6–2–5 in the key of C Major would be: Cmaj7, Amin7, Dmin7, G7. You may notice there is only one dominant chord in a key, built on the 5th scale degree. This chord, the G7 in the key of C, creates tension that resolves to the on chord, Cmaj7. Any chord in the key can have its arrival preceded by a dominant chord. This is called a secondary dominant and that's how the A7 chord will be explained in the following sequence:

1	6	2	5
Cmaj7	**A7**	**Dmin7**	**G7**

The secondary dominant A7 is the dominant of 2, or the "5" of 2. Many tunes feature this sequence so try to learn it in as many keys as possible. Some "standards" employing the 1–6–2–5 include *Oleo, Rhythm-a-ning, The Theme, Moose The Mooch, Ready And Able* and *Tipping* (all in the rhythm changes "A" section) and *Have You Met Miss Jones, Turnaround In Blues* (last two bars) and *St. Thomas*. Try these three four-chord 1–6–2–5 patterns to hear the sound of A7 resolving to Dmin7, as well as G7 resolving to Cmaj7. The first sequence is made up of roots and guide tones, the second features added tensions, and the third uses upper-four-string voicings.

It's a rhythm thing: when the roots of jazz were being formulated, the guitarist's role was first an foremost as a member of the rhythm section. The album *Pioneers of the Jazz Guitar* contains more solid work from early greats than you can shake a swing-time stick at – with some sweet soloing besides. From a later era, Freddie Green's rock-steady chops on The Count Basie Band's 1957 recording *The Complete Atomic Basie* remains a stunning example of how to play the changes with major groove.

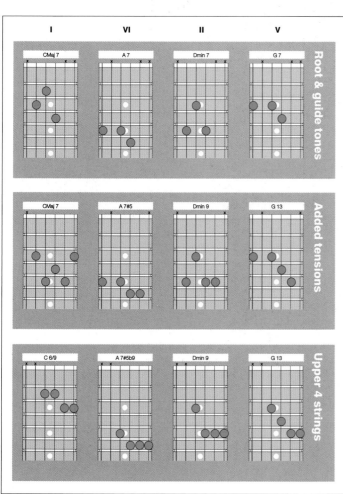

I	VI	II	V
CMaj 7	A 7	Dmin 7	G 7

Root & guide tones

| CMaj 7 | A 7#5 | Dmin 9 | G 13 |

Added tensions

| C 6/9 | A 7#5b9 | Dmin 9 | G 13 |

Upper 4 strings

MOVING FURTHER

Understanding just a few concepts like diatonic harmony, related 2s and 5s, subflat 5s, and chord families can help you produce some harmonically complex chord sequences. This may take a while to understand thoroughly, but don't let this discourage you from trying out some new and interesting patterns.

Diatonic harmony produces tonic, sub dominant and dominant chords built on the root, 4th and 5th degree of the major scale. Since they share common tones 3 and 6 they are said to have "diatonic" harmony. The 2 chord has sub-dominant harmony and the 7 chord has dominant harmony. A 2–5 pattern is important because it implies a key. A dominant chord can be preceded by its related 2 chord, a 5th above the root. Since the 3 and 7 of a dominant chord are shared by another dominant chord a tri-tone away, they are considered substitutes for on another: G7=Dflat7. Chords with upper tensions 9, 11 and 13 don't effect the basic quality of sound. Cmin7, Cmin9 and Cmin11 are all minor family chords and are interchangeable. The major family includes C6, Cmaj7, Cmaj9, C6/9. The dominant family includes C7, C9 and C13.

SONG FORMS

Finally, let's play some tunes! There are three basic forms you should master: jazz blues, minor blues and rhythm changes – illustrated in turn in **exercises 1–3**. These will help you learn tunes from *The Real Book* (a "fake book" owned by every jazz player, containing hundreds of popular jazz standards). For example, the jazz blues form is used in many tunes by Charlie

Parker, Wes Montgomery, Sonny Rollins, Thelonius Monk and many others. Learn these in a few more keys and you'll get a lot of mileage out of this section with a little practise and perseverance. Notice that no rhythms are given here. For now, use basic chord forms or chords you've just learned and strum through each of these exercises in your own style. Next, we'll put some rhythms to them to start playing some more familiar songs.

ESSENTIAL RHYTHMS

Let's talk about how to play the five essential rhythms that will not only help you with the three basic forms, but with many others as well. These will allow you to function in a variety of musical styles.

Exercise 4 is a rhythm called "four to the bar." This perfectly exemplifies the 4/4 time signature, and is a rhythm you'll hear in plenty of classic jazz. Four to the bar is traditionally played with all downstrokes on the quarter notes, sometimes with the occasional upstroke on an eighth note for emphasis, to suggest a solid rhythm, with chord changes according to the tune. It often works best when you are supplying the time (no bass player or drummer) or for playing rhythm guitar charts in a big band – think Freddie Green. Sometimes chords change as fast as one per beat, which takes some fancy finger work, but here we'll strum two bars against muted strings to get the rhythm down, then play two bars with a chord change every two beats. As in the previous exercise, use basic chord forms or those you have already learned elsewhere. After you've got the feel of it, try playing four to the bar against the jazz blues in Ex.1.

Exercise 5 is a "jazz waltz." As you might guess it's in 3/4, but a jazz waltz also works great in 6/8, just double it up. Also, note the importance of the rests for the feel of the rhythm. Repeat

the two bars until you get a feel for it. After you've got this down, try it on the standard tunes *Alice In Wonderland, Bluesette, Someday My Prince Will Come* and *Windows*.

The "bossa nova" rhythm in **exercise 6** works great for sambas as well as bossas – a samba being faster. While there are many variations of Latin and Brazilian rhythms used in jazz, this is a great one to start out with and is multi-functional. Listen out for these rhythms in the standard tunes *Blue Bossa, One Note Samba, Wave* and *Triste*, all of which you can learn yourself. (Get deeper into these rhythms in the *Latin* chapter.)

The easy way to approach a "ballad" is to play the root on beats 1 and 3 and on beats 2 and 4 play the notes of the chord that are left on the D, G and B strings, as exemplified in **exercise 7**. Simple, but effective.

Exercise 8 gives an example in "odd time," in this case 5/4, probably the most-used odd time signature in jazz. Think of it as a jazz waltz in 3/4 plus two extra quarter notes: 3+2=5. Many odd time signatures can be played using this concept. *Take Five* is a classic jazz tune in 5/4 which most of you will recognize, and a good one to learn on your own once you get this rhythm down. Again, note the major contribution of the rests to the rhythmic feel of this exercise.

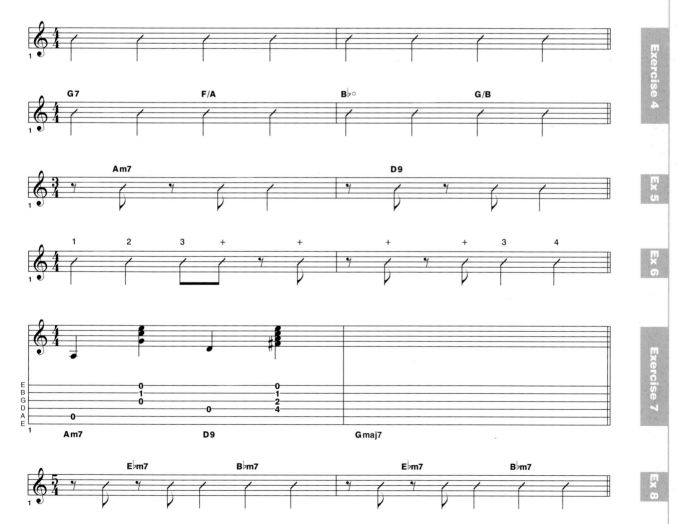

IMPROVISATION

Finally it's time to move on to what many guitarists think of as the essence of jazz: soloing and improvisation. We'll start by talking about soloing "over" and "through" the chord changes.

Learn the C major scale in all positions and you've also learned the location of it's related modes. They are: D Dorian, E Phrygian, F Lydian, G Mixolydian, A Aeolian, B Locrian. We'll learn more about modes a little later in the chapter, but for now let's use it as a C major scale. Since a 2–5–1 in C major is built from the notes of the 2nd, 5th and root of the scale, simply play notes of the C Major scale over all three changes. The scale generates the harmony and the chords imply the scale. Chords are scales and scales are chords – simple.

While playing a C major scale may not make you sound like Pat Martino (or insert your favorite jazz player here!) it will be a fairly easy and melodic way to start playing "through" changes – improvising in the scale of the key of the tune, while the changes go on behind your solo.

Another way that jazz players solo to chords is to use a different scale for each chord. Chord-scale relationships is a way to start playing "over" the changes instead of through them. One is not better than the other, just different.

Playing over the changes reflects the sound of each chord in a 2–5–1 progression. For the 2 chord, Dmin7, play in the D dorian scale – simply a C major scale starting on the 2nd scale degree: D, E, F, G, A, B, C, D. Over the 5 chord, G7, play G mixolydian, which starts on the 5th degree of the C major scale. Its scale spelling is: G, A, B, C, D, E, F, G. Over the 1 chord, Cmaj7, you're back to the notes of the C major scale. That's a basic look at modes as applied to the theory of improvisation used in jazz guitar soloing. We'll explore some ways to use each mode a little better in the next section.

Right now, however, let's break down some more elements essential in jazz soloing. We have already talked about guide tones – the 3rds and 7ths which define the quality of the chord – and chord scales – which reveal the melodic relationships between scale, chord and harmony. So let's move on to arpeggios and how to use melodic embellishments.

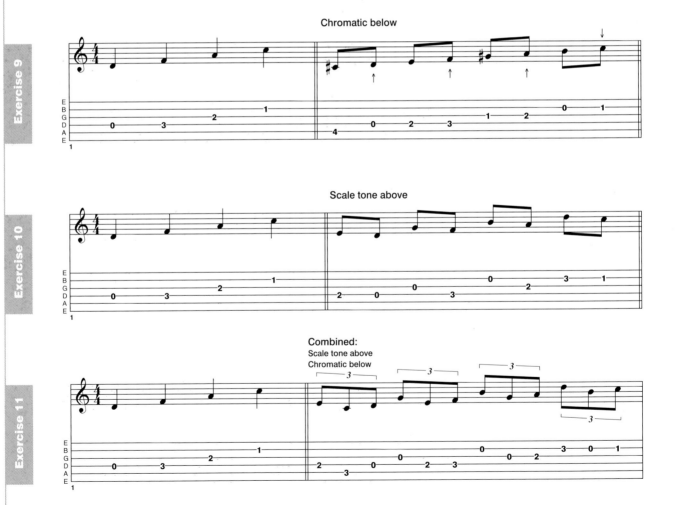

soloing

MELODIC EMBELLISHMENT

Arpeggios outline the targeted chord tones (root, 3rd, 5th, 7th and above) and melodic embellishment approaches the chord tones chromatically, scale-wise, from above and below. In the following exercises I've used a Dmin7 arpeggio and have shown several ways to approach each chord tone to produce a more melodic effect. By combining notes that are chromatically above and below the targeted chord tones, our playing becomes more melodic and still defines the harmonic sound of the chord, in this case Dmin7. **Exercise 9** takes a "chromatic below" approach to the chord tone (guide tones are indicated by arrows in the exercise). **Exercise 10** uses a scale tone above approach, while **exercise 11** combines the two in one approach, and **exercise 12** combines them in another. **Exercise 13** uses a double chromatic below, and **exercise 14** a double chromatic above.

Now do the same for G7 and Cmaj7 and you'll hear what we're getting at. When combined with other concepts (guide tones, chords, scales and arpeggios) melodic embellishments will get us closer to some of the ways jazz lines are created.

As a young musician, Pat Martino was influenced by John Coltrane, Wes Montgomery, Stan Getz and Johnny Smith, then earned gigs as a rock and jazz sideman before taking his own fluid, virtuoso solo work into the realms of fusion and beyond.

Combined:
Chromatic below
Scale tone above

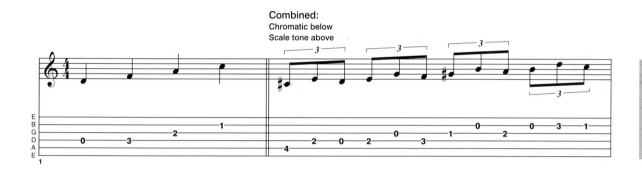

Exercise 12

Double chromatic below

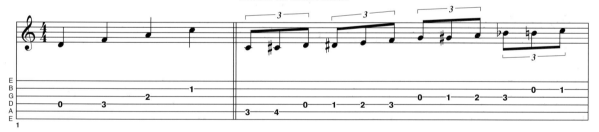

Exercise 13

Double chromatic above

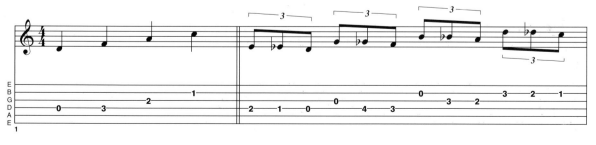

Exercise 14

DEVELOPING A JAZZ LINE

You now have a handle on many of the essential building blocks of jazz soloing, so let's examine a series of different ways of combining these melodic approaches to chords and scales in order to develop a variety of solo lines with different moods and feels, starting with the extremely simple and building to some more complex approaches. Still in our familiar key of C major, we'll use our four-bar 2–5–1 progression of Dmin7, G7 and Cmaj7 over eleven great ways of building your solo lines.

Play them individually to hear how each approach works, then try stringing selected examples together – or even all of them – for a long solo that shifts between techniques. When you get the hang of it, record the chord progression for as many bars as you like and try playing along.

There isn't a whole lot to say about each exercise; you just need to play through them to hear and feel how each approach works. **Exercise 15** starts us off simply hitting the guide tones; **exercise 16** takes it a step further, linking 3rds and 7ths. **Exercise 17** uses "octave displacement" to run down from the 2 toward the 5, then jumping to the octave and running down to the 1, while **exercise 18** uses an example of "altered tension" in the flatted 9th.

Exercise 19 picks up the pace with eighth notes (squeezing three into a triplet for starters, to boot), while **exercise 20** keeps it breezy to outline minor 7th arpeggios over the changes. **Exercise 21** gets your fingers stretching a little further with "interval leaps," and **exercise 22** outlines some short hops in lines made up of jumps between 5ths.

There are few better places to turn for great improvisational work than Joe Pass and Jim Hall, two of jazz's all-time great all-arounders. Above left, Pass goes it solo for *Virtuoso*, while Hall joins pianist Bill Evans on the impressive *Undercurrent*, right.

Exercise 15

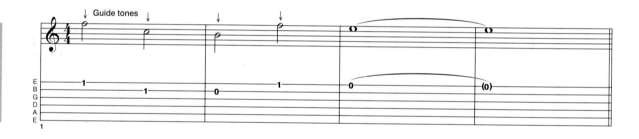

Exercise 16

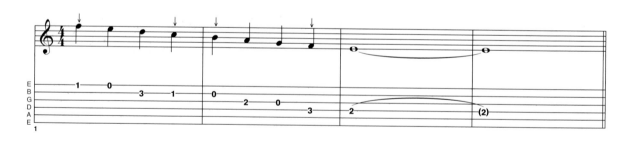

Exercise 17

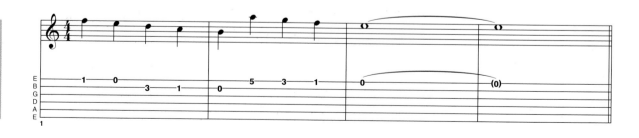

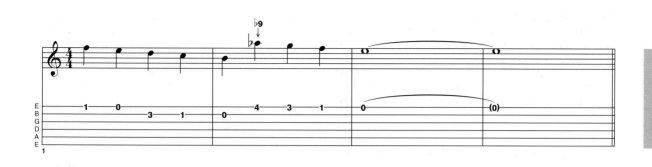

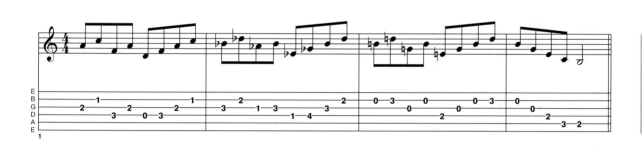

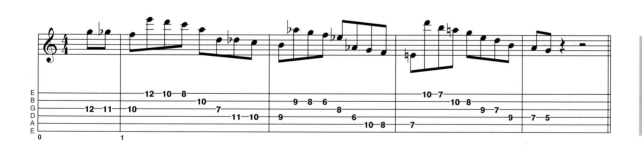

Wrapping bop influences and stunning technique in thoroughly modern sounds with atmosphere to spare, Pat Metheny remains at the forefront of the modern jazz pack. Residing further toward the heart of fusion, British guitarist Allan Holdsworth runs the gamut from rock to jazz, hitting all stops in between and certainly sounding like no one else on earth along the way.

We'll wrap up our eleven techniques for developing jazz lines with three more effective approaches, still using our 2–5–1 progression in C major (Dmin7, G7, Cmaj7). **Exercise 23** shows you a "chord over chord" technique, which layers chords on top of each other. **Exercise 24** uses "motifs," melodic riffs similar in shape and feel, which move with the changes.

Finally, **exercise 25** uses "chromatic" lines – runs that move short intervals for a tight, occasionally off-key sound that still falls in at all the right reference points and makes a great change from sweet, strictly melodic runs.

Although these are "only" eighth notes, these lines move pretty swiftly at faster tempos, especially with some of the unfamiliar tonal leaps required, so take your time and go at them slowly at first, building speed with practise.

Exercise 23

Exercise 24

Exercise 25

soloing

ESSENTIAL SCALES AND MODES

Before concluding our exploration of jazz guitar with an extended exercise of Bebop lines, let's look at a few techniques which we don't have room to cover here in any great depth, but which will help you extend your playing beyond the obvious clichés and simple melody lines. If this chapter has whet your appetite to explore jazz guitar further, you can expand on these concepts on your own, or seek out more in-depth instruction.

The four essential scales to know are the major scale,, melodic minor, diminished scale and the whole tone scale. Knowing their spelling and scale formulae will aid you greatly in knowing how to use them. We'll look at them in our old friend C major, but once learned they can be transposed to any key to give you a full arsenal of improvisational tools.

Here are the chords built from a C major (Ionian) scale and their corresponding modes. As we briefly discussed earlier in this section, you find these modes in any particular key by playing the major scale in that key, but starting on each subsequent note rather than on the root (or "one"), thus:

Cmaj7	**C Ionian**
Dmin7	**D Dorian**
Emin7	**E Phrygian**
Fmaj7	**F Lydian**
G7	**G Mixolydian**
Amin7	**A Aeolian**
Bmin7b5	**B Locrian**

So the following relationship would give you a modal approach to soloing over our familiar 2–5–1 changes in C major.

Dmin7	**G7**	**Cmaj7**
use: **D Dorian**	**G Mixolydian**	**C Major Scale**

C melodic minor is an easy variation to learn, simply: C, D, Eb, F, G, A, B, C.

Two modes that are extremely useful are built from the 4th and 7th degrees of the scale. They are: F Lydian b7 and B altered dominant. Play F Lydian b7 over F9#4 chord types; play B altered dominant over B7#9, B7flat9, B7flat5, B7#5

The C diminished scale runs C, D, Eb, F, Gb, Ab, A, B, C. Play the B diminished half step, whole step scale over these chord types: B7flat9, B7#9, B7flat5, B13.

The C whole tone scale is: C, D, E, F#, G#, Bb, C. Play it over C+, C7+5, C9#11 and chords of that type.

Remember chords are scales and scales are chords. One implies the other. For example, look at D Dorian – the notes of the scale reveal the chord qualities:

D	E	F	G	A	B	C	D	E	F	G	A	B	C	D
R		-3		5		b7		9		11		13		

D Dorian sounds great over a Dmin7, Dmin9, Dmin11 and even Dmin13 chord (sometimes the 13th will appear an octave lower as the sixth). Now look at a G altered dominant scale over a G7 chord:

G	Ab	Bb	Cb	Db	Eb	F
Root	b9	#9	M3	b5	#5	b7

Play this scale over G7, G7flat9, G7#9, G7flat5, G7#5, or any combination of these.

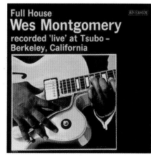

Wes Montgomery (performing live, left, and on record, below left) is considered by many to be the true father of modern jazz guitar, executing octave runs faster than most guitarists can play single lines. George Benson (seen on the album *It's Uptown*, below right) set new standards of bop guitar virtuosity before moving on to even broader fame as a jazz and soul vocalist.

Exercise 26

bop solo lines

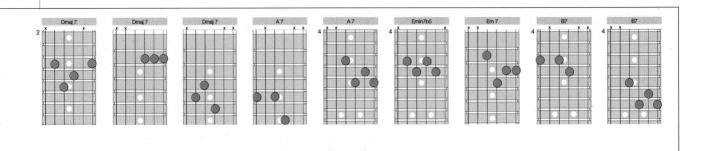

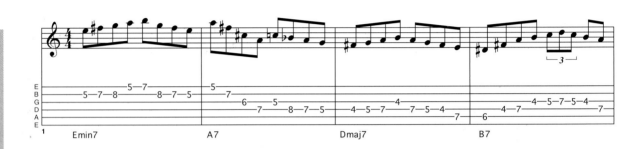

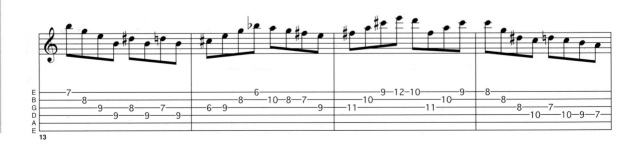

2–5–1–6 BOP LINES

Exercise 26 offers eight Bop lines over a 2–5–1–6 progression in a new key, D major (the chords from the first four bars repeat throughout each four-bar line, though you can try your own variations). Have someone play the chords or tape them to hear the sound of the line and its various degrees of tension.

Not only are they eight useful lines to study, but they can also be played in one continuous etude. As always, start off slowly at first then build speed as you get the hang of it – though speed in itself isn't the objective; we're looking to build melodic and harmonic awareness and compile a handy bag of lines (derived from scales and modes) to use as improvisational building blocks to apply to your other playing.

The chords shown in the nine diagrams to the left are variations on chords you will have encountered already in this chapter, transposed to appropriate positions for this exercise. They will help you with some useful voices to get started, but try working out others for yourself to use in your own backing track.

As an added challenge, refer back to the Essential Scales And Modes page to help you analyze some of these licks. I hope you have fun with this exercise and it helps you to master some of those great lines that you've heard your favorite artists play.

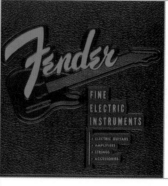

"Much of the pioneering work on electric guitars was done in the United States, and as with most inventions there were several people working independently along similar lines. But a handful of significant explorers did more than most to devise what we now know as the electric guitar. Chief among these were George Beauchamp and Paul Barth, who put together a basic magnetic pickup for guitar. Their research culminated in 1931 with an experimental one-off instrument, the wooden Rickenbacker 'Frying Pan' guitar."

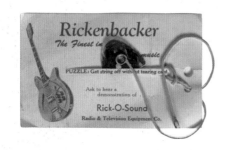

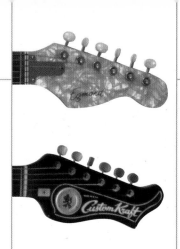

chapter 5

TOTALLY GUITAR
MANUFACTURERS

A definitive guide to the story of the electric guitar, this comprehensive A-to-Z directory covers the stories of 130 leading brands, with pictures of all the key axes and a host of celebrated players. Revel in seven decades of great instruments and musicians and learn why the electric guitar is the most important icon of modern music.

Hagstrom 299

GUITARS AND BASSES

ACOUSTIC

Known primarily for amplifiers, the Acoustic Control Corporation of Los Angeles introduced Black Widow solidbody guitars with a protective red "spider" back pad in 1972, endorsed by jazzman Larry Coryell. Most were built in Japan, but around 200 were made by Semie Moseley in California before their demise in 1975.

AIRLINE

This 1950s/1960s brandname was used by the Montgomery Ward mail-order company on instruments supplied by a number of manufacturers. Some were produced by Kay, others by Valco, the company that made National and Supro guitars. Most of the Valco-made Airlines are similar to Supro models, though some have unconventional body shapes.

ALAMO

Remembered for colorful, exotic shapes, Alamo guitars were made under the direction of Charles Eilenberg for Southern Music in San Antonio, Texas, beginning with lap-steels and amps around 1950. Student-grade solidbodies appeared around 1960, with a change to hollow-core bodies from 1963 to 1970; amps continued into the 1980s.

ALEMBIC

While the California maker is best known for bass guitars, its use of exotic woods, multi-laminate through-neck construction and pioneering active electronics generally influenced many guitar-makers during the 1970s and after. Alembic started in southern California in 1969 as an electronics workshop among the community that gradually grew up around the Grateful Dead. Alembic worked in the warehouse where the Dead rehearsed in Novato, California, about 30 miles north of San Francisco. At first the idea was for Alembic to make improved recordings of Dead concerts. This developed into a general interest in the improvement of studio and live sound quality, and Alembic branched out into three main areas: a recording studio; a developer of PA systems; and a workshop for guitar repair and modification.

The combination of the woodworking talents of Rick Turner, a one-time Massachusetts folk guitarist and guitar repairer, and the electronics knowledge of Ron Wickersham, who had worked at the Ampex recording-equipment company, soon turned the workshop into a full-fledged guitar-making operation. In 1970 Alembic moved to San Francisco, and became a corporation with three equal shareholders: Rick Turner, Ron Wickersham and recording engineer Bob Matthews.

At first they customized instruments, what they called "Alembicizing." The first official Alembic instrument made to the new company's own design was a bass built for Jack Casady around 1971. A few years later L D Heater of Portland, Oregon, began US distribution of Alembic instruments, and production increased. By 1974 Alembic's guitar workshop was at Cotati, about 40 miles north of San Francisco, handling

An Acoustic Black Widow from about 1971 (near right, with a 1974 ad featuring Black Widow endorser Larry Coryell); an Airline fiberglass-body model (center) made by Valco around 1964; and an Alamo Titan produced in Texas in 1962 (far right). Ron and Susan Wickersham (Kaman strings ad, opposite page) were two of the original founders of Alembic. The main Alembic guitar shown (opposite page) is a Series I dating from 1978.

Professionals. Larry Coryell and Acoustic's Black Widow Guitar.

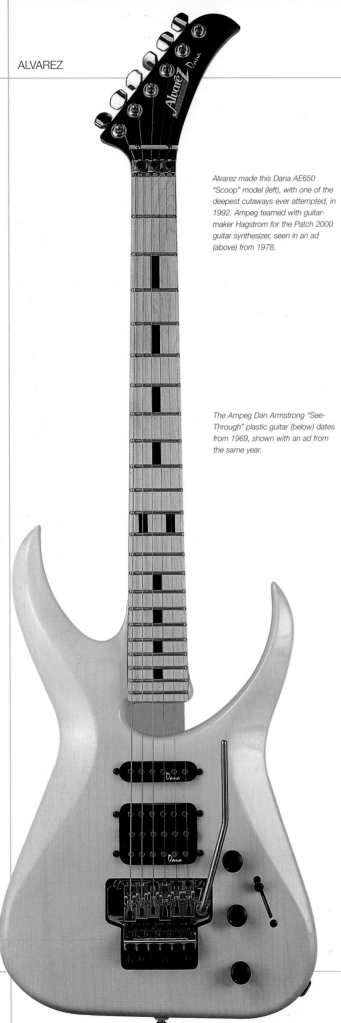

Alvarez made this Dana AE650 "Scoop" model (left), with one of the deepest cutaways ever attempted, in 1992. Ampeg teamed with guitar-maker Hagstrom for the Patch 2000 guitar synthesizer, seen in an ad (above) from 1978.

The Ampeg Dan Armstrong "See-Through" plastic guitar (below) dates from 1969, shown with an ad from the same year.

woodwork, metalwork and pickups, while at the Alembic office in nearby Sebastopol Wickersham dealt with electronics production. All guitar production moved to Cotati in 1977 and to Santa Rosa two years later.

Alembic had gradually standardized a regular line of short-scale, medium-scale and long-scale basses, with equivalents in guitars, primarily the Series I and Series II. Alembic has always produced many more basses than guitars. The instruments featured a high quality multi-laminate through-neck construction using attractive, exotic woods (such as walnut, myrtle, zebrawood, padauk, vermilion and cocobolo), heavy tone-enhancing brass hardware and active-electronics systems with external power supplies. All this came at a price, and Alembic virtually established the idea of the specialist, high quality, high price guitar.

Alembic continues today in Santa Rosa, California, primarily as a prestigious high-end bass specialist, but offering some guitars. Current six-string models include the Orion and California Special.

ALVAREZ

Alvarez was a brand for acoustic guitars until 1991 when US distributor St. Louis Music used it to replace Westone on its electrics. The change brought a significantly reworked Korean-made line, and only Trevor Rabin's signature model remained much the same, with styling derived from the earlier Westone Pantera. Many of the all-new Alvarez

the revolutionary dan armstrong guitar from ampeg

This 1970 Ampeg ad has Keith Richards discovering the joys of six strings and a transparent body.

electrics were devised by guitar-maker/designer Dana Sutcliffe. They included the Scoop, a radical solidbody sporting long, slim and sharp horns and the right cutaway sweeping around the end of the neck. It was claimed this enhanced sustain and resonance... but Sutcliffe later admitted it was actually due to a carving accident.

Other Alvarez models included the equally rock-orientated Paramount and Successor, while the later LA Scoop and Nashville Scoop were more Fender-flavored. Alvarez then made safer designs; by 2000 only the Classics offered anything individual in a much-reduced line.

AMPEG

In the late 1940s New York bassist Everett Hull had tackled the problem of amplifying double-basses by producing an amplification system that consisted of a microphone which fitted inside the bass's pointed "peg," the spike that supports the instrument at its base. This "amplified peg" gave Hull's new company its name – Ampeg – and their adaptation of existing double-basses to amplified sound proved a moderate success for the fledgling operation.

Through the following decades Ampeg grew and became principally known for its excellent line of instrument amplifiers. The company first tried to get into the electric guitar market in 1963, importing four Burns guitar models from Britain – Jazz Split Sound, Nu-Sonic, Split Sonic and TR-2 – identical to the UK originals apart from an Ampeg logo on the pickguard. Few were sold, making these Ampeg-Burns rare catches today. The Ampeg-Burns deal ended in 1964.

By 1968 Ampeg were still keen to grab some of the burgeoning electric guitar business, and local New York City guitar repairman Dan Armstrong was hired to design a new line of guitars. Armstrong decided to carve the bodies from blocks of clear Lucite (perspex), intending to provide a distinctive looking instrument as well as to exploit the sonic potential of the material.

Ampeg offered the See-Through guitar with six slide-in/slide-out pickups designed by Bill Lawrence: Rock, Country and Jazz, each in treble and bass versions. Two of these units were supplied as standard with every new guitar; the others were available to keen See-Through players as accessories that could be purchased through their friendly local Ampeg dealer.

Despite all this invention, Ampeg's imaginative See-Through models lasted little more than a year in production, hindered by conservative players and an expensive manufacturing process. Pro users of the See Through have been few, although an honorable exception was Keith Richards.

In 1999, Ampeg's Japanese-made ADAG1 clear-plastic-body reworking of the original See-Through was launched, and the following year a wood-body version appeared, the AMG1AB, using maple-faced mahogany.

Ampeg made a small number of its Dan Armstrong models in black plastic, including this 1969 example (near left). Most were in clear Lucite (perspex), most famously played by Keith Richards (left). Ampeg had earlier imported to the US a selection of Burns models from England. They included the Burns Split Sonic rebadged as the Ampeg De Luxe Wild Dog model, as seen in this ad (above) from 1963.

guitar manufacturers

Shiro Arai's Aria company has used a number of brandnames. One of the earliest was Aria Diamond, as on this 12-string ADSG-12T model (right) from around 1968, and the Japanese catalog (far right) of the same year.

Another Aria brandname was Aria Pro II, as used from the mid 1970s. This Aria Pro II PE-160 (below, right) made in 1977 came with an unusual carved dragon motif on the body.

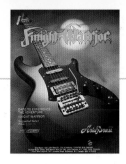

This ad for the Aria Pro II Knight Warrior model dates from 1984, with the heavy-duty vibrato of the period.

ARIA

Aria has been one of the seminal companies in the globalization of guitar-making, with a history that includes major involvement in the 1970s "copy era." Along the way, Aria produced an extraordinary number of guitar models in a variety of different styles and guises. The sheer magnitude of Aria's guitar lines and the worldwide markets in which they have been sold is daunting.

The company was founded in Japan as an importing operation by classical guitarist Shiro Arai during the early 1950s. Arai began manufacturing classical guitars around 1956 and entered the market for electric guitars in 1960. The company developed a mix of solidbody and hollowbody models (including one style with a "violin"-shape body) and these bore the Arai, Aria, Aria Diamond and Diamond brandnames. The factory also manufactured instruments for other companies.

The turning point came at the NAMM instrument trade show in the US in 1968 where Gibson was exhibiting its newly reissued Les Pauls. This inspired Arai in 1969 to build the first Japanese-made bolt-on-neck copy of the Gibson classic, formally kicking off the "copy era" of the 1970s. Copies of the Ampeg Dan Armstrong clear Lucite (perspex) guitar and Fender's Telecaster quickly followed, and this soon mushroomed into the copying of virtually all popular and significant American guitar models. In the mid 1970s Aria added another electric-guitar brand, Aria Pro II, including

models with fancy inlay. The Aria brandname continued to be used in a number of different markets. Many of the better models were built at the Japanese Matsumoku factory, until that closed its doors to guitar-building in 1987. Copies continued until 1978, the year Aria picked up its first big-name endorser in Herb Ellis, whose PE-175 was a Gibson-inspired archtop electric. Full-body and thinline electrics would be mainstay Aria offerings from this time.

However, 1977 saw the introduction of Aria's first truly original design, the Matsumoku-made PE Prototype series. These were either set-neck or bolt-on-neck single-cutaway guitars with carved tops and a sweeping curve that came down from the body's upper shoulder into the cutaway opposite. The Japanese PE Prototypes, many with luxurious appointments, some with vibratos and P.J. Marx pickups, were succeeded by Korean-made versions that began to appear in 1988.

More original Aria designs debuted in 1979, including offset-double-cutaway guitars with pointy horns, and a signature hollowbody for British jazzer Ike Isaacs. The first RS Rev Sound series were through-neck guitars made in an Alembic style, with active electronics, and a few double-necks. They lasted until 1982. The TS Thor Sound (also called Tri-Sound) guitars were passive or active, in set-neck, bolt-on-neck and through-neck configurations, and lasted until 1983. Lines offered in Europe included the shortlived YS and NK (Noise Killer) series. In 1981 Aria added to its catalog the CS

Gerry Cott (left), guitarist with Bob Geldof's band The Boomtown Rats, shows off his Aria Pro II PE-1000 in this 1979 ad. Alongside are two more Aria Pro II models: a Rev-Sound RS-850 (left) from 1981; and a 1983 Thor-Sound TS-500 (near left) from the Black'n'Gold line that featured models with black finish and gold-plated hardware.

Jazz guitarist Herb Ellis was honored with the "signature" Aria Pro II PE-175 archtop electric of 1978.

Cardinal Sound series with passive electronics (lots of switches on some models) and either bolt-on- or set-necks. Most of these were available for a few years.

In 1982 Aria helped start a wave of popularity for exotic guitar shapes. The company introduced its B.C.-Rich-inspired Urchin series (which lasted to 1984), the mini-Flying-V-like XX series and the mini-Explorer-style ZZ series, the latter two with fancy paint jobs and available in one form or another through 1987. From 1982 until 1986 various models from different series were rolled into a Black'n'Gold line with appropriate black finishes and gold hardware.

In 1983 Aria introduced a revamped RS Rev Sound line with Stratocaster-like styling and bolt-on necks. In a number of variations, these models would dominate Aria's offerings into the 1990s. The earliest of these second-generation Rev Sounds had elegant thin horns and came either with active or passive electronics, although after 1985 most were passive. Models such as the Bobcat, Wildcat and Straycat suggested the directions that Aria would soon be taking.

By the mid 1980s the RS profile would thicken up to take on even more of a Fender style. Other popular mid-1980s models in this long-running series included the Knight Warrior and Road Warrior. In 1985 the definition of RS was changed to Rock Solid, then the Cat series in 1986. Original Aria locking vibratos were joined by Kahlers in 1986. These guitars lasted through 1987 and the end of Matsumoku's Japanese factory. A

number of other Japanese-made offset-double-cutaway lines were also offered during this period, and these models included such delights as the MM Mega Metal, IC Interceptor, IG Integra, GT and XR series. Many of these were in fact variations on the superstrat, but none was as popular as the Cats.

In 1987 Aria briefly offered a US Custom series of American-made guitars. That same year Aria shifted its general production of electric guitars to Korea, where it continued the superstrat theme, beginning with the SL series and followed by a mind-dizzying list of essentially similar models over the next few years. Mainly these were differentiated by timbers, figured tops, level of appointments and sometimes subtle differences in body contouring.

A few of the better models continued to be made in Japan, but the need to remain at a lower price-point meant that the majority of production was now based in Korea. In 1988, lasting for just a year, came the CT, LB Libra, VA Vanguard, and WR Warrior series. These were supplanted in 1989 by yet more superstrats including the Polaris, VS, and AW series.

Those superstrats were in turn replaced by the FS, JS, XL Excel, VP Viper and MA Magna series in 1990, many of which remained in the catalog for a few years. In 1991 the high-end AQ Aquanotes appeared, which would later evolve into the CR Cobra line. These were followed by the current and decidedly low-end STGs in 1993. Most of

Aria Pro II's first "pointy"-shape guitars were marketed as the Urchin series in 1982, with clear influence from the US brand B.C. Rich. The catalog from 1982 (above) includes the Urchin Deluxe (right). The Titan Artist series began in 1981; this TA-60 (far right) dates from 1989.

these were gone by the mid 1990s. Aria has during its history never had a great many "signature" models in its lines, reflecting the company's relatively low-key presence among leading pro players. It has always seemed as if Aria guitars have been more popular with amateur and semi-pro guitarists, even though the quality of some of the instruments would seem high enough to attract pros. However, during 1991 Aria made a line of Ventures signature models, revived in 1999. The Ventures have always been more successful in Japan than anywhere else, so it was not too surprising that an oriental manufacturer would court the group and its many fans.

In 1994 Aria's US distributor NHF Industries unveiled a single-cutaway model originally called the Nashville 93. This model was styled by British designer Trev Wilkinson, and was at first produced in the United States. However, Gretsch soon objected to Aria's use of the "Nashville" name, which the US company had used for some time on one of its models. So it was that the Aria guitar was renamed as the 615 Custom – at least reflecting Nashville's telephone area code. Lower-grade 615s were manufactured in Korea until 1998.

Also launched in 1994 was the Strat-like Fullerton series, with further Wilkinson input. The top models were made in the US, most others in Korea. At the end of the decade the Aria Pro II line was anchored by PEs (renamed Pro Electrics), Fullerton and STG solidbodies, plus the long-running TA thinlines and FA "jazz" guitars.

Aria Pro II continued with angular shapes for the ZZ series, which included this 1985 ZZ Deluxe (main guitar, left) and the ZZ Bladerunner (featured in 1985 ad, above left). By the time this sparkle-finish M-650T appeared (left) in 1999, Aria had like many guitar-makers embraced "retro" fashion. More mainstream tastes were indulged with the Fullerton series (1998 ad, below).

Baldwin in the US bought the Burns company of England in the 1965. This ad (above) from that year shows three models from the line, including the green sunburst Double Six 12-string (main guitar, right). Baldwin's catalog (above right) is from 1967 – could it be any other time? – and has a groovy lady posing with a Marvin model. The smaller guitar picture on this page (right) is from Bartolini, a wonderful example of the accordion-influenced plastic-covered guitars made in Italy during the 1960s.

guitar manufacturers

When it first appeared in 1976 the Bich from B. C. Rich was a ten-string guitar. This 1982 ad features the six-string version, still boasting the bizarre cut-out and pointy body.

BALDWIN

In the 1960s this Ohio-based specialist maker of pianos and organs briefly dabbled with electric guitars. In 1965 they bid unsuccessfully for Fender but bought the Burns company of England for $250,000. Burns already had some American experience through distributor Lipsky and by badging some models with the Ampeg brand.

After Baldwin took control there were "transition" examples; a few guitars even carried both Burns and Baldwin brands. In 1966 the existing Nu-Sonic, GB65 and GB66 models were dropped and various changes made. Most significant was a new "flattened-scroll" headstock, replacing the original Burns type on most models. The Baby Bison and Vibraslim were redesigned with a new, short Rezo-tube vibrato.

In 1967 Baldwin introduced the Gibson 335-like 700 series, with Italian-made bodies. By 1968 bar-magnet pickups were being fitted to the Marvin and Bison models. In 1970 Baldwin discontinued Burns production, concentrating their particular management skills on Gretsch, which they had acquired in 1967.

BARTOLINI

The early-1960s guitar boom overtook many Italian accordion makers, who survived by catering for the new craze. Bartolini was one of numerous brands appearing on the flamboyant results. Styling varied but multiple pushbutton selectors and an abundance of sparkle or pearloid plastic were shared by most, echoing the accordion ancestry.

B. C. RICH

B.C. Rich founder Bernardo Chavez Rico was a pioneer in through-neck, pointy-shaped solidbody guitars with onboard "active" pre-amps and a host of knobs and switches. Rico's instruments became favored by heavy guitarists such as Tony Iommi, Rick Derringer, Nikki Sixx, Blackie Lawless and Lita Ford. It's ironic to note, therefore, that Rico began as a flamenco and classical guitarist making acoustic guitars in his father's Los Angeles shop in the mid 1950s.

The first guitars branded B.C. Rich were acoustics, beginning around 1966, while the first electrics were fancy Gibson copies in 1969. Rico's first original through-neck, heel-less design appeared as the single-cutaway Seagull model, around 1971 – and it had an extra little point on the upper bout which indicated B.C. Rich's future direction that would include points just about everywhere. Early pickups were Gibsons and Guilds, followed by DiMarzio humbuckers from 1974 to 1986. The Seagulls were endorsed by Dominic Troiano and Dick Wagner.

Then came the studies in graceful angularity for which B.C. Rich is known, including the Mockingbird and novel ten-string Bich (1976), the Warlock (1981), and Ironbird, Wave and Stealth models (1983). Fancy woods and bright paint jobs were typical, and Craig Chaquico was an endorser in 1980. A few bolt-neck B.C. Riches were built in the late 1970s, including the Nighthawk (Eagle-style) and Phoenix (Mockingbird). Strat-

Three examples of the B.C. Rich approach to guitar style on this page: a typically "pointy" Bich NJ model from 1999 (left); a rather more subdued Eagle of 1981 (center); and a classic Mockingbird Standard made in 1979. Craig Chaquico, guitarist with Jefferson Starship, is pictured on a 1982 magazine cover (below) holding down a chord on another Mockingbird.

style guitars (ST, Gunslinger, Outlaw) debuted in 1987. B.C. Rich began making guitars outside the US in 1976 with a small number of B.C. Rico-brand Eagles produced in Japan. Oriental production resumed in 1984-86 with the Japanese-made NJ Series (for Nagoya, Japan). These instruments were versions of popular designs as well as some Standard thinlines that came in a Gibson 335-style. There was also the US Production Series, which consisted of US-assembled Korean kits. The Korean-made Rave and Platinum Series followed in 1986, and in the same year the NJ Series shifted production to the Cort factory in Korea.

Marketing of the B.C. Rich guitars not made in the United States was taken over in America in 1987 by a company called Class Axe, based in New Jersey. Class Axe introduced its own design, the Virgin, that year. In 1989 Bernie Rico began a three-year break, licensing to Class Axe the rights to B.C. Rich. During his vacation, Rico built a number of handmade guitars with the Mason Bernard brand.

During 1994 Rico resumed the building of B.C. Rich guitars, now in Hesperia, California. These included extra-fancy versions of classics (arched tops, figured woods, abalone trim), variations of other popular guitars (Junior V, Tele-style Blaster), signature models (Jeff Cook, Kerry King), and new designs (super-pointy Ignitor; contoured-top, Tele-style Robert Conti six- and eight-strings). Rico died in 1999; his son Bernie Jr is continuing the company today.

More angular vulgarity from B.C. Rich is apparent in a doom-laden 1982 ad (above right) for the Warlock model. Some B.C. Rich guitars were made in Korea during the late 1990s, including this conservative EMI model of 1997 (near right). The multi-point 1995 US-made Ignitor (main guitar, right) is much more in the classic Rich style.

guitar manufacturers

Paul Bigsby's most famous guitar is this early semi-solidbody electric (left) which he custom-made for country guitarist Merle Travis in 1948.

Paul Bigsby's lasting contribution to guitar-playing is his vibrato bridge, an example of which is fitted to this remarkable double-neck (below), the first electric of its kind, made by Bigsby in 1952 for another country musician, sessionman Grady Martin. He is pictured with the instrument on the sleeve of a 1954 solo release.

BIGSBY

Paul Bigsby of Downey, California, was a major influence on country music in the late 1940s and early 1950s. He is often credited with building the first solidbody electric guitar. In fact, the ground-breaking instrument he built for Merle Travis in 1948 had a solid through-neck section with hollow body "wings." Nonetheless, the instrument is of enormous historical importance, being closer to what we now think of as a solidbody electric guitar than anything that had existed before. Bigsby is, however, most famous for his bolt-on hand vibrato unit for guitar, also developed for Travis.

Bigsby also offered replacement necks that sported his distinctive six-in-line headstock, and helped musicians create an identifiable "country sound" with his innovative pedal-steel guitars, first used by Speedy West and quickly adopted by others. All Bigsby's custom creations are now rare. In addition to the thin Les-Paul-shape Travis-style guitar, Bigsby offered the Electric Standard (similar except for a scrolled upper shoulder) and Billy Byrd double-cutaway guitars.

Bigsby made at least one thick-bodied guitar (for Jack Parsons) and built electric mandolins, the first in 1951 for Tiny Moore. He also made double-necks, including one for Nashville great Grady Martin; most were guitar/mandolins, but at least one was a guitar/bass. In 1956 Bigsby designed two guitars and a steel for amplifier maker Magnatone. He continued to offer guitars until 1965, and died three years later.

B O N D

Bond's shortlived mid-1980s Electraglide guitar had a novel "stepped" fingerboard. Bond was set up in Scotland by guitar-maker Andrew Bond, Ian Flooks of the Wasted Talent artist agency, and two others. The company had a new factory built at Muir Of Ord, near Inverness, and the first Electraglides began to appear in 1984.

Where a normal guitar fingerboard has a row of frets, the Bond's "pitchboard" was a one-piece construction, with a step and gentle incline between each "fret" position. Some players found there was not enough room to bend strings. It was also impossible to "dress" frets conventionally for personal playability. It quickly became apparent that the success of a conventional frets-and-fingerboard construction is partly due to its potential for modification to suit different string types and different players.

There were other unusual aspects of the twin-cutaway Bond. Composite plastic was used for most of the instrument, as popularized a few years earlier by Steinberger, and the Electraglide was without normal control knobs. Instead it used touch-switches with color-coded LEDs for volume, active tone, pickup switching and phase, and employed a small digital read-out facing up to the player to reveal setting levels. Again, these novelties served mainly to underline the strengths of a conventional control system. The instrument certainly looked futuristic, and was clearly different in many approaches – but it did not necessarily address players' concerns, and might have worked better as

The Bond Electraglide (near right), with novel stepped fingerboard and digital read-outs, was made in Scotland in 1984; the Brian Moore M/C1, with custom fingerboard inlay by Ray Memmels, was made in New York in 1999.

a custom instrument made in small numbers. Amid production problems, Bond collapsed during 1985 having made around 1,400 guitars. In its brief life the company found that many players couldn't be bothered to adapt to the new guitar's oddities, though it did attract Mick Jones, who loved the way it played, as well as John Turnbull and Dave Stewart.

BRIAN MOORE

One of a new breed of makers that emerged in the 1990s, Brian Moore aimed to achieve a fine balance between conventional wood and newer composite materials. Patrick Cummings, ex-Gibson general manager, teamed up with Brian Moore, ex-Steinberger plastics expert, to produce high-end, exclusive guitars, starting in 1994 and based in Brewster, New York. The first model was the M/C1 (Moore/Cummings). Its composite semi-hollow body had a center-block inside to acoustically "tune" the instrument, and an arched figured-wood top. Recent instruments have been virtually all wooden. The Korean-made iGuitar, a synth-access hybrid, and the more conventional iSeries debuted in 2000.

BURNS

These legendary British guitars of the 1960s include a handful of classics, and have a style all their own. Jim Burns was born in north-east England in 1925. His first production guitar, the Ike Isaacs Short Scale model, appeared on the market in 1958

A remarkable achievement in British guitar engineering was the rare four-pickup Bison (main guitar), this example of which was made in 1961. A "simplified" three-pickup Bison replaced it during 1962.

The first model from the Ormston Burns company was the 1960 Artiste, soon with added vibrato known as the Vibra Artiste (below left). The 1963 Burns catalog page shows the Split Sonic model.

313

ORMSTON BURNS

THE FINEST IN MUSICAL ENGINEERING *Burns* LONDON

The most desirable Burns guitar among collectors is the 1964 Marvin (main guitar). Co-designer Hank Marvin is seen holding one with the rest of The Shadows in a 1964 portrait (top of page), above a 1960s catalog. This 1977 Burns UK Flyte (right) was apparently modeled on the supersonic Concorde airliner.

with the Supersound brandname. Only about 20 were made. In 1959 Jim joined forces with Henry Weill. Burns-Weill guitars were somewhat crudely constructed and among the earliest British-made production solidbodies. The line included the small-bodied Fenton and the RP (named for British session player Roy Plummer). The angular body shape and Art Deco headstock of the RP soon earned it the nickname "Martian cricket bat." Few Burns-Weill guitars were made; by late 1959 the partnership was over.

In 1960 Jim Burns formed Ormston Burns Ltd (though many guitars were branded "Burns London"). The first guitar was the Artiste, with advanced features for its time including a heel-less set neck and 24 frets. With a Burns vibrato tailpiece it soon became the Vibra Artiste. The Sonic was a popular twin-pickup small-bodied solid aimed at beginners.

The first high-end Burns was the Bison, launched in 1961. The body's long, sweeping horns curved upwards, inwards and forwards to create a unique sculpture in wood. Originally the Bison appeared as a set-neck, four-pickup guitar liberally adorned with gold-plating, plus ebony fingerboard, a new bridge/vibrato unit boasting maximum sustain and smooth operation, a patented "gear box" truss-rod system (later adopted by Gretsch), and low-impedance Ultra Sonic pickups linked to new circuitry that included a novel Split Sound effect. Only 50 were built before a revised version was introduced in 1962 with bolt-on neck, rosewood fingerboard, three pickups, simplified vibrato and chrome-plated hardware. While not as eye-catching as its predecessor it was a more playable, practical instrument, and arguably the epitome of Burns design, character, quality and innovation.

More new models appeared in 1962 including the Jazz Split Sound and Split Sonic guitars, with Bison-style circuitry linked to three Split Sound pickups. Cheaper partners were the two-pickup Jazz and three-pickup Vista Sonic. In 1963 Burns ventured into semi-acoustics with the twin-pickup TR2. Its on-board "active" transistorized pre-amp, for wider tone colors, was an idea ahead of its time. The TR2 was superseded in 1964 by the similarly-styled but passive Vibraslim line.

The next Burns classic was the Marvin, introduced in 1964, designed in conjunction with Hank Marvin. The Marvin copied the construction, scale-length and circuitry of Hank's famous Fender Strat. But the headstock had a distinctive "scroll" top, and a two-bar handrest and three-piece pickguard completed the visual distinctions. The Marvin's new Rez-o-Matik pickups were modeled on Fender, although unlike the Strat all three were angled. The main innovation was a new Rezo-tube vibrato unit which had a knife-edge bearing and six tubes to anchor the strings rather than Fender's single metal block. The vibrato was largely responsible for the Marvin's tone, somewhat sweeter and deeper than the Fender. Only about 400 original Marvins were produced. The Bison was restyled to match the new Marvin, losing much of its distinctive

character in the process. Also launched at this time was the Double Six 12-string. Players have included Mike Pender, Chris Britton and Hank Marvin plus, later, Mark Knopfler and Gaz Coombes. Further down the line, the Sonics were replaced by the Nu-Sonics; Vista Sonics and Split Sonics were gone by 1965. Additions included the GB65, GB66 and Virginian semis, the latter with the round soundhole of a flat-top acoustic.

In September 1965, the Baldwin Piano & Organ Company bought Burns for $250,000 (see Baldwin). The last Burns to appear prior to the Baldwin takeover was the Baby Bison, coincidentally produced for export only. Baldwin acquired sole rights to the Burns brand, so Jim Burns used his middle name, Ormston, as a brand for his late-1960s instruments, including a semi-solid six-string that prompted the line of Hayman guitars he helped develop in 1969 (see Hayman).

In 1973 the Burns UK company was formed. First and best-known model was the Flyte, endorsed by Dave Hill and Marc Bolan. The body design was apparently based on the Concorde aircraft, and two poor Mach One Humbuster pickups were fitted alongside the Dynamic Tension bridge/tailpiece. The Mirage and Artist followed in 1976, later joined by the final Burns UK model, the LJ24. This better guitar came too late to revive the company, which collapsed later that year.

The new Jim Burns company was launched in 1979. Despite commercial pressure to revive the best of the past, the company decided to produce new models. First was

Three more Burns: a peculiar Jim Burns Scorpion (this page, far left) from 1979; a Nu-Sonic from 1996 (center); and a Club series Marquee model from 1999.

Burns fan Gaz Coombes (left) of Supergrass plays a recent Nu-Sonic.

the odd Scorpion. The body had two carved Scorpion-like lower horns and a headstock that might have represented the sting in its tail. Next came the Steer, reminiscent of the Virginian, and the budget Magpie.

In 1981 the company finally acknowledged demand for vintage styles and issued revised versions of the Marvin and Bison. But economies were made and the revivals lacked much of the character and quality of the original 1960s instruments. In 1983 the Bandit model appeared, a small-bodied solid that came with unusual multi-angled styling. This last effort was the best made by the operation, but by 1984 the erratic and misguided Jim Burns company had ceased trading.

Jim himself returned to inactivity and obscurity, while many of his early creations continued to attract more interest on the "vintage" market. In 1991 a British company, Burns London, began producing authentic reproductions and updates of 1960s classics. These included 30/50 Anniversary editions of the Bison and others in 1994. The following year saw the Nu-Sonic, an old name on a Telecaster-style instrument. In 1999 a new Club series was launched with the Marquee model.

In its heyday of the 1960s, Burns represented the best of British guitar design and construction. While not always equal to some of the competition in sound, Burns quality and playability was rarely in question. Jim Burns died in 1998, but his original designs stand as testimony to the man regarded by many as the British Leo Fender.

Those who know that The Shadows were first called The Drifters will understand the reference in the model name of this Burns London Drifter (right) of 1999. The Carvin SGB-3 shown (far right) was made by the California company around 1959, while the catalog page is from 1974.

CARVIN

Uniquely relying and thriving almost exclusively on mail-order marketing, Carvin guitars had their roots in the Kiesel-brand Bakelite lap-steels and amps made in Los Angeles by Lowell C. Kiesel, beginning in 1947.

A distribution problem led in 1949 to a change of brandname – Carvin was named for Lowell's sons Carson and Gavin – and relocation to Covina, California, plus a switch to mail-order. Since mail-order Carvins are basically custom-made, a variety of options has been available since the beginning.

Carvin began to re-market Harmony and Kay Spanish guitars outfitted with Carvin pickups in 1954, offering its original, Kiesel-designed SGB solidbody with a distinctive body point from 1955 to 1961. Early endorsers of the Carvin instruments included country stars such as Joe Maphis and Larry Collins. From 1962-68 a more Fender-style body with a steep lower cutaway was used; Bigsby vibratos became standard-issue in 1963. This model was later played by John Cippolina. German Hofner-made necks were used from 1964-76.

In 1968 Carvin relocated to Escondido, California, changing its model designations to SS, briefly using Japanese Strat-style bodies, then switching to German-made bodies the following year. Gibson-style double-cutaway AS55B and AS51 "Thin Acoustical Guitars" began about this time. During 1976 the operation moved to a larger

INSTRUMENTS   1974

The Ultimate Weapon

More Carvin guitars and guys. The 2-MS double-neck (main guitar) was built around 1965, the pointy V220T 20 years later. Meanwhile, Jason Becker (below) of the David Lee Roth band fingers a DC200C in 1990.

Busy endorser Craig Chaquico of Jefferson Starship prepares to blast out on his "main guitar," Carvin's pointy V220, in this 1986 ad. He liked the amps, too.

factory, where it began producing its first hex-pole pickups. The newly-located Carvin company also produced new electrics, the CM96 or DC150 Stereo Gibson-style solidbodies, now with Carvin-made necks.

Carvin guitar construction switched to set-necks in 1978. During 1980 the company's distinctive sharp-horned offset-double-cutaway body shape appeared on the DC200 model, which was designed by Mark Kiesel. The following year this was offered as the DC200K in koa, marking the beginning of Carvin's use of more exotic timbers, available as standard on high-end models but also offered as options on a number of other models in the line.

Carvin's DC production models continued to proliferate with different pickup configurations. From around 1985-88 a DC160 version of the DC150 appeared in quilted maple. By 1989 the typical Carvin three-tuners-a-side headstock was replaced with a pointy-droopy six-in-line version, and several double-neck options were available. That year the flamed-maple DC400 version of the DC200 also debuted.

In 1985 Carvin made its first venture into exotic shapes with the four-point V220, similar to a Dean ML and endorsed by Craig Chaquico. This was followed in 1987 by the Ultra V, inspired by the Jackson Randy Rhoads. In 1988 Carvin changed construction again to through-neck style, and this became Carvin's favored form of manufacturing. The original Explorer-style headstocks on these changed to pointy-

For the finest in neck through body guitars —step up to Carvin!

Jason Becker
—David Lee Roth Band

Stanley Jordan's touch/tapping style of playing found an unusual home on Casio's PG-380 guitar synthesizer, as publicized in this 1989 ad.

droopy six-tuners-in-line in 1989. A more pointy X220 replaced the V220 in 1990. Pointy guitars were gone from the Carvin line by 1993.

From 1987 to 1990 Carvin offered another thinline electric, the SH225, a double-humbucker guitar with very rounded equal cutaways. In 1989 only a rounded-horn version of the offset-cutaway model was offered, the DC145. By the late 1980s Carvin products were used by a host of pros including Elvin Bishop, Jeff Cook, Larry Coryell, Marshall Crenshaw, Lita Ford, Ray Gomez, Alex Lifeson, Steve Lynch and Rick Nielsen, among many others. Later endorsers of Carvin's various models would also include Jason Becker and Al DiMeola.

In 1991 Carvin augmented its catalog (and factory showroom) by setting up and opening two new retail outlets. These were based in Hollywood and Santa Ana, California, and would be followed later by several European stores. That year a 12-string version of the DC200, the DC120, appeared.

In 1993, with "vintage" guitar designs prevalent throughout the rest of the guitar industry, Carvin added the classic Telecaster-style shape to its repertoire with the TL60 model. This was joined the following year by the f-holed AE185. The trend was "solidified" with the solidbody Tele-like SC90 in 1996, the same year that Carvin introduced its flagship Allan Holdsworth signature guitar. The instrument was distinguished by a two-and-four headstock and an extra dip on the lower bout.

CASIO

Best-known for digital watches and keyboards, this Japanese company took a tentative step into guitar synthesis in 1987 with the MG-500 and MG-510 MIDI six-strings.

Roland had paved the way, but in 1988 came Casio's superior PG-380 offering a more player-friendly, full-fledged alternative. This Fender-influenced, Floyd Rose-equipped solidbody had all the technical bits arranged in a very accessible manner. Famous names such as Stanley Jordan and Curtis Mayfield obviously agreed. The less expensive PG-300 debuted in 1990, with Strat-style pickup layout and vibrato. Casio's final guitar synth came three years later with the simplified and shortlived G-393.

CHANDLER

Originally a supplier of guitar components, and based in California, Chandler expanded operations during 1991 to include complete instruments. These included custom-built examples and a selection of standard production models initially offered in kit form.

Additions to Chandler's fully-assembled line in the following year included the Rickenbacker-like 555 as well as the ultra-offset Austin Special. This single-cutaway solidbody equipped with lipstick pickups was based on a guitar originally made for Keith Richards by US luthier Ted Newman-Jones.

More recent models include the Fender-derived Telephathic and Metro, offered in various guises, along with the equally California-flavored Futurama and Spitfire.

Carvin's Allan Holdsworth signature guitar (pictured on this page, far left), this one made in 1997; Casio's PG-380 guitar synthesizer (center) from 1988; and a Chandler Austin Special from 1992. The ad from the same year highlights the Texan charm of that guitar, as well as alluding to the Rickenbacker-like qualities of Chandler's 555 model.

The leading electric guitar design of the 1980s, the superstrat, takes shape in this 1986 ad (near left) for a Japanese-made Charvel Model Six.

CHARVEL

Charvel grew from a small supplier of guitar parts in the late 1970s to a major producer of rock guitars in the 1980s. In 1974 Wayne Charvel set up a guitar repair business in Azusa, northern Los Angeles, California (and soon moved to nearby San Dimas). Charvel began supplying much-needed hardware replacement parts, and from this humble beginning the line would expand to include bodies, necks, pickups and, ultimately, complete guitar kits.

Financial problems struck in 1977, and late the following year Wayne Charvel signed over his name and the entire operation to employee Grover Jackson. (Charvel himself went on to run several shortlived companies in the 1980s, and launched the Wayne brand in 1999.)

Grover Jackson continued to offer a customizing service at Charvel for instruments brought in by customers, while continuing to develop and hone his own ideas on guitar design. The results eventually appeared in limited form in 1979 with the first Charvel-brand guitars. One of the early efforts was seen under the fast-moving fingers of a rising guitar star, Edward Van Halen.

At the start of the 1980s Jackson added a new line under his own name (see Jackson). The Charvel brand was reserved for bolt-on-neck guitars with essentially Fender-style bodies and necks – as well as Gibson- or Vox-inspired alternatives and an original four-point "star" shape. Options in 1981 also included various DiMarzio pickups as well as distinctive flashy custom paint jobs.

Business grew as Grover Jackson's efforts led to high-profile associations with key emerging guitar heroes. In 1986 a joint venture with distributor IMC of Fort Worth, Texas, resulted in a less-expensive made-in-Japan Charvel line sporting Jackson's by now established drooped "pointy" headstock. Jackson/Charvel relocated a few miles east to Ontario, California, around this time.

The new Charvel line remained Fender-styled: Models One, Two, Three and Four each employed a bolt-on neck and Strat-like body shape. Models Five and Six featured 24-fret through-neck construction allied to a slimmer-horned body. This and the pointy headstock would become characteristics of the new "superstrat" styling, as would Model Six's sharkfin-shape fingerboard markers. Pickup layouts included a single bridge humbucker, as well as the two-single-coils-plus-bridge-humbucker strongly identified with the new rock-oriented superstrats. Vibratos too were considered to be mandatory equipment back then.

By 1988 the line had expanded, but the following year saw a major revamp signified by a new Charvel logo in a "script" style as on Jacksons. Models were split into named series including Contemporary, Classic, Fusion and Professional. The market for superstrats was now clearly defined, and the new Charvels – fine examples of high-

Charvel's first Japanese line featured models still largely Strat-based, such as this 1986 Model Four (near right), as well as in the new superstrat style, like this 1986 Model Five (center). Superstrats prevailed: this Fusion Custom (far right) was made in 1988.

end Japanese mass-manufacture – were intended to fill every niche. A Korean-made line, new for 1989, was branded Charvette By Charvel and clearly aimed at entry-level players. However, by 1991 all instruments regardless of origin were branded Charvel once more. Some new 1990 models catered for traditional as well as extreme tastes: the Strat-style STs and Tele-like TE contrasted the Avenger's offset-V shape that echoed Jackson's Randy Rhoads.

One of the first determined moves into original yet retro-flavored design came in 1991 with the Surfcaster semi-solidbody, something of a mutated Jazzmaster-meets-Rickenbacker-meets-Danelectro. The Surfcaster had started life as a custom Jackson model, but the Charvel versions initially came in six-string (vibrato or fixed-bridge) and 12-string models. Then the CX series took over from the Charvettes, maintaining Charvel's low-end presence. A new overtly Fender-style headstock was soon amended to a design intended to calm trademark lawyers.

In 1994 Charvel's San Dimas series was introduced, named for the location of the old Charvel facility. This marked a return to US manufacture (though three years earlier there had been a limited-edition remake of the original late-1970s model), while the budget CHS series was launched in 1995. However, the acquisition of Jackson/Charvel by the Japanese electronic musical instrument company Akai in 1997 marked the end of Charvel-brand instruments.

Eddie Van Halen built the guitar he used on his band's 1978 debut album (above) using a body and neck bought from Charvel among other parts. Charvel's Contemporary Spectrum model (1989 example, far left) retained some Fender-style touches, while retro fever hit the company for this 1991 Surfcaster (center, with 1992 ad). The 1994 San Dimas (near left) marked a return to US manufacture for Charvel, but the brandname was dead by 1997.

321

CORAL

In 1966 the entertainment conglomerate MCA bought Danelectro. MCA maintained the company's base in its existing premises in Neptune, New Jersey, along with founder Nat Daniel, but one of the changes that the new owner made was the addition of a new Danelectro-made brand in 1967, which they called Coral. The name came from one of MCA's record labels. (See the Danelectro entry for models that continued at this time with the Danelectro brand.)

The first Coral-brand instruments shared the Jaguar-like shape and short Strat-style head of contemporary Danelectros, but were solidbodies with a Coral logo and the unusual "crackle" finishes of the Dane D series. Models included the two- or three-pickup Hornet and 12-string Scorpion.

Joining these Corals in 1967 was the vaguely US-map shaped Coral Sitar, endorsed by Al Nichol and Tom Dawes. Like the earlier Danelectro Bellzouki 12-string, it was co-designed by session-man Vinnie Bell who had spotted a demand in New York studios in the mid 1960s for trendy sitar sounds, popular since George Harrison used a real sitar on The Beatles' 1965 track 'Norwegian Wood.'

Bell prompted Danelectro to devise an electric guitar that would make a sitar-like sound. The secret was the flat plastic "bridge" that gave a buzzy sound – and made intonation almost impossible. There was also a bank of 13 extra "drone" strings tuned in half-steps. A similarly-shaped Coral Bellzouki 12-string was also introduced. New, too, were the f-hole thinline hollowbody Firefly, flat-top Vincent Bell Combo, and Long Horn Series (f-hole hollow versions of the older Danelectro Long Horns). Coral died along with Danelectro in 1969.

CORT

The Korean guitar-making powerhouse of Cort was established in 1973 by Jack Westheimer of Chicago, Illinois. Westheimer, formerly the US importer of Teisco, used the factory to produce Cortez-brand acoustic guitars, made in Japan since 1960. Cort also produced some Cortez-brand copies of American electric guitars during the 1970s, and supplied guitars for other companies too. Around 1978 Cort developed an efficient way to produce through-neck versions of popular guitar designs; some were sold with the Arbor brand.

In 1983 Cort built a new, modern factory in Korea and began to use timbers and electronics imported from North America. By 1985 Cort was producing lines for Kramer and B.C. Rich. Soon after the new factory opened the Cort brandname itself appeared on various beginner-grade copies of American guitars.

Then Cort bought a license to Ned Steinberger's headless guitar design and has offered a version ever since. By 1986 Cort was offering exotic guitars such as the Effector, with built-in effects, the Sound, with built-in amp and speaker, a star-shaped

Steve Howe on stage with Yes in 1973 (right) about to play a Coral Sitar on the guitar "tree" he had built to enable a fast changeover between different guitars. Howe had first used the Coral Sitar on 'Siberian Khatru,' a track on the band's 1972 album Close To The Edge (below).

guitar manufacturers

Vinnie Bell worked with Danelectro on the design of the Coral Sitar and appeared in this shameless ad (left) in 1967. New York sessionman Bell played the Sitar on many 1960s pop hits, including 'Green Tambourine' by The Lemon Pipers (1967 album, opposite page).

model, plus Strat-style and Explorer-style models with elaborate pearl dragon inlays. Original designs followed two years later including the pointy-horned Strat-style Solo series and the exaggerated extended-horn double-cutaway Starfires.

By 1989 there was the curly-maple-topped, scalloped and contoured deep-double-cutaway Viva Deluxe guitar, plus a Heavy Metal model that came with a built-in octave-splitting effect. In addition to various copies, the Viva and Starfire (offered as the S-Series) would anchor the line through the 1990s.

During 1992 Cort's line was reorganized into the Performer Series, now including Stratocaster-style guitars that were called the Stature, Mega, Statos, Retro and STAT. These models were offered with various options in materials and the pickup layouts. Also debuting at this time were the thinline Source (in a Gibson ES-335-style) and the full-bodied Yorktown Deluxe archtop (this in Super-400-style). From 1994 for around three years Cort offered the Artist Series, which included a high-end Viva CM with Bartolini pickups, as well as a swamp ash superstrat, the A2000.

Around 1997 Cort began to work with well-known guitar-makers to develop new designs. Luthier Jerry Auerswald came up with the EF (Environmentally Friendly) Series made from the synthetic "luthite." A year later the Solo Series superstrats were introduced, as well as the Signature Series. This included the TRG, an archtop with cats-eye soundholes designed by Nashville luthier Jim Triggs; the LCS-1, a Gibson-

style archtop endorsed by Larry Coryell; and the MGM-1, a carved PRS-like solid endorsed by Matt "Guitar" Murphy.

By 1999 the Cort line had continued to move to higher-end instruments with several archtops endorsed by Joe Beck, some very fancy Solo models including the birdseye-maple HBS Hiram Bullock Signature, plus a sleek deep-cut Viva Gold II and the dramatic Music Man Silhouette-style S Series. New for 1999 was the streamlined Telecaster-style CL Series, including the CL1500 with a carved, quilted-maple top, sound chambers and f-holes.

CUSTOM KRAFT

This was a brand applied to entry-level guitars and amplifiers made for Bernard Kornbloom's St. Louis Music, based in Missouri. The line got underway during the mid 1950s with some archtops made by Kay. From 1961 until the middle of the decade many Custom Krafts were variants of Kay hollowbodies (including versions of Kay's Thinline series). At first these were joined by Japanese-made solidbodies.

In 1963 the Valco-made Ambassador solidbodies debuted. These seemed to be somewhat inspired by Burns, but in fact were variants of some of Valco's existing National and Supro models. Valco purchased Kay in 1967; the following year the Mod line of hollowbodies appeared. Despite the demise of Valco/Kay in 1968, Custom Krafts continued to 1970, increasingly using non-US parts.

On this page: a Coral Sitar from 1967 (far left) complete with "buzzy" bridge and drone strings; a Cort Larry Coryell signature model from 1999; and a Custom Kraft

Ambassador Vibramatic made by Valco in the US in 1966. The company's ad from the following year (above) attempts to link Custom Kraft with the popular British sound.

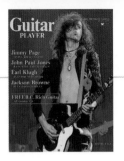

Jimmy Page on-stage with Led Zeppelin (below right), and on magazine cover (left) playing the Danelectro Standard he favored for slide work. The Standard 3021 pictured (right) was made around 1965, and is very similar to that used by Page.

DANELECTRO

Probably no other instruments so humble have garnered as much reverence as Danelectro guitars of the 1950s and 1960s, thrust into immortality primarily through association with the mail-order catalog of Sears, Roebuck.

Before competition from Japanese and other importers, Danelectros – or "Danos" as they're often called – were the beginner guitars of the post-war Baby Boom generation. A Danelectro is reported to have set Jerry Garcia on the road to eventual stardom, but the guitars also found their way into recording studios because of an individual sound that attracted pro players. Danelectros can be heard on records that range from 'Sugar, Sugar' by The Archies to 'I'm A Believer' by The Monkees and 'The Sound Of Silence' by Simon & Garfunkel. The instruments have been played by artists as diverse as Jimi Hendrix, Jimmy Page and Los Lobos.

Danelectro's founder was Nathan I. (Nat) Daniel. He began his career in 1933 building amplifiers for a department store in New York City. Some time during the following year Daniel was recruited by Epiphone man Herb Sunshine to build the earliest Epiphone Electar amps. Until 1942 Daniel would continue to supply Epiphone with a number of products.

The Danelectro company was founded in 1946 and began supplying amps for mail-order company Montgomery Ward in 1947, and for Sears in 1948. In 1954 Danelectro expanded into solidbody electric guitars, introducing its own Danelectro-brand models. That same year, in the Fall Sears catalog, Danelectro-made guitars branded Silvertone replaced the solidbodies that had previously been made for the mail-order company by Harmony. These Dano-origin Silvertones were small, Les-Paul-shaped guitars that came with either one or two single-coil pickups concealed underneath a melamine pickguard. The Danelectro-brand versions were covered in white tweed vinyl and were distinguished by wide "bell"-shape headstocks, while the similar Silvertone models came in maroon vinyl but were topped by equally distinctive wide "Coke bottle"-shape headstocks. Most Danelectro guitars of the time sported simple metal bridge/tailpiece assemblies with a moveable rosewood saddle.

In 1955 the small ginger-colored Model C "peanut" appeared with a Coke-bottle headstock. The pickguard had shrunk in size and the pickups were now exposed, first wrapped in brown vinyl tape, followed by unplated and then chrome-plated "lipstick" pickups – the covers actually purchased from a lipstick-tube manufacturer.

The similar U-1 and U-2 models replaced the Cs in 1956, the main difference being their availability in a line of new colors (black, copper, royal blue, coral red, surf green and so on). A Danelectro innovation was the six-string bass, introduced as the short-scale UB-2 model around 1956. This was effectively a guitar that was tuned an octave lower than usual. Dano six-string basses of various designs also began to appear on

Danelectro's popular electrics included the early U-1 and U-2 models, seen in the company's two-sided flyer from 1956 (above). The company sold a number of instruments to the Sears mail-order catalog with the Silvertone brand. This 1958 Silvertone G01301L (right) was the Sears version of Dano's masonite-and-pine U-2.

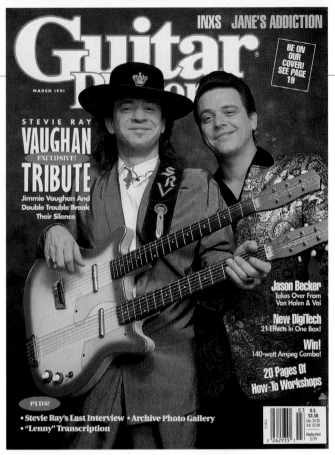

Danelectro's Bellzouki, introduced in 1961, was one of the first 12-string electric guitars generally available. This two-pickup version (far right) dates from around 1965. The publicity material is from Danelectro's 1967 catalog.

records, including such gems of Dano twanginess as Duane Eddy's 'Because They're Young.' A three-pickup U-3 regular guitar was added in 1957, and that same year saw the U series Danos also available with the Silvertone brand. However, by the close of the 1950s the Silvertone line had reduced to just a few Danelectro models, replaced largely by Harmony- and Kay-made guitars. Single-pickup Silvertone U models got a new, skinny "dolphin"-shape headstock that had six tuners in-line. This style would last on Danelectro instruments through 1961.

In 1958 Danelectro relocated the guitar and amplifier factory to new premises in Neptune, New Jersey. It was at this time that the company introduced its legendary semi-hollowbody guitars, the Standard (with one or two pickups and Coke-bottle headstock), the Deluxe (two or three pickups) and the oddly-named Hand Vibrato (with "duck foot"-shape headstock, and vibrato).

These are now known as Danelectro's "short-horn" models because of their widely flared double-cutaway horns which are shorter than those of the later "long-horn" style. The various models came with laminated masonite (hardboard) tops and backs over wooden frames of either poplar or pine; sides were covered in vinyl. These instruments would typify the Danelectro line through 1966, but three other classic Danos had been introduced in 1959. These comprised a short-horn guitar/bass double-neck in white-to-brown sunburst, the wood-grained, hollowbody Convertible

More fabulous Danelectro guitars on this page include a "short-horn" double-neck (near right) combining guitar and four-string bass, this one made in 1960. Stevie Ray Vaughan clutches one with guitar and six-string bass on a 1991 magazine cover (above, right). Danelectro was a pioneer of the six-string bass, effectively a guitar tuned an octave lower than normal. This 1958 Long Horn Model 4623 (far right) is owned by Duane Eddy, who did much to popularize the sound of the six-string bass. The ad for long-horn and short-horn guitars dates from 1959.

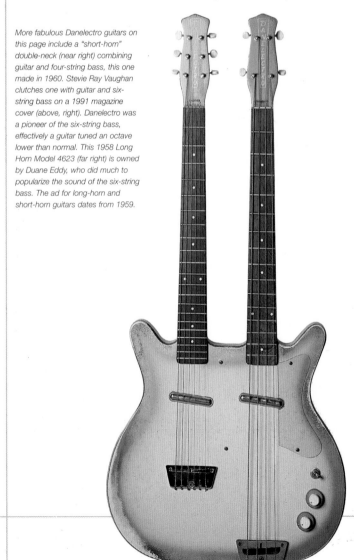

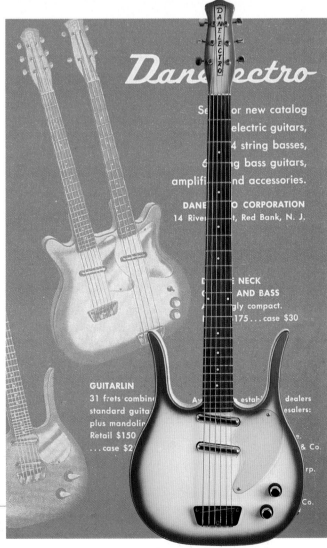

Top Guitarist VINCENT BELL is famed among the pros for innovation. That's why he says "DANELECTRO has presented the most new ideas over the years. They are usually first with the new sounds. It's top value for my money!"

the all-new
DANE line

Danelectro

...anced custom features for easier, better play
...nmatched Danelectro More-for-the-Dollar value

Danelectro's advertising was something else, exemplified by this 1967 ad for the Electric Sitar.

that came with or without pickup, and the white-to-bronze sunburst Long Horn Bass with its distinctive "lyre"-shape long-horn body.

In 1958 studio guitarist Vinnie Bell became associated with Danelectro and it was in 1961 that the Bellzouki model he helped to design was introduced. It was an electric 12-string guitar – at this time one of the few such production models available. Its body looked something like a Greek bouzouki, hence the name. The one-pickup version had a teardrop shape, while the two-pickup model added four extra points. Both had a "mustache" pickguard under the strings and a duck-foot head.

Meanwhile, by 1962 the only Danelectro guitar offered by Sears was the new amp-in-case guitar, a single-pickup short-horn in black metalflake. The brilliantly simple idea was that built into the guitar's case was a three-watt amp and 6″ speaker, providing the guitarist with a portable electric guitar outfit. This was joined in 1963 by a two-pickup version in red sunburst that came with a deafening five-watt amp, 8″ speaker and tremolo. The six-tuners-in-line headstocks now looked like meat cleavers. In 1967 the amp-in-case guitars changed to a new Fender Jaguar-style shape.

During 1963 Danelectro rolled out the little Pro 1 solidbody guitar which, with its asymmetrical, square-ish shape, looked something like a poor guitarist's Guild Thunderbird. It did however introduce Nat Daniel's neck-tilt adjustment. It was followed on to the market by the exotic Guitarlin model which sported the long-horn lyre-shaped body and a fingerboard that sported no less than 31 frets. In 1966 the entertainment conglomerate MCA bought Danelectro and, while they kept Daniel in charge, made big changes. Alongside the Danelectro-brand guitars, the new owner would also introduce a new Coral brand, named for one of the MCA's record labels, but still manufactured in the Danelectro factory (see Coral).

The 1967 Danelectro Slimline guitars were semi-hollowbody models with a Jaguar-style shape, distinctive vinyl side-trim, stubby Strat-like head and two or three pickups, with or without vibrato. A 12-string version was also offered. The Hawk line was similar, with one or two pickups but without the vinyl side trim.

Also similar to the Slimlines, the 1967 Dane Series had four basic sub-groups: A (one or two pickups); B (two or three pickups); C (crackled two-tone "gator" finish); and D ("gator" finish plus deluxe pickguard in a swirled plastic and brushed-chrome control panel). Finally during 1967 a new Danelectro-brand Electric Sitar debuted (see Coral for the better-known model). The Danelectro sitar was a one-pickup instrument with rounded, sitar-like body shape and matching headstock style.

By 1968 demand for guitars had declined and in 1969 MCA closed the Danelectro factory. Guitar-maker Dan Armstrong obtained some leftover parts and in 1969 sold them with his own pickups as Dan Armstrong Modified Danelectros. Later, some Danelectro models would became collectable cult items, especially after players of the

Three more Danelectro guitars on this page: a 31-fret Guitarlin from 1966 (near right) in the distinctive "long-horn" style; an Electric Sitar (center) made in 1967; and a reissued U-3 from 1999.

guitar manufacturers

Evets acquired the Danelectro name in 1995 and started to revive guitars three years later. The "new" Danelectros did much to shape retro fashion in the late 1990s. This catalog cover from 1999 displays a sparkle finish on a reissued U-3.

stature of Jimmy Page were seen using the instruments. Page would often opt for a Standard short-horn on stage for slide work, exploiting the bright, cutting sound of the guitar's pickups that was enhanced by the cheap but effective construction.

Nat Daniel died in 1994. In 1995 the Evets Corporation obtained rights to the Danelectro name, introducing a line of effects pedals in 1997 followed by guitars in 1998. The new Danelectros were similar in look and construction to the vintage models, with reproduction "lipstick" pickups and similar hardware, although by 1999 the line had begun to expand into retro sparkle finishes and new electronic switching. There were also a number of new designs such as the Hodad (1999) and Mod (2000), consistent with the spirit if not the letter of the legend that is Danelectro.

D'ANGELICO

New York City guitar-maker John D'Angelico is best known for his superb acoustic archtop instruments built from the early 1930s to the early 1960s. Some owners of these fine instruments would inevitably fit the guitars with "floating" pickups to allow amplified playing. Other customers would sometimes take more drastic action, such as Chet Atkins who unleashed his toolkit to permanently fix a Gibson pickup into the top of his D'Angelico instrument. This is enough to make guitar collectors weep today, because D'Angelicos are among the most valuable "vintage" guitars. However, due to continuing demand from a number of guitarists who would visit his busy Manhattan

shop, John D'Angelico decided to offer during the 1950s and early 1960s a line of budget archtops with permanently built-in pickups and controls. These are sometimes referred to as G-7 models, though it's unclear if D'Angelico actually allocated model names to the electrics. Most had plywood bodies that D'Angelico would buy in from local suppliers such as United Guitars or Codé of New Jersey, but the necks at least were made by D'Angelico himself.

D'AQUISTO

Jimmy D'Aquisto worked with the New York archtop guitar-maker John D'Angelico from 1959. Following D'Angelico's death five years later, D'Aquisto began making guitars in his own right.

Gradually D'Aquisto developed his own style, and while primarily working in the acoustic archtop field he did make a number of flat-top guitars as well as some fully electric instruments. The electric models culminated in the luthier's Les Paul-shaped semi-hollowbody Centura Electric model. This stylish guitar debuted in the early 1990s. It included typical D'Aquisto touches such as a wooden tailpiece and pickguard, as well as the maker's customary employment of the finest neck and body timbers. D'Aquisto also designed electrics for Hagstrom (the Jimmy model) and for Fender (the D'Aquisto Deluxe, Elite and Standard models). D'Aquisto died in 1995 at the age of just 59. He once described his guitars as "a way that I can make the world a bit better."

On this page: a recent original design from the relaunched Danelectro company, this is a Hodad (far left) from 1999; the D'Angelico electric archtop shown (center) was made around 1960; and the D'Aquisto Centura Electric dates from 1991.

Dean managed to cause almost as much controversy with its blatantly sexist ads, such as this 1983 example (right), as it did with its Gibson-inspired guitars. (left)

DEAN

Dean rode to fame in the late 1970s making fancy versions of Gibson-style designs, originally with flamboyant "wishbone" headstocks. Dean was founded in 1976 by Dean Zelinsky of Evanston, Illinois. Production of the Z (Explorer-like), V (Flying V-style) and a hybrid of the two, the much-emulated ML, began in 1977. Dean guitars had figured tops and loud DiMarzio pickups.

The Les-Paul-inspired E'Lite and Cadillac appeared in 1979-80, followed by a downsized Baby series in 1982, as favored by Rik Emmett and Sammy Hagar. The 1983 Bel Aire's bolt-on neck came from ESP in Japan and was one of the first guitars (along with the Kramer Pacer) sporting the humbucker/single-coil/single-coil pickup layout that practically defined the coming "superstrat" genre.

Debuting in 1985 were the Hollywood models from ESP in Japan, the Signature series from Korea, and the "heavy metal" Mach V (Japan) and VII (US). Manufacture of Dean's conventional Fender-style guitars shifted to Korea in 1986, including 1987's Eighty-Eight, Jammer and Playmate series.

In 1990 Zelinsky licensed the Dean name to Tropical Music of Miami, Florida, and a year later Korean Strat-style solidbodies debuted. A Reissue Series of early Dean designs was produced in 1993-94 in California, supervised by Zelinsky, becoming American Customs made in Cleveland, Ohio, in 1994. In 1995 a new Dean factory

Dean clearly absorbed Gibson influences into its original trio of models – the Explorer-like Z (1978 example, near right), the Flying-V-style V, and a combination of the two, the ML – all detailed in this 1977 ad (below). Dean's Explorer-

meets-V ML model would itself spawn a good number of imitators in the pointy-guitar world. Dean's Golden E'lite (center) dates from 1983. Fender revived the De Armond name in the 1990s for a line of Guild-alikes, including this M-75 (far right) which was produced during 1998.

opened in Plant City, Florida, managed by Armadillo Enterprises, offering US-made American Customs and the US Series with Korean bodies, all variations on classic Dean designs. Models made in the US and Korea (American Spirit) were offered in 1997, including a Korina series and new Icon models inspired by PRS's designs.

In 1998 Dean continued mining its heritage with the US Custom Shop series, the Flame, Ultima and US Phantom series, and the European Custom and Premium series, as well as an electric resonator guitar.

DE ARMOND

De Armond has been famous as a brandname for pickups and effects-pedals, starting back in the 1940s. In 1997 it was acquired by Fender, who subsequently decided to apply it to a line of Korean-built electrics to represent a less expensive alter ego of Guild, which had been in Fender ownership since 1995.

The De Armond guitar line debuted in Europe in 1998, the American launch following a year later. Including solidbodies, semi-solids and archtop electrics, the line consists of models based on well-known Guild designs, some re-created more closely than others, and employing similar or identical names to the originals.

The Starfire Special closely resembles its early-1960s single-cutaway inspiration, complete with reproduction De Armond single-coil pickups and Bigsby-style vibrato tailpiece, while the standard Starfire replicates the later equal-double-cutaway version.

The humbucker-equipped M75 solid recalls Guild's own Les Paul-style equivalent, and is also offered as the M75T with sparkle-finished front, single-coils and vibrato.

The Jet-Star approximates the style of the odd 1960s Guild Thunderbird, but with simplified fixtures and fittings – no built-in stand or Hagstrom vibrato here. The single-cutaway X155 archtop electric embodies classic Guild features, including a stepped pickguard, harp tailpiece and two humbuckers.

Cheaper Indonesian-made versions of the various solidbodies have since been introduced to the De Armond line. These models can be generally identified by their bolt-on-neck construction and more basic appointments.

Additions during 2000 included the T400 thinline hollowbody, and two flavor-of-the-moment seven-string solidbodies, the S67 and Seven Star.

DOMINO

Cheap Japanese-made Dominos replaced the Orpheum line for Maurice Lipsky of New York around 1967, lasting about a year. The asymmetrical California models were imaginative, but other near-copies of popular Eko, Vox, Guild and Fender solidbody and hollowbody electric guitars and basses presaged the "copy era" in the US.

DWIGHT

Epiphone, like some other makers, occasionally made special versions of existing models for particular retailers. Dwight was a US outlet whose sole claim to guitar fame

Two guitars from Domino are pictured here: a California Rebel from 1967 (far left) and a solidbody Baron (center) made in the same year. The Dwight-branded guitar (near left) is a specially badged version of an Epiphone Coronet made in 1962.

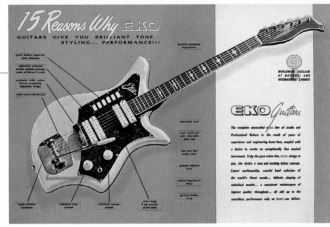

An object lesson in how to excite gadget-freaks with a pushbutton-laden multi-pickup guitar, as taught by Eko in a catalog from 1964.

was a special custom-branded edition of the New York company's solidbody Coronet that it commissioned during the early 1960s. It had a Dwight headstock logo and "D"-badged pickguard, but was otherwise identical to the Epi Coronet.

EGGLE

Here was a serious attempt to establish a quality UK guitar brand. Patrick Eggle began his professional guitar-making career in 1990 with the shortlived Climaxe instruments, but a year later Patrick Eggle-brand guitars burst on to the scene from a factory that was based in Coventry, England.

The Patrick Eggle Guitar Company was formed by Eggle and businessman Andrew Selby. The guitars themselves – the small-body fixed-bridge PRS-like Berlin and the similar Berlin Pro, one of the first guitars to be fitted with a Wilkinson VS-100 vibrato – were well conceived and good value.

But problems arose when the company tried to maintain production levels, discovering the marked differences between building one guitar a month and 20 a week. So there followed a liaison with Swiss-based maker Gary Levinson, with the Coventry factory making Eggles as well as Levinson's own Blade-brand guitars. In the midst of the problems, Eggle himself left early in 1994. At first he produced Redwing guitars, but soon retreated to custom-making.

The Eggle/Levinson operation itself folded early in 1995, but a new Eggle company

was back in business within a month. Despite having noted hardware designer Trev Wilkinson on board, this too failed, and Eggle was sold to Birmingham-based distributor Musical Exchanges at the end of 1996, from where Patrick Eggle Guitars operates today. Wilkinson remains as creative director, and has his own Fret-King brand. Current Eggles include a number of Berlin derivatives, plus New York, Austin, Milan and Artist models, with sales centering on the high-end Berlin Pro.

EGMOND

This Dutch maker provided affordable, low-end electrics for many aspiring axe heroes in Europe. Some Egmonds exported to the UK were branded with distributor Rosetti's name. A 1950s example was the Solid 7, actually a thin hollowbody with a floating assembly incorporating two pickups and controls. At just £19 ($32) it was the first electric for many players, including Paul McCartney. Models in the 1960s included the Fender-influenced solidbody Airstream 2 and 3, the semi-solid Sheer-Line 7, the Jazzmaster-like Rosetti 3 and the relatively luxurious three-pickup Princess 3. By the early 1970s the Egmond operation had closed.

An Eggle Berlin Pro from Britain is shown here (near right), made in 1991, the first year of production. The ad (below) was published during the company's direct-sale period in 1995. This Dutch-made Egmond (center) is a model 3 from 1965, while the fabulous Italian Eko is a 700/4V of 1964 – an early showing for multi-cutaway design.

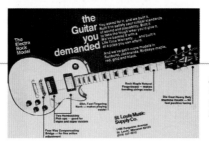

An object lesson in how to attract trademark lawyers with a very close visual copy of a Les Paul, as taught by Electra in a 1975 ad.

EKO

Among Italy's best-known guitar-makers, and one of the country's biggest exporters, Eko was established in the late 1950s by Oliviero Pigini & Co of Porto Recanati. Pigini at first made accordions, with Eko electric guitars following around 1960.

In 1961 Eko teamed up with American distributor LoDuca of Milwaukee, Wisconsin, and the new duo was marketing electrics by 1962. The models included sparkle- and marble-plastic-covered solidbodies and "violin"-shape guitars. During the 1970s Eko sold vaguely Gibson-like guitars primarily in Europe. The brand appeared on a line of Korean-made copies in the late 1980s. During the late 1990s a series of retro-flavor electrics revived Eko's 1960s designs.

ELECTAR

Electar was a brandname on Epiphone's early electric guitars and amplifiers from around 1935 to 1939. New York-based Epiphone had roots in banjo-making but began making guitars in the late 1920s. Its Electar models gave it an early start in the new electric guitar business. Some Electar guitars have large Rickenbacker-like horseshoe pickups, but the company's Master pickup, in use by 1939 and designed by Herb Sunshine, was among the first with individually adjustable polepieces, enabling the relative volume of each string to be set. Around 1939 Epiphone logically began to use its own brandname for electric guitars.

ELECTRA

A top 1970s "copy" brand in the US, Electra succeeded Custom Kraft and Apollo for importer St. Louis Music, beginning in 1971 with an Ampeg Dan Armstrong copy. Primarily made in Japan by Matsumoku, these early copies of designs made famous by Gibson and Fender quickly improved. By 1974 they had gained in quality enough to be endorsed by Nashville ace Paul Yandell. Innovations included US pickups and, in 1976, the MPC line with onboard modular effects, as endorsed by Peter Frampton. Original designs followed a 1977 industry lawsuit over copying, and included the Phoenix line, plus "pointy" shapes by 1983. St. Louis Music replaced the brand with Westone guitars around 1983.

ELECTRO

A brandname originally used by Rickenbacker for its earliest electric guitars. These included the cast aluminum "Frying Pan" lap-steel model of 1932, the world's first electric guitar with magnetic pickup to be put into production. From about 1934 the company added Rickenbacker (or "Rickenbacher") to its logo plates, the same year its manufacturing operation was named the Electro String Instrument Corporation. Rickenbacker alone took over as the company's sole brandname in the 1950s, but the Electro name was briefly revived in 1964 for two solidbody models, the ES-16 (based on the Rickenbacker Model 1000) and ES-17 (based on Rickenbacker's 425).

Three similar brandnames, three very different guitars on this page: Electar was Epiphone's early brand for electric guitars, and this Century model (far left) dates from around 1937; Electra was a brand used on guitars imported to the US by St. Louis Music, including this pointy Lady XV1RD (center) from 1983; and Electro was an early Rickenbacker-related brand revived in the mid 1960s for two models, including this ES-17 of 1964 (near left).

Epiphone's archtop guitars have been popular not just as full-fledged electrics, but as acoustics with "floating" pickups, as demonstrated by Duke Robillard in this 1998 ad.

This Epiphone Zephyr (near right) was made around 1941 and was one of three archtop electrics made by Epiphone at the time, alongside the Century and Coronet models. The ad in the background dates from 1950 and shows sessionman Al Caiola with a Zephyr Deluxe Regent.

An Epiphone Zephyr Emperor Regent made in 1954 is shown (below, far right), at the time a startling mix of old and new, with traditional archtop body topped by an up-to-the-minute bank of six tone-modifying switches.

EPIPHONE

Many younger readers may only know Epiphone as a brand primarily of bargain-price entry-level versions of Gibson- and Fender-style models. But back when archtops ruled the earth, in the years before and after World War II, Epiphone was one of the most respected guitar companies, making midrange to high-end instruments often used in big-band jazz orchestras.

The Epiphone company dates back to the 1870s in Smyrna, Turkey, where Greek-born founder Anastasios Stathopoulo crafted his own-label fiddles, lutes and Greek lioutos. Stathopoulo moved to the United States in 1903 and continued to make instruments, including mandolins, in Long Island City, Queens, New York.

Anastasios died in 1915 and his son Epaminondas took over. He was generally and helpfully known as "Epi." Two years later the company became known as the House Of Stathopoulo and, following World War I, began making banjos. In 1924 the company's Recording line of banjos was introduced and four years later the official name was changed to the Epiphone Banjo Company.

Epiphone began producing guitars around 1928, introducing its first round-soundhole Recording archtop models, and in the early 1930s the company's famous Masterbilt line of f-hole archtops debuted. By the end of the decade Epiphone was a major competitor to Gibson, which by now was generally acknowledged as the leading

guitar manufacturers

ЄPIPHONЄ

guitars
basses
amplifiers

Epiphone Inc. - 210 Rush Street - Kalamazoo,

EPIPHONE

By the mid 1990s the Emperor was redesigned with two pickups, but had the benefit of an endorsement by jazzman Joe Pass.

manufacturer of archtops. The Epiphone operation was renamed Epiphone Inc in 1935 and introduced a line of electric archtops and amplifiers, initially called Electraphone but quickly changed to Electar.

Many of the early Electar amps were made by Nat Daniel who would later found Danelectro. Early Electar guitars were non-cutaway archtops (and lap-steels) that had pickups with large handrests over the strings. By 1939 Epiphone-brand electric archtops included the Century, Coronet and Zephyr (fitted with a large distinctively shaped oval pickup). In 1939 Epiphone's Herb Sunshine was one of the first to conceive of adjustable polepieces on pickups to achieve a better balance of sound, and these soon began to appear on Epiphones.

Epi Stathopoulo died in 1943 and control of Epiphone went to his brothers Orphie and Frixo. Pre-war electric archtops continued following World War II, joined by the Kent model in 1949. Epiphone introduced in 1948 its first single-cutaway archtop acoustics, versions of the earlier Emperor and DeLuxe, and added Tone Spectrum pickups to them in 1949. Among the pros who played Epiphones during these early years were George Van Eps, Tony Mottola, Al Caiola and Oscar Moore.

However, Epiphone's challenge to Gibson was about to fall apart. In 1951 a strike shut down Epiphone's New York factory for four months, and Epiphone relocated its factory to Philadelphia, Pennsylvania. During the Philadelphia tenure the company

Epiphone was bought by Gibson in the late 1950s. Production was shifted to Kalamazoo, Michigan, starting in 1958. The "new" electric Emperor had a more conventional control layout, seen on this 1959 example (left). By the time this 1964 Emperor (right) was made, mini-humbucking pickups were standard.

experimented with some interesting prototypes of solidbody electric guitars, but none ever got so far as to be put into production. During 1955, Epiphone introduced an archtop instrument equipped with a DeArmond pickup and endorsed by Harry Volpe. However, in 1957 Frixo Stathopoulo died – and this sad occasion would in effect mark the end of Epiphone's independence.

Gibson purchased Epiphone and relocated it to Kalamazoo, Michigan, turning the brand into its second-tier line. In 1958 Gibson started to manufacture and market its new Epiphone lines. These included the first Epiphone solidbody electric guitars, similar in style to Les Paul Specials and Juniors: the equal-double-cutaway, slab-bodied, two-pickup Crestwood; and the low-end one-pickup Coronet. Both models were fitted with small pickups now known as "New York" types because they were devised and originally used when the company occupied its east-coast premises. The pickups had arrived with various other leftover parts from Epiphone with the purchase. All Gibson-made Epiphones had set-necks in the new owner's customary style.

Also in 1958, Gibson reworked the old Century electric archtop into a thinline electric fitted with one P-90 pickup. This was followed by the twin-humbucker, double-cutaway Sheraton thinline in 1959. This model would later appeal to Noel Gallagher in Oasis, while a John Lee Hooker signature Sheraton would be introduced to the Epiphone line just over 40 years later, in 2000. Back in 1959, the Epi solidbody line

The Sheraton was the second most expensive f-hole electric in Gibson's new Epiphone line. This natural-finish E212TN version was made in 1962. In the fishy 1966 ad (above) the company wondered why celebrities didn't endorse Epi guitars. Maybe because they were too busy helping to promote Gibsons instead.

This jolly gathering (above) is for the cover of Epiphone's 1964 catalog, where the night will be long, the guitars loud... and ties preferred.

guitar manufacturers

was expanding. The Crestwood was renamed the Crestwood Custom, restyled with a trimmer, more rounded body that sported New York pickups until a change was made to mini-humbuckers in 1963.

The Coronet remained, but now came with a P-90 single-coil pickup. New in 1959 was the Wilshire, effectively a Coronet fitted with two P-90s. Both models adopted the new "rounded" Crestwood body style in 1960, the same year seeing the introduction of the single-cutaway Olympic (single pickup), Olympic Double (two pickups) and double-cutaway Olympic Special. Some Epiphones of the period came with a simple flat-spring vibrato, although after 1961 the rosewood-clad Maestro vibrato was also offered, mainly on Crestwood Customs.

Epiphone thinlines continued to expand with the single-pointed-cutaway Sorrento (two mini-humbuckers) in 1960, double-cutaway Professional (mini-humbucker) and Casino (two P-90s) in 1961, the non-cutaway Granada (one Melody Maker pickup) and double-cutaway Riviera (two mini-humbuckers) in 1962, and the double-cutaway Al Caiola Custom (two mini-humbuckers) in 1963. The Caiola Standard with two P-90s followed in 1966. In 1964 Epiphone introduced the Howard Roberts Standard with one sharp cutaway, oval soundhole and a mini-humbucker.

Popularity of the thinlines increased in the 1960s when first Paul McCartney acquired a Casino for Beatle studio work, followed by John Lennon and George

Harrison who each used new Casinos on-stage in the final fab-four concerts of 1966. The group's new Epis were also all over the band's latest *Revolver* LP, and the Beatle connection has ensured that the Epiphone thinlines in general and the Casino model in particular enjoy a continuing popularity among pop groups who find themselves keen on reactivating a Merseyside-style mix.

In 1963 the Epi solidbodies were redesigned to feature a longer upper horn as well as a scalloped "batwing" six-tuners-in-line headstock. A three-pickup Crestwood Deluxe joined the line, and in 1966 a Wilshire 12-string was offered.

Gibson was purchased from Chicago Musical Instruments (CMI) in 1969 by Norlin, an international conglomerate. Kalamazoo-made Epiphone solidbodies continued to be available through 1970, although by that time plans were already underway to transfer production to Japan. The first Japanese-made Epiphones came on to the market around 1970. These bolt-on-neck electrics included the 1802 Stratocaster-style solidbody and the 5102T ES-335-style thinline, each fitted with a pair of black-and-white "Art Deco" single-coil pickups. Ironically, Gibson-owned Epiphone thus offered copies similar to those of Aria… the Japanese company that had started the "copy era" by replicating Gibson's Les Paul Custom.

In 1972 Gibson renamed the 1802 as the ET-270 and the 5102T as the EA-250. The company also added two bolt-on-neck "copies" of its venerable Crestwoods, the

Three more Epiphones on this page: a first-type Crestwood solidbody from 1959 (far left); a Crestwood Custom from 1964 (center); and a Sorrento hollowbody from 1968.

ET-278 (bound fingerboard) and ET-275, both with two humbuckers, vibrato and Gibson-style headstock. This Epiphone line-up remained unchanged into the early 1970s. By 1975 the Stratocaster-style guitar was gone, and the ET-278 (which was now fitted with a stoptail bridge) and the ET-275 acquired new finishes and fresh appointments.The EA-250 thinline remained in the line. These were joined by another Crestwood, the ET-290N in natural maple with a maple fingerboard, and a high-end, walnut-topped EA-255 thinline, these last two both with gold hardware.

In 1976 Epiphone added the distinctive new Scroll models to its catalog. These were distinguished by a carved "scroll" on the upper cutaway horn, and were joined by the set-neck SC550 (block-shape fingerboard inlays) and SC450 (dots), and the bolt-on-neck SC350. All of these came fitted with two humbuckers and pre-Gibson-style Epiphone headstock, differing in finishes and trim. They were available through 1979.

From around 1977-79 Gibson marketed the Epiphone "Rock'n'Roll Star Solid Body Line Up" in Japan, guitars similar to the Scrolls but with equal cutaways and no scrolls, bearing the old Epi names Olympic Custom, Olympic and Wilshire. From 1979-81 Gibson offered the Epiphone Genesis series, again made in Japan. Featuring set-neck, mahogany body with carved maple cap, twin humbuckers and the old Epiphone-style headstock, the Genesis models had various appointments and levels of trim and included the Custom (block inlays, gold hardware), Deluxe (crown inlays, chrome

A Crestwood Deluxe from 1966 (near right) alongside Paul McCartney's very own Epiphone Casino, made in 1962 and used on many Beatle records such as 'Paperback Writer.' Epiphone's 1961 ad (below) sets out the advantages of the company's new Tremotone vibrato bridge.

Paul McCartney was attracted to Epiphone's Casino in the 1960s because it came with the Bigsby vibrato that he'd heard used so well by Duane Eddy. But years after the break-up of The Beatles he still counted it among his favorites, often playing it in concert (below) as well as in the studio.

The West Side blues-and-soul man Otis Rush pictured with an Epiphone Riviera on a 1969 album sleeve.

Epiphone's Professional model (1963 example, left) had five Tonexpressor controls, and its special amplifier could be adjusted from extra controls on the guitar. This did not prove very popular.

Epiphone designed the Caiola Custom (1964 example, below right) in collaboration with studio guitarist Al Caiola (he played the Bonanza theme among many others) as a slightly more conventional version of the earlier Professional. The Caiola ad dates from 1967.

hardware) and Standard (dot inlays). An even more basic model called simply The Genesis was added to the Epiphone line in 1981, but the entire series was gone by the end of that year. Following the demise of the Genesis series, in 1982 Gibson briefly offered some Japanese-made Epiphone hollowbody electrics: the Emperor, the Sheraton, the Casino and the Riviera.

Competition had taken its toll on Gibson during the 1970s, particularly the success of Japanese manufacturers. Beginning at this time Gibson began slowly transferring production to a new factory in Nashville, Tennessee, where labor costs were lower than in Kalamazoo. With idle production capability in Kalamazoo, Gibson decided to make Epiphones in America again.

Calling back laid-off workers, in 1982 Gibson unveiled the Kalamazoo-made Epiphone Spirit version of the same-name Gibson model. This was a set-neck, equal-double-cutaway guitar that was clearly inspired by Gibson's own Les Paul Special shape. The Gibson Spirit featured an Explorer-style headstock, whereas the Epi had a typical Gibson-style "open-book" head. The Epiphone Spirit came with either one or two humbuckers. The Spirit was joined in the new catalog by the Epiphone Special, which was in effect an SG available with one or two humbuckers. Very few of these Specials were made, and the American-made Epiphones were gone from the line by the end of the year. As Gibson's Kalamazoo factory wound down to a close, one final Epiphone

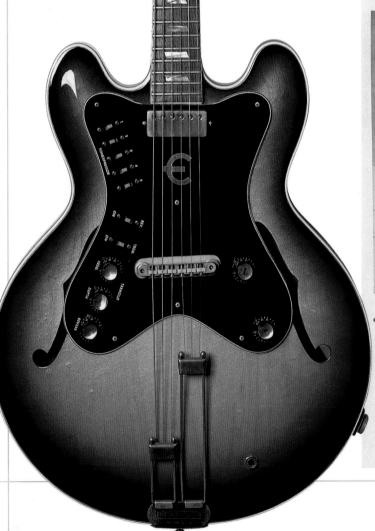

The inimitable Stacie Jones gets herself back to the garden for a Korean Epi Coronet in 1996.

solidbody was made, a US-map-shaped guitar. This featured a Gibson-style neck glued into a body cut out in the shape of the continental United States. It was intended to be a promotional item but was well received, so Gibson decided to re-brand the "map" guitars with the Gibson logo.

This was the (temporary) end of Epiphone guitar production, and for the time being at least marked the cessation of an operation that stretched back to the late 1920s, deep into early American guitar history.

In 1984 Gibson closed down its guitar-making at Kalamazoo, selling part of the facility to former employees who formed the Heritage guitar company. During this period Gibson offered a few Japanese-made Epiphone electric thinlines, including the round-cutaway Emperor II and double-cutaway Sheraton, both fitted with two humbuckers. A year earlier a few Epiphone solidbody models had been sourced from the Samick factory in Korea.

By the early 1980s Gibson's parent company Norlin seemed to have lost interest in guitar-making altogether. However, in 1984 Gibson was turned over to a broker and at the beginning of 1986 the company was purchased by Henry Juszkiewicz, Dave Berryman and Gary Zebrowski. They promptly revived the Epiphone brand, primarily as a vehicle for Korean-made low-end instruments, although a select few Epi models would be made at Gibson's Nashville plant in subsequent years. The new 1986

Epiphone By Gibson line included versions of both Gibson and Fender stalwarts: copies of the Flying V (V-2) and the Explorer, plus five S-series Stratocaster-style guitars. By the end of the year these early Korean-made Epiphones were being replaced by a considerably expanded line. Included were three new bolt-on-neck Les Pauls, all now equipped with Steinberger KB locking vibratos. The Les Paul 3 had the popular humbucker/single-coil/single-coil pickup layout. The Les Paul 2 was similar but with two humbuckers, while the Les Paul 1 had a single lead humbucker. Also offered were two Epiphone Firebirds, through-neck guitars with Steinberger KB vibrato and optional layouts of EMG Select pickups.

Six Strat-style guitars were offered in late 1986, including four superstrats with Kramer-style "hockey stick" (or "banana") six-tuners-in-line headstocks plus locking Steinberger KB vibratos. The top-of-the-line X-1000 had through-neck construction, EMG Select pickups in a humbucker/single-coil/single-coil layout, and chevron-shape fingerboard inlays. The X-900 was similar except the body was more like a wide Ibanez Roadstar, with triangular sharktooth inlays. The S-800 was basically a bolt-on-neck version of the X-900.

The S-600 was another similar bolt-on-neck guitar shaped more like contemporary Kramers. The S-400 (maple fingerboard, humbucker/single-coil/single-coil pickup layout, and locking vibrato) and S-310 (three single-coil pickups and traditional fulcrum

Three more Epiphones on this page: a Coronet made in 1965 (far left); a Riviera 12-string (center) from 1968; and an ET-270 from 1973 (near left).

A 1979 ad for Epi's Japan-made double-cutaway Genesis series.

vibrato) also had the Kramer body styling. Most of this line-up continued to be available into 1989. Epiphone tapped a host of celebrities to endorse its new lines, including Les Paul, Chet Atkins (for a new Country Gentleman II thinline) and Howard Roberts (new HR Fusion II and HR Fusion III thinline models), as well as Billy Burnette, Julio Fernandez, Zakk Wylde, Vinnie Zummo and Ed Ott.

Gibson planned a new series of Japanese-made guitars in 1987 to be called the Nouveau By Gibson line, with several new designs including a superstrat similar to the X-1000, an archtop and a model patterned in the style of a PRS solidbody. Whether these ever got beyond the prototype stage is unknown, but in 1988 the PRS-like solidbody did provide the basis for the Epiphone Spotlight series, sporting through-neck construction, fancy carved maple cap, EMG Select pickups and "chevron"-shape fingerboard inlays. A traditional-style vibrato was offered, although some versions featured the locking Steinberger KB unit. The Spotlight models lasted only a year in the line before high costs made them impractical.

While earlier Epiphones had flirted with the idea of copying popular designs, in 1988 Gibson hit on the formula that would bring success to the Epiphone brand in the 1990s and beyond. Two new proper set-neck Les Paul copies were introduced, the Custom and the Standard (plus a bolt-on-neck Les Paul 2, now with stoptail). In 1989 Epiphone revamped the whole line. The Les Paul Custom and Standard, plus the old

Strat-style S-310, were joined by the G Series of Gibson SG copies, the G-400 being a set-neck copy of Gibson's SG 62, and the G-310 being a bolt-on-neck version of a 1967-style SG. Also new was the Epiphone Flying V, a copy of Gibson's 1967-style V, and the T-310. This was a Telecaster-like copy, but underlining its Gibson association was a "hockey stick" Explorer-like head.

Though fast becoming passé, three superstrats with Floyd Rose locking vibratos continued to be offered: the bolt-neck 435i and 635i (humbucker/single-coil/single-coil pickup layout) and the neck-through-body 935i (humbucker and one single-coil pickup), all with Explorer-style headstock.

During the 1989 makeover Gibson returned to making a few special Epiphones in Nashville. This time it was the USA Pro, a superstrat-style replacement for the previous X-1000, though with a bolt-on neck, plus locking Floyd Rose vibrato system and a Gibson lead humbucker and neck single-coil pickup.

Another American-made Epiphone was introduced in 1990, the USA Coronet. This presented a clever combination of old and new, reviving the defunct 1960s Epiphone shape and set-neck design, and adding a new reverse-Explorer headstock plus a five-way pickup selector switch, as well as a circuit board that provided humbucker, single-coil, out-of-phase and series/parallel sounds. The USA Coronets came with gold hardware and stoptails or black hardware and Floyd Rose locking vibrato systems. In

An Epiphone Scroll 250 from 1977 (near right) next to a gold-finished USA Coronet made at Gibson's Nashville plant in 1990. The catalog highlights another American-made Epi from that period, the USA Pro.

guitar manufacturers

1991 two more new Epiphone "copies" debuted, the EM-2 and EM-1, being Korean-made, bolt-on-neck versions of Gibson's new M-III, slightly offset-cutaway solidbodies with a dramatically extended horn and reverse-Explorer headstock.

The Epiphones were plainer than the original Gibson models. However, they used the same electronic switching system, a combination of a two-way toggle and five-way switch to control the humbucker/single-coil/humbucker pickup layout. This offered either humbucking or single-coil tonalities depending on the position of the two-way switch. The EM-2 featured a locking Floyd Rose vibrato, whereas the EM-1 had a traditional "fulcrum" vibrato.

In 1991 Epiphone briefly added to the bottom of its line an inexpensive bolt-on-neck Les Paul, the LP-300, and the Stratocaster-style S-300, which would last only a year. Epiphone also continued to add pro endorsers, including Mick Cribbs, Tracii Guns, Dan Toler, Frank Hannon, Pete Pagan, John Ricco and Tom Keifer.

A management change occurred in 1992 when Jim Rosenberg was hired from electronic instrument manufacturer E-Mu Systems to take charge of Epiphone. It was at this time that Epiphone revived the trend of marketing musical instruments through mail-order catalogs. By 1993 a new low-end bolt-on-neck LP-100 model Les Paul had joined the line, while the i Series superstrats were gone. Epiphone added another EM-3 Rebel Custom in 1994 to the line derived from the Gibson M-IIIs (the EMs now

also called Rebels). This was still a bolt-on-neck guitar, but appointments such as the pick-shape fingerboard inlays were more like the Gibson original. It also had a new Steinberger Jam-Trem vibrato system. New too in 1994 was the Epiphone Explorer, a copy of the famous Gibson model. By 1995 the EM Rebel models had been dropped and American Epiphone production had ended.

More Gibson "copies" were introduced, while reissues of earlier Epis proliferated too, including the Casino, Riviera, Emperor Regent, Sheraton and Sorrento. A signature Supernova model appeared in 1997 for Noel Gallagher, though it lacked the Oasis guitarist's subtle British flag graphic that brightened up the body of his own Sheraton.

The most striking aspect of recent Epiphones has been the veritable explosion of Les Paul variants. Appointments range from exotic, transparent and sparkle finishes to good looking flamed-maple and birdseye-maple caps. There are seven-string versions, one with f-holes, and there's even a Metal Edition, as well as a signature model for Slash of Guns N'Roses that comes with a suitable snake graphic.

In the company's thinline series, a swathe of old names still manages to conjure up the heritage of 1950s and 1960s designs. These make available a vintage-style alternative to parent company Gibson's thinlines, always more fashionable in this area. Nonetheless, new signature Epiphone thinlines launched in 2000 underlined their continuing appeal to some players. There was the already mentioned John Lee Hooker

Some guitars from the more recent Epiphone lines on this page include two "copies" of established Gibson faves: a Les Paul from 1998 (far left) and a Flying V from 1999 (center). The nifty Les Paul with f-holes marks an interesting twist: it's called the ES model and the one shown (near left) dates from 1999.

This striking ESP ad published in 1982 (right) features a metal-inclined model from the Navigator line.

Noel Gallagher from Oasis (opposite page) playing one of his Epiphone Sheratons with Union Jack graphic. This Gallagher-endorsed Epiphone Supernova (left) was made in 1997.

1964 Sheraton, available with two bridge/tailpiece options, and the Jorma Kaukonen Riviera Deluxe, a wonderful cherry and gold concoction. In fact, there are now almost enough guitars to compete with Gibson... just like in the old days.

ESP

This high-end Japanese maker began in 1975 by offering handmade guitars with the Navigator brandname. A move to guitar parts came in 1978; ESP-brand instruments soon followed. Many maintained Fender styling, and were joined in the 1980s by graphic-finished superstrats and models for metal players. ESPs were made in the US and Germany as well as Japan; quality (and prices) stayed high. The less expensive Edwards line appeared in the late 1980s, then the even more affordable Korean-made Grass Roots series (more recent budget Koreans had an LTD logo). Influential endorsers have included Kirk Hammett and James Hetfield, both with popular signature models.

This ESP Ltd M-250 model (left) was made during 1998 and is from the company's more affordable Korean-made series. Ron Wood has been a long-standing and important endorser of ESP instruments, and he is portrayed in this 1993 ad (below) with one of the more traditional products of the Japanese-based company.

Fender's Broadcaster is historically the most important electric guitar ever made. It was the first instrument to commercialize the concept of the solidbody electric guitar – and put Fender on the map. This example (main guitar) was made, like all Broadcasters, in 1950.

This ad (below) was the first to feature and name the Esquire, the earliest version of Fender's new solidbody electric in its pre-production form. It's clear from this 1950 ad that Fender's main business was still in amps and steel guitars, but it effectively marks the birth of marketing for the solidbody electric.

FENDER

No other company has contributed more to the look and sound of the solidbody electric guitar than Fender. Clarence Leo Fender's original firm changed the course of popular music by revolutionizing the design and manufacture of electric guitars.

So successful did Fender become that in 1965 the business was sold to the giant CBS conglomerate for $13 million, an unprecedentedly large figure. Yet the whole affair had started around 20 years earlier when Leo made some electric steel guitars with a few thousand dollars that he'd earned from a record-player design. From these humble beginnings grew one of the largest, most influential and splendidly original musical instrument manufacturers in the world.

Despite spectacular later successes, during its early years the southern California company came perilously close to failing. It was Leo Fender's sheer determination, combined with his luck in surrounding himself with clever, dedicated people, that helped pull the Fender company through difficult times.

Leo was born in 1909, in a barn near the Anaheim/Fullerton border in the Los Angeles area. His parents ran a "truck farm," growing vegetables and fruit for the market, and had put up the barn first before they could afford to build a house. A friend once recalled that when Leo was small his father had told him that the only thing worthwhile in the world was what you accomplished at work – and that if you weren't

"PRO-AMP" Tremendous Power Superb Tone 15" Speaker

"CUSTOM" 3 NECK GUITAR The choice of leading professionals and teachers. Available with legs.

"ESQUIRE" The newest thing in Spanish guitars— Fine Action New Tone Perfect Intonation

Fender *...e electric instruments*

Amplifiers • Guitars
Covers • Cases

TELEVISION EQUIPMENT CO.

...TREET   SANTA ANA, CALIF.

Exclusive Distributor

346

Gretsch made Fender change the name of its Broadcaster guitar because the New York company already used it for drum products (1949 Gretsch catalog, right).

working you were lazy, which was a sin. It seems that Leo would judge himself and everyone else around him by that measure... and himself hardest of all.

Although he went on to study accountancy and began his working life in the accounts sections of the state highway department and a tire distribution company, Leo's hobby was always electronics, and in his 20s he built amplifiers and PA systems for use at public events such as sports and religious gatherings as well as dances. In about 1939 Leo opened The Fender Radio Service, a radio and record store at Fullerton in the Los Angeles area. Leo had lost his accounting job earlier in that decade of depression. His new shop brought instant introductions to many local musicians including professional violinist and lap-steel guitarist "Doc" Kauffman. Doc had worked on electric guitar designs for another local company, Rickenbacker.

Lap-steel guitar playing, or Hawaiian guitar playing, had been fashionable in the United States since the 1920s and was still tremendously popular at the time Leo opened his new store. A lap-steel guitar is one that sits horizontally on the player's lap, and its strings are stopped not by the frets, but with a sliding steel bar held in the player's non-picking hand. As the most prevalent type of guitar in America at the time, lap-steels were thus the first guitars to "go electric" in the 1930s. Several innovative companies, with Rickenbacker in the lead, had started to experiment with electro-magnetic pickups, attaching them to guitars and connecting them to small amplifiers.

During the 1930s and later the term "Spanish" was used to identify the other (less popular) hold-against-the-body type of guitar.

Leo had by this time already begun to look into the potential for electric guitars and to play around with pickup designs. Leo and Doc built a solidbody guitar in 1943 to test these early pickups, as well as a design for a record-changer good enough to net them $5,000. Some of this money went into starting their shortlived company, K&F (Kauffman & Fender), and the two men began proper production of electric lap-steel guitars and small amplifiers in November 1945.

Another significant person with whom Leo started working at this early stage was Don Randall, general manager of Radio & Television Equipment Co ("Radio-Tel") which was based in Santa Ana, some 15 miles south of Fullerton. Radio-Tel, owned by Francis Hall, became the exclusive distributor of K&F products in 1946 – around the time that Leo and Doc Kauffman decided to split. In 1946 Leo called his new operation Fender Manufacturing (renamed the Fender Electric Instrument Co in December 1947). Leo continued to make lap-steels and amps as he had with K&F, but gradually developed new products. He also expanded into larger premises in Fullerton, separate from the radio store and described by one observer as two plain, unattractive steel buildings.

Yet another important member of the growing Fender team, Dale Hyatt, had joined the company in January 1946. Hyatt later became a crucial member of the Fender

The Esquire model name had been used for Fender's earliest solidbody prototype, but was soon revived for the single-pickup production version. This Esquire (far left) was made in 1953. The two-pickup Broadcaster's name was changed to Telecaster after Gretsch complained about prior use. At first Fender removed "Broadcaster" from its decals, making "Nocaster" models (see headstock picture, right), but during 1951 had the new Telecaster name in place. The Telecaster shown here (near left) was made in 1953. Gene Vincent's guitarist Russell Wilaford, replacing a just-departed Cliff Gallup, plays a Telecaster (above) on the set of The Girl Can't Help It movie in 1956.

sales team, but one of his early tasks, in late 1947 or early 1948, was to take over the radio store business because Leo was trying to get things started at the new buildings in Pomona Avenue. Next to join Fender's company was George Fullerton, who was to become what one colleague describes as Leo's faithful workhorse. Fullerton started working at Pomona Avenue in February 1948.

Karl Olmsted and his partner Lymon Race had left the services in 1947 and decided to start a much-needed tool-and-die company in Fullerton, making specialist tools, as well as dies that customers could use to stamp out metal parts on punch presses. They were looking for work, and Leo had reached the point where he needed dies to be made for production work. He'd been making parts by hand, cutting out raw metal. But of course Leo now needed to make several identical copies of each component. Race & Olmsted continued to make Fender's tooling and most metal parts for the next 30 years and more, progressing to more complicated, sophisticated and high-production tooling as time went on.

Fender's electric lap-steels enjoyed some local success, and Leo began to think about producing a solidbody electric guitar of normal shape and playing style: an "electric Spanish" guitar. Normal Spanish archtop hollowbody "f-hole" acoustic guitars with built-in electric pickups and associated controls had been produced by makers such as Rickenbacker, National, Gibson and Epiphone at various times since the

The first famous user of the Fender Stratocaster was Buddy Holly, seen (above) with his Strat on the first Crickets LP, released in late 1957.

Two early Stratocasters are shown on this page. This first-year 1954 example (below left) in non-standard color has serial number 0001; behind is the cover of Fender's catalog of the same year. The fine 1957 Strat (main guitar) is the standard sunburst model of the time.

Fender's 1958/59 catalog (left) was the first to show a custom color guitar, the Fiesta Red Stratocaster above the man's head.

1930s, but without much effect on player's habits. And while demand was rising from danceband guitarists who found themselves increasingly unable to compete with the volume of the rest of the band, most of the early electric hollowbody guitars were effectively experimental. They were only partially successful from a technical standpoint, and electric guitars were still some way from becoming a great commercial sensation. Leo's plans would change all that.

A number of guitar makers, musicians and engineers in America were wondering about the possibility of a solidbody instrument. Such a design would curtail the annoying feedback often produced by amplified hollowbody guitars, at the same time reducing the guitar body's interference with its overall tone and thus more accurately reproducing and sustaining the sound of the strings.

Rickenbacker had launched a relatively solid Bakelite-body electric guitar in the mid 1930s – the type that Leo's friend Doc Kauffman had played – while around 1940 guitarist Les Paul built a personal test-bed electric guitar in New York which used parts

from a variety of instruments mounted on a solid central block of pine. In Downey, California, about 15 miles to the west of Fender's operation in Fullerton, Paul Bigsby had a small workshop where he spent a good deal of time fixing motorcycles and, later, making some fine pedal-steel guitars and vibrato units. He also ventured into the solidbody electric guitar and mandolin field, hand-building a limited number of distinctive instruments. He'd started this in 1948 with the historic Merle Travis guitar, an instrument with through-neck construction and hollow body "wings."

It's difficult to judge whether the design of Fender's first solidbody electric guitar was influenced very much by those earlier instruments of Bigsby's. George Fullerton says that he and Leo knew Paul Bigsby and had seen Merle Travis playing his Bigsby guitar. On the other hand, it's possible that Fender and Bigsby just made something similar at the same time.

Leo started work in the summer of 1949 on the instrument which we now know as the Fender Telecaster, effectively the world's first commercially marketed solidbody electric guitar, and still very much alive today. The guitar, originally named the Fender Esquire and then the Fender Broadcaster, first went into production in 1950. Early prototypes borrowed their headstock design from Fender's lap-steels, with three tuners each side, but the production version had a smart new headstock with all six tuners along one side, allowing strings to meet tuners in a straight line and obviating the

An enviable 1950s Strat collection: a "Mary Kaye" Strat from 1958 (far left) with blond body and gold-plated hardware; an early example of the Fiesta Red finish on a 1959 Strat (center); and a gold-finish model (near left) dating from 1958.

349

traditional "angled back" headstock. Fender's new solidbody electric guitar was unadorned, straightforward, potent, and — perhaps most significantly — ahead of its time. As such it did not prove immediately easy for the salesmen at Fender to sell, as Don Randall of Radio-Tel found when he took some prototypes to a musical instrument trade show in Chicago during the summer of 1950. In fact, Randall was aghast to find that competitors generally laughed at the new instrument, calling the prototypes canoe paddles, snow shovels and worse.

A very few pre-production one-pickup Esquire models without truss-rods were made in April 1950, with another tiny production run of two-pickup Esquires two months later. General production of the better-known single-pickup Esquire with truss-rod did not begin until January 1951.

But in November 1950, a truss-rod was added to the two-pickup model, its name was changed to Broadcaster, and the retail price was fixed at $170. The Broadcaster name was shortlived, halted in early 1951 after Gretsch, a large New York-based instrument manufacturer, indicated its prior use of "Broadkaster" on various drum products. At first, Fender simply used up its "Fender Broadcaster" decals on the guitar's headstock by cutting off the "Broadcaster" and leaving just the "Fender" logo; these no-name guitars are known among collectors today as Nocasters. The new name decided upon for the Fender solid electric was Telecaster, coined by Don Randall. The

This Fender Musicmaster was made in 1957, and it has an anodized aluminum pickguard. Fender also made a two-pickup version, called the Duo-Sonic, and a Duo-Sonic with vibrato, known as the Mustang.

Fender's cheaper models have been popular with more recent musicians looking for an affordable instrument. Liz Phair, whose folk-grunge Exile To Guyville album appeared in 1993, is seen (below) playing a Duo-Sonic.

Fender began an enjoyable and often inventive series of ads in the late 1950s where a guitar was placed in an unlikely setting, with the tag-line: "You won't part with yours either..." This one (left) with a nautical Jazzmaster was published in 1960.

Telecaster name was on headstocks by April 1951, and at last Fender's new $189.50 solidbody electric had a permanent name.

At Fender, practicality and function ruled. There was no hand-carving of selected timbers as one would find in the workshops of established archtop guitar makers. With the Telecaster, Fender made the electric guitar into a factory product, stripped down to its essential elements, built up from easily assembled parts, and produced at a relatively affordable price. Fender's methods made for easier, more consistent production – and a different sound. Not for Fender the fat, Gibson-style jazz tone, but a clearer, spikier sound, something like a cross between a clean acoustic guitar and a cutting electric lap-steel.

One of the earliest players to appreciate this new sound was Jimmy Bryant, best known for his staggering guitar instrumental duets with pedal-steel virtuoso Speedy West. Bryant soon took to playing the new Fender solidbody. He was respected by professionals in the music business for his session work, including recordings made with Tennessee Ernie Ford and Ella Mae Morse among others. Bryant also made television appearances on country showcases, and would highlight Fender's exciting new solidbody for the growing TV audience.

It was western swing, a lively dance music that grew up in Texas dancehalls during the 1930s and 1940s, that popularized the electric guitar in the US, at first with steel

guitars. Many of its steel players used Fender electrics, notably Noel Boggs and Leon McAuliffe, but there were also some electric-Spanish guitarists in the bands, like Tele-wielding Bill Carson.

Business began to pick up for the Fender company as news of the Telecaster spread, and as Radio-Tel's five salesmen began to persuade instrument store owners to stock the instrument. Early in 1953 Fender's existing sales set-up with Radio-Tel was re-organized into a new Fender Sales distribution company, which was operational by June. Based like Radio-Tel in Santa Ana, Fender Sales had four business partners: Leo, Don Randall, Radio-Tel owner Francis Hall and salesman Charlie Hayes. Hayes was killed in a road accident and in late 1953 Hall bought the Rickenbacker company, so in 1955 Fender Sales became a partnership owned by Leo and Don Randall. It was Randall who actually ran this pivotal part of the Fender business.

The sales side of Fender was, therefore, in capable hands. Another important addition to the Fender team occurred in 1953 when steel guitarist Freddie Tavares, best known for his swooping steel intro over the titles of the *Looney Tunes* cartoons, joined the California guitar maker, principally to help Leo design new products. Also in 1953 three new buildings at South Raymond Avenue and Valencia Drive were added to the company's manufacturing premises. As well as just two electric guitars, the Telecaster and Esquire, Fender had at this time a line of seven amplifiers (Bandmaster,

Three Jazzmasters on this page. This early example in standard sunburst finish (far left) was made in 1959, while the 1963 model (center) is in lurid Foam Green. This 1966 instrument (near left) was originally finished in Blue Ice Metallic, but a gradual "yellowing" of its outer skin has transformed it to more of a green. It also displays the change to bound fingerboard and block-shape fingerboard inlays made to the Jazzmaster during 1965 and 1966. The Jazzmaster hang-tag (below) would be fastened to the guitar's tuner button in music stores.

The first Stratocaster to arrive in Britain was specially imported in 1959 by singer Cliff Richard for Hank Marvin, guitarist in Richard's group The Shadows. The Fiesta Red Strat, in its present refinished state, is pictured below. Hank Marvin plays it on-stage with Richard in the 1960s (main picture, below), and it is just visible on the 1961 LP sleeve (right).

guitar manufacturers

Two further late-1950s ads in the "You won't part with yours" series feature a Jazzmaster on a Porsche in the California hills (far right) and somewhere above (near right).

Bassman, Champ, Deluxe, Princeton, Super, Twin Amp), five electric steel guitars (Custom, Deluxe, Dual, Stringmaster, Student) and its revolutionary electric bass guitar, the Precision, that had been introduced two years earlier.

Another newcomer was Forrest White. He had joined the company after Leo asked if he'd be interested in helping sort out some "management problems" at Fender. White was shocked by the disorganized mess he found at the Fender workshops, and agreed to come in and work for Leo, beginning in May 1954. White soon began to put the manufacturing operations into order.

Now Leo had able men – Forrest White and Don Randall – poised at the head of the production and sales halves of the Fender company. He had a new factory, and a small but growing reputation. All he needed now, it seemed, was more new products. And along came the stylish Fender Stratocaster, the epitome of tailfin-flash American design of the 1950s.

Leo was listening hard to players' comments about the "plain vanilla" Tele and Esquire, and during the early 1950s he and Freddie Tavares began to formulate the guitar that would become the Stratocaster. Some musicians were complaining that the sharp edge on the Telecaster was uncomfortable, so the team began to fool around with smoothed contouring on the body. The Stratocaster was eventually launched during 1954 – samples around May and June were followed by the first proper

production run in October. It was priced at $249.50 (or $229.50 without vibrato) plus $39.50 for a case. The new Fender was the first solidbody electric with three pickups, and also featured a new-design built-in vibrato unit (or "tremolo" as Fender called it) to provide pitch-bending and shimmering chordal effects for the player. It was the first self-contained vibrato unit: an adjustable bridge, tailpiece and vibrato system all in one. Not a simple mechanism for the time, but a reasonably effective one. It followed the Fender principle of taking an existing product (in this case the Bigsby vibrato) and improving on it. Fender's new Strat vibrato also had six saddles, one for each string, adjustable for height and length. The complete unit was typical of Fender's constant consideration of musicians' requirements and the consequent application of a mass-producer's solution.

The Strat came with a radically sleek, solid body, based on the shape of the earlier Fender Precision Bass, contoured for the player's comfort and finished in a yellow-to-black sunburst finish. Even the jack socket mounting was new, recessed in a stylish plate on the body face. The Strat looked like no other guitar around – and in some ways

Three Strats, all featuring the new rosewood fingerboard introduced during 1959: a 1964 example (far left) in Sonic Blue; another made in 1961 (center) in Burgundy Mist Metallic; and a sunburst model dating from 1964 (near left).

*Esquires and Telecasters also gained
a rosewood fingerboard during 1959,
as featured in this page (right) from
Fender's 1963/64 catalog .*

*Three custom color Telecasters are
shown on this page. This one in
Fiesta Red (near right) dates from
1960, while the Shoreline Gold
model (center) was made in 1963.
The pale green Tele from around
1964 (far right) was originally finished
in Sonic Blue but has since "faded"
to a green color. It has been fitted
with a Parsons-White B-Bender that
can raise the pitch of the B-string to
provide string-bends that emulate
pedal-steel type sounds.*

guitar manufacturers

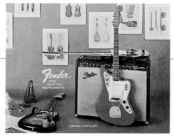

Temptation... Jaguars and
Jazzmasters on a 1960s hang-tag
(far left) and a luscious Jaguar with
gold-plated hardware on the cover of
Fender's 1963/64 catalog (near left).

seemed to owe more to contemporary automobile design than traditional guitar forms, especially in the flowing, sensual curves of that beautifully proportioned, timeless body.

The Stratocaster's new-style pickguard complemented the body lines perfectly. Indeed, the overall impression was of a guitar where all the components ideally suited one another. It's not surprising, therefore, that the Strat is still made today, over 45 years since its birth in the Fender company's functional buildings in Fullerton, California. The exemplary Fender Stratocaster has become the most popular, the most copied, the most desired, and very probably the most played solid electric guitar ever.

On its 40th anniversary in 1994 an official Fender estimate put Stratocaster sales so far at between a million and a million-and-a-half guitars – and that's without the plethora of unsubtle copies or more subtly "influenced" guitars that subsequently appeared from hundreds of other guitar-makers. The Stratocaster has appeared in the hands of virtually every great guitarist over the years. Back in the 1950s it was a more specialized market, but nonetheless the Strat fired the music then of players such as Buddy Holly, Carl Perkins and Buddy Guy.

Fender's next model introductions came in 1956 with a pair of new "student" electrics. These had a shorter string-length than was usual for Fender. The "three-quarter size" one-pickup Musicmaster and two-pickup Duo-Sonic were described in the company's literature as "ideal for students and adults with small hands." They were

clearly designed for players on a tight budget, for those who were starting out on electric guitar and were flocking to the music-retailer "schools" that were springing up everywhere in the US at the time.

Fender then created a decidedly high-end instrument. The Jazzmaster first appeared on Fender's pricelists in 1958, and at $329 was some $50 more expensive than the Strat. At that sort of price Fender couldn't resist tagging its new Jazzmaster as "America's finest electric guitar... unequaled in performance and design features." Immediately striking to the guitarist of 1958 was the Jazzmaster's unusual offset-waist body shape and, for the first time on a Fender, a separate rosewood fingerboard glued to the customary maple neck. The vibrato system was new, too, with an ill-conceived "lock-off" facility aimed at preventing tuning problems if a string should break.

The sound of the Jazzmaster was richer and warmer than players were used to from Fender. The name Jazzmaster was not chosen at random, for Fender aimed the different tone at jazz players. But jazz guitarists found little appeal in this new, rather difficult solidbody guitar, and mainstream Fender players largely stayed with their Strats and Teles.

All in all, the Jazzmaster was a distinct change for Fender, and constituted a real effort to extend the scope and appeal of its guitar line. Ironically, and despite significant early success, this has been partly responsible for the guitar's lack of long-term

Fender's Custom Telecaster, new in
1959, had a bound body. This
example (far left) was made in 1963.
Two Fender Jaguars are shown next
to it: a sunburst model from 1963,
and one finished in Candy Apple Red
from the following year.

popularity relative to the Strat and Tele, mainly as a result of players' dissatisfaction with the guitar's looks and sounds. Nonetheless, the Jazzmaster remained near the top of the Fender pricelist until withdrawn around 1980.

Most Fender guitars of the 1950s came officially only in sunburst or varieties of the original "blond" (some rare early Esquires were black). But a few guitars, specially made at the factory effectively as one-offs, were finished in solid colors. The rare surviving examples indicate that this practice was underway by 1954, but few players then seemed interested in slinging on a colored guitar, and Fender's main production remained in sunburst and blond instruments.

The company's early production of special-color guitars was certainly casual, often no doubt the understandable reaction of a small company to lucrative if unusual orders from a handful of customers. But this informal arrangement was given a rather more commercial footing in the company's sales literature of 1956 when "player's choice" colored guitars were noted as an option, at five per cent extra cost. In the following year these Du Pont paint finishes were described in Fender's catalog as "Custom Colors" (a name that has stuck ever since) and in the pricelist as "custom Du Pont Duco finishes," still at five per cent on top of normal prices.

Fender also announced, early in 1957, a Stratocaster in see-through blond finish and with gold-plated hardware. Don Randall says the gold plate was influenced by

The Mustang was a relatively low-end Fender that first appeared in 1964; the example pictured (below left) dates from around 1971. Another Fender popular with grunge acts in the 1990s, a Mustang is seen with Steve Turner of Mudhoney (above).

Thurston Moore of Sonic Youth was also a 1980s fan of "other" Fenders, such as this much modified Mustang (below left) that he used alongside Jaguars and Jazzmasters.

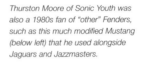

Joining the Fender line in 1965 as a high-end model was the Electric XII 12-string. The two shown here both date from 1966, the one on this page finished in Candy Apple Red, the other (opposite) in the more subtle shade of Olympic White.

Shown (below, right) is a second prototype for Fender's ill-fated Marauder project, which never saw production. This 1966 Marauder has multiple switches and angled frets. The original prototype was even odder, with pickups concealed below the pickguard (as pictured in Fender's 1965/66 catalog, below).

seeing the new White Falcon model by Gretsch. In fact Fender had trouble getting the gold-plate to stay on the its components. But the gold-hardware blond Strat was in effect Fender's first official Custom Color guitar – although the term has always been more popularly applied since to solid-color varieties. The blond/gold Strat was later known as the "Mary Kaye" model thanks to musician Kaye regularly appearing with such a model in Fender catalogs.

Fender eventually came up with a defined list of its choice of available Custom Colors. In the early 1960s, when many more Custom Color Fenders were being made, the company issued color charts to publicize the various shades. There were three original charts: the first, in about 1960, featured Black, Burgundy Mist Metallic, Dakota Red, Daphne Blue, Fiesta Red, Foam Green, Inca Silver Metallic, Lake Placid Blue Metallic, Olympic White, Shell Pink, Sherwood Green Metallic, Shoreline Gold Metallic, Sonic Blue and Surf Green; the second, around 1963, had lost Shell Pink and gained Candy Apple Red Metallic; and the third, in 1965, lost Burgundy Mist Metallic, Daphne Blue, Inca Silver Metallic, Sherwood Green Metallic, Shoreline Gold Metallic and Surf Green, and gained – all Metallics – Blue Ice, Charcoal Frost, Firemist Gold, Firemist Silver, Ocean Turquoise and Teal Green.

The automobile industry was clearly having a profound effect upon US guitar manufacturers in the 1950s, not least in this ability to enhance the look of an already

Fender's 1965/66 catalog included this page with three harmless Jaguars (right) and two Marauders (left) with pickups hidden underneath the pickguard. The Marauder never actually went into production.

During 1967 George Harrison painted his Strat (centre left) in a suitably psychedelic/rockabilly style. He played it in the Magical Mystery Tour movie and regularly after The Beatles split. Preferring a Tele at the end of the 1960s was country picker Clarence White on The Byrds' Sweetheart Of The Rodeo (left).

stylish object with a rich, sparkling paint job. Fender used paints from Du Pont's Duco nitro-cellulose lines, such as Dakota Red or Foam Green, as well as the more color-retentive Lucite acrylics like Lake Placid Blue Metallic or Burgundy Mist Metallic. Decades later the guitars bearing these original Fiesta Reds, Sonic Blues, Shoreline Golds and the like have proved very desirable among collectors, many of whom rate a Custom Color Fender, especially an early one, as a prime catch. This is despite the prevalence of recent "refinishes" which have become so accurate that even alleged experts can be fooled into declaring some fake finishes as original. Some players find it difficult to understand why collectors can pay a very high premium simply for the promise that a particular layer of paint is "original."

At Fender in the late 1950s a few cosmetic and production adjustments were being made to the company's electric guitars. The Jazzmaster had been the first Fender with a rosewood fingerboard, and this material was adopted for other models around 1959. The company also altered the look of its sunburst finish at the time, adding red to give a three-tone yellow-to-red-to-black effect. By 1959 Fender employed 100 workers in nine buildings occupying some 54,000 square feet.

The last "new" Fender electrics of the 1950s were the bound-body Custom versions of the Esquire and Telecaster, new for 1959. Forrest White got advice on the process of binding from Fred Martin, head of the leading American flat-top acoustic

guitar manufacturer Martin. The Customs each listed at just $30 more than the regular unbound versions, but far fewer of these were sold.

As Fender entered the 1960s, the company boasted an extended list of products in addition to its electric guitars. The company's July 1961 pricelist, for example, noted 13 amplifiers (Bandmaster, Bassman, Champ, Concert, Deluxe, Harvard, Princeton, Pro Amp, Super, Tremolux, Twin Amp, Vibrasonic, Vibrolux), five steel guitars (Champ, Deluxe, Dual, Stringmaster, Studio Deluxe), two pedal-steel guitars (400, 1000) and two bass guitars (Jazz, Precision).

The next new electric six-string design to leave Fender's production line was the Jaguar, which first showed up in sales material during 1962. It used a similar offset-waist body shape to the Jazzmaster, and also shared that guitar's separate bridge and vibrato unit, though the Jaguar had the addition of a spring-loaded string mute at the bridge. Fender rather optimistically believed that players of the time were so obsessed with gadgets that they would prefer a mechanical string mute to the natural edge-of-the-hand method. They were wrong. There are many elements of playing technique that simply cannot be replaced by hardware.

Despite the surface similarities, there were some notable differences between the new Jaguar and the now four-year-old Jazzmaster. Visually, the Jaguar had three distinctive chrome-plated control panels, and was the first Fender with 22 frets on the

Three Stratocasters are shown on this page with the new larger headstock that began to appear during 1965. Two date from 1966: one finished in Lake Placid Blue Metallic (far left); the other in Black (center). The black guitar is said to have been given by Jimi Hendrix to sessionman Al Kooper in the late 1960s. The 1968 example in Olympic White (near left; since yellowed) has the optional maple fingerboard offered at the time.

A Grand NEW Guitar from Fender The *Antigua*

Fender developed unusual colors for some of its new Coronado models. Antigua was a white-to-brown shaded finish, as featured in this Fender leaflet (left) of 1968. Stranger still was the Wildwood effect (1968 flyer, right) achieved by injecting dyes into beech trees for spectacular streaked and striped colors.

We planted a whole forest... to give you Fender *Wildwood*

Wildwood Guitar, Bass and 12-String

fingerboard. The Jaguar also had a slightly shorter string-length than usual for Fenders, closer to Gibson's standard, making for a different playing feel.

The Jaguar had better pickups than the Jazzmaster. They looked much like Strat units but had metal shielding added at the base and sides, partly as a response to criticisms of the Jazzmaster's tendency to noisiness. The Jag's electrics were even more complex than the Jazzmaster's, using the same rhythm circuit but adding a trio of lead-circuit switches. Like the Jazzmaster, the Jaguar enjoyed a burst of popularity when introduced. But this top-of-the-line guitar, "one of the finest solidbody electric guitars that has ever been offered to the public" in Fender's original sales hyperbole, has never enjoyed sustained success.

As the 1960s got underway it was clear that Fender had become a remarkably successful company. In a relatively short period Fender's brilliantly inventive trio of Telecaster, Precision Bass and Stratocaster had established in the minds of musicians and guitar-makers the idea of the solidbody electric guitar as a viable modern instrument. The company found itself in the midst of the rock'n'roll music revolution of the late 1950s and early 1960s... and were happy to ensure that players had a good supply of affordable guitars available in large numbers.

Fender had captured a huge segment of the new market. Many buildings had been added to cope with increased manufacturing demands, and by 1964 the operation

Two Coronado models: first, a Wildwood II six-string (near right) from 1968, with Fender's special injected-wood finish; second, a Coronado XII (center) in Teal Green, dating from around 1968. A new low-end model was the Bronco, with a standard red finish. This example (far right) was made in about 1972.

employed some 600 people (of whom 500 were in manufacturing) spread over 29 buildings. Forrest White once said that his guitar production staff were making 1,500 instruments a week at the end of 1964, compared to the 40 a week when he'd joined the company ten years earlier. As well as electric guitars, Fender's pricelist in 1964 offered amplifiers, steel guitars, electric basses, acoustic guitars, electric pianos, effects units and a host of related accessories.

Don Randall remembers writing a million dollars' worth of sales during his first year in the 1950s, which rose to some 10 million dollars' worth in the mid 1960s (translating to some $40 million of retail sales). By that time the beat boom, triggered by The Beatles and the so-called British Invasion of pop groups, was taking the United States by storm. Electric guitars were at their peak of popularity, and Fender was among the biggest and most successful producers. Players as diverse as surf king Dick Dale, bluesman Muddy Waters and pop stylist Hank Marvin – plus thousands of others around and between them – were rarely seen without a Fender in their hands.

Exporting had also become important to Fender's huge success, and had started back in 1960 when sales chief Don Randall first visited the leading European trade show at Frankfurt, Germany. Fenders had become known in Europe, not only through the spread of pop music, but also because of the many GIs stationed throughout the continent, many of whom played guitars... and Fenders. Britain was an especially

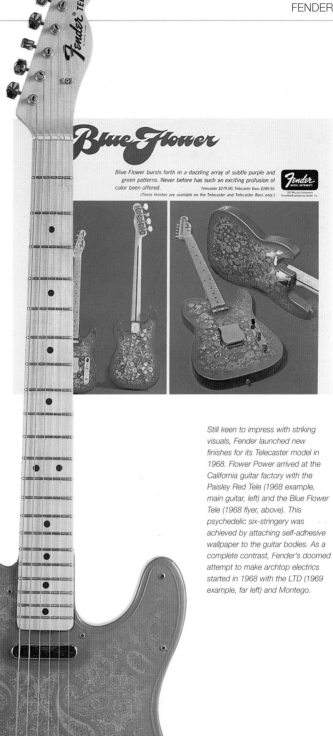

Still keen to impress with striking visuals, Fender launched new finishes for its Telecaster model in 1968. Flower Power arrived at the California guitar factory with the Paisley Red Tele (1968 example, main guitar, left) and the Blue Flower Tele (1968 flyer, above). This psychedelic six-stringery was achieved by attaching self-adhesive wallpaper to the guitar bodies. As a complete contrast, Fender's doomed attempt to make archtop electrics started in 1968 with the LTD (1969 example, far left) and Montego.

important market in the 1960s because of the worldwide success of its pop groups. Up to the start of the 1960s it had been virtually impossible for British musicians to buy Fenders, because of a government ban from 1951 to 1959 on the importation of American merchandise.

But in 1960 Jennings (see Vox) became the first official British distributor of Fender gear, joined by Selmer in 1962. By summer 1965 both Selmer and Jennings had been replaced as the British Fender distributor by Arbiter which, other than a lapse for a few years in the 1980s, has been Fender's UK agent ever since. Western Europe was clearly the biggest export market, but Fender also did well in Scandinavia, South Africa, Rhodesia (now Zimbabwe), Japan, Australia, Canada and elsewhere.

All in all, Fender was extremely successful. Then, in January 1965, the Fender companies were sold to the mighty Columbia Broadcasting System Inc, better known as CBS. A music-trade magazine reported in somewhat shocked tones: "The purchase price of $13 million is by far the highest ever offered in the history of the [musical instrument] industry for any single manufacturer, and was about two million dollars more than CBS paid recently for the New York Yankees baseball team. The acquisition, a sterling proof of the music industry's growth potential, marks the first time that one of the nation's largest corporations has entered our field. With sales volume in excess of half a billion dollars annually, CBS currently does more business than the entire

Country star Buck Owens (above) played a custom-made sparkle-finish Telecaster for years. Three more Fenders made in 1969 are shown on this page. The Thinline Telecaster (near right) was a respectable attempt at producing a semi-solid Tele, but the two others were made by adapting parts left over from existing instruments. The Custom (center) was hacked from an Electric XII and with Mustang parts, while the Swinger (far right) was a low-end short-scale guitar.

guitar manufacturers

[musical instrument] industry does at retail. Actual purchase of Fender was made by the Columbia Records Distribution Division of CBS whose outstanding recent feats have included the production of *My Fair Lady*."

Leo Fender was by all accounts a hypochondriac, and the sale of Fender was prompted by his acute health worries, principally over the sinus complaint that had troubled him since the mid 1950s. Leo was apparently also uncertain about how to finance expansion.

The sale of Fender to CBS has provoked much retrospective consternation among guitarists and collectors, some of whom considered so-called "pre-CBS" instruments – in other words those made prior to the beginning of 1965 – as superior to those made after that date. This was a rather meaningless generalization, and it is a pity that such an assumption became so entrenched.

According to some insiders, the problem with CBS at this time was that they seemed to believe that it was enough simply to pour a great deal of money into Fender. And certainly Fender's sales did increase and profits did go up – Randall remembers income almost doubling in the first year that CBS owned Fender. Profit became paramount, said Forrest White, who remained as manager of electric guitar and amplifier production. Clearly there was a significant clash of cultures. The new CBS men, often trained engineers with college degrees, believed in high-volume production,

Fender's rosewood Telecaster (the example here was made around 1969) used a wood usually reserved for fingerboards for the entire instrument. The result was a striking if heavy guitar, and one was played by George Harrison (above, on 1969 magazine cover) during the famous Apple rooftop concert featured in the group's Let It Be movie of 1970.

363

At the start of his success, Jimi Hendrix (first two albums, both 1967, above) was using a battered sunburst Fender Stratocaster. Soon he began to acquire more Strats, usually opting for a black- or white-finished model on stage (he's seen with a white rosewood-fingerboard Strat, opposite). From around the middle of 1968, Jimi's preference moved to maple-fingerboard models.

This Olympic White Stratocaster (main guitar) dating from around 1968 was sold at Sotheby's saleroom in London in April 1990 as the instrument that Hendrix used at the Woodstock festival in 1969, among other performances. It was sold by Jimi's drummer, Mitch Mitchell, and fetched a record price of £180,000 (about $270,000).

whereas Fender's old guard – the team that had done much to put Fender where it was at the time – were long-serving craft workers without formal qualifications.

Leo's services were retained, CBS grandly naming him a "special consultant in research and development." In fact, he was set up away from the Fender buildings and allowed to tinker as much as he liked – with very little effect on the Fender product lines. A couple of years after the sale to CBS, Leo changed doctors and was given a huge dose of antibiotics which cured his sinus complaint. He completed a few projects for CBS but left when his five-year contract expired in 1970. He went on to design and make instruments for Music Man and G&L.

But Leo was not the first of the old team to leave CBS. White departed in 1967; he died in November 1994. Randall resigned from CBS in April 1969, and formed Randall Electric Instruments, which he sold in 1987. Fullerton left CBS in 1970, worked at Ernie Ball for a while, and with Leo formed the G&L company in 1979, although Fullerton sold his interest in 1986. Hyatt, who resigned from CBS in 1972, was also part of the G&L set-up, which was sold to BBE Sound Inc after Leo Fender's death in March 1991.

Back at Fender Musical Instruments, the Electric XII – a guitar that had been on the drawing board when the CBS sale took place – finally hit the music stores in the summer of 1965. Electric 12-strings had recently been popularized by The Beatles and The Byrds, who both used Rickenbackers, so Fender joined in the battle with its own

This 1973 natural-finish Strat features the new neck truss-rod system introduced along with a three-bolt neck fixing by Fender to some models during 1971. The new "bullet" truss-rod adjuster is visible on the headstock by the nut.

 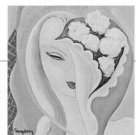

rather belated version. An innovation was the Electric XII's 12-saddle bridge which allowed for precise adjustments of individual string heights and intonation, a luxury hitherto unknown on any 12-string guitar. But the 12-string craze of the 1960s was almost over and the Electric XII proved shortlived, lasting in the line only until 1968.

One of Fender's first CBS-era pricelists, dated April 1965, reveals a burgeoning line of products in addition to the company's 11 electric guitar models (namely the Duo-Sonic, Electric XII, Esquire, Esquire Custom, Jaguar, Jazzmaster, Musicmaster, Mustang, Stratocaster, Telecaster and Telecaster Custom).

The other lines included three bass guitars (the Jazz, Precision, and VI), six flat-top acoustic guitars (the Classic, Concert, King, Malibu, Palomino and Newporter) and 15 amplifiers (Bandmaster, Bassman, Champ, Deluxe, Deluxe Reverb, Dual Showman, Princeton, Princeton Reverb, Pro Reverb, Showman, Super Reverb, Tremolux, Twin Reverb, Vibro Champ, Vibrolux Reverb). These were accompanied by various Fender-Rhodes keyboards, a number of steel and pedal steel guitars, and a solidbody electric mandolin, as well as reverb and echo units.

Uniquely for Fender, a guitar appeared in its 1965/66 literature that never actually made it into production. Naturally a company makes many designs and prototypes which do not translate to commercial release, but for an instrument to get as far as printed sales material, and then be withdrawn, implies a serious error of judgement

somewhere along the line. It was the first sign that CBS might be losing its grip. The guitar was the Marauder, and its obvious distinction was summed up by Fender as follows in the hapless catalog entry: "It appears as though there are no pickups. There are, in reality, however, four newly created pickups mounted underneath the pickguard." The design had been offered to Fender by one Quilla H. Freeman, who had a patent for his idea of hiding powerful pickups under a guitar's pickguard.

Forrest White later remembered that there were problems with weak signals from the pickups, and George Fullerton said he thought there was also a dispute between Freeman and CBS concerning the patent. Whatever the circumstances, we know that Freeman later took the hidden-pickups idea to another California company, Rickenbacker, who also got no further than prototypes.

A second proposed version of the Marauder was worked on at Fender during 1966. Eight prototypes were built of the new version, this time with three conventional, visible pickups, plus some complex associated control switching. Four of these trial guitars also had slanted frets. It was in this state that the Marauder project finally died.

During 1966 CBS completed the construction of a new Fender factory, which had been planned before its purchase of the company. It cost the new owner $1.3million, and was situated next to Fender's buildings on the South Raymond site in Fullerton. Meanwhile, some cosmetic changes were being made to various Fender models. In

The Telecaster Thinline gained humbucking pickups in 1971, as on this example from around 1977 (near right). Two other "new" Teles from the period were the Telecaster Custom with neck humbuckers (1977 example, center) and the twin-humbucker Telecaster Deluxe (1976 example, far right).

guitar manufacturers

This unusual Rhinestone Strat, made in 1975, has a bonded metal and fiberglass body by British sculptor Jon Douglas, specially ordered by Fender's UK distributor. Some, like this one, have rhinestones set into the heavy relief design. Only a very small quantity was produced. A later unauthorized version made in the 1990s has an identifying plaque on the back of the body.

Fender's second attempt at a semi-solid instrument was the Starcaster (below right), this one dating from around 1978. Despite the quality, it was not popular. A Starcasting minstrel is pictured on the cover of Fender's 1976 catalog.

1965 the Stratocaster gained a broader headstock, effectively matching that of the Jazzmaster and Jaguar. Also during 1965 the fingerboards of the Electric XII, Jaguar and Jazzmaster were bound, while the following year the same trio was given block-shaped fingerboard inlays rather than the previous dot markers. Generally, CBS seemed to be fiddling for fiddling's sake.

A firm innovation – at least for Fender – came in the shape of a new line of hollowbody electrics. These were the first such electrics from Fender who until this point were clearly identified in the player's mind as a solidbody producer. Evidently the strong success of Gibson's ES line of semi-solidbodies and to a lesser extent models by Gretsch and others must have tempted CBS and its search for wider markets.

German maker Roger Rossmeisl had been brought into the company by Leo Fender in 1962 to design acoustic guitars, and Rossmeisl also became responsible for the new electric hollowbodies. Launched in 1966, the Coronado thinline guitars were the first to appear of Rossmeisl's electric designs for Fender and, despite their conventional, equal-double-cutaway, bound bodies with large, stylized f-holes, they employed the standard Fender bolt-on neck and headstock design. Options included a new vibrato tailpiece, and there was also a 12-string version that borrowed the Electric XII's "hockey-stick" headstock. Rossmeisl was also among the team which came up with a lightweight version of the Tele in 1968. The Thinline Telecaster had three hollowed-out

THE COLLECTED WORKS OF FENDER

guitar manufacturers

cavities inside the body and a modified pickguard shaped to accommodate the single, token f-hole. It was also around this time – and quite apart from Fender – that Byrds guitarist Clarence White and drummer Gene Parsons came up with their "shoulder strap control" B-string-pull device that fitted into a Telecaster. It was designed to offer string-bends within chords to emulate pedal steel-type sounds.

It was at this time that Rossmeisl was let loose with a couple of guitar designs that were even less like the normal run of Fenders than the Coronado models had been. Rossmeisl's specialty was the so-called "German carve" taught to him by his guitar-making father, Wenzel Rossmeisl. This applies a distinctive "dished" dip around the top edge of the body, following its outline. Rossmeisl adopted this feature for the new hollowbody archtop electric Montego and LTD models, all eminently traditional but still obstinately using Fender's customary bolt-on neck. From all reports there were very few of these made, and the models are rarely seen today.

Toward the end of the 1960s came firm evidence that CBS was trying to wring every last drop of potential income from unused Fender factory stock that would otherwise have been written off. Two shortlived guitars, the Custom and the Swinger, were assembled from these leftovers.

As the close of the 1960s loomed, Fender took a boost when an inspired guitarist by the name of Jimi Hendrix applied the Stratocaster's sensuous curves and glorious tone to his live cavorting and studio experiments. Salesman Dale Hyatt once said, only half-jokingly one suspects, that Jimi Hendrix caused more Stratocasters to be sold than all the Fender salesmen put together.

One of the few top bands apparently absent from Fender patronage during the 1960s was The Beatles, who at least on-stage contented themselves with a mix of primarily Gretsch, Rickenbacker, Gibson, Epiphone and Hofner guitars. In fact, George Harrison and John Lennon had each acquired a Stratocaster in 1965 for studio use, and Paul McCartney bought an Esquire a year or two later. But the public face of the band remained distinctly Fender-less, which led Don Randall to try to persuade manager Brian Epstein to get his boys into Fender. Probably during 1969, Randall managed to secure a meeting with Lennon and McCartney at the band's Apple headquarters in London. The results were the band's Fender-Rhodes pianos, a Jazz Bass and a VI six-string bass, as well as George Harrison's Rosewood Telecaster – all visible at various times during the *Let It Be* movie.

The 1970s are believed by many players and collectors to be the poorest years of Fender's production history, and there can be little doubt that quality control slipped and more low-standard Fenders were made during this decade than any other. But some fine Fender guitars were made in the 1970s as well. It's just that there were more average guitars made than good ones – and it often seems as if the good

Three more Stratocasters on this page: a 25th Anniversary model in fetching silver finish from 1979 (far left); a 1980 example of the Strat (center), a shortlived official use of the common abbreviation; and a regular Stratocaster model from 1980 finished in Capri Orange, one of several lurid "International Colors" offered briefly at this time.

instruments that do turn up were produced in spite rather than because of the company's policies and activities during that decade.

The 1970s would be a time when CBS management cut back on the existing Fender product lines and offered hardly any new models. The last Esquire of the period was made in 1970, the year in which the Duo-Sonic also died. The Jaguar disappeared around 1975, and by 1980 the Bronco, Jazzmaster, Musicmaster and Thinline Tele had all been taken out of production.

Elsewhere in Fender's guitar lines, the original acoustic flat-tops had all gone from the catalog by 1971. Ten years later the steels and pedal-steels had all disappeared, with only amplifiers (some 14 models) offering anything like the previous market coverage. Most of the original Custom Colors had been discontinued during the late 1960s and early 1970s.

So it was that by the start of the 1980s the guitarist who wanted to buy a new Fender electric had little choice beyond the company's ever-reliable Strats and Teles. And apart from a few shortlived exceptions, these came mostly in sunburst, blond, black or natural. It was hard to resist the feeling that the newly-important calculations of the balance sheet had become firmly established at Fender, and had taken precedence over the company's former creativity. A few new electric Fender models did get introduced in the 1970s, but mostly these were variations on familiar themes. Part

Fender launched its first Vintage reissue series of guitars in 1982, a masterstroke that allowed it to capitalize on its own valuable history. This example of the Vintage 57 Stratocaster (main guitar) was made in 1987. There was also a Vintage 62 Stratocaster that had a rosewood fingerboard among other features associated with early-1960s Strats.

The shortlived Standard Stratocaster (1982 example, below left) returned to a more traditional look and feel for the Strat, abandoning features such as the "large" headstock, three-bolt neck fixing and headstock-located bullet truss-rod adjuster. The ad from 1983 shows a close-up of that year's Elite Stratocaster (details opposite).

Most Guitar Makers Would Be Happy With A Page In History.

Fender's catalog of 1982 (below) featured famous Fender players on the cover (left to right): Buddy Holly, James Burton, The Ventures, Steve Cropper, Jimi Hendrix, Eric Clapton. The page from inside shows Fender's new low-end Lead III model pictured in a punky dressing room, somewhat in contrast to the cover stars.

Three more new-in-the-1980s Fenders on this page: a '52 Telecaster vintage reissue, this one (far left) made in 1984; a Stratocaster Elite (center) dating from 1983, with pushbutton pickup selectors and finished in Blue Stratoburst; plus a Elite Telecaster from 1983 with two new-design humbucking pickups.

of Fender's distinction had come from using bright-sounding single-coil pickups; the warmer, fatter-sounding humbucking types were always considered then as a Gibson mainstay. Nonetheless, in keeping with changing market trends, the Telecaster was given a humbucking pickup at the neck position to create the Telecaster Custom in 1972, and similar dabbling led to a sort of Tele-meets-Strat-meets-Gibson: the two-humbucker, Strat-necked Telecaster Deluxe of 1973.

The company made another attempt at thinline hollowbody electrics with the ill-fated Starcaster in 1976, again aimed at competing with Gibson's ever-popular ES line. The Starcaster had left the Fender list by 1980.

By 1976 Fender had a five-acre facility under one roof in Fullerton and employed over 750 workers. Some new "student" models appeared at this time to replace the Musicmaster, Bronco, Duo-Sonic and Mustang. The Lead I and Lead II guitars of 1979 were simple double-cutaway solids, though not especially cheap at $399. They were followed by the single-cutaway Bullet series which began production in 1981. Fender did briefly attempt to have these models produced in Korea, to eliminate tooling costs, but after a number of problems manufacturing resumed in the US.

In the early 1980s the CBS management appears to have decided that Fender needed some new blood to help reverse the decline in the company's fortunes. During 1981 key personnel were recruited from the American musical instrument operation of

A radically different design was the shortlived Performer (main guitar), this one made in 1986.

This D'Aquisto Deluxe (below left) was made at Fender's Custom Shop in 1997. The 1986 ad shows sessionman Tommy Tedesco with the earlier and similar Japanese-made D'Aquisto Elite model.

How Tommy Tedesco gets a date.

You'll find that Tommy Tedesco's played on more records, television and movie scores than any other guitarist in the world. And you'll usually find him with his Fender D'Aquisto Elite in his hands.

Because when it comes to dates, Tommy's been one of the most popular guys in Hollywood for over 30 years. And when it comes to guitars, his first call is a Fender.

Fender Master Series

guitar manufacturers

One of the Stratocaster's leading advocates during the 1980s was Edge of U2, who did much to keep the instrument in public view.

the giant Japanese company Yamaha, including John McLaren, Bill Schultz and Dan Smith. It appeared that they were brought in to turn around the reputation of Fender, to get the operation on its feet and making a profit once again.

One of the new team's recommendations was to start alternative production of Fenders in Japan. The reason was relatively straightforward: Fender's sales were being hammered by the onslaught of orientally-produced copies. These Japanese copyists made their biggest profits in their own domestic market, so the best place to hit back at them was in Japan – by making and selling guitars there. So, with the blessing of CBS, negotiations began with two Japanese distributors to establish the Fender Japan company. A joint venture was officially established in March 1982.

In the States the new management team was working on a strategy to return Fender to its former glory. The plan was for Fender in effect to copy itself, by recreating the guitars that many players and collectors were spending large sums of money to acquire: the Fenders made back in the company's glory years in the 1950s and 1960s. The result was the Vintage reissue series, begun in 1982. The guitars consisted of a maple-neck "57" and rosewood-fingerboard "62" Strat, as well as a "52" Telecaster. These Vintage reproductions were not exact enough for some die-hard Fender collectors, but generally the guitars were praised and welcomed. Production of the Vintage reissues was planned to start in 1982 at Fender US (Fullerton) and at Fender

Fender joined in the mid-1980s trend for weird body shapes with the shortlived Katana model (far left), this one made in 1985. A longer stay in the Fender line was enjoyed by the 12-string Strat XII (1990 example, center). Fender Japan launched a Paisley Stratocaster and a Blue Flower Stratocaster in 1988, two finishes first used in the 1960s – on Telecasters. This Blue Flower Strat (near left) dates from 1989.

Fender's Custom Shop began to operate officially in 1987, and the company was soon publishing ads like this one (near right) to underline the traditional role of a custom shop making one-off "fantasy" guitars. Fender acquired the rights to products bearing Floyd Rose's name in 1991 (ad from that year, far right).

Japan (Fujigen). But changes being instituted at the American factory meant that the US versions did not come on-stream until early 1983. Fender Japan's guitars at this stage were being made only for the internal Japanese market, but Fender's European agents were putting pressure on the Fullerton management for a low-end Fender to compete with the multitude of exported models being sold in Europe and elsewhere by other Japanese manufacturers.

So Fender Japan made some less costly versions of the Vintage reissues for European distribution in 1982, with the Squier brand (see Squier). At the end of 1983, with the US Fender factory still not up to the scale of production the team wanted, Fender Japan also built a Squier Stratocaster for the US market. This instrument, together with the earlier Squier Stratocasters and Telecasters, saw the start of the sale of Fender Japan products around the world, and a move by Fender to become an international manufacturer of guitars.

A shortlived pair from the US factory at this time was the Elite Stratocaster and Elite Telecaster, intended as radical new high-end versions of the old faithfuls. Unfortunately the vibrato-equipped Elite Strat came saddled with a terrible bridge, which is what most players recall when the Elites are mentioned. In-fighting at Fender had led to last-minute modifications of the vibrato design and the result was an unwieldy, unworkable piece of hardware. The Elite Strat also featured three pushbuttons for pickup selection,

Fender's American Standard series re-established the good name of the Stratocaster and Telecaster with efficacious updates. The Stratocaster American Standard (1991 example, near right) first appeared in 1985; the Telecaster American Standard (1991 example, far right) in 1988. Both remain popular and important models in Fender's line. The company's first signature model was the Eric Clapton Stratocaster; this example (center) dates from 1990.

guitar manufacturers

The 40th Anniversary Telecaster was the Fender Custom Shop's first limited-edition guitar. This exquisite 1989 example (main guitar) is number 221 of 300.

Fender's Yngwie Malmsteen signature Strat has a scalloped fingerboard – "scooped" rather than flat between each fret, to enable faster playing.

which were not to the taste of players brought up on the classic Fender pickup switch. There were good points – the new pickups, the effective active circuitry, and an improved truss-rod design – but they tended to be overlooked. The Elites were also dropped by the end of 1984.

Three new-design Fender lines were introduced in 1984, made by Fender Japan and intended to compete with some of Gibson's popular lines. The overall name for the new instruments was the Master Series, encompassing electric archtop D'Aquisto models, with design input from American luthier Jimmy D'Aquisto, and semi-solid Esprit and Flame guitars. Significantly, they were the first Fender Japan products with the Fender rather than Squier headstock logo to be sold officially outside Japan, and the first Fenders with set-necks. Their overtly Gibson image was to be their undoing. Most players wanted recognizable Fenders from Fender. This recurring theme has jarred with all Fender's attempts to introduce new-design guitars.

For a variety of reasons, CBS decided during 1984 that it had finally had enough of this part of the music business, and that it wished to sell Fender Musical Instruments. CBS invited offers and at the end of January 1985, almost exactly 20 years since acquiring it, CBS confirmed that it would sell Fender to an investor group led by Bill Schultz, then president of Fender Musical Instruments. The contract was formalized in February and the sale completed in March 1985 for $12.5million. It's interesting to

Swedish heavy metal guitarist Yngwie Malmsteen is pictured in this 1990 ad with one of his Fender signature Stratocasters.

compare this with the $13million that CBS originally paid for the company back in 1965 (which translates to around $90million at 1985 prices).

The problems facing the new owners were legion, but probably the most immediate was the fact that the Fullerton factories were not included in the deal. So US production of Fenders stopped in February 1985. However, the new team had been stockpiling bodies and necks, and did acquire some existing inventory of completed guitars as well as production machinery. The company went from employing over 800 people in early 1984 down to just over 100 in early 1985.

Fender had been working on a couple of radical guitar designs before CBS sold the company, and these instruments became victims of the crossfire. One was the Performer, which started life intended for US production. But with nowhere to build it in the States, Fender had it manufactured at the Fujigen factory in Japan.

The Performer had a distinctive body shape, twin slanted pickups, 24 frets, and an arrow-shape headstock quite different from the usual Fender Strat derivative, a reaction to the newly popular "superstrat" design popularized by American guitar makers such as Jackson and including a drooped "pointy" headstock. All in all, Fender's Performer was a thoroughly modern instrument with few nods to the company's illustrious past, but this brave move was killed by the CBS sale. The Japanese operation became Fender's lifeline at this time, providing much-needed

product to the company which still had no US factory. All the guitars in Fender's 1985 catalog were made in Japan, including the new Contemporary Stratocasters and Telecasters which were the first Fenders with the increasingly fashionable heavy-duty vibrato units and string-clamps.

One estimate put as much as 80 per cent of the guitars that Fender US sold from around the end of 1984 to the middle of 1986 as Japanese-made.

Fender finally established its new factory at Corona, about 20 miles east of the now defunct Fullerton site. Production started on a very limited scale toward the end of 1985, producing only about five guitars a day for the Vintage reissue series. But Dan Smith and his colleagues wanted to re-establish the US side of Fender's production with some good, basic Strats and Teles that would be seen as a continuation of the best of Fender's American traditions. That plan translated into the American Standard models: the Strat version was launched in 1986; the Tele followed two years later.

The American Standard was an efficacious piece of re-interpretation. It drew from the best of the original Stratocaster but was updated with a flatter-camber 22-fret neck and a revised vibrato unit based on twin stud pivot points. Once the Corona plant's production lines reached full speed, the American Standard Stratocaster proved extremely successful for the revitalized Fender operation. By the early 1990s, the instrument was a best-seller, and was notching up some 25,000 sales annually. In

Three Fenders made in the 1990s are shown on this page: a Strat Plus of 1990 (near right), the first with Fenders low-noise Lace Sensor pickups; the Prodigy II (1991 example, center) acknowledged the superstrat trend, and was one of the first Fender's worked on at the company's new Mexican factory; and this Strat Ultra (far right), with doubled-up single-coil pickup at the bridge, was made in 1991.

Jeff Beck's early career saw him a dedicated Les Paul player (as on 1971's Rough And Ready album, near left), but by the time of Wired (1976, far left) he had switched to Strats, which he still uses.

many markets today, including the United States, the American Standard Stratocasters and Telecasters remain the best-selling US-made Fender models.

In 1987 the Fender Custom Shop was officially established at the Corona plant. The Custom Shop was started so that Fender could build one-offs and special orders for players who had the money and the inclination. While this role remains – customers have ranged from Chet Atkins to Lou Reed – the Custom Shop now has a much wider part to play in Fender's expanding business.

The Shop's activities today effectively divide into three. First there are the one-offs, or Master Built guitars as the Custom Shop calls them. These are exactly what most people would understand as the work of a custom shop: instruments made by one person with acute attention to detail and a price to match. The second type is the limited edition, a special numbered run of anything from a handful to several hundred of a specific model. Third, the Custom Shop makes a general line of "catalog" models which it calls Stock Team (or, more personally, Custom Team) items, normally introduced after a style of model has proved popular in one-off requests.

One of the first jobs for the Custom Shop was to make a yellow Vintage reissue Strat for Jeff Beck. At this stage Beck vetoed Fender's wish to produce a Jeff Beck signature edition Strat, and the design intended for that purpose evolved into the Strat Plus. A Jeff Beck signature Strat not dissimilar to the Plus finally appeared in 1991. Signature

instruments now form an important part of the Fender line. The first was the Eric Clapton Stratocaster. Clapton had asked Fender to make him a guitar with the distinct V-shape neck of his favorite 1930s Martin acoustic guitar, as well as what he described as a "compressed" pickup sound. Various prototypes were built by George Blanda at Fender, and the final design eventually went on sale to the public in 1988.

Lace Sensor pickups and an active circuit delivered the sound Clapton was after and, curiously, the production model even offers a blocked-off vintage-style vibrato unit, carefully duplicating that feature of Clapton's original. A number of Fender signature models have followed over the years and continue to appear. Some are made in the Custom Shop, others at the Corona factory or further afield, and each one is generally endowed with features favored by the named artist. They range from the posthumous Stevie Ray Vaughan Stratocaster to the Waylon Jennings "tribute series" Telecaster, the Dick Dale surfing Strat to the worn-and-torn Muddy Waters Tele, and the Jerry Donahue Telecaster to the Hendrix Voodoocaster Strat, with many more besides.

In 1988 the Custom Shop produced the 40th Anniversary Telecaster, its first limited-edition production run. At that time most players and collectors (and Fender itself) believed that the first Broadcaster/Telecaster had been produced in 1948, hence the timing of the anniversary model. John Page, head of Fender's Custom Shop, says that it took some 18 months to build the full edition of 300 guitars – and then many

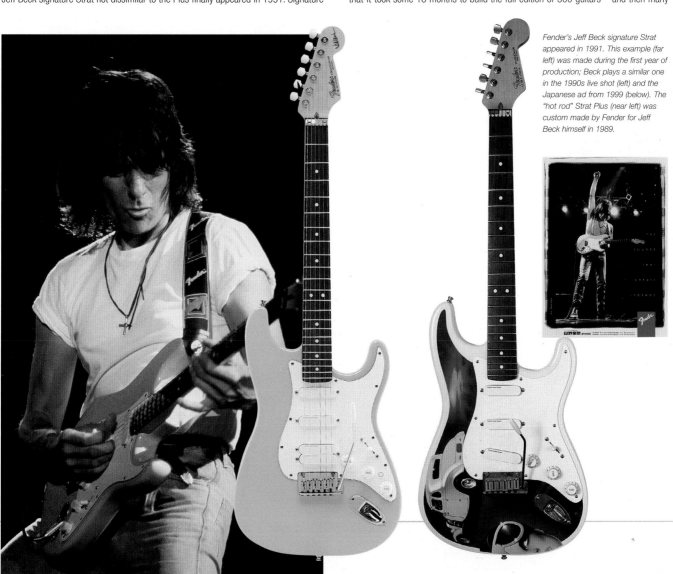

Fender's Jeff Beck signature Strat appeared in 1991. This example (far left) was made during the first year of production; Beck plays a similar one in the 1990s live shot (left) and the Japanese ad from 1999 (below). The "hot rod" Strat Plus (near left) was custom made by Fender for Jeff Beck himself in 1989.

James Burton exchanged the red Tele seen on this 1969 duo album (left) for a Paisley Red model that he used with Elvis Presley in the 1970s. A more recent fan of the Telecaster's friendly playability has been Thom Yorke (right) of Radiohead.

Fender dealers were upset because the company only made 300. So the Shop's next limited run, the HLE Stratocaster (Haynes Limited Edition), was upped to 500 units. Other numbered runs continued to appear from the Custom Shop and became an important part of the Shop's job.

A logical extension to the limited editions occurred in 1992 with the Shop's first catalog of standard Custom Shop products – which it now groups together under the general headings of Stock Team and Custom Team guitars. No production limit is put on these models other than the confines of the Shop's capacity. They include models such as the Carved Top Strat, the Set Neck Strat and the Robben Ford guitars, in series such as Custom Classics, Showmasters, and Time Machines. The expansion of the Custom Shop's business prompted a move in 1993 to new buildings (but still close to the Corona factory) to gain extra space and improve efficiency.

Following the success of the Vintage reissue series, first introduced in 1982, Fender Japan marketed a number of models that re-created many of the guitars from Fender's past. These included reproductions of the Paisley, Blue Flower, Rosewood and Thinline Telecasters, the Jaguar and Jazzmaster, the Mustang, and of course a plethora of Strats recalling various periods.

Fender US came up with a new design in 1991 called the Prodigy, a shortlived attempt to compete with successful guitars from popular makers of the time such as

Three signature Telecasters are shown on this page: a James Burton from 1991 (near right); a Danny Gatton from 1991 (center); and a 1990 prototype of the Jerry Donahue model (far right) that went into production two years later.

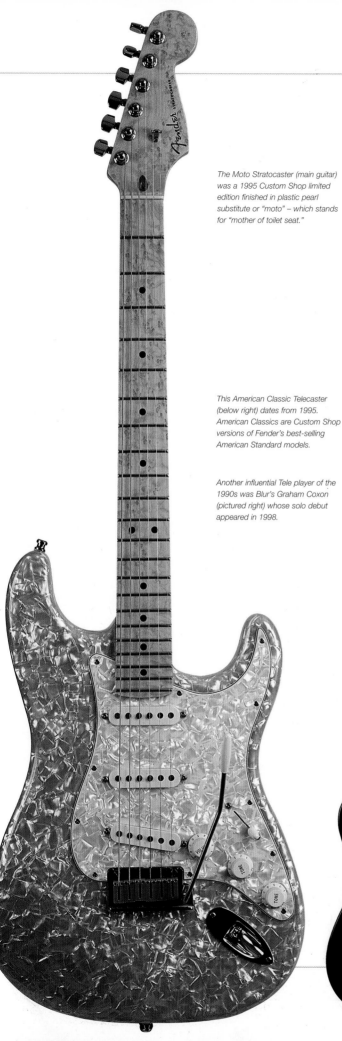

The Moto Stratocaster (main guitar) was a 1995 Custom Shop limited edition finished in plastic pearl substitute or "moto" – which stands for "mother of toilet seat."

This American Classic Telecaster (below right) dates from 1995. American Classics are Custom Shop versions of Fender's best-selling American Standard models.

Another influential Tele player of the 1990s was Blur's Graham Coxon (pictured right) whose solo debut appeared in 1998.

Charvel. It had an offset-waist body with sharper horns than a Strat, two single-coils and a humbucker, and an optional locking vibrato. The Prodigy was among the first Fender guitars to receive attention at the company's new factory in Ensenada, Mexico, which had been established in 1987. Ensenada is some 180 miles south of Los Angeles, just across the California/Mexico border. Fender amps started to appear from the Mexico factory in 1989, with guitars following soon after.

By early 1992 the Mexican factory was producing around 175 Fender Standard Stratocasters per day. One estimate in the late 1990s had Mexico assembling around 150,000 Fenders a year, compared to some 85,000 at Corona. The workforce was around 1,000 at the Mexico factory and 700 at Corona. During 1999 Fender launched the first two original-design guitars to be manufactured at its Mexican plant, the Toronado and the Cyclone models.

During the late 1990s Fender put a good deal of effort into offering a greater variety of pickups on some models. The first wave of its own US-made units had begun with the "hotter" Texas Special Strat-type single-coils, first seen on the Stevie Ray Vaughan model in 1992. Also, the company became more inclined to use pickups from popular outside makers, including well-known brands such as DiMarzio and Seymour Duncan. Fender also used the increasingly popular Fishman Powerbridge, with "acoustic"-sounding piezo inserts, on the Power Tele models that it launched in 2000. Fender

This Relic Stratocaster was made in Fender's Custom Shop in 1998, complete with an aged appearance that included wear, knocks and tarnishing. Instant new vintage!

One of Fender's Custom Shop builders was told that some vintage replicas he'd made for Keith Richards (on-stage in the 1990s, below) "looked too new." This led to the idea for Fender's Relics, "New Old Stock" and Closet Classic models, new guitars that are given various degrees of an aged and distressed vintage look.

manufactures some of its own pickups at the Fender Mexico plant for use on guitars assembled there. In addition to the expected single-coil units, there have been humbuckers – and so it seemed to Fender an obvious move to develop and make humbuckers at Corona. The first guitars with the new Fender US-made humbuckers were the California "Fat" models of 1997: the Fat Strat had a bridge humbucker while the Fat Tele came with a neck humbucker.

In the mid 1990s Fender began again to revisit one of its favorite locations: the past. A common request from some artists was for the Custom Shop to make them a replica of a favorite old guitar, usually because the original was too valuable to risk taking on the road. After Keith Richards told the Shop that some replicas made for him for a Stones tour looked too new ("bash 'em up a bit and I'll play 'em") the Shop began to include wear-and-tear distress marks to replicate the overall look of a battered old original. Then Master Builder J.W. Black came up with the idea of offering these aged replicas as standard Custom Shop catalog items, called Relics.

The Shop made two aged 1950s-era samples: a Nocaster (the in-between Broadcaster/Telecaster with no model name) and a "Mary Kaye" Strat (blond body, gold-plated parts). Soon the Custom Shop was reacting to the demand generated from these samples by offering a line of three Relic Strats and a Relic Nocaster. The Relics have proved remarkably successful and the line has expanded. John Page, boss of the

guitar manufacturers

Japanese-made Jaguar and Jazzmaster models appeared in this 1995 ad (left). By 2000 Fender Japan was primarily supplying its domestic market, exporting just a handful of small-run basses, as Fender's Mexican plant and new US factory – plus offshore suppliers – took care of general demand.

Custom Shop, said that the Mary Kaye Relic Strat was the Shop's single best-selling model of the late 1990s, and the general popularity of the Relics was continued into the early 21st century.

At the time of writing, the Custom Shop has reorganized the line to offer three types of "re-creations" in its renamed Time Machine series. First are the N.O.S. "New Old Stock" guitars, intended as pristine replicas that are produced as closely as possible to original brand new instruments that would have come off the Fender production line during the particular period concerned. Next, there are the Closet Classics, which are meant to be like guitars bought new years ago, played a bit, and shoved under the bed or in a closet. Third is the Relic style, as already discussed, with "aged" knocks and wear added by the Shop.

The Time Machine guitars obviously appeal to a relatively small but growing number of affluent Fender fans keen to acquire a new Fender that has the feel and sound of

an oldie and that, in the case of the Relics, is made to look as if decades of wear-and-tear have stained the fingerboard, scuffed the body and tarnished the hardware. The Time Machine series is a brilliant marketing move by Fender, because these guitars are the nearest that the company has got in new instruments to the almost indefinable appeal of vintage guitars, something that most modern manufacturers – and certainly most collectors – had thought was firmly locked away in the past.

Meanwhile there were truly new guitars. Well... almost new guitars. Larry Brooks in the Custom Shop had built a hybrid guitar for grunge supremo Kurt Cobain in 1993 after the guitarist had come up with some ideas for a merged Jaguar and Mustang: the Jag-Stang. A number of also-ran Fender models beyond Stratocasters and Telecasters were proving popular at this time with grunge guitarists: Cobain himself played Jaguars and Mustangs; Steve Turner played a Mustang; J Mascis had a Jazzmaster. And the reason was straightforward. These guitars had the comforting Fender logo on the head, but could be bought more cheaply secondhand than Strats or Teles. The ethics of such deals suited grunge guitarists perfectly.

Cobain, meanwhile, decided to take cut-up photographs of his Jag and Mustang and stick them together this way and that, trying out different combinations to see what they would look like combined. The Custom Shop then took his paste-ups as a basis, assembled the design, and contoured it here and there to improve balance and feel.

Three more 1990s Fender models are displayed on this page: a Telecaster Electric-Acoustic hybrid guitar from 1996 (far left); the Kurt Cobain-designed Jag-Stang (1997 left-handed example, center); and a Big Apple Strat (near left) that dates from 1997, the first US-made Stratocaster with two humbuckers.

FENDER

These 1997 ads promoted some recent signature models. Richie Sambora of Bon Jovi (right) displays the Japan-made limited edition of his Strat, while Stevie Ray Vaughan's brother Jimmie (far right) endorses Fender's Tex-Mex Strat, made – suitably enough – at the company's Mexican factory.

After Cobain's untimely death in 1994, the guitarist's family collaborated with the Fender company to release a Japan-made production version of the instrument, which was named the Fender Jag-Stang. Cobain's guitar hit the market in 1996.

Fender opened a brand new guitar- and amp-making factory in November 1998, still in Corona, California. The company described the impressive state-of-the-art factory as arguably the most expensive and automated facility of its type in the world. Since starting production at the original Corona factory back in 1985, Fender had grown to occupy a total of 115,000 square feet of space in ten buildings across the city. Such a rambling spread proved increasingly inefficient, and Fender had begun to plan a new factory during the early 1990s. With this new facility Fender are now clearly geared up for even more expansion, and the new $20million 177,000-square-feet plant affords the continuously successful Fender a potentially growing production capacity for the future. The new factory, with a staff of 600, also means that Fender's long-standing fight with California's stringent environmental laws are at an end, as the new purpose-built paint section works without toxic emissions.

The new factory may be only 20 miles or so from Fullerton and the site of Leo Fender's original workshops, but it is a universe away from those humble steel shacks that provided the first home for Fender guitar production. However, with his love of gadgetry Leo would undoubtedly have been enthralled by the new plant, not least its

Concentrate while you read this. In 1997 Fender made this completely reversed version of Jimi Hendrix's late-1960s Strat (which was a normal right-handed Strat Jimi turned upside down to accommodate his leftness). A right-handed player would find this to be a "normal" left-handed guitar turned upside down, suitably re-strung. Instant Jimi! There's even a reversed headstock logo to enhance the irresistible peek in the mirror.

Fender's 1997 ad (below) promotes the Jimi Hendrix Stratocaster surrounded by some of the great guitarist's sartorial effects.

guitar manufacturers

This John Jorgensen Hellecaster (main guitar) was made in 1997. The shortlived signature model mixed Electric XII-like split pickups with a Hendrix-style reversed headstock. The 1999 Japanese ad (far left) gets close to an American Classic Strat.

Two new retro-flavored designs grace this pair of models (below right) launched during 1999: here a red Cyclone and a black Toronado.

FENDER
CLASSIC SERIES

新しいフェンダー・クラシック・シリーズは、選び抜かれたトラディショナル・ルーフィンテージ・モデルへのリビュート。厳定の機能とオリジナルの特色を忠実に再現。

automated conveyor system that enables the storage and supply on demand to the production line of a vast inventory of guitar components.

As the 21st century gets underway, the Fender Musical Instruments Corporation is as aware as ever of the value of Leo's surname. But many musicians, collectors and guitar dealers measure the worth of Fender purely in terms of past achievements – which must be a continuing frustration for a modern company whose new ideas are often resisted for being "un-Fender."

Fender has reached the enviable point today where it dominates the world's electric guitar market. It has achieved its current successes in a variety of ways, not least by trying to provide a model or models that will appeal to every conceivable type of guitar player at every level of skill and affluence.

Fender chairman and CEO Bill Schultz took a moment in 1999 to describe his firm's outlook in simple business-like terms: "Our goal couldn't be more straightforward. Simply put, we're going to be the world's best guitar and guitar-amp company."

The history of Fender and of Fender electric guitars – which continues as you read these words – has been a remarkable mixture of inspiration and invention, of luck and mishap. But the company's best guitars ensure that the Fender name lives on into this new millennium. Fender guitars will no doubt help further generations of players turn strings and frets and pickups into remarkable music.

Fernandes adopted the Sustainer system on a number of instruments, promoted in this 1992 ad (left). Among the more esoteric archtop models from Framus was its Attila Zoller model (1963 ad, right).

FENTON-WEILL

Henry Weill's British company made amplifiers, but Jim Burns formed a partnership with Weill in 1959 to make guitars. After Burns's quick departure, Weill continued, adopting the Fenton-Weill brand for Twinmaster, Fibratone, Twister and other models, also making for Dallas, Vox, Hohner and Rose-Morris. The guitars stopped in 1965.

FERNANDES

At home in Japan, Fernandes has long been one of the biggest brands. Guitar megastar Hotei is a Japanese devotee. Fernandes originated in the early 1970s on copies, but a decade later the catalog had expanded to include flattering imitations not just of Gibsons and Fenders but also Alembic, B.C. Rich and others.

Through the 1980s more players noticed Fernandes, praising accuracy, construction and quality. Name endorsers included Frank Dunnery, Brad Gillis, John Mayall, Steve Stevens and Mick Taylor. Despite Fender's legal successes and its own Japanese-made "copies," Fernandes remained busy in the US and Europe, battling with the likes of Tokai for the role of top copyist.

The 1990s brought a retro flavor to Fernandes, and a new feature: the Sustainer. This was a development of an American electro-magnetic sustain device that had appeared in 1987, refined and incorporated into guitars by Hamer and others. Fernandes developed the system. By the late 1990s it offered regular guitar

A Fenton-Weill Triplemaster from 1962 (near right); a Fernandes FR5S (center) with Sustainer, made in 1993 as a special for a trade show; and a Framus Hollywood 5/132 (far right) produced in Germany around 1959.

Framus is among the few makers to offer a nine-string guitar. This Melodie (left) from 1965 has three pairs of two strings, doubled as on a 12-string, alongside three standard singles for the higher-pitched strings.

This Framus Strato Deluxe from 1965 (below right) has the maker's unusual "Organtone" effect, operated by the small bent handle below the bridge. The 1975 ad is for the Framus Jan Akkerman model.

performance plus controllable, never-ending sustain at any volume. The feature was fitted to numerous Fernandes models from the start of the 1990s, with Billy Gibbons a reported convert. The Fernandes line continues to boast a variety of standard, retro-style and superstrat electrics.

FRAMUS

Even though guitars have been made in Germany for centuries, Framus would become one of the most successful German companies during the fabled guitar boom of the 1960s. During that decade, Framus guitars were especially noted for features such as multi-laminated necks and complex electronics.

Frankische Musikindustrie (Framus) had been founded in the Erlangen area of Germany by Fred Wilfer in 1946, at first making only acoustic instruments. However, in 1954 the Framus operation relocated to Bubenreuth, and began adding pickups. Framus soon began making slimline semi-acoustic electric guitars around 1958, the best known being the single-cutaway Billy Lorento hollowbody (for the jazz guitarist later known as Bill Lawrence).

The late 1950s also brought the flat-topped, Les Paul-shaped Hollywood series of semi-solids, which later had single- or double-cutaway styling. They were succeeded in the early 1960s by Strato solidbodies. A great many solids carried this model name, regardless of shape or configuration, and Stratos came with numerous variations of

385

pickups and hardware. By the mid 1960s the shape had changed to a more Fender Jazzmaster-like style, both for solidbody Strato and hollowbody Television models. By 1965, high-end Framus models had an Organtone effect, a spring-loaded volume control with a hook (or "spigot") operated by the little finger. For the exceptionally coordinated player it could simulate an organ swell effect. Better models often had mutes, plus many switches for questionable circuitry tricks.

Double-cutaway thinline hollowbodies offered in the mid 1960s included the Fret Jet and New Sound, both with multiple switches on the upper horn. Exotic examples from this era included the nine-string Melody, and the Electronica with "18 different string outputs" and onboard pre-amp.

Around 1969, Framus collaborated with Bill Lawrence – who was by now a pickup designer – on the BL series of offset-double-cutaway solidbodies with thick waist and chunky upper horn. In the early 1970s Framus also built Fender and Gibson copies, returning to original thinking around 1974 with the Jan Akkerman semi-hollowbody and the broad, solidbody Nashville series.

In 1977 Framus introduced the Memphis, a sort of anthropomorphic wedge-shape solidbody, and several other distinctive models. Framus limped on into the early 1980s before becoming Warwick, a brand more successful with bass guitars. Warwick revived the Framus brandname in 1995 for a line of high-end German-made six-strings.

The G&L ad from 1981 pictured (above, left) shows the first guitar and bass models introduced by the company that Leo Fender started after he'd left Music Man.

This G&L Comanche was made in 1989 and features Leo Fender's distinctive split-pickup design, echoing the style of the pickups that Leo devised for the Precision Bass at his original company.

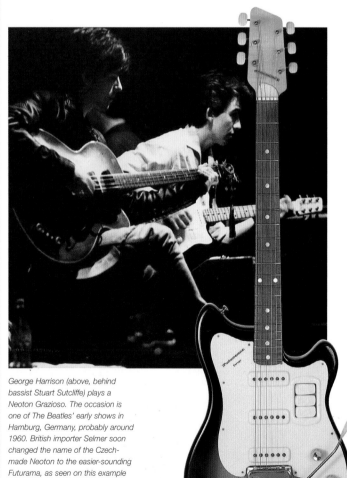

George Harrison (above, behind bassist Stuart Sutcliffe) plays a Neoton Grazioso. The occasion is one of The Beatles' early shows in Hamburg, Germany, probably around 1960. British importer Selmer soon changed the name of the Czech-made Neoton to the easier-sounding Futurama, as seen on this example (right) that dates from about 1960.

guitar manufacturers

Leo Fender introduced his G&L Broadcaster in 1985 (ad from that year, right) but the Fender company suggested otherwise, and the model was renamed as the ASAT (said by some to stand for "Another Strat, Another Tele," though G&L deny this).

FUTURAMA

These cheap imported guitars for early British would-be rockers were first made by Neoton, which was based in Prague, Czech Republic (then Czechoslovakia). The Fender-style Neoton Grazioso arrived in Britain in 1957, marketed by Selmer. At around £55 ($90) it proved popular with many soon-to-be-famous players such as George Harrison, Albert Lee and Gerry Marsden.

Selmer soon changed the uncommercial Grazioso name to the more evocative Futurama brand. During 1963 Selmer switched sources, using the new brand on guitars made by Hagstrom of Sweden. The Futurama Coronado model represented the best in Futurama quality, but Selmer had dropped the brandname by 1965.

G & L

G&L provided the final vehicle for Leo Fender's ideas on guitar design, continuing the tradition established by one of the industry's most famous names. Leo sold Fender to CBS in 1965. After leaving his Music Man operation, he started G&L in Fullerton, California, in 1979.

The name for the company, G&L, was in fact an abbreviation of "George and Leo," partner George Fullerton having worked with Leo at Fender. George Fullerton sold his interest in the G&L company in 1986. The first guitar model from the new company was the F-100, and this went on to the market during 1980. The two-humbucker F-100 model displayed several design touches that were unmistakably the work of Leo Fender. G&L then addressed the less expensive end of the market with its first SC series, debuting in 1982 with a body reminiscent of Fender's Mustang. High-end models continued to appear, many being variations on a now-established G&L template. Most striking of the high-end G&Ls was the limited-edition Interceptor which had an unusual X-shaped body.

In 1985 Leo refined his original Telecaster for the G&L Broadcaster. Body shape and control plate were familiar; other aspects remained staunchly G&L. Fender objected, so in 1986 G&L's Broadcaster became the ASAT, which went on to be a popular model.

During the late 1980s all-new rock machines included the Invader, Rampage and Superhawk. The Interceptor was modified with extended body horns and a Kahler vibrato, but in 1988 became a more conventional superstrat. In the same year the Comanche appeared, one of Leo's last designs. Signature versions of some models bore Leo's autograph logo on the body. The limited-edition Commemorative marked Leo's death in March 1991.

In late 1991 G&L was sold to BBE Sound of Huntington Beach, California. A Japan-only Tribute series of Japanese-made G&Ls appeared in 1998, including an ASAT. In the US the Comanche model was revived the same year, reintroducing for this as well as other models Leo's distinctive split-coil pickups, now called Z-coils.

Two more G&L guitars: the classic ASAT (far left, this one made in 1989), and a Cavalier (near left) from 1984. Seattle grunge-man Jerry Cantrell of Alice In Chains is seen playing his decorated G&L Rampage on stage around 1993.

387

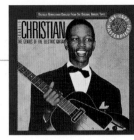

Charlie Christian, the original electric guitarist of jazz, is seen playing a Gibson ES-150 (main picture, in New York 1939, and album sleeve, top of page). This example of the ES-150 (left) dates from 1937. Introduced during the previous year, it was Gibson's first electric guitar (other than an earlier lap-steel model).

Gibson's 1937 catalog features its new ES-150 electric guitar and associated amplifier, along with pictures of players of the 150 and of Gibson's related lap-steel electrics of the period.

GIBSON

Gibson is one of the greatest and most significant fretted instrument manufacturers, and has been in existence for more than 100 years. Orville H. Gibson was born in 1856 in upstate New York, near the Canadian border. He began making stringed musical instruments in Kalamazoo, Michigan, probably by the 1880s, and set himself up as a manufacturer of musical instruments there around 1894.

Orville Gibson had a refreshingly unconventional mixture of ideas about how to construct his mandolin-family instruments and oval-soundhole guitars. He would hand-carve the tops and backs, but would cut sides from solid wood rather than using the usual heating-and-bending method. Also unusual was the lack of internal bracing, which he thought degraded volume and tone. Gibson would often have his instrument's bodies decorated with beautiful inlaid pickguards and a distinctive crescent-and-star logo on the headstock. The only patent that Orville ever received – which was granted in 1898 – was for his mandolin design that featured the distinctive one-piece carved sides, as well as a similarly one-piece neck.

In 1902 a group of businessmen joined Orville Gibson to form the Gibson Mandolin-Guitar Manufacturing company. The instruments that the new operation produced illustrated the diverse range of fretted stringed instruments available in the United States during the early decades of the 20th century. The mandolin was clearly the most popular, and Gibson would soon find itself among the most celebrated of mandolin makers, thanks in no small part to the enormously influential F-5 model that would appear in 1922. Gibson also instigated a successful teacher-agent system to sell its mandolins. This was in contrast to the normal distribution operated by most instrument companies that would be based on a network of retailers.

Orville had left the Gibson company in 1903, receiving a regular royalty from the company for the following five years and then a monthly income until his death in 1918. A year earlier the company had moved to new premises on Parsons Street, Kalamazoo (which it occupied until 1984).

Once Orville left Gibson, changes began to be made to his original construction methods, apparently for reasons of efficiency, for ease of production and, indeed, for improvement. Orville's sawed solid-wood sides were replaced with conventional heated-and-bent parts, and his inlaid, integral pickguard was replaced around 1908 with a unit elevated from the instrument's surface: the "floating pickguard." It was devised by Gibson man Lewis Williams, and the general design is still in use today by many producers of archtop guitars.

The guitar began to grow in importance during the late 1920s and into the 1930s, largely replacing the previously prominent tenor banjo. It became essential that any company demanding attention among guitarists should be seen as inventive and

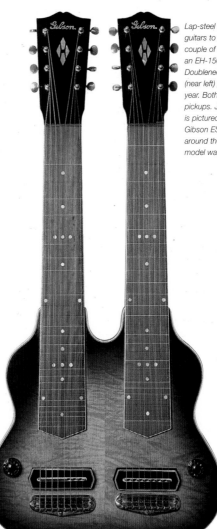

Lap-steel instruments were the first guitars to go electric, and here are a couple of Gibson's earliest models: an EH-150 (far left) of 1938, and a Doubleneck Electric Hawaiian model (near left) probably made in the same year. Both have "Charlie Christian" pickups. Jazz guitarist Jimmy Raney is pictured (this page) playing a Gibson ES-150 in a 1955 ad – around the time that the 19-year-old model was finally discontinued.

forward-thinking in this vital new area. Gibson obliged with many six-string innovations, including Ted McHugh's adjustable truss-rod that did an excellent job of strengthening the instrument's neck. Truss-rods are virtually obligatory on today's guitars.

Thanks to the creativity of gifted employees such as Lloyd Loar, Gibson also established individual landmarks like the L-5 guitar of the early 1920s. With its novel f-holes and "floating" pickguard, this model virtually defined the look and sound of the early archtop acoustic guitar. It soon established itself and was played in a variety of musical styles, none more appealing than the "parlor jazz" music epitomized by the incomparable guitarist Eddie Lang.

Lloyd Loar was an experienced musician who had started to work at Gibson in 1919 as a designer, and his best-known achievements were the Master Models series that included that ground-breaking L-5 guitar. Loar left Gibson in 1924 and around 1933 formed a company with ex-Gibson man Lewis Williams, primarily to manufacture electric instruments, which they called Vivi Tone or Acousti-Lectric.

The still barely understood potential of electric instruments fascinated Loar, who had devised an early experimental electric pickup while at Gibson in the 1920s. But Loar and Williams's offerings appear to have been too radical and ahead of their time to make any commercial impact, and within a few years of its inception their company had closed. Loar died in the early 1940s at the age of 57.

The ES-300 (1941 example, near right) was Gibson's most expensive pre-war electric guitar. This ES-350 (far right) was made in 1952, still with an old-style control layout. The ad (above) for the new ES-5 model was published in 1950.

Two more Gibson-wielding jazzmen, both of whom usually favored ES-175 models: Kenny Burrell, in a 1956 ad (near left), and Herb Ellis, seen in an ad from 1957 (far left).

As players demanded more volume from their guitars, Gibson dutifully increased the size of its acoustic instruments, introducing the superb, huge archtop Super 400 model in 1934. Later in the decade came Gibson's "jumbo" J-series flat-tops. It was around this time that Gibson introduced its first electric guitars, the Electric Hawaiian E-150 cast aluminum steel guitar in 1935, and the following year the EH-150 steel plus an f-hole hollowbody, the ES-150, Gibson's first archtop electric.

The non-cutaway ES-150 electric guitar was a very significant addition to the catalog for Gibson. It effectively marked the start of the company's long-running ES series – the initial letters standing for "Electric Spanish." It's worth noting that, in this context, the term "Spanish" of course had nothing at all to do with nylon-string round-soundhole guitars. Instead, it was being used to distinguish this type of guitar from its Hawaiian-style cousin, the one generally played on the lap.

The ES-150 was famously taken up by Charlie Christian, the genius who showed jazz players what an electric guitar was for. Playing clear, single-note runs as if he were a horn player, Christian virtually invented the idea of the electric guitar solo. The "bar" pickup of the earliest ES-150 models, which was designed by Walt Fuller at Gibson, has subsequently become known as the "Charlie Christian" pickup as the guitarist was by far its best-known user, even though Christian's career was cut tragically short by his early death in 1942 at the age of just 25. Gibson tentatively built on these low-key

electric experiments, adding the budget ES-100 archtop in 1938, and following this with its most expensive pre-war electric model, the ES-300, in 1940. When America entered the war two years later Gibson effectively put a halt to its guitar production. As instrument manufacturing gradually recommenced afterwards, Gibson rightly concluded that the electric guitar was set to become an important part of its reactivated business.

Around this time Gibson also manufactured instruments with a number of brandnames in addition to the most famous one. A good deal of the instruments bearing these names were acoustics, but electrics did appear with the following brands: Capital (made for Jenkins mail-order); Cromwell (for a variety of mail-order houses); Kalamazoo (a low-end in-house brand); Old Kraftsman (made for Spiegel mail-order); and Recording King (for Montgomery-Ward mail-order).

A controlling interest in Gibson was purchased in 1944 by the Chicago Musical Instrument Company (CMI), founded some 25 years earlier in Chicago, Illinois, by Maurice Berlin. Gibson's manufacturing base remained at its original factory, purpose-built in 1917 at Kalamazoo, which was roughly equidistant between Detroit and Chicago. The latter city was the location for Gibson's new sales and administration headquarters at CMI. It was at this time that Gibson began to pioneer electric guitars with cutaways. A cutaway offered easier access to the now audible and musically

Gibson's ES-175 that debuted in 1949 (this example, far left, was made in 1953) has proved popular with jazzmen, including Jim Hall (pictured). Another new model for 1949 was the three-pickup ES-5: this attractive natural-finish model (near left) was made in 1952.

GIBSON

Steve Howe, long-standing guitarist in Yes (1971 album, right), has a large guitar collection, but among his firm favorites is this ES-175D (below) that dates from 1964. Like many active players, Howe regularly modifies his instruments to enhance playability and to suit personal taste.

Wes Montgomery, among the greatest of jazz guitarists, is seen on this 1973 magazine cover with a Gibson L-5CES. Montgomery sometimes played custom-made single-pickup versions of this model.

useful area of the upper fingerboard, previously of little use to quiet acoustic players who tended to limit their fret-based ramblings primarily to the headstock end of the neck. Talented and imaginative guitarists openly welcomed the artistic potential of the cutaway... and began to investigate the dusty end of the fingerboard.

Significant new archtop electric guitars debuted in the late 1940s. The ES-350 of 1947 and two years later the ES-5 and sharp-cutaway ES-175 were all aimed at players who were prepared to commit themselves to fully integrated electric instruments designed and built as such by Gibson.

Gibson's ES-350 of 1947 was the first of the company's new-style cutaway electrics (and at first it bore the "Premier" tag of the pre-war cutaway acoustics). The 350 was followed in 1949 by the new single-pickup ES-175, Gibson's first electric with a "pointed" cutaway style and a pressed, laminated top. This construction contributed a distinctively bright, cutting tone color to the 175. A two-pickup version, the ES-175D, was added in 1953.

The ES-175 became a popular instrument and was Gibson's first really successful electric guitar. It has made a particular impact among electric jazz musicians, including such luminaries as Joe Pass, while also attracting eclectic modern players like Steve Howe and Pat Metheny.

The ES-5 also debuted in 1949 and was the first electric guitar with three pickups

– it was effectively a three-pickup ES-350. However, before long, players found that it was less controllable than they wanted. As with all Gibson's immediate post-war electric guitars, the ES-5 had no pickup switching. Instead, each pickup had a separate volume control, which meant that the only way to achieve a balance between the pickups was to set the three volume knobs at relative positions.

So it was that in 1956 Gibson issued the ES-5 model with redesigned electronics, this time with a new name: the ES-5 Switchmaster. Three individual tone knobs were added alongside the three volume controls, and near the cutaway a four-way pickup selector switch was added, hence the new model name. The switch, explained a Gibson catalog of the time, "activates each of the three pickups separately, a combination of any two, or all three simultaneously."

At a time when Fender had just launched its stylish three-pickup Stratocaster, and Epiphone was offering models with a six-button "color tone" switching system, Gibson probably felt the ES-5 Switchmaster was a potential market leader. But it never caught on. And anyway, by now Gibson had produced proper electric versions of its great archtop acoustics, the L-5 and the Super 400.

In 1951 Gibson became serious about the electric guitar, launching the Super 400CES and the L-5CES (the initials stand for Cutaway, Electric, Spanish). For the 400CES, Gibson built on its existing Super 400C acoustic model, and for the L-5CES

Gibson's two new high-end electric archtops, first issued in 1951: the Super 400CES (1953 example, far left) and the L-5CES (1951 example, near left). The letters stand for Cutaway Electric Spanish. Elvis Presley's guitarist Scotty Moore was an early fan of the Super 400CES. Moore is seen with the Gibson in this 1956 photograph (far left) that he sent to amplifier-maker Ray Butts to illustrate his handiwork in action.

Gibson's first solidbody electric guitar was the Les Paul Model of 1952, endorsed by the popular guitarist in this launch-year ad (center). The striking pair of gold-top instruments on this page – a regular right-hand model and a special-order left-hand version – also date from the Les Paul's debut year of 1952.

Gibson
Les Paul model

It's a Sensation!

Designed by Les Paul—produced by Gibson—and enthusiastically approved by top guitarists everywhere. The Les Paul Model is a unique and exciting innovation in the fretted instrument field; you have to see and hear it to appreciate the wonderful features and unusual tone of this newest Gibson guitar. Write Dept. 101 for more information about it.

Gibson, Inc., Kalamazoo, Mich.

guitar manufacturers

Gibson boss Ted McCarty holds a custom-made gold-finished hollowbody guitar (above, right) that provided the inspiration for the company's gold-top Les Paul model and all-gold ES-295.

An ES-295 (main guitar) made in 1952, the model's first year of production. This was in effect a gold-finished version of the ES-175D.

combined elements of its acoustic L-5C and electric ES-5 guitars. The new electric models had modified and stronger internal "bracing" to make them less prone to feedback when amplified.

The generally large proportions of the 18″-wide acoustic bodies of the earlier models were retained for these impressive new electrics in the Gibson line. For the 400CES model, the acoustic 400's high-end appointments remained – such as split-block-shape fingerboard inlays, a "marbleized" tortoiseshell pickguard, and a fancy "split-diamond" headstock inlay.

At first the electric 400 and L-5 came with a pair of Gibson's standard single-coil P-90 pickups, but in 1954 changed to more powerful "Alnico" types with distinctive rectangular polepieces. The Alnico nickname comes from the magnet type used in these pickups. A "rounded"-cutaway body style lasted from the launch of the two electrics in 1951 until 1960, when a new "pointed" cutaway was introduced. Gibson reverted to the original rounded design in 1969.

An immense variety of players has at different times been drawn to the power and versatility of Gibson's two leading archtop electrics. The Super 400CES has attracted bluesman Robben Ford, country players like Hank Thompson and Merle Travis (whose custom 400 was described in 1952 as Gibson's "most expensive guitar ever"), rock'n'roller Scotty Moore, and a number of fine jazz guitarists including George

Following on from the original gold-top Les Paul model came the high-end black-finish Les Paul Custom. This example (left) dates from the first year it was made, 1954. Bill Haley & His Comets did much to popularize rock'n'roll in its early years, and Haley's guitarist Frank Beecher is seen in this 1957 Gibson ad (below) with his favored Les Paul Custom. Haley himself is playing an acoustic Gibson Super 400C.

Benson and Kenny Burrell. The L-5CES has also had its fans and adherents over the subsequent years, including jazzmen such as Wes Montgomery and John Collins, as well as the fine country-jazzer Hank Garland.

Ted McCarty had joined Gibson back in March 1948, having worked at the Wurlitzer organ company for the previous 12 years. In 1950 he was made president of Gibson. Gibson was finding it hard in the post-war years to get back into full-scale guitar production, and McCarty's first managerial tasks were to increase the effectiveness of supervision, to bolster efficiency, and to improve internal communication.

Gibson began to work on a solidbody design soon after Fender's original Telecaster-style model had appeared in 1950. McCarty had a good team working on the project, including production head John Huis, as well as employees Julius Bellson and Wilbur Marker, while the sales people were regularly consulted through manager Clarence Havenga. It took them all about a year to come up with satisfactory prototypes for a new Gibson solidbody – at which point McCarty began to think about guitarist Les Paul, who was just about the most famous guitar player in America.

In the 1940s Les Paul had been a member of the supergroup Jazz At The Philharmonic, and had played prominent guitar on Bing Crosby's hit 'It's Been A Long Long Time.' Crosby encouraged Paul to build a studio into the garage of the guitarist's home in Hollywood, California, and it was here that he hit upon his effective "multiple"

recording techniques. These early overdubbing routines allowed Paul to create huge, magical orchestras of massed guitars, arranged by the guitarist to play catchy instrumental tunes. Les Paul and his New Sound was signed to Capitol Records, with the first release 'Lover' a hit in 1948.

Paul found even greater popularity when he added vocalist Mary Ford to the act. They had married in 1949, and the following year the duo released their first joint record. Guitars and now voices too were given the multiple recording treatment, and big hits followed for Les Paul & Mary Ford including 'The Tennessee Waltz' (1950) and 'How High The Moon' (1951). The duo performed hundreds of personal appearances and concerts, and were heard on NBC Radio's *Les Paul Show* every week for six months during 1949 and 1950. Their networked TV series *The Les Paul & Mary Ford Show* began in 1953, beamed from their extravagant new home in Mahwah, New Jersey. As the 1950s got underway, Les Paul & Mary Ford – "America's Musical Sweethearts" – were huge stars.

Les Paul's obsessive tinkering with gadgetry was not restricted to the recording studio. The teenage Lester, drawn to the guitar, had soon become interested in the idea of amplification. In the late 1930s his new jazz-based trio was broadcasting out of New York on the Fred Waring radio show, with Paul at first playing a Gibson L-5 archtop acoustic, and later a similar Epiphone. The guitarist exercised his curiosity for electric

Gibson added more Les Paul models to its line, including relatively low-end models such as the single-pickup Junior (near right, 1956 example) and two-pickup Special (center, 1955 example), both with uncarved "slab" body and simple appointments. The Byrdland (1957 example, far right) was among Gibson's first "thinline" electric archtops, with a more comfortable, less deep body.

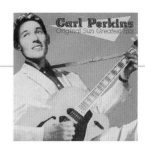

Rockabilly star Carl Perkins played Fenders and Les Pauls as well as the Switchmaster seen on the sleeve of a CD reissue of his classic Sun sides.

Another of Gibson's new thinline models was the ES-350T (main guitar). This fine natural-finish example was produced during 1957.

Rock'n'roller Chuck Berry favored Gibson's ES-350T, and is seen (below) taking the instrument on one his classic on-stage "duck walks."

instruments and his flair for technical experimentation by adapting and modifying the Epiphone guitar.

Around 1940, Les Paul used to go at weekends into the empty Epiphone factory in New York in order to fiddle with what he would call his "log" guitar. The nickname was derived from the 4″ by 4″ solid block of pine which the guitarist had inserted between the sawed halves of the body that he'd just dismembered. He then carefully re-joined the neck to the pine log, using some metal brackets, and mounted on the top a couple of crude pickups he'd made for himself.

Later he modified a second and third Epiphone, which he called his "clunkers," this time chopping up the bodies to add metal strengthening braces, and again topped off with Paul's own pickups. Despite their makeshift origins, the semi-solid "log" and the modified "clunker" Epiphones often accompanied Les Paul and Mary Ford on stage and in recording studios throughout the 1940s and into the early 1950s.

Paul was not alone in his investigations. Several unconnected explorations into the possibility of a solidbody electric guitar were being undertaken elsewhere in America at this time, not least at the California workshops of Rickenbacker, National, Bigsby and Fender. A solidbody electric was appealing because it would dispose of the involved construction of an acoustic guitar, and instead use a body or section of the body made of solid wood (or some other rigid material) to support the strings and pickups. Also, it

The ES-5 was redesigned in 1955 with a new pickup selector switch for easier operation, and renamed the ES-5 Switchmaster. This example with its exquisitely flamed maple top was made in 1957.

397

would curtail the annoying feedback produced by amplified acoustic guitars, and reduce the body's interference with the guitar's overall tone, thus more accurately reproducing and sustaining the sound of the strings.

During the 1940s, Paul had decided that he would take his "log" idea to a major guitar manufacturing company in order to try to generate some real interest in its commercial potential. He decided – accurately, as it turned out – that Epiphone would not continue in its present form as a strong force in the guitar world. So around 1946 Paul took his crude log guitar to Gibson's parent company, CMI in Chicago, with the intention of convincing them to market such a semi-solid guitar. No doubt with all the courtesy that a pressurised city businessman could muster, the boss of CMI showed Les Paul the door. A startled Paul recalls that they laughed at his guitar, dismissing him as "the guy with the broomstick."

But some years later, as we've seen, Gibson was developing ideas for a solidbody electric guitar in the wake of Fender's new instrument, and Gibson president Ted McCarty decided to contact the now hugely popular Les Paul. A meeting took place, probably in 1951. McCarty's intention was to interest Paul in publicly playing Gibson's newly designed guitar in return for a royalty on sales – an arrangement generally referred to now as an "endorsement" deal. It was certainly not a new arrangement for Gibson: the company's Nick Lucas flat-top acoustic model of 1928 had exploited the

During 1957 Gibson began to fit its new humbucking pickups to the instruments in its electric lines. This ES-5 Switchmaster (1961 example, near right) has three humbuckers, and also features the new "sharp" cutaway that Gibson began applying to its archtop electrics from 1960. The Les Paul Custom turned into a three-pickup instrument when it was switched to the new humbuckers, as this example made in 1957 (main guitar, far right) illustrates.

guitar manufacturers

Robert Fripp (pictured below) regularly played an original three-humbucker Les Paul Custom from his early days in the first King Crimson (1969 album sleeve, left).

popularity of Lucas, known as "the crooning troubadour," to produce the contemporary guitar industry's first "signature" instrument.

Gibson's meeting with Les Paul around 1951 was the first opportunity the guitarist had to see the prototype of what would soon become the Gibson Les Paul solidbody electric. A deal was struck: Paul's royalty on Les Paul models would be five per cent, and the term of the contract was set at five years. Paul's respected playing and commercial success added to Gibson's weighty experience in manufacturing and marketing guitars made for a strong and impressive combination.

The new Les Paul guitar was launched by Gibson in 1952, probably in the spring of that year, and was priced at $210 (this being around $20 more than Fender's Telecaster). Today, this first style of Les Paul model is nearly always called the "gold-top" because of its distinctive gold-finished body face. The gold-top's solid body cleverly combined a carved maple top bonded to a mahogany "back," uniting the darker tonality of mahogany with the brighter sound of maple.

Gibson had made a one-off all-gold hollowbody guitar in 1951 for Paul to present to a terminally ill patient whom he had met when making a special hospital appearance. This presentation guitar presumably prompted the all-gold archtop electric ES-295 model of 1952 (effectively a gold-finished ES-175) and was probably the inspiration for the color of the first Les Paul model. Almost all the other design elements

Gibson's new humbucking pickups were developed at the company's headquarters in Kalamazoo, Michigan, as illustrated in this 1950s catalog (above). The Les Paul gold-top received humbuckers in place of its original P-90 pickups during 1957, the year in which this example (below left) was made. The left-handed gold-top (main guitar) was also made in 1957, and is owned today by Paul McCartney. Gold-tops continue to be popular, as seen in this hectic Neil Young/Pearl Jam gathering (below).

guitar manufacturers

Scotty Moore used mainly Gibson guitars – including a Super 400CES and an ES-295 – to drive the sound of Elvis Presley's great Sun records.

of the first Gibson Les Paul have precedents in earlier Gibson models. For example, the instrument's layout of two P-90 single-coil pickups and four controls (which comprised a volume and tone pair for each pickup) was already a feature of Gibson's CES electric archtops that had been launched the previous year.

The general body outline and glued-in mahogany neck also followed established Gibson traditions, and the "crown"-shape inlays on the rosewood fingerboard had first appeared on the 1950 incarnation of the ES-150 model. Several Gibson acoustics had already appeared with the same scale-length as the new Les Paul.

The model came with a new height-adjustable combined bridge/tailpiece which was bar-shaped, joined to long metal rods that anchored it to the bottom edge of the guitar. This was designed by Les Paul, intended for use on archtop guitars (and Gibson also sold it as a separate replacement accessory). It proved unsuitable for the new solidbody, and was quickly replaced by a new purpose-built "stud" bar-shaped bridge/tailpiece, phased in around 1953. This was mounted to the top of the body with twin height-adjustable studs, hence the nickname.

The original gold-top sold well at first in relation to Gibson's other models. Electric guitars were clearly catching on. In 1954 Gibson's historian Julius Bellson charted the progress of the company's electric instruments. Consulting records, Bellson estimated that back in 1938 electric guitars had made up no more than ten per cent of Gibson

guitar sales, but that the proportion of electrics to the rest had risen to 15 per cent by 1940, to 50 per cent by 1951, and that by 1953 electric guitars constituted no less than 65 per cent of the company's total guitar sales.

In a move designed to widen the market still further for solidbody electrics, Gibson issued two more Les Paul models in 1954, the Junior and the Custom. The cheaper Junior was designed for and aimed at beginners, although over time it has proved itself well enough suited to straightforward pro use.

Although the outline of the Junior's body was clearly Les Paul-like, the most obvious difference to its partners was the flat-top "slab" mahogany body, finished in traditional Gibson sunburst. It did not pretend to be anything other than a cheaper guitar: it had a single P-90 pickup, simple volume and tone controls, and the unbound rosewood fingerboard bore plain dot-shape position markers. It featured the stud bridge/tailpiece as used on the second incarnation of the gold-top.

By contrast, the high-end two-pickup Custom looked luxurious. It came with an all-black finish, multiple binding, block-shape position markers in an ebony fingerboard, and gold-plated hardware. It was, naturally, more expensive than the gold-top.

The Custom had an all-mahogany body, as favored by Les Paul himself, rather than the maple/mahogany mix of the gold-top model, and this gave the new guitar a rather more mellow tone. The Custom was promoted in Gibson catalogs as "The Fretless

Existing Gibson electrics began to be fitted with humbucking pickups from 1957, including the Byrdland (1959 example, far left) and Super 400CES (1962 example, near left). The 400 also shows the "sharp" cutaway introduced in 1960, a contrast to the earlier "rounded" cutaway as seen on Scotty Moore's 400 (above).

Jimmy Page of Led Zeppelin (albums from 1969, far left, and 1971) plays one of his Les Paul Standards on-stage (below) in the 1970s.

guitar manufacturers

Wonder" thanks to its use of very low, flat fretwire, different than the wire used on other Les Pauls at the time. It was the first Les Paul model to feature Gibson's new Tune-o-matic bridge, used with a separate bar-shaped tailpiece and offering for the first time on Gibsons the opportunity to adjust individually the length of each string, thus improving intonation (tuning accuracy). These new units were gradually added to other models in the Gibson line.

In 1955 Gibson launched the Les Paul TV model, essentially a Junior in what Gibson referred to as "natural" finish – actually more of a murky beige. Also that year the original line-up of Les Paul models was completed with the addition of the Special, effectively a two-pickup version of the Junior finished in the TV's beige color (but not called a TV model).

A number of well-known players from a variety of musical styles were drawn to Gibson Les Paul models during the 1950s. These musicians included rock'n'roller Frannie Beecher, bluesmen such as Guitar Slim, Freddy King and John Lee Hooker, as well as rockabilly rebel Carl Perkins.

Gibson launched three hollowbody electrics during 1955 in a new "thinline" thinner-body style, aiming to provide instruments more comfortable than their existing deep-bodied archtop cutaway electrics which were generally around 3.5″ deep. The ES-225T, the ES-350T and the Byrdland had shallower bodies, around 2″ deep, and the

During his time with Led Zeppelin, Jimmy Page mainly used these two Les Paul Standards. His "number one" (main guitar) is probably a 1958 model, while "number two" (far left), a gift from Joe Walsh, is from 1959. Both have replaced tuners. Gibson issued a Page signature model Les Paul in 1995 (ad, above). Original 1950s Les Pauls tend to have a strip of binding in the cutaway that follows the contour of the body (below, top picture) while some Les Pauls made after that period have a deeper strip of binding (below, lower picture) that continues down to the line where the guitar's maple cap meets its mahogany "back."

403

latter two also boasted a shorter scale-length and a shorter, narrower neck, all designed for an easier, more playable feel. Top of the new line was the Byrdland, a kind of thinline L-5CES. It was inspired by country guitarist Billy Byrd and sessionman Hank Garland, hence the combined model name.

An important player who grasped the possibilities of these new friendlier electrics from Gibson was Chuck Berry, the most influential rock'n'roll guitarist of the 1950s. Berry chose a brand new natural-finish ES-350T to fuel his startlingly fresh hybrid of boogie, country and blues. In hindsight, it's remarkable that this great player did not appear in any Gibson advertising at the time – but then nor did any other black guitarists of the period.

Jazz players still kept Gibson's name prominent in the archtop electric field. Of the guitarists in the poll for the prestigious US jazz magazine *Down Beat* in 1956, Gibson could count six of the top ten as being loyal to the company: Barney Kessel (most often seen with an ES-350); Tal Farlow (also principally a 350 man); Les Paul (no prizes for guessing his six-string choice); Herb Ellis; Jimmy Raney; and Jim Hall (the last three all favoring Gibson ES-175s).

New humbucking pickups were developed by Seth Lover in the Gibson workshops. The idea was to cut down the hum and electrical interference that plagued standard single-coil pickups, Gibson's ubiquitous P-90 unit included. Lover contemplated the

Eric Clapton teamed his 1950s Les Paul Standard with a 50-watt Marshall combo for some startling work on John Mayall's 1966 album, Blues Breakers (sleeve, above), often referred to now as the peak of recorded white blues.

Keith Richards had been one of the first British guitarists to bag a Standard, having returned to Britain with one after The Rolling Stones' summer 1964 US tour. He's pictured (below left) searching for a pick with which to attack his Les Paul.

guitar manufacturers

This trio of rare and desirable Les Paul Standards illustrates the variety of visual effects brought about by the original wood used by Gibson in their production, and the way in which the paints used in the finish can change over time. This 1958 Standard (left) has a virtually plain, unfigured maple top, but with most of the original sunbursting color intact. This spectacular 1959 example (near right) is the kind that collectors dream about. The maple is highly figured, and the sunburst colors are rich and clear. The 1960 Standard shown (far right) is of a type called an "unburst" by some collectors. It has some attractive figuring in the timber used for the top, but the sunburst colors have all but faded away, leaving behind a uniform honey color. However, beyond all considerations of aesthetics and appearance, they all sound superb.

The close-up of this Standard with pickguard removed (below) reveals how the fading of sunburst colors is due to exposure to light. Where the finish has been protected under the pickguard, traces of the red paint remain. One imagines that Eric Clapton (pictured left) had little concern for the color of his Les Paul, though the supplier of the jacket might have argued otherwise.

Peter Green was in the original line-up of Fleetwood Mac (albums from 1968 and 1969, right) and did much to define the potential of the Gibson Les Paul Standard in the hands of a great guitar player.

Pictured on-stage with Fleetwood Mac in the late 1960s is Peter Green (above). The 1959 Les Paul Standard that he played with the group (main guitar) is now owned by guitarist Gary Moore. The neck pickup was famously reversed by Green and is said to aid the instrument's particular tone. Moore has, wisely, never had this modification "corrected."

guitar manufacturers

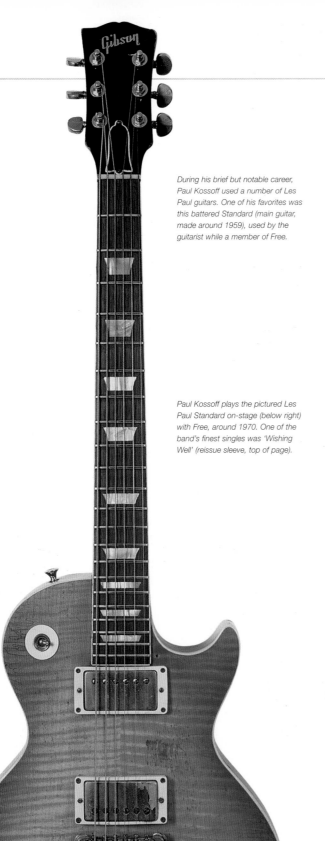

During his brief but notable career, Paul Kossoff used a number of Les Paul guitars. One of his favorites was this battered Standard (main guitar, made around 1959), used by the guitarist while a member of Free.

Paul Kossoff plays the pictured Les Paul Standard on-stage (below right) with Free, around 1970. One of the band's finest singles was 'Wishing Well' (reissue sleeve, top of page).

humbucking "choke coil" found in some Gibson amplifiers, installed to eliminate the hum dispensed by their power transformers.

From those beginnings, Lover extrapolated a pickup design that employed two coils wired together electrically "out of phase" and with opposite magnetic polarities. The result was less prone to picking up extraneous noise, in the process giving a fatter, thicker tone than single-coil types. Ray Butts came up with a similar principle around the same time while working for Gretsch.

During 1957 Gibson started to fit its electric guitars with the new humbuckers. The Les Paul Custom was promoted to a three-pickup guitar in its new humbucker-equipped guise. Today many guitarists and collectors make a point of seeking out the earliest type of Gibson humbucking pickup, which is now known as a "PAF" because of the small "patent applied for" label that is attached to the underside. The PAF labels appear on pickups on Gibson guitars dated up to 1962 (even though the patent had been granted in 1959). Some who prefer the sound of PAF-label humbuckers say that later humbuckers sound different because of small changes made to coil-winding, magnet grades and wire-sheathing.

Gibson purchased the old Epiphone brand of New York in 1957, relocating the operation to its base at Kalamazoo, Michigan. The following year Gibson released the first of its new Epiphones, effectively creating for itself a second-tier line. Some of

407

these "new" guitars continued existing Epiphone models, but others were new Epiphone equivalents of Gibson models – for example the Casino, very similar to a Gibson ES330 (but with an Epiphone logo, of course).

In fact, 1958 proved to be one of the most significant years in Gibson's entire history. During that heady 12 months the company issued the radical new Explorer and Flying V solidbodies, changed the finish of its Les Paul model to a gorgeous sunburst, introduced the brand new semi-solid ES-335 and ES-355 guitars, changed the body outlines of the Les Paul Junior and Les Paul Special to a useful double-cutaway shape, and brought out its first double-neck electric guitars. All these various designs would to a greater or lesser extent become classics over the coming years, and today some of them qualify as the most revered electric guitars ever made.

The Gibson Modernistic series of guitars was first seen in public during 1958. Fender's flamboyant designs such as the Stratocaster and the new-that-year Jazzmaster had been leaving Gibson's rather staid electric models behind as rock'n'roll burst forth. Guitar makers became increasingly aware that, beyond the usual considerations of quality and playability, there was an immense and largely untapped value in sheer visual appeal.

So the designers at Gibson temporarily set aside their customary preoccupation with curvaceously elegant forms to come up with the boldly adventurous Flying V and

Another collector's-dream Les Paul Standard (main guitar), this one made during 1960.

A few Standards were fitted with Bigsby vibratos, like this 1959 example (below left), pictured alongside some Gibson hang-tags of the period.

guitar manufacturers

Another remarkable instrument from Paul McCartney's working collection, this left-handed Les Paul Standard was made in 1960.

Paul McCartney is seen in the photo (below) holding the pictured guitar during the late 1980s.

Explorer. Here was a pair of stark, linear creations. The body of the Flying V had an angular, pointed, arrow-head shape, while that of the Explorer was an uncompromising study in offset rectangles.

Most Explorers have a long, drooping headstock with the tuners in a line on one side – a design that would later inspire the superstrat's "pointy" headstock of the 1980s. But a small number of early Explorers (sometimes referred to as Futura models) had an unusual V-shaped head.

Both Flying V and Explorer were made from Korina, which was a timber tradename for an African relative of mahogany, sometimes known as limba. Gibson used a different control layout on the V and Explorer than the one they generally employed on two-humbucker electrics: on the Modernistics, the player was offered a volume knob per pickup but just one overall tone control.

"An asset to the combo musician with a flair for showmanship," insisted Gibson's 1950s publicity for the new Modernistic pair. The company urged its dealers: "Try one of these 'new look' instruments – either is a sure-fire hit with guitarists of today!" But customers ignored the designs as too futuristic, too un-Gibson and too un-guitar. One story has a number of the new oddball Gibsons reduced to hanging as signs outside guitar shops: if you can't sell them, flaunt them.

The small numbers produced would turn the Modernistics into future collectables

of the rarest kind. In fact, only 98 of the original Flying V were made, with a further 20 or so assembled in the early 1960s from existing parts.

Gibson's factory records for the original Explorer are not so clear, but the best estimates among collectors and other experts put production at just 22 instruments, with a further 16 assembled later. A good number of reissues and redesigns of both the Flying V and Explorer has followed, especially during their bouts of popularity with metal guitarists and others in subsequent decades.

Among players drawn to the Flying V in its various guises were Albert King in the 1950s, Jimi Hendrix in the 1960s, Marc Bolan and Andy Powell in the 1970s, Mick Mars and Michael Schenker in the 1980s, and Jim Martin and Tim Wheeler in the 1990s. Perhaps more importantly (or disgracefully, depending on your viewpoint) this late-flowering popularity of Gibson's Modernistic duo of Flying V and Explorer has been the trigger for any number of outlandishly shaped solidbody guitars, especially during the late 1970s and 1980s.

A third guitar in the original 1958 Modernistic series, the Moderne, was planned but never actually reached general production or distribution, even though a patent for the design was filed in summer 1957 along with similar documents claiming the Flying V and Explorer designs. No prototype or other incarnation of the original Moderne has ever turned up, despite much searching by desperate collectors. Some keen Gibson

The Modernistic series launched by Gibson in 1958 included guitars with radical body shapes. This prototype Flying V (far left) was produced – probably in 1957 – so that Gibson's case manufacturer could design a special fitted case for the unusual guitar. Even models from the Flying V's first production run are rare, such as this 1959 example (main guitar). Despite the lack of popularity at the time, Flying Vs have attracted a number of players since, including Tim Wheeler of Ash, pictured (above) with a recently reissued model.

fans have even described this virtually fictional guitar as the company's "holy grail." If a Moderne should ever surface, it would surely be the ultimate collectable Gibson instrument. It might even prove to be the first million-dollar guitar.

Also in 1958, Gibson made a radical design-change to three of the Les Paul models, as well as a cosmetic alteration to another that would later take on enormous importance. The single-pickup Les Paul Junior and TV models were revamped with a completely new double-cutaway body shape, apparently as a reaction to players' requests for more access to the top frets than the previous single-cutaway design allowed. The new cutaways did the trick. The Junior's fresh look was enhanced with a new cherry red finish. The TV adopted the new double-cutaway design as well, along with a rather more yellow-tinged finish.

When the double-cutaway design was applied to the two-pickup Les Paul Special during the following year, the construction was not an immediate success. Gibson had overlooked the fact that the cavity for the neck pickup in the Special's new body severely weakened the neck-to-body joint. In fact, the neck could potentially snap off at this point. The error was soon corrected when Gibson's designers moved the neck pickup further down the body, resulting in a stronger joint. The new double-cutaway Special was offered in cherry or the new TV yellow (although the yellow Special was never actually called a TV model).

Sales of Gibson's Les Paul gold-top had gradually declined during the late 1950s, and so in a bid to improve sales in 1958 Gibson changed the look by applying its more traditional cherry sunburst finish. This sunburst Les Paul is generally known as the Les Paul Standard, although Gibson did not refer to it as such in their literature until 1960, and the guitar itself never bore the name.

Gibson must have deduced that the unusual gold finish of the original Les Paul model was considered too unconventional. To some extent they were proved right. Sales of the gold-top had declined from a high of 920 in 1956 to just 434 in 1958, the year of the new Standard. After the sunburst model appeared, sales then climbed to 643 in 1959. But when they dipped again in 1960, Gibson decided that this change of finish had not been enough, and that the only way to attract new customers was to completely redesign the Les Paul.

So the sunburst Standard was dropped, having existed for a little short of three years. Here again was one of Gibson's sleeping giants: almost ignored at the time, this instrument would become an ultra-collectable object in later years. Players and collectors came to realize that the guitar's inherent musicality, as well as its short production run (some 1,700 examples were made between 1958 and 1960), added up to a modern classic. This re-evaluation was prompted originally in the middle and late 1960s when a number of guitarists discovered that the Gibson Les Paul had

The other Gibson Modernistic guitar launched in 1958 was the Explorer. This first-year example (far left) has the rare early "split" headstock. This was soon changed to a "drooped" style, as seen on the Explorer (near left) made in the early 1960s from leftover parts, and with nickel-plated rather than gold-plated hardware. Eric Clapton is pictured in a 1975 Music Man amps ad playing an original Explorer, as heard briefly on the 1975 album EC Was Here.

ERIC CLAPTON in concert

enormous potential for high-volume blues-based rock. It turned out that the Les Paul's inherent tonality coupled with its humbucking pickups – played through a loud tube amp – made a wonderful noise.

Of course, this newly discovered sonic potential of the Les Paul was something that neither Gibson nor Les Paul could possibly have planned. Leading early members of the Loud Les Appreciation Society were Mike Bloomfield in America and Eric Clapton in England. Demand for the old instruments rocketed. (As we shall see, Gibson would reintroduce original-design Les Pauls in 1968.)

The original sunburst Gibson Les Paul Standard – the "burst" in guitar-speak – has since achieved almost mythological status. The revised model appeared on Gibson's November 1959 pricelist, where it was shown to have a retail cost of $280. That's equivalent to about $3,500 at today's prices, but even this is far short of the five-figure sums that genuine originals now fetch on the active collector's market. Oddly, however, the value of these instruments is not only determined by their sound or playability or rarity – but often by their individual look.

Gold-top Les Pauls mostly had maple tops made from two or more pieces of wood, safely hidden under the gold paint. Now that this maple top was on show through the transparent sunburst finish of the Standard, Gibson's woodworkers were more careful in selecting wood of good appearance, and would usually bookmatch the timber. This

More great Gibsons were first offered during 1958. The semi-solid ES-335 (1959 example, with vibrato, near right) had the thinline body style, detailed in this 1960 catalog page (above). The company's first electric double-necks were the EDS-1275 Double 12 six-string/12-string (1960 example, far right) and EDS-1235 Double Mandolin.

There have been many notable users of Gibson 300-series semi-solids through the years, including blues-boom guitarist Alvin Lee of Ten Years After, and Suede fretman Bernard Butler, who left the group to go solo later in the 1990s.

is where a piece of wood is sliced into two, then matched together like an open book, the pieces opened out down a central join to give symmetrically similar patterns.

The most celebrated "bursts" are those that display through the top's finish the most outrageous wood pattern. This is often called "flame," but more correctly "figure." Figure is caused by a kind of genetic anomaly in the growing tree that makes ripples in the cells of the living wood. The visual effect of figure is also determined by the situation of the original tree, and the way in which the timber is cut from it. Quarter-sawing – cutting so that the grain is generally square to the face of the resulting pieces – usually produces the most attractive results. The illusion can exist of roughly parallel rows of three-dimensional "fingers" or "hills and valleys" going across the face of the timber. In extreme cases this can look spectacular.

Another factor that can make sunburst Standard models look quite different from one another is color-fading. The colored paints used to create the sunburst effect, especially the red element, can fade in varying ways over time, depending primarily on how the guitar has been exposed to daylight during its lifetime. Some apparently sharp-eyed collectors claim to be able to tell exactly how long a particular guitar spent in the shop window. In some cases the original shaded sunburst will have almost totally disappeared, leaving a uniform and rather pleasant honey color on such guitars, now affectionately known as "unburst" examples.

A further innovation of 1958, and one that proved to be more successful at the time, was Gibson's new ES-335 guitar. This was a development of the company's thin-body "thinline" design that had begun with the Byrdland and the ES-350T three years earlier. When it came to the new 335, however, Gibson deployed a radical double-cutaway design, as well as the use of a novel solid block within the otherwise hollow body to create a new "semi-solid" structure.

Gibson's idea was effectively to combine a hollowbody guitar with a solidbody, not only in terms of construction but also in sonic effect. A problem for hollowbody electric guitar designers had been the screeching "feedback" that often occurred when the guitar was played with its amplifier set at high volume. The 335's solid maple block inside what Gibson described as its "wonder-thin" body tamed the feedback and combined pure solidbody sustain with the woody warmth of a hollowbody. This quality would endear the 335-style Gibson to a wide range of players, especially bluesmen such as B.B. King, but also to a number of other guitarists from jazz stylist Larry Carlton to Britpop pioneer Bernard Butler.

The "dot neck" 335 – one with dot-shape fingerboard markers and made between 1958 and 1962 – has become a prime collectable guitar. In 1962 Gibson replaced the dots with block-shape markers. Not that this makes the guitar sound less good, but collectors feel the dot-neck feature marks a "better" period of quality and

Here are three 1959-made examples of the instruments in Gibson's new double-cutaway semi-solid series: the ES-335 (far left); the stereo ES-345 (center); and the deluxe ES-355 (near left).

Punks often sought cheaper, straightforward guitars, so it's hardly surprising that Mick Jones of The Clash regularly used a double-cutaway Les Paul Junior.

manufacturing standards, and therefore denotes a more desirable instrument. Players tend to be less selective and will generally tend to choose a 335 from any period, that plays well and feels good, and that is financially within reach.

The earliest 335 models were officially named ES-335T, the "T" at the end standing for "thinline" to emphasize and underline one of its most important features. Soon, however, a "D" was added by Gibson, meaning double pickups, as well as an extra "N" for natural-finish examples, resulting in the rather overwhelming model description of ES-335TDN. The sunburst 335 was originally made in greater numbers than the natural version, which was dropped in 1960. From that year the 335 was also available in a cherry red finish, known as the ES-335TDC.

A more high-end version of the 335 model also appeared in 1958, a cherry-finish guitar that was named the ES-355. This guitar was distinguished by multiple binding on the neck, body and headstock, the latter also bearing Gibson's luxurious split-diamond inlay. The 355 generally gleamed with gold-plated hardware, as well as boasting an ebony fingerboard and a Bigsby vibrato as standard.

The idea of a stereo guitar had originally been investigated by Jimmie Webster at Gretsch in New York. He had filed a patent for a stereo pickup system in 1956, leading to Gretsch's as-ever wonderfully titled Project-O-Sonic guitars of 1958. Gibson's first take on the stereo idea, the ES-345, appeared in the following year, along with optional

stereo wiring for the ES-355. "Stereophonic" and its more common diminutive "stereo" had become buzzwords in the late 1950s, as first stereo pre-recorded tapes and then stereo records hit the market.

Gretsch's pioneering system had worked by effectively splitting each pickup on a two-pickup guitar into two, so that one pickup could feed the output from the instrument's lower three strings to one amplifier, while the other pickup sent the higher three strings out to another amp.

Gibson would certainly have known about and examined the Gretsch system, and when it came to their own stereo guitars adopted a rather more straightforward system in 1959. Gibson's two-pickup circuitry simply directed the output of each complete pickup to a separate amplifier. In contemporary advertising, Gibson assured the guitarist of the day that it would soon be customary to plug in to a pair of amps and produce "a symphony of warm, full stereophonic sound."

Another new Gibson feature in the search for fresh electric tonalities was the Varitone control, offered on the ES-345 and some ES-355s. This switch selected one of six preset tone options, in combination with the pickup selector expanding to 18 possible tonal shades.

However, Gibson's Varitone and stereo capabilities were never especially popular among guitarists. Often, players would simply disconnect the confusing Varitone and,

Gibson changed the Les Paul Junior and Special from the old single-cutaway style (as detailed in this 1957 catalog, below) to a new double-cutaway body shape, introduced during the late 1950s. This Junior (near right) dates from 1958, while the Special (center) was made in 1959. This L-5CES (far right) was made in 1964 and bears the "sharp" cutaway of that period.

Angus Young of AC/DC has long played SGs, and in this ad from 1987 he's being used to promote Gibson's new SG 62 reissue.

despite the stereo option, would just get on with playing what was undoubtedly a very good guitar in conventional "mono" mode.

Gibson's doubtless exhausted development team added one more innovation to the line during 1958: the company's first double-neck guitars. Always something of a compromise between convenience and comfort, the double-neck electric guitar was a relatively new idea, the first one having been custom-made by Paul Bigsby in California in 1952. The concept would have been obvious to Bigsby because he also made pedal-steel guitars, on which multiple necks are common.

A double-neck instrument is designed so that it can offer the player two different guitars in one instrument. An instant changeover from one neck to another saves the guitarist having to swap between separate instruments. Clearly, this is especially useful for the stage musician. The most obvious drawback to the double-neck electric is the increased weight of the resulting instrument, as well as the general awkwardness involved in reaching beyond a neck in an ideal playing position to the other that is invariably too high or too low for comfort.

Gibson launched two double-necks in 1958. The EDS-1275 Double 12 had what became the most common combination for electric double-necks, mixing a six-string and a 12-string neck. It looked something like an extended ES-175 with its twin pointed cutaways. The more unusual EMS-1235 Double Mandolin had one standard

More new designs from Gibson were the SG solidbodies, at first still called Les Paul models. These transition examples have since become known as SG/Les Pauls: this white SG/Les Paul Custom (main guitar) dates from 1962, and the cherry-finish SG/Les Paul Junior (far right) was made in 1961. A notable player of SG-style Gibsons was John Cipollina of Quicksilver Messenger Service, pictured above with his decorated SG around 1972.

six-string neck, plus a short-scale neck with six strings tuned an octave higher than a guitar, supposedly to mimic the sound of a mandolin.

These first Gibson double-necks were produced only to special order, their hollow bodies made with carved spruce tops and maple backs and sides. The instruments are rare today. Around 1962 Gibson changed the double-necks to a solidbody style, which made them look more like extended SG models. They remained custom-order-only instruments. The most famous player to opt for a Gibson double-neck was Jimmy Page who regularly used one on stage.

Gibson's first low-end solidbody – aside from earlier Les Paul Juniors – was the Melody Maker, launched in 1959. At first it had a simple "slab" single-cutaway body, though this was modified to a double-cutaway body two years later. An option was a short scale-length, another feature aimed at the smaller fingers of beginners. The last change to the Melody Maker came in 1965 when it adopted the style of Gibson's SG solidbody. This type of body design would last until the Melody Maker was dropped from the Gibson line during the early 1970s.

Considering all the Les Paul models as a whole, sales declined in 1960 after a peak in 1959. As we've seen, by 1961 Gibson had decided on a complete re-design of the line in an effort to try to reactivate this faltering model. The company had started a $400,000 expansion of the factory in Kalamazoo during 1960 which more than

This SG Standard (main guitar), made around 1965, was acquired by Eric Clapton early in 1967, probably to replace his stolen Les Paul Standard. Soon Clapton had a Dutch group of artists called The Fool paint the guitar. Clapton used the guitar widely with Cream, both on-stage (pictured far right) and on recordings such as the Disraeli Gears and Wheels Of Fire albums. Some of the original hardware has been replaced, and areas of paintwork have been restored. From 1974 the instrument was owned by Todd Rundgren.

Two more SGs are shown here (below left): an SG Special from 1966 finished in Pelham Blue that has aged to green; and an SG/Les Paul Standard from 1961 in regular cherry finish.

Eric Clapton on-stage with his painted SG (below) tests the sustain of humbuckers-and-Marshall during a Cream performance in 1967. Clapton recorded the band's Disraeli Gears album (far left) in New York in May 1967 using the SG. Dutch art group The Fool, who decorated the SG, made their own LP (near left).

Charlie Whitney used his Gibson double-neck on tour with Family. The band's set often featured songs from the second album, Entertainment, released in 1969, including their anthem 'The Weaver's Answer.'

doubled the size of the plant by the time it was completed in 1961. It was the third addition to the original 1917 factory, other buildings having been added in 1945 and 1950. But this new single-story brick-and-steel building was more than twice the size of the previous additions combined, resulting in a plant of more than 120,000 square feet that extended for two city blocks at Parsons Street in Kalamazoo. Clearly, Gibson was expecting its business to expand rapidly in the coming years.

One of the first series of new models to benefit from the company's newly expanded production facilities was the completely revised line of Les Paul models. Gibson redesigned the Junior, Standard and Custom models, adopting a new, distinctly modern, sculpted double-cutaway design. The "Les Paul" name was still used at first, but during 1963 Gibson began to call these new models the SG Junior, the SG Standard and the SG Custom. (Confusingly, the SG name had been used earlier on old-style Les Pauls: the old-design TV and Special had been renamed as the SG TV and the SG Special in 1959.) The transition models – those produced between 1961 and 1963 – had the new SG design but the old Les Paul names, and these are now known to collectors and players as SG/Les Paul models.

Les Paul's name was dropped for a number of reasons. Partly it was because the connection with the guitarist was less of a commercial bonus for Gibson than it had been. His popularity as a recording artist had declined: he'd had no more hits after

1955. Crucially, Les Paul and Mary Ford had separated in May 1963 and were officially divorced by the end of 1964, and Paul did not want to sign any fresh contract with Gibson that would bring in new money while the divorce proceedings were underway. So his contract with Gibson was terminated in 1962, and the following year Les Paul models became SG models ("Solid Guitar").

From 1964 until 1967 inclusive there were no guitars in the Gibson line that bore the name of Les Paul, either on the actual guitars themselves or in the company's catalogs, pricelists and other advertising material.

Production did increase at the Gibson factory of the new SG-style designs, with the output of Gibson Les Pauls from the Kalamazoo plant settling at just under 6,000 units every year for 1961, 1962 and 1963. SG-style solidbodies have attracted a number of players over the years, including John Cipollina, Eric Clapton, Tony Iommi, Robbie Krieger, Tony McPhee, Pete Townshend, Angus Young and Frank Zappa.

Gibson produced a number of new electric archtop signature models in the 1960s named for jazz guitarists such as Barney Kessel and Tal Farlow, both best known for their fine playing which had come to the fore in the previous decade. The body of the Gibson Barney Kessel (1961) featured an unusual double "sharp" cutaway. More successful as an instrument was the Tal Farlow model (1962), visually distinguished by an ornate swirl of extra binding at the cutaway. Back in the solidbody department,

Double-neck instruments provide the on-stage guitarist with a (relatively) portable opportunity to swap between six-string and 12-string (or bass) necks on one guitar. Family's guitar player Charlie Whitney used this Gibson solidbody EDS-1275 (right, made in 1966) throughout the band's career, and the road-weary guitar has been modified and restored over the years. Whitney is pictured with his Gibson in front of Family vocalist Roger Chapman around 1971. On the opposite page is a white EDS-1275 made in 1964, used by Steve Howe on many Yes tours. The main picture shows Rush guitarist Alex Lifeson with his similar double-neck, on-stage in 1979.

Gibson was determined to take on its chief rival, Fender, and came up with the Firebird guitars (and matching Thunderbird bass). Launched in 1963, the Firebirds clearly recognized the solidbody style of the West Coast firm while retaining the style and workmanship for which Gibson was known. Gibson called upon car designer Ray Dietrich to out-Fender Fender.

Dietrich devised the new Firebird line with sleek, asymmetrical bodies that looked a little as if Gibson's old Explorer design had been modernized with some additional curves. The new elongated body shape featured a "horn-less" upper portion that had the effect of making the lower cutaway appear to protrude further. This unbalanced "lop-sided" effect has since gained the original Firebirds the nickname "reverse body" among collectors and players.

There were four models in the 1963 Firebird line. The Firebird I had a single pickup and was the only model without a vibrato unit. The Firebird III had two pickups and a "stud"-style bridge, while the Firebird V had two pickups and a Tune-o-matic bridge. The glorious top-of-the-line Firebird VII had three pickups.

They were the first Gibson electrics to employ through-neck construction. They were also unusual in that they featured a "flipped Fender" headstock which was fitted with banjo-style tuners. This meant that players had to adjust tuning in an unfamiliar way, reaching around to the back of the headstock. But at least the design of the

Two albums from the jazz guitarists whose Gibson signature guitars are pictured here: Tal Farlow's 'Tal' from 1956 (above left) and an eponymous Barney Kessel record of the 1950s.

Another signature Gibson made in collaboration with a jazz great was the Tal Farlow model (main guitar, made in 1964). The instrument was similar to an L-5CES, but with a decorated scroll near the cutaway recalling early Gibson instruments, and a slightly shallower body.

This Barney Kessel Custom (near right) was made by Gibson during 1961, and unusually features double-cutaways on a deep body. This Custom version has gold-plated hardware, while the Regular model had nickel plating.

Eric Clapton plays his Gibson ES-335TDC (pictured right, made in 1964) at London's Royal Albert Hall in November 1968 during Cream's last tour. He may have used the 335 to record 'Badge' the same year.

Johnny Winter (1969 album, right) has regularly used a "reverse body" Firebird, as seen on a magazine cover from 1974 (far right).

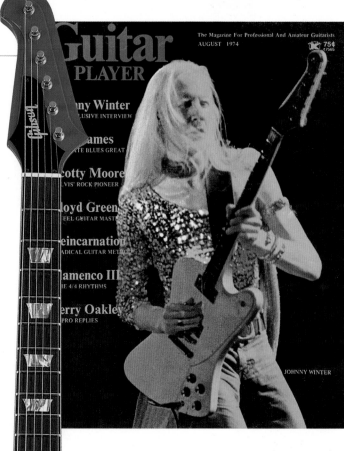

headstock showed a clean outline to the audience. The Firebirds were all fitted with special smaller-than-normal humbucking pickups which were without adjustable polepieces. Standard finish for the Firebirds was sunburst. However, Gibson went further than adopting just a Fender vibe for the new line.

The company also borrowed Fender's custom color idea, applying to the new line of guitars a range of paints more often employed to brighten up the look of the latest automobiles. One of Gibson's ten new Firebird colors was in fact identical to a Fender color. However, Gibson used the Oldsmobile name for it – Golden Mist – while Fender had opted for the Pontiac term, Shoreline Gold.

Despite the striking appearance of the Firebirds, and their prominent use in the 1960s and later by players such as Brian Jones and Johnny Winter, the ploy didn't work. Gibson's sales of electric guitars during the 1960s had to rely on classic 1950s designs such as the great semi-solid ES-335. Fender understandably complained about similarities to its patented "offset waist" design feature, pointing primarily to the Jazzmaster and Jaguar in its line, and so Gibson tried to fix things by reworking the Firebirds in 1965.

Gibson came up with a new Firebird shape that flipped the old one into a slightly more conventional if still quite Fender-like outline, known now as the "non-reverse" body. Gibson also dropped the through-neck construction in favor of its customary set-

Gibson's color chart for the Firebird models illustrates the ten optional finishes beyond sunburst, as well as instruments from the Firebird guitar and matching Thunderbird bass lines. Two of these "reverse body" Firebirds are pictured on this page: a sunburst Firebird I (far left) made in 1964, and a Firebird V (main guitar) manufactured during the following year and finished in Cardinal Red.

Phil Manzanera used this Firebird VII (pictured left, made around 1964) with Roxy Music both on-stage (above) and in the studio (first album, released in 1972, top of page).

Jimi Hendrix was best known for playing a Strat, but during the last half of 1967 this Flying V was his favorite guitar. Jimi painted the guitar himself. It's a pity he didn't paint the cover of *Electric Ladyland* (1968, left), a remarkably kitsch document that Jimi apparently hated.

guitar manufacturers

neck. The new Firebird I had two single-coil pickups, the Firebird III three single-coil pickups, the Firebird V two mini-humbuckers, and the Firebird VII three mini-humbuckers. Still unsuccessful, the Firebirds were grounded by 1969. Since then, the non-reverse Firebirds have been used even less by well-known players than the marginally more favored reverse versions. However, Oasis's new rhythm guitarist Gem Archer was to be seen on the band's 2000 dates occasionally strapping on a non-reverse Firebird, which must have pleased a number of vintage guitar dealers.

Back in the 1960s, Gibson enjoyed good sales in Britain amid the mushrooming of pop music talent there. Distribution of Gibson in Britain had been patchy until Selmer, a wholesale company that was based in London, started officially to import Gibson guitars to the UK during 1960. In fact, British musicians had virtually been starved of any American-made guitars between 1951 and 1959, thanks to a government ban on importation during that period.

Selmer was in the right place when the ban was lifted. The company's famed retail store in London's Charing Cross Road was at the heart of an area alive with music publishers, small studios and instrument retailers, a mecca for both the budding and successful musician. Jeff Beck bought his first Les Paul Standard from the Selmer store; Steve Howe purchased his favorite ES-175D there; and Robert Fripp acquired his prized Les Paul Custom at the store in 1968.

As noted earlier, Gibson had since the 1930s used the Kalamazoo brand – named for the location of its factory in Michigan – for cheaper products unworthy of the full Gibson marque. In 1965 the Kalamazoo brand was revived as Gibson decided to feed a strong demand for bargain electric guitars. At first the entry-level Kalamazoo electrics had Fender-style offset cutaways, although later in the 1960s a shape more like Gibson's own SG was adopted. A handful of different models appeared in this KG series, but they were all dropped by the turn of the decade.

There was a newly revised version of the Flying V launched by Gibson during the second half of the 1960s. The reworked model had more conventional hardware than the original late-1950s V, without the through-body stringing. Gibson also redesigned the control layout for these models first issued during 1967, with the three knobs now forming a triangular group rather than the three-in-a-line style of the original. These new-style Vs would stay in the Gibson catalog until the late 1970s.

Guitar sales in general in the United States – including acoustic as well as electric instruments – had climbed throughout the early 1960s, hitting a peak of some 1,500,000 units in 1965, after which sales declined and fell to just over a million in 1967. CMI's sales of Gibson guitars and amplifiers hit a fiscal peak of $19million in 1966, but then began to fall in line with the general industry trend, and were down to $15million-worth by 1968. As well as the general decline in demand for guitars,

Gibson revised the Firebird body design in 1965 to the "non-reverse" shape seen on these two examples: a Firebird I from 1965 (far left) and a Firebird III made in 1966. The catalog from the same period illustrates the other two models in the line, the Firebird VII and Firebird V.

Gibson's production had been hit by a number of strikes in the 1960s, including a 16-day stoppage in 1966. Gibson president Ted McCarty and his number two, John Huis, left that year after purchasing the Bigsby musical accessories company of California, which they re-established in Kalamazoo.

In February 1968, after a number of short-stay occupants in the president's chair, Stan Rendell was appointed as the new president of the Gibson operation. Rendell immediately set about his task of improving the company's fortunes.

Meanwhile, as we've seen, the blues-rock boom had made players aware of the potential of old Les Paul guitars. Musicians began to hunt for the instruments, and prices for secondhand examples began gradually to climb. Gibson at last decided to do something about their deteriorating position in the electric guitar market, and specifically about the increasing demand for their old-style Les Paul guitars.

Les Paul's musical activities had been very low-key since the mid 1960s, but in 1967 he began a new association with Gibson that resulted in a reissue program for Les Paul models. By the time Stan Rendell became president of Gibson in early 1968 the decision to re-commence manufacturing Les Paul guitars had been made by the CMI management in Chicago, principally by Maurice Berlin and Marc Carlucci, and a new contract was negotiated with Paul. For some reason, Gibson decided to re-introduce the relatively rare two-humbucker Les Paul Custom, and the gold-top Les

Paul with P-90 pickups and Tune-o-matic bridge. They were launched at a June 1968 trade show in Chicago. Gibson's ads publicizing the revived guitars admitted that the company had virtually been forced to re-introduce the guitars: "The demand for them just won't quit. And the pressure to make more has never let up. Okay, you win. We are pleased to announce that more of the original Les Paul Gibsons are available." The new Les Pauls sold well, and Gibson clearly had a success in the making. The only mystery so far as many guitarists were concerned was why they'd waited so long.

An important change to Gibson's ownership occurred in 1969. The new owner, Norlin Industries, was formed that year with the merger of Gibson's parent company, CMI, with ECL, an Ecuadorian brewery. The Norlin name was arrived at by combining the first syllable of ECL chairman Norton Stevens' name with the last syllable of that of CMI founder Maurice Berlin.

Norlin was in three businesses: musical instruments, brewing, and "technology." The takeover was formalized in 1974 and Maurice Berlin, a man widely respected in the musical instrument industry, was moved sideways in the new structure, away from the general running of the company.

Many people who worked at Gibson during this period feel that there was a move away from managers who understood guitars to managers who understood manufacturing. Some of the instruments made during the period soon after Gibson

Gibson reintroduced original-design Les Paul models in 1968 after a number of years when guitars with the SG design had replaced them. Shown on this page are the two "new" models, both made in 1968: the revived gold-top (near right, this one with some non-standard features on the headstock) and a Custom (center). The Les Paul Deluxe model was introduced in 1969. This example from about 1975 (far right) is in a custom blue sparkle finish.

guitar manufacturers

A 1972 ad for the Les Paul Recording model, highlighting the multiple controls that left most musicians somewhat baffled.

The Les Paul Recording model replaced two earlier models with low-impedance pickups, the Les Paul Personal and Professional, in 1971. This example of the Recording (main guitar) was made around 1972. A British catalog of the period details the Recording and its matching bass guitar, the Les Paul Triumph.

were taken over have a bad reputation today. The new owners are generally felt now to have been insensitive to the needs of musicians. Clearly this was a sign of the times, as economic analysts were busily advising many of the big corporations that they should diversify into a range of different areas, pour in some money... and sit back to wait for the profits.

There was a shift in emphasis at Gibson toward the rationalization of production, and this meant that changes were made to some of the company's instruments built during the 1970s (and, to some extent, to those made into the 1980s). Generally, such alterations were made for one of three reasons. The first and apparently most pressing requirement was to save money. Second, Gibson wished to limit the number of guitars returned for work under warranty. Lastly, there was a distinct desire to speed up production of Gibson guitars at the Kalamazoo factory.

The guitar design department at Gibson gave a change of style and name to the recently re-introduced Les Paul gold-top model in 1969, when the Les Paul Deluxe took its place. The Deluxe was the first "new" Les Paul model for 14 years, and was prompted by calls for a gold-top with humbucking pickups rather than the single-coil P-90s of the existing reissue model.

Gibson ended up using small Epiphone humbuckers for the Les Paul Deluxe model that were surplus to requirements. At first the Deluxe was only available with a gold

Les Paul Triumph Bass

Les Paul Recording Guitar

The first Les Paul model with an f-hole was the Les Paul Signature (1976 example here), a gold-finished guitar with low-impedance pickups.

427

top, but gradually sunbursts and other colors were introduced, and it lasted in production until the mid 1980s.

Back in the 1950s and 1960s one of guitarist Les Paul's more out-of-step tastes had been for low-impedance pickups. Today, low-impedance elements are more often used as part of a pickup design, thanks to improvements in associated components, but back then Paul was largely on his own. The vast majority of electric guitars and guitar-related equipment was (and still is) high-impedance.

The chief advantage of low-impedance is a wide and all-encompassing tonal characteristic. This might appear at first to be an advantage, but in fact the tonal range offered isn't necessarily to everyone's taste. Another disadvantage is that low-impedance pickups must have their power boosted at some point before the signal reaches the amplifier (unless the player is plugging the guitar straight into a recording studio mixer, as Les Paul did).

When Paul had gone to Gibson in 1967 to discuss the revival of Les Paul guitars, he'd talked with great passion about his beloved low-impedance pickups, and how Gibson should use them on some of their instruments. So in 1969 along came the first wave of Gibson Les Paul guitars with low-impedance pickups: the Les Paul Professional and the Les Paul Personal. The Personal was, as the name implied, in keeping with one of Paul's own modified Les Paul guitars, even copying his odd feature

of a microphone socket on the top edge of the body. The Personal and Professional had a complex array of controls, seemingly aimed at recording engineers rather than guitarists. These included an 11-position Decade control, "to tune high frequencies," a three-position tone selector to create various in- and out-of-circuit mixes, and a pickup phase switch. The Personal also provided a volume control for that handy on-board microphone input. Both guitars required connection with the special cord supplied, which had an integral transformer to boost the output from the low-impedance stacked-coil humbucking pickups to a level suitable for use with normal high-impedance amplifiers.

Predictably, the guitars were not a great success, and did not last long in the Gibson line. Their rather somber brown color, achieved with a natural mahogany finish, could not have helped in an era when most of the competition was busily turning out simple guitars finished in bright colors.

The company did have another go at low-impedance instruments during 1971. First, Gibson decided to scale down the body size of the Professional/Personal style, virtually to that of a normal Les Paul, and to give it a contoured back. Second, the company located the still-necessary transformer into the guitar itself, and provided a switch on the guitar to give either low-impedance output or normal high-impedance output. Third, Gibson re-titled the guitar to the more appropriate Les Paul Recording. It

guitar manufacturers

The Les Paul Artisan (near right, from 1982) had a fancy fingerboard; the S-1 (far right, from 1976) unusually for Gibson had a bolt-on neck. Meanwhile, Al DiMeola promotes the L-6S (above).

would remain in the line until 1980. Another low-impedance-equipped model came along in 1972, the L-5S. The name of this single-cutaway solidbody alluded to Gibson's great old electric hollowbody model, the L-5CES – but beyond that, any obvious kind of connection was unclear.

There seemed to be even less chance of guitarists being attracted to low-impedance pickups on an instrument that didn't even have the cachet of the Les Paul name. So it was that a few years into its life the new L-5S was changed from low-impedance pickups to regular humbuckers – but that still made no difference to its popularity. Even the use of the new L-5S by the fine jazzman Pat Martino had apparently little impact on other musicians. Gibson's final fling with low-impedance pickups was reserved for the company's thinline style, and was launched during 1973 as the two-pickup gold-colored Les Paul Signature.

Some of the new Signature model's controls were similar to those found on previous low-impedance models, but an extra feature on the Signature was the inclusion of two jack sockets. One was on the side of the body, for normal high-impedance output; the other on the face of the body was for connection to low-impedance equipment such as recording mixers. (A similar facility was offered on the final version of the Recording model.) The Signature models never really fired players' imaginations, and by the end of the 1970s they were out of production. By now Gibson

A luxurious high-end guitar, even by Gibson's sometimes lofty standards, was The Les Paul. The instrument was made in very limited numbers from 1976 to 1979 at Gibson's original factory at Kalamazoo, Michigan. Work there on these special new Les Pauls was at first overseen by local luthier Dick Schneider. Very fine rosewood and maple was used for many of the parts of The Les Paul that would not normally be made from wood, and the result was a very beautiful and, at $3,000, a very expensive instrument. Two magnificent examples from the run of under 100 The Les Pauls are shown on this page: number 48 (main guitar, alongside its highly-figured back), completed on March 8th 1978; and number 51 (far left) which was finished two days later.

employed around 600 people at its Kalamazoo factory, and was producing something like 300 guitars every day. Demand for guitars had increased during the early 1970s, and so management decided to build a second Gibson factory at Nashville, Tennessee, some 500 miles south of Kalamazoo. Recent strikes at Gibson had cost Norlin dear, and the new plant of 100,000 square feet was also constructed with a view to decreasing costs through advantageous labor deals.

Work began in 1974 on the new facility, five miles to the east of Nashville, and the factory eventually opened in June 1975. Gibson's original intention was to keep both Kalamazoo and Nashville running. Nashville was designed to produce very large quantities of a handful of models, while Kalamazoo was more flexible and had the potential to specialize in small runs. Nashville was thus the obvious choice to produce the models in Gibson's solidbody line required in the greatest volume at the time – the Les Paul Custom and Deluxe models – along with various other solidbody models.

As if to highlight the contrast between the capabilities of the two plants, Gibson introduced two new Les Paul models in 1976. First was the Les Paul Pro Deluxe, effectively a Deluxe with P-90 pickups and an ebony fingerboard. It was produced in large quantities at Nashville.

The other new model was The Les Paul, a spectacular limited-edition model that was notable for Gibson's employment of various fine woods for virtually the entire instrument. Many parts that on a normal electric guitar would be made from plastic were hand-carved from rosewood. These included the pickguard, backplates, control knobs and truss-rod cover.

Raw bodies and necks of attractive maple and an ornate ebony and rosewood fingerboard for the The Les Paul were produced at Gibson's Kalamazoo factory. Further work on the multiple colored binding, abalone inlays and handmade wooden parts was continued at the workshop of freelance luthier Dick Schneider, who was based about a mile from the factory in Kalamazoo.

Very few of The Les Pauls were made, with probably well under 100 produced from 1976 to 1979, primarily in the first year. During this time Schneider moved away from Kalamazoo, and later examples of The Les Paul were therefore produced entirely at the Gibson factory. As the limited stocks of Schneider's handmade wooden parts ran out, so normal plastic items were substituted, along with less ornate binding.

Each example of The Les Paul had a numbered oval plate on the back of the headstock. Number 25 was presented to Les Paul just prior to the 1977 Grammy Awards ceremony where Paul and Chet Atkins received a Grammy award for their *Chester & Lester* album. The $3,000 price tag on The Les Paul made it four times the cost of the next most expensive Les Paul model on the 1976 pricelist. During the previous year, Gibson had in fact introduced a number of other new models and a

Three guitars with Gibson's new active circuitry are shown on this page: an RD Artist from 1979 (near right); a Les Paul Artist (center) made in 1979; and an ES Artist (far right) that dates from 1980.

reissue. These included a revitalized Explorer, plus two new solidbodys: the all-maple single-cutaway L-6S, as endorsed by Carlos Santana, and the Les Paul-shape bolt-on-neck Marauder with humbucker and angled single-coil pickups. The S-1 was a sort of three-pickup Marauder that also sported that model's V-shape headstock, and it joined the line in 1976. None of these lasted long.

The 25/50 Les Paul was intended to celebrate Les Paul's 25th year with Gibson (presumably it had been planned for 1977) and his 50th year in the music business. The silver and gold themes generally associated with these anniversaries were reflected in the guitar's chrome- and gold-plated hardware, while Chuck Burge in Gibson's R&D (research and development) department designed the special intricate inlay in pearl and abalone on the guitar's headstock.

The guitar bore a three-digit edition number on the back of the headstock as well as a standard serial number. Once again Les Paul himself was presented with a special example: this time he received guitar number one at a party given in his honor by Gibson, who launched the Les Paul 25/50 Anniversary model during 1978. Despite its relatively high price the Kalamazoo-made 25/50 sold well, bringing into sharp focus for Norlin the ready market for more costly Les Paul models

Gibson's new RD models first appeared in 1978, and incorporated a package of complex "active" electronics. This kind of circuit had been popularized by Alembic at

This V-II (far left) from 1981 updated the Flying V with "boomerang" pickups and a sandwiched walnut-and-maple construction. Gibson's Heritage Series Standard 80 (main guitar, 1980) was an early attempt to recapture previous glories. The ads here are for the gold-top's 30th Anniversary model (1982, above) and 1979's The SG (below).

the start of the 1970s and was designed to boost the signal and widen the tonal range of a guitar. The circuit was powered by an on-board battery. The body of the RD series was an even curvier version of the previous decade's Firebird "reverse body" design.

This kind of "hi-fi" guitar was prompted by the apparent competition from synthesizers, which had become big business during the late 1970s. Gibson's parent company Norlin figured that a hook-up with Moog, one of the synthesizer field's most famous names of the time, might re-capture some of the ground that guitars seemed to be losing to the new keyboards.

In fact one of the RD models – the Standard – was a regular electric, without the active circuit, which was reserved for the Custom and Artist models. Gibson's RD line did not, however, prove popular and was soon gone from the catalog. Many guitarists disliked what they considered the "unnatural" sounds of active circuitry, and this was a major factor in the downfall of the RD series. Gibson believed that the radical styling was more to blame for the lack of popularity, and moved to combine the RD technology with some of its traditional body designs.

In 1979 Gibson did this, expanding the RD concept into two of its more mainstream electric series, the ES thinlines and the Les Pauls. Gibson had to re-design the large RD circuit board to fit into these more confined body designs. Each of the new Artist models had three knobs, for volume, bass and treble, and three switches for brightness, expansion and compression. However, these models also failed to grab many guitarists, and the Artists did not last for very long: the Les Paul Artist hobbled on to 1981, while the ES Artist managed to last until 1985.

A happier project was the Les Paul Heritage Series, one of the first conscious attempts by Gibson to try to make Les Pauls in a way that many players thought was no longer possible. A reasonably healthy market had been building since the late 1960s in so-called "vintage" guitars (which used to be called merely "secondhand," or "used," or just plain "old guitars").

This trend was fueled by the general feeling that Gibson "didn't make them like they used to," combined with the prominent use of older instruments by many of the most popular guitarists of the day. While to some extent this was flattering in general to the Gibson name (and to others such as Fender and Gretsch whose guitars were also associated with the vintage trend), it did not help a manufacturer whose main priority was to continue to sell new guitars and especially its new models.

Some US dealers such as Strings & Things and Music Trader who specialized in older instruments had already begun to order selected new models with vintage-style appointments from Gibson's Kalamazoo plant, which since the onset of the Nashville factory was beginning to lean more heavily toward shorter, specialized runs of guitars. For the Heritage Series Les Pauls, Gibson's team used a 1954 pattern sample for the

Nobody seemed ready for the sheer ugliness of Gibson's Corvus model (1983 example, near right; ad, below, from 1984). Better was the Les Paul Spotlight Special (1983, center) with its central walnut block between some beautiful maple. This prototype Explorer (far right) was made in 1980 as a pattern for the limited-edition Explorer Heritage reissue of 1983.

carving of the body top, changed the then-regular neck construction to three-piece mahogany, disposed of then-current production oddities such as the "volute" carving below the back of the headstock, and moved a little closer to older pickup specifications. Especially attractive maple was selected for the tops of these new Les Paul models, which were touted as limited editions and were not included on the company's general pricelist.

Launched in 1980, the two Heritage Series models were the Heritage Standard 80 and the Heritage Standard 80 Elite, the latter with an ebony fingerboard and an even more desirable "quilt" figured maple top.

Whether as a result of the influence of the Heritage models or a general awareness of market demands, Gibson began at this time to rectify some of the general production quirks instituted in the 1970s, removing from its standard models the volute, for example, and gradually reverting to one-piece mahogany necks.

An oddity issued in 1980 was the Les Paul-shape Sonex 180 which had what Gibson called a Multi-Phonic body. This was in fact a wooden core with a plastic outer skin, following a relatively shortlived 1980s trend for experimental non-wood guitars. The Sonex lasted less than four years in the Gibson line. The idea for a combination of wood and non-wood materials would find a firmer foundation with Parker in the 1990s. Also during 1980 Gibson issued one of its first signature guitars for a black player, the

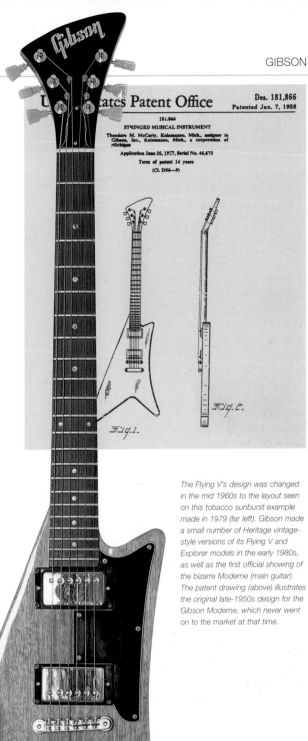

The Flying V's design was changed in the mid 1960s to the layout seen on this tobacco sunburst example made in 1979 (far left). Gibson made a small number of Heritage vintage-style versions of its Flying V and Explorer models in the early 1980s, as well as the first official showing of the bizarre Moderne (main guitar). The patent drawing (above) illustrates the original late-1950s design for the Gibson Moderne, which never went on to the market at that time.

double-cutaway thinline B.B. King model, in Standard and Custom versions. Both had stereo wiring and were without f-holes, the Custom adding a Varitone six-way tone selector. The King models were based on the Gibson ES-355 that had been the great bluesman's favored instrument since 1959. The Standard was dropped in 1985, but the Custom soon became known as the Lucille – "Lucille" is King's nickname for his cherished 355 – and is still in Gibson's line at the time of writing.

The Victory MV models of 1981 were yet further attempts by Gibson to compete directly with Fender, the exaggerated Strat-like bodies clearly influenced by the California competitor. The Victorys were gone from the line by 1984.

During the early 1980s Gibson continued to attempt to update its image, as it had during the previous decade, but in the process was coming up with some wildly inappropriate new designs – none more so than the ugly Corvus line of 1982. The Corvus was available (though largely unpurchased) with one, two or three pickups, and had a peculiar body shaped like a misguided can-opener. While it would be kind to say that other companies were also trying odd-shaped models at this time, the Corvus models must be some of the most pointless guitars ever created. These too were gone from the Gibson pricelist by 1984.

Despite such aberrations, Gibson was also becoming more and more aware of the value of its old, hallowed "traditional" designs. We've already seen how this had

Since 1959 B.B. King has played one of Gibson's ES-355 models, affectionately known to the great bluesman as Lucille (and seen on album sleeves from 1992 and 1967, top of page). Gibson first issued a signature King model in 1980 (promoted in the 1981 ad, above), and one remains in the Gibson line today – this B.B. King Lucille (main guitar) was produced in 1998. Gibson's reissue program was stepped up in the early 1980s, and increasingly accurate repros have since appeared. This '59 Flametop Reissue (far right, this page) was made in 1987.

prompted the Heritage Les Paul series in 1980. During the next few years – and with even less publicity – Gibson also put into production a small number of Heritage-series versions of the old Flying V and Explorer, modeled as close as possible on the originals, including the use of korina wood.

More unusually, Gibson also produced a recreation of the third "missing guitar" of the original late-1950s Modernistic series. The peculiar Moderne had never been put on sale back then, but in 1982 it finally appeared as part of the limited-edition korina-body Heritage series, looking as if the lower half of a Flying V body had been lopped off and curved away underneath. The club-shape headstock of the Moderne was unusual too, and the overall impression was that Gibson's initial decision in the 1950s had been correct.

Gibson, aware of the continuing demand at the monied end of the market for "vintage" Les Pauls, realized that the Heritage Series of 1980 had only been a half-hearted approach to recreating the most celebrated old Les Pauls.

So in 1983 a proper reissue program was instituted by Gibson. These reissue guitars have been known over the years by a number of different titles, including Reissue Outfits, Replicas and, at the time of writing, the Historic Collection. Gibson's reissue series stepped backward and forward at the same time, using old specs but made with modern methods. By 1985 the company's pricelist showed a gold-top

Reissue and a sunburst Standard Reissue, effectively high-quality versions of the existing sunburst-finish and gold-top Les Paul models, the former with a selected "curly" maple top.

Gradually since then Gibson has tried gradually to improve the authenticity and accuracy of its reissues, driven by the persistent demands of fastidious customers who seek "perfect" duplication of those hallowed 1950s originals. In a way, that will never happen, of course. Trying to recapture the past is an expensive and largely impossible business. But that does not stop some guitar manufacturers making an attempt.

At present the basic reissue sunburst Standard is referred to as the 1959 Les Paul Flametop because of its general proximity to a 1959-style model with "flamed"-maple top. Little "corrections" have been made since the reissue model's introduction in 1983, including moves to a smaller-sized vintage-style headstock; the use of especially attractive figured maple for the top; the adoption of carving that matches the original body contours; re-tooling of the neck for similar reasons of authenticity; a slight reduction in the neck pitch; holly veneer for the headstock face; "correct" routing of the control cavity; early-style Tune-o-matic bridge; and the reinstatement of a longer and wider neck "tongue" at the neck/body joint.

Other reissue Les Pauls in the Historic Collection on Gibson's 2000 pricelist included the 1958 Plaintop and Figured Top, the 1960 Flametop, the 1952, 1954,

Three more Gibson guitars on this page: a Chet Atkins Country Gentleman (far left) made in 1998; a Les Paul Studio Lite (center) made in 1992; and (near left) a Les Paul Studio Lite/M-III from 1993.

1956 and 1957 Goldtops, the 1954 and 1957 Custom Black Beautys (two or three pickups), and single- or double-cutaway Juniors and Specials. At a high price, these bring accurate reproductions of the classic Les Paul originals within the grasp of mere (wealthy) mortals.

During the early 1980s Norlin decided to sell Gibson. Sales fell by 30 per cent in 1982 alone, to a total of $19.5million, against a high in 1979 of $35.5million. Of course, Gibson was not alone in this decline. The guitar market in general had virtually imploded, and most other American makers were suffering in broadly similar ways. Their costs were high, economic circumstances and currency fluctuations were against them, and Japanese competitors increasingly had the edge.

A hostile takeover of Norlin by Rooney Pace occurred in 1984, and chairman Norton Stevens was off the board. Norlin had relocated some of its administration personnel from Chicago to Nashville around 1980. All the main Gibson production was now handled at the Nashville plant. Kalamazoo had become a specialist factory making custom orders, banjos and mandolins, and as far as Norlin was concerned its closure became inevitable.

The last production at Kalamazoo was in June 1984, and the plant closed three months later, after more than 65 years' worthy service since the original building had been erected by Gibson. It was of course an emotional time for managers and workers,

many of whom had worked in the plant for a considerable time. Three of them – Jim Deurloo, Marv Lamb and J.P. Moats – rented part of the Kalamazoo plant and started their new Heritage guitar company in April 1985. Although the emphasis at the Nashville plant had been on large runs of a small number of models, this had to change when it became Gibson's sole factory.

Norlin had put Gibson up for sale around 1980, and by summer 1985 they finally found a buyer. In January 1986 three businessmen – Henry Juskiewicz, David Berryman and Gary Zebrowski, who had met while classmates at Harvard business school – completed their purchase of the Gibson operation for a sum undisclosed at the time, though since confirmed as $5million.

The inevitable "restructuring" of the Gibson business occurred, and as seems so often to be the case in such undertakings many employees lost their jobs. However, today the company appears to be relatively healthy again. As well as tailoring the reissue program to sensible and defined areas, the new owners – with guitar-fan Juskiewicz at the helm – also continued to attempt innovations and to introduce new models. However, such new designs still apparently had little effect on players who thought that Gibson meant classics.

Luck played a part, however: Chet Atkins had severed allegiance with the Gretsch company, and now switched to Gibson. A number of "signature" electric thinline

Gibson may have originated the "drooped" headstock style back in the late 1950s for the Explorer, but during the 1980s it was better known on guitars from makers like Charvel. Here are three guitars that reclaimed the feature for Gibson: a Spirit II XPL (near right) made in 1985; an Alpha Q-3000 (center) made in Gibson's Custom Shop in 1985; and a US-1 that dates from 1987.

guitar manufacturers

436

hollowbodies appeared from 1986, not dissimilar in style to some of the well-known Gretsch Chet Atkins models, but with distinct Gibson touches. Models include the Country Gentleman and the Tennessean.

The superstrat-like US-1 model debuted during 1986 and introduced musicians to a new idea from Gibson in the construction of solidbody guitars. For the new US-1, the company decided to employ a core of "chromite" (balsa wood) at the heart of the guitar, primarily for the material's low weight and its resonant qualities. Chromite had the effect of reducing the weight of the maple-top US-1, and Gibson also applied the new material to the Les Paul Studio Lite model in 1991.

New in 1991 was the solidbody M-III line, a series of radically styled double-cutaway guitars fitted with flexible circuitry. The M-III guitars used the popular humbucker/single-coil/humbucker pickup layout, in the process aiming to provide Stratocaster-like and Les Paul-style tones from a five-way switch.

Unfortunately, Gibson's customers felt the design and the electronics of the new M-III guitars were, again, too "un-Gibson," and they did not rush to buy the instruments. So it was that in a move reminiscent of the marriage of RD and Artist ten years before, Gibson decided to apply the electronics from the strange M-III to the more familiar environment of the Les Paul design. This resulted in two new models, the Classic/M-III and the Studio Lite/M-III. However, even this made little difference to players'

Three more relatively recent Gibsons on this page: an SG-90D (far left) from 1988; an M-III Standard (center) made in 1991; and an ES-135 (near left) that dates from 1993. The 1993 Historic Collection ad (above left) marks a change of name for Gibson's program of reissuing its most famous vintage instruments.

allegiances, and the original M-IIIs as well as these Les Paul versions were gone from the Gibson line by the late 1990s.

Gibson's first official Custom Shop had started in the 1960s at Kalamazoo, building one-offs to customers' requirements, although of course non-standard orders had been undertaken from the company's earliest days. The Custom Shop idea was revived in the 1980s at Nashville, running from 1983 to 1988, and has now been running again since another new start in 1992.

The present Custom Shop at Gibson continues the traditional role of making oddities for wealthy players, but also provides more mainstream inspiration for the current Custom Shop Collection series that includes everything from a Zakk Wylde signature Les Paul to Tony Iommi's SG model.

The most recent new solidbody from Gibson was the single-cutaway humbucker/single-coil/humbucker Nighthawk, launched in 1993 in Standard, Special and Custom guises, but dropped by the end of the decade. Semi-hollow versions, the Blueshawk and B.B. King Little Lucille, followed in 1996 and 1999.

A relatively simple cosmetic alteration provided Gibson with its Gothic series that first appeared in 1999, with matt black finish and matt black hardware. Two of the models chosen for this line of instruments aimed at the solid rocking guitarist were obvious: the Flying V and the Explorer. However, the all-black 335 was a more

surprising choice, and did not last in this particular category of Gibson's Designer Collection, which also finds room to contain models such as the Explorer 1976 and EDS1275 double-neck reissues.

Reissue "repros" of more vintage glories were featured in Gibson's 2000 catalog, including Firebirds, Flying Vs, 175s, 295s, 335s, Explorers, CESs and SGs. These are in addition to a long list of Les Paul reissues, some of which were mentioned earlier. One interesting addition to the burgeoning line of Gibson's "new/old" Les Pauls was the Aged 40th Anniversary model, which first appeared in 1999. Essentially, this was yet another move toward a more accurate reproduction of those hallowed 1959-period flame-top Les Paul Standards. The engineers at Gibson responsible for this particular attempt explained that they had virtually started again from scratch (which is what they usually say), finding new sources of materials and components.

But the major difference with the 40th Anniversary recreation was, however, the aged finish. There's no doubt that this was influenced by the success that Fender had found with its Relic series, introduced in the mid 1990s after the company had almost jokingly displayed a couple of aged repros of early models at a trade show – and received an incredibly positive reaction (for which read many orders from dealers visiting the show). So it was that a trained team at Gibson set about giving the 40th Anniversary model a look that suggests it has actually been gigged and used for 40

Forwards and backwards with Gibson in the 1990s: a Nighthawk Special (near right) from 1993; the first '60 Corvette (center) made by the Custom Shop in 1995, with the look of a 1960 Chevrolet Corvette transferred to a six-string; and a signature Wes Montgomery (far right) that steals a pickup from an L-5CES, this one made in 1997.

guitar manufacturers

New signature models have continued to appear from Gibson's Nashville factory. Joe Perry, guitarist with glossy metal band Aerosmith, was honored by a Les Paul signature model (main guitar), this one made in 1997. The Tak Matsumoto ad (below left) is from the following year, while a rash of metallic signatures breaks out on a Japanese ad from 1999 (above left) for the Gibson Custom Shop.

guitar manufacturers

years. Thus the paint colors were made to appear faded, the nickel parts on the instrument such as the pickup covers were realistically tarnished, the lacquer "skin" was cracked and effectively dulled, and there were all manner of dings and knocks over the guitar. Like Fender and its Relics, Gibson aimed to recreate the almost indefinable allure of a vintage guitar with this model – at a stiff price, of course.

More signature models have also appeared from Gibson, including an L-5CES named for Wes Montgomery (1993) that reproduces the great jazzman's custom requirement of a single pickup, as well as Les Pauls for Jimmy Page (1995), Joe Perry (1996), Slash (1997), Ace Frehley (1997) and Peter Frampton (2000). As these latest models come off the Gibson production line in Nashville it's curious to observe that the company's classic designs, many of which are dozens of years old, seem more than ever before to reflect the needs of contemporary musicians.

At the start of the 21st century the Gibson group of companies enjoyed annual revenues of around $200million and had 1,200 employees. It must be apparent to them that, among the greatly increased competition of today's guitar market, Gibson is uniquely placed to serve up its own true, traditional flavor – but with all the benefits of the improvements made in modern manufacturing. Gibson guitar designs look set for many new adventures, in the hands of succeeding generations of inspired musicians, and in the care of its industrious creators.

Gibson has continued to build its reissue program in recent years, recreating many of its most revered models of the past in new, modern versions. This Historic Collection Firebird VII (main guitar) is a fine example. It left the company's Nashville factory during 1999, although the vibe is unashamedly of the early 1960s.

Two more recent Gibson models are pictured below. This Les Paul DC Standard (below left) is a double-cutaway version of the company's most famous solidbody, made in 1998. The Flying V Gothic (below) is a black-finished ultra-rock machine, this one dating from 1999.

guitar manufacturers

GITTLER

"Less is more" was the philosophy behind the unique minimalist guitars of inventor Allan Gittler. Born in 1928, Gittler made his first electric guitar – basically a wooden neck – while living in New York City in 1974. This quickly evolved into a stainless steel headless "skeleton" built around a central rod or "spine" on to which were mounted machined-tube frets. There was also a small pickup housing and a volume control, plus knurled knobs to tune strings that were tied at the nut. A moveable "arm" served as an armrest or legrest. In 1982, Gittler changed his name to Avraham Bar Rashi and emigrated to Israel, where his guitars were built by the Astron company from 1986-87. As a concession to guitarists who needed more neck, some featured a metal extension behind the frets. Bar Rashi's more recent pear-shaped guitars were still minimalist, fashioned from plywood, with frets made of nylon fishing line and wing-nuts for tuners.

GODIN

This large Canadian maker has popularized "synth-access" guitars, and is also among those offering "hybrid" instruments that mix electric and acoustic qualities.

The company is located in Canada and the US, headed by Robert Godin. Godin first set up his LaSiDo shop in La Patrie, Quebec, in the early 1980s to build replacement electric-guitar necks and bodies. Soon LaSiDo was building instruments and parts for a number of big-name guitar brands – this continues today – but also developed its

The Canadian-based Godin company produced this G-1000 (main guitar) during 1996. Earlier attempts by Godin at solidbody electrics had leaned heavily on Strat-style and Tele-style shapes, but for the Artisan and then this G-1000 a more original design was employed. Allan Gittler's peculiar guitar (below, far left) is little more than a skeleton that retains merely the essential elements of an instrument. This example was made in Israel by Astron Engineering around 1986. The skeleton itself is made from stainless steel, and this one has "open" frets, although some examples were made with an optional "back" to the neck, situated behind the wishbone-shape fret system. The adjustable "spar" seen sticking out at an angle from behind the tiny body serves as an armrest or legrest. The instruments were not made beyond the 1980s.

own models, for which Godin is the sole electric brand. LaSiDo is still best known as a maker of acoustics and electro-acoustics (making brands such as Seagull, Norman, Simon & Patrick etc). Godin came to prominence with its innovative Acousticaster model of 1987, a Telecaster-size bolt-on-neck electro-acoustic with unusual harp-shape "sound fork" under the bridge, designed to improve the guitar's response.

Moves by Godin into the market for solidbody electric guitars proved relatively unsuccessful for the company until the launch of its LG-X model in 1994. This was a "synth-access" guitar – in other words an instrument with special built-in pickup and circuitry that enables it to be linked directly with (and control) a remote synthesizer module, thus giving the guitarist access to synth sounds. Guitar synthesizers had foundered in the 1980s due to poor compatibility with the synthesizers available, but this new MIDI-based system offered better performance.

The Les Paul-style LG-X now heads a small series of similar instruments, some also with piezo "acoustic"-sounding bridge pickups. The LG-XT of 1998, for example, incorporated the piezo-loaded L.R. Baggs vibrato X-bridge, and as such offers the adventurous player the potential for a variety of different sounds and applications from one instrument. Godin's first synth-access guitar had in fact been the Multiac, launched in 1993, which was a thinline nylon-strung electric-acoustic, and it's joined in the Godin line today by the Multiac Classical and Multiac Steel, plus the budget-price

Solidac. The LGX-SA was a further Godin aimed at players who prefer a solidbody feel. Despite this innovation and industry, the mass-produced, well-made Godin line lacked "classic" styling. So in the late 1990s attempts were made to introduce some guitars with retro-inspired designs. These included the Radiator, launched in 1999, which illustrated a desire by Godin to go beyond its specialist status and move into the mainstream market. Certainly Godin guitars are unusual in offering hybrid pickups and synth-access, but they are almost an underground force within the guitar industry, and at present lack star-name users to attract younger players to their undoubtedly innovative instruments. Godin now also has factories in Berlin, New Hampshire, and Princeville, Quebec, as well as at the original location in La Patrie.

GODWIN

During the 1970s Sisme, Italian owner of Godwin organs, aimed also to attract guitarists with the ambitious Super Professional Guitar-Organ. It looked impressive, with a vast array of controls, and was big on weight and body dimensions, essential to accommodate the copious electrics. As with the ill-fated Vox guitar organ, frets were wired to tone generators and string contact completed the circuit, creating the "organ" sound. Results could be convincing but performance was, predictably, erratic. In marked contrast, the company later issued a straightforward, Les Paul-like Godwin six-string, which also went nowhere.

Two more Godin guitars are shown on this page. This LG-XT (near right) from 1998 is a modern "hybrid," mixing normal electro-magnetic electric sounds with "acoustic"-like tones from its piezo bridge pickups. The Radiator (1999 example, center) was Godin's retro model. This Godwin Guitar-Organ (far right) from around 1976 required serious study of its multiple controls in order to coax a convincing organ sound.

GORDON-SMITH

The longest-running British manufacturer, Gordon-Smith has operated since 1975 when Gordon Whittam and John Smith started making guitars. Whittam established the shortlived Gordy brand in 1984, but John Smith remained, producing models such as the Graduate, Gypsy and the start-up GS series. Smith's original symmetrical double-cutaway shape based on the Les Paul Junior became established as a good quality workingman's guitar, low on style but offering a notoriously Gibson-like tone with added upper-frequency sparkle. Smith continues today, designing his own vibratos, making his own pickups, and employing a unique one-piece neck construction.

GOYA

Levin in Sweden provided some of the first acoustic guitars imported into the US, branded Goya and sold from 1952 by Hershman of New York and David Wexler of Chicago. By 1959 Hershman's Goyas also included Swedish-made Hagstrom sparkle- and swirled-plastic-covered electric hollowbodies.

Hershman switched to Italian-made solidbody and hollowbody electric guitars and basses, including the Rangemaster models with Burns-style pickups and controls, until about 1970. In 1966 the Goya name had passed to Avnet (Guild). It later went to Kustom and then Martin, who imported Japanese Goya solidbodies around 1980 but mainly used the name on imported acoustics.

Goya was a brandname used for guitars imported to the US from various sources. At the end of the 1950s it appeared on the Swedish company Hagstrom's sparkle-top electrics (1959 ad, above), while this Rangemaster of 1968 (near left) came from Italy, probably originating at Eko. This Gordon-Smith Gypsy "60" SS hollowbody (far left) dates from 1997.

GRETSCH

Making a distinctive mark with some visually arresting guitars, Gretsch has attracted some key players in its long history, including Chet Atkins, Duane Eddy and George Harrison. The company's founder, Friedrich Gretsch, emigrated to the United States from Germany in 1872 at the age of 16.

After working for a manufacturer of drums and banjos in New York City, Gretsch set up his own Fred Gretsch Manufacturing Company there in 1883 to make drums, banjos, tambourines and toy instruments.

Friedrich's son Fred, the eldest of seven children, took over at age 15 on his father's premature death in 1895. During the next five years Fred Sr, as he became known, added mandolins to the company's drum-making and banjo-making operations. In 1916 construction was completed of a large ten-story building at 60 Broadway, Brooklyn, just by the Williamsburg Bridge. This imposing building continued to house the factory and offices of the Gretsch company for many years.

In the early 1930s the guitar began to replace the banjo in general popularity, and about 1933 the first Gretsch-brand guitars appeared, a line of archtop and flat-top acoustics. They were offered alongside Gretsch's burgeoning wholesale list of other makers' instruments, including guitars from the "big two" Chicago manufacturers, Kay and Harmony. The first Gretsch-brand archtop electric was introduced around 1939,

One of Gretsch's earliest electric guitars was the Electromatic Spanish hollowbody model, pictured in the 1950 catalog (left) alongside a number of more popular lap-steel electrics. The Electro II (main guitar, 1954 example) helped to set Gretsch's more modern cutaway electric archtop style, and would soon evolve into the Country Club model. The Country Club was one of the instruments that started a notable line of color options that Gretsch began to offer at this time. This 1955 Country Club (opposite page, left) is finished in Cadillac Green, further enhanced by gold-plated hardware. The Duo Jet was Gretsch's first "solidbody" electric (actually semi-solid), this one (opposite, center) made in 1955. Another Gretsch color, Jaguar Tan, is seen on this Streamliner (opposite, right), also made in 1955.

The old-fashioned look of this Corvette, made in 1955, would soon give way to Gretsch's new cutaway electric models.

guitar manufacturers

Jimmie Webster was the guitar-playing brain behind many Gretsch guitars and gadgets. He's pictured in the early 1950s (right) playing with his tapping-like "touch" system on a Gretsch Electro II model.

the shortlived Electromatic Spanish model, which was made for Gretsch by Kay. At this time Fred Sr was still nominally president of Gretsch, but in fact had effectively retired from active management in the early 1930s to devote himself to banking. He officially retired from Gretsch in 1942.

Fred Sr was replaced as company president in 1942 by his third son, William Walter Gretsch, generally known as Bill, who headed Gretsch until his premature death at the age of 44 in 1948. Bill's brother Fred Gretsch Jr, already the company's treasurer, then took over as president. It was Fred Jr who would steer the company through its glory years during the 1950s and 1960s.

After World War II was over, Gretsch placed a new emphasis on supplying guitars for professional musicians. The first new Gretsch electric guitar of the post-war era revived the Electromatic Spanish model name, this archtop debuting in 1949 alongside a number of Synchromatic acoustic guitars. The single-coil pickup of the Electromatic Spanish was the first of many made for Gretsch by Rowe Industries of Toledo, Ohio, a company run by Harry DeArmond. A few years later that DeArmond pickup would receive its official Gretsch name, the Dynasonic.

Cutaway-body electrics followed in 1951, the Electromatic and Electro II, in effect proving that Gretsch now took seriously the expanding electric guitar business. Helping to launch the models was a new Gretsch man, Jimmie Webster, a qualified piano-tuner

and inspired guitarist. Webster used an unusual "touch" playing system, similar to that popularized much later by Eddie Van Halen. Webster became an important ambassador for Gretsch, probably doing more than anyone else in the coming years to spread the word about Gretsch guitars, as well as doing much in the process to promote electric guitars and guitar-playing in general.

Gretsch certainly noticed the new solidbody electric guitar that Fender began marketing during 1950, mainly because the upstart California company chose to call it the Broadcaster. This was a model name that Gretsch still used – although spelled "Broadkaster" – for a number of its drum products. (Gretsch had made drums since its earliest days, and was important for its pioneering work in new manufacturing techniques, as well as instigating the significant switch among jazz drummers to smaller-size drums in the kit during the 1940s.)

At Gretsch's request, Fender dropped the Broadcaster name, changing it to Telecaster (which was a more appropriately modern name, anyway). When Fred Jr saw that Fender and Gibson were actually beginning to sell these new-style solidbody guitars, he acted swiftly. In 1953 Gretsch launched its first solidbody, the single-cutaway Duo Jet. In fact, the guitar was a semi-solid with routed channels and pockets inside, but the visual effect was certainly of a solidbody instrument. In its early years the new Duo Jet had, unusually, a body front covered in a black plastic material, as

George Harrison bought this 1957 Gretsch Duo Jet (main guitar) early in 1961, and is pictured that year (above) posing proudly with his first treasured American guitar alongside his fellow Beatles (drummer Pete Best was still in the group at that time). Harrison used the Duo Jet throughout the group's rise to fame, only retiring it when he acquired a double-cutaway Gretsch Country Gentleman in summer 1963.

guitar manufacturers

Two keen Gretsch players: Bo Diddley with a keen jacket and a Jet Firebird, rather more sedate than some of the custom-shape guitars that Gretsch made for him around 1960. Jeff Beck used a Duo Jet to record his 1993 album Crazy Legs, a tribute to Gene Vincent – and more especially to Vincent's Duo Jet-toting guitarist Cliff Gallup.

used on some Gretsch drums. It also had Gretsch's unique two-piece strap buttons (an early take on the idea of locking strap buttons) and the Melita Synchro-Sonic bridge.

The Melita was the first bridge to offer independent intonation adjustment for each string, beating Gibson's Tune-o-matic version by at least a year. Three more solidbodies in the style of the Duo Jet were added to the Gretsch line in 1954 and 1955: the country-flavored Round Up, the Silver Jet, and the red Jet Fire Bird. The Silver Jet came with a silver sparkle finish on the front of its body, and this was another product of Gretsch's helpful drum department.

That same year in the hollowbody lines the non-cutaway Electromatic Spanish became the Corvette, the cutaway Electro II became the Country Club, and the Electromatic became the Streamliner. The Country Club would go on to be the most enduring model name in Gretsch's history.

Another significant addition to the Gretsch line in 1954 was the option of colored finishes for some models, beyond the normal sunburst or natural varieties. We've already noted the company's use of drum coverings on the Silver Jet and the black Duo Jet, but equally flamboyant paint finishes were on the way.

Automobile marketing was having a growing influence on guitar manufacturers in the early 1950s, and the theme was especially evident in Gretsch's colorful campaign of 1954, with a Cadillac Green option for the Country Club and a Jaguar Tan (a sort of

dark gold) for the Streamliner. The paints came from DuPont, a company that also supplied most of the car companies at that time (and later Fender too). Gretsch drew yet again on its experience in finishing and lacquering drum products in different colors, artfully applying know-how that already existed within the operation to help make its guitars stand out in the market.

There had been isolated precedents for colored-finish guitars, such as Gibson's all-gold ES-295 and gold-top Les Paul of 1952, as well as Fender's infrequent and as-yet unofficial custom colors. But for a few years Gretsch made the use of color into a marketing bonus almost entirely its own. Through the middle 1950s Gretsch added a number of pleasant two-tone options – yellows, coppers, ivories – contrasting a darker body back and sides against a lighter-colored body front, for example on archtop electrics such as the Streamliner (launched 1954), Convertible (1955) and Clipper (1956). This two-tone style was yet further evidence of inspiration from long-standing techniques used in the drum department.

The success of Gibson's new Les Paul guitar – well over 2,000 were sold in 1953 alone – alerted other manufacturers, including Gretsch, to the value of a "signature" model endorsed by a famous player. Today the practice is very familiar, but back in the 1950s it was a new, exciting and potentially profitable area of musical instrument marketing. Around 1954 Jimmie Webster succeeded in securing talented Nashville-

Three desirable Gretsch Jet models are pictured on this page: a Duo Jet (far left) from 1958; a Jet Fire Bird (center) made in 1960; and a Silver Jet (near left) that dates from 1955.

447

based country guitarist Chet Atkins for this role, a move that in time would completely turn around Gretsch's fortunes.

After various discussions and meetings between the company and the guitarist, the Gretsch Chet Atkins Hollow Body 6120 model appeared in 1955. Atkins wasn't keen on the Western paraphernalia that Gretsch insisted on applying to the guitar – including cactus and cattle inlays, and a branded "G" on the body – but relented because he was so keen to get a signature guitar on to the market.

In fact, the decorations on the Hollow Body model were gradually removed over the following years. Gretsch had also given ground by adding a Bigsby vibrato to the production model, in line with Atkins's request. There was a Chet Atkins Solid Body, too, essentially a Round Up with a Bigsby vibrato – although, despite the name, the Solid Body still had Gretsch's customary semi-solid construction. Atkins had little to do with the Solid Body model, and it was dropped after a few years.

The Hollow Body, however, became Atkins's exclusive instrument for his increasingly popular work. It remained one of the most famous Gretsch models for many years, and Gretsch did good business from the new endorsement deal. Its 1955 catalog trumpeted: "Every Chet Atkins appearance, whether in person or on TV... and every new album he cuts for RCA Victor, wins new admirers to swell the vast army of Chet Atkins fans." The new Chet Atkins model effectively put Gretsch on the map. Not

This Chet Atkins Hollow Body (main guitar) was made in 1955, the model's launch year, and has all the Western paraphernalia: G-brand on body; engraved fingerboard markers; steer's head on the headstock. Gretsch used Atkins's name extensively, not just on guitars but on accessories such as strings too.

The Solid Body (far left, 1956 example) was the less popular semi-solid version of the first Chet Atkins models, despite Atkins appearing in ads such as this 1955 promo (below left). The catalog from that same year shows both the Hollow and Solid Chet models with special Gretsch Western straps attached.

Chet Atkins has worked constantly in Nashville recording studios (with Country Gent guitar, below) making records with everyone from The Everly Brothers to Elvis Presley. His own albums (1960 example, left) have been a brilliant source of inspiration to other guitar players.

This 1955 Chet Hollow Body model (right) is an early production sample that was sent to Chet Atkins by Gretsch. The control layout and bridge are not standard.

Two great fans of Gretsch guitars were Stephen Stills and Neil Young, who included their White Falcons among the guitars used for this 1970 Crosby Stills Nash & Young album, Deja Vu (left).

content with the coup of attracting Chet Atkins to the company, however, Jimmie Webster also devised Gretsch's brand new high-end sensation, the White Falcon. First marketed by Gretsch in 1955, it was an overwhelmingly impressive instrument. The guitar's single-cutaway hollow body was finished in a gleaming white paint finish, as was the new "winged" design headstock, and both bore gold sparkle decorations again borrowed from the Gretsch drum department.

All of the White Falcon's metalwork was finished in gold plate, including the deluxe Grover Imperial tuners with "stepped" buttons and the stylish new tailpiece – since nicknamed the "Cadillac" because of its V shape similar to the auto company's logo. The fingerboard markers of the White Falcon had suitably ornithoid engravings, and the gold plastic pickguard featured a flying falcon about to land on the nearby Gretsch logo. It was, simply, a stunner.

"Cost was never considered in the planning of this guitar," boasted the Gretsch publicity. "We were planning an instrument for the artist-player whose caliber justifies and demands the utmost in striking beauty, luxurious styling, and peak tonal performance and who is willing to pay the price." To be precise, $600. The next highest in the line at the time was a $400 Country Club. Gibson's most expensive archtop electric in 1955 was the $690 Super 400CESN – but by comparison that was a sedate, natural-finish product of the much more conventional Kalamazoo-based company.

The luxurious White Falcon first appeared in 1955, and this first-year example has all the classic early Falcon features. The guitar has proved a great posing instrument over the years, with players such as Billy Duffy of The Cult (above left, with a 1970s model) drawn to the Falcon's magnetic charm. The Gretsch catalog from 1961 (above) has a pair of Falcons: regular mono on top; stereo version below.

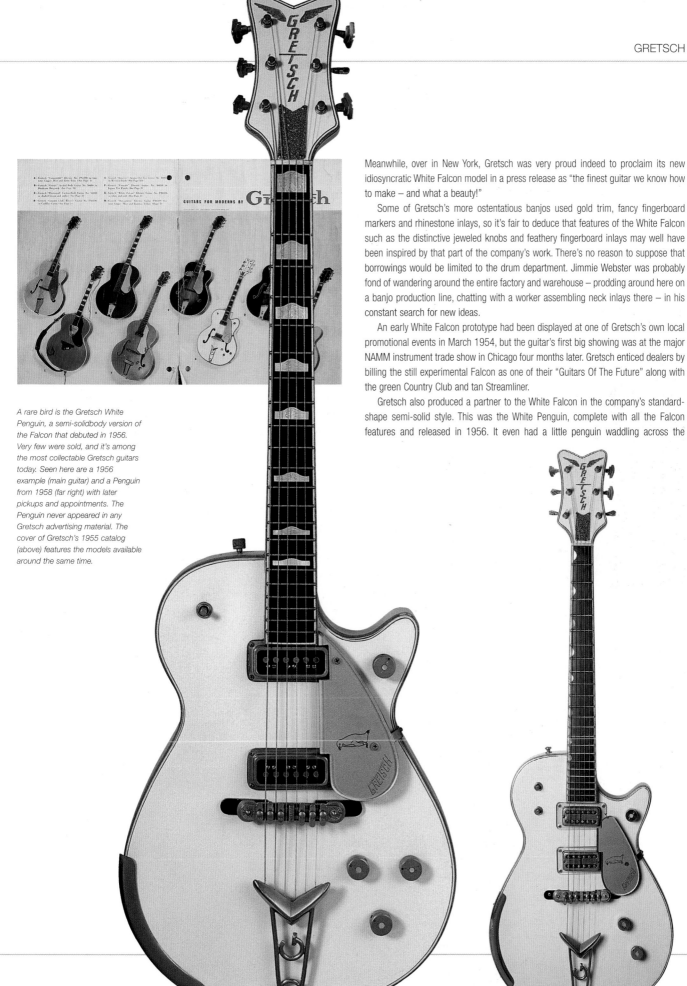

A rare bird is the Gretsch White Penguin, a semi-solidbody version of the Falcon that debuted in 1956. Very few were sold, and it's among the most collectable Gretsch guitars today. Seen here are a 1956 example (main guitar) and a Penguin from 1958 (far right) with later pickups and appointments. The Penguin never appeared in any Gretsch advertising material. The cover of Gretsch's 1955 catalog (above) features the models available around the same time.

Meanwhile, over in New York, Gretsch was very proud indeed to proclaim its new idiosyncratic White Falcon model in a press release as "the finest guitar we know how to make – and what a beauty!"

Some of Gretsch's more ostentatious banjos used gold trim, fancy fingerboard markers and rhinestone inlays, so it's fair to deduce that features of the White Falcon such as the distinctive jeweled knobs and feathery fingerboard inlays may well have been inspired by that part of the company's work. There's no reason to suppose that borrowings would be limited to the drum department. Jimmie Webster was probably fond of wandering around the entire factory and warehouse – prodding around here on a banjo production line, chatting with a worker assembling neck inlays there – in his constant search for new ideas.

An early White Falcon prototype had been displayed at one of Gretsch's own local promotional events in March 1954, but the guitar's first big showing was at the major NAMM instrument trade show in Chicago four months later. Gretsch enticed dealers by billing the still experimental Falcon as one of their "Guitars Of The Future" along with the green Country Club and tan Streamliner.

Gretsch also produced a partner to the White Falcon in the company's standard-shape semi-solid style. This was the White Penguin, complete with all the Falcon features and released in 1956. It even had a little penguin waddling across the

Rockabilly maestro Brian Setzer has long been a Gretsch lover, and he's pictured above with some of his collection. Gretsch honored the guitarist in 1993 with a signature guitar. This 1955 White Falcon was once owned by Setzer, with some of his extra glitz on the headstock.

pickguard. Very few White Penguins were sold, and the model has since become regarded as one of the most collectable of all Gretsch guitars.

Gretsch benefited from some big success stories among two early rock'n'roll guitarists, both of whom used Chet Atkins Hollow Body guitars to power their sound. Eddie Cochran was an accomplished guitarist who landed a cameo spot in the 1956 movie *The Girl Can't Help It* and then made some blasting rock'n'roll with his Hollow Body at the center of a churning mix of rockabilly, country and blues.

Duane Eddy turned out a string of hit records from the late 1950s, based on his deceptively simple instrumental style that will forever be known by the word that was attached to so many of the guitarist's albums: Twang! That twangy tone came when Eddy concentrated on playing melodies on the bass strings of his Hollow Body. He made full use of the pitch-bending potential of the guitar's Bigsby vibrato, as well as exploiting his amplifier's tremolo effect and the studio's echo facilities.

Ray Butts, a music store owner and electronics wizard from Cairo, Illinois, met Chet Atkins in 1954 and showed the guitarist his new combination amplifier that offered echo from a built-in tape loop, an unusual facility at the time. Atkins and players such as Carl Perkins and Scotty Moore became customers for Butts's amp. Then Atkins, who didn't like Gretsch's DeArmond pickups, asked Butts to come up with an improved type of pickup. Butts devised a humbucking model, around the same time that Seth Lover

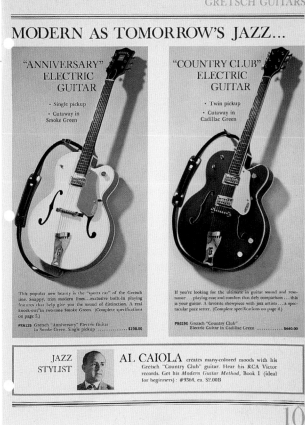

Three more fine Gretsch guitars are shown on this page: a single-cutaway Chet Atkins Country Gentleman (far left) from 1961; a "Single" Anniversary model (center) made in 1959; and a "Double" Anniversary (near left), with two pickups, that dates from 1961. Gretsch's control layouts are often unusual. The one-pickup guitar here has a single volume control near the cutaway and a tone-selector switch opposite. The two-pickup guitars here have a master volume control on the cutaway, a tone-selector switch for each pickup, and a volume control per pickup in the "normal" position, near the bridge. The 1959 catalog (above) also shows these layouts, on a one-pickup Anniversary and a two-pickup Country Club.

LIVING STEREO · RCA VICTOR

Jimmie Webster was a keen advocate of stereo guitars and stereo records. He made Unabridged (left) in 1958, playing a Gretsch White Falcon Stereo. It was one of the earliest guitar albums to be recorded in stereo.

over at Gibson in Michigan formulated his humbucker. Gretsch was fitting the new Filter'Tron pickups to most electrics by 1958.

Two new models in the Chet Atkins series were the dark brown Country Gentleman and the red Tennessean. The Country Gent, new in 1957, was the first Gretsch hollowbody to be made with a thinline body – about two inches deep, unlike most of the company's existing hollowbodies which were around three inches deep. The thinline concept had been popularized by Gibson in the preceding years.

The Country Gent was also the first Gretsch Chet Atkins model to be offered with a slightly wider 17″ body, like the company's White Falcon, Country Club and Convertible. The Hollow Body (and indeed the new Tennessean) was closer to 16″ wide. The Gent had what are generally referred to by players and collectors as "fake" f-holes. These have a visual representation of f-holes on the body, to help the general look of the guitar, but are without actual apertures. The Gretsch f-holes would not revert to true holes until the early 1970s.

Atkins had tried to convince Gretsch that in order to cut feedback – and moreover to enhance the guitarist's beloved sustain – it would be useful to make the Country Gent's hollow body more "solid" at certain points by adding wooden reinforcement inside. In fact, what Atkins wanted was a guitar that had a solid wooden section running through the center of the body from neck to tailpiece – exactly as Gibson had done on

its ES-335 model that debuted in 1958. Gibson also needed this solid center to mount the bridge and humbucking pickups that it used at the time, but as Gretsch employed a floating bridge and non-height-adjustable humbuckers they had no need for this facility. Gretsch was content merely to add twin strengthening braces under the top of the Country Gentleman's body.

The new Space Control bridge appeared around this time, another Jimmie Webster design. It was simpler than the Melita, and lacked intonation adjustment. Also new were "Neo-Classic" half-moon-shape markers at the edge of the fingerboard, which appeared around 1957.

In 1958 Gretsch marked the 75th anniversary of the company's founding with a pair of special Anniversary model guitars. These were offered in one- and two-pickup versions that have since been nicknamed as the Single Anniversary and Double Anniversary models. Remarkably, they lasted in the Gretsch catalog until as late as 1977. Meanwhile, the tireless Jimmie Webster collaborated with Ray Butts to come up with the first stereo guitar system, "Project-O-Sonic." At first they achieved a stereo effect by splitting the output of the pickups, sending the sound of the top three strings to one amplifier and the bottom three to another.

This stereo circuitry was first launched as an option on the Country Club and White Falcon models during 1958. Various modifications appeared over subsequent years,

Jimmie Webster devised Gretsch's new stereo guitar system. The two guitars pictured on this page are a White Falcon Stereo (near right) from 1958 and a Country Club Stereo (far right). Webster is seen (above) in about 1962 with a later-style White Falcon Stereo model.

but stereo seemed too complex to capture many players' imaginations. Another questionable piece of Webster weirdness was "T-Zone Tempered Treble," which translates to the more simple description "slanted frets." Webster claimed that they improved intonation. The White Falcon and the new high-end Viking model bore the skewed frets from 1964, the fingerboard helpfully marked with offset dot markers in the slanted zone to warn innocent players.

The Country Gent, Hollow Body and White Falcon changed to a double-cutaway style during 1961 and 1962. Gibson was as ever the primary inspiration for this decision: since 1958 the Kalamazoo guitar-maker had increasingly employed double cutaways to successful effect. With such a body design, players could more easily reach the higher frets of the fingerboard and make fuller use of this upper register when soloing. George Harrison, who'd previously used a Duo Jet, was a very visible player of the double-cutaway Country Gentleman in the 1960s.

Gretsch's solidbody line moved to a double-cutaway style too, from 1961. Also that year, Gretsch decided that it needed a cheaper solidbody that could compete with Gibson's Les Paul Junior, and so came up with the low-end Corvette (a name borrowed from an early archtop model). This was the company's first true solidbody guitar, and came complete with HiLo'Tron single-coil pickup. The Gretsch Corvette started life with a "slab" body like the Junior, but subsequently gained beveled-edge contours, aping

GEORGE HARRISON
of the BEATLES
and his
GRETSCH CHET ATKINS COUNTRY
GENTLEMEN GUITAR

Gretsch changed many of its models to a double-cutaway style from about 1961. The Country Gent followed the trend: this example (main guitar) was made in 1963. By far the most influential player of the model was George Harrison, seen in a Gretsch publicity shot from 1964 (above). The Chet Atkins Hollow Body also gained a double-cutaway body at the time; this one (far left) dates from 1962.

The 1963 catalog (left) showed the
solidbody Corvette in its amended
contoured style, alongside a double-
cutaway Duo Jet.

Gibson's new SG design. During the early 1960s, Gretsch went on to toy with a number of peculiar solidbody designs – and the Bikini was certainly among the oddest. It consisted of a hinged, folding body-back which could accept slide-in, interchangeable guitar and bass necks. The body-backs were in both single- and double-neck styles. Few Bikinis were made.

The colorful Princess model of 1962 was, according to the boys at Gretsch, "engineered to meet the needs and standards of young women all over the world." Gretsch had, in fact, simply finished the later-style Corvette in special pastel color combinations designed to appeal to the delicate female sensibility.

Another opportunist solidbody based on the Corvette was the Twist of 1962, exploiting the contemporary dance craze. It sported a pickguard with a twisting red and white "peppermint" design. The Astro-Jet of 1963 was a very strange looking guitar, almost as if it had been left out too long on a hot Brooklyn summer day and melted into several disfigured lumps. It also had an apparently randomly styled headstock, with four tuners on one side, two the other.

During the guitar boom of the middle 1960s Gretsch decided to move its drum department out of the Brooklyn factory to another location a few blocks away, while a good deal of the company's wholesaling operations were either ceased or moved to the Chicago office. All this was to allow the whole of the seventh floor in Brooklyn to be turned over to guitar making, not least because of the popularity afforded Gretsch by George Harrison's prominent use of a Country Gentleman.

No Harrison signature model ever appeared, but Gretsch did produce a shortlived Monkees model to cash in on the TV pop group of the 1960s. Through a marketing deal the group featured Gretsch instruments including drums and the company's 12-string thinline electric introduced in 1966. The six-string Monkees model that Gretsch issued that same year had the group's distinctive guitar-shape logo on the pickguard and truss-rod cover.

By the mid 1960s models such as the high-end White Falcon came fitted with a gamut of guitar gadgets created by the ever-fertile mind of Jimmie Webster. They included the weird slanted frets in the upper register that we've already seen. Additionally there was a "standby" on/off switch, which on a stereo-equipped model meant a total of two control knobs and six switches, as well as a couple of levers behind the back pickup to operate padded string-dampers.

Also, the vibrato tailpiece would sport a telescopic adjustable arm, while a Floating Sound frame-like device sat on a "fork" passing through the body and contacting the back. It was positioned in front of the bridge with the strings passing through it and was supposed to enhance tone and increase sustain. Webster's inspiration came from the tuning forks he used regularly as a piano tuner. Thus the top-of-the-line Gretsch

Three Gretsch Corvette-style guitars are pictured on this page: an early-type Corvette (near right) from about 1961; a pastel-colored Princess (center) made in 1962; and a custom-finished "Gold Duke" Corvette (far right) from 1966.

models of the day were probably the most gadget-laden instruments on the market, assaulting players' imaginations with a plethora of possibilities. But some musicians were simply scared off.

Shockwaves had been sent through the guitar manufacturing industry in 1965 when the Fender companies were sold to the Columbia Broadcasting System corporation for $13million. D.H. Baldwin, an Ohio-based musical instrument company specializing in the manufacture of pianos and organs, was like many actively seeking to purchase a guitar-making operation at this time. In 1965 it had bid unsuccessfully for Fender. So Baldwin bought the Burns guitar company of England (see Baldwin) and then, in 1967, Gretsch.

Baldwin began to diversify away from its original core of music and into financial services, including banking and insurance. The company's Annual Report for 1969 noted a 12 per cent drop in Gretsch sales, conveniently attributing over half the fall to a three-month strike that began in October 1969.

By 1970 plans were underway by Baldwin to move the Gretsch factory out of its 54-year-old home in Brooklyn to a site in Booneville, Arkansas, well over 1,000 miles away. Baldwin already operated a number of factories there, enjoying cheaper and more amenable labor. Of course, the move did not please an already disgruntled workforce at Gretsch, and very few personnel made the move south-west in September

The peculiar Astro-Jet (main guitar, from 1966, plus side view, above) made few friends for Gretsch. Other models in the line had gained a double-cutaway shape, including the Silver Jet (1969 example, far left). A double-cutaway Jet Fire Bird and Duo Jet feature in the 1961 catalog.

Jazzman George Van Eps promotes his Gretsch seven-string guitar in this 1969 ad (left). The Monkees received Gretsch gear (1967 magazine cover, right) in return for Gretsch marketing an endorsed guitar (pictured below, center).

1970. The Brooklyn building continued to house Gretsch sales until that too was moved, first to the Illinois office and then in 1972 to Baldwin's HQ in Cincinnati, Ohio. Thus by the summer of 1972 the very last Gretsch connection had been severed with 60 Broadway, Brooklyn, New York City.

Before production moved in 1970 from Brooklyn to Booneville there was a period when Gretsch made a number of limited-run instruments for various retailers, players, teachers and so on. Not that Gretsch had ever been shy of custom work, most famously exemplified by the handful of odd-shaped solidbodies it made for Bo Diddley around 1960. Some Gretsch personnel have suggested that the company was more likely to do custom work in the summer months – when other business was slower. And collectors have always noted Gretsch as a brand where, as a result of its flexible approach to custom orders, almost anything is possible.

Small-order batches in the 1960s included specially modified models for Gretsch dealers such as Sam Ash (Anniversary-style with cat's-eye shape soundholes), Sam Goody (twin-cutaway archtop with "G"-shape soundholes) and Sherman Clay (gold- and silver-finish Corvettes, later nicknamed the Silver Duke and the Gold Duke).

Special small-run "signature" guitars were also made, including a limited number for New York-based player/teacher/store-owner Ronny Lee, as well as some six- and seven-string models named for guitarist George Van Eps (the seven-string version of

Coming in at the high end of the Gretsch line was the new Viking model (1967 example, near right). The Monkees gained TV fame and a Gretsch signature guitar (center), this one made in 1967. An early example of the seven-string guitar was Gretsch's Van Eps model (far right). The one pictured dates from 1977.

This 1969 catalog page promotes the new Van Eps seven-string and the double-cutaway version of the Streamliner model.

which remained in the catalog for ten years). Around 1940 the Epiphone company had built Van Eps a custom guitar based on his unusual requirement for a seven-string model, adding a low-A below the existing E-string (over 40 years before Steve Vai came up with a similar idea).

Van Eps once explained that the reason for the additional low A-string was based on his love of deep basslines, and because he approached the guitar as a complete instrument within itself, almost a mini-orchestra.

Gretsch produced the Van Eps single-cutaway archtop models from 1968, in six-string as well as the seven-string versions. This underlined once again the company's compliant approach, enabling the manufacture of small numbers of limited-appeal instruments – even if it did mean tooling-up for the unique 14-pole humbuckers necessary for Van Eps's seven-string.

The first new Gretsch model of the Baldwin era was the undistinguished twin-cutaway thinline Rally, although it did have an unusual built-in active treble-boost circuit. More interesting, though hardly devastating, was a new line of Chet Atkins models. In 1972 the Deluxe Chet and the Super Chet were launched. The big, deep-body, single-cutaway archtop style was the result of a collaboration between Chet Atkins and Gretsch men Dean Porter and Clyde Edwards. The highly-decorated Super Chet sported an unusual row of control "wheels" built into the pickguard's edge, while

the plainer Deluxe Chet had conventional controls. The Deluxe did not last long, but the Super stayed in the line for some seven years.

Two new low-end guitars came along in 1975, the Broadkaster solidbody and semi-hollow electrics. As usual Gretsch was to some extent following Gibson's lead – and on this occasion the path was an unpopular one. Gibson had launched the Marauder, its first solidbody guitar with a Fender-style bolt-on neck, in 1974; likewise, the Broadkaster solidbody was the first Gretsch with a bolt-on neck, while also displaying strong Strat-style influences. Neither of these new Gretsch guitars drew much praise.

More new Chet Atkins signature models appeared in 1977. These were the effects-laden Super Axe, plus the gadget-less Atkins Axe. The distinctive look of these big new solidbody guitars with their sweeping, pointed cutaway was the subject of a patent issued to Gretsch designer Clyde Edwards for "ornamental design." Both were gone from the line by 1980.

There were a couple more solidbody electrics added to the Gretsch line in 1977, the TK 300 and the Committee. The TK 300 was another cheap bolt-on-neck solidbody, this time with a strange, asymmetric body, while the Committee followed a trend of the period for using through-neck construction. But these were uninspiring guitars by any standards, and appeared to be almost totally lacking in the character which had once been at the heart of Gretsch design. The last new Gretsch guitars to appear under

The Chet Atkins Super Axe (1977 example, far left) was the last Atkins signature model to appear from Gretsch. Meanwhile the White Falcon continued, seen here in mono (1975 example, center) and stereo (1980 example, near left).

The new Committee model, with the popular laminated through-neck construction style of the time, seen on the cover of a 1978 catalog.

Baldwin ownership were the unappealing Beast solidbodys, launched in 1979. While nobody realized it at the time, they marked the end of an era with a depressingly low note. If Baldwin's performance in handling its fresh acquisition was measured by the aptitude and success of the new Gretsch guitar models that it launched during the 1970s, then the score would be low.

Baldwin fared little better in the business affairs surrounding Gretsch. Although sales picked up a little in the early 1970s, Baldwin was disturbed to find that the business was still not returning a profit, despite various cost-cutting exercises.

In early 1979, Baldwin bought the Kustom amplifier company, and by the end of the year had merged Gretsch with Kustom, moving the sales and administration office for the new combined operation to Chanute, Kansas. Probably during 1980 Baldwin finally decided that they would stop production of Gretsch guitars. Very few instruments were manufactured beyond the start of 1981 (which, somewhat ironically, was two years short of Gretsch's 100th anniversary).

A man called Charlie Roy was running the Gretsch/Kustom operation, which he bought from Baldwin in 1982, moving the offices to Gallatin, Tennessee, just outside Nashville. By now Chet Atkins's endorsement deal had come to a natural end, and he soon transferred allegiance to Gibson. (Gibson began making a number of Chet Atkins signature models from 1986.) Baldwin once again took control of Gretsch in about

1984, when the deal with Roy ceased. Around this time there was a last-ditch plan to revive Gretsch guitar production at a piano-action factory that Baldwin owned in Ciudad Juarez, Mexico. However, only a small trial batch of instruments was assembled, after which the idea was dropped.

Baldwin then sold Gretsch to yet another Fred Gretsch. This one was the grandson of Fred Sr, and we shall call him Fred III. He had originally worked for his grandfather at Gretsch from 1965 until 1971, when he began to run his own business, importing and wholesaling musical instruments. Fred III acquired the Synsonics brandname in 1980 from Mattel, which led to some success with acoustic and electronic percussion as well as electric guitars.

Fred III bought Gretsch from Baldwin at the very beginning of 1985. Gretsch drum production – which had never ceased – continued in Arkansas for a year, then moved to Fred's own premises in South Carolina. It was then that Gretsch guitar manufacturing was started again.

With the help of old Gretsch hand Duke Kramer, Fred III decided to introduce updated versions of the classic Gretsch models of the past, no doubt having noticed the increasing prices that certain Gretsch instruments had been fetching for some time on the "vintage" guitar market. The unique character of Gretsch – in sound, looks and playability – was appealing to yet another new generation of players. Kramer drew up

Some of the last new models from the Gretsch/Baldwin operation are shown here: a Country Roc (near right) from 1975; a Committee (center) made during 1978; and a Beast BST-1000 (far right) that dates from 1979.

Brian Setzer spearheaded the 1990s rockabilly revival with his Orchestra, Gretsch guitars to the fore as ever, and albums such as this 1998 release, Dirty Boogie.

specifications for the proposed new models, and visited many American makers with a view to US production. But negotiations were unsuccessful, and so Gretsch decided to go "offshore," in guitar-biz-speak – meaning that they contracted a manufacturer based a good distance beyond the shores of the United States. After some searching, Gretsch selected Terada in Japan as its new factory.

However, in 1989 Gretsch offered an unusual forerunner to its forthcoming guitars with a series of Korean-made electrics intended to capitalize on the popularity of the fictional-family supergroup, The Traveling Wilburys. The cheap and somewhat primitive guitars were loosely based on the group's old Danelectro instruments, and various models were issued, all boldly finished in what Gretsch called "original graphics" with a travel theme appropriate to the band's name.

Gretsch delivered its first proper models later in 1989. Clearly it could no longer use Chet Atkins's name, now a Gibson property, so while some of the model names were familiar, others were necessarily modified.

Nine new Gretsch models were launched. There were five hollowbodies: the Tennessee Rose, recalling a Tennessean; the Nashville; Nashville Western with G-brand and Western appointments; Country Classic, recalling a Country Club; and Country Classic double-cutaway. There were four solidbodies: the Duo Jet; Silver Jet; Jet Firebird; and Round Up. This initial selection was soon joined by a pair of White Falcon

models offered in single- or double-cutaway styles. Since then the revitalized Gretsch operation has, like so very many of its contemporaries, placed increasing emphasis on revisiting the past. This has resulted in the reissue of various oldies that bear re-activated pickup and hardware designs, including the reincarnation of Filter'Tron humbucker and DeArmond single-coil pickups.

The company has also launched a number of signature models that honor well-known Gretsch players through the years. The musicians appearing in Gretsch's hall of fame include Brian Setzer (whose signature model debuted in 1993), Malcolm Young (1997), Keith Scott (1999), Duane Eddy (1999) and Stephen Stills (2000).

During recent years Gretsch has added more models to its line, including a Black Falcon, an Anniversary reissue and a variety of fresh color options, as well as a less expensive Korean-made series that revived the old Electromatic name. At first this was offered for sale only in Japan, but by 2000 was available elsewhere.

A line of selected new Custom USA classics manufactured in the United States has also appeared in the Gretsch catalog. At the time of writing this line included a number of models such as the Nashville G6120-1955, the White Falcon G6136-1955 and the Country Club G6196-1955, apparently good vintage-style recreations, albeit at a very high price. With the addition of this small-scale line of American-manufactured models, the story of the Gretsch electric guitar has come full circle.

A new Gretsch company was in operation by 1989. Among the new offerings was a signature model for Brian Setzer (1995 example, far left, with a Japanese ad from the previous year). Still aware of the bonus of applying drum finishes to guitar bodies, this Blue Pearl sparkle Jet (near left) was made in 1995. More signature models were made for Bryan Adams's guitarist Keith Scott (1999 ad, above left) and Duane Eddy (1998 ad, above).

G R I M S H A W

On the UK's embryonic electric guitar scene of the late 1950s, Emile Grimshaw's London-based company provided more or less the only practical British-made instruments available for serious players.

Soon-to-be stars such as Joe Brown and Bruce Welch favored the SS De Luxe, a short-scale, slim semi-solidbody. The SS had quite adventurous styling for its type and the era, with a figured sycamore body that featured offset cutaways and unusual "teardrop"-shape soundholes. The guitar conjured a very modern image compared to most of the available competition at the time.

Grimshaw was already well established, having started in business two decades earlier. Although primarily producing numerous acoustic models, the company catered for the 1960s beat boom with an increasing assortment of electrics. Most were hollowbodies, but the Meteor was an early solidbody alternative.

The early 1970s brought more solidbodies to the Grimshaw line in the shape of the GS7 and GS33 models, while the GS30 was one of the first unabashed Les Paul-alikes, and all the more popular among players as a result.

Later models such as the Telecaster-style GTC and the SG-based GSG Custom were more copies, but by the end of the 1970s the brand had effectively succumbed to the onslaught of Japanese imports armed with the same intentions.

Underlining Guild's early benefit from an influx of ex-Epiphone workers, this Guild Stratford X-350 (this page, right) made in 1954 was similar in pickup and control layout to Epiphone's Zephyr Emperor Regent model. On the opposite page are three more Guilds: the top electric archtop of its time, a Stuart X-550 from 1958 (left); a Duane Eddy from 1962 (center); and a Bert Weedon Model made in 1966.

Guild first produced its Johnny Smith Award model in 1956, although Smith (seen in 1957 ad, below) apparently did not like it. Guild renamed it the Artist Award during 1961 – the same year that a Gibson Johnny Smith model appeared.

Grimshaw made this striking Electric Deluxe model (near right) in London during the late 1950s.

guitar manufacturers

Jazz guitarist Johnny Smith's allegiance with Guild may have been shortlived, but more regrettable is that his playing career, flecked with masterful, emotive performances, was not much longer itself.

GUILD

For players who've discovered them, Guild guitars have since their inception in the early 1950s always offered a high-quality alternative to the market leaders. Founded in New York City by jazz guitarist Alfred Dronge, Guild was born just as the Epiphone company was embroiled in a labor dispute and was relocating to Philadelphia. Many former Epiphone employees joined the new company and brought their skills to Guild, especially in making carved archtops.

So it's no surprise that Guild's first guitars, introduced around 1953, were non-cutaway and single-cutaway archtops – either electric, or acoustics with an optional pickup. Guild's archtops would always command respect, although the company quickly began to make its reputation with high-quality acoustic flat-tops. The full-bodied, rounded "F"-series and dreadnoughts that debuted in 1954 were played through the years by stars such as Eric Clapton, Ralph Towner and Charlie Byrd (who chose an instrument from the classical Mark series).

Among Guild's 1953 non-cutaway electric archtops were the one-pickup X-100 and two-pickup X-200, replaced the following year by the one-pickup Granada (and renamed the Cordoba X-50 in 1961) which was offered until 1970. Single-cutaway models included the shortlived one-pickup X-300, two-pickup X-400 and three-pickup X-600, plus the luxuriously appointed Stuart X-500 which remained Guild's flagship archtop until 1994. Other long-running single-cutaway electric archtops introduced the following year were the one-pickup Savoy X-150, two pickup Manhattan X-175, and two-pickup hollowbody Aristocrat M-75, a model that lasted until 1963 and then reappeared a few years later as the semi-hollow BluesBird, transforming into the solidbody M-75 BluesBird in 1970.

In 1956 Guild moved its factory to Hoboken, New Jersey, and picked up its first pro endorsement by jazz great Johnny Smith, beginning a string of artist models. The single-cutaway, single-DeArmond-equipped Johnny Smith Award was introduced that year – renamed the Artist Award in 1961 – and became another high-end mainstay of the Guild line. In 1962 jazz ace George Barnes entered the fold with his single-cutaway, twin-humbucker George Barnes AcoustiLectric model, followed by the "George Barnes Guitar In F" model in 1963, both offered until the early 1970s.

Twangy instrumentalist Duane Eddy also came on board in 1962 with his single-cutaway, twin-DeArmond Duane Eddy Deluxe (lasting to 1987) followed by the Standard in 1963 (until 1974). From 1963-65 the single-cutaway Bert Weedon Model, with two DeArmonds and a Bigsby vibrato, was available, endorsed by the British sessionman and author of the influential teaching book *Play In A Day*.

Guild entered the thinline market in 1960 with its Starfire series, initially single-cutaways (Starfire I with one single-coil pickup, II with two single-coil pickups, III with

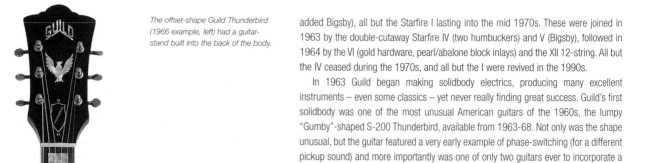

The offset-shape Guild Thunderbird (1966 example, left) had a guitar-stand built into the back of the body.

Guild's 1979 ad (below) features a specially built see-through plastic version of the company's "bell-bottom" S series solidbody of the period. Two Guild f-hole electrics are shown on this page: a Starfire III made in 1961 (below, center), and an Artist Award from 1976 (right).

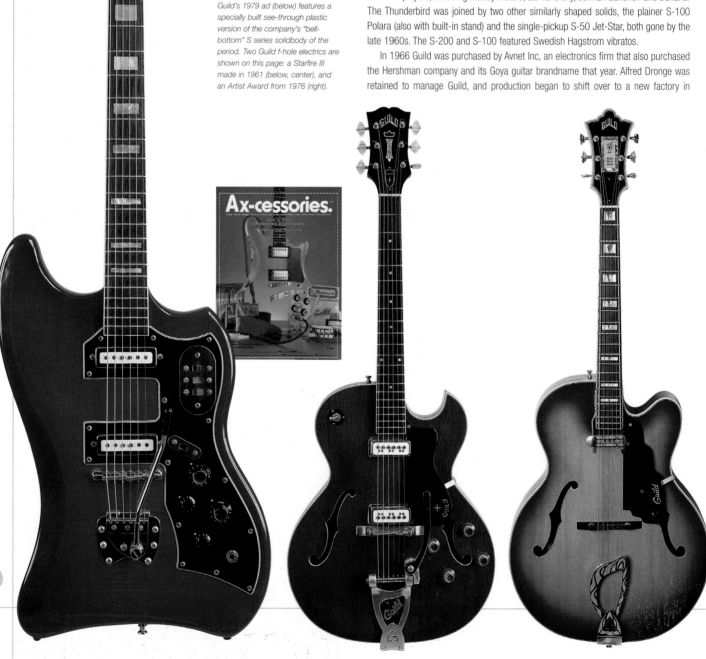

added Bigsby), all but the Starfire I lasting into the mid 1970s. These were joined in 1963 by the double-cutaway Starfire IV (two humbuckers) and V (Bigsby), followed in 1964 by the VI (gold hardware, pearl/abalone block inlays) and the Xll 12-string. All but the IV ceased during the 1970s, and all but the I were revived in the 1990s.

In 1963 Guild began making solidbody electrics, producing many excellent instruments – even some classics – yet never really finding great success. Guild's first solidbody was one of the most unusual American guitars of the 1960s, the lumpy "Gumby"-shaped S-200 Thunderbird, available from 1963-68. Not only was the shape unusual, but the guitar featured a very early example of phase-switching (for a different pickup sound) and more importantly was one of only two guitars ever to incorporate a metal stand built into the back.

Despite these oddities, the Thunderbird had enough appeal to win over an eclectic bunch of players, including Muddy Waters, Zal Yanofsky, Jorma Kaukonen and Banana. The Thunderbird was joined by two other similarly shaped solids, the plainer S-100 Polara (also with built-in stand) and the single-pickup S-50 Jet-Star, both gone by the late 1960s. The S-200 and S-100 featured Swedish Hagstrom vibratos.

In 1966 Guild was purchased by Avnet Inc, an electronics firm that also purchased the Hershman company and its Goya guitar brandname that year. Alfred Dronge was retained to manage Guild, and production began to shift over to a new factory in

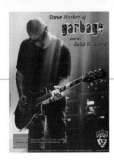

Westerly, Rhode Island. Guild production continues there today. When Hoboken production ended in 1971 the corporate HQ was moved to Elizabeth, New Jersey.

In 1970 Guild revisited the solidbody market and introduced a new S-100 Polara, more conventionally styled with a slightly offset double cutaway, and twin humbuckers. It's often referred to as "Guild's SG" because of its similarity to the Gibson, though it was closer to Hagstrom's mid-1960s solidbody design. Two low-end companions were also introduced at this time, the S-90 and S-50. An S-100 Deluxe joined the line in 1973 with optional stereo output, followed by the S-100C in 1974, a version with an oak leaf carved into the front. The previously mentioned M-75 solidbody was offered from 1970-80, along with a Deluxe version and, beginning in 1975, the M-85CS.

In 1972 Dronge was killed in an aircraft crash and was succeeded by Leon Tell. Guild briefly participated in the "copy era" in 1973-74 by offering Japanese-made Madeira-brand copies of its own S-100 as well as of Fender and Gibson designs.

The SG-like S series was retired in 1976, supplanted by a new S design with offset double-cutaways and a "bell"-shaped lower bout. With different appointments (some sporting DiMarzio pickups) these included the S-60, S-65, S-70, S-300, and S-400, all offered through 1982.

From 1980-83 the M-80 was available, a double-cutaway version of the M-75. In 1981 Guild introduced its first Strat-style solids, the S-250 and S-25 (both with set-necks) and its first "pointy" guitars, the X-82 Nova and X-79 Skylark. The X-82 Nova was essentially a hybrid Explorer/Flying V similar to Dean's ML model, while the X-79 Skylark was more radically pointed and had a dramatically extended upper horn and sloped lower bout, and a matching headstock shape. Both lasted into the mid 1980s. In 1983 the X-80 Skyhawk joined the line, essentially an X-79 variant. The Madeira brand was revived briefly on a series of original and copy designs in the early 1980s.

During 1983, Guild began offering a number of fairly popular Strat-style models, often with a bewildering variety of model names for the same or similar guitars, and all distinguished by set-necks and Guild's first six-tuners-in-line headstocks. The S series differed primarily in details such as pickup types and layouts and included Flyer, Thunderbolt and Aviator models among others.

In 1984 and '85 Guild offered perhaps its most exotic solidbodies with the X-88 Crue Flying Star (a very pointy variant on the X-82, named for Motley Crue's Mick Mars), the X-100 Bladerunner (almost "X"-shaped, with large holes cut out of the body, designed by luthier David Andrews) and the X-90 Citron Breakaway (shaped something like a Jackson Randy Rhoads V but with detachable wings to make it a travel guitar, designed by luthier Harvey Citron).

In 1985 the single-cutaway solid Bluesbird and semi-hollow Nightbird electrics debuted. It was also during this mid-1980s period that Guild introduced one of its more

Two more Guild guitars are shown on this page. This M-75 BCG BluesBird (far left) was made in 1977, showing the design used for the BluesBird during the 1970s (compare the 1990s example at the top of the page). The S-100 Carved (near left, this one made in 1974) is in Guild's offset-SG-like style used for a number of models in the 1970s. The Carved had an unusual design of acorns and leaves in the top. Soundgarden's Kim Thayil (below) repopularized the S-100 in the 1990s.

collectable models, the Brian May MHM1, promoted as a "copy" of the Queen guitarist's homemade axe, even though it wasn't an exact replica.

A period of turmoil began for Guild. In 1986 Avnet sold Guild to an investment group headed by banker Jere Haskew from Chattanooga, Tennessee. Around this time Guild introduced Telecaster-style guitars in two versions, the fancy T-250 and the T-200 Roy Buchanan, endorsed by the great Tele ace. These were Guild's first bolt-on-neck guitars. In 1987-88 Guild returned to imports with a line of high-quality Japanese-made solidbodies carrying the Burnside brandname, including both Strat- and Tele-style guitars and original "pointy" designs (often with flashy paint jobs). Some had set-necks, others were bolt-ons.

In 1987 Guild experienced financial difficulties, yet managed to introduce some fine electrics including the high-end semi-hollow Nightbird I and II, the solidbody Liberator series and the well-made but otherwise conventional Detonator superstrat. The Liberator Elite was a spectacular set-neck guitar with a carved flamed-maple body cap and fancy rising-sun inlays.

In 1988 Guild went into bankruptcy and ceased solidbody guitar production, though it continued to make the semi-hollow and hollowbody electrics (which often appear to be solids) for a couple more years. In 1989 the company was sold to the Fass Corporation of New Berlin, Wisconsin (subsequently US Music Corporation). While

Guild collaborated with Brian May for a series of instruments based on his famous home-made guitar, Big Red, beginning with the MHM-1 in 1984, as featured in the 1986 ad (above). Closer to the original was the Brian May Signature (1993 example, main guitar, right), followed by three more May models in 1994.

Guild joined the pointy-body trend with the X-79 model (left), this example dating from 1984.

The "bell-bottom" body shape of the S series (S-70D from 1980, right) took Guild solidbodies into the early 1980s. Later that decade Guild's particular take on superstrat fashion led to its Flyers (1986 ad, above).

Brian May with his original homemade guitar – Big Red – on stage with Queen (below). May continued to use the instrument regularly for his solo projects following Queen's demise, including the 1998 album Another World (left).

brian may

another world

guitar manufacturers

domestic electric production was in hiatus, the Madeira brand was again revived in 1990-91 for a brief run of Strat- and Les Paul-style guitars.

After a period when Guild concentrated on its traditional strengths – mainly flat-top acoustics – the company ventured back to solidbodies in 1993-94 by reviving the Brian May guitar with the limited-edition Signature, this time a little closer to the original. It was followed in 1994-95 by three more May models: the Pro, Special and Standard, differing in appointments. In 1994 Guild reissued its venerable SG-style solidbody, the S-100 of the 1970s, after its high-profile use by Kim Thayil.

In late 1995, Guild was sold to Fender. The new owner decided to bring Guild designs to a wider market with an additional line of less expensive equivalents marketed with the DeArmond name, after Harry DeArmond whose Rowe company made many of Guild's early pickups (see DeArmond).

At the other end of the price scale the Guild electric line was rationalized. The Brian May models were dropped from the catalog, and the accent was now much more on traditional design. Late-1990s models included revivals of the 1960s-style single-cutaway Starfire semi-hollowbodies, alongside the continuing Bluesbird and S-100 solidbodies. Famed archtop builder Bob Benedetto was brought in during 2000 to redefine Guild's Artist Award and Stuart archtops, as well as to launch a new custom-shop Guild Benedetto line, including the small sealed-body Benny model.

GUYATONE

One of the oldest Japanese guitar brands, Guyatone dates from the 1930s when Mitsuo Matsuki set up in Tokyo. The Guyatone brand was based on Matsuki's nickname "Guya," someone who takes care of tools. Guyatone's first solidbody electric debuted in 1955, the "Les Paul Model," styled more like early Nationals and Supros. Exporting began in the late 1950s. Budget Guyatones (some branded Star or Antoria) proved popular in the UK, where little else was available. Hank Marvin was an early customer.

By the mid 1960s the catalog had expanded, with some inspiration from Mosrite, plus originals like the "holed" LG-160T Telstar. The high-end LG-350T Sharp 5 was featured by the Japanese group of that name.

Around 1968 the electric guitar market crashed in Japan. Many companies failed, including Guyatone. It re-emerged as the Guya Co Ltd. When the Japanese "copy era" began during the early 1970s Guyatone was quick to contribute a succession of Fender and Gibson clones. The mid 1970s brought some Guyatone originals and a revival of the Sharp 5. One guitar even came with a basic drum machine on-board.

Matsuki died in 1992. The LGX-II of 1993 employed a novel combination of Gibson and Fender features and was endorsed by the late Rory Gallagher. The Sharp 5 was reissued again in 1996, as was the LG-2100M. Another reissue of a 1960s model was the LG-160T that appeared in 2000 complete with distinctive body hole.

Three recent Guild instruments are shown on this page: a Blues 90 (near right) made in 2000, with P-90-style pickups; an X-700 Stuart archtop electric (center) from 1995; and a reissue Starfire IV semi-solidbody dating from 2000.

guitar manufacturers

HAGSTROM

Hagstrom of Älvdalen, Sweden, was a major global operator during the great guitar boom of the 1960s. The company had been founded as an accordion importer in 1921 by Albin Hagstrom. Guitar-making began in 1958 with the sparkle-plastic-covered hollowbody De Luxe and Standard models.

These single-cutaway guitars could in theory at least be played "acoustically," or electrically with modular plug-in assemblies featuring one, two or four single-coil pickups. Their popularity was later boosted when bands such as Roxy Music and ABC displayed them in publicity material. (The guitars were imported into the US from 1959 to 1961 by Hershman, with the Goya brand.)

In 1962 Hagstrom introduced the Kent-brand line of Strat-influenced solidbodies featuring vinyl-covered backs and Lucite (plastic) covered fronts. These were sold in the US by Merson as Hagstroms (the Kent name was already in use by Buegeleisen & Jacobson) and in the UK by Selmer as Futurama guitars. The patented Hagstrom vibrato was licensed to Guild and Harmony and appeared on some of their 1960s solidbodies. The asymmetrically shaped two-pickup Impala and three-pickup Corvette (later Condor) with pushbutton controls appeared from 1963-67.

Kents later lost the Lucite, became distinctly more Strat-like, and gained the Hagstrom brand. By 1965, body-horns had become more pointed, hinting more at

The 1967 Guyatone LG-350T on this page (far left) is a Sharp 5 version, endorsed by the Japanese pop group of the time, while the 2000 ad is for the reissued LG-160T Telstar. This sparkly Hagstrom P46 Deluxe (main guitar) was made in 1959; one is seen in the hands of Bryan Ferry of Roxy Music (1972 promo pic, above). Hagstrom was noted for its thin necks (1965 ad, top of page).

Elvis Presley appeared on his famous December 1968 "comeback" TV special playing a Hagstrom Viking, providing an unexpected PR bonus for Hagstrom's US agent, Merson.

Gibson's SG, and making a classic Hagstrom style. The line included 12-string models (Frank Zappa used one) and Viking thinlines. Hagstrom's most popular model, the Les-Paul-like Swede, was offered from 1973 to 1982. Equipped with a synthesizer pickup it was also offered as the Patch 2000 in the late 1970s (see Ampeg). A fancier Super Swede was made from 1978-83. In 1968 Hagstrom had hired New York luthier James D'Aquisto to design an archtop model, the Jimmy, with f-holes or oval soundhole. A number were produced in 1969, but supply problems delayed main production until the late 1970s. Hagstrom considered Japanese sourcing in the early 1980s, but ceased production in 1983 to concentrate on retailing.

HALLMARK

Headed by ex-Mosrite man Joe Hall, this shortlived company was based in Arvin, California. The only Hallmark model was the Swept Wing, its large, thin body having a distinctive offset-arrow outline. A semi-solid version debuted in 1967, followed by a solidbody, and there were six-strings, 12-strings, basses and double-necks.

HAMER

One of the new-generation American makers of the 1970s, Hamer has survived with an enviable reputation. Established around 1975, Hamer grew out of Northern Prairie Music, a respected repair workshop in Wilmette, Illinois, that included co-founders Paul Hamer and Jol Dantzig. Hamer and chief ideas-man Dantzig preferred Gibson designs

and construction. Their early instruments reflected this with liberal use of mahogany, the Gibson scale-length, a 22-fret glued-in neck and twin humbuckers. First up was the Standard, strongly Explorer-based but no clone: high-end features included a bound, bookmatched maple top, and pickups from new maker DiMarzio.

The Sunburst of 1977 had the outline of Gibson's late-1950s double-cutaway Les Paul Junior. It became a classic Hamer, sharing the features and deluxe appointments of the Standard and adding Fender-like through-body stringing and a fixed bridge. By 1980 it was joined by the more basic Special, the same year that Hamer relocated to larger premised in Arlington Heights, on the north-west side of Chicago.

The 1981 Prototype was the first with original styling, though far from radical. The odd triple-coil pickup did attract Andy Summers of The Police, however. Multi-string basses became a Hamer specialty, including eight- and 12-string versions. Although Cheap Trick's Rick Nielsen was Hamer's highest-profile fan, his unusual taste in guitars precluded a signature production model, so Hamer's first signature guitar was the Steve Stevens model, launched in 1984.

In 1988 Hamer was acquired by Ovation's manufacturer, Kaman. Paul Hamer had left a year earlier, and it was around this time that significant changes were made to the line. Most Gibson-influenced models disappeared, largely replaced by superstrat designs catering for the new breed of fast-gun guitarists. More unusual were the 36-

Three more Hagstrom guitars on this page: a plastic-topped Kent PB24G (near right) made in 1963; a multi-control Impala (center) from 1965; and a Swede model, this 1980 example being part of a Patch 2000 guitar synthesizer outfit.

Rick Nielsen of Cheap Trick

HAMER GUITARS U.S.A.

Dept. C, 544 Wood Street, Palatine, Illinois 60067

Send 50¢ for color brochure.

Hamer's first production model was the Standard, generously promoted in this 1979 ad (left) by Cheap Trick's lead guitar nut, Rick Nielsen. The guitar was clearly influenced by Gibson's Explorer, but had its own style and inherent class.

Still with Gibson flavors – and an influential design in itself – was Hamer's double-cutaway Sunburst model (main guitar). This example was made in 1979.

Hallmark's only contribution to electric guitar design is this bizarre instrument, aptly named the Swept Wing. This solidbody version was made during 1967, and the ad dates from the same year.

NEW
From Hallmark
SWEPT WING GUITAR
Electric Acoustic
(other models available)

fret Virtuoso and seven-string Maestro, while the Sustainiac infinite-sustain system was a novel option on the Chaparral. A stylistic balance returned with the reissued Sunburst in 1989, amid a fashionable revival of guitars with two humbuckers and a fixed bridge. Since then this original Hamer has been reborn several times, including high-end Archtops and cheaper Specials.

The line became further diversified during the 1990s, with Fender derivatives as well as the Korean-made Slammer series, launched in 1993, bringing the US designs to more affordable levels. The Duo Tone was Hamer's hybrid guitar, launched in 1994. In 1998 Hamer revived the 1980s Phantom name but using the shape of the Prototype model. A year later the company issued a suitably deluxe 25th Anniversary model.

HARMONY

Before guitars turned global during the 1960s one of the largest mass-manufacturers of bargain and midrange guitars was the Harmony company of Chicago, founded by German immigrant Wilhelm J.F. Schultz in 1892.

By about 1905 the company had become a large supplier of instruments to the Sears, Roebuck mail-order catalog, with a variety of "parlor" guitars. In 1914 Sears introduced Supertone-brand guitars, virtually all Harmony-made, and purchased

Harmony in 1916. Schultz died in 1925 and was succeeded by Jay Kraus. In 1928 Harmony introduced a line of acoustics endorsed by Roy Smeck. During the Depression of the 1930s fancier trim was replaced by stenciled designs, typical of cheaper Harmony guitars through the 1950s.

Harmony's first archtop acoustic guitar models appeared during the mid 1930s. However, in 1940 Sears sold Harmony to a group of investors headed by Kraus. Sears changed the in-house brandname used for its guitars to Silvertone, and these were no longer exclusively made by Harmony.

Harmony came relatively late to electric guitars, with an amplified Spanish archtop and Hawaiian lap-steel appearing in 1939. From around 1948 Harmony increasingly applied pickups to full-sized archtops, which continued through the 1960s. Harmony's first solidbody electric debuted in 1953: the small copper-finished, Les-Paul-shaped Stratotone had a neck and body made from one piece of wood.

The Stratotone line expanded in 1955 with the black Doublet and the yellow or green Newport, with aluminum and vinyl strips on the sides. In 1955 electric Roy Smeck guitars appeared, a Spanish archtop and a lap-steel. In 1956 Harmony introduced the one-pickup H65, its first cutaway archtop.

Harmony thinlines began with the single-cutaway Meteor hollowbodies in 1958. By this time the electric models featured single-coil pickups by DeArmond, and bolt-on

Three Hamer guitars here: this Chaparral Elite (near right) of 1990 has a Sustainiac pickup fitted at the neck position, linked to the on-board infinite-sustain system; this Phantom A5 (center) of 1984 boasts a triple-coil pickup, first used by Hamer on its earlier Prototype model; and this Duo Tone of 1994 (far right) is Hamer's hybrid guitar, mixing electric and "acoustic" pickup sounds.

guitar manufacturers

The Stratotone model in its earliest guise was Harmony's first solidbody electric. The yellow Newport H42/1 example (below, left) dates from 1957, as does the ad above it where Harmony aims the two-pickup version squarely at country players. This later Stratotone Jupiter H-49 (main guitar) was made in 1960.

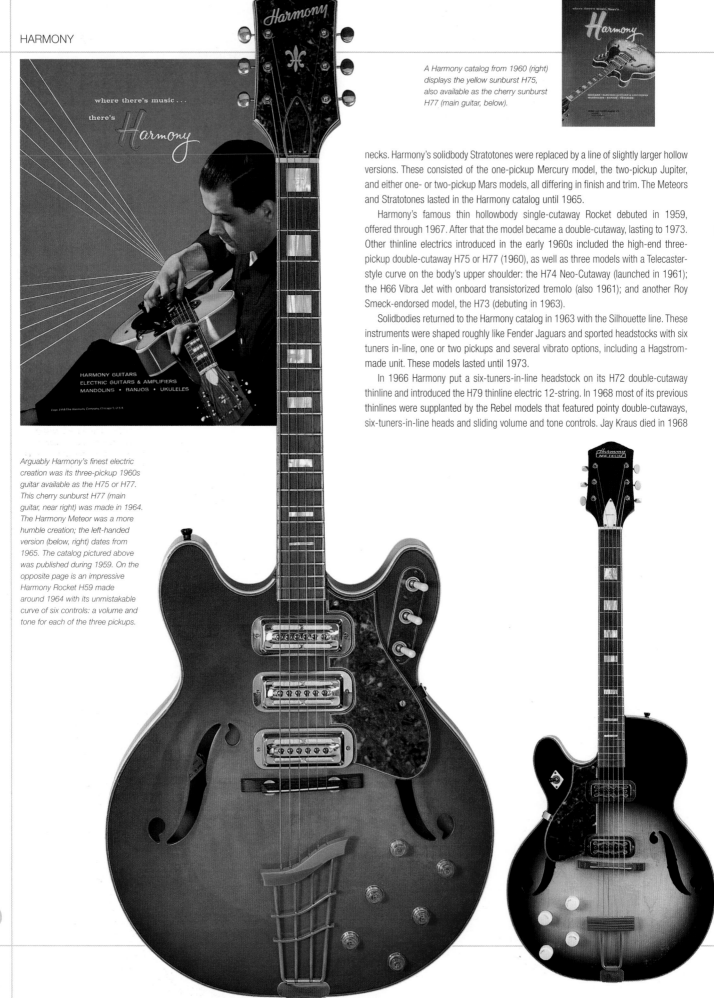

A Harmony catalog from 1960 (right) displays the yellow sunburst H75, also available as the cherry sunburst H77 (main guitar, below).

necks. Harmony's solidbody Stratotones were replaced by a line of slightly larger hollow versions. These consisted of the one-pickup Mercury model, the two-pickup Jupiter, and either one- or two-pickup Mars models, all differing in finish and trim. The Meteors and Stratotones lasted in the Harmony catalog until 1965.

Harmony's famous thin hollowbody single-cutaway Rocket debuted in 1959, offered through 1967. After that the model became a double-cutaway, lasting to 1973. Other thinline electrics introduced in the early 1960s included the high-end three-pickup double-cutaway H75 or H77 (1960), as well as three models with a Telecaster-style curve on the body's upper shoulder: the H74 Neo-Cutaway (launched in 1961); the H66 Vibra Jet with onboard transistorized tremolo (also 1961); and another Roy Smeck-endorsed model, the H73 (debuting in 1963).

Solidbodies returned to the Harmony catalog in 1963 with the Silhouette line. These instruments were shaped roughly like Fender Jaguars and sported headstocks with six tuners in-line, one or two pickups and several vibrato options, including a Hagstrom-made unit. These models lasted until 1973.

In 1966 Harmony put a six-tuners-in-line headstock on its H72 double-cutaway thinline and introduced the H79 thinline electric 12-string. In 1968 most of its previous thinlines were supplanted by the Rebel models that featured pointy double-cutaways, six-tuners-in-line heads and sliding volume and tone controls. Jay Kraus died in 1968

Arguably Harmony's finest electric creation was its three-pickup 1960s guitar available as the H75 or H77. This cherry sunburst H77 (main guitar, near right) was made in 1964. The Harmony Meteor was a more humble creation; the left-handed version (below, right) dates from 1965. The catalog pictured above was published during 1959. On the opposite page is an impressive Harmony Rocket H59 made around 1964 with its unmistakable curve of six controls: a volume and tone for each of the three pickups.

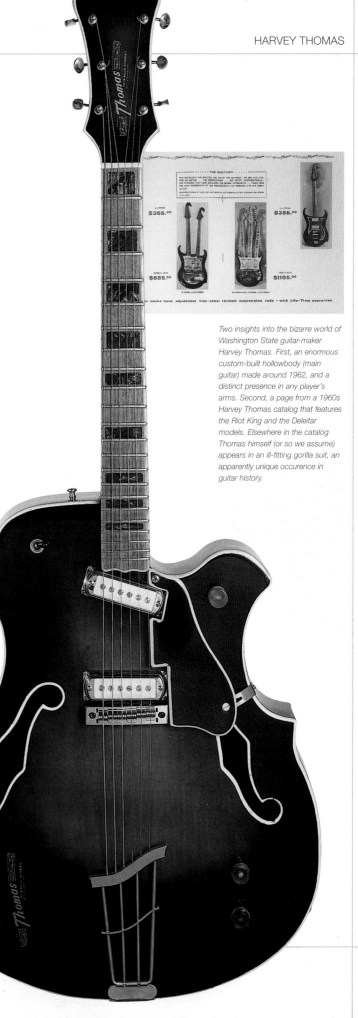

Harmony was a vast company as it entered the 1960s, offering everything from bargain flat-tops with stenciled cowboy scenes to electric archtops (1959 ad, right) and solidbody Stratotones.

and management passed to a trust. Hit hard by imported competition from oriental makers and others, Harmony had dropped its electric lines by 1975, the year in which Harmony purchased Ampeg to handle its distribution.

In 1976 Harmony was auctioned off, the name going to the Global company. During the 1980s some imported low-end double-cutaway solidbodies appeared with the Harmony logo. The brand entered the 1990s on inexpensive beginner guitars, including near-copies of Strats.

HARVEY THOMAS

Based in Kent, Washington State, Harvey Thomas built instruments with gloriously little evidence of design influences from outside the four walls of his workshop.

Thomas's individuality was manifested in distinctive solidbody instruments such as the unusual cross-shaped Maltese model (an example of which would later attract Ian Hunter), the oddball triangular Mandarin, and the deranged mutations of the Mod and the Riot King. Thomas also offered a custom-building service to his customers, resulting in even stranger creations, including ax- and map-shape guitars, as well as a few enormous hollowbody electrics.

Thomas worked near the Spanish Castle outside Seattle, as frequented by a young Jimi Hendrix and immortalized in his song 'Spanish Castle Magic.' Thomas had nothing to do with Thomas Organs, a common misconception.

Two insights into the bizarre world of Washington State guitar-maker Harvey Thomas. First, an enormous custom-built hollowbody (main guitar) made around 1962, and a distinct presence in any player's arms. Second, a page from a 1960s Harvey Thomas catalog that features the Riot King and the Deleitar models. Elsewhere in the catalog Thomas himself (or so we assume) appears in an ill-fitting gorilla suit, an apparently unique occurence in guitar history.

HAYMAN

This dependable British brand provided many amateur 1970s groups with workmanlike tools. Jim Burns, a few years after he sold Burns to Baldwin in 1965, joined forces with ex-Vox man Bob Pearson and distributor Dallas Arbiter to develop a new brand of electric guitars – which became Hayman. Naturally enough, Jim drew on several of his contacts from the Burns-brand days, including Jack Golder's timber firm and Derek Adams's polyester-finishing skills.

Hayman guitars were launched in 1970 with two chunky, distinctive six-strings, the three-pickup 1010 solidbody and two-pickup 2020 semi-solid. The 3030 followed in 1971. Scale-length and 21-fret maple neck followed Fender formats, but the zero-fret and characterful headstock were pure Burns.

Jim left Dallas-Arbiter in summer 1971 and Pearson continued to develop new models. The low-end Hayman Comet appeared in 1974, while the following year's Modular had plug-in modules for changing control circuitry. The White Cloud was the final Hayman, a three-single-coil solidbody produced in small numbers.

At its peak in 1974 Dallas's factory in Shoeburyness, Essex, was producing 200 Haymans a month. But Dallas ran into financial problems in 1975, and Hayman guitars did not survive the sale to CBS/Arbiter that formed Dallas Arbiter. However, Jack Golder continued the spirit of Hayman with his new Shergold brand.

HEARTFIELD

Launched in 1989, Heartfield lasted about four years and represented a joint design effort by Fender Musical Instruments in America and Fender Japan.

Like many of Fender Japan's guitars, the line was manufactured at the Fujigen factory. The Heartfield instruments included the chunky, short-horned RR series, among the first guitars to feature retro styling, which became a growing trend throughout the 1990s. Some versions incorporated novel "touch" selectors governing active circuitry that included stompbox-style distortion.

The EX and Elan lines were more conventionally styled and attired, while the Talon series targeted the rock market with aggressive Ibanez-inspired styling, including a locking vibrato system and other hot-rod hardware.

HERITAGE

Established in 1985, Heritage occupies part of the former Gibson factory in Kalamazoo, Michigan, and numbered among the staff are many ex-employees of that company. Some early Heritage guitars displayed Fender tendencies, but predictably enough the most popular of the company's models echo various facets of Gibson design, often using what seem deliberately similar model designations.

The H-535 and H-555 are equal-double-cutaway thinline semi-solids in ES-335 and ES-355 style, while the H-575 is a Gibson ES-175 style single-cutaway archtop

The three guitars on this page are: a solidbody Hayman 3030 (near right) from 1973; a prototype (center) made at the Fujigen factory in 1989 for Heartfield's Talon series; and a Heritage H-150CM from 1998.

electric. Naturally, Les Paul-like solidbodies abound, including the H-150CM, a fancy-fronted limited edition. Other models such as the Prospect Standard semi and the latest Millennium series continue to emphasize the "Gibson alternative."

HOFNER

In the late 1950s and early 1960s German-made Hofner guitars served a growing army of young three-chord hopefuls in the UK. However, a good deal of this intense popularity was the result of the fact that Hofner guitars were, quite simply, available, rather than that they possessed any notable inherent quality.

Hofner saw the potential of the fast-growing market for electric guitars before many of its competitors. The company had been founded in the 1880s by Karl Höfner in Schoenbach, Germany, initially producing violins, cellos and double basses. Guitars were first introduced in 1925, by which time Karl's sons Josef and Walter had joined their father, and the business had developed into one of the largest in the Schoenbach area. After World War II the Höfner family moved to the Erlangen district, an area in what became West Germany and was home to a good number of musical instrument makers. Hofner production began again in 1949, and two years later the company and its factory was relocated to Bubenreuth.

Archtop acoustic guitars were added to the line sold in Germany during the early 1950s, and these were very soon partnered by alternative versions that had floating

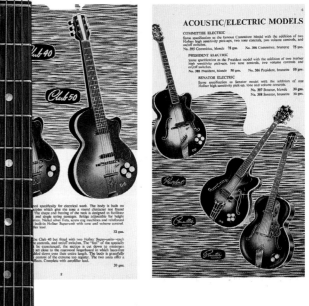

This Hofner Club 50 was made around 1958, a two-pickup version of the instrument that started John Lennon's electric-guitar adventures. Hofners had a great effect on British guitarists in the 1950s. Sessionman Bert Weedon played an electrified Committee model (far left) before adopting proper electric models. The German-made Hofner guitars were imported into the UK by Selmer, beginning with acoustics in 1953, and adding electrics two years later. Selmer's 1957 catalog (above) features the Clubs, plus Committee, President and Senator electrics.

pickups attached. Hofner electric guitars with built-in pickups followed on to the German market in 1954, and these thinline, small-bodied, single-cutaway instruments reflected the growing influence among guitarists as well as guitar-makers of Gibson's Les Paul model. Although without f-holes, these Hofners were in fact hollow, and consequently relatively lightweight.

The first Hofner "solids" were launched in Germany in 1956, but these too were more semi-solid than solidbody. Also at this time Hofner's first bass guitar, the 500/1, appeared in the manufacturer's catalog, another small hollowbody instrument. It is better known today by its descriptive nickname, the "violin" bass, and even more as the "Beatle" bass for its most famous player, Paul McCartney, who played one on-stage throughout his mop-top career.

In 1953 Hofner acoustic archtop guitars were first brought into Britain by the busy importer and distributor Selmer. This London-based company began to offer a selection from Hofner's comprehensive lines, and most models were specifically made or modified to Selmer's requirements.

Selmer soon began to realize the value of the instruments coming from its new German supplier. The UK distributor chose to ignore the detailed numbered model designations of the instruments they'd commissioned for the British market, instead giving them distinct model names that were more likely to attract British players. Thus

Selmer would begin to launch such models as the Golden Hofner, the Committee, the President, Senator and Club, the Verithin, and the Colorama and Galaxie.

As already noted, Hofner had introduced its first electric guitars with built-in pickups on to the German market in 1954, and these appeared in the UK in 1955, marketed as the Club 40 and Club 50. They were small, single-cutaway six-string hollowbody models without f-holes, in a loosely Les Paul style, offered with one pickup (the Club 40) or two pickups (the Club 50). They were joined in 1958 by the rather more fancy Club 60, which was distinguished by its bound ebony fingerboard and more decorated position markers. The affordable Club line (£28-£50, about $45-$80) quickly became essential to many aspiring beat-groups, including an embryonic Fab Four wherein John Lennon thrashed a battered Club 40.

Selmer's timing with the introduction of Hofners to Britain was perfect. As the 1950s progressed, Britain was beginning to embrace rock'n'roll – but there was a very limited choice of electric guitars available, mostly due to a ban on US imports that was in effect from 1951 to 1959. British players welcomed the variety, quality and value offered by the Hofner line, and the brand soon became a leading name in the UK, seen in the hands of famous artists such as Bert Weedon and Tommy Steele.

The electric archtop Committee, which appeared in 1957, was designed in conjunction with an advisory group of six leading UK players: Frank Deniz, Ike Isaacs,

Two popular Hofner hollowbody electrics both made in 1959 are shown here: a Committee (near right) and a President (far right). The ad, published in the same year, features an array of bandsmen, sessioneers and would-be rock'n'rollers, including Dickie Bishop and Denny Wright, both of whom played with skiffle king Lonnie Donegan at various times.

(sidebar, rotated) guitar manufacturers

The Golden Hofner was Hofner's high-end hollowbody electric, launched in 1959. The two examples shown here were made in 1961: this Bigsby-equipped model (main guitar) is a thinline Thin model; the other (below, far left) the full-depth version. The Golden Hofner Thin is owned by Bert Weedon, the author of the Play In A Day teaching guide, first published in 1957, that provided the initial inspiration for many later famous guitarists. The large ad (left) with Golden Hofner is from 1959.

Jack Llewellyn, Freddie Phillips, Roy Plummer and Bert Weedon. With an ornate, high-end image, the Committee featured two pickups, a flowery headstock inlay, a harp-style tailpiece, multiple binding all around, and figured maple veneer on the body's sides and back (which also sported a fancy inlaid fleur-de-lis). As with most Hofner hollowbody guitars, finish options were sunburst and natural – or, as Selmer preferred to call them, brunette and blonde.

Slotting into the electric archtop line below the Committee were the more austere two-pickup President and single-pickup Senator, although the general image of the President was improved by triple-dot position markers and the company's six-"finger" Compensator tailpiece.

The Golden Hofner was launched in 1959 and was by far the most luxurious Hofner, going to extremes in size, opulence and price. This top-of-the-line hollowbody electric boasted a hand-carved body, ebony fingerboard, fancy inlay and binding, and gold-plated hardware – including an engraved, shield-shaped tailpiece.

The ornate Golden Hofner also bore the Committee-style inlaid fleur-de-lis on the back of the body, and was described with some justification in Hofner advertising as "a masterpiece of guitar perfection."

By the time the Golden Hofner model was launched in 1959 the Hofner catalog had increased considerably, with a wide variety of large-bodied archtops, thinline versions,

Two classic Hofner guitars are shown on this page: a Galaxie (main guitar) from around 1965; and a Verithin, made about 1961.

guitar manufacturers

smaller semis and an assortment of solidbodies. In Britain at the time Selmer offered eight UK-only electric models in addition to the Golden Hofner: the Committee, President, Senator, Club 40, Club 50, Club 60, and Colorama.

The single-cutaway Colorama solidbodies had first appeared on the British market during 1958, offered in one- or two-pickup models. Later versions of the Colorama modified the body shape to equal-double-cutaways, first seen in 1960, and then to Fender-like offset cutaways, a style that debuted during 1963.

Gibson's successful thinline electrics of the period had prompted Hofner to offer slim versions of its existing archtop electric bestsellers. The Verithin model, first introduced in 1960, offered an even thinner cross-section to the body, as well as some notably Gibson-like touches such as an equal-double-cutaway design and a bright cherry-red finish. This stylish approach and, as ever with Hofner at the time, keen pricing proved very popular in the UK, and the Verithin model became something of a classic among cost-conscious British beat groups.

As 1950s rock'n'roll gave way to the beat group music of the early 1960s, Hofner continued to maintain a healthy share of electric guitar business in Britain. Most Hofner instruments targeted beginners and second-time buyers, and while the guitars could not match Fender or Gibson for quality, Hofners invariably offered a great deal of character, some impressive visuals and fair performance, and as such they attracted

many soon-to-be-famous guitarists during their formative years, including Ritchie Blackmore, Joe Brown, David Gilmour and Roy Wood.

Hofner's second line of solidbody models for the UK appeared during 1963, the Stratocaster-inspired Galaxie series. This instrument was offered bedecked with slider switches and roller controls, in keeping with popular trends at the time.

Sales of Hofner's guitars peaked in the UK during the 1960s, but the transition into rock music by the end of the decade saw Hofner's British popularity diminishing as competition increased at all price levels. Hofner appeared to be reluctant to move with the changing times, and of course the ever-stronger Japanese challenge and the 1970s "copy era" only increased the pressure.

Ironically, Hofner instruments from the late 1970s to the mid 1980s are usually of better quality than the earlier guitars, but have attracted far less attention.

Hofner battled on through the 1980s and 1990s and into the 21st century, with sales mainly limited to the company's apparently timeless "Beatle" basses. Undeterred, Hofner did introduce a number of new models, some of which reflected changing market trends, while others recreated former glories. But today, for guitar collectors of a certain age in Britain, it's the UK-only electric archtops that Hofner produced from 1957 to 1965 that are the most desirable, mainly for the image and artist-association – but also, of course, for pure and simple nostalgia.

Three more Hofner guitars: a German-market 175 (far left) with special vinyl-covered body, made around 1968; a 459/VTZ "violin" guitar (center, made in about 1965), inspired by the better-known violin-shape "Beatle" bass; and an A2L hollowbody from 1983.

H O N D O

A pioneer of Korean guitar-making, Hondo began in 1969 as a joint venture between Samick of Korea and International Music Corporation (IMC) of Fort Worth, Texas. Primitive solidbody electrics (1972) became low-end Hondo II copies of Fenders and Gibsons (1974). Better models included the Longhorn, an active-electronics take on Danelectro's Guitarlin, made in Japan by Tokai.

In 1982 came the Chiquita Travel model and a Steinberger-like Lazer headless, modeled on Johnny Winter's guitar, plus the weird "pointy" H-2 and Coyote. More Fender/Gibson copies (Fame, Revival) and Fleischman originals appeared in 1984.

IMC purchased an interest in Jackson/Charvel in 1985, and supplanted the Hondo line with Charvels after 1987. In 1991 IMC co-founder Jerry Freed repurchased Hondo, importing beginner instruments. Hondo has been owned by MBT International (J.B. Player) since 1995.

H O P F

The Hopf name has been associated with German musical instrument making since the 17th century, although the company was officially established in 1906. After World War II, Hopf's manufacturing resumed at a new factory located in Taunusstein, near Wiesbaden, with Dieter Hopf responsible for stringed instruments. The first Hopf electric guitars appeared during the late 1950s, and soon models included the Spezisl archtop-electric and Harmony H-75-like Galaxie semi-acoustic. The Saturn 63 had a Fender Jazzmaster-style body with metal-rimmed teardrop soundholes, and was featured in publicity material for the fabled Star Club in Hamburg. Later Hopfs included the budget Twisty, while the more high-end Telstar had abundant roller controls, toggles and slide switches. Hopf steadily decreased electric guitar production during the 1970s and ceased manufacturing in the mid 1980s.

H O Y E R

Hoyer instruments date back to the 19th century, made in the Erlangen area of Germany. Archtop electrics from the 1950s and 1960s were big-bodied and often fancy in typical German fashion, while semi-solids were usually Gibson-like. Early solidbodies were more individual: the mid-1960s model 35, for example, balanced Fender-like features with distinctively German ideas.

Copies prevailed in the 1970s, although solids like the straight-sided HG 651 and UK-designed Foldaxe maintained some original thinking. This mix continued into the 1980s, with Fender- and Gibson-inspired guitars partnering a few oddities.

Some high-end models appeared briefly with the breakaway Walter Hoyer brand around 1984, but both operations had ceased manufacturing by 1990. In 1998 Hoyer returned with some traditional-style semi-solids and archtop electrics, Les Paul-shaped solids and a revived HG 651, appropriately renamed the Bo.

This Hondo H-2 (near right) was made in Korea in 1983, in a similar style to Ibanez's X series of the period. Two German guitars made around 1965 grace the rest of the page: a Hopf Saturn 63 (center) and a Hoyer 35 (far right).

IBANEZ

No Japanese guitar manufacturer has had more global impact than Hoshino Gakki Ten, a company best known for its primary brandname, Ibanez. Its instruments have been seen in the hands of some of the world's top players, and for half a century Hoshino has contributed classic designs, efficient instruments for working musicians, and countless players' first guitars.

Hoshino was founded in 1909 in Nagoya, Japan, by Matsujiro Hoshino as a supplier of books and stationery, also retailing musical instruments. The company began importing instruments in 1921. Later in the 1920s, Yoshitaro Hoshino succeeded his father and in 1932 the first acoustic instruments appeared carrying the Ibanez brand. However, the company's buildings were destroyed during World War II, and Hoshino did not resume business until 1950.

Yoshitaro's son Junpei became president in 1960 and opened a new factory called Tama Seisakusho (Tama Industries). By 1964 Hoshino was making and exporting guitars with brandnames such as Ibanez, Star, King's Stone, Jamboree and Goldentone. While it's an oversimplification that ignores the many original creations, one can characterize Ibanez guitars historically in terms of stylistic influences, breaking the maker's long history down into three main areas: the 1960s; the 1970s; and the 1980s and later. The 1960s reflected the design influence of Jim Burns of England;

These two early Ibanez electrics illustrate the two body shapes that the brand at first adopted: a Jazzmaster-like outline, as on this Model 882 (far left) from about 1963; and a Burns-inspired shape and multiple-pickguard arrangement, as on this unnamed model (near left) made around 1964.

the 1970s were heavily dominated by Gibson-style guitars; and the remainder of the century was given over primarily to offset-double-cutaway guitars derived from Fender's Stratocaster design.

In the early 1960s Hoshino first reached the US when it sold acoustic guitars to Harry Rosenblum, founder of Elger Guitars and owner of Medley Music in Ardmore, Pennsylvania. Interested in obtaining an American distribution arm, Hoshino purchased a half interest in Elger around 1962. By that time Hoshino still only made acoustic guitars, but was offering a line of solidbody electrics sourced from other Japanese factories such as Fujigen Gakki, Kasuga, Chu Sin Gakki and others.

These early Ibanez instruments were small-body short-scale low-end guitars aimed at beginners. They came in two basic shapes, one of which was similar to a pointy-horned Burns Bison, the other more like a Fender Jazzmaster, and they were fitted with up to four small single-coil pickups.

Around 1964 Hoshino revised the Burns-style guitar with an interpretation somewhat closer to the original, including three-part pickguards, and replaced the little Jazzmaster-shaped body with one that was slightly more Stratocaster-like. But throughout most of the 1960s Hoshino's principal focus was on acoustic guitars.

Hoshino's serious interest in electric guitars strengthened after Shiro Arai of Aria encountered the newly-reissued Gibson Les Paul Custom – effectively Gibson's own

"copy" of the original – at a US trade show in 1968. Arai took back to Japan the notion of making Les Paul copies, launching what would become the "copy era." By 1969, bolt-neck Ibanez "Les Pauls" had joined those of other Japanese manufacturers, followed around 1971 by an Ibanez version of the Ampeg Dan Armstrong "see-through" Lucite guitar.

Around this time other Japanese manufacturers began to produce full lines of Fender, Gibson and Martin copies, increasingly closer to the originals, as did Hoshino by 1973. It was during the early 1970s that Hoshino began selling Ibanez- and CSL-brand guitars in the UK through distributor Summerfield Brothers, and Jason-brand guitars in Australia. Technical advice from Maurice Summerfield in the UK and Jeff Hasselberger in the US made Ibanez copies even better, with necks lowered into the body and squared-off fingerboard ends.

By 1974, the Ibanez line had exploded with both bolt-on-neck and set-neck variations on Gibson designs, including instruments in the style of the SG (including double-necks), Flying V (called the Rocket Roll), Firebird, Les Paul, Explorer (the Destroyer), Moderne, ES-345 and ES-175, plus a full complement of Fender copies. A number of these were marketed in the UK with the Antoria brand.

No sooner had these full-blown copies arrived than Hoshino began to innovate. In 1974 Ibanez introduced maple fingerboards on Les Paul and thinline copies, plus a

484

Three guitars from Ibanez's copying period: a 2347 (near right) from about 1974, copying a Gibson SG, including a very Gibson-like headstock shape; a 2364 (center) made in 1975 and copying an Ampeg Dan Armstrong "see-through" guitar; and a 2351 (far right) dating from 1976, copying a Gibson Les Paul, and with the "pre-lawsuit" Guild-like headstock shape.

rosewood-capped "Les Paul" with elaborate fingerboard inlays – before Gibson adopted such features. Ibanez had introduced original designs by 1974 (which, combined later, would yield its most popular and respected 1970s model, the Artist).

The 1974 models from Ibanez included four "Artist" electric guitars. Two were double-cutaway thinline types and two were solidbodies. They had fatter horns than the later Artist, but appeared with bolt-on necks with the "castle" headstock shape associated with the later-style Artist. Another solidbody debuted at this time, bearing two small sharply-pointed cutaways, but with an early version of the later Artist's glued-in heel-less neck joint.

Company literature dates the appearance of the carved-top, equal-double-cutaway Ibanez Artist to 1975, although it does not seem to have been advertised until the following year. The new Artist's fast, heel-less, glued-in neck and twin humbuckers competed with Yamaha's similar SG-2000. The Artist models would proliferate through 1982, to include versions with active onboard EQ and various options of switching and appointments. The two players most associated with the Artist were John Scofield and Steve Miller. The Artist solidbody line would be revived during 1997 – but not before the model name had seen more use.

In 1975 a number of Ibanez guitars appeared which are now considered some of the most collectable. They included the Custom Agent (a Les Paul-alike with a Gibson F-5 mandolin-style head and pearl belly inlays), the Artwood Nouveau (Strat-style with a dragon-carved body) and the Artwood Twin (a copy of the double-neck instrument played by John McLaughlin, built for him by luthier Rex Bogue).

These special guitars led to a variety of Les-Paul-style single-cutaway and Artist-style double-cutaway carved ash models, with features including "tree-of-life" inlays. Most of these were produced in limited runs and were referred to as Artist and/or Professional models, although common names had little to do with consistency of features and design. Musicians playing these guitars at the time included Randy Scruggs, Carl Perkins and Bob Weir.

An original-design Ibanez model, the Iceman, debuted In 1976. It was popularized when a custom-made model faced with broken mirror parts was played by Paul Stanley. The Iceman featured a medallion-like body shape with a point on the end and a large, Mosrite-style extended lower-cutaway horn. It was offered in both set-neck and bolt-on-neck versions.

It was at this time that original US distributor Harry Rosenblum sold his interest in Elger to Hoshino, although Hoshino's American subsidiary did not change its name to Hoshino USA until 1981. The strategy of copying US classics was very successful for everyone marketing Japanese guitars in the 1970s, especially Hoshino, and the American companies being copied became increasingly alarmed at the erosion of their

Three more Ibanez guitars are shown on this page, these from the company's transitional period when it was mixing copies and more original styles: a Performer 230 (far left) Les Paul-inspired model, the first "lawsuit" redesign with subtle but important body and headstock changes, plus fancy decoration; a limited-edition Artist Professional model (center) from 1977 with tree-of-life fingerboard inlay; and a Firebrand 2348 (near left), a somewhat more blatant copy of a "non-reverse" Gibson Firebird.

The great jazz popularizer George Benson (on-stage, below) was honored with Ibanez signature models in 1977. Benson is seen promoting a GB-10 model in this 1979 ad (far left) and posing with one for the cover of his fine album of 1987 (near left) made with Earl Klugh.

market share. In 1977 Norlin, the parent company of Gibson, filed a federal lawsuit against Elger. It claimed trademark infringement based on the copying of Gibson's headstock design – even though Ibanez had changed to a more Guild-like shape the previous year. It's from this action that copy guitars are sometimes nicknamed "lawsuit" instruments. The suit was settled out of court and, in the US at least, this particular "copy era" ended.

Ibanez's move away from copies was relatively quick and certainly dramatic. First to appear in 1978 was the Performer series, which essentially consisted of set-neck or bolt-on-neck Les-Paul-style instruments with an extra Telecaster-style curve on the upper shoulder, plus that Guild-style headstock. These were followed by the Concert series, which combined more of a Stratocaster-style offset-double-cutaway body with the carved top of a Les Paul.

Ibanez quickly settled on the Studio and Musician series, both of which featured rounded slightly-offset double-cutaways with short, pointed horns that clearly had taken their cue from the designs of Alembic. The Musicians were through-neck guitars with figured ash or walnut "wings" and, on the top models, onboard active pre-amps and equalization, again Alembic-like.

In 1977 Ibanez began what became a long tradition of artist-endorsed models, introducing the Artist Autograph line including versions of the ash-bodied Professional,

now renamed the Bob Weir, a limited-edition Iceman called the Paul Stanley, and two new fancy twin-humbucker single-cutaway archtops named for jazz sensation George Benson, the full-sized GB-20 and the smaller GB-10. The Weir and Iceman models did not make it into the 1980s, but the Benson models, including several variations, would remain Ibanez's flagship archtops.

A sign of Ibanez's shift from Gibson-like designs to Fender styles was the introduction in 1979 of the Roadster. This Stratocaster-style guitar had a bolt-on-neck, non-vibrato bridge and three single-coils. It came with either ash or mahogany bodies, and flamed-maple tops peering through semi-opaque finishes. A year later Ibanez helped start the Dyna factory in Japan to produce Fender-style guitars and introduced the new Stratocaster-style oil-finished Blazer, soon altered to feature slightly "hooked" body horns. The Blazer became popular and would help to set the pattern for Ibanez's upcoming Roadstar II series.

Ibanez reintroduced in 1981 a version of its Explorer-style guitar, the Destroyer II, this time with a rather more stylized, "pointy" body shape. Some models sported fancy tops. Two more endorsement guitars appeared, the LR10 Lee Ritenour Model, an equal-double-cutaway thinline semi-hollowbody in ES-335 style, and a full-size single-cutaway archtop hollowbody, the JP20 Joe Pass Model. In 1982 Ibanez revived its Flying V-style model as the Rocket Roll II, along with the Iceman II, some with flamed-

One of the signature models for George Benson, this is a small-body GB-10 (far left) made in 1978. Ibanez's Musician series was Alembic-influenced, as can be seen on this Musician MC500 (center) made in 1978. The Professional 2617 shown here (near left, made in 1978) is another limited edition, but exemplifies the company's new and popular Artist double-cutaway style.

maple tops. Also during 1982 the Blazers were replaced with what would become the enormously successful Roadstar II series, hitting the market as both Strat-style guitars and heavy metal pyrotechnics enjoyed a popular revival.

By 1983 Roadstar IIs ranged from the ash-bodied RS-100, a three-single-coil descendent of the Roadster, to the RS-1000 with carved birdseye-maple top, plus two through-neck models with twin humbuckers or three single-coils. Locking vibrato systems appeared in 1984, as did the company's first model with a humbucker/single-coil/single-coil pickup layout, the RS-440.

Steve Lukather endorsed a Roadstar, the basswood-and-maple RS-1010SL, launched in 1985. This model had two special humbuckers and a Pro Rocker locking vibrato system. Jazz-fusion legend Allan Holdsworth also helped to design his own Roadstar: the twin-humbucker AH10 and AH20 appeared briefly from 1985. The Roadstar II shape continued through 1986, although at the end the prefix changed to RG – which is confusing, because subsequent RGs had different styling. The birdseye models were gone, but the hardtail RG-600 still sported a bound flamed-maple top as well as low-impedance active pickups.

The V-shaped Rocket Roll was rolled into a new X series of heavy-metal-style guitars in 1983. These included a new Destroyer, combining the V and Explorer shapes into a model similar to a Dean ML, and the dramatic stretched-x-shape X-500. Ibanez

Steve Miller (above) was one of the most visible players of Ibanez's Artist models in the late 1970s and early 1980s. One of the best-known Ibanez guitars from the late 1970s is the odd-shape Iceman. This Iceman IC210 (main guitar) dates from 1979. Ibanez shifted from Gibson influence to Fender flavors with the Roadster series, new in 1979; this Roadster RS100 (far right) was made that year.

The Artist series from Ibanez ran from the mid 1970s to the late 1980s. These good quality guitars rivaled Yamaha's top SG models as the finest Japanese-made electrics of the period. This Artist ad (right) was published in 1982.

launched a brief foray into synth-access guitars in 1985-86 with the IMG-2010 guitar (sometimes referred to as a "controller") that had a space-age minimalist shape. The IMG featured a clever electronic vibrato system that reproduced the analog effect without tracking problems.

The move away from the Roadstar II era began in 1985 as Ibanez introduced the Pro-Line series, which had old Roadstar styling but new "superstrat" features. The guitars had the now ubiquitous superstrat appointments – that is, humbucker/single-coil/single-coil pickup layouts and locking vibrato systems – plus a row of small pushbuttons for recalling pickup settings.

Also debuting in 1985 was the RG series, distinct from the renamed Roadstar-style RGs by virtue of a more modern superstrat design with deep, pointed double cutaways. These guitars came in a wide array of pickup and trim configurations, in vibrato or stop-tail versions, with or without pickguards, and some with flamed-maple tops. They had a remarkable run and would anchor the Ibanez solidbody line right throughout the 1990s. The RG7620 (vibrato) and RG7621 (fixed bridge) seven-strings catered to the late-1990s rage for the extra low-tuned string, with the cheaper 7420 and 7421 models following in 2000.

Four new guitars appeared in 1987 – three basic bolt-on-neck Pro-Line models and the shortlived, more radical looking Maxxas line. The Pro-Lines included the Pro-540R Radius, a pointy-horned offset-double-cutaway instrument with a wedge-shape cross-section, quickly adopted by solo virtuoso Joe Satriani, and the Pro-540S Saber. This had a similar shape but featured a wafer-thin contoured body. Both would achieve considerable success in the 1990s.

Ibanez's involvement with endorsers had accelerated and expanded during the 1980s. By the end of the decade the redesigned Pro-Line Power model was endorsed by fusion ace Frank Gambale, and the JEM series appeared in 1988, designed in conjunction with former Frank Zappa guitarist Steve Vai. The JEM77 had deeply offset, sharp double-cutaways, vine-pattern inlays, humbucker/single-coil/humbucker pickup layout, locking vibrato system, floral pattern finish and a "monkey grip" cut-out body handle. A number of colorful versions, some with aluminum pickguards, subsequently appeared. A celebratory 10th Anniversary JEM with engraved pickguard and fancy trim was issued by Ibanez during the late 1990s.

The technically brilliant Vai had first come to notice in terms of his choice of instrument when he opted for a custom-made Charvel in the mid 1980s, a guitar known as the Green Meanie. Vai modified the instrument regularly. His tool-kit-assisted changes included the addition of a rout beneath the vibrato plate to allow for upbends as well as downward travel, much further chamfering of the cutaways to allow yet more access to the upper frets, and the inclusion of the influential pickup combination of

Three Ibanez models made in the 1980s are pictured on this page: an Artist 2618 (far left) from 1981; an Axstar AX45 (center) made in 1985; and a Rocket Roll II (near left) produced in 1982.

humbucker/single-coil/humbucker. When the Meanie was stolen, Vai remembered a Maxxas model that Ibanez had sent to him as a Christmas gift, and got in touch with the Japanese company. A prototype Vai model followed, based on drawings of the old Charvel, and along came the JEM series.

The JEM777 was first issued in a limited run of 777 examples, each in Loch Ness green and signed by Vai. The JEMs were often wildly finished, sometimes with vibrant color schemes and strange fingerboard inlays, as well as a floral version of the JEM77 that had a "tree-of-life" inlay.

Ibanez faced a dilemma common to other Japanese makers in the late 1980s. Successful marketing had made the company one of the largest guitar producers in the world, but inherent costs and currency exchange rates made it increasingly difficult to market guitars manufactured in Japan at the lower price points customers had come to expect. In order to continue offering high-end options, in 1988 Ibanez opened a US custom shop operation in Los Angeles, California. At first the shop dealt with custom graphics, but by 1989 had introduced the American Master Series, high-end through-neck versions of regular models, including the basswood MA2HSH and maple-topped-mahogany MA3HH, which lasted to 1991.

In 1990 the US shop began making the Exotic Wood series with fancy, unusual timbers. Two years later the USA Custom Graphic series appeared with colorful

More 1980s Ibanez guitars on this page: a Destroyer II DT555 (near right) from 1984 (another model from the DT line was endorsed by Def Leppard's Phil Collen – see 1984 ad, above); a highly sculpted X Series XV500 (center) made in 1985; and the guitar part of Ibanez's shortlived IMG2010 guitar synthesizer (far right) from 1986.

John Petrucci of Dream Theater (1992 album, left) used a number of American-made Ibanez USA Custom models in the 1990s (pictured, right). Later in the decade a signature Petrucci model would appear, the JPM100.

imaginary painted landscapes. Custom models can feature highly figured woods and extremely elaborate PRS-style multi-color inlays.

By 1994 Ibanez had moved its American production to the PBS factory in Pennsylvania operated by innovative luthier Dave Bunker. This lasted until about 1997, when PBS folded. Ibanez began producing the low-end bolt-on-neck EX series in Korea from 1989 to 1994. These EXs were superstrats – with deep, sharp double-cutaways – and reflected Ibanez's well-known RG series. The better EX models came with special touches such as bound fingerboards and triangular-shape fingerboard inlays.

At the start of the 1990s Ibanez introduced a new Artist series of set-neck double-cutaway electrics, twin-humbucker guitars only vaguely reminiscent of the old Artists. They included the semi-hollow f-hole AM200, the all-mahogany solidbody AR200, and maple-capped AR300, all lasting until mid-decade.

In 1990 Ibanez began to shuffle its Japanese solidbody lines. The wedge-cross-section Radius was endorsed by Satriani and transformed into the JS Joe Satriani Signature series, a variety of twin-humbucker models in finishes ranging from oiled mahogany to custom graphics. In 1998 came the JS 10th Anniversary Chrome Limited Edition, made of synthetic "luthite" material and finished in chrome. Ibanez's relationship with Steve Vai yielded the seven-string Universe series in 1990, essentially a JEM without the "monkey grip" handle. By 1992 the UV77 was available with pyramid

inlays and swirled, multi-colored "bowling ball" finishes. Yet more changes occurred in the Ibanez catalog during 1991. The thin-bodied Saber guitars were renamed the S-series, adding a seven-string model and proliferating as the decade progressed. By 1997 variants included the S Classic SC620 with a bound, flamed-maple top, and the S Prestige S2540 NT made of figured sapelle mahogany.

Frank Gambale got his own Signature FGM series in 1991, a version of the thin Saber with humbucker/single-coil/humbucker pickups, locking vibrato system and "sharktooth" inlays. In 1994 the Gambale line split into vibrato and stop-tail models, and three years later these were replaced by the FGM400, a high-end version with a quilted maple top and block inlays that lasted until 1998.

Reb Beach helped design the Voyager model, offered from 1991 until 1996. Behind its vibrato was a wide, wedge-shaped cutout designed to make extreme double-action

This Roadstar II RG240 (far left) dates from 1986; the Pro Line PL2550 shown here (center) was made in 1987; and this recent seven-string member of the long-running RG series, the RG7620 (near left), dates from 1998.

IBANEZ

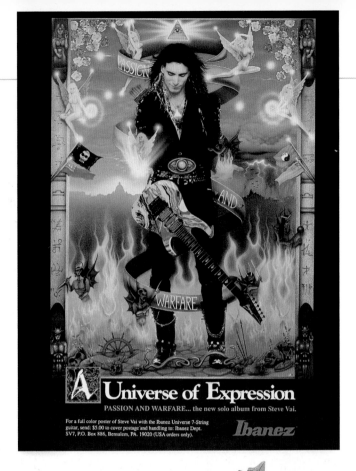

Steve Vai (pictured below) played a custom Charvel called the "Green Meanie" before collaborating with Ibanez for the Jem (main guitar) and then the Universe series. On this 1995 cover (right) an alienized Jem promotes Vai's Alien Love Secrets album, while the 1990 ad (far right) featured a multicolored Universe.

vibrato work easier. The RBM1 had a maple neck; the RBM2 had a koa top and Bolivian rosewood neck. These were replaced in 1994 by the mahogany-bodied RBM10 and oil-finish RBM400, available through 1996.

Ibanez's respected Benson electric archtops were joined by the Artstar series, beginning with the AF2000 in 1991. These were conceptually related to the late-1980s Artist line, with full-size hollow bodies and a single rounded cutaway, twin humbuckers, a headstock shaped somewhat like the old Artist "castle," and a trapeze tailpiece. A new Artstar AS200 semi-hollowbody thinline also debuted in 1991, with a larger body than the contemporary Artist AM200. These too would continue to be available in various versions through the following decade.

While the Radius guitars had earlier been transformed into the Satriani Signatures, their success inspired the less expensive R series in 1992. These lasted only a year, except for the R540 LTD which, with its humbucker/single-coil/humbucker pickups and sharktooth inlays, lasted to 1996.

By the early 1990s guitar manufacturers with any longevity had begun to realize that they were not only competing with other makers, but with their own "vintage" models which were increasingly prized by players and collectors alike. This resulted in two trends: the introduction of "retro" guitars with pseudo-1960s styling; and the reissuing of the company's own vintage classics. For Ibanez this was reflected in 1994

Guitar virtuoso Joe Satriani (below) is a long-time Ibanez player. This 1987 ad (right) is from around the start of their association, when Satriani endorsed the Radius 540R model – which formed the basis for signature models in the later JS series. This special JS 10th Anniversary (main guitar) dates from 1998, its synthetic "luthite" body finished in chrome.

Joe Satriani recorded this impressive solo album (left) in 1987 with an Ibanez Radius 540R. Later, Ibanez produced Satriani signature models, called the JS series and based on the Radius model. Korn were among the bands who brought a new popularity to seven-string guitars, seen in this 1999 ad (right).

with the retro Talman series and the reissue of its radical Iceman guitars. The Talman had an offset cutaway shape, like a lumpy Jazzmaster. The initial line was made in Japan and featured synthetic Resoncast (MDF) bodies. Some had Sky "lipstick" single-coil pickups and photogravure pseudo-figured-maple on bodies and necks. In 1995 the line expanded to include models with pearloid pickguards, metallic finishes and retro-looking fulcrum vibratos. In 1996 Talman production was shifted to Korea where the line changed to wood-body construction. The Talmans were gone by 1999.

The 1994 Iceman series included two bolt-on-neck reissues, the IC300 with a bound body and fingerboard, and the IC500 with fancier pearloid binding. In 1995 Ibanez added the limited-edition Paul Stanley PS10LTD, with a carved maple top and set-neck, and the general-production PS10II. In 1996 the Paul Stanley PS10CL replaced the IC500, and a year later the glued-neck ICJ100 WZ with abalone binding supplanted the Stanley-endorsed models.

The Ghostrider was new in 1994. An equal-double-cutaway solidbody with a bound top, two humbuckers and three-tuners-a-side headstock, it provided an early-to-mid-1980s feel with a late-1950s name, and lasted two years. While pointy-double-cutaway superstrats were still the principal fare for Ibanez, the retro vibe brought back traditional Strat-shaped guitars in 1994 with the RX series. These ranged from the RX750 with a padauk/mahogany/padauk sandwich body and the RX650 with a

Three more Ibanez models are shown on this page: a Radius 540R (near right) from 1989; a Saber 540S (center) also made in 1989; and a Universe UV7 (far right) from 1990.

figured-maple top, to models with Strat-style pickguards – all in various pickup configurations. The RX series continued through 1998 when it was renamed the GRX series and downsized. In 1999 the series was augmented with a beginner-level equal-double-cutaway guitar, the twin-humbucker GAX70.

Ibanez added yet another pro endorsement in 1994 with the Paul Gilbert series. The first guitar was the PGM500, basically a deep-cutaway RG with a reverse headstock, humbucker/single-coil/humbucker pickup layout and fixed bridge assembly. The most distinctive decorative feature was its white finish with painted-on black f-holes. This was available for two years.

The first Gilbert model was joined by the PGM30 in 1995, the same guitar except for the addition of a double-locking vibrato system. This guitar would become the principal Gilbert model. In 1998 the Gilbert line was briefly enhanced for about a year by the transparent red PGM900 PMTC, essentially a Talman with twin humbuckers, stop tailpiece and the distinctive fake f-holes.

Another celebrity series was introduced in 1996, endorsed by jazz guitarist Pat Metheny, a long-time Ibanez player. The first model was the fancy PM100, a uniquely shaped offset-double-cutaway f-hole hollowbody archtop with a small pointed cutaway on the bass side and a deeper, pointed cutaway on the treble side. It was joined in 1997 by the PM20, a more traditional single-rounded-cutaway archtop with a rosewood fingerboard and ivoroid trim, still with one neck humbucker. In 1997 Ibanez brought back the Blazer, its Fender-influenced double-cutaway of 1980. The new Blazers revived the "hooked-horn" body, "blade" headstock, pearloid pickguard and a humbucker/single-coil/humbucker pickup arrangement. The BL1025 had a Wilkinson vibrato; the BL850 had a Gotoh unit. These late-era Blazers were available until 1999.

The last new endorsement of the 1990s came from another long-time Ibanez player, John Petrucci. The JPM100 of 1998 was another pointy deep-double-cutaway guitar with the RG profile, but finished in a camouflage pattern.

At the start of the 21st century the Ibanez line looked much as it had for more than a decade. Solidbodies were represented by the pointy RG guitars and their many different six- and seven-string variations, the Satriani versions of the old wedge-section Radius, the thin S series Sabers, and the Strat-style GRX series, plus the reissued Iceman and Artist models. Semi-hollowbody thinlines included the Artstar series, and hollowbody "jazz" electrics included the venerable George Benson and more recent Pat Metheny. Signaling future directions, new for 2000 was the Double Edge Bridge, a locking vibrato with built-in L.R. Baggs piezo pickups for a switchable "acoustic" sound.

A Millennium series of high-price limited editions included a clear plastic Satriani, a swirly-painted Vai Jem and a George Benson Masquerade. Still favored by many top pros, Ibanez guitars reflect a long heritage of commitment to quality and innovation.

Ibanez did the retro thing with its Talman series, as these two examples show: a Talman TC530 (far left) from 1993, and a Talman TV750 (center) from 1994. This S Classic SC420 (near left), updating the Saber series, dates from 1999.

JACKSON

Grover Jackson's brand came to symbolize the "superstrat" rock guitar of the 1980s. His update of Fender's classic Stratocaster design offered more frets, deeper cutaways, a drooped "pointy" headstock, altered pickup layouts and a high-performance vibrato system. Jackson attracted many of the emerging fast-gun players like Randy Rhoads, George Lynch and Vivian Campbell, as well as more mainstream guitarists such as Jeff Beck, Gary Moore and Frank Stepanek.

Guitarist Jackson liked to tinker with guitars, and he joined Wayne Charvel's guitar-parts supply operation in San Dimas, California, in September 1977. However, the company was experiencing some financial problems, and in November 1978 Jackson bought the outfit for almost $40,000. Initially the small three-man workshop continued making necks, bodies and other components, as well as repairing and modifying instruments. Charvel-brand bolt-on-neck instruments debuted in 1979 (see Charvel).

In late 1980, Grover Jackson met a 24-year-old up-and-coming guitarist called Randy Rhoads. Together they designed a custom guitar that was based on the overall design of Gibson's Flying V. In 1981 they collaborated again on a more radical variant of the original design, this time with an offset body style. For these clear departures from the Charvels, Jackson began to use his own name as a brand. In fact, the two brands would remain clearly distinct from one another until early 1986. Charvels were

Randy Rhoads is pictured on-stage with Ozzy Osbourne (opposite page) and one of the custom guitars made for him by Grover Jackson. It became the Jackson Randy Rhoads model of 1983. This example (main guitar) from that first year was the 30th built, and the first to be equipped with a Floyd Rose vibrato.

Two early Jackson guitars are shown below. The earliest guitar (below left) was probably the first Jackson Strat-style instrument, made in 1982 for Mark St John, then a member of Kiss. Note the early freehand Jackson logo. The other guitar (below, from 1983) is the first Jackson Soloist, and the first Jackson with a graphic finish. It marks the birth of the "superstrat" design that defined the look of rock guitars in the 1980s, achieving wide acclaim for Jackson in the process and spurring many makers to adopt the style.

guitar manufacturers

made mostly in a Fender-like style, and had bolt-on-necks. Jacksons, however, were more original, and featured through-neck construction. Guitars from either brand made a feature of flashy graphics and custom paint-jobs.

With the tragic death of Rhoads in 1982 and the subsequent interest in his unusual Jacksons, the value of player-association was underlined. So it was that early in 1983 the first Jackson-brand production model appeared, the Randy Rhoads.

More exaggerated-shape custom designs were built especially for players such as Australian band Heaven's guitarist Kelly (a curved Explorer-style design) and Dave Linsk of Overkill (a Flying V-like "Double Rhoads"). At first, Jackson would reserve his own brandname for these custom instruments built to the various designs of the individual musicians concerned. Gradually, however, favorites emerged, and all Jackson's significant body styles – which would later be given specific model names – were developed at the company's San Dimas workshop between 1983 and 1986.

These were: the Randy Rhoads (offset V, from 1983); the Soloist (superstrat, from 1983); the Kelly ("curved" Explorer-style, from 1984); the Double Rhoads and later King V (Flying V-style, from 1985). More or less from the start, these models were offered with two levels of trim – Student (with rosewood fingerboard, dot markers, unbound neck/headstock) and Custom (with ebony fingerboard, "sharkfin" markers, bound neck/headstock) – although variations often appeared. Jackson gradually

developed and modified the original Strat-style guitars he'd made with the Charvel brandname, at first as the blatantly-named Strat Body, but more importantly as the Jackson Soloist. From about 1983 the Soloist came to define what we now know as the superstrat, the most influential electric guitar design of the 1980s. With input from players regularly shaping the changing design, Jackson built on the classic Strat-style guitar, squaring the body's sides while making the contouring bolder and overall shape slimmer, and "stretching" the horns.

While his early superstrat-inclined guitars continued with 22 frets, Jackson began to capitalize on the extra upper-fret access provided by his through-neck and deeper cutaways by increasing the number of frets to 24, giving players a wider range. The revamped body carried powerful combinations of single-coil and humbucker pickups, evolving to the "standard" superstrat combination of two single-coils plus bridge humbucker, partnered by a locking heavy-duty vibrato system. Jackson also instigated the drooped "pointy" headstock. So was the superstrat born: a new tool for high-speed,

Another early Jackson Soloist (near right) superstrat, with Custom trim, this one made in 1985. This Double Rhoads Custom (center, from 1984) was named for its two Rhoads "wings," and scaled down later became the King V series. It was designed by Dave Linsk of Overkill, and has a unique finish, lightning-bolt inlays, slight cutaway, and rear-mounted jack. The custom-made reverse-Firebird-style guitar (far right) was called Instant Sex, built in 1988 by Jackson for Robin Crosby of Ratt.

guitar manufacturers

A motley crew of Jackson/Charvel endorsers lined up for this ad published in 1985 (left), with the accent on the graphic finishes that the joint company pioneered. Steve Vai is there, fourth from the right. Twelve years later Joey Z of Life Of Agony promoted the US-made JJP model in this Jackson ad (right).

high-gain guitarists, able to meet, match and foster their athletic excesses.

The Charvel logo was transferred to a Japan-built line in 1986, with the Jackson brand retained for the high-end US-made line. By 1987 production of the US Jacksons switched to a large new facility at Ontario, California. By late 1987 the King V was a production model. Two years on, the Strat Body's name was changed to the less contentious Vintage Style, while the line expanded to include the Dinky.

Also new in the Jackson line at this time was the strange Phil Collen signature six-string, its radically carved and contoured body far removed from the established idea of a rock guitar. A more affordable Collen model, the PC3, appeared in 1997.

In 1985 Jackson himself had started a joint venture with Texas-based distributor International Music Corporation. Jackson left in 1989. He later went on to design a number of instruments for Washburn and others. After Jackson's departure, three different Jackson lines emerged: Custom Shop; US series; and Jackson Professional.

The Custom Shop editions were US-made special pieces at prices too rarefied for most mortals to even consider. The limited-production US series models each came with the option of ten different hand-painted airbrush graphic finishes. The Japanese-made Jackson Professional line was intended to bring Jackson to a wider market with high-quality versions of the American originals. These included the unusual Phil Collen model, along with the new Fusion Pro and ultra-pointy Warrior Pro. Prices of the

Professional line were relatively elevated for Japanese factory-built instruments. Despite such price variety, the choice of models remained limited, although the company wasn't slow to pick up and exploit changing trends. As part of the 1992 Professional series, the PRS-style Infinity model insisted on retaining Jackson's most distinctive features, the pointy headstock and the heavy-duty vibrato system. The retro-influenced JIX model appeared in the Jackson catalog during 1993, as did the Kelly Standard version of a Custom Shop line. High-end limited editions and variations on continuing themes appeared throughout the 1990s.

Jackson has concentrated on established strengths, while continuing to expand into lower-price markets. The Concept series launched in 1993 featured relatively affordable Japanese-built versions of the best-known Jackson designs, while the Performer line of 1994 was manufactured in Korea to attain even cheaper prices. By 2000 the X Series was made in India.

The acquisition of Jackson by the Japanese electronic musical instrument company Akai in 1997 saw the demise of the operation's sister-brand, Charvel. But the Charvel Surfcaster survived as a Jackson production model, introduced to the line during the following year (it had begun life earlier as a Jackson custom-shop guitar). Jackson continues today to refine its body shapes, for example in 2000 when it melded the Kelly and Rhoads styles to create the new Kelly Star KS2 model.

Three more Jacksons are pictured on this page: a Stealth TH2 from 1997 (far left); a PC3 (center) made in 1998; and a Surfcaster model, also dating from 1998.

JAMES TYLER

These high-end instruments are held in high esteem by many LA and Nashville sessionmen, and typify the virtuoso rock-style guitar. They are high-class, high-performance mostly Stratocaster-like guitars, available in spectacular custom colors including "psychedelic vomit" and even "haz-mat-sewage-fiasco shmear."

Tyler is virtually a custom maker, heading a team of three other builders based in Van Nuys, California. There is a line of firm models available too that includes the superstrat-style and Telecaster-like Studio Elites, the Stratocaster-style Classic (also with Michael Landau and Dan Huff signature versions), the Les Paul-based top-of-the-line Mongoose model, and the rather more originally styled Ultimate Weapon. By 1999 the operation was producing some 150 instruments a year.

JOHN BIRCH

During the 1970s this UK maker produced a line of solidbodies demonstrating individual ideas. Models such as the J1 and J2 employed through-neck construction, distinctive multi-pole pickups and often comprehensive circuitry. Styling, however, seldom strayed beyond conventional designs.

Custom requirements were also accommodated at the Birch workshop and many famous British names employed him to build what often amounted to some very unusual instruments. Such customers have included Tony Iommi, Roy Wood, Ritchie

Blackmore and Dave Hill. This became Birch's best known work, often providing the most bizarre creations to bear the maker's brand.

Birch quit the guitar business in the mid 1980s, but returned during the early 1990s with new instruments, pickups and synth-access systems.

KAPA

Capitalizing on the early-1960s guitar boom, Kapa guitars were the brainchild of Dutch immigrant Kope Veneman of Hyattsville, Maryland, and were launched around 1963. Known for ultra-thin necks and an unusual 12-string vibrato, Kapa launched its first offset-shape solidbodies with the Challenger model name.

Thinner-body Continental models appeared in 1966. However, names were used indiscriminately on many models. The Hofner-style pickups were mostly made by Kapa itself. Kapa's popular Minstrel teardrop-shape guitars were introduced in 1968, and Japanese thinlines and solidbodies (plus oriental hardware) began to appear in 1969. A very few all-Japanese guitars appeared near Kapa's end, in 1970, when parts and equipment were sold to Micro-Frets and Mosrite.

KAWAI

This Japanese manufacturer is best known for pianos, keyboards and synthesizers. Its electric guitars started in the 1960s, targeting the lower end of the market and often attempting to impress with chromed control panels, banks of multiple switches and

A conservatively-finished James Tyler Studio Elite (near right) made in 1999; a fine example of John Birch's often bizarre custom work, this 1976 AJS Custom (center) was named for the initials of its original bat-obsessed owner; and a Kapa Continental 12-string made in Maryland in 1966.

eye-catching body shapes. The late 1970s brought much improved quality, and the KS series from that period featured a distinctive slotted headstock. Other models aped Alembic's multi-laminated through-neck style, but the crescent-shaped Moon Sault solidbody was a design clearly out on its own.

The early-1980s Aquarius line from Kawai was rather more Fender-orientated. The company has since catered mainly for domestic customers in Japan, and has reissued the Moon Sault and some other oldies.

KAY

Of the huge Chicago-based guitar power-houses, only Kay approached the size and influence of Harmony on the lower to middle ranges of the mass market. Kay was founded in 1890 as the Groehsl Company, a mandolin manufacturer, adding guitars and banjos around 1918.

In 1921 the company name was changed to Stromberg-Voisinet and two years later Henry Kay "Hank" Kuhrmeyer joined the company. The guitars themselves were called Strombergs, while the company was referred to as Voisinet (thus distinguishing it from a Boston company that was producing Stromberg-brand archtop acoustics).

By the mid 1920s Voisinet was supplying some of mail-order company Montgomery Ward's fancier instruments, often using pearloid, a popular Kay material. Voisinet (Kay) also supplied many guitars for the Spiegel catalog and other distributors, including

The Kawai Concert shown (far left) dates from around 1968. The Japanese Kawai company built instruments for a number of other brands, including the obscure Telestar, whose 1960s catalog (above, left) has a painfully hip cover. Two Kays are shown on this page: a 1954 Thin Twin K161 (center, with 1953 ad), known as the Jimmy Reed model; and a monstrous Solo King (near left) from about 1958.

501

Continental, Chicago Musical Instruments (CMI) and Oahu. In 1928 Voisinet introduced some very early production "electric" guitars, the Stromberg Electros. Despite their ground-breaking status, they were not what we think of now as electric guitars: crucial electro-magnetic pickups were still a few years away. The Stromberg Electros were in fact acoustic flat-top instruments fitted with a transducer to pick up the vibrations of the body's top (but not the strings). They were supplied with a primitive amplifier. The unusual Electro models were nonetheless greeted with some enthusiasm, especially among Chicago's hillbilly radio performers. But few were made, and with the onset of the Depression they disappeared from the market.

Stromberg-brand instruments, often with a decal decoration, continued to be sold until around 1932. In 1931 Kuhrmeyer became president. The KayKraft brand debuted on both regular Spanish and distinctive two-point Venetian guitars. Through the 1930s the line was anchored by KayKrafts, cheaper Arch Krafts, and small-bodied guitars often of plywood. By 1934 the company was known as the Kay Musical Instrument Company. The Kay brand began to appear around 1936.

Kay resumed making electrics in 1936 with a pickup-equipped flat-top for Ward. Unique violin-shaped guitars were made in 1938, and in 1939 the high-end Television archtop appeared. Kay also made a few guitar models for National and Gretsch during the 1930s. In 1940 Sears' new Silvertone brandname was first applied to a Kay-made

This Kay Jazz II K776 (near right) was produced in around 1962. A similar model was used by Eric Clapton in his early band, The Roosters. This Kay Up-Beat K8995J (main guitar, far right) was made about 1960.

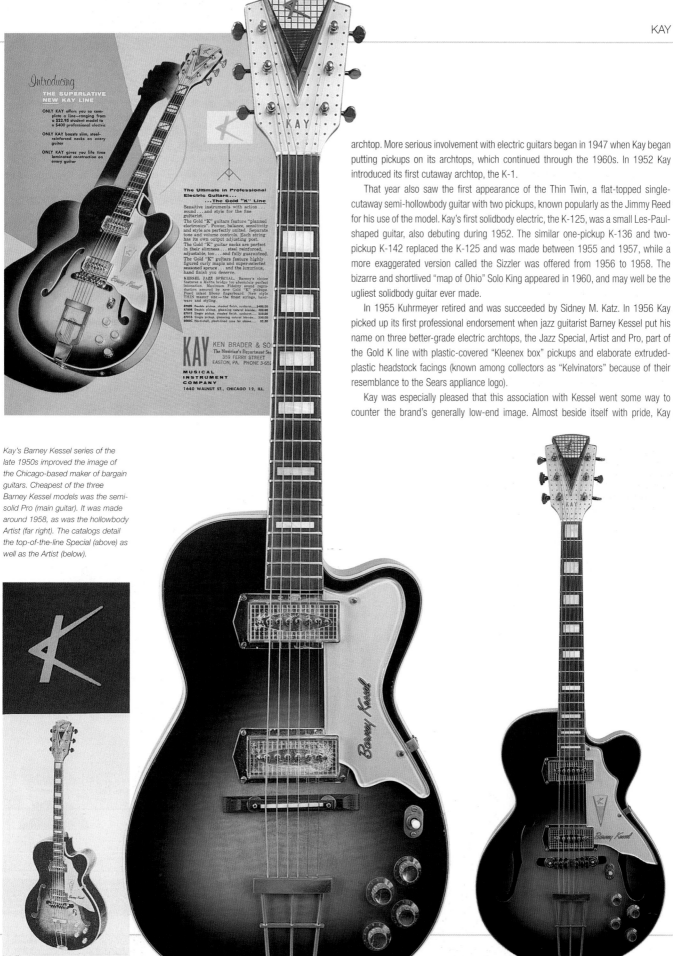

Kay's Barney Kessel series of the late 1950s improved the image of the Chicago-based maker of bargain guitars. Cheapest of the three Barney Kessel models was the semi-solid Pro (main guitar). It was made around 1958, as was the hollowbody Artist (far right). The catalogs detail the top-of-the-line Special (above) as well as the Artist (below).

archtop. More serious involvement with electric guitars began in 1947 when Kay began putting pickups on its archtops, which continued through the 1960s. In 1952 Kay introduced its first cutaway archtop, the K-1.

That year also saw the first appearance of the Thin Twin, a flat-topped single-cutaway semi-hollowbody guitar with two pickups, known popularly as the Jimmy Reed for his use of the model. Kay's first solidbody electric, the K-125, was a small Les-Paul-shaped guitar, also debuting during 1952. The similar one-pickup K-136 and two-pickup K-142 replaced the K-125 and was made between 1955 and 1957, while a more exaggerated version called the Sizzler was offered from 1956 to 1958. The bizarre and shortlived "map of Ohio" Solo King appeared in 1960, and may well be the ugliest solidbody guitar ever made.

In 1955 Kuhrmeyer retired and was succeeded by Sidney M. Katz. In 1956 Kay picked up its first professional endorsement when jazz guitarist Barney Kessel put his name on three better-grade electric archtops, the Jazz Special, Artist and Pro, part of the Gold K line with plastic-covered "Kleenex box" pickups and elaborate extruded-plastic headstock facings (known among collectors as "Kelvinators" because of their resemblance to the Sears appliance logo).

Kay was especially pleased that this association with Kessel went some way to counter the brand's generally low-end image. Almost beside itself with pride, Kay announced in advertising material in 1957: "Kay and the nation's number one jazz guitarist Barney Kessel, winner of the *Down Beat*, *Metronome* and *Playboy* polls, have together developed a professional guitar which will establish new standards in quality of sound, workmanship and design."

Unfortunately, the liaison did not last. Kessel's name was dropped from the instruments during 1960, but the guitars continued with abridged headstock designs. Other popular Kay electrics of the time included the mid-size Upbeat and thinline single-cutaway Swing Master. In 1960 the hollowbody Les-Paul-shaped thinline Value Leader, Style Leader and Pro arrived in various finishes and pickup configurations, with metal "Art Deco" pickguards.

Versions without the metal were offered by St. Louis Music with their own Custom Kraft brandname. From this point onwards, Kay increasingly employed bolt-on necks on most of its electric guitars.

The Vanguard line of solidbodies followed in 1961. These had slab bodies shaped something like a Fender Jazzmaster. A more attractive solidbody was introduced the following year, the Strat-style K-300. Three new electric thinline hollowbodies also joined the Kay line in 1961: the pointy single-cutaway Speed Demon and Galaxie, and double-cutaway Jazz II. In 1965 the Vanguards were redesigned with a "German carve." Kay's six-tuners-in-line "bushwhacker" headstock also debuted in 1965. In

1964 Kay had relocated to a huge ultra-efficient factory in suburban Elk Grove Village, Illinois. Three more solidbodies were introduced during 1965 – the Artiste, Titan I, and Apollo – with the new bushwhacker head, short cutaways, heavy contouring and a shape that crossed a Strat with a Jazzmaster.

In 1966 Kay was purchased by Louis J. Nicastro's Seeburg Corporation, best known for its juke boxes. Katz remained in control of the new musical instrument division. Most of the guitars from the early 1960s were eliminated, but the frumpy early Vanguards became the budget Value Leader line. The mid-1960s models expanded. The somewhat high-end K400 Series Professional solidbodies were introduced, with equal cutaways similar to a Gibson SG and a tapered lower bout like a Strat. The Speed Demon name was applied to a couple more similarly-shaped solidbodies.

Seeburg's tenure as a guitar-maker was brief. In 1967 Kay changed hands again, purchased by long-time competitor Valco (formerly National and National-Dobro), headed by Robert Engelhardt who was keen to obtain the new manufacturing capacity.

The Kay line remained unaffected, although a number of hybrid Supro-brand guitars including the solidbody Lexington began sporting Kay components and Japanese-made parts. The Valco-Kay marriage was also shortlived. In 1968 the market for electric guitars collapsed. It was in that year that the Valco-Kay operation declared bankruptcy and closed its doors. During 1969 Valco-Kay's assets were auctioned off

Three more Kay guitars are shown on this page: a Double Cutaway K592 (near right) made around 1964; a K30 (center) from about 1976; and a Busker (far right) with built-in amp and speaker, dating from 1986.

guitar manufacturers

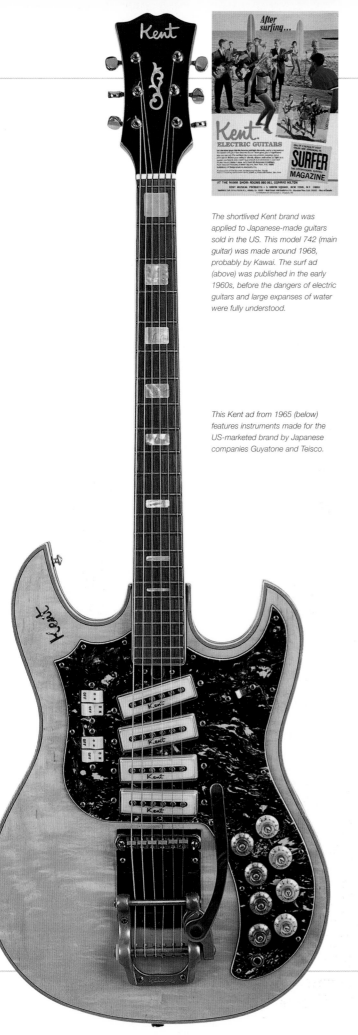

The shortlived Kent brand was applied to Japanese-made guitars sold in the US. This model 742 (main guitar) was made around 1968, probably by Kawai. The surf ad (above) was published in the early 1960s, before the dangers of electric guitars and large expanses of water were fully understood.

This Kent ad from 1965 (below) features instruments made for the US-marketed brand by Japanese companies Guyatone and Teisco.

and rights to the Kay name passed to Sol Weindling and Barry Hornstein of WMI, importer to the US of Teisco Del Rey guitars from Japan. In the early 1970s both the Teisco Del Ray and Kay brands appeared on Teisco-made instruments, but by about 1973 WMI was using only the Kay brand. The bolt-neck K-20T Gibson SG "copy" appeared that year, and most 1970s Kay guitars were low-end copies of popular American models. In 1980 the Kay name was sold to Tony Blair of AR Musical Enterprises of Indianapolis, Indiana. From that point on the Kay name was used on guitars for the beginner market, with production continually migrating to developing countries in order to maintain the low price point.

KENT

The Kent brandname appeared on some of the earliest Japanese-made musical equipment imported to the US. New York distributor Buegeleisen & Jacobson used it on microphones and pickups in the late 1950s, and around 1962 on beginner-level solidbody guitars made by Guyatone and Teisco with small slab bodies and up to four pickups. The Kent line eventually included guitars, basses, amps, mandolins and banjos. The most interesting Kents came in 1967, symmetrical and asymmetrical hollowbodies and solidbodies with burled-maple tops and wide, almost baroque black-and-white plastic strips covering the sides. Kent-brand guitars do not appear to have survived the 1960s.

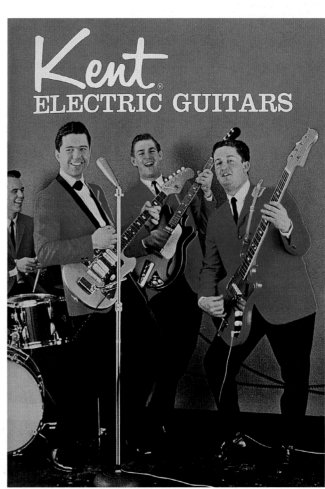

KLEIN

Steve Klein is best known to electric guitarists for his unusual ergonomic "Kleinberger" headless-guitar design. As well as the normal requirements to provide a fine, playable instrument with a good sound, the Klein electric is also intended to enable correct posture for the seated player.

Klein himself continues to market acoustic guitars made in Lafayette, California, but is no longer associated with the electric guitar company, having sold out to employee Lorenzo German in 1995. German's Klein Electric Guitars operation is now located in Byron, California, north-east of San Francisco.

The Steinberger-style headless one-piece rosewood neck of the Klein electric instrument is joined to an unusually-shaped and distinctive curving body. It was originally devised by Klein with the help of Carl Margolis, musician Ronnie Montrose and designer Ned Steinberger.

The Klein electric is at the time of writing available in two three-pickup versions: the solidbody basswood or alder DT; and the swamp ash or alder BF with hollowed body chambers. The chambered model is a new development since Klein's own involvement ceased. Pickups are by Seymour Duncan, or optionally Joe Barden.

Both models come as standard fitted with either a Steinberger S-trem or Transtrem vibrato bridge, although they are also available with a DeLorenzo vibrato or hardtail

This Klein (main guitar) is a BF model, with "chambered" swamp ash body, made in 1998. Pickups are Kent Armstrong lipsticks plus a DiMarzio, and the bridge is equipped with an RMC piezo pickup.

Klein has attracted a number of name players to its distinctive instruments. This 1990s ad (below) features two: ex-Police guitarist Andy Summers (left) and avant-garde stylist David Torn.

TWO INNOVATIVE PLAYERS
TWO INNOVATIVE PRODUCTS

ANDY SUMMERS

PEARCE
AMPLIFIER SYSTEMS

KLEIN
ELECTRIC GUITARS

AVAILABLE DIRECT

DAVID TORN

BLAKE BOGDANOVICH

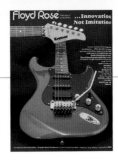

bridge. Klein also offers limited production of a four- and five-string bass in the same general design. The "ergonomic" qualities of the Klein guitar stem from the unusual body shape. The whole object is designed so that when the player sits with the guitar, the neck will be situated at an optimum angle and in a way that allows the fretting hand to access the fingerboard easily and comfortably.

This contrasts with a regular electric guitar where the player's fretting hand is moved away from his body to play on the lower frets, and into his body to reach the upper frets. With the Klein, it is claimed, the player's hand and arm moves freely and travels the minimum distance to reach any particular fret on the fingerboard.

Klein guitars have been used by an impressive array of artists that includes Bill Frisell, Joni Mitchell, Lou Reed, Andy Summers, David Torn and Joe Walsh. Custom-built oddities have included an electric harp-guitar for the late Michael Hedges and an electric sitar for Steve Miller.

KLIRA

This German maker provided value-for-money electrics during four decades. Klira was established in Schoenbach, West Germany, in 1887 by violin maker Johannes Klier, succeeded by his son Otto Josef in 1914. The company relocated in 1950 to Bubenreuth (also the base for Hofner and Framus), the emphasis shifting from violins to guitars. Klira first offered electrics in 1958 with a line of amplified archtops with unusually shaped soundholes. Most Klira electrics were designed by Heinrich Weidner. Solidbodies debuted in 1960, budget Fender-influenced models often covered in sparkle plastic or textured vinyl. The mid 1960s represented the peak of Klira's electric production, with many exports.

Klira also made very cheap Triumphator-brand instruments, which were sold in Germany only through the Quelle mail-order operation. In the 1970s Klira offered mainly copies, although there was some retention of individual character. However, electric guitar production slipped dramatically, and by the end of the 1980s Klira guitar manufacturing had ceased.

KRAMER

Kramer began in the late 1970s as part of the movement to improve guitar technology with aluminum necks, but before its demise at the end of the 1980s it had become one of the largest guitar companies in the United States.

Kramer guitars were made by the BKL Corporation, founded in 1976 in Neptune City, New Jersey, by former Travis Bean associate Gray Kramer, music retailer Dennis Berardi and ex-Norlin executive Peter LaPlaca. Financial backing came from real-estate developer Henry Vaccaro. Kramer himself, however, left the company shortly after it was originally set up. The first Kramer guitars – the 450G model and the 350G model – were designed in conjunction with luthier Phil Petillo and featured fancy

A Klira 320 Star Club (far left) made around 1965; a Kramer 450 (center) from 1977; and a Kramer 650 also made around 1977.

hardwood bodies with slightly offset double-cutaways and bolt-on "T-bar" aluminum necks. These necks had wooden inserts in the back, synthetic ebonol fingerboards and "tuning fork"-shape headstocks.

Kramer switched from its own pickups to DiMarzio-made units with the DMZ series beginning in 1978. In 1980 Kramer briefly launched a series of exotic shapes, including the B.C.-Rich-inspired XL series, the V-shaped XKG models, and the legendary battle-axe-shaped Gene Simmons Axe.

During 1979 Kramer ran into financial problems and until 1982 management was assumed by Guitar Center of Los Angeles. They recommended a switch to more economical wooden necks, and these were introduced as an option in 1981.

This was another big year for Kramer, seeing the introduction of the popular minimalist aluminum-necked headless Duke model, somewhat similar to a Steinberger, the "pointy" Voyager series, which was more in the style of Dean's influential ML guitar, and the first series of Kramer's Stratocaster-style Pacers and the high-end Stagemaster models. German-made Rockinger vibratos also began to be offered that year on Kramer guitars. Aluminum necks were losing popularity in the early 1980s, and the last few Kramers with these were produced in 1985.

In 1982 Kramer began a long-time association with locking-vibrato innovator Floyd Rose, becoming the exclusive distributor while introducing the asymmetrical pointy

Floyd Rose Signature model. The link with Rose brought Edward Van Halen into the Kramer camp, the brand's most important endorser who further boosted Kramer's success. In 1983 the Pacer series was slimmed down, with the Deluxe model becoming one of the first guitars to feature the "superstrat" pickup layout of humbucker/single-coil/single-coil. This became a very popular configuration and, along with Stratocaster-based body shapes and drooped "pointy" headstocks, would dominate the rest of the 1980s.

In 1984 the popular single-slanted-humbucker Baretta with "banana" headstock debuted. That year Kramer also introduced the Ripley Stereo, with electronics by luthier Steve Ripley that had individual volume and stereo fader controls for each string. In 1985 a revised Voyager, the Vanguard (reminiscent of the Jackson Randy Rhoads) and the Explorer-like Condor appeared.

A sign of Kramer's growing muscle were the company's 1985 endorsers Brad Gillis, Jeff Golub, John McCarry, Ed Ojeda and Neal Schon. Also that year Kramer purchased Spector Guitars & Basses, instruments designed by Stuart Spector and Alan Charney and available in American- and Japanese-made versions.

Along with other major US guitar companies, Kramer began importing its own budget versions of its main designs, starting with the Japanese-made Focus line in 1984, followed by the Korean-made Striker series in 1985 and Korean Aero-Stars in

guitar manufacturers

Two Kramer guitars are pictured on the opposite page: a Duke Special (far left) from 1982, and a DMZ-2000 Custom (near left) made in 1979.

Three more Kramers are shown here: a Voyager Imperial (main guitar) from 1982; an RSG-1 Ripley Stereo (center) dating from 1984; and an American Sustainer (far right) made in 1989, with a Floyd Rose Sustainer pickup in the neck position. This 1989 ad (below) highlights the Kramer Nightswan, endorsed by Vivian Campbell, who would later join Def Leppard.

1986. Kramer's strangest models, the spaceship-shaped Enterprize and Triaxe, appeared in 1986 only. That year also saw the limited-edition through-neck Paul Dean Signature. By the end of 1986 Kramer was the largest American guitar company.

By 1987 Kramer's golden age of superstrats had begun, with revamped Pacers, Baretta models and luxurious carved-top, through-neck Stagemasters, plus a host of other broadly similar models.

Elliot Easton joined the ranks of Kramer endorsers with the release of the EE Pro guitars, Vivian Campbell began his endorsement of the NightSwan models, and during 1988 Richie Sambora got his own Kramer model too.

The Kramer Sustainer with the Floyd Rose distortion-generating pickup also appeared in 1988. It was around this time that Kramer founder Dennis Berardi started a management company that handled a Russian band, Gorky Park. Kramer introduced a Korean-made balalaika-shaped Gorky Park model in 1989.

Following the introduction in 1989 of the Metalist and Showster lines that used some metal parts to improve sustain, the Kramer empire suddenly collapsed in bankruptcy. New management under James Liati took over, but by late 1990 Kramer was gone. In 1995 Henry Vaccaro (see Vaccaro) intended a revival of the aluminum-neck models, but in 1997 the rights to the Kramer name and most of its model designations were sold to Gibson.

The LaBaye 2-By-4 guitar and a band called The Robbs feature in this ad. Its publication in 1967 appears to have marked the big moment both for the guitar and for the band.

This bizarre Krundaal Bikini (main guitar) was made by Wandre in Italy around 1962. It was one of the first self-contained electric guitars: the pod attached to the body contains a built-in amp and speaker.

Another oddity from the 1960s was this LaBaye 2-By-4 Six (below right), made in 1967 and with a bare minimum body, many years before Steinberger. Vox launched its own small-body guitar, the Winchester, the same year, seen with bearded designer Dick Denney in the picture.

KRUNDAAL

Wandre Pioli of Cavriago, Italy, made guitars in the 1960s, including a number of eccentric models, and with a variety of brandnames (see Wandre).

Some of Pioli's instruments even had two or three different names spread across them, which makes for even more confusion when attempting to map this maker's history. Foremost of Pioli's brandnames was Wandre, but other brands appearing on his guitars included Avalon, Krundaal, Noble and Orpheum. Any of these US importers' names indicate a Pioli instrument. Krundaal may have been the parent company of Davoli, Pioli's Italian pickup supplier, and seems to have appeared only on a very unusual amp-in-guitar model called the Bikini, produced around 1960.

LABAYE

LaBaye inventor Dan Helland reasoned that a guitar is just pickups and strings… so if you put those on a 2x4 block of wood, that would be a guitar.

Helland, a guitar teacher and photographer living in Green Bay, Wisconsin, decided to turn that idea into a reality. He was financed by music store owner Henry Czachor and decided to hook up with the Holman-Woodell guitar factory in Neodesha, Kansas. Holman-Woodell also made Wurlitzer-brand guitars.

The new company produced around 45 of the now-legendary LaBaye 2-By-4 Six, Twelve and Four guitars and basses for display at the 1967 NAMM music trade show

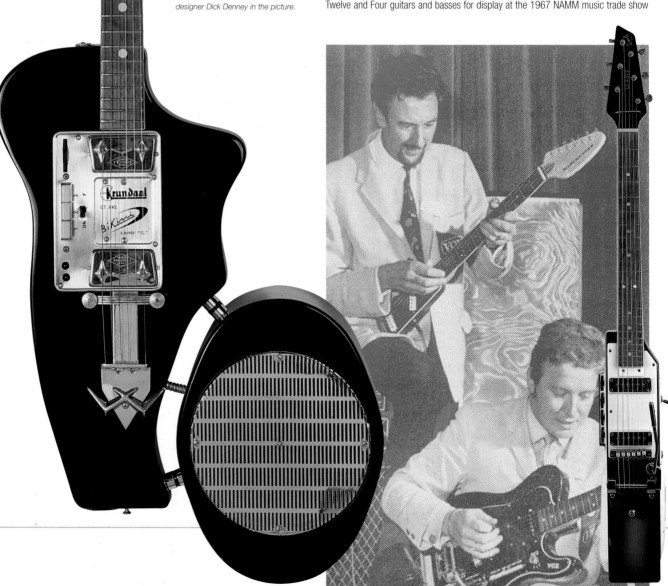

guitar manufacturers

in Chicago, Illinois. Finished either in solid colors or sunburst, the instruments had a standard Holman neck attached to a 2x4 log with two Holman pickups, thumbwheel controls and a Wurlitzer vibrato.

Some samples were put into the hands of the guitarist and bassist for Tommy James & The Shondels, who used them briefly on tour. A local Milwaukee band called The Robbs also performed with LaBayes.

Despite high hopes and an ad in *Guitar Player* magazine, no orders were received, and the LaBaye 2-By-4s became history... almost. Holman-Woodell apparently had hoped for a larger contract and was left with some 2-By-4 bodies which it released around 1968 with the 21st Century brand – and achieved hardly any more success than LaBaye. In the 1980s Mark Mothersbaugh of Devo was pictured with a LaBaye on an album sleeve, though it's unclear if he actually played it.

MAGNATONE

Best known for amplifiers that propelled Buddy Holly's glassy rhythms and Lonnie Mack's pulsing sound in the 1950s, Magnatone also made a series of unusual electric guitars. The amps descended from a line introduced around 1937 by Dickerson Brothers of Los Angeles. Dickerson evolved into Magna Electronics and, in turn, the Magnatone brand, run by Art Duhamell in Inglewood, California, from about 1947. Innovative steel guitars of the early 1950s with stamped metal and chrome-and-

colored-Lucite bodies led to Magnatone's first single-cutaway Spanish Mark III solidbody in 1956, followed by the hollowed-out, set-neck, double-cutaway Mark IV and Mark V, professional-grade guitars designed by Paul Bigsby in 1957.

Following a merger with Estey organs in 1959, the Mark models were succeeded by the bolt-on-neck double-cutaway Artist Series, which were similar to Rickenbacker's 600 model and were thus probably designed by Paul Barth, who had formerly been an executive with National and then Rickenbacker.

In 1961 Barth certainly contributed Magnatone's "golden-voiced Magna-Touch" line. These instruments were Telecaster-like in body shape, and had a hollow-core construction similar to that employed by Danelectro. These models lasted until 1965 when the best-known Magnatones debuted, the Starstream Series of Zephyr, Tornado and Typhoon. These guitars were small offset-double-cutaway beginners' solidbodies (some with metalflake finishes) inspired by Fender's Stratocaster.

In 1966 the Starstreams were redesigned with a hooked three-tuners-each-side headstock, endorsed by country legend Jimmy Bryant, and joined by the pointy-horned double-cutaway Semi-Acoustic Thinbody guitars. That same year Magna relocated to Harmony, Pennsylvania, making huge solid-state amps. A few Italian-made Magnatone hollowbodies appeared following the move, but guitars faded away. The end came in 1971 when Magna was purchased by a toy company.

Two Magnatone guitars are pictured on this page: a Mark V from around 1959 (far left, with a 1959 ad) and a Zephyr X-5 made in about 1965.

...don't
bug me
baby...

...I've switched to MAG

There's just no substitute for Magnatone w

The highest highs and the mellowest lows,

doors. For guitar, cello, bass, violin and ac

Ask your dealer for a demonstration today!

For free catalog write: *Patent Pending ®*   **MAGNA ELECTRONIC**
Dept. 105-D
Inglewood, California

Maton (logo, left) has been one of the few Australian makers of electric guitars. Martin (ad, right) is better known for flat-top acoustics, but had some attempts at making electrics.

MARTIN

Starting in the early 1830s, the C.F. Martin company has established itself as the producer of some of the finest flat-top acoustic guitars in the world.

Based in Nazareth, Pennsylvania, Martin has dominated the American flat-top scene, but interestingly made a couple of brief – and ultimately unsuccessful – forays into the electric guitar market.

At the end of the 1950s Martin decided to add single-coil DeArmond pickups and associated controls to its existing 00-18, D-18 and D-28 flat-top guitars in order to create the "electric-acoustic" 00-18E, D-18E and D-28E models. Unfortunately the results were not good, whether played electrically or acoustically, and this now seems like an example of an idea before its time.

Martin's next attempt at electric guitars went further into competitors' territory. In 1961 the company launched its thinline f-hole hollowbody F-50, F-55 (both single-cutaway) and F-65 (equal-double-cutaway), aping successful models of the period by Gibson and Gretsch. Martin found little success, however, even when it revised the headstock shape for the similar GT series in 1965.

The last stab at electrics came in 1979 with the E series, Martin's first and equally unsuccessful attempt at producing solidbody electrics. The blockish E-18, EM-18 and E-28 ended Martin's electric experiments when they were dropped in 1983.

MATON

One of the few high-profile Australian makers, Maton for years offered viable alternatives to imports. Bill May set up as a guitar-maker in 1944, joined later by his brother Reg, in Canterbury, Victoria. Their first electrics appeared in 1949, with solidbodies added by 1959 and thinline semis in the 1960s. Maton boldly promoted such features as Magnametle pickups and Break-Thru Sound Barrier switching. By the 1980s acoustic guitars dominated. May, who retired in 1986, died in the early 1990s. Maton returned to electrics in 1999 with the Mastersound, reviving a 1960s model said to have been used briefly by George Harrison.

MELOBAR

Walt Smith from Sweet, Idaho, thought slide-guitar players should abandon their "lap" instruments and stand up. So he invented the Melobar guitar with a neck mounted at 45-degrees to the top.

The first Melobars were metal ten-string acoustics introduced in 1964, made in the California workshop of Ed and Rudy Dopyera of Dobro. Solidbody electric Melobars debuted in 1967, double-cutaway guitars with an extended lower horn. The first 400 were made by Semie Moseley featuring Mosrite pickups.

Early Melobars were played on Jefferson Airplane's *Crown Of Creation* LP and by Poco's Rusty Young. Other guitarists favoring Melobars have included Brian Jones,

A Martin GT-75 (near right) made in 1967, this one with a non-standard red finish; a Martin EM-18 (center) from 1981; and a Maton Wedgetail (far right) produced around 1968.

guitar manufacturers

Jimmy Page, Ry Cooder, David Lindley, Keith Richards and Bonnie Raitt. Around 1982 Smith introduced a new Melobar, the PowerSlide 88, with a slanted wooden neck down to the bridge, one or two pickups, and a choice of body shaped like a Stratocaster, Flying V or Explorer, made either of wood or a polyurethane foam material.

Smith died in 1990 and was succeeded by his son Ted. By the late 1990s Melobar models included the birch or fiberglass acoustic resonator Melobro, the Steel Gitr Double-Neck (slide and regular necks), six- and eight-string Lap Steel Guitars, and the Skreemer (Flying V-style).

MESSENGER

Among the more mysterious and interesting guitars produced during the 1960s were the aluminum-through-neck Messengers. They were built by Bert T. Casey and Arnold B. Curtis of Musicraft Inc, originally based in San Francisco, California.

Beginning in 1967, the six- and 12-string guitars (and basses) had medium-depth hollow bodies with "cats-eye" f-holes, colorful translucent finishes and sometimes fancy timbers. Oddly, the expensive Messenger instruments featured inexpensive DeArmond single-coil pickups, which were wired for mono or stereo output (one pickup per channel) at the flick of a switch.

By early 1968 the company had relocated to Astoria, Oregon, and were busily touting an "improved" magnesium neck – before promptly disappearing from sight.

The strange Melobar (main guitar, made around 1973) was an electric-guitar-shaped instrument for steel players. Rusty Young of country-rockers Poco is seen attacking one in the picture (above) around 1978. Another unusual guitar was the Messenger ME-11 (far right, made in 1967) which had a structural "backbone" of magnesium alloy.

During the late 1960s, increasing attention began to be paid to the methods which could be adopted to improve electric guitar technology. Among the more curious results were Micro-Frets guitars, the brainchild of self-educated genius Ralph J. Jones. After working on various prototypes, Jones put Micro-Frets instruments into production in Frederick, Maryland, during 1967.

Micro-Frets guitars featured three curious patented innovations. First, the front and back of the instrument were made of two hollowed-out pieces of wood joined at the side, a technique that Jones dubbed "Tonesponder."

Second, the (very thin) bolt-on necks proudly sported the Micro-Nut, a metal device that allowed for the adjustment of the length of each individual string at the nut as well as the tail, theoretically providing more accurate intonation.

Third, from 1968 or so Micro-Fret guitars could be outfitted with a Calibrato vibrato, which was specially designed by Jones to keep all six strings harmonically in tune during use, even after taking into account the different string gauges. It was also intended to be less likely to render the guitar out of tune after use.

Most Micro-Frets guitars were frumpy-shaped variations on two basic designs: equal-double-cutaway (such as Spacetone and Signature models) or offset-double-cutaway (Wanderer, Golden Melody). The earliest Micro-Frets guitars had a side gasket

Four Micro-Frets guitars are pictured on these pages: an Orbiter (this page, main guitar) made in about 1968, with onboard wireless transmitter and Calibrato vibrato; a Golden Melody (this page, far right) from around 1970; a Huntington (opposite page, near right) made about 1971; and a Signature (opposite page, center) that dates from around 1968. The Micro-Frets catalog (above) details a number of other models in the line.

guitar manufacturers

where the body halves joined, DeArmond-like pickups, an early-Bigsby-style vibrato design, and a bi-level pickguard with thumbwheel controls built into a scalloped edge on the top portion.

Other early guitar models included the Huntington (with a scrolled upper horn), Covington, Golden Comet, Orbiter (extended upper horn and pointed lower bout) and Plainsman. In 1968 Micro-Frets announced one of the earliest wireless systems, using an FM transmitter. Jones apparently got the idea from newly-invented garage door openers. Wireless became a shortlived option on most models, with an antenna protruding from the upper horn.

By around 1970 the side gasket had disappeared and a variety of Jones-designed pickups were used. The bi-level pickguards now had regular knobs mounted on the lower portion. Models from this era include the Calibra I, Signature and Stage II. By 1971 Micro-Frets also offered its first true solidbody, the Swinger, plus the Signature Baritone and Stage II Baritone.

While most Micro-Frets finishes were reasonably conventional, a wild green-to-yellow "Martian sunburst" was also offered. Oddly, some models came with plastic decals of cats or pumpkins affixed. Jones died around 1973, and by 1974 the brand was gone. A very few guitars with the Diamond S brand were subsequently assembled in Virginia using leftover Micro-Frets parts.

MIGHTY MITE

Mighty Mite was involved in the "replacement parts" phenomenon that began in the mid 1970s. Guitar players increasingly wanted to improve their guitars by replacing stock factory parts such as pickups, tuners and bridges with "retrofit" or "aftermarket" units provided by independent manufacturers.

Mighty Mite was started in Santa Monica, California, by Randy Zacuto, who at the time was the west-coast distributor of DiMarzio pickups. By 1976, Mighty Mite had a full line of replacement parts that included Screamer humbucking pickups, Matchatone guitar tuners and Metrognome metronomes, and brass knobs, bridge parts, pickguards and jack plates.

About a year later Mighty Mite relocated to Camarillo, California, and increased its offerings. By 1978 the products were being distributed internationally and included full pickguard assemblies, and pickups with colored bobbins. At the end of the 1970s the company was providing unfinished bodies, necks and complete guitar kits.

Mighty Mite's line eventually expanded to include its most famous pickup, a three-coil monster called a Motherbucker, and some exotically-shaped, finished mahogany bodies (Mercury, Buick etc) with fancy figured flat caps routed to house the Mother. Mighty Mite faded from the scene in the early 1980s, but the tradename is still actively used on parts distributed by the Cort Corporation of Northbrook, Illinois.

Mighty Mite started as a supplier of guitar parts (1979 ad, above) but also provided complete guitar kits. This parts-guitar (near left) from around 1980 has a Mighty Mite Mercury body, Mighty Mite three-coil Motherbucker pickup, and a Warmoth neck.

MODULUS GUITARS

Modulus is a pioneer of composite "carbon-graphite" materials for guitar-making, and an active proponent of the ecologically responsible use of timber. The original company was called Modulus Graphite and was started by Geoff Gould in 1978 with the intention of making composite necks in California.

Geoff Gould and Rick Turner while still at Alembic had come up with the idea of molded carbon-graphite fiber-and-resin necks, primarily intended for use on Alembic and Music Man basses.

By the early 1980s Modulus Graphite began producing basses, then guitars. These graphite-neck high-end instruments were generally allied to classic-style US solidbody designs, aimed at players who realized that the new material offered an even sustain across the range as well as a road-friendly resistance to environmental change.

These instruments continued to appear from the Modulus Graphite workshop in San Francisco, California, in a low-key manner until late 1995 when Rich Lasner bought the Modulus name from founder Geoff Gould. Lasner, who dropped the "Graphite" suffix to rename the new operation Modulus Guitars, had previously worked as an instrument designer for Yamaha, Ibanez and Peavey.

Lasner took the Modulus legacy of carbon-graphite construction to produce new Genesis models, with a wood-shrouded graphite-spined neck construction. Like a

Mosrite's Mark I Ventures model (this example, main guitar, made around 1966) was built in collaboration with the American instrumental group (sleeves featuring Mosrites, above). The two other guitars on this page are a Modulus Graphite Flight 6 Monocoque (below, left) made in 1983, and a Modulus Guitars Genesis from 1998 (below, right).

guitar manufacturers

number of modern makers, Modulus recognizes the combined virtues of graphite's strength and wood's tonal qualities. Modulus relocated to Novato, California, in 1997.

Modulus is concerned about the ecologically responsible use of timber. The company emphasizes the need to ensure that timber sources are sustainable, and employs non-traditional alternative woods such as granadillo, chechen, red cedar and soma. Modulus says its goal is that all the wood it uses should be "earth-friendly and properly harvested," and Modulus cooperates with pressure groups such as SoundWood and Eco Timber. While the guitar industry in general has been slow to follow these ideas, they are likely to become more significant.

MOSRITE

One of the most colorful American guitar-makers, Semie Moseley enjoyed an erratic career producing distinctive, boldly-designed instruments. Moseley was born in Durant, Oklahoma, in 1935, and later moved to Bakersfield, California. At age 13 he was playing guitar with an evangelical music group.

Moseley joined Rickenbacker in the late 1950s, but soon formed his own guitar-making business, encouraged and assisted by the Reverend Ray Boatright. Their combined surnames, with a little modification in the spelling, provided the name for their new Los Angeles-based Mosrite company. From the outset Mosrites had unusual features, including a distinctive "M"-topped headstock. Moseley soon produced what

The ad for Mosrite's original Ventures model (above left) dates from 1966. Johnny Ramone of The Ramones is pictured (left) playing his Mosrite Ventures around 1979. The two unusual Mosrite instruments on this page – a six-string (far left) and 12-string (near left) – were custom-made by Semie Moseley for the Strawberry Alarm Clock group in 1967. The painting was done by California artist Von Dutch, well known in the hot-rod and custom-bike worlds at the time.

was to become the definitive Mosrite design, essentially a reversed Stratocaster-like body with stylistic and dimensional changes that gave a wholly new and refreshing outline. The design was streamlined and full of visual "movement," but still managed to be comfortable and well-balanced.

This radical design was noticed by Nokie Edwards, guitarist with The Ventures, America's leading instrumental group of the time. Production of the Mosrite Ventures models commenced during 1963 at a new factory in Bakersfield, funded by the band in return for exclusive distribution. The new Mk I guitars each carried a Ventures logo on the headstock. Output soon increased from 35 to 300 instruments per month. None of the subsequent models achieved the popularity of the Ventures guitars, which are now the most collectable. Mosrite closed in 1969.

The next 20 years saw false starts and financial setbacks for Moseley. In 1976 his unsuccessful Brass Rail model had a brass fingerboard for extra sustain.

Demand increased in Japan for original Ventures models, and a dealer there commissioned recreations, but it wasn't until 1984 that Moseley was able to establish a production facility in Jonas Ridge, North Carolina, making reissues and other models. His last production instrument was the 40th Anniversary model of 1992. Moseley died that year; his widow Loretta continued the business. By 1995 all Mosrites were Japanese-made, including Johnny Ramone and Nokie Edwards signature models.

Mosrite guitars have always been extremely popular in Japan – as have The Ventures – and Japanese copies of Mosrites flourished, none more blatant than those of Firstman (catalog from about 1967, above). Three more Mosrite guitars are pictured on this page: a remarkably crafted custom-made instrument (near right) built by Semie Moseley in 1980 for a business partner; a Ventures-like Model 88 (center) made in 1988; and a Ventures reissue, the Japanese-made Excellent 65 (far right), this one produced during 1998.

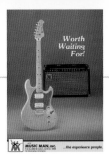

Two promos from Music Man's different eras are shown here this 1977 ad (left) announces the company's first guitar, the StingRay, while the 1991 ad (below) highlights Edward Van Halen's involvement with the design of the new EVH model.

MUSIC MAN

Originally connected with Leo Fender, US-made Music Man guitars are now among the leading alternatives to the "big two" brands, Fender and Gibson.

Two ex-Fender employees, Forrest White and Tom Walker, together with Leo Fender, set up a new company in Fullerton, California, in 1972, naming it Music Man two years later. At first production concentrated on a line of amplifiers based on designs by Walker, but a move into instruments followed in 1976. The distinctive Music Man logo had two guitarists whose legs formed a large "M."

When CBS purchased the Fender companies it had given Leo a contract with a ten-year non-competition clause. This expired in 1975. In April of that year Leo was announced as president of Music Man Inc. The first guitar to appear was the StingRay, introduced in mid 1976, along with a fine bass guitar with the same model name. They reflected typical Fender styling, but displayed significant and subtle refinements of construction and components. A three-bolt neck/body joint was successfully employed, contradicting the poor reputation it had gained when Fender used it amid inferior manufacturing standards in the 1970s.

The StingRay followed trends of the time, favoring twin humbuckers and a fixed bridge, while active circuitry was optional. The instrument was not necessarily what was expected of Leo Fender, and the notorious resistance of guitarists to anything new

Music Man's first guitar was the StingRay (far left), this one made around 1978. The Silhouette (main guitar) was the first guitar model from Music Man's new owner, Ernie Ball. This example was made in 1988 with a special one-off finish.

Albert Lee is a fine player whose work includes his own band Heads Hands & Feet (1972 album, far left) and many sessions, including contributions to Emmylou Harris's Quarter Moon In A Ten Cent Town (1978, sleeve near left). Lee is pictured (below) playing his signature Music Man model.

guitar manufacturers

meant that it never enjoyed much more than a low-key reaction. But Leo, typically, saw little point in merely reworking his past achievements, and aimed to offer genuine improvements in quality, consistency and performance.

The Sabre guitar was added two years later with a body outline slightly different to that of the StingRay. It shared the large, six-tuners-on-one-side headstock and one-piece maple neck construction, and likewise came in two versions – I or II – the former with a 12″-radius fingerboard and jumbo frets, the latter employing a more "vintage" 7.5″ radius and standard-size frets. Once more, neither single-coil pickups nor a vibrato unit were present, while active electrics came as standard, together with more comprehensive circuitry and refinements to hardware. Regardless of such changes and the more streamlined image, the Sabre fared no better with players.

Behind the scenes, all was not well. Part of the business arrangements of the operation meant that Music Man instruments were manufactured by Leo's CLF Research company, but after Music Man tried unsuccessfully to buy CLF in 1978 Leo decided to break away and set up his own guitar-making business, G&L, in 1979. The first instruments bearing his new brandname appeared in 1980.

Music Man continued to manufacture instruments in Fullerton for a time after this upheaval, but later other production sources were used, including Jackson. Despite such turmoil, a limited model selection continued until 1980 when the StingRay guitar

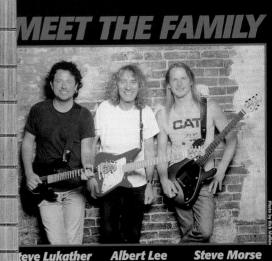

Music Man has marketed some impressive signature guitars. These have included Steve Lukather's model, the Luke (1998 example, far left), and the odd-shape Albert Lee (the guitar, not our Albert). This Lee model (main guitar) dates from 1994. The 1993 ad (above) shows earlier endorser Steve Morse included in the Music Man family, with some string-gauge tips for budding music men and women.

disappeared from the catalog, the remainder lasting into the early 1980s. However, in March 1984 Music Man was acquired by the Ernie Ball company, production being transferred north, near to Ball's string and accessory works in San Luis Obispo, California, and the second chapter in the Music Man story began.

Music Man's basses had been more popular than the guitars thus far, so it was the four-string models that first went into production with the new owner.

The prototype of an all-new guitar, the Silhouette, was previewed in 1986, and production commenced the following year. Designed in 1985 by ex-Valley Arts man Dudley Gimpel, with the help of country-rock guitarist Albert Lee, this solidbody was Fender-inspired. But other features included a compact, stylishly-contoured body and a headstock that echoed the Music Man bass design, the tuners now arranged in a convenient four-and-two formation.

Options included the 24-fret maple neck with rosewood or maple fingerboard, a fixed bridge or locking vibrato system, and various pickup formats. The most recent variant is the Silhouette Special, launched in 1995, its 22-fret neck and Wilkinson vibrato unit being the most obvious of a number of changes made to the (continuing) standard model. Among the high-profile players of the Silhouette have been Ron Wood and Keith Richards in what appears to be a rare example of these two favoring contemporary new-design guitars rather than vintage-style oldies.

Back in the 1980s, the Silhouette was joined by the Steve Morse signature model in 1987. The model employed a novel four-pickup configuration favored by this players' player. A very popular Music Man six-string model was the EVH, offered for a few years from 1991 and designed in close collaboration with the influential high-speed guitarist Edward Van Halen.

Features of the EVH included Van Halen's own-design body, a custom-profile neck and specially devised DiMarzio-made humbuckers. The original Floyd Rose-equipped model was joined by a fixed-bridge option, reflecting Van Halen's changing requirements. However, in the mid 1990s the guitarist changed allegiance to Peavey for a new signature model, and so Music Man subsequently altered the name of its EVH model to the Axis. Since then the original Music Man EVHs have become quite collectable, especially examples with pretty woods.

Causing some confusion in retrospect, Music Man had used the Axis model name earlier for a number of prototypes of what would become the Albert Lee model. One of these angular prototypes was made for Paul McCartney, enjoying the distinction of being the first left-handed solidbody six-string instrument made by the new Music Man operation. The remarkable Nigel Tufnel had a typically more refined version, too, that featured no less than four humbuckers, a rev counter, tailpipes, Woody Woodpecker logo and, rather subtly, note names inlaid into the fingerboard to increase Tufnel's

Three more Music Man guitars are pictured on this page: an EVH (near right) made in 1992, as endorsed by Edward Van Halen; a hybrid Axis Super Sport (center) from 2000; and a Silhouette Special (far right) made in 1998.

already frightening speed. Other 1990s additions to the Music Man guitar line included two more signature editions that were added during 1993, the Luke and the Albert Lee.

The Luke was designed to the specifications of Steve Lukather, while the Albert Lee had that odd-looking, angular body shape. New in 1997 at Music Man was a cheaper Axis variant, the Axis Sport, which had the P-90-like MM90 pickups, the first pickups to be made in-house at Music Man. During 1999 Music Man followed the hybrid trend by offering a piezo-pickup option for the Axis.

While the choice is far from vast, the Music Man line offers a high-quality, top-performance selection that represents some of the best of the new generation of American-made instruments.

NATIONAL

The National brand appeared on some early electric guitars of the 1930s, but the company is especially remembered for its unusual "map shape" electrics of the 1960s.

John Dopyera and his brothers Rudy and Ed emigrated from what was then Czechoslovakia and set up the National String Instrument Corporation in Los Angeles, California, in the mid 1920s, at first to produce a metal-body tenor banjo that John had invented. In 1927, National launched its now-famous acoustic "tricone" resonator guitar. Suspended inside its metal body were three resonating aluminum cones that acted a little like loudspeakers. The result was a loud, distinctive instrument. A few rare

Two classic fiberglass-body National guitars are shown here: an Art Deco-inspired Studio 66 (far left) from 1961, and a Varsity 66 (main guitar) made in 1964. The two pictures at the top of the page are views of Nationals being made at the Valco factory in 1962, and the catalogs also date from the 1960s.

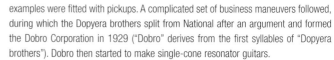

VERSATILITY · BEAUTY · ELEGANCE

The Kim Sisters and N—— ——ric G——

examples were fitted with pickups. A complicated set of business maneuvers followed, during which the Dopyera brothers split from National after an argument and formed the Dobro Corporation in 1929 ("Dobro" derives from the first syllables of "Dopyera brothers"). Dobro then started to make single-cone resonator guitars.

Dobro and National were merged again in 1935, and it was at this time that National-Dobro marketed a National electric guitar, the Electric Spanish f-hole archtop model (along with a similar Dobro-brand version, plus cheaper Supro-brand electrics). The magnetic pickups on these early electrics were designed by Victor Smith.

In 1936 the company relocated to Chicago. It continued to make a number of National archtop electrics, unusually including some that were without f-holes, as well as one of the earliest guitars with two pickups, the Sonora model of 1939.

During 1942 Victor Smith, Al Frost and Louis Dopyera (another of the Dopyera brothers) bought the National-Dobro company and changed the name to the Valco Manufacturing Company.

After World War II, more Valco electrics appeared bearing the National brand, as well as low-end Supro-brand models and catalog-company contracted brands such as Airline. Post-war National archtop electric models included the Aristocrat – at first with an unusual arrangement of control knobs and jack either side of the large bridge/pickup unit, and later with bodies supplied by Gibson – and the single-cutaway

The two Nationals on this page both have fiberglass bodies. This Newport 84 (main guitar) was made in 1964 and has a regular magnetic pickup plus a bridge-mounted "contact" pickup (the connecting wire is visible). The Glenwood 95 (right) was also made in 1964. The glamorous if unknown Kim Sisters (above) model some National Glenwoods in an ad published during 1966.

National made some early and significant electric guitars in the 1930s, but the brand is best known for its appearance on the "map shape" fiberglass- and wood-body guitars of the 1960s, some examples of which are pictured below.

Club Combo introduced in 1952. Valco then started its experiments with materials. It was not the first brand to offer guitars built from synthetic materials, earlier innovations including Rickenbacker's Bakelite models of the 1930s. But the brightly colored and unusually shaped fiberglass Valco-made guitars of the 1960s were without doubt among the most eye-catchingly different instruments of the era.

Valco was never short of impressive sounding names for its guitar innovations, and came up with "Res-O-Glas" and "Hollow-Glas" for the material used in its new line of non-wood instruments, introduced in 1962. This was in fact one of the first composite materials used for guitar manufacturing, a technique that would in later decades become more prevalent with the advent of "carbon-graphite."

The material used for the National (and Supro) guitars of the 1960s was described at the time by Valco in advertising material as "polyester resins with threads of pure glass." More simply, this was fiberglass. Valco intended that the material, which it trumpeted as "more adaptable and workable than conventional wood," would provide a longer lasting instrument. Two molded body halves were joined together with a strip of white vinyl binding around the edge.

Valco also produced wood-body National models alongside the Res-O-Glas guitars. The various plastic Newport and Glenwood models and wood-body Westwood guitars have become known as "map shape" Nationals among collectors, because the body

suggests a stylized outline of part of the map of the United States. By 1964 National had nine map-shape guitars in its catalog, ranging from the wood-body Westwood 72 to the most expensive model in that line, the plastic-body Glenwood 99.

Like some contemporary Supro models, a number of National guitars, including map-shapes, had in addition to the conventional magnetic pickup(s) an innovative "contact" pickup built into the bridge. The facility was also included on non-map-shape Nationals, including the various Val-Trol models introduced in the late 1950s. The bridge-pickup scheme was another National idea before its time; similar piezo bridge pickups would find success in the "hybrid" guitars of the late 1990s.

However, these brave plastic and pickup experiments ended with Valco itself in the late 1960s. Control in Valco had passed to one Robert Engelhardt, who went on to buy its competitor, the Kay guitar company, in 1967. When Kay went out of business during the following year, Valco – and its National and Supro brands – went down with it.

The National brand has resurfaced since, including a 1970s line of unremarkable imported electrics. In 1988 National Reso-phonic Guitars was founded in San Luis Obispo, California, and began producing resonator guitars, with a line of ResoLectric electric models following in the 1990s. Meanwhile, National's "map shape" design was revived in 1996 for wood-body guitars with the Metropolitan brandname, made by Robin in Houston, Texas, and marketed by Alamo Music Products.

Three more National "map shape" guitars are pictured on this page: a fiberglass-body Newport 82 (far left) made in 1964; a wood-body Westwood 75 (center) made in 1963; and a 1962 wood-body Westwood 77 (near left), another model that had Valco's extra bridge pickup.

OVATION

Known for revolutionizing electric-acoustic guitars with "Lyracord" fiberglass bowl-back instruments in 1966, Ovation tried for years to market innovative solidbody electric guitar designs, but with little success.

Ovation was founded by aeronautical engineer and helicopter manufacturer Charles H. Kaman in Bloomfield, Connecticut (relocating to New Hartford in 1967). The guitar company used aeronautical materials to solve what they considered as problems with the instability of natural wood. Ovation acoustics got an early push when played by Josh White and Charlie Byrd, but it was Glen Campbell's TV show *Goodtime Hour* in 1969 that made the brand.

It was on that show that Ovation's first under-bridge-saddle transducer was introduced. This device paved the way for a revolution in "amplified acoustic" or "electro-acoustic" guitars, as well as the later trend toward "hybrid" instruments that mixed bridge transducers and conventional magnetic pickups.

While waiting for the bowl-backs to catch on, Ovation had in 1968 introduced its first semi-hollow thinline electrics, the Electric Storm series: Thunderhead, Tornado and Hurricane 12-string. They had German Framus-made bodies, Schaller hardware and pickups, and Ovation necks. In 1971 a low-end black Eclipse model was added. These were all discontinued by 1973. Ovation entered the solidbody electric guitar market

Ovation went into battle with these two odd-shape solidbodies: the Breadwinner (1975 example, far left) and the higher-end Deacon (main guitar, also made in 1975). Steve Marriott is seen with a Deacon in this 1976 (ad), a year after Marriott's band Humble Pie had finally split.

with its battle-axe-shape Breadwinner model in 1972, followed by the more high-end Deacon with high gloss finish, neck binding and fancier inlays.

Featuring onboard FET pre-amps, the Breadwinner and Deacon were among the earliest American production guitars with active electronics. A 12-string model was available by 1976. While the Breadwinner lasted until 1979 and the Deacon to 1980, they never achieved much popularity. Toward the end of its life the Deacon had extra contouring added to its body, but this didn't help sales.

Meanwhile, the company's various acoustic guitar models continued to mature and evolve, most notably with the introduction in 1976 of the graphite-topped Adamas series, which had a multiple series of soundholes in the body. Ovation's successful Collector Series debuted in 1982, and its domestic and imported electro-acoustic lines continued to proliferate and thrive.

During 1975 Ovation introduced more solidbodies, this time the more conventional-looking double-cutaway Preacher, Preacher Deluxe and single-cutaway Viper models. The Preacher had passive electrics, while the Preacher Deluxe featured active circuitry and fancier appointments. A 12-string version of the Deluxe was also offered. The Viper came with two or three pickups.

In 1979 the curious Ultra Kaman, or UK II, made its debut. This single-cutaway guitar featured an aluminum-framed body that was filled out with lightweight urethane foam. It boasted precise tone and volume control. The aluminum/foam concept was derived from the necks of Ovation's low-end Applause acoustics. Alas, none of these efforts caught on with the market and in 1983 Ovation's American-made solidbodies ceased production. The only "stars" to play Ovation solidbodies briefly were Jim Messina, Roy Clark and Glen Campbell.

Around 1985 Ovation attempted solidbodies one more time with the introduction of its Hard Body series, consisting of Korean-made necks and bodies assembled and finished in the US using Schaller hardware and DiMarzio pickups. The GP was a flame-top, equal-double-cutaway with a set-Oneck; the GS a bolt-on-neck Strat-style guitar, with one or two humbuckers or humbucker/single-coil/single-coil pickup layout. These lasted only a year or so.

A few hundred more solidbody guitars were briefly imported from Japan, and a shortlived, entry-level, Korean-made Celebrity By Ovation line of superstrats was offered around 1987. None of the various models was successful. A few experimental guitars that were fitted with Steve Ripley's "stereo" electronics were tried (as on Kramer's Ripley Stereo) but the project went nowhere.

Giving up on its own efforts, Kaman purchased Hamer Guitars of Chicago in 1988. Ovation-brand solidbodies were always well considered and carefully designed, but so often seemed out of step with the times.

Three more Ovation solidbodies are pictured on this page: a Preacher (far left) from around 1976; a UK II (center) made in 1979; and a Viper III (near left) from about 1978.

guitar manufacturers

Two guitars from the Parker lines are shown on this page: a Fly Artist (far right) from 1997 with Parker's revolutionary wood/composite construction; and a less expensive bolt-on-neck wood-body NiteFly (main guitar) made in 1996. Reeves Gabrels, whose credits include work with David Bowie, is an enthusiastic Parker player, and is seen in this 1997 ad (above) with a NiteFly.

PARKER

In the mid 1990s Parker popularized the "hybrid" guitar – an instrument fitted with piezo as well as magnetic pickups – and revolutionized the way in which electric guitars can be built.

Parker is a partnership between guitar-maker Ken Parker and electronics expert Larry Fishman. The project required considerable finance, provided primarily by Korg USA, a company better known for its electronic musical instruments.

A purpose-built factory was established near Boston, Massachusetts, to manufacture the unusually-shaped Parker Fly. The facility was designed to make Parkers in an entirely different way to any other electric guitars. Every part of the Fly, with the exception of its Sperzel locking tuners, is unique to Parker, including the tangless stainless-steel frets which are glued into the fingerboard, and the unusual "flat-spring" vibrato with built-in piezo-electric pickups.

Parker said that all this was intended to make its new Fly a more versatile guitar – not merely something that looked different from the rest. The theory involved in the new design was that the only reason for a guitar's solid wooden body is strength, and that the wood's effect on the sound of the instrument is secondary.

However, Parker knew that acoustic guitars depend much more for their sound on the timbers used, especially that employed for the body's top. So the company intended

Ken Parker, co-founder of Parker Guitars, is pictured in this ad published in 1998.

that its Fly models would have thin, lightweight but highly resonant wooden bodies strengthened by a composite material (glass and carbon fibers in an epoxy matrix) that forms a very thin "external skeleton" around the wood. The necks are constructed in a similar fashion. It's almost as if the body of a Parker instrument is just the top of an acoustic guitar, specially strengthened.

Most Fly guitars have two different kinds of pickup fitted. The first is recognizable as a traditional magnetic type that provides normal electric-guitar sounds, while piezo elements in the bridge give the instrument "acoustic"-like tones.

While these two different types of pickup had been offered on individual guitars before, no previous instrument had provided the player with a means to combine magnetic and piezo pickups in a way that allowed the use of either type independently or both mixed together.

The Parker's Fishman-designed pickup-mix facility effectively provides musicians with two guitars in one, merging electric and electro-acoustic sounds. Many other makers have subsequently emulated this "hybrid" style, and some guitar-industry people are arguing that it provides one of the most exciting possible future directions for the electric guitar.

The first Parker introduced was the poplar-body Fly Vibrato Deluxe, in 1993, followed by the mahogany Fly Classic (introduced 1996), the spruce Fly Artist (1997),

the rare figured-maple Supreme (1998) and a nylon-string version, the Spanish Fly (1999). The Concert model (1997) is a piezo-only guitar without vibrato. The MIDI Fly (1999) uses a sophisticated synth-access system, while the lower-price NiteFly (1996) has many of the regular Fly's attributes but with a bolt-on reinforced-wood neck and a more conventional soft maple body (ash and mahogany from '99).

New non-vibrato Parker guitars appeared in 2000. These included the basswood-body black-hardware Hardtail model, which includes a Sperzel D-Tuner on the D-string and is aimed at the modern rock market, as well as the Jazz model that has gold-plated hardware and a mahogany body.

Parker players – a diverse bunch that includes Pops Staples, Reeves Gabrels and Dave Navarro – seem drawn as much by the comfort and playability of the various models as by the light weight and hybrid sounds.

PEAVEY

Beginning as an amplifier manufacturer founded in 1965 by Hartley Peavey in Meridian, Mississippi, Peavey Electronics was notable in pioneering new construction techniques for electric guitars in the late 1970s, and has offered a large, varied and mostly mid-priced line of instruments ever since.

Peavey guitars originated with Hartley's idea that he could create a relatively inexpensive alternative to Gibson and Fender offerings. Working with Chip Todd, he

A Parker synth-access MIDI Fly (far left) made in 1999, alongside a 2000 ad featuring Orgy's Amir Derakh; and a Peavey T-60 (near left) that was produced during 1979.

devised the T-60 guitar ("T" for Todd). This instrument effectively combined a Gibson-like rounded body shape and twin humbuckers with a Fender-style maple fingerboard and slightly offset double-cutaways.

The T-60 debuted in 1978, lasted a decade and was notable for three innovations. First was a tone control that doubled as a coil-tap, devised for Peavey by the Los Angeles-based pedal-steel guitarist Orville "Red" Rhodes. The second development was a patented "bi-laminated" maple neck that had opposing grain directions to provide extra stability. Finally, this was the first guitar constructed using computer-controlled carving machines, a technique borrowed from gun-stock-making that is now standard practice among mass-production guitar-makers.

The 1980s were exceptionally fertile for Peavey guitars. The T Series had a facelift in 1982, including a new T-25 Special with a phenolic fingerboard. The profile was slightly reshaped and Super Ferrite blade-style pickups were added; these lasted only about a year. Peavey's first traditional-style vibratos debuted in 1983, and the company flirted with "pointy" body shapes in the mid 1980s with the electric-shaver-shaped Razer, B.C. Rich-style Mystic and V-shaped Mantis.

Peavey also began to introduce more conventionally shaped offset-double-cutaway models between 1983 and 1986. These included the Horizon, Milestone and Patriot series, the latter with a solid-state amp included in the instrument's molded plastic

case, a tribute to Danelectro. Peavey's Hydra double-neck debuted in 1984, and a Kahler-equipped Jeff Cook model appeared the following year. Peavey began using Kahler locking vibratos on other models in 1985.

The popular Stratocaster-style Predator series was introduced by Peavey during 1985. (The line was revived in 1990, and a seven-string version was added to the series in 2000.) An Explorer-inspired "pointy" Vortex model also appeared in 1985, and the Stratocaster-style Impact series debuted the following year. All these had disappeared from the line by the late 1990s, although the Impact was briefly revived as the figured-top Impact Milano and Torino models during 1994.

Peavey guitars always offered high quality at their respective price points, but in the late 1980s the company began markedly improving the quality of its instruments. During 1987 the popular Nitro series of superstrats and the active and passive Falcon series of near-Strats appeared (both with versions lasting until 1990), as well as Peavey's first venture into through-neck construction, the Impact Unity model. In 1988 Peavey began using Alnico pickups and unveiled the superstrat Tracer series, some models of which survived to 1994.

In 1988 Peavey began working with another celebrity, introducing the violin-waisted Vandenberg Signature model that had been designed with Dutch guitar-slinger Adrian Vandenberg. During the following year the company introduced the high-end Destiny

Three more Peavey guitars are pictured here: a T-25 Special (near right) with plastic fingerboard, this example dating from 1982; a Razer model (center) made in 1984; and a Vandenberg Signature (far right) from 1989, designed in collaboration with Adrian Vandenberg, who at the time played with Whitesnake.

superstrat as well as the Generation Telecaster-style model, both of which came with carved figured maple caps. These were offered until 1994.

In 1990 Peavey introduced its first Les-Paul-inspired model, the single-cutaway Odyssey, available until 1994 and including a quilt-top version. The 1990s saw the continuation of the offset-double-cutaway style – Axecellerator, Defender, Detonator, Firenza (formerly Impact), G-90 and Raptor – and the Tele-style designs – Cropper Classic, for Memphis great Steve Cropper, and Reactor. A PRS-style guitar, the Ltd model, appeared in the Peavey line during 2000.

Peavey guitars can be said to have finally arrived with the landing of the Eddie Van Halen EVH Wolfgang series in 1996, the acclaimed guitarist having transferred his allegiance to Peavey from Music Man. Van Halen had already worked with Peavey on the 5150 amplifier series (the 5150 name coming from the title that Van Halen then used for his own recording studio). Peavey's various offset-double-cutaway Peavey Van Halen models, with their distinctive chunky upper horn, remain high-end, desirable guitars thanks to their endorsement pedigree.

PREMIER

Made by the Multivox amplifier company in New York, Premier guitars progressed from acoustic flat-top instruments with crude stick-on pickups in 1938 to archtops with Premier's distinctive scroll-shape shoulders by 1947. (Completely unrelated Rickenbacker-sourced Bakelite-body electric guitars were branded Premier by the British drum company in the 1940s.) Premier's parent company, Sorkin, also produced a number of Marvel-brand low-end electric guitars from the late 1940s.

Late-1950s hollowbodys, including the single-cutaway Bantam, featured another distinctive Premier decoration, sparkle plastic trim. The company's Scroll solidbody models, featuring solid rosewood necks, debuted around 1958. A stereo guitar and a number of other electronic options were added to the line around 1960.

Thinline guitars and an unusual wireless instrument joined the Premier catalog during 1961, while the plastic-covered Custom line with scroll bodies replaced the original Scroll models. The Customs stayed in the Premier line from their introduction in 1963 until around 1970. After a few years of production the Custom models began to use some imported components, including European and Japanese parts. Another Sorkin brandname was adapted for electric guitars in the 1960s when some Strad-O-Lin solidbodies were made available.

Japanese-made Les Paul-style copies were offered briefly in the mid 1970s, but after this the Premier brand disappeared from view. Sorkin's other main product, Multivox amplifiers, continued to be produced until around 1984. The rights to the Premier brand were owned at this time by Entertainment Music of New York, and it did resurface on some low-end oriental Fender-style guitars during the early 1990s.

A Peavey EVH Wolfgang (far left) produced in collaboration with Eddie Van Halen, this one made in 1997; a Peavey Cropper Classic (center) from 2000; and a Premier Scroll (near left) made around 1960. The ad (below) for Premier Scrolls dates from 1959.

The second full-color catalog from PRS (right) issued in the mid 1980s featured flame-maple-top Custom models on the cover.

P R S

Back in the mid 1970s, few would have imagined that a lanky, big-haired kid repairing guitars in an impossibly small workshop in Annapolis, Maryland, would one day be running the number-three guitar company behind Fender and Gibson. Yet that is the remarkable story of Paul Reed Smith, "the Stradivari of the electric guitar" as one satisfied customer would later call him.

The details of this ascent are more fabulous still. Coming from a musical family, Smith started both his musical and guitar-making career during high school. Initially playing bass before moving on to guitar, Smith built his first instrument toward the end of senior high school by fixing the neck of a Japanese "Beatle bass" copy to a strangely-shaped solid body.

Smith then managed to get a job repairing guitars at the Washington Music Center before deciding to go to St. Mary's College in Maryland to study mathematics. The opportunity in the second half of his first year to undertake an independent study project proved to be a turning point. Smith made his first proper guitar, a single-cutaway solidbody in the style of Gibson's Les Paul Junior, which earned him credits and respect from his teachers.

In that summer of 1975 he turned the top floor of his parents' house into a workshop and, with the help of his brother, set about making more guitars. The bug

Two very early PRS Custom guitars are pictured on this page: number 0002 (far left) and 0005 (main guitar). The company's ads have continually stressed the importance of name players, including Dickie Betts of The Allman Brothers (above) and Brad Whitford of Aerosmith (below).

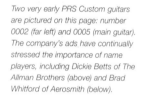

Ted Nugent pictured with a Metal graphic-finish PRS around 1985.

had bitten, and Smith's return to college proved to be shortlived. By the start of 1976 he had left and moved into his first workshop in West Street, Annapolis.

Smith made his first electric guitar at his new shop, a solidbody Gibson Byrdland-style instrument for Ted Nugent. This was quickly followed by a guitar for British rocker Peter Frampton. The all-mahogany guitar for Frampton was an interesting instrument which, although built in early 1976, set the foundation for Smith's future.

Its double-cutaway outline apes Gibson's post-1958 Les Paul Special, but features the arched, carved top of a Les Paul Standard. For the first time on a Smith guitar there were mother-of-pearl birds inlaid by hand down the fingerboard, a distinctive feature that would later help to shift a lot of PRS guitars. But why birds? Smith's mother was a keen bird-watcher, and he says that he simply grabbed one of her bird-watching guides and stole the pictures out of it, drawing a couple of others with friends Billy Armiger and Tim Campbell.

Along with the motif of an eagle landing that was inlaid into the headstock – a feature that would return to PRS guitars some years later – Frampton's guitar also featured the combination of a 24-fret-neck and twin humbucking pickups that would be the basis of Smith's instruments until the beginning of the 1990s.

Smith's dream, however, was to make a guitar for Carlos Santana, one of his guitar-playing idols. Getting to meet players like Santana proved one of Smith's hidden talents. He achieved this by hanging out backstage at the local arenas, begging roadies to let their employer see his instruments. The deal was simple: if you don't fall in love with the instrument, you get your money back. It worked.

Apart from Nugent and Frampton, Smith got orders from Al DiMeola (a 12-string with a built-in phase shifter), and from Frampton's and Bruce Springsteen's bass players, not to mention many local musicians. It also became apparent to Smith from a very early point that big-name guitar players sell guitars to others. DiMeola said after owning a PRS that he felt Smith had the ability to custom-make the guitar of anyone's dreams. Slowly, the word was beginning to spread.

In 1980, after selling his first maple-topped hand-made guitar to Heart guitarist Howard Leese, Smith got to make an instrument for Carlos Santana. This would be the first of four hand-made Smith guitars that Santana used in the coming years.

The association with Santana, and the maple-topped instruments themselves, proved to be vastly important turning points – although as is so often the case that is not how they appeared at the time.

The figured "curly" maple that Smith used for these early maple-top guitars originally came from the drawer-fronts of a friend's dresser. This crucial timber helped to summon up visions of those late-1950s Les Pauls that have influenced so many players and makers. By the time Carlos Santana owned a Smith guitar he was already

This PRS Guitar (far left; the all-mahogany-body model was soon renamed as the Standard) dates from 1986 and is finished in a striking Magenta Pearl. The Metal (1985 example, center) was a shortlived graphic-finish Standard. The Signature (1986 prototype, near left) was PRS's first ultra-high-end model, with hand-signed logo and outrageously flamed maple top.

on his first comeback. Nearly 20 years later, still playing a PRS guitar, he would be topping the *Billboard* charts again with *Supernatural*, another comeback album. Smith said in 1999 that he couldn't have been successful without Santana's support, because the guitarist gave his instruments instant credibility.

Musicians such as Santana, Howard Leese and Al DiMeola all disregarded the overwhelming opinion of the time about which guitars pro players should be using. Their mark of approval was crucial to Smith's early operation. Smith knew that by successfully building a guitar that Santana liked, he had a shot at starting a professional guitar-making operation.

However, building Santana's guitar nearly didn't happen at all. But when, eventually, Santana received his first instrument, the guitar player remarked that its special quality was "an accident of God" and that Smith would never be able to do it again. Santana then said the second guitar Smith made for him was, too, an accident of God. There was a third one, and then a double-neck. When he finally got that, Santana said that maybe this wasn't an accident of God. Finally it seems Santana concluded that Smith might actually be a guitar-maker.

But by 1984 Smith was struggling to survive. He still held some ambition to become a professional guitar player, but with the counsel of his close friends and loyal assistant John Ingram, Smith realized that it was his guitar-building that was making headway,

not his playing. He'd set about designing what we know today as the PRS Custom, and after trying unsuccessfully to persuade various big-name manufacturers to make his design under license, he realized he'd have to do it himself.

Armed with a couple of prototypes, Smith headed out on the road and raised orders worth nearly $300,000. Making the guitars to fulfill these orders was another matter. But by the fall of 1985 Smith and his wife Barbara, guided by the business know-how of Warren Esanu, had set up a limited partnership to raise the capital necessary to start a factory in Virginia Avenue, Annapolis. At last, just about a decade after making his first electric guitar, Smith had his production company, PRS Guitars, up and running and in business.

Apart from a few lucky musicians and their fans, nobody knew Paul Reed Smith when the company first displayed its wares at the important American NAMM trade-shows held during 1985. It was a time of hi-tech musical fashion. The major trends swirling around the guitar industry during that period mainly involved aggressive, futuristic-looking, modern rock guitar designs. In those surroundings, the PRS Custom must have seemed very out of place.

With the Custom, here was an instrument clearly inspired by classic 1950s Gibson and Fender guitars. Often called evolutionary rather than revolutionary, the PRS guitar was substantially more expensive than the high-line Gibson or Fender instruments, but

A Studio Maple Top from 1990 (near right), with humbucker/single/single pickup layout, and a bolt-on-neck Classic Electric (far right, with ad) made in 1988. The Classic Electric was soon renamed the CE.

This PRS semi-solidbody Limited Edition (near right) was made in 1989, one of only 300 examples, each of which had an unusual figured cedar top.

The Artist I (1991 example, far right, with original flyer) continued the Signature theme as a high-end model using exclusive, top-grade materials, but also had new pickups and a changed neck/heel design.

ARTIST SERIES

"Occasionally a mahogany board comes into our shop that is extra dense and resonant. Sometimes the figure and cut in a particular block of curly maple is absolutely exceptional. These rare pieces become the Artist Series. My favorite stains...violin glues...Abalone inlays...vintage tones...Our Very Best."

- Exceptionally figured Curly Maple top
- One-piece Mahogany body and neck
- Select Rosewood fingerboard
- Wide-Fat ARTIST SERIES neck
- Inlaid Signature Headstock and Abalone birds
- 25 inch scale
- Thin finish for enhanced resonance
- PRS ARTIST SERIES pickups
- Five-position Rotary, Volume and Tone
- PRS Tremolo System
- Certificate of Authenticity
- Options: Semi-hollowbody, Gold hardware, PRS Stop-tail, Quilted Maple top, Studio package, Hum/Single/Hum pickups

AVAILABLE COLORS: Amber, Teal Black, Indigo, Dark Cherry Sunburst

PRS PAUL REED SMITH GUITARS

Made in the USA.   © 1992 PRS

it began to gain interest from players and press. The fabulously-colored carved-maple tops harked back to the classic late-1950s Gibson Les Paul, while the guitar's outline melded the double-cutaway shape of Smith's earlier instruments with elements of a Fender Stratocaster-style shape, creating a unique hybrid design that was both classic-looking yet original enough to be noticed.

This mix of Gibson and Fender – effectively the two major cornerstones of electric guitar design – was crucial to the concept.

PRS's scale-length of 25″ (635mm) sat half-way between Gibson's shorter 24.56″ (626mm) scale and Fender's longer 25.5″ (648mm). The 10″ (254mm) fingerboard radius also sat between Gibson's flatter 12″ (305mm) camber and the smaller 7.25″ (184mm) radius of vintage Fenders. That wasn't all. With an unusual rotary pickup selector switch, the twin PRS humbuckers created five distinct sounds: a combination of thick humbucking Gibson-like tones and thinner single-coil mixes that approximated some of the Stratocaster's key voices.

Augmenting the pickup switch was a master volume control and, instead of a conventional tone control, a "sweet switch" which rounded off the guitar's upper frequencies. (By 1991 the sweet switch had been replaced on all models in favor of a standard tone control.) The early 1980s had seen the double-locking Floyd Rose vibrato become one of the most popular design features used on contemporary electric

guitars. However, as a working musician Smith didn't like the fact that you needed a set of Allen wrenches to change strings.

So, with the help of local guitar-playing engineer John Mann, Smith designed his own vibrato system that updated the classic Fender vibrato and employed unique cam-locking tuners, yet still offered fashionable "wide-travel" pitch-bending with near perfect tuning stability.

The Custom used classic "tonewoods," including top-quality curly maple for the distinctly carved top, mahogany for the back and set-neck, and Brazilian rosewood for the fingerboard. The instrument also brought some innovations. Instead of employing conventional plastic binding, the edge of the maple top was left natural-colored, contrasting the colored finish of the guitar's top. Along with all this detail, the guitar's double-octave, 24-fret fingerboard was made to feel "as comfortable as an old T-shirt," like a guitar that had been played in.

It was a design that embodied all of Smith's experience to date, made by a guitar player for other guitar players. Although there have been numerous design changes over the years, the PRS Custom is one of the few electric guitars designed outside the 1950s that can genuinely lay claim to the term "design classic."

Launched at the same time as the Custom was the Standard. Originally just called the PRS, it featured an all-mahogany body, and as such was the workingman's PRS,

Three examples of PRS's EG models, the company's first attempt at "affordable" guitars, are shown on this page, all made during 1991: an EG 3 (near right); an EG 4 (center); and an EG II (far right).

though otherwise it had the same specification. The Metal, a Standard with a graphic paint job, bowed to current fashion but was quickly dropped in favor of the more classic-looking instruments.

Further models followed that only subtly changed the specification of the main pair of PRS models. The Special, which first appeared during 1987, pandered more to contemporary heavy-rock playing trends, while the Studio, which debuted in the PRS line in 1988, offered a pickup layout that featured a humbucker and two single-coils, and came with or without a maple top.

These early years were fraught with the problems of production. Smith had a decade of experience in custom one-off building and repairing, but the production of a number of instruments to the high quality of his pre-factory hand-made guitars provided a steep learning curve. Yet apart from the guitars themselves, Paul Reed Smith became a natural figurehead. His own playing experience enabled easy communication with top-line players – he would sometimes guest with name bands – and early on his in-store clinics became a successful if time-consuming part of his job. For many years PRS was quite happy to let people believe that it was Paul Reed Smith himself who made every guitar.

To support these high-end instruments a sequence of simple and distinguished advertisements became another hallmark of the brand. This parallel invention did not

The fabulous fingerboard inlay work by Pearl Works on the Dragon I overshadowed the developments made at PRS for the guitar's design. Changes included the Stop-Tail bridge and the first set-neck 22-fret fingerboard. The 1992 Dragon I was produced in a limited run of 50 instruments; this one (main guitar) is number 31. The Dragon II (far right, 1993, limited run of 100) had a more elaborate inlay. The four fingerboards pictured above show (left to right): Dragon I inlay with pearl wings; Dragon III inlay; Dragon I inlay with blue wings; Dragon II inlay.

go unnoticed: the ads' designer Dennis Voss and photographer Michael Ward won an Award of Merit for Graphic Excellence in 1985.

Smith seemed on every level to surround himself with mentors and teachers. Early on in PRS's history, Eric Pritchard had given Smith valuable advice on numerous engineering and technical matters. Pritchard not only helped to design the locking PRS tuners but also many of the production tools that were used to fabricate PRS guitars for years. Many friends remarked how Smith possessed an uncanny ability to absorb information, like a sponge.

In 1987 Smith introduced a theme that has since become an important part of PRS Guitars: the limited-edition "ultimate quality" guitar. A friend had remarked to Smith that he didn't charge enough for his work. The result was the Signature, basically a Custom but with absolutely top quality woods and maple tops.

In all, some 1,000 Signature models were made. Each was hand-signed on the headstock by Smith himself, before the Artist Series took over the top-of-the-line position in 1991. Smith would at this time go on long sales tours, away from the factory, and obviously wasn't available then to sign the Signature models. An interim solution was to have Smith sign decals which could go under the finish, and Smith says the production team even threatened to sign the guitars themselves. So the Signature came to an end. Nonetheless, the new Limited Edition model appeared during 1989,

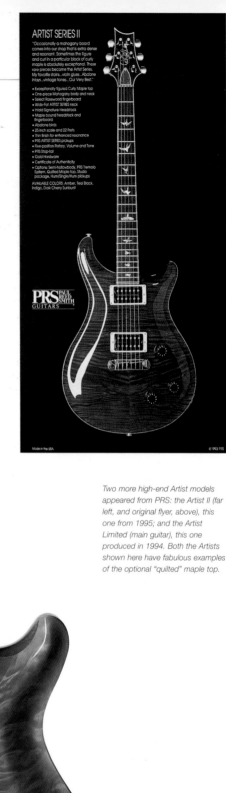

Two more high-end Artist models appeared from PRS: the Artist II (far left, and original flyer, above), this one from 1995; and the Artist Limited (main guitar), this one produced in 1994. Both the Artists shown here have fabulous examples of the optional "quilted" maple top.

One of Paul Reed Smith's original customers from the pre-factory days, Ted Nugent stayed faithful to the new PRS instruments as this 1994 ad (right) demonstrates.

the first production PRS to feature as standard a non-vibrato, tune-o-matic bridge and stud tailpiece. The guitar also featured hollow tone chambers, although the top was sealed, without any f-holes. Along with curly maple, unusual but highly-figured woods for tops such as cedar and redwood created one of the most unusual PRS guitars from this period. Of Signature quality and price, the Limited Edition was only planned as a small 300-piece run, though fewer were actually made. Both the Signature and Limited Edition proved that there was a highly lucrative market for limited-edition PRS guitars.

By 1988 some dealers, not to mention new export markets like the UK, were calling for PRS to make a less expensive guitar. The result was the first PRS bolt-on-neck instrument, the Classic Electric (quickly abbreviated to CE after Peavey objected to the use of "their" word Classic).

Originally the CE, with its alder body and maple neck and fingerboard, brought a more Fender-like style to the PRS line which up to that point had exclusively featured set-neck guitars. Initially the market was confused, and the company realized that players wanted a cheaper PRS Custom, not a different-sounding instrument. So a black-face headstock quickly followed, as did a maple-top option and, of course, the majority of PRS options such as bird inlays.

The CE evolved into a highly successful guitar. Its body changed to mahogany in 1995, a year after 22-fret versions had been added. It wasn't until 2000 that the standard, non-maple-top CE 22 and CE 24 were phased out, not for lack of popularity or sales, but for simple economic reasons. The start-up CE made little profit for the company and, with pressures on production space caused by increased demand, the CE was an obvious candidate for shelving.

Yet especially in the UK and Europe the CE didn't really satisfy the demand for a lower-priced PRS. This market pressure led the company to produce the bolt-on-neck EG, the first flat-fronted PRS guitar and the first with a 22-fret fingerboard. However, the company soon realized that they were losing money on every EG that was shipped. Smith has said in retrospect that he was unhappy with the sound of the original EGs.

In 1991 a new version appeared, again with a flat front but a rounder, more PRS-like outline. This new EG line was quite a departure. The bodies were crafted on computerized routers by a Baltimore engineering company, Excel (who would manufacture the majority of PRS's hardware parts during the 1990s). However, by 1995 the EG line was discontinued, and at the time of writing they mark the final attempt at a cheaper PRS guitar. There are rumored plans of a PRS guitar that is to be made outside the US ("offshore" in business-speak), as well as another attempt at producing a low-cost US-made electric guitar.

Wood quality was paramount from the start of PRS Guitars, as it had been in Smith's "apprentice" days making one-off custom instruments. Early on, Smith had

The first major change to the Custom model was its move in 1993, inspired by the Dragon I, to 22 frets as the Custom 22 (1994 example, far left). Other models were also made available with 22 frets at this time, including the CE. This CE 22 Maple Top (near left) was made in 1998.

The CE models widened the appeal of PRSs to some players, as these 1990s ads show. They feature Alex Lifeson of Rush (top) and Brian "Damage" Forsyth of Kix.

PRS's McCarty models were developed with Ted McCarty, Gibson president from 1950 to 1966. McCarty is pictured (right) with Paul Reed Smith at the PRS factory. The PRS McCarty solidbodies were endorsed by players such as Larry Lalonde of Primus (centre right) and Ross Childress of Collective Soul (far right).

drawn the conclusion that the better the quality of the raw material, in terms of its weight and condition, the better the guitar would sound.

Unlike many makers at the time, Smith believed that an electric guitar's tone was not all derived from its pickups and electronics. His feeling was that the electric guitar was an acoustic structure, and that the pickups and signal chain could not amplify what wasn't there in the first place. It led him on a quest for the finest woods and knowledgeable timber suppliers, such as Michael Reid whom Smith had first met in 1980. Reid became a valued part of PRS's production chain.

The fabulously curly and quilted maple tops were especially important to PRS Guitars. The company set up a grading system: the Classic grade, used for the CE Maple Top guitars, is about a "7" on PRS's 1-to-10 rating system. The set-neck guitars use a Regular grade – now more commonly known as a Custom grade – of around 7 to 9 on the system.

PRS's "10-tops" are an option on certain production guitars like the Custom, and are obviously 10 on that scale. The Signature series and subsequent limited-edition models use what Smith describes as "something spectacular."

Curly maple is a highly "figured," or patterned, timber. Under the vibrant, stained and colored finishes used by PRS, it helps to create a guitar that for many is as much a work of art as a working musical tool. Conversely, the opulent appearance of a PRS curly maple top has drawn many a derogatory phrase, from "over-pretty" to "furniture guitar." Although curly maple has been synonymous with guitars such as the Gibson Les Paul since the late 1950s, PRS refueled the demand almost as soon as its guitars appeared in the mid 1980s.

Once a curly log is discovered it needs to be correctly processed before it gets close to being part of a PRS guitar. Imagine a rectangular block of maple. Along the sides run "wave" shapes. By slicing the blank in two – as you would to cut a bun before buttering it – you slice through the wave, and open the blank like a book. You then see the curl, like lines across a page.

The type of wave, and the extremes of width and distance between its "peaks" and "troughs," will influence the look of the curl. A slightly curved wave will result in a mild curl; a triangular wave will be more spectacular; and a square wave will be the strongest. Because the relative hardness between the peaks and the troughs of the curl differs, certain color-staining and sanding techniques can emphasize the curl.

The way in which a log is cut will also affect the final look of the curl. A quarter-sawn rectangular blank, with grain running parallel to the long sides, creates a pronounced and symmetrical curl. If the blank is slab-sawn, with grain running parallel to the shorter top face of a rectangular blank, the curl twists and looks more diverse – and the grain will not be symmetrical across the halves of the bookmatched top, unlike

The Dragon III (1994 prototype, near right) had another highly detailed fingerboard inlay. PRS's two new McCarty guitars marked a distinct development: shown here are a McCarty Model (center, from 1994) and a McCarty Standard (far right, made in 1998).

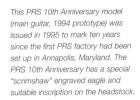

the curl. The curl of a slab-sawn example will be less curly and more "wiggly." The look of a curly-maple top will be further altered by the type of maple used. PRS use two main types of maple for guitar tops: West Coast and East Coast. East Coast maple, also known as red maple, is what PRS started with. Later they added West Coast maple, also known as big-leaf maple, which can be had from a variety of sources including British Columbia, Washington state, Oregon and Southern California.

In 1991 PRS announced the Artist I, which outwardly seemed a continuation of the Signature series. In fact, the Artist I signaled a fundamental change in the design of PRS guitars. Many of the top pros who'd been attracted to PRS guitars loved the look and feel of the instruments but felt there was room for tonal improvement.

It seemed clear to some that PRS provided a natural progression beyond vintage Gibson Les Paul instruments – but the sound lacked the low-end associated with those classic guitars. So, along with its ultimate-grade timbers, the Artist I introduced a stronger neck construction and many different production techniques, primarily

This PRS 10th Anniversary model (main guitar, 1994 prototype) was issued in 1995 to mark ten years since the first PRS factory had been set up in Annapolis, Maryland. The PRS 10th Anniversary has a special "scrimshaw" engraved eagle and suitable inscription on the headstock.

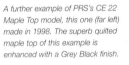

A further example of PRS's CE 22 Maple Top model, this one (far left) made in 1998. The superb quilted maple top of this example is enhanced with a Grey Black finish.

541

Carlos Santana (below; 1999 Supernatural album, right) has been a long-time PRS player. The main guitar pictured here is the first instrument that Paul Reed Smith built for Santana in 1980 at the guitar-maker's West Street, Annapolis, workshop.

guitar manufacturers

intended to improve the "acoustic" tone of PRS guitars. While the Artist got Smith closer to the sound he and a significant number of his top-flight customers were looking for, it still wasn't close enough. Yet PRS's next sonic development was virtually missed by the guitar-playing public.

When the Dragon I was launched in 1992 in a limited edition of just 50 pieces, the market was staggered by the exquisite computer-cut inlay down the fingerboard. But this feature, which brought the company a good deal of media interest, disguised the fact that the guitar featured a shorter 22-fret neck with a "wide-fat" profile, a new non-vibrato Stop-Tail bridge, and new pickups.

While the Dragon I was heading for guitar collections around the world, those lucky enough to own and play one realized the tonal improvement. This led the following year to the introduction of the PRS Custom 22, basically a Dragon without the inlay. Indeed, while 24-fret options still remain on the Custom, Standard and CE, the majority of future PRS guitars would follow the shorter and fatter neck concept. Smith says that a big neck equals big tone, and few players would disagree. As a consequence, PRS's other major models of the time – the Standard and CE lines – were also offered in 22-fret formats from 1994.

These gradual changes in specification are typical of PRS. With a couple of exceptions the guitars have always used pickups designed and made by PRS.

Originally, the Custom, Standard and Signature used what PRS called the Standard Treble and Standard Bass humbuckers.

These pickups looked like any other uncovered humbucker, but actually used magnetic "slug" polepieces in the non-adjustable inner coil, as well as a rear-placed feeder magnet. This helped to achieve a more accurate single-coil tone when split by the company's five-position rotary switch.

Catering for the more aggressive rock market, PRS developed pickups such as the Chainsaw, and the HFS ("Hot, Fat and Screams") as used initially on the Special. The Vintage Treble and Vintage Bass humbuckers first appeared on the Classic Electric, and the pairing of an HFS at bridge and Vintage Bass in neck position endures today on the 24-fret CE Maple Top, Standard and Custom. The first Dragon guitar featured the Dragon Treble and Dragon Bass pickups (which also appeared on the Custom 22), but since the McCarty Model and its new McCarty pickups the 22-fret PRSs have featured covered pickups which, tonally, chase a more "classic" sound.

In 1988 PRS launched the unique Electronics Upgrade Kit designed to improve the "fatness" and midrange definition of pre-1993 PRS instruments. It could have been called the "all we've learned since we started" kit as it reflected changes made over the years to minor components, such as lighter-weight tuner buttons and thumb screws, nickel-plated-brass screws for saddles and intonation, a simulated tone

Three more PRS guitars are illustrated on this page: a Santana "reissue" model (far left) from 1995; an Artist III (center) made in 1997; and an Artist IV prototype (near left) that was produced in 1995.

control for early switch-equipped guitars, and high-capacitance hook-up wire. The Dragon I, meanwhile, had been a risk that worked. The Dragon II followed in 1993 (along with the 22-fret Artist II) and the Dragon III in 1994 (joined by the Artist Ltd). Both new Dragons were limited to just 100 pieces and each featured along the fingerboard a more flamboyant dragon inlay than the last.

Announced in 1999, the most fabulous Dragon guitar was unleashed with a "three-dimensional" inlay, this time over the complex curves of the body. The Dragon 2000, limited to 50 pieces, may for some have been just another collectors' guitar, but it illustrates the desire of PRS to stretch the boundaries of guitar-making in their ultra-high-end models.

Little known until 1994 was the involvement with PRS of Ted McCarty. He had been president of Gibson between 1950 and 1965, the period that many considered as the company's golden years. Smith says he "discovered" McCarty's name when doing some research in the local patent office. Just after starting his production company, Smith cold-called McCarty for advice. With great foresight, Smith subsequently enlisted him as a consultant. McCarty, meanwhile, "downloaded the hard disk" for Smith, explaining how Gibson made its instruments back in the 1950s.

But when it came to PRS's next landmark guitar, it was again player pressure that spurred the idea onward, notably from Texas guitar-slinger David Grissom. Leaving the

The prototype (near right) for PRS's Rosewood Ltd was made in 1995, and like the production models has a spectacular tree-of-life inlay on the fingerboard, and a solid rosewood neck. This Fender-flavored Swamp Ash Special (center) dates from 1997, as does this Golden Eagle (far right), with carving by Floyd Scholz and planned as a limited run of ten. It also provides the rare sight on a PRS of three humbuckers.

opulence of the Dragon and Artist guitars behind, 1994's McCarty Model changed the formula in a seemingly subtle way, creating a PRS guitar that got closer still to the sound and feel of Gibson's classic late-1950s Les Paul.

PRS said the McCarty Model was essentially a Dragon with a thicker body, thinner headstock, lighter tuners and different pickups. In reality it was much more than that. It proved a turning point for PRS Guitars.

The company had grown up and the McCarty Model quite quickly became the "player's PRS." Certainly when compared side-by-side with a mid-1980s Custom, the differences in sound and feel were startlingly obvious. Physically, the McCarty had a shorter, fatter neck, while the difference in body thickness, while subtle, is there: the McCarty feels slightly less petite. Generally speaking, the McCarty has more of a Gibson-like, "vintage" vibe to it. It has a broader sound than an early Custom's typically aggressive, thinner tone, but still with plenty of PRS character, particularly a focused midrange and a chunkier feel.

The McCarty Model also featured for the first time on a major PRS guitar a three-way Gibson-style pickup-selecting toggle switch instead of PRS's unique five-way rotary switch. (Later, a pull/push switch was added to the tone control in order to coil-split the humbuckers.) Mirroring the Custom/Standard relationship in the PRS line, the mahogany McCarty Standard without a maple cap was introduced at the same time as

the maple-top McCarty Model. In 1998 the McCarty Model was offered with twin Seymour Duncan P-90-style "soapbar" single-coil pickups as the McCarty Soapbar, cashing in on the popularity of P-90s toward the end of the decade.The all-mahogany McCarty Soapbar returns to the construction and style of Smith's early pre-factory pre-maple-top guitars which usually favored mahogany construction and P-90 pickups.

Another "soapbar" guitar, the Custom 22 Soapbar, appeared in 1998, unusually for a PRS featuring a maple set-neck and three soapbar pickups controlled by a five-way lever switch, giving a unique "hot" Strat-style tone. Ten years old as a production company in 1995, PRS Guitars released the 10th Anniversary model that year which featured "scrimshaw" engraved bird inlays and headstock eagle.

After many, many requests, PRS also started making in 1995 a reproduction of the pre-factory Santana guitar, with its old-style double-cutaway outline, 24.5″ (622mm) scale-length and flatter 11.5″ (292mm) fingerboard radius. Ironically, although this seemed a backward design step, it was among the first PRS guitars to be made using the company's recently installed computer-assisted routing machines. These began to replace the innovative jigs and tools that had helped to fabricate PRS guitars for the previous decade.

Santana always liked his pre-factory PRS guitars, although Smith says that the guitarist tried "really hard" to like the new, modern PRS design. Eventually, PRS made

This Custom 22 Soapbar (far left) left the PRS production line in 1999, at the time of a vogue for guitars with pickups in the style of Gibson's P-90 "soapbar" units. The two other PRSs pictured here are examples of the company's Private Stock custom shop instruments. Private Stock #86 (center) is a luxurious Santana II with ultimate-quality timbers; Private Stock #62 (near left) is a McCarty Hollowbody with a spectacularly figured one-piece maple top.

Santana some replicas of his now well-used originals. PRS wanted to make its new Santana guitar a production model, and to use Santana's name. A deal was subsequently arranged, and a large percentage of Santana's royalties go to charity. Santana remains the only guitar player to have a "signature" PRS guitar.

The growth of PRS guitars is aptly reflected by its expanding workshop space. Compared to Smith's tiny West Street rooms in Annapolis, the first Virginia Avenue factory must have seemed massive to the handful of staff who manned it in early 1985. At first there were just eight people working there. PRS had one-third of the building to start with, sharing with a furniture-stripping shop, a brass business and a sail-maker, but after three or four years PRS had taken over most of the premises. As time progressed a separate woodshop was added, a short walk from the main facility.

This was all certainly a far cry from the beginnings of PRS Guitars. During the ten years preceding the move in 1985 to Virginia Avenue, it was taking Smith and his co-workers on average a little over a month to produce every guitar. By 1988, a crew of 45 people were making around 15 guitars every day, and by 1995 Virginia Avenue housed about 80 workers who were crafting between 25 and 30 guitars daily. The last PRS guitar was shipped from the Virginia Avenue plant at the end of December 1995. The company estimates that in its first ten years it produced around 23,000 set-neck guitars and about 14,000 bolt-on-neck models. PRS relocated to its brand new

Ted McCarty once again collaborated with PRS in the development of the company's new hollowbody guitars – the deep-body Archtop and the shallower Hollowbody. McCarty is pictured (above, right) with Paul Reed Smith at the launch of the new instruments at a 1998 trade show. Shown here are the three Archtop models: a prototype of the spruce-top Archtop (main guitar) from 1997; a maple-top Archtop II (this page, far right) made in 1998; and an ultra-high-end Archtop Artist (opposite page, brown guitar) also dating from 1998.

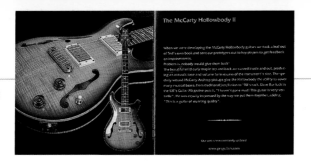

The McCarty Hollowbody II

When we were developing the McCarty Hollowbody guitars we took a leaf out of Ted's own book and sent our prototypes out to key players to get feedback on improvements.

Problem is, nobody would give them back!

The beautiful solid curly maple top and back are carved inside and out, producing an acoustic tone and volume far in excess of the instrument's size. The specially wound McCarty Archtop pickups give the Hollowbody the ability to cover many musical bases, from traditional jazz/fusion to '60s rock. Dave Burluck in the UK's Guitar Magazine puts it, "I haven't gone mad! This guitar is very versatile". He was equally impressed by the way we put them together, adding, "This is a guitar of stunning quality".

Our website is constantly updated

www.prsguitars.com

PRS's 1998 catalog (right) provided visual evidence of the Hollowbody models' more shallow body depth.

manufacturing base at Stevensville, on Kent Island, just across the Chesapeake bridge from Annapolis, and production resumed in the first week of January 1996. With some 25,000 square feet now at the company's disposal – which was nearly double that of the Virginia Avenue facility and its outbuildings – PRS employed around 110 staff by the end of 1998 and aimed to produce around 700 guitars every month.

Having invested in computer-assisted routing machines in 1995, more were installed at the new factory to bring a higher level of consistency to guitars that were already renowned for their craftsmanship. Pushing production efficiency further forward, robotic buffing machines appeared soon after the factory move. But even with these new tools, PRS guitars still felt "hand-made," comfortable instruments rather than sterile, machine-made items. Even with the high-tech equipment, there is more hand-work in the sanding, coloring and finishing of a PRS guitar than most other production instruments.

The first new models to come off the line in 1996 were the Rosewood Ltd and the Swamp Ash Special. The former continued Smith's pursuit of the ultimate tonewood for necks, featuring a solid East Indian rosewood neck with Brazilian rosewood fingerboard, the latter inlaid with a fantastically detailed tree-of-life design.

Although mahogany is used for the majority of PRS's set-neck guitars, there's little doubt that Paul Reed Smith would choose rosewood if the cost was not prohibitive.

Smith's personal "number one" guitar – an amber-colored Dragon I – was the first PRS to feature a rosewood neck, and the option of an Indian rosewood neck was subsequently offered for the McCarty. During 1999, a limited run of McCartys with expensive Brazilian rosewood necks was made.

While the Rosewood Ltd was a limited edition of 100 pieces, it was dramatically different to the Swamp Ash Special, which was intended like the original Classic Electric and Studio to bring a more Fender-like tone to the PRS line. The 22-fret Swamp Ash Special, as its name implies, uses a lightweight ash body with bolt-on maple neck and fingerboard, and pairs two McCarty humbuckers with a centrally-placed single-coil-size humbucker.

Also launched by PRS during 1996 were two more luxurious Artist models, the III and IV. These were intended to replace the previous Artist II and Artist Limited.

PRS's custom shop, producing what the company calls Private Stock guitars, was established in 1996. It aimed to recreate the circumstances of Smith's old workshop: almost anything a customer wants, PRS will make as a Private Stock instrument – at a price. While some guitars are based on existing production techniques, others need to be built fully or partially from the ground up. PRS estimates the ratio of hand-work to machine-work on a Private Stock guitar is around 50/50 in the initial stages, but a double-neck, for example, would be all hand-made. For many customers the starting

Two PRS Hollowbody models are shown on this page: a quilted-maple Hollowbody II (center) from 1999; and a flame-maple Hollowbody II made during 1998.

A page from PRS's luxurious 1998 catalog highlights the McCarty Soapbar model launched that year.

The McCarty Soapbar

The old "Soapbar" single-coil pickups had a clarity of tone - without sounding thin and weak - that had defined the sound of Rock and Roll and small combo Jazz guitar playing in the 1940's and 1950's.

We wanted to try some in our McCarty Model, but the search for the "right" Soapbar proved difficult. It seems other companies settled for second best. Our R & D Department worked with the experts at Seymour Duncan and designed a pickup with all the slick vintage punch of the original with a spanking definition that's right up to the minute.

Andrew Fleming is the 10's Guitarist magazine says. "A fabulously retro take on PRS's established Strat meets Les Paul theme. An absolute cracker." Tom Wheeler says it "looks like an heirloom instrument and a '55 Chevy showcar all at the same time."

Check out our Price List for more cool colors like the Ocean Turquoise shown opposite.

Our web site has our complete Accessory Shop online.
www.prsguitars.com

---

point for a Private Stock has tended to be a McCarty with custom bird inlays, Brazilian rosewood fingerboard and double-stained "killer" top.

The first Private Stock guitar was completed in April 1996. By the spring of 1999 some 87 pieces had been built, each carrying a sequential Private Stock number as well as a standard serial number. Around half have been high-end McCartys, but there have been Archtops, double-necks, 12-strings and others. As with the Guitars Of The Month that prompted the Private Stock scheme, new ideas and designs that come up can effectively provide prototypes for future PRS production models. A bass design was unveiled at a trade show during 1998, for example, and positive reaction led to a new PRS bass joining the line in 2000.

A Private Stock example of a hollowbody archtop PRS guitar was shown at another trade show, this time in 1997, and the following year PRS brought out a new line of hollowbody McCarty guitars, marking a company well into its stride.

The Archtop looked like any other PRS, save for the twin f-holes and substantially deeper body. A guitar like this would not have been commercially possible if it wasn't for PRS's use of computer-assisted machinery. This hollows out the central mahogany block, leaving thin sides, a pocket for the neck and, importantly, a block under the bridge. Not only was the front carved but the back too and, like a violin, the top and back were carved on the inside as well. Launched at the same time, the PRS

Hollowbody used the same construction as the Archtop, except that the body was less deep: about three inches at its center as opposed to four inches. The majority of production-built semi-solidbody or fully hollow guitars from other makers tend to use laminated maple tops, back and sides. PRS's use of solid timbers matches the kinds of specification usually limited to hand-carved (and more expensive) guitars.

The Archtop featured a new version of the PRS Stop-Tail tailpiece with adjustable saddles to cater for the larger string gauges used by the jazz players for whom the instrument was intended. Also, new pickups were developed for these instruments' more "classic" tones. The basic models came with spruce front and mahogany back and sides. The Archtop II and Hollowbody II added figured maple tops and backs, while the Archtop Artist was an ultimate high-end model – PRS called it "a piece of art that doubles as a musical instrument."

This hollow guitar line had been developed by Joe Knaggs, PRS's master luthier who builds the majority of the company's custom one-off Private Stock line. The Archtop in particular was intended to enable PRS to offer a more jazz-oriented instrument. However, it quickly appeared that the more Gibson ES-335-like Hollowbody was the most popular of the new line, and by late 1998 it accounted for nearly half of PRS's total production. All the Hollowbody and Archtop models are offered with an optional piezo-pickup bridge system, developed in conjunction with noted US acoustic

Another PRS with P-90-style pickups was the McCarty Soapbar, this one (near right) dating from 1999. PRS updated the Santana model in 1998 with a three-way toggle switch replacing the original pickup selector mini-switches. This example (center) was made in 1999. Some PRS models continued to be available in original 24-fret style, as shown by this CE 24 (far right) from 1998.

pickup manufacturer L.R. Baggs. The extremely efficient piezo system allows these guitars to sound like amplified acoustic instruments as well as offering all the usual magnetic pickup tones. By 2000 the Hollowbody craze had settled, while the Archtop had become a minor part of PRS sales.

The introduction of left-handed PRS models came in 1999 for the McCarty and Custom 22 (with Stop-Tail or vibrato bridge). Typically, these were carefully detailed models with every feature properly left-handed, from the positioning of the headstock logo right down to the labeling of the control knobs.

Some 25 years after Smith built his first proper electric – that single-cutaway flat-front Les Paul-alike – PRS launched the Singlecut, the closest the company had got to both the look and tone of those classic vintage Les Pauls. The company's first ads for the new-for-2000 model, which wasn't in the McCarty line, featured a profile picture of Ted McCarty and the caption, "Ted McCarty introduced the single cutaway, carved-top solidbody to the world in 1952. We learned a lot from Ted while we were working on ours." This illustrated where PRS was heading.

Over the years many companies have either blatantly copied the Les Paul or used it as clear inspiration. Yet the PRS Singlecut will be seen by many as the closest anyone has come to the hallowed tone of Gibson's late-1950s Les Paul without actually breaching any trademarked design features. Apart from the single-cutaway shape, the guitar follows the specification of PRS's McCarty model with, typically, many subtle changes. These include a slightly thicker body, and new covered pickups simply called PRS 7s. Smith believes these are the closest yet to the tone of original Gibson PAFs, but with modern-day performance standards. On the Singlecut's launch early in 2000, initial sales proved immensely strong, but whether the Singlecut will prove as popular in the long term as the Custom and McCarty Model remains to be seen.

However, the launch of that new guitar was rather over-shadowed by the leading PRS player Carlos Santana, who simply refused to fade away. In February 2000, at the age of 52, Santana won a phenomenal eight Grammy Awards for his 1999 *Supernatural* album, equaling Michael Jackson's previous record for *Thriller* in 1983. At the time of writing, *Supernatural* had notched up sales in excess of 11 million copies. As the awards ceremony closed, there was Santana propelling his hallmark Latin-tinged music on his beautifully distinctive PRS guitar.

Paul Reed Smith is the first to acknowledge Santana's importance to the company. But the lanky, big-haired kid from Maryland, now in his early 40s, must have been extremely proud to witness Santana – some two decades after he'd first plucked a PRS – still making incredible music in front of the world's most important music-industry people, on a guitar that was originally conceived in an impossibly small workshop in Annapolis. Maybe it was an accident of God after all.

Three more PRS guitars are pictured on this page: a Custom 24 (far left) from 1998; a Dragon 2000 (center) made in 1999; and a Standard 24 (near left) that dates from 1998.

*The cover of this 1956 catalog
commemorates the 25th anniversary
of Rickenbacker's first electric guitar,
the prototype "Frying Pan" lap-steel.*

R I C K E N B A C K E R

Rickenbacker is best known for some great designs devised in the 1950s, as well as its popularization of the electric 12-string guitar through prominent use by acts such as The Beatles and The Byrds during the 1960s.

Adolph Rickenbacker was born near Basel, Switzerland, in 1886, but while still young was brought to the United States. Around 1918 he moved to Los Angeles, California, and in the 1920s established a successful tool-and-die operation there, stamping out metal and plastic parts. One especially enthusiastic customer for these was the National guitar company of Los Angeles.

At National, George Beauchamp and Paul Barth put together a basic magnetic pickup for guitars. Their experiments culminated in a pickup with a pair of horseshoe-shape magnets enclosing the pickup coil and surrounding the strings. Beauchamp and Barth had a working version in mid 1931. Another National man, Harry Watson, built a one-piece maple lap-steel guitar on which the prototype pickup could be mounted. This was the famous wooden "Frying Pan" guitar, so-called because of its small round body and long neck. It was the first guitar to feature an electro-magnetic pickup, and in that sense the basis for virtually all modern electric guitars.

Beauchamp, Barth and Adolph Rickenbacker teamed up to put the ideas of this exciting prototype electric guitar into production. They formed the curiously named Ro-

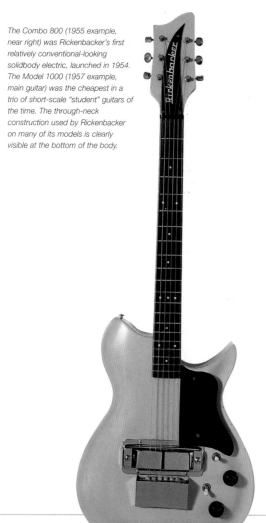

*The Combo 800 (1955 example,
near right) was Rickenbacker's first
relatively conventional-looking
solidbody electric, launched in 1954.
The Model 1000 (1957 example,
main guitar) was the cheapest in a
trio of short-scale "student" guitars of
the time. The through-neck
construction used by Rickenbacker
on many of its models is clearly
visible at the bottom of the body.*

Jean "Toots" Thielemans, guitarist with the George Shearing Quintet, on a 1960 magazine cover. It was at this time that John Lennon saw Thielemans's Rickenbacker and became interested in owning one.

Pat-In company at the end of 1931 – just before Beauchamp and Barth were fired by National. In summer 1932 Ro-Pat-In started manufacturing cast aluminum production versions of the Frying Pan electric lap-steel guitar, complete with horseshoe electromagnetic pickups. Ro-Pat-In's Frying Pans were effectively the first electric guitars with electro-magnetic pickups put into general production.

Early examples of the Frying Pan lap-steels tend to have the Electro brandname on the headstock, and so are usually referred to by players and collectors today as the Electro Hawaiian models. By 1934 "Rickenbacker" had been added to the headstock logo (sometimes the name is spelled "Rickenbacher"). Also that year the name of the manufacturing company was changed from the bizarre Ro-Pat-In to the more logical Electro String Instrument Corporation.

Around this time Electro also produced some Spanish wood-body archtop electrics. The Electro Spanish appeared around 1932 – among the earliest of its kind – and the Ken Roberts model, named for a session guitarist, followed about three years later. Bakelite was the first synthetic plastic, and Electro started using it in 1935 for its Model B Hawaiian lap-steel and the Electro Spanish (also called the Model B). The latter was arguably the first "solidbody" electric guitar.

During World War II Electro worked for the government, extending the Los Angeles factory in the process. After the war Adolph Rickenbacker decided not to continue

Three more early Rickenbackers are shown on this page: a "tulip" shape Combo 450 (far left) from 1957 with classic "cooker" knobs; a Combo 850 (center) made in 1957 with the new "crescent" shape cutaways; and a 460 (near left) from 1961, with the new five-knob control layout and "cresting wave" body shape.

Two early examples of what became Rickenbacker's best-known design: a 360 (main guitar) made in 1959, and a 330 (far right) from 1958. The 1960s ad (below) promoted Rickenbacker's 21-fret neck with "easier, faster reach." The 1989 catalog (above) shows a 381.

many of his musical instruments, including most of the poorly-received Spanish electrics. During 1946 he turned 60, and began to think about selling the musical instrument part of his business.

The eventual buyer was Francis Cary Hall, who had moved with his family to California when he was around 11 years old. He'd opened a radio repair store, Hall's Radio Service, in the 1920s. This led logically to a wholesale company distributing electronic parts, the Radio & Television Equipment Co (Radio-Tel), which F.C. Hall set up in Santa Ana, Orange County, in 1936.

After distributing Fender guitars and amplifiers for a time, Hall began to reconsider his position. Given his experience, Hall could see the potential for an instrument business where he not only distributed the product but also manufactured it. So in late 1953 Hall bought the Electro String Music Corporation from Adolph, with its guitar factory still at South Western Avenue, Los Angeles.

Around the beginning of 1954 German-born guitar-maker Roger Rossmeisl, previously at Gibson, was hired by Electro to come up with new designs for Rickenbacker electric guitars. That same year Electro launched its first "modern" electrics, the double-cutaway carved-top Rickenbacker Combo 600 and Combo 800. They were aptly named, combining the horseshoe pickup and almost square neck of the earlier Hawaiian lap-steels with the up-and-coming solidbody electric Spanish

Nightclub entertainer Suzi Arden with the first Rickenbacker 12-string guitar, which she acquired in 1963 – the year before George Harrison got his.

style. The first Combo models began to feature on the headstocks a brand new "underlined" Rickenbacker logo of the type still in use today.

Electro's next move was to abandon the clumsy horseshoe pickup and apply a more suitable pickup to its Spanish electrics. First to receive the new pickup was the Combo 400, launched in 1956. Another first was its through-neck construction, a feature that would become a familiar aspect of many of Rickenbacker's solidbody instruments.

New Combo 650 and Combo 850 models appeared in 1957, introducing a body shape with a "sweeping crescent"-shape across the two cutaways. In various incarnations and dimensions this has been in continual use by Rickenbacker to the present day.

In 1958 a series of new models was introduced that formed the basis for Rickenbacker's success during the 1960s and onwards. The thin-hollowbody designs were largely the responsibility of Rossmeisl.

For these new electric hollowbody Capri guitars he further developed an unusual "scooped-out" construction. Rather than make a hollow guitar in the traditional method he would start with a semi-solid block of wood – usually two halves of maple joined together – and cut it to a rough body shape, partially hollowing it out from the rear. A separate wooden back was added once all the electric fittings had been secured, and the neck was glued into place. The first new Rickenbacker Capri was the small-body short-scale three-pickup 325 model, a guitar that would have a great effect on the company's success when it was taken up a few years later by John Lennon.

A full 12-model Capri line-up was launched during 1958, though the Capri name itself was soon dropped. There were four short-scale models: 310 (two pickups), 315 (plus vibrato), 320 (three pickups) and 325 (plus vibrato); four full-scale models: 330 (two pickups), 335 (plus vibrato), 340 (three pickups) and 345 (plus vibrato); and four "deluxe" full-scale models with triangle-shape fingerboard inlays: 360 (two pickups), 365 (plus vibrato), 370 (three pickups) and 375 (plus vibrato).

Two classic Rickenbacker design elements began to appear at this time. New "toaster-top" pickups were devised, nicknamed for their split chrome look, and unusual two-tier pickguards, made at first in an arresting gold-colored plastic. These comprised

A relatively conventional hollowbody, this 375F (far left, 1964) was top of the Thin Full-Body line, and a heavily-carved Thick-body 381V69 (near left) from 1990. Steppenwolf guitarist John Kay (above) with his 1988 signature model, the 381JK.

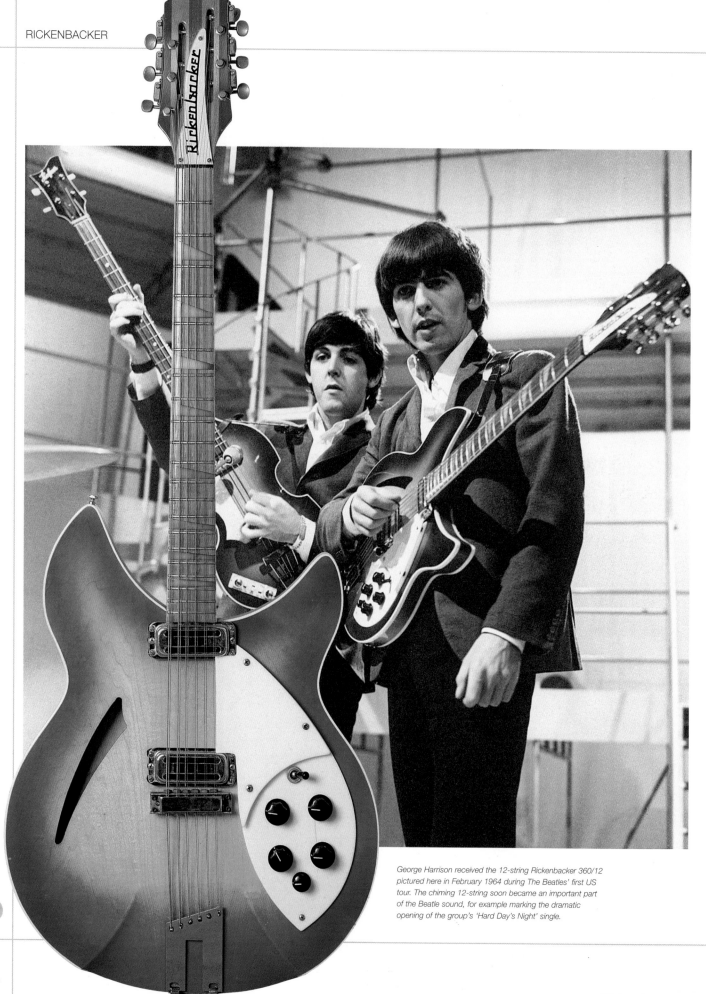

guitar manufacturers

George Harrison received the 12-string Rickenbacker 360/12 pictured here in February 1964 during The Beatles' first US tour. The chiming 12-string soon became an important part of the Beatle sound, for example marking the dramatic opening of the group's 'Hard Day's Night' single.

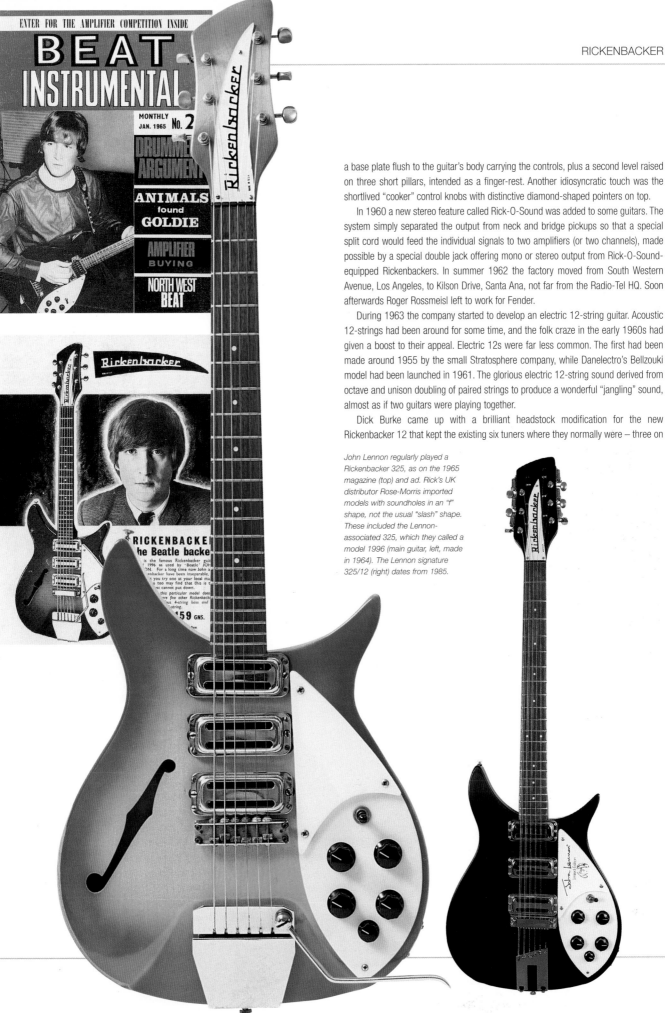

a base plate flush to the guitar's body carrying the controls, plus a second level raised on three short pillars, intended as a finger-rest. Another idiosyncratic touch was the shortlived "cooker" control knobs with distinctive diamond-shaped pointers on top.

In 1960 a new stereo feature called Rick-O-Sound was added to some guitars. The system simply separated the output from neck and bridge pickups so that a special split cord would feed the individual signals to two amplifiers (or two channels), made possible by a special double jack offering mono or stereo output from Rick-O-Sound-equipped Rickenbackers. In summer 1962 the factory moved from South Western Avenue, Los Angeles, to Kilson Drive, Santa Ana, not far from the Radio-Tel HQ. Soon afterwards Roger Rossmeisl left to work for Fender.

During 1963 the company started to develop an electric 12-string guitar. Acoustic 12-strings had been around for some time, and the folk craze in the early 1960s had given a boost to their appeal. Electric 12s were far less common. The first had been made around 1955 by the small Stratosphere company, while Danelectro's Bellzouki model had been launched in 1961. The glorious electric 12-string sound derived from octave and unison doubling of paired strings to produce a wonderful "jangling" sound, almost as if two guitars were playing together.

Dick Burke came up with a brilliant headstock modification for the new Rickenbacker 12 that kept the existing six tuners where they normally were – three on

John Lennon regularly played a Rickenbacker 325, as on the 1965 magazine (top) and ad. Rick's UK distributor Rose-Morris imported models with soundholes in an "f" shape, not the usual "slash" shape. These included the Lennon-associated 325, which they called a model 1996 (main guitar, left, made in 1964). The Lennon signature 325/12 (right) dates from 1985.

Rickenbackers became popular in Britain in the 1960s as a result of The Beatles' use of the instruments. Importer Rose-Morris gave its special f-hole guitars different numbers: for example, this 360/12 (near right) made in 1964 was known in the UK as a model 1993. Pete Townshend of The Who was an enthusiastic user (and abuser) of Rickenbackers. Pete's influence lives on. This 1998PT signature model (main guitar, far right) was made in 1988. Paul Weller's debt to 1960s music in general and Townshend's in particular was underlined by The Jam guitarist's prominent use of Rickenbacker guitars (above).

One of the most influential Rickenbacker players in the 1980s and beyond was Peter Buck of REM, seen on-stage here (left) with 12 strings at his disposal.

each side – but added two parallel channels into the face, as if the slots of a classical guitar had been cut only half-way through. Burke attached the second set of six tuners at 90 degrees to the first set, the keys facing "backwards" – again, like a classical guitar, with strings attached into the tuners' spindles in the channels. The design overcame the problems that many makers of 12-string guitars have discovered, not least the unbalancing effect of a heavy long head with six tuners each side.

Rickenbacker made at least three experimental 12-string guitars in 1963. The first model went to showband singer, fiddle-player and guitarist Suzi Arden, whose Suzi Arden Show, a regular at the Golden Nugget in Las Vegas, was kitted out with Rickenbacker equipment.

Rickenbacker set up a special display at the Savoy Hilton hotel in New York City in February 1964 to show some equipment to The Beatles. The group's arrival in the US to play Ed Sullivan's TV show and three concerts had caused unrivalled scenes of fan

mania. Despite missing the display due to illness, George Harrison ended up with a great prize, one of the company's experimental 12-string electrics, in model 360 style.

John Lennon also came away with a new guitar, a black 325 model with new five-control layout, replacing the somewhat road-weary 325 that he'd used for most of the group's early career. The company also promised to send to Lennon a special one-off 12-string version of the 325, just as soon as they'd made it. And Beatles manager Brian Epstein requested a second 360-style 12-string for another of his now famous charges, Gerry Marsden of Gerry & The Pacemakers.

For the two *Ed Sullivan Show* appearances in New York Lennon used his old 325, but for a further appearance, broadcast from Miami, Lennon gave his new five-knob 325 its public debut. The Sullivan shows were outrageously popular, each receiving an unprecedented American TV audience of some 70 million viewers. No doubt Rickenbacker boss F.C. Hall allowed himself a smile as he watched the group perform in the New York TV studio.

After their thoroughly successful invasion of the United States, The Beatles returned to Britain, and Harrison used his 12-string to great effect on some new recordings, including the distinctive opening chord of the title song from *A Hard Day's Night*, ringing out in typically jangling fashion. A rush for Rickenbacker 12-strings followed. Rickenbackers proved popular with other British pop guitarists during the second half

Rickenbacker's "deluxe" large-body models were redesigned in 1964 with a more rounded body shape, the lack of binding on the front softening the outline still further. This 360 (near right) from 1975 shows the new look. Roger McGuinn (right) of The Byrds did much to promote the jingle-jangle Rickenbacker 12-string sound in the 1960s. The company issued this signature 370/12RM model (far right) in 1988.

of the 1960s, including such influential guitarists as Denny Laine, Hilton Valentine and, with most notable effect, Pete Townshend.

During 1964 Rickenbacker officially added three 12-strings to its line, the 360/12 (two-pickup 360-style), 370/12 (three pickups) and 450/12 (two-pickup solidbody). The company also began at this time to supply export versions of certain models to distributor Rose-Morris in the UK, lasting until 1969. This would be unremarkable but for the fact that the British company requested instruments with real f-holes rather than Rickenbacker's customary "slash"-shape soundholes, and models with this feature have since become collectable.

From 1964 Rickenbacker introduced an alternative body style for the "deluxe" models (360, 360/12, 365, 370, 370/12 and 375) with a streamlined, less angular look to the front of the body, as well as binding on the soundhole and, now, only on the back edge of the body. Designed to be more comfortable for the player, the new streamlined design was the main production style used for the models mentioned from 1964. Old-style versions (body bound front and back, "sharp" edges) remained available on special order. A year earlier Rickenbacker had also introduced a striking new tailpiece, in the shape of a large "R."

The name of the sales/distribution company was changed in 1965 from the old Radio & Television Equipment Co to the more appropriate Rickenbacker Inc, and the sales office moved within Santa Ana in 1966. The name of the manufacturing company remained as Electro String.

A "light-show" guitar was introduced in 1970 with a clear plastic top through which a psychedelic array of colored lights would shine, flashing in response to the frequencies of the notes being played. Roger McGuinn had a special 12-string light-show Rickenbacker built with slanted frets and three pickups, which he used for 'Eight Miles High' at the end of Byrds shows in the early 1970s. It was perhaps the most bizarre Rickenbacker ever made – which makes it a rare beast indeed, given the number of odd and peculiar instruments that were made at and escaped from Rickenbacker's Santa Ana factory.

Around this time demand for Rickenbackers began to decline. Fortunately for Rickenbacker, its bass guitars gained in popularity in the early 1970s. Production began to pick up again at Santa Ana, concentrating on four-string models.

A new body shape appeared in 1973, although it was really only new to Rickenbacker's six-string guitar lines. The 480 used the body styling made famous by the company's electric bass guitars, which had first appeared in 1957, with a distinctive elongated upper horn.

A few custom double-neck guitars had been made for individual Rickenbacker customers in the 1960s, but in 1975 the company's first production double-necks

Three Rickenbackers are pictured on this page: an Astro kit guitar (near right) from 1964, sold as a self-assembly pack of parts; a 336/12 Convertible (center) made in 1967, with a Converter "comb" to switch between six-string and 12-string operation; and a 331 "light show" guitar (far right) from 1971, with sound-triggered lights visible through the transparent plastic top. Whatever it was that Rickenbacker's team was on at the time, modern guitar designers surely need a dose or two.

appeared. There were two types: the 4080 also used the electric bass body, while the 362 enlarged upon the familiar 360 style.

In 1983 Rickenbacker made a low-key attempt to recreate some of its older models, which the company noticed were increasingly popular among "vintage" collectors. A new generation of guitarists had also started to take up Rickenbackers, and this helped the company's climb back to popularity during the 1980s. Among the most notable and visible players of Rickenbackers at the time were Peter Buck and Johnny Marr. The jangling, rhythmic thrust of Rickenbackers was once more to be heard at the heart of some of pop's most vibrant offerings.

The business operation of Rickenbacker was changed in 1984 when F.C. Hall's son John, who'd worked at Rickenbacker since 1969, officially took control. He formed a new company, Rickenbacker International Corporation (RIC), which purchased the guitar-related parts of his father's Rickenbacker Inc and Electro String companies. In 1989 Rickenbacker moved its factory from Kilson Drive after some 27 years, consolidating factory and offices at the corner of South Main and Stevens in Santa Ana.

A new idea during the late 1980s was the production of numbered limited-edition signature models. Rickenbacker have so far made eight artist guitars in editions of between 250 and 1,000: Pete Townshend (1987), Roger McGuinn (1988), John Kay (1988); Susanna Hoffs (1988), John Lennon (1989); Tom Petty (1991); Glenn Frey

Another peculiarity from the Santa Ana workshops of Rickenbacker was this 360SF model (main guitar) from 1968, with slanted frets. The company's publicity insisted that the skewed frets matched "natural finger angle," but the rest of the world stayed resolutely parallel. The 481 (far right, from 1976) used the body shape best known on Rickenbacker's basses, with a distinctive elongated bass horn. Still at home in the 1990s, Rickenbacker continued to enchant pop players looking for a certain sound, such as Adam Devlin of The Bluetones (above).

Two Rickenbacker catalogs are pictured here: one from 1981 (right) shows the three double-necks of the period, including six-and-12 and six-and-bass versions; the other (below) from 1990 details the V-series reissues of the 325 models.

Three more Rickenbacker guitars: a 1987 360/12 (near right) in Tuxedo, a finish option of the time; a 362/12 double-neck (far right) from 1975; and a 660/12TP Tom Petty signature model (opposite) made in 1993.

(1992) and Carl Wilson (2000). Also, a proper Rickenbacker vintage reissue program is now underway. The idea of an organised line of appropriate reissue models celebrating Rickenbacker's best-loved instruments began in 1984 with three guitars. These were the 325V59 (now called the 325V59 Hamburg for the period in which John Lennon used his model), the 325V63 (now the 325V63 Miami, as Lennon first used his in a Miami TV studio) and the 360/12V64. The "V59"-type suffixes indicate the vintage of the original – 1959 in this example. At the time of writing the reissue series is up to nine models, adding a 350V63 Liverpool, 350/12V63 12-string, 360V64, 381V69, 381/12V69 and 1997SPC.

In 1992 Rickenbacker devised the new 24-fret 650 series. These share the body style of the earlier 400 and 600 "cresting wave" models, but have wider necks and high output pickups to compete with more mainstream instruments. Still in the line today, they complement Rickenbacker's continuing business with its set of classic and apparently timeless designs.

Tom Petty has long been a user of Rickenbacker guitars, although as this 1982 album sleeve (right) shows, he has not been averse to other axes, including Fenders.

RICK TURNER

Ex-guitar repairer and folk guitarist Rick Turner was one of three original 1970 shareholders in Alembic, the pioneering California guitar-maker, along with electronics expert Ron Wickersham and recording engineer Bob Matthews. While at Alembic, Turner moved from customizing instruments to full-scale production, making distinctive guitars (primarily electric basses) that developed the use of active electronics and exotic timbers. Turner was also involved with Geoff Gould of Modulus Graphite in the birth of the graphite neck.

Turner left Alembic in 1978 and soon formed his own operation, Turner Guitars, steering more toward guitars than basses. The new Turner 1C guitar had a small body with an almost violin-like outline and a rotating pickup to change tonal response, and is best known for its use by Lindsey Buckingham. Turner had designed it initially to use Alembic scrap parts, and also as a direct contrast to the generally unpopular Alembic through-neck six-string guitars.

After a break in production Turner returned in the 1990s and along with Turner-brand custom instruments now offers from Santa Cruz, California, a line of Renaissance-brand electric, electric-acoustic and bass designs. The retro Model T with its replica of the Rickenbacker-style horseshoe pickup of the 1930s remains a testament to this highly eclectic and respected luthier.

ROBIN

Robin is now a resolutely American brand, but its early guitars were manufactured for the company by Tokai in Japan.

First to appear in 1982 were some Stratocaster-shaped six-string models, many of which featured humbucking pickups, but all employed distinctive "reversed" headstock in the style of Gibson's Explorer guitar.

Next to be added to the Robin catalog were a number of less conventional designs including the Raider that had a "left-handed" look about it, despite being resolutely right-handed. The Ranger was styled somewhat like an early Fender Precision Bass, and this has proved to be one of Robin's most effective and enduring design ideas, with several subsequent variations. The Ranger has since attracted the attention of guitarists such as Jimmie Vaughan.

Later in the 1980s the Robin's Medley superstrat, manufactured in the United States, targeted the rock guitarist, as did the much more distinctive Machete. The Machete featured an offset body with a unique stepped construction and Robin's V-shape headstock with four tuners one side, two the other.

During the mid 1990s these continuing models were joined by the single-cutaway Avalon and Savoy series, adding Les Paul-like elements to a line which has remained virtually unchanged to the time of writing.

This Rick Turner Model T (center) was made in 1999, while the Robin Machete Custom dates from 1989. The 1991 Robin ad (below) pictures Tim Kelly of Slaughter with his Machete Deluxe.

A cheery if unknown Syd Delmonte plays a Roger archtop with floating pickup in this 1959 ad for the German maker's UK importer, Boosey & Hawkes.

ROGER

This was the brand used by German luthier Wenzel Rossmeisl during the 1950s and 1960s. It was originally named for Wenzel's son, Roger, who would go on to do some significant work at Rickenbacker and at Fender.

Most Roger guitars were ornate, large-bodied acoustics available with add-on pickups and controls. They often featured deep "dished" shaping around the body edges, Wenzel's trademark that is now known as the "German carve." His son used it on his US designs, inspiring Semie Moseley of Mosrite.

The only "proper" Roger electric guitar was the model 56, which was a single-cutaway semi-solidbody dating from around 1960. It had a plain "slab" body, and its pickups and controls were mounted on a large floating assembly.

ROLAND

Established in 1974, this Japanese company championed the guitar synthesizer, developing the combination of a specialized guitar (or "controller" in Roland-speak) and a standalone synthesizer unit that produced the sounds.

The first such duo debuted in 1977, consisting of the heavy GS-500 multi-control Les Paul-shape solidbody, and the large GR-500 synthesizer unit. Wired frets provided infinite sustain, and the sounds produced were wide-ranging and impressive. However, players seemed not to be keen on the fact that one had to use the guitar supplied by

Roland. Three years later a new two-piece outfit replaced the earlier combo. This time Roland offered guitars with simplified controls: there was a G-808 or G-303 original-design solidbody, teamed with the much more compact GR-300 floor unit. This was later joined by the Fender-like G-505 and G-202 six-strings plus an even more basic GR-100 floor box. Operation was easier, but inevitably the performance was less versatile. Many players still didn't take to Roland's guitars, which were nonetheless high quality instruments mostly made for Roland by Fujigen in Japan.

Guitarists still disliked the next guitar synthesizer from Roland, the futuristic G-707 guitar, launched in 1984 with "coat hanger" stabilizer, and the enormous GR-700 pedalboard. The hi-tech image seemed to alienate any remaining guitarists not already wary of guitar synths in general and Roland's in particular.

Roland switched shortly afterwards to providing a "hex" pickup that can be added to existing guitars and plugged into new GR synth units. Roland continues to provide this successful solution that does the required job with great flexibility.

SAMICK

The Korean piano manufacturer Samick began making acoustic guitars in 1965, and is today one of the world's largest guitar manufacturers, producing a dizzying array of models. Samick had an early boost when it began making the Hondo brand in 1969. Quality and quantity progressed throughout the 1970s, and since 1984 many of the

This Roger 54 (near right) was made in about 1960. The 1984 Roland G-707 guitar synthesizer "controller" (center) was the last in Roland's attempts to make guitar-plus-synth outfits. The 1993 ad featuring Eric Johnson displays Roland's solution – still in use today – for synth-inclined guitarists who didn't want to buy a new guitar: the GK-2 synth pickup fits to any guitar, driving the GR-1 synth unit. This Samick DCV9500 (far right) was produced in 1999.

world's most recognized guitar brands have turned to Samick for budget alternatives to their premium US-made guitars. Samick began to use its name as a guitar brand in the early 1990s, and in 1993 purchased the small Valley Arts guitar company of Los Angeles, California, effectively to serve as its custom shop. By 1998 Samick had an enormous line ranging from general "copies" to more original designs. These included a Les Paul-alike with a Zemaitis-style round mother-of-pearl inlaid top, and set-neck offset-double-cutaway guitars with carved, quilted-maple tops and abalone trim.

SCHECTER

Established in 1975, Schecter initially provided high-quality replacement parts. Later there followed complete guitars, although choice was limited to "improved" Fender-style instruments. Endorsers in the 1980s included Pete Townshend, but the brand suffered a bumpy economic ride in the US, and Japanese-made models kept it going. By the end of the decade US-built instruments were back, the California line partnering the existing offshore Schecter East series. Designs remained firmly Fender-inspired. These themes more or less remained through the early 1990s, but later there were some major changes. Schecter suddenly caught the retro bug with the Tempest and Hellcat (optionally available with ten strings), while the Avenger echoed the shape of Teisco's Spectrum 5. In 1999 the Korean-made Diamond series brought Schecter to a much wider audience, and was among the first to offer affordable seven-string guitars.

S.D. CURLEE

S.D. Curlee was the first US company to license its own designs, and thus make some money from others' copies. S.D. Curlee guitars had a unique neck-through-bridge construction, natural oil finishes, and used exotic woods such as walnut or purpleheart. Begun by Randy Curlee in Matteson, Illinois, in 1975, Curlee was originally conceived to offer interchangeable exotic-wood bodies. The licenses resulted in guitars branded Aspen and S.D. Curlee International (made in Japan by Matsumoku) as well as Global and Hondo (made in Korea). Production wound down by 1981, though a few "pointy"-style guitars were imported in 1982 before the brand ceased.

SHERGOLD

Jack Golder was responsible for a line of electrics that provided many 1970s British would-be guitar stars with good quality instruments. Golder left Burns after Baldwin's takeover in 1965, setting up Shergold Woodcrafts in Essex with Norman Houlder.

Shergold guitars did appear then, but Golder mostly did timber work for British brands like Burns UK and Hayman. When Hayman folded in 1975 Golder revived the Shergold brand for reworked Haymans, including the Meteor and Modulator, as well as new models like the Masquerader. Golder stopped production in 1983, but continued to enjoy custom work. He resumed commercial manufacturing in 1991 with limited editions of the Masquerader, but died the following April.

The three guitars illustrated on this page are: a retro Schecter Hellcat-10 ten-string (far left) from 1998; an Aspen AE-700 (center) made in 1976 in Japan under license from the US-based S.D. Curlee company; and a Shergold Custom Masquerader (near left) that dates from 1980.

Danelectro's ingenious "all-in-one" outfit, made for catalog company Sears's Silvertone brand, consisted of a guitar case with built-in amp and speaker, plus accompanying guitar. This 1457 set with two-pickup guitar (also shown below, left) joined an earlier single-pickup version.

SILVERTONE

It's likely that more American musicians began their interest in guitar-playing on a Silvertone – as sold by Chicago's Sears, Roebuck & Co – than on any other beginner guitar. Supplanting the Supertone brand when Sears divested itself of the Harmony guitar company in 1940, Silvertone was a former brand for radios, record-players and records. It was first applied to guitars in 1941. A Silvertone version of the Kay Thin Twin and Sears' first Les-Paul-style Harmony solidbody appeared in 1954. That same year the first of several Danelectro-made Silvertone solidbodies appeared, followed by masonite-and-vinyl hollowbodies in 1956 (see Danelectro).

The single-pickup amp-in-case guitars debuted in 1962 (see Danelectro). The Silvertone brand appeared throughout the 1960s on solidbodies that were made by Kay (such as the Vanguard model) and Harmony (for example the Silhouette).

By 1965 Sears was offering numerous Japanese Teisco-made Silvertone models, although these were sold through the company's stores rather than its catalog. The first Japanese Silvertones to feature in the catalog were made by Kawai and appeared in 1969. By the early 1970s the Silvertone name was dropped from guitars.

SPECTOR

Stuart Spector started his instrument company during 1976, and this American builder's basses were the first to feature the bulbous-horned body styling designed by Ned Steinberger (and subsequently borrowed by many competitors). The early Spector six-string guitars were similarly shaped, including characteristic concave-back/convex-front carving and through-neck construction.

In 1986 the Spector name was sold to Kramer. The US-made NS-6 was the only Spector six-string produced under the new ownership, partnered by Korean-made equivalents that were better than most from this source at the time.

Kramer folded in 1990, but Stuart Spector didn't regain the rights to his name for another seven years, in the interim trading as SSD (Stuart Spector Design). This period produced the bolt-on-neck Blackhawk model, which at first was manufactured in the US and was later also available as the cheaper Czech-made CR model. This proved to be Spector's final six-string model, disappearing in 1998 when the company decided to concentrate on its more successful bass guitars.

SQUIER

Beginning in the early 1980s, Japanese-made Fender instruments exported into Europe (and later elsewhere) bore the Squier brandname. The name was borrowed from a string-making company, V.C. Squier of Michigan, that Fender had acquired in

This Silvertone guitar (near right) was part of an amp-in-case set (see top of page) made by Danelectro, this one from about 1964. The Silvertone 1437 (center) was made for Sears by Teisco in Japan, and is similar to a Teisco WG-4L. It was made around 1965. This Ned Steinberger-designed Spector NS-6A (far right) was made in Korea during 1989.

In this 1983 ad (left) Fender introduced to the US market its new Squier-brand guitars – effectively authorized copies of the Fender Strat, Tele and Precision. At the time, these new Squiers were made in Japan, but since then the brand has been produced by a number of international manufacturers.

the mid 1960s. Victor Carroll Squier had been born in 19th-century Boston, the son of an English immigrant, and became a violin-maker, moving to Battle Creek, Michigan, where he founded his string-making firm in 1890.

Fender's policy was that the new 1980s Squier guitar brandname should cater for lower price points. That way, the company reasoned, it would be able to maintain its ever-expanding market coverage but, crucially, without unnecessarily cheapening the valuable Fender brandname itself. The new Squier logo – alongside a small but all-important line that read "by Fender" – appeared on an increasing number of models as the 1980s progressed.

Fender had established its Fender Japan operation with two Japanese partners – distributors Kanda Shokai and Yamano Music – during March 1982. Fender Japan at first used as its manufacturer the Fujigen factory, based in Matsumoto, some 130 miles north-west of Tokyo. Fujigen produced Fender-brand instruments for the Japanese market, plus Fender- and Squier-brand instruments for general export. Fujigen also made Fender's Japanese Vintage series instruments during the early 1980s as well as the Squier-brand versions that were initially sold only in Europe.

However, escalating production costs meant a move to cheaper manufacturing sources for Squier-brand guitars. Korea came on line in 1985, and India made a brief contribution in the late 1980s for some early "Squier II" instruments (or Sunn

equivalents – another borrowed brandname, this time from an amplifier company that had been purchased by Fender).

Fender's factory in Ensenada, Mexico – established in 1987 – also came into the picture when it produced some Squier guitars during the early 1990s. More recently a number of guitar-making factories in China and Indonesia have become new sources for the manufacture of Squier instruments, providing low-end electric guitars that have the desirable prestige of a legitimate Fender connection.

A return to Japanese production yielded impressive results with Squier's shortlived late-1990s Vista series. Courtney Love came up with a Rickenbacker-influenced design to inspire Squier's Venus model, while the Jagmaster was prompted by Gavin Rossdale's humbucker-modified Jazzmaster. Last in the Vista series was the Super-Sonic model which apparently was inspired by a 1960s photograph of Jimi Hendrix unusually playing an upside-down Fender Jaguar. The late-1990s midrange Pro Tone line offered evidence of improving Korean quality.

At the time of writing Fender had redirected most of its Squier brand to provide no-nonsense entry-level Korean guitars. Many are obvious Strats and Teles, although the reverse-head Stagemaster offers something a little more distinctive. The continuing success story of Squier makes it a very significant "support" brand for Fender, often exhibiting qualities beyond its apparent status as a secondary line.

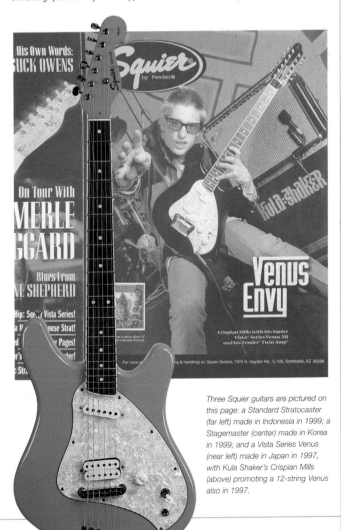

Three Squier guitars are pictured on this page: a Standard Stratocaster (far left) made in Indonesia in 1999; a Stagemaster (center) made in Korea in 1999; and a Vista Series Venus (near left) made in Japan in 1997, with Kula Shaker's Crispian Mills (above) promoting a 12-string Venus also in 1997.

STANDEL

Best known for amplifiers in the 1960s, this California company started by Bob Crooks in the previous decade made some distinctive electric guitars. An early association with Semie Moseley resulted in rare Mosrite-influenced guitars, but the final Standels of the late 1960s were high-quality archtops and semis made by Harptone in New Jersey.

STARFIELD

Ibanez's parent company Hoshino launched the Starfield brand in 1992. It was an attempt to combine character and convention, with Hoshino trying to achieve an elusive ideal: to be different but to stay commercial.

The retro-flavored selection included Altair and Cabriolet models, offered as part of the Japanese-made SJ series or as more expensive American Series alternatives, the latter ostensibly US-made, with better woods and higher-grade hardware.

Featuring a squat, rounded Stratocaster-derived outline, the Altair came in Classic, Trad and Custom variations, later joined by an SJ Classic-only 12-string. Cabriolets comprised the American Standard and Special versions, plus the SL Limited, and all employed an offset, mutated Telecaster-like shape.

None of these models enjoyed the success expected, and by 1994 Hoshino had introduced cheaper Korean-made Starfields in an attempt to rescue the line, but to no avail. Starfield sank soon afterwards.

STEINBERGER

Ned Steinberger proved that conventional materials are not essential to the production of a first-class instrument. Art-school graduate Steinberger moved to New York in the 1970s, and designed the NS bass for maker Stuart Spector in 1977. Steinberger produced his own bass, the L-2, in 1981. It combined plastic materials with a radical new "body-less" and headless design.

A six-string Steinberger guitar, the GL, followed in 1983. As with the bass, the usual headstock was discarded, and tuners were moved to the end of the minimal body. The one-piece hollow neck and body was made of a fiber and resin composite, sealed initially with a removable "lid" on top to which the equally innovative active EMG pickups were mounted.

For a short time in the hi-tech obsessed decade of the 1980s, the Steinberger design seemed to encapsulate the future of the electric instrument. But despite use by many top players, including Eddie Van Halen and Allan Holdsworth, it proved too uncompromising for mainstream acceptance.

Subsequently, wooden-body instruments appeared made both in the US and offshore, and in 1991 the conventionally-shaped Sceptre model appeared – with a headstock. It was the designer's last project for the now Gibson-owned Steinberger company. In retrospect it is more likely to be Steinberger's hardware – notably his

This Standel Custom Deluxe (far left) from 1966 has strong Mosrite flavors; the Starfield Altair SJ Custom (near left) was made in 1992; and this Steinberger GM4T (right) dates from 1989. Mike Rutherford of Genesis (above), who helped design the GM models, is here playing an earlier mini-body Steinberger.

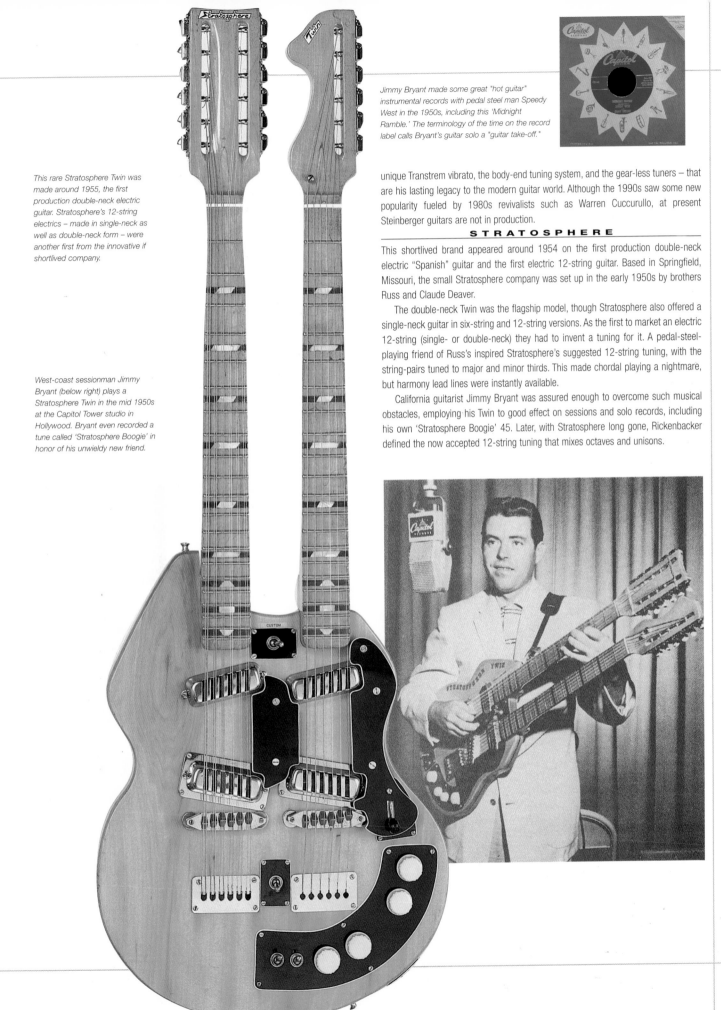

This rare Stratosphere Twin was made around 1955, the first production double-neck electric guitar. Stratosphere's 12-string electrics – made in single-neck as well as double-neck form – were another first from the innovative if shortlived company.

West-coast sessionman Jimmy Bryant (below right) plays a Stratosphere Twin in the mid 1950s at the Capitol Tower studio in Hollywood. Bryant even recorded a tune called 'Stratosphere Boogie' in honor of his unwieldy new friend.

Jimmy Bryant made some great "hot guitar" instrumental records with pedal steel man Speedy West in the 1950s, including this 'Midnight Ramble.' The terminology of the time on the record label calls Bryant's guitar solo a "guitar take-off."

unique Transtrem vibrato, the body-end tuning system, and the gear-less tuners – that are his lasting legacy to the modern guitar world. Although the 1990s saw some new popularity fueled by 1980s revivalists such as Warren Cuccurullo, at present Steinberger guitars are not in production.

STRATOSPHERE

This shortlived brand appeared around 1954 on the first production double-neck electric "Spanish" guitar and the first electric 12-string guitar. Based in Springfield, Missouri, the small Stratosphere company was set up in the early 1950s by brothers Russ and Claude Deaver.

The double-neck Twin was the flagship model, though Stratosphere also offered a single-neck guitar in six-string and 12-string versions. As the first to market an electric 12-string (single- or double-neck) they had to invent a tuning for it. A pedal-steel-playing friend of Russ's inspired Stratosphere's suggested 12-string tuning, with the string-pairs tuned to major and minor thirds. This made chordal playing a nightmare, but harmony lead lines were instantly available.

California guitarist Jimmy Bryant was assured enough to overcome such musical obstacles, employing his Twin to good effect on sessions and solo records, including his own 'Stratosphere Boogie' 45. Later, with Stratosphere long gone, Rickenbacker defined the now accepted 12-string tuning that mixes octaves and unisons.

SUPRO

As guitar manufacturers took their first tentative steps toward the production of electric guitars in the 1930s, Supro emerged as the primarily electric budget-price line of the Los Angeles-based National-Dobro company. National-Dobro was the recombined National and Dobro companies.

The Supro brand first appeared on a cast aluminum "frying pan" Hawaiian lap-steel, a Spanish electric archtop and a number of other instruments during 1935. It would also be the principal brandname that was used by the National-Dobro operation for its amplifiers throughout the 1960s.

Following a relocation of the parent company in 1936 to Chicago, the Supro name was used on some of the earliest lap-steel guitars to feature an amp-in-case design, such as the battery-powered Portable 70. This was an idea that would resurface, if briefly, in 1955.

Supro went on to appear on a variety of lap-steel instruments through the 1960s, and was occasionally used on resonator guitars. The Supro Capitan electric archtop and Rio electric flat-top debuted in 1941, with more electric archtops such as the El Capitan and Ranchero resuming production after World War II.

In 1942 Victor Smith, Al Frost and Louis Dopyera bought National-Dobro and changed its name to the Valco Manufacturing Company. In 1948 one of the brand's

Two Supro guitars are pictured on this page: a wood-body Dual Tone (far left) from 1958; and a 1960 Belmont (main guitar), the wooden body of which has been "shrink-wrapped" in red-pearloid plastic. Supro was one of several guitar brands by Valco; the other main one was National. This Supro catalog cover (above) dates from 1959.

guitar manufacturers

TEISCO

most distinctive features appeared, the under-bridge Bridge-Tone transducer pickup. It was usually used in conjunction with magnetic pickups.

Supro's first solidbody electrics debuted in 1952, the Spanish-shaped Ozark and single-cutaway Ozark Cut-Away Jet, both with small slab bodies, floating pickups attached to a large housing containing the wiring harness, and a characteristic bolt-on neck that sat very high on the body at the joint. The single-cutaway Supro Dual-Tone solidbody debuted in 1954, receiving top-mounted pickups the following year. Supro's first cutaway electric archtop also appeared in 1955. Beginning in 1957 the Bridge-Tone pickup was included on many solidbodies.

In 1962 the company modified its name to Valco Guitars Inc, and the guitar line changed from wood construction to fiberglass bodies in various colors with plastic-faced "Gumby" headstocks. (See also National.) Robert Engelhardt bought Valco in 1964, changed to a more Fender-style wood-bodied guitar design in 1965, and offered Supro's first double-cutaway thinlines in 1966.

The following year, with the guitar boom at full volume, Valco bought its competitor, the Kay Musical Instrument Company... and went bankrupt in 1968. At the end, the Supro logo was applied to a variety of Kay-made acoustic instruments. The Supro name was purchased at auction in 1969, but went unused until it reappeared briefly during the early 1980s on guitars assembled from old parts.

The leading producer of 1960s Japanese-made beginner guitars, Teisco was unusual in using mainly its own brandname.

Atswo Kaneko and Doryu Matsuda had introduced Teisco lap-steel instruments in 1946, followed by Gibson-style guitars. By 1960 Jack Westheimer began importing Fender-like Teisco models to the United States.

The Teisco Del Rey brand debuted in 1964, including the TRG-1 model that featured an amplifier and small loudspeaker built into the guitar.

In 1965 Sid Weiss's WMI company of Illinois also brought Teisco Del Reys into America, including 1966's flared-cutaway pushbutton Spectrum 5 model – now a desirable, collectable guitar. Teisco developed financial problems, and was purchased by Kawai in Japan in 1967. New Kawai-made models for 1968 included the odd-shape May Queen. In 1969 WMI bought Kay, and by 1972 were using that brand rather than Teisco. Kawai revived the Teisco brand in the early 1990s.

This fiberglass-body Supro Sahara (far left) dates from around 1964; the vinyl-faced Teisco SD-4L (center) was made in about 1963; and this Teisco Del Rey May Queen (near left) is from around 1968. The Teisco Del Rey catalog (at the top of this page) was published in the US in 1966.

TEUFFEL

Teuffel's catalog from 1998 (right) lays out the unique charms of the minimalist Birdfish model.

T E U F F E L

This high-end German maker has a unique, modern approach to design. Teuffel's Birdfish appeared in 1995 and looks like a well-engineered sculpture, with a minimalist metal frame body, removable pickups and add-on resonator tubes.

The recent Coco model is almost conventional in comparison – but only by founder Ulrich Teuffel's remarkable standards.

T O K A I

In the 1980s Tokai's blatant replicas of classic American guitars highlighted the threat posed to US makers by primarily Japanese-made "copy" guitars.

Tokai was based in Hamamatsu, Japan, and produced its first electric guitars in 1967, the Humming Bird models. Styling varied, but the "reverse-body" models were heavily influenced by Mosrite, although they had their own style of savagely pointed horns. Tokai's quality at this time was adequate – better than some of the Japanese competition, but not so good as makers like Yamaha.

As with many Japanese manufacturers, Tokai's standards improved considerably during the 1970s, and the large Hamamatsu factory became responsible for a great deal of sub-contract work for other Japanese guitar brands.

Tokai did not yet export its own-brand guitars, but this changed dramatically in the 1980s. The Tokai lines included over 100 models by that time, many of which were

This bizarre metal-frame Birdfish model (near right) was produced by Teuffel in Germany in 1999. The Mosrite-influenced Tokai Humming Bird (far right) was made in Japan in 1968. The 1983 Tokai ad highlights the brand's notorious role in copying classic US models, here targeting Fender's Stratocaster.

This first-year 1984 ad (left) from Tom Anderson Guitarworks features a fine example of one of the maker's beautifully figured instruments.

reproductions of popular instruments from the best American brands. Copy guitars were a well-established and commercial force in the world guitar market, but Tokai significantly increased the accuracy and quality.

Tokais began to arrive in Europe around 1981 and in the US by 1983, and were an immediate success, assisted in America by the dollar's soaring value compared to the yen, making Japanese instruments good value. The success triggered a fight from Fender, the company targeted most directly by the copying. Fender's answer was to establish its Fender Japan operation, to produce "authorized copies." This proved to be a very successful move which naturally dented the sales of Tokai and other Japanese copyists – although Japanese-made guitars continued to be popular.

Tokai catered for the Japanese market with a variety of models that ranged from the Triangle-X and Zero Fighter "reverse-body" originals to the Fender-influenced Versatile Sound selection. In the US the first line from the new Robin brand took advantage of Tokai's continuing sub-contract work. Prior to a change brought by legal challenges, Tokai itself used a very Fender-style logo. Other Tokai clones included recreations of Gibson's Les Paul, ES-series semis, Flying V and Explorer, plus various limited-production variations incorporating deluxe options.

Some Tokai originals appeared too: the 1985 Talbo had a distinctively designed aluminum body (Tokai ALuminum BOdy) while the same year's MAT series (Most Advanced Technology) was seemingly Fender-style, but with necks and bodies made from various combinations of fiberglass and carbon graphite.

By the mid 1990s Tokai had stopped exporting, and at home in Japan was limited to various synthetic-body Talbo models. In 1999 a revised version of the Talbo in a conventional material appeared, the Talbo Woody.

TOM ANDERSON GUITARWORKS

A small-scale operation making respected high-performance electrics, this company was started during 1984 by Tom Anderson, who had previously worked for Schecter.

Tom Anderson Guitarworks is currently based in Newbury Park, California, producing some 800 guitars a year. During the 1990s the brand became synonymous with high quality. The modernized Stratocaster-style outline often employs a maple "drop top" (a method of laminating a thin maple top over the body's Strat-like contouring). Fitted to this are Anderson's own pickups and highly versatile switching, and there is an option list wider than that of many custom shops.

Models include the Pro Am Classic, the Grand Am Lam, the Drop Top T, the Hollow Drop Top and the Cobra, all in a broadly Fender- or superstrat-style. Anderson was one of the first makers to embrace the Buzz Feiten tuning system, a standard fitting since 1996. Feiten's system is a brave attempt to "correct" the compromise of equal-tempered tuning. Players of Anderson instruments include Vivian Campbell.

Three guitars are shown on this page: a 1984 Tokai Talbo A80D (far left); a Tom Anderson Guitarworks Grand Am Lam T (center) made in 1989; and a second Anderson guitar, a Hollow Drop Top (near left), made ten years later.

TRAVIS BEAN

Although not the first to feature aluminum necks, Travis Bean's guitars caused quite a stir in 1974. Based in Sun Valley, California, Bean decided he could solve stability problems and enhance sustain with light metal necks.

The first and most famous Travis Bean model was the equal-double-cutaway, two-humbucker TB1000, initially offered as the slab-bodied Standard but soon joined by the carved-top, block-inlaid Artist. The triangular-shaped Wedge looked and felt clumsy, but the "budget" TB500 was better. With offset cutaways and pickguard-mounted controls, this slim-bodied solid offered Fender-like flavors, as did Bean's powerful single-coil pickups.

Jerry Garcia was a famous endorser, but many players didn't like the cold feel of aluminum. Business pressures made Bean himself shut up shop in 1979. Guitarists such as Stanley Jordan and Slash have since helped raise the brand's profile, and in 1998 Travis Bean returned to the fray with a remake of the TB1000.

VACCARO

Vaccaro was originally intended to revive the late-1970s aluminum-necked Kramer guitars. It was started by former Kramer principal Henry Vaccaro in 1996, using the Kramer name with revamped designs by original luthier Phil Petillo. Investment glitches led to the sale of the Kramer name to Gibson in 1997. A new Vaccaro line in 1998 had

a trimmed-down, completely wood-sheathed T-bar neck (and lighter "tuning-fork" head), vintage-style pickups and sparkle finish options. The first line included an SG-style Groove Jet, flared-cutaway X-Ray, Fender-ish Generator X, and Les-Paul-Junior-like Astrolite, followed in 1999 by the less expensive V-2 X-Ray and Generator X.

VALLEY ARTS

Valley Arts originated from a retail operation, expanding during the 1970s to build its own high-end Custom Pro instruments. These mainly followed familiar Fender designs but with variations determined by a comprehensive list of options.

Larry Carlton was an early endorser, and the liaison resulted in a 1990s signature model. Unusually for "Mr. 335" it was a small-bodied solid. It combined Telecaster-like and Stratocaster-like styling, but hardware was more Gibson-based. The Standard version came with a pickguard; the Custom had a carved top.

The Standard Pro series introduced in the late 1980s offered less expensive US instruments, while the same period saw the addition of Japanese-made models such as the M series. This lowered prices further, as has the involvement since 1993 of the major Korean manufacturer Samick.

More recent lines have included such models as the California Pro and the IML series, which were joined during 1996 by the Studio Pro series, along with signature models such as Ray Benson's oversized-Telecaster-style Texas T.

A Travis Bean TB1000 (near right) and ad (below) for Bean's aluminum neck, both 1977; a 1999 aluminum-neck Vaccaro Stingray (center); and a Valley Arts Custom Pro (far right) from 1993. The 1990 ad features Valley Arts founder Mike McGuire with endorser Steve Lukather.

VEGA

Best known for banjos, Vega nonetheless made some electric guitars including in the 1950s a novel 12-pickup stereo instrument.

Vega's roots go back to the 1880s, but the company began officially in Boston in 1903 when two Swedish brothers, Julius and Carl Nelson, renamed their company Vega (for the brightest star in the constellation of Lyra, hence the star-shape logo often used on Vegas). At first they concentrated on banjo production, and designed an unusual amplified banjo in the late 1920s.

Vega made small Martin-style "parlor" acoustics, and from the 1930s offered conventional archtop guitars, including some electrics. The Duo-Tron of 1949 had the controls and jack built into the tailpiece.

Much more unusual was the shortlived 1200 Stereo model of 1959, which followed Gretsch and Gibson's "stereo guitar" idea. Vega's instrument fed the bass notes from six individual circular pickups to one amplifier, and six treble-string pickups to another, adding electronic vibrato for good effect.

However, Vega had already begun to run out of steam, and the 1960s were a lean period. By 1970 Vega had been sold to Martin, who acquired the company for its banjo business. Around 1980 Martin sold Vega to a Korean firm, and more recently the name has been used by the Deering company for a line of banjos.

This Vega 1200 Stereo (main guitar) was made around 1959 and, unusually, features 12 separate polepiece pickup units. The idea was that the six "treble pickups" would feed one amplifier, the six "bass pickups" another, giving a kind of stereo spread. But the instrument was shortlived, joining earlier stereo instruments by Gretsch and Gibson in the guitar industry's out-tray. The 1959 ad (above) features a more conventional Vega, the Westerner model, as chosen by overlooked endorser Rusty Draper. This Vega E-300 Duo-Tron (left, below) was made in 1951. With its neck-mounted pickup and tailpiece-mounted controls, it offered an instrument somewhere between an acoustic with floating pickups and a full-fledged electric guitar.

guitar manufacturers

VEILLETTE-CITRON

Joe Veillette started making acoustics in the early 1970s, soon setting up Veillette-Citron in Brooklyn which he ran with partner Harvey Citron from 1975 to 1983. Their high-end guitars were of the time, employing "organic" Alembic influences such as multi-laminated through-neck construction, exotic woods and brass hardware. The line was later rationalized to the less elaborate Standard, Classic and Limited Edition. It was at this time that Veillette's fascination began with low-tuned "baritone" guitars, using long non-standard scale-lengths. The Shark was a baritone designed in collaboration with John Sebastian, based on a Guild Thunderbird. It was later joined by a matching S series guitar. Veillette and Citron parted company not long after and each now offers an established catalog. Veillette-brand electrics and baritones began in 1993 with a revised Shark, and now emanate from Woodstock, New York.

VELENO

The shiny chrome plating on these carved-aluminum hollowbody guitars was well suited to the glam tastes of early 1970s rockers – which is why they were owned by Gregg Allman, Martin Barre, Marc Bolan, Eric Clapton, Mark Farner, Ace Frehley, Pete Haycock, Alvin Lee, Jeff Lynne, Ronnie Montrose, Dave Peverett and Lou Reed. John Veleno was a St. Petersburg, Florida, engineer and guitar teacher who began hand-making his unusual aluminum guitars around 1970, personally marketing them to

This Veleno Original (main guitar) was made around 1972. Veleno guitars were constructed almost entirely from aluminum. This one has a gold anodized finish. The publicity flyer from Veleno (opposite page), produced around 1975, profiles a number of Veleno players: Dave Peverett of Savoy Brown (center); Pete Haycock alongside his co-guitarist in Climax Blues Band (above Peverett); Todd Rundgren (right) with a custom "ankh"-shape Veleno; and Mark Farner (below) on-stage with Grand Funk Railroad. Two instruments related to New York-based maker Joe Veillette are shown (below left) marking his fascination with low-tuned "baritone" guitars: a Veillette-Citron Shark Baritone (far left) made about 1981; and a Veillette version of the Shark Baritone (near left) that was produced during 1998.

guitar manufacturers

The Eagles (no, the other ones) show off a handful of Vox's Fender-style models from the 1960s.

touring guitarists who passed through Florida. By 1971 Veleno's early six-tuners-in-line headstock changed to the more common three-and-three V-shape with ruby insert, for the model known as the Original.

Available in chrome, gold and other anodized colors (some with a black anodized neck), Veleno Originals primarily featured two humbuckers (by Guild, Gibson or DiMarzio) with coil-taps and phase-switching. Only between 145 and 185 Veleno Originals were made, probably until early 1977.

Inspired by a post-concert conversation with B.B. King and working with Mark Farner, Veleno also developed a mini-guitar known as the Traveller (two were made by Veleno, around ten by his son). Veleno made one bass, and built two Egyptian "ankh"-shaped guitars for Todd Rundgren in 1977 before abandoning the guitar business to become a wedding photographer.

VIGIER

The characterful instruments of French maker Patrice Vigier first appeared in 1980 with the Arpege model, a challenging design that used unusual materials. It typifies the more distinctive end of Vigier production in that it had a radical shape, was produced using non-standard construction methods, and employed "delta metal" (a type of bell brass) for the fingerboard. Another early oddity from Vigier was the Nautilus memory guitar of 1982, a multi-control instrument that enabled the recall of various player-set tonal and other control settings. From 1984 Vigier began to offer carbon-fiber necks. Their proprietary 10/90 neck system was made using 10 per cent graphite and 90 per cent maple. In the same way as some later makers, Vigier's intention was that this dual construction would offer a useful balance in the neck's strength and feel.

Vigier also offered a more derivative Fender-influenced line, the Excalibur series, which also featured 10/90 necks, and these helped Vigier turn its relatively wild early ideas into more marketable instruments.

Vigier's Excalibur Surfreter of 1997 was an unusual "fretless" guitar, as used occasionally by Gary Moore. The company had offered a fretless Arpege since 1980. Vigier celebrated the year 2000 with a lush $30,000 20th Anniversary guitar, produced in a very limited edition of two.

VOX

Vox amplifiers were a great British 1960s success, but the company's stylish guitars made less impact. Vox products were originally made by Jennings in Dartford, Kent, set up by Tom Jennings in the 1950s. The factory was not equipped at first to make guitars, so most early Vox electrics – aimed at beginners on a budget – came from other UK or Italian sources.

In 1962 the first Vox original appeared from Dartford. The Phantom had an unusual body styled by The Design Centre in London. Equipped with three single-coil pickups,

A Vigier Arpege V6-V (far left) from 1984, alongside two Vox guitars: an Apache (center) made around 1961; and a Mk VI (near left) that dates from about 1965. Brian Jones of The Rolling Stones (above) plays a non-standard two-pickup Mk VI.

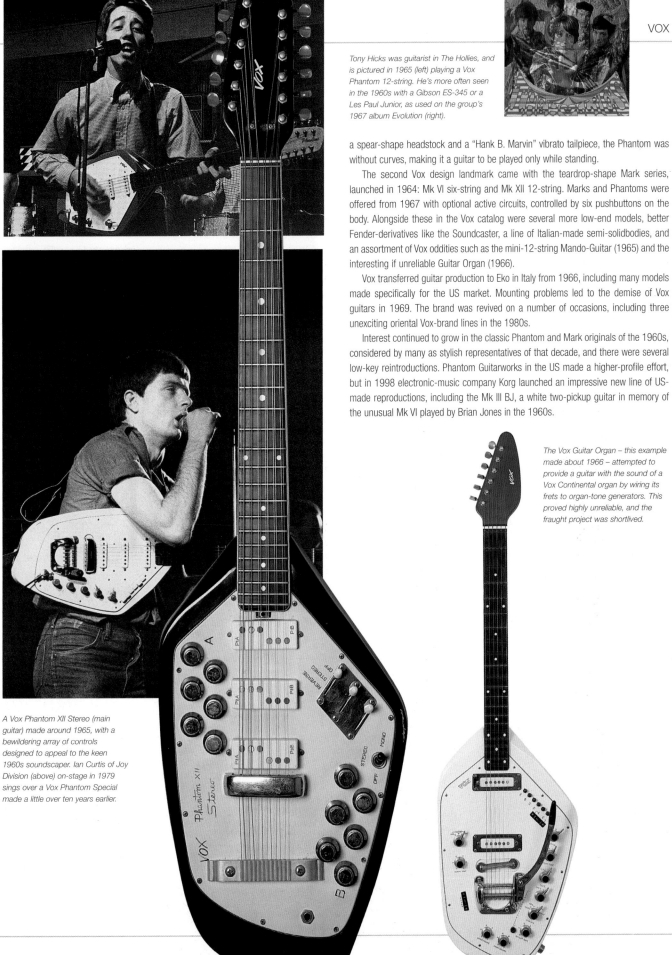

Tony Hicks was guitarist in The Hollies, and is pictured in 1965 (left) playing a Vox Phantom 12-string. He's more often seen in the 1960s with a Gibson ES-345 or a Les Paul Junior, as used on the group's 1967 album Evolution (right).

a spear-shape headstock and a "Hank B. Marvin" vibrato tailpiece, the Phantom was without curves, making it a guitar to be played only while standing.

The second Vox design landmark came with the teardrop-shape Mark series, launched in 1964: Mk VI six-string and Mk XII 12-string. Marks and Phantoms were offered from 1967 with optional active circuits, controlled by six pushbuttons on the body. Alongside these in the Vox catalog were several more low-end models, better Fender-derivatives like the Soundcaster, a line of Italian-made semi-solidbodies, and an assortment of Vox oddities such as the mini-12-string Mando-Guitar (1965) and the interesting if unreliable Guitar Organ (1966).

Vox transferred guitar production to Eko in Italy from 1966, including many models made specifically for the US market. Mounting problems led to the demise of Vox guitars in 1969. The brand was revived on a number of occasions, including three unexciting oriental Vox-brand lines in the 1980s.

Interest continued to grow in the classic Phantom and Mark originals of the 1960s, considered by many as stylish representatives of that decade, and there were several low-key reintroductions. Phantom Guitarworks in the US made a higher-profile effort, but in 1998 electronic-music company Korg launched an impressive new line of US-made reproductions, including the Mk III BJ, a white two-pickup guitar in memory of the unusual Mk VI played by Brian Jones in the 1960s.

The Vox Guitar Organ – this example made about 1966 – attempted to provide a guitar with the sound of a Vox Continental organ by wiring its frets to organ-tone generators. This proved highly unreliable, and the fraught project was shortlived.

A Vox Phantom XII Stereo (main guitar) made around 1965, with a bewildering array of controls designed to appeal to the keen 1960s soundscaper. Ian Curtis of Joy Division (above) on-stage in 1979 sings over a Vox Phantom Special made a little over ten years earlier.

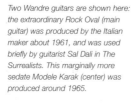

Two Wandre guitars are shown here: the extraordinary Rock Oval (main guitar) was produced by the Italian maker about 1961, and was used briefly by guitarist Sal Dali in The Surrealists. This marginally more sedate Modele Karak (center) was produced around 1965.

Three Washburns are pictured here: a Stage A-20V (this page, far right) from 1981; a 36-fret George Washburn EC-36 (opposite page, left) made in 1988, with "monkey grip" body handle; and a Force G-40V (opposite page, right) with triple pickup, also from 1988.

WANDRE

Among the most eccentric European guitars of any period in guitar history were those made by Wandre Pioli from Cavriago, Italy.

Pioli began producing primarily hollowbody electric (and some acoustic) guitars in 1959 with a unique aluminum neck-through-tailpiece design, unusual laminated materials, wild multi-color paint jobs and often exotic shapes.

More conventional single-cutaway models included the Blue Jeans, Tri-Lam, and BB (for Brigitte Bardot), but the Bikini of 1960 was a very unusual minimalist guitar with attached amplifier and speaker (see Krundaal).

Around 1961 Wandre guitars were distributed in the UK by Vox parent company Jennings, including the blob-shaped Framez, the "deep cutaway" Rock Oval and the thin Electronica Oval-Basso.

Between 1963 and 1966 Wandre guitars were sold in the US by Chicago distributor Don E. Noble. The line featured a changed vibrato design, as well as a new solidbody, the Rock 6. In the mid 1960s some Wandres were made available in the UK with the Dallas brand, and later guitars were of more conventional design.

Around 1967 Pioli introduced the Psichedelic Sound, a take on Gibson's thinline style, as well as the Cobra variation on a Fender design and the bat-shaped Black Tulip. In 1970 Pioli sold his factory and turned to making art leather clothing.

guitar manufacturers

Kiss's Ace Frehley snuggling up to his shortlived signature model in a 1986 ad.

WASHBURN

Washburn is a famous old American brandname that lives on thanks mainly to instruments of oriental origin.

George Washburn Lyon was an associate in Chicago's big Lyon & Healy company, founded in 1864. Guitar-maker Patrick J. Healy was one of the true founders of the acoustic guitar industry in the United States, but it was George Washburn Lyon's middle name that provided the brandname for the prodigious quantity of flat-top acoustic instruments produced by Lyon & Healy.

By the 1920s competition had grown and business was down. Lyon & Healy sold the Washburn name to distribution company Tonk Bros in 1928. After World War II, Tonk did not revive the Washburn name, which went unused until a small company called Beckmen used it in the early 1970s. Beckmen soon sold the name to a Chicago-based importer, Fretted Industries Inc.

Fretted Industries was owned by guitar-maker Rudy Schlacher and musician Rick Johnstone. Both were experienced in retailing and realized the commercial potential in employing the Washburn name on reasonably-priced instruments. Japan was the obvious source for production.

The new line included electric guitars, the first to carry the Washburn brand. Launched in 1979, the Wing series employed high-waisted body styling with twin small-horned cutaways, through-neck construction, two humbuckers and a conventional circuit with four controls plus selector. First models were the Hawk and Falcon, soon joined by the cheaper bolt-on-neck Raven and the high-end Eagle.

The following year brought the Stage solidbodies which targeted the rock market in more overt fashion, shaped like a chopped-down Gibson Explorer and in various formats including a 12-string.

By 1983 Washburn's electric line had increased considerably. Fender-influenced Force solids partnered 335-style HB hollowbodies and the Flying V-based Tour models. Various Stages continued, while Wings had withered to the Hawk, Falcon and Eagle plus the new T Bird. The headless-neck fashion hit in 1984 and Washburn responded with Bantam mini-body guitars, including a double-neck. Washburn also followed the trend for locking vibrato systems.

As the 1980s progressed a distinctly metal theme began to dominate Washburn's catalog. By 1986 the Wings had gone but the Stages remained. The Force models became more superstrat than Strat-like, and the Tour V now had an offset body like a Jackson Randy Rhoads.

The new Heavy Metal models sported an overt, sharp-pointed body, while unsubtle graphics and the newly released Wonderbar heavy-duty vibrato bridge were common features throughout the line. Artist-endorsed models were becoming increasingly

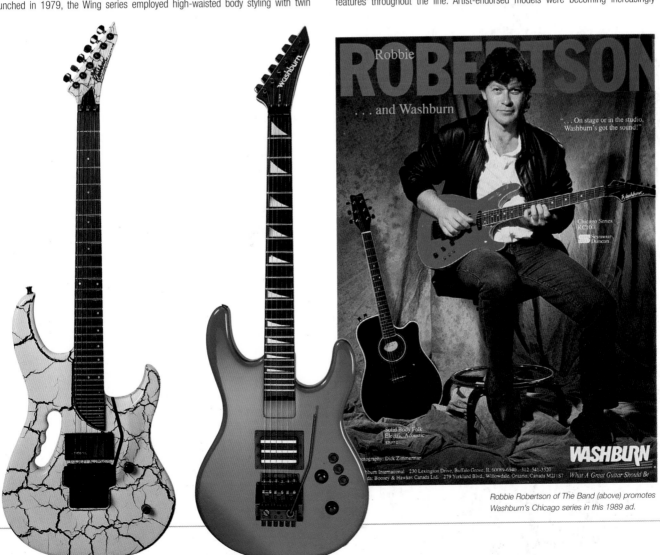

Robbie Robertson of The Band (above) promotes Washburn's Chicago series in this 1989 ad.

common, and included among these "signature" Washburns was the strange angular
form of the shortlived AF40V Ace Frehley guitar.

The first Korean-made Washburns were the Rebel series of cheap superstrats,
debuting in 1986. Existing designs were also transferred to Korea, a source used by
many brands at this time. Further models to originate from the new production base
included the PRS-influenced RS8 and RS10, part of the Tour series.

By now the Washburn catalog consisted of just the Tour and Force series, between
them covering a variety of instruments where common model names had little to do
with consistency of features or design.

Some guitars continued to be manufactured for the company in Japan. Included
among these orientally-sourced instruments were the Stephens Extended Cutaway
(EC) series, first introduced during 1987. Also known as Spitfires, these George
Washburn-brand solidbodies catered for players who adopted the popular two-handed
tapping technique of the time, the guitars' extreme carved cutaway allowing access to
a 29-fret or unprecedented 36-fret fingerboard. Through-neck construction and active
circuitry were other features of this high-quality, US-designed super-superstrat.

The late 1980s also brought the superstrat-style Chicago series, plus Les Paul-style
models marketed as the Classic series. Fretted Industries officially changed its name
to Washburn International in 1987. Increased prominence for Washburn in the early

*This Nuno Bettencourt N-8 double-
neck was made in 1996. One-time
Extreme guitarist Nuno is featured
(above) in two Washburn ads: with
the N-8 and single-neck N-4 (1996,
top) and with a Chicago series KC70
in 1990. Paul Stanley's signature
models (1999 PS-500 far right; 1999
ad for PS-2000) were based on the
Kiss man's Ibanez Iceman shape.*

Watkins drew on its amplifier expertise for the early-1960s Circuit 4 model (catalog, right).

1990s came with Nuno Bettencourt's signature model. It was a popular move, prompting a succession of versions made in the US, Japan and Korea.

It was during the early 1990s that the G.W. Lyon brandname was employed on a line of low-end guitars while, in a bid to plunder the more recent past, Washburn also revived a reduced Wing series.

The Mercury solid series appeared in 1992, and this comprehensive line of guitars included models made in the US. It was revamped two years later and again in 1995. Other 1990s newcomers have included the Fender-style Silverado and Laredo, and the Steve Stevens signature six-string.

In 1996 the Dime series first appeared, as used by Dimebag Darrell and based on his previously favored Dean guitar. A number of variants have since been issued, including the Culprit of 1999 that was like a sliced-up Explorer.

Also in 1996 the US-made MG series was launched, designed by Grover Jackson, and the Peavey Wolfgang-like Billy T series appeared, evolving into 1997's Maverick series, some of which were made in Indonesia. Washburn's P series debuted in 1997, endorsed by Nuno Bettencourt, some made in the US, some in Korea. With such output from a variety of production sources the Washburn name remains prominent and continues to enjoy a credibly high profile worldwide – no mean achievement in today's increasingly competitive marketplace.

WATKINS

Watkins provided cheap guitars for many fledgling British beat groups of the 1960s. The London-based company headed by Charlie Watkins originally specialized in amplification. But with Charlie's brother Sid in charge their first instrument, the Rapier Deluxe, was launched around 1959, the original of what is by far the most famous and what proved to be the longest-running Watkins model.

Styling and construction of the single-cutaway solidbody Rapier owed more to Gibson than Fender, with a 22-fret set-neck and three-tuners-a-side headstock. Body and headstock were altered around 1961 to an approximation of Fender's market-leading Stratocaster, with two (Rapier 22) or three pickups (33). The four-pickup Rapier 44 later completed the line with more comprehensive controls.

The new WEM brandname (Watkins Electric Music) first appeared on the high-end Sapphire series of 1965. The most expensive WEM instrument of the 1960s was the shortlived 5th Man, introduced in 1967, a gimmick-laden guitar with built-in effects including Sting treble-boost and Project IV sustain.

In the late 1960s Wilson, another new Watkins brand, appeared on models such as the twin-cutaway SA semi-acoustics and cheap Ranger solidbodies. By 1976 the line was much reduced, and in the 1980s the Hand Made Mercury was the flagship model with a Strat-style shape, but by 1985 instrument manufacturing had ceased.

Dimebag Darrell of Pantera spurred Washburn to a number of signature models, which included the charming finishes highlighted in this 1996 Japanese ad (far left). The Dime Culprit CP2003 pictured (center) was made in 1999. The best-known Watkins models are the various Rapiers; this Rapier 33 (near left) was made in England about 1964.

581

WELSON

This was the brandname of the Orlando Quagliardi company. Based in Castelfidardo, Italy, and dating back to 1919, like so many accordion makers it turned to electric guitars in the early 1960s.

Some single-cutaway semi-solids appeared in the UK branded Vox. Odd-shaped Welson solidbodies adorned in garish plastics followed. The body styling was retained, without plastic, for later examples such as the Dyno II and Vedette. In contrast, late-1960s semis were straightforward Gibson-inspired equal-double-cutaway models.

A selection from the 1966 line was marketed in Germany branded for amplification company Dynacord. This badge-engineering continued with semis for the American Thomas and Wurlitzer catalogs in the early 1970s. The Welson line later included the SG-style Red Flame. The Black Pearl model was a Les Paul-alike, and one of the final Welsons was the late-1970s multi-laminated Blue Flame.

WESTONE

Starting in 1981, Westone was chosen as the in-house brandname for high quality guitars made by the Matsumoku factory of Matsumoto City, Japan, and the instruments were sold internationally.

They included the Concord, Paduak, Prestige and Thunder solidbodies, and Rainbow semi-hollows. Following its purchase of an interest in Matsumoku, St. Louis

Music of Missouri decided by 1984 to replace its Electra brand with Westone. Original designs like the minimalist Dynasty and svelte Pantera (played by Leslie West) yielded to conventional superstrats.

Around 1988 the Matsumoku factory was sold to Singer Sewing Machines and all guitar production ceased. Westone manufacturing switched to Korea, the brandname changing to Alvarez in 1991. The Westone name was revived in 1996 by original UK importer FCN, initially appearing on Korean superstrats, replaced by British-made originals the following year.

WURLITZER

Better known for its keyboards and juke boxes, Wurlitzer of Elkhart, Indiana, also distributed musical instruments – and decided to cash in on the boom of the 1960s with its own line of guitars. Wurlitzer contracted the Holman-Woodell guitar factory in Neodesha, Kansas, to manufacture the two-pickup solidbody Stereo Electric models in 1965: the Cougar, which was a relatively conventional Fender-style guitar, the Wildcat, of more exaggerated shape, and the Gemini, a pointy, asymmetrical design.

Pickups and hardware for the Wurlitzers were made by Holman. A high volume of returns, mainly due to poor painting, led Wurlitzer to cancel the contract around the end of 1966. A line of Italian Welson-made hollowbodies replaced the Holmans for another year or so, after which Wurlitzer decided to leave the guitar-making business.

The three guitars shown on this page are: a Welson Jazz Vedette (near right) made around 1967; a Westone Paduak II (center) from 1982; and a Wurlitzer Cougar 2512 (far right) produced during 1966.

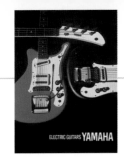

This Yamaha catalog from 1966 features models from Yamaha's distinctive early line, the SG "flying samurai" guitars.

YAMAHA

Although better known for a plethora of assorted products – from motorcycles to synthesizers – the Japanese Yamaha company has produced some excellent electric guitars over the years. Perhaps the most famous is the SG-2000, once favored by Carlos Santana. For a company with such a diverse product line, the standard and quality of its electric guitars has been remarkably high throughout its history.

Yamaha was started in the 1880s, began making acoustic guitars during 1946, and first offered solidbody electrics around 1964, although its first major line of such instruments debuted in 1966.

The 1966 solidbodies consisted of the two-pickup S-201 and three-pickup S-302 (later renamed the SG-2 and SG-3, and soon joined by a 12-string). These were bolt-on-neck models with pointed offset horns and Jazzmaster-style dual circuitry. They were soon followed by the crescent-shape SG-2C and SG-3C, and the instruments that became the best-known of Yamaha's early electrics, the SG-2A, SG-5A, SG-7A and SG-12A. These are known as "flying samurais" for their unique asymmetrical "reverse body" shape with dramatically extended lower horn.

The bolt-on-neck SA-15 semi-hollowbody adopted a similar outline, while several more such models, including the SA-50, employed more traditional double-cutaway styling. There were also full-size, single-pointed-cutaway archtop AE series electrics. In 1972 Yamaha's solidbody line changed to a design with a single sloping cutaway. Still called SG models, these came either with a flat body or with a "German carve" edge relief. The following year these instruments were joined by an equal-double-cutaway series that employed a body shape which would culminate in Yamaha's most renowned SG-2000 solidbody guitar.

By 1973 the semi-hollow line had been enhanced with the fancier SA-60 and SA-90 sporting more powerful humbuckers. Two new single-rounded-cutaway hollowbody guitars were offered, the AE-12 (sunburst) and AE-18 (natural). Around 1976 the shortlived SX-800 and SX-900 solidbodies joined the line. These had two equal almost flat cutaways and sharp pointed horns.

Yamaha achieved its first big success with the SG-2000, introduced in 1976 and endorsed by Carlos Santana. It represented a big leap forward for Yamaha, and was the guitar that at last reversed the impression that Japan only produced cheap copies. It had a through-neck construction, carved top, twin humbuckers, and a bridge mounted on a brass block for added sustain.

Yamaha discovered that while its solidbody models had been of undisputedly high quality, they nevertheless had been too unconventional to provoke general popularity. However, when Yamaha tried the equally high-quality but conservatively designed SG-2000 – in effect a double-cutaway Les Paul-style guitar – they suddenly had a

Three proud Yamahas: an SG-5A "flying samurai" (far left) from 1967; an SA-15 (center) made about the same time; and an SG-60T (near left), with "German carve" body, dating from 1973.

successful instrument. This was an important lesson not only for Yamaha but also for a number of other Japanese electric guitar manufacturers.

Tracking the very many different Yamaha SG models that followed the 2000 is highly confusing. In America they were called SBGs to distinguish them from Gibsons. Furthermore, specifications on domestic Japanese models were quite different from those on export models with the same number. Yamaha stopped exporting the SBGs to the US in 1988, although the SBG-500 and 700 were reintroduced in 1998.

Demand for copies of American guitars picked up in Japan in 1977 just as one particular "copy era" wound down in the US. Yamaha obliged on its domestic market with high quality SR Strat-style models (SuperR'nroller) and SL Les Paul-alikes (Studio Lord). Also new in 1977 were the Strat-shape SC series, featuring blade-style single-coils, and Yamaha introduced the set-neck SF series (Super Flighter) with twin humbuckers and offset cutaways.

In 1982 Yamaha revised the SC series to reflect the old "reverse" SG body shape, now with three single-coil pickups in a Strat-style layout.

Two years later Yamaha revamped its solidbody line again, adding more SGs and a number of Tele-style SJ-series models. There were also new Strat-based six-strings called the SE series as well as variations with twin humbuckers. New Yamaha endorsers included Cornell Dupree, Barry Finnerty and Carlos Rios. By 1984 the costs

of manufacturing electric guitars in Japan had soared, and Yamaha moved most of its guitar production to a new, modern factory that was based in Kaohsiung, Taiwan. At this point Yamaha continued to make only a very few of its electric guitar models in Japan. These included the evergreen SGs as well as 1985's EX-2 and VX-2 Flying V-style models with carved-relief tops and locking vibratos.

Yamaha's new Taiwan-made line was the Strat-style SE series, introduced in 1985, with bolt-on necks, locking or traditional vibrato systems and various pickups. In 1986 Yamaha briefly offered the minimalist G-10 synth guitar controller. By 1988 top-of-the-line, through-neck models came with either passive or active electronics.

Yamaha's RGX Series debuted in 1987, sleek offset-double-cutaway superstrats with scalloped, sharp, pointed cutaways, locking vibratos and a variety of pickups, with through-neck and active models. By 1988 the RGX Custom (through-neck and ash body) and Standard (flame-maple cap) topped the line.

A year later Yamaha introduced the flamed-top, set-neck Image series: Custom with LED position markers for playing in the dark; Deluxe with vibrato; and hardtail Standard. Designed at Yamaha's Kemble facility in the UK, these equal-double-cutaway solidbodies lasted only a couple years.

By 1990 Yamaha had opened a custom shop in Los Angeles, California. The SE series was history, and most RGX guitars were renamed RGZ, now joined by the new

Yamaha's most famous instrument was the SG-2000; this 2000S (near right) was made around 1984. From its launch in 1976, the 2000 showed that Japanese-made guitars of high quality and conservative design could sell. The 1983 catalog page (below) shows the US-market SG-2000, renamed the SBG-2000. This Gibson-style SA-1100 (center) was made in 1990, while the SC-400 (far right) from 1981 reflects Yamaha's early "reverse" body style.

Two more Yamahas are shown on this page. A luscious example from the wide-ranging and popular Pacifica series, this Pacifica 604 (main guitar) was made in 1994, while the RGX Custom (below) produced in 1989 is typical of Yamaha's superstrat period.

The ads here feature contrasting musicians who have both found appeal in Yamaha's guitars. Jazzman Martin Taylor (top) is seen with a "hybrid" AEX-1500 and various AES hollowbodies in 1999, while Blues Saraceno shows off his custom plaid-finished RGX model.

Rich Lasner-designed Pacifica line and the fancy Weddington series. The Pacifica instruments continued the enthusiasm for Fender-style guitars, ranging from through-neck types with carved flame-maple tops and internal sound chambers, to bolt-on-neck models that came with various pickup combinations and vibratos. Many of the Pacifica line offered excellent value and have sold very well.

The Weddington Custom (with carved quilted-maple top), Classic (carved maple top) and Special (with a flat-top mahogany body) were twin-humbucker Les-Paul-style solidbodies with an Aria PE-like sweeping curve down from the upper shoulder into the cutaway opposite.

Most of Yamaha's higher-end RGZ guitars and the Weddington instruments were gone from the line by 1995, to be replaced in 1996 by several American-made Pacifica USA models that employed bodies and necks supplied by Warmoth.

By 1999 the Pacifica series included an ash-bodied Telecaster-style solidbody that gained Yamaha a valuable endorsement from guitarist Mike Stern. The AES series of solidbodies and semi-hollowbodies were also among the new models in the Yamaha catalog. These nodded to the "neo-vintage" revival with their exaggerated rounded single-cutaway and retro-shape pickguards, a generally 1960s image that brought Yamaha almost full circle. This continued in 2000 with the launch of SGV models, direct revivals of the "reverse"-body SGs from almost 35 years earlier.

Two guitars from Yamaha's retro-style AES line are pictured: this 1998 AES-800 (near right) has hum-cancelling P-90-like pickups, while the 1999 AES-500 (center) has humbuckers. Also shown (far right) is a Yamaha Pacifica 511MS Mike Stern model, made in 1998, with an ad from that same year announcing Stern's new endorsement.

A leading proponent of Zemaitis guitars was The Pretenders' James Honeyman-Scott, who recorded especially dramatic guitar parts for their second album (right) of 1981.

ZEMAITIS

Tony Zemaitis made the highest-profile British guitars of the 20th century, and is best known for the "metal front" and "pearl front" solidbodies that he built for players like Ron Wood. Zemaitis was based at Chatham, Kent, retiring in 2000 after 35 years as a professional guitar-maker.

Zemaitis first came to wide attention in the early 1970s when Wood and Ronnie Lane began using his instruments, and from then his list of clients – both for acoustic and electric guitars – began to read like rock'n'roll royalty, including Hendrix, Clapton, Harrison, Richards, Gilmour, Honeyman-Scott and many others.

His electrics are flamboyant guitars for stage use, symbolizing glorious 1970s rock'n'roll decadence. They boast plenty of handwork, hand-made bridges, and engraved metal or mosaic-like pearl inlays. Some metal-front Zemaitis guitars featured work by shotgun engraver Danny O'Brien. The idea for the metal fronts started when Zemaitis shielded Strat pickups with metal foil and decided to take the idea further.

Most guitars were custom-ordered, but there was a dalliance around 1980 with the shortlived Budget student model. Zemaitis instruments became desirable to later generations seeking 1970s styles, with more recent players including Gilby Clark and Richie Robinson. The electrics have become highly-prized and valuable guitars, and in Japan have reached almost mythical status.

Among the largely British clientele drawn to Tony Zemaitis's singular creations was Marc Bolan of T Rex. The metal guru is pictured (above) playing a metal-front Zemaitis. Two typical examples of the classic Zemaitis metal-fronts are shown on this page (left).

Grimshaw
GUITARS

"Retrofit: Any component that is added to a guitar after it leaves the place in which it was made, and one that fits directly onto the intended guitar with no alteration to the instrument."

chapter 6

TOTALLY GUITAR
GLOSSARY/INDEX

Over the next dozen pages is all the hard information you'll need to speak fluent guitar. No matter what your accent, you'll find here the specific meanings of the simplest as well as the most esoteric terms in guitar-speak, from action to fan-strutting, grunge tuning to master volume, nut to snakehead, and tremolo to zero-fret.

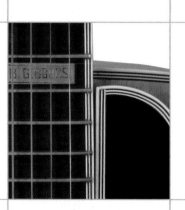

Abalam Trade name for abalone laminated to thin plastic sheet, the result of a new cutting technique which yields more of the useable shell and less waste.

abalone Shellfish used for inlay material on guitars. Comes in many iridescent hues, most prized being the green heart. Becoming rare.

AC Short for "alternating current," an electric current that can change the direction in which it flows. This is the type of electricity that flows from common domestic wall outlets (commonly 120V in the US, 230-240V in the UK). See also *DC*.

acoustic General term for any hollowbody acoustic guitar. An acoustic musical instrument is one that generates sound without electrical amplification. Also, a term related to sound and hearing.

acrylic Paint containing acrylic resin, widely used in guitar finishes as a more eco-friendly substitute for cellulose lacquers.

action Often used to describe only the height of the strings above the tops of the frets; thus "high action," "low action," "buzz-free action" etc. In fact, the term can refer to the entire playing feel of a given instrument; thus "good action," "easy action" etc.

active (active electronics, active circuit) Circuitry in some guitars that boosts signal and/or widens tonal range with necessary additional (usually battery) powering. Refers to a pickup or circuit that incorporates a preamp. See also *preamp*.

active crossover See *crossover*.

active powered Not necessarily amplified, but using (active) electronics to assist or improve functioning.

ADAT Type of multi-track digital audio tape.

ADT Artificial (or automatic) double tracking. Used to reinforce an existing signal, for instance making one singer sound like two.

alder Medium weight hardwood commonly used for solid guitar bodies, for example some of those made by Fender.

alerce South American tree related to the larch.

alnico Magnet material used for pickups and speakers (generally of more "vintage" design). It is an alloy of aluminum, nickel, and cobalt. Also, a nickname for a single-coil Gibson pickup with flat-sided polepieces.

alphabeto 17th century Italian notation system using an alphabet of chord symbols.

alternating current See *AC*.

amp(lifier) Electrical circuit designed to increase the level of a signal; but more usually, an audio system for boosting sound before transmission to a loudspeaker. The system could be a power amp, or backline instrument amplifier, or line amp.

amp rack Sturdy frame or rack designed for mounting power amps. It is usually deeper than regular instrument racks, and often very heavy.

amplification Making a signal bigger (may refer to voltage, analogous to signal level and loudness, or current). General term for amps, speakers and associated gear.

analog (UK: analogue) System which reproduces a signal by copying its original amplitude waveform. Examples include the groove of an old vinyl recording, the electrical signal on a magnetic tape recording, or the voltage levels of an analog synthesizer. As opposed to digital, where the signal is recorded as a series of numbers.

anode (plate) Part within a vacuum tube (UK: valve) which collects current.

anodized (UK: anodised) Finish given to metal by electrolysis. Often refers, erroneously, to Fender's gold-tinted aluminum pickguards of the 1950s (which are alodined).

anti-surge "Delayed" fuse (body marked "T") that withstands brief current surges without breaking. Note that it doesn't prevent current surges.

apoyando In classical performance, a right-hand technique (also known as the rest stroke) in which the playing finger passes "through" the string, coming to rest on the adjacent string.

archtop Guitar with arched body top formed by carving or pressing. Usually refers to hollowbody or semi-acoustic instruments; thus "archtop jazz guitar". As opposed to the other principal type of acoustic guitar, the flat-top.

arpeggio Broken chord in which the notes are played sequentially rather than together.

arrangement Music that emerges after allocating different parts of a composition to various instruments and/or voices. Also, the adaptation to guitar of music originally intended for instruments other than guitar. See also *transcription*.

ash Medium to heavy hardwood commonly used for solid guitar bodies, for example by Fender.

ashtray Nickname for the bridge cover originally supplied but often missing from vintage-style Fender Telecaster guitars.

atonal Type of composition, usually of the 20th century, which has no allegiance to a tonal center.

attack Speed at which a sound (or filter, or envelope) reaches its maximum level. For instance, percussive sounds usually have fast attacks, while smooth, liquid sounds have slow attacks.

attenuate Reduce in strength.

attenuator Electronic circuitry that reduces level, usually in fixed steps of useful round-figure amounts, such as -10dB, -20dB. Also the knob or switch that controls such a setting.

aux return Abbreviation of auxiliary return. Inputs on a mixer used for adding back the signal from/with the FX.

aux send Abbreviation of auxiliary send. Output typically from a mixer to FX and other locations.

B+ Symbol used to indicate high voltage supply in an amplifier circuit schematic. Also "HT" (for High Tension), the latter particularly used in the UK.

baby blue Popular (unofficial) name for Fender's early Sonic Blue Custom Color.

backlash Any "give" in a tuner's operation where the string-post does not immediately move when the tuner button is turned.

backline Musical instrument amps (usually for guitars) placed in a line across the back of the stage, or stacked up in a wall or crescent for visual effect. In modern stage sets, can also include racks of sampler channels and their sub-mixers, or indeed anything on the stage.

backplate Panel fitted over a cavity in the rear of a guitar body, allowing access to pots and wiring or vibrato springs.

baffle Front panel or baseboard of a speaker cabinet onto which direct-radiating drivers and smaller horn flares are mounted.

Bakelite First plastic, invented 1909. Used for some guitars, parts and components from the '30s to the '50s.

balanced Signals or in/out connections where a pair of

ac to bullet

conductors (hot and cold) are separate from the ground (earth) shield, carrying opposing versions of the same signal at exactly the same level, and also having near identical impedances compared to ground (earth). Greatly helps to avoid noise problems in compatible circuitry and equipment, and longer cable lengths can be used than with unbalanced leads.

ball-end Metal retainer wound onto the end of a guitar string and used to secure it to the anchor point at the bridge.

bandurría Spanish folk instrument with a pear-shaped body and steel strings.

banjo tuners Rear-facing tuners found on some guitars, notably on some early Martin OM and Gibson reverse-body Firebird models.

bass pickup See *neck pickup*.

B-bender String-pulling device giving a pedal-steel effect on regular electric guitar. The best known models are by Parsons-White, and Joe Glaser.

bias For a tube (valve) guitar amp, a critical "tune-up" setting (and also of a tape machine or other piece of equipment), generally involving some auxiliary voltage or current that helps the circuitry to work properly.

biasing Setting the bias of the tubes (valves) within an amp for optimum performance. See *bias*.

Bigsby Simple single-spring non-recessed vibrato device developed by Paul Bigsby. Now sometimes

used as a generic term for similar designs by other makers.

binding Protective and decorative strip(s) added to edges of the body and/or fingerboard and/or headstock of some guitars.

birdseye Type of maple with small circular figure.

blackface Used to denote "vintage" Fender amps manufactured between approximately 1963 and 1967, so-called because of their black control panels. Also used to describe the sound produced by these amps. (Black control panels were occasionally returned to in later years, but any post-'67 Fender amps would not accurately be termed blackface.) See also *brownface*, *silverface*.

blade pickup (bar pickup) Pickup (humbucker or single-coil) that uses a long single blade polepiece for each coil, rather than the more usual individual polepieces for each string.

block markers Square-shape or rectangular-shape position markers in the fingerboard.

blond (blonde) Natural finish, usually enhancing plain wood color; or (on some Fenders) a slightly yellowed finish.

blue-bell Describes the blue painted bell-shaped magnet cover on original Celestion-manufactured Vox 12-inch speakers.

Bluesbreaker Nickname for the Marshall 2x12 combo used by Eric Clapton on the John Mayall album of the same name. Originals are highly sought after, and the model was re-issued by Marshall in the late 1980s.

board (UK: desk) Mixer, mixing console, mixdown unit.

boat neck Alternative name for V-neck (describes shape). See *V-neck*.

bobbin Frame around which pickup coils are wound.

body Main portion of the guitar, onto which are (usually) mounted the bridge, pickups, controls etc. Can be solid, hollow, or a combination of the two.

bolt-on neck Describes a (usually solidbody) guitar with neck bolted rather than glued to the body. Typified by most Fender electric guitars. In fact, such a neck is most often secured with screws.

bookmatched Wood split into two thin sheets and joined together to present symmetrically matching grain/figure patterns.

bossa nova Means "new trend" in Portuguese. Musical style derived from the influence of Brazilian samba rhythms on West Coast jazz in the early 1960s.

bottleneck Style of guitar playing using a metal or glass object to slide up and down the guitar strings instead of fretting individual notes. The broken-off neck of a bottle was originally used, hence the name.

bound See *binding*.

bout Looking at a guitar standing upright, the bouts are the outward curves of the body above (upper bout) and below (lower bout) the instrument's "waist."

boutique amp High-end, generally hand-built and hand-wired guitar amplifier produced usually in limited numbers by an independent craftsman.

box Slang term for (usually hollowbody "jazz") guitar.

BPM Beats per minute – the tempo of the music.

braces (bracing) Wood structures beneath a hollowbody guitar's front and back intended to enhance strength and tonal response.

Brazilian rosewood Hardwood derived from the tropical evergreen Dalbergia nigra and used in the making of some guitar bodies, necks and fingerboards. Now a protected species, meaning further exportation from Brazil is banned.

bridge Unit on guitar body that holds the saddle(s). Sometimes also incorporates the anchor point for the strings.

bridge block On acoustic guitars, this refers to the drilled section of a bridge through which the strings are threaded.

bridge pickup Pickup placed nearest the bridge. At one time known as the lead or treble pickup.

bridgeplate On electric guitars, this is the baseplate on to which bridge components are mounted; on acoustic guitars, the reinforcing hardwood plate under the bridge.

bronze Metal used as outer wrap on modern flat-top acoustic strings. As a material for this purpose it has replaced the less durable brass.

brown (brown sound) Soft distortion produced by a guitar amp when run at slightly lower mains voltages than its specs require. (Derived from the term "brown-out," the partial loss of power to a city's supply grid – itself a contrast to "blackout," a total loss of power.)

brownface Used to denote Fender amps manufactured between approximately 1960 and 1963, so-called because of their brown control panels. See also *blackface*, *silverface*.

bullet Describes the appearance of the truss-rod adjustment nut visible at the headstock on some Fender and Fender-style guitars.

burst Abbreviation of sunburst (finish), but often used specifically to refer to one of the original sunburst-finish Gibson Les Paul Standard models made between 1958 and 1960.

button Knob used to turn tuners (machine heads).

cab Abbreviation of (speaker) cabinet, commonly used for enclosure containing drivers for one or more frequency ranges.

cable Another name for a cord (lead) to supply mains power, or to connect amps and speakers, or to connect instruments and amplifiers. Can also be used generally for the sheathed connecting wires, with or without connectors.

camber See *radius*.

cans Slang term for headphones.

cante Means folk-singing in Spanish; one of the components of flamenco.

capacitor (cap) Frequency-dependent electrical component. Within an electric guitar tone control, for example, it's used to filter high frequencies to ground (earth) making the sound progressively darker as the control is turned down. Used similarly in guitar amplifiers, as well as for filtering noise from power supplies by passing AC signal to ground.

capo (from capo tasto or capo dastro) Movable device which can be fitted over the fingerboard behind any fret. It shortens the strings' length and therefore raises their pitch. Used to play in different keys but with familiar chord shapes.

carbon graphite Strong, stable, man-made material used by some modern electric guitar makers. Has a very high resonant frequency.

cathode biased In a tube amp, an output stage which is biased according to the voltage drop across a resistor connected to the cathode of the power tube(s). Often considered a source of "vintage" tone, it is a feature of the tweed Fender Deluxe, the Vox AC-30 and others. See also *fixed bias*.

cavity Hollowed-out area in solidbody guitar for controls and switches: thus "control cavity."

CE Mark applied to equipment sold in EU (European Union) countries, theoretically indicating that the equipment meets (largely unspecified) Euro regulations.

cedar Evergreen conifer of the Mediterranean; the timber is used particularly in the making of classical guitar necks. In flat-top and other building the term often refers to "western red cedar," which is not a cedar at all but a North American thuya or arbor vitae.

cellulose See *nitro-cellulose*.

center block Solid wooden block running through the inside of a semi-acoustic guitar's body.

ch Abbreviation of channel. Can be used of a splitter, mixer, crossover, power amp, and so on.

chamfer Bevel or slope to the edges of a guitar's body.

changer Unit at the bridge end of a pedal steel guitar neck with "fingers" to which strings are attached and that connect to the player's choice of pedals and levers.

Charlie Christian Pioneering electric guitarist whose name was popularly applied to one of Gibson's first pickups, since reissued on the ES-175 Charlie Christian model.

chassis Steel or aluminum casing that houses the electronics of an

amp or an effects unit.

checkerboard binding Binding made up of small alternate black and white blocks running around the circumference of a guitar body. Normally associated with high-end Rickenbacker guitars.

cherry Shade of red stain used in translucent guitar finishes and most commonly associated with Gibson who used it extensively from the '50s onwards. Hence often referred to as Gibson Cherry Red.

choke Small transformer within some guitar amps which helps to filter AC noise from the circuit.

choking String colliding with a higher fret as the string is played and/or bent.

chops Slang for player's technical proficiency.

class A Amplifier with output tubes set to operate throughout the full 360-degree cycle of the signal. Class A is sometimes considered "sweeter" sounding harmonically, but is less efficient power-wise than class AB. (The term is often incorrectly used to describe guitar amps which are in fact cathode-biased class AB circuits with no negative feedback, and therefore share some sonic characteristics with class A amps.) See *class AB*.

class AB Amplifier with output tubes set to cut off alternately for a portion of the signal's 360-degree cycle, thereby sharing the load and increasing output efficiency. (In reality, this is the operating class of the majority of guitar amps, and certainly of many classics by Marshall, Fender, Mesa/Boogie and others.) See *class A*.

clay dot Refers to the material used for the dot inlays on Fender guitars from circa 1959 to 1963.

coil(s) Insulated wire wound around bobbin(s) in a pickup.

coil-split Usually describes a method to cut out one coil of a humbucking pickup, giving a slightly lower output and cleaner, more single-coil-like sound. Also known, incorrectly, as coil-tap.

coil-tap (tapped pickup) Pickup coil which has two or more live leads exiting at different

percentages of the total wind, in order to provide multiple output levels and tones. Not to be confused with coil-split.

combo Abbreviation of combination, meaning a combination in one cabinet of an instrument amplifier and speaker system. Also, old-fashioned/obsolete term for a band or group of musicians.

compensation Small distance added to each string's speaking length to make the guitar play in-tune. This additional string length compensates for the sharpening effect of pressing the strings down onto the fingerboard.

comping Playing style, usually associated with jazz, which sustains the tempo and rhythm of a piece while simultaneously stating its chord changes.

compound radius See *radius*.

compressor Sound processor that can be set to smooth dynamic range and thus minimize sudden leaps in volume. Overall perceived loudness is in this way increased without "clipping."

concert Name originated by Martin to designate a specific style of large-bodied flat-top acoustic guitar. Also, in classical guitar terminology a concert guitar is one intended for the public performance of "serious" music.

concert pitch Standardized instrument tuning used in most Western music (at least since 1960) where the A above middle C has a fundamental frequency of 440Hz. This can be measured using an electronic tuner or checked against a tuning fork.

concerto Extended work for a solo instrument and an orchestra.

conductor wires Wires attached to the start and finish of a pickup coil which take the output signal to the controls. A four-conductor humbucker, for example, actually has five output wires: four conductor wires and a fifth (bare) wire which comes from the pickup's grounding plate and/or cover and must always be connected to ground (earth).

conical radius See *radius*.

contoured body Gentle curving of the front and/or back of a solid guitar body, and usually designed to aid player comfort.

control(s) Knobs and switch levers on outside of guitar activating the function of electric components that are usually mounted below the pickguard or in back of the body.

control cavity See *cavity*.

cord (cable, UK: lead) Cable to supply unit with power, or to connect amplifiers and speakers, or to connect instruments and amplifiers.

counterpoint Music that consists of two or more independent melody lines.

coupling Exchange of mechanical energy between an instrument's string(s) and soundboard.

course Usually means a pair of strings running together but tuned apart, usually in unison or an octave apart, as on a 12-string guitar, mandolin, or baroque guitar. Technically, the term can also refer to a single string (or, rarely, a group of three strings).

cross-head screw Screw that has two slots in a "cross" shape in its head.

cross-head screwdriver Screwdriver with a cross-shaped point to fit a cross-head screw. Sometimes known as a Phillips (head) screwdriver.

crossover Circuit, sometimes built into amps and/or speakers, that splits a signal into two or more complementary frequency ranges.

current Flow of electrons in an electrical circuit, measured in amps.

custom color Selected color finish for a guitar, as opposed to natural or sunburst. Term originated by Fender in the late '50s, now widely used.

cutaway Curve into body near neck joint, aiding player's access to high frets. A guitar can have two ("double," "equal," "offset," "twin") cutaways or one ("single") cutaway. Sharp ("florentine") or round ("venetian") describe the shape of the horn formed by the cutaway.

cypress Conifer native to southern Europe, east Asia and North America and widely planted for decorative purposes and for wood. Used in the 19th century for the bodies of cheaper guitars taken up by the flamencos.

damping Deadening of a sound, especially by stopping the vibration of a string with, for example, the palm of the hand.

DC Short for "direct current." Electric current flowing only in one direction. Tube (valve) amps utilize DC voltages for the vast portion of their internal operation.

DC resistance "Direct current" resistance: a measurement (in ohms) that is often quoted in pickup specs to give an indication of relative output.

dead string length Portion of the string beyond the nut and behind the saddle.

decal (UK: transfer, sticker) Small sheet with logo, brandname or trademark, usually on headstock. Licked by the good Captain, baby.

desk See *board*.

DI Abbreviation of direct injection. Means of isolating, adjusting and balancing a line-level instrument signal (from keyboards, guitars etc) so it can be connected to the PA's stagebox or to a recording mixer at a suitable level and without creating buzzes.

digital System of recording or processing which stores and processes analog information by converting it into a series of numbers (binary 1s and 0s).

digital modeling See *modeling amp*.

dings Small knocks, dents or other signs of normal wear in a guitar's surface. A true indicator of aged beauty if you're selling; a cause for mirth and money-saving if you're buying.

diode Electronic component used within some guitar amps as a solid-state rectifier to convert AC current to DC. Also occasionally used in solid-state overdrive circuits. See also *rectifier*.

dissonance Perceived sonic clash between two or more notes that are sounded together.

distortion Signal degradation caused by the overloading or intentional manipulation of audio systems (such as guitar amplifier). Often used deliberately to create a harsher and grittier or sweeter and more compressed sound.

dive-bomb See *down-bend*.

Dobro Product of the Dopyera Brothers or the successors to their brandname, subsequently adopted as a generic term for a guitar with metal resonator(s) inside.

dog-ear Nickname for some P-90 pickups, derived from the shape of the mounting lugs on the cover. See also *soap-bar*.

dot markers Dot-shape position markers in fingerboard.

dot-neck Fingerboard with dot-shape position markers; nickname for Gibson ES-335 of 1958-62 (and reissues) with such markers.

double-locking vibrato See *locking vibrato*.

double-neck (twin-neck) Large guitar specially made with two necks, usually combining six-string and 12-string, or six-string and bass.

down-bend Downward shift in the strings' pitch using a vibrato. In extreme cases this is known as dive-bombing.

down-market See *low-end*.

DPDT switch Double-pole double-throw switch, usually miniature or sub-miniature variety used for guitar coil-tap or other such switching.

Dreadnought Large flat-top acoustic guitar designed by Frank H. Martin and Harry Hunt and named for a type of large British battleship. Now used to describe any acoustic of this body style.

dropped headstock (pointed headstock, droopy headstock) Long, down-pointing headstock popularized on 1980s superstrats.

dynamics Expression in music using a range of volume (intensity) shifts.

ears Jazz slang for player's speed and ability to learn and interpret new tunes.

earth (UK term; also known as ground, especially in US) Connection between an electrical circuit or device and the ground. A common neutral reference point in an electrical circuit. All electrical components (and shielding) within a guitar (and amplifiers, signal processors, etc) must be linked to earth as the guitar's pickups and electrics are susceptible to noise interference. See also *shielding*.

ebonized Wood darkened to look like ebony.

ebonol Synthetic material made of compressed paper and resin, used as fingerboard material by some manufacturers, notably Steinberger.

ebony Dense, black hardwood used for fingerboards and bridges.

effects (effects units, FX) Generic term for audio processing devices such as distortions, delays, reverbs, flangers, phasers, harmonizers and so on.

effects loop Patch between the preamp and power amp (or sometimes within preamp stages) of guitar amp, processing unit or mixer for inserting effects that will operate on selected sound signals.

electric Term simply applied to any electric guitar; in other words, a guitar intended to be used in conjunction with an amplifier.

electro-acoustic (electro) Acoustic guitar with built-in pickup, usually of piezo-electric type. The guitar usually has a preamp and includes volume and tone controls.

electro-acoustics Academic name for key parts of PA where electronics and acoustics come together, meaning inter-disciplinary work with mikes, mike amps, power amps, speakers, cables, cans and acoustics.

electron tube See *tube*.

electronic tuner Typically battery-powered unit that displays and enables accurate tuning to standard concert pitch.

end-block Thick wooden block used to join sides of guitar at the lower bout.

EQ See *equalization*.

equalization (EQ) Active tone control that works by emphasizing or de-emphasizing specific frequency bands. General term for tone control.

étude Means "study" in French. Classical piece intended to help develop technical skills, and sometimes also of musical value.

European spruce Sometimes called German spruce, picea abies tends to come from the Balkans. Spruce originally meant "from Prussia." Used for soundboards.

face See *plate*, *soundboard*.

fan-strutting Wooden struts beneath lower soundboard of guitar, arranged approximately in the shape of an open fan.

Farad Measure of electrical capacitance, and usually (for electric guitar capacitors) quoted in microfarads (mF or μF) or picofarads (pF).

feedback Howling noise produced by leakage of the output of an amplification system back into its input, typically a guitar's pickup(s).

f-hole Soundhole of approximately "f" shape on some hollowbody and semi-acoustic guitars.

figure Natural pattern on surface of wood; thus "figured maple".

fine-tuners Set of tuners that tune strings to very fine degrees, usually as fitted to a locking vibrato or a specialized bridge.

finger String holder actuated by footpedal or knee lever to alter the pitch of a pedal steel guitar.

fingerboard (fretboard, board) Playing surface of the guitar that holds the frets. It can be simply the front of the neck itself, or a separate thin board glued to the neck.

finish Protective and decorative covering on wood parts, typically the guitar's body, back of neck, and headstock.

five-position switch See *five-way switch*.

five-way switch (five-position switch) Selector switch that offers five options, for example the five pickup combinations on a Strat-style guitar.

fixed bias In guitar amps, a technique for biasing output tubes using a pot to adjust negative voltage on the tube's grid as compared to its cathode. (Note that the name is somewhat misleading as "fixed-bias" amps generally have a bias which is adjustable, whereas cathode-biased amps are set and non-adjustable.) See *cathode biased*.

fixed bridge Non-vibrato bridge.

fixed neck See *glued neck*.

flame Dramatic figure, usually on maple.

flame-top Guitar, often specifically a Gibson Les Paul Standard, with sunburst maple top.

flat-blade screwdriver See *slot-head screwdriver*.

flat-top Acoustic guitar with flat top (as opposed to arched) and usually with a round soundhole.

floating bridge Bridge not fixed permanently to the guitar's top, but held in place by string tension (usually on older or old-style hollowbody guitars).

floating pickup Pickup not fixed permanently to the guitar's top, but mounted on a separate pickguard or to the end of the fingerboard (on some hollowbody electric guitars).

floating vibrato Vibrato unit (such as the Floyd Rose or Wilkinson type) that "floats" above the surface of the body.

flowerpot inlay Describes an inlay depicting a stylized vase and foliage used by Gibson on, notably,

its L-5 model.

14-fret/12-fret Refers to the point at which a flat-top acoustic guitar's neck joins the body.

French polishing Traditional varnishing technique that uses a small fabric pad to rub shellac dissolved in alcohol into the wood of a guitar body.

frequency Number of cycles of a vibration occurring per unit of time; the perceived pitch of a sound. See also *Hertz*.

fretboard See *fingerboard*.

fretless Guitar fingerboard without frets; usually bass, but sometimes (very rarely) guitar.

frets Metal strips positioned on the fingerboard of a guitar (or sometimes directly into the face of a solid neck) to enable the player to stop the strings and produce specific notes.

fretwire Wire from which individual frets are cut.

friction peg Traditional tuning peg held in position by the friction of the wooden peg in its hole. Now only on flamenco guitars, though still commonly seen on other stringed instruments such as violins and cellos.

frontline Arrangement of amplifiers and speakers when placed at the front of the stage, in front of musicians, as was sometimes done in the '50s and early '60s. See also *backline*.

FX Abbreviation for effects. Also known more formally as signal processors – boxes that can be used to alter sound in a creative and/or artistic manner.

gain Amount of increase or change in signal level. When dBs are used, increased gain is shown as +dB; reduction is shown -dB; and no change as 0dB.

gauge Outer diameter of a string, always measured in thousandths of an inch (.009", .042" etc). Strings are supplied in particular gauges and/or in sets of matched gauges. Fretwire is also offered in different gauges, or sizes.

gig Live musical event.

glued neck (glued-in neck, set neck, fixed neck) Type of neck/body joint popularized by Gibson which permanently glues the two main components together.

golpeador (golpe) Thin protective plate used to protect the top of a flamenco guitar from the player's finger-tapping.

greenback Describes a particularly desirable Celestion 12" guitar speaker that had a green magnet-cover.

ground (also known as earth, particularly in the UK) Connection between an electrical circuit or device and the ground. A common neutral reference point in an electrical circuit. All electrical components (and shielding) within a guitar (and amplifiers, signal processors, etc) must be linked to earth as the guitar's pickups and electrics are susceptible to noise interference.

ground wire Wire connected from vibrato, bridge, tailpiece, switch, pickup cover, grounding plate etc to ground (earth).

grounding plate Metal baseplate of pickup that is connected to ground (earth).

grunge tuning Tuning all strings down one half step (one semitone) for a fatter sound.

gut Cured animal intestines used for classical strings before development of nylon.

hang-tags Small cards and other documents hung on a guitar in the showroom, and prized when still available with vintage instruments.

hardtail Guitar with non-vibrato bridge (originally used primarily to distinguish non-vibrato Fender Stratocasters from the more common vibrato-loaded models).

hardware Separate components (non-electrical) fitted to the guitar: the bridge, tuners, strap buttons, and so on.

harmonic Usually refers to a ringing, high-pitched note produced by touching (rather than fretting) strategic points on the string while it is plucked, most noticeably at the fifth, seventh and 12th fret. In fact, "harmonics" also occur naturally during the playing of the acoustic or electric guitar (or any stringed instrument) and are part of any guitar's overall voice.

harmonic bar Fitted inside an acoustic guitar, usually one above the soundhole and one below.

harmonic distortion "Ordinary" distortion occurring in analog (audio) electronics, speakers and mikes, involving the generation of harmonics.

headless Design with no headstock, popularized by Ned Steinberger in the early 1980s.

headstock Portion at the end of the neck where the strings attach to the tuners. "Six-a-side" type (Fender-style) has all six tuners on one side of the headstock. "Three-a-side" type (Gibson-style) has three tuners on one side, three the other.

heel Curved deepening of the neck for strength near body joint.

herringbone Describes a black-and-white decorative inlay for acoustic guitars, as popularized by the Martin company.

Hertz (Hz) Unit of frequency measurement. One Hertz equals one cycle per second. See *frequency*.

hex pickup Provides suitable signal for an external synthesizer.

high-end (up-market, upscale) High- or higher-cost instrument, usually aimed at those seeking the best materials and workmanship.

hockey stick Refers to the shape of the headstock on Fender's Electric XII 12-string guitar.

hook-up wire Connecting wire (live or ground) from pickup to pots, switches etc.

horn Pointed body shape formed by cutaway: thus "left horn," "sharp horn," etc. See also *cutaway*.

hot In electrical connections, means live. Also used generally to mean powerful, as in "hot pickup."

hot-rodding Making modifications to a guitar, usually its pickups and/or electronics.

HT Symbol denoting high voltage in amplifier circuits (short for High Tension) and particularly used in the UK. See *B+*.

humbucker (humbucking) Noise-canceling twin-coil pickup. Typically the two coils have opposite magnetic polarity and are wired together electrically out-of-phase to produce a sound that we call in-phase. See also *phase*.

hybrid Technically, any instrument that combines two or more systems of any kind. But now most often indicates a guitar that combines original-style magnetic "electric" pickups with "acoustic"-sounding piezo-electric pickups.

iced-tea Description of the color of a Les Paul Standard which has faded with time and UV exposure.

impedance Electrical resistance to the flow of alternating current, measured in Ohms (Ω). A few electric guitars have low-impedance circuits or pickups to match the inputs of recording equipment; the vast majority are high impedance. Impedance matching is important to avoid loss of signal and tone. Also commonly encountered with speakers, where it is important to match a speaker's (or speaker cab's) impedance to that of the amplifier's speaker output (commonly 4Ω, 8Ω or 16Ω).

in-between sound Legendary tone achieved on older Fender Strats fitted with three-way Centralab switch by jamming the switch between settings so that pairs of pickups operate at once. Made easier from early '80s when Fender fitted a five-way version of the switch, a quarter of a century after the model was launched.

Indian rosewood Hardwood from tropical evergreen tree, known as East Indian rosewood or Dalbergia latifolia. Used for acoustic guitar bodies, fingerboards or necks, especially now that Brazilian rosewood is not freely available.

inertia block See *sustain block*.

inlay Decorative material cut and fitted into body, fingerboard, headstock etc.

insulation Plastic, cloth or tape wrap, or sheath (non-conductive), around an electrical wire, designed to prevent wire(s) coming into contact with other components and thus shorting the circuit.

intonation State of a guitar so that it is as in-tune with itself as physically possible. This is usually dependent on setting each string's speaking length by adjusting the point at which the strings cross the bridge saddle, known as intonation adjustment. Some bridges allow more adjustment, and therefore greater possibilities for accurate intonation, than others.

jack (UK: jack socket) Mono or stereo connecting socket, usually ¼" (6.5mm), used to feed guitar's output signal to amplification.

jackplate Mounting plate for output jack (jack socket), usually screwed on to body.

jack socket See *jack*.

jewel light Fender-style pilot light with faceted cut-glass "jewel" screwed on over a small bulb.

juerga Spontaneous flamenco event.

jumbo Large-bodied flat-top acoustic guitar. Also used as a name for extra wide and high frets on a guitar fingerboard.

kerfed lining Lining that has been partly cut through at intervals to make it flexible enough to follow the shape of a hollowbody guitar's sides.

Kluson Brand of tuner, originally used on old Fender, Gibson and other guitars, and now reissued.

knurled Serrated or cross-hatched patterning to provide grip on metal (or plastic) components; thus "knurled control knobs" (as fitted to a Telecaster-style guitar).

lacquer See *nitro-cellulose*.

laminated Joined together in layers; usually wood (bodies, necks) or plastic (pickguards).

lead Shorthand for lead guitar: the main guitar within a group; the one that plays most of the solos and/or riffs. Also (UK) term for cord; see also *cable*, *cord*.

lead pickup See *bridge pickup*.

leaf switch See *toggle switch*.

LED Abbreviation of light emitting diode, a small light often used as an "on" indicator in footswitches, effects and amplifier control panels. Sometimes also used as a component within circuits.

legato Term used in musical notation to instruct the musician to play smoothly.

lever switch Type of pickup selector switch historically used by Fender – for example the five-way lever switch. A single, pivoted lever moves between contacts to direct the input-to-output path. See *pickup switch*, *selector*, *toggle switch*.

ligado Left-hand technique involving hammering-on and pulling-off. Especially important in flamenco playing.

linear taper See *taper*.

lining Continuous strip of wood used to join sides of hollowbody guitar to top and back. See also *kerfed lining*.

locking nut Unit that locks strings in place at the nut, usually with three locking bolts.

locking trem See *locking vibrato*.

locking tuner Special tuner that locks the string to the string-post and thus aids string-loading.

locking vibrato Type of vibrato system that locks strings at nut and bridge saddles (hence also called "double-locking") in an effort to stabilize tuning.

logarithmic taper See *taper*.

logo Brandname and/or trademark, usually on the headstock.

low-end (down-market, bargain, budget) Low- or lower-cost instrument, often aimed at beginners or other players on a restricted budget.

lower bout See *bout*.

lug Protruding part or surface. On electrical components, a lug (sometimes called a tag) allows a connection to be made.

lute Medieval and Renaissance

stringed musical instrument.

luthier Old word for maker of violins and/or guitars.

machine head See *tuner*.

magnetic pickup Transducer using coils of wire wound around a magnet. It converts string vibrations into electrical signals.

mahogany Very stable, medium weight hardwood favored by most guitar makers for necks, and by many for solid bodies.

mains Term for high AC voltage (particularly in the UK) as supplied by domestic wall socket – that is, the "main" domestic supply.

maple Hard, heavy wood, often displaying extreme figure patterns prized by guitar makers. Varying kinds of figure give rise to visual nicknames such as quilted, tigerstripe, curly, flame.

master volume/tone Control that affects all pickups equally. In amplification, a master volume control governs the output level – or operating level of the power section – when partnered with a gain, drive or volume control that governs the level of the individual preamp(s).

microfarad See *Farad*.

microphonic Used of a pickup, this means one that is inclined to squeal unpleasantly, usually due to incomplete wax saturation, to loose coil windings, or to insecure mountings that create so-called microphonic feedback.

MIDI Abbreviation of Musical Instrument Digital Interface. The industry-standard control system for electronic instruments. Data for notes, performance effects, patch changes, voice and sample data, tempo and other information can be transmitted and received.

mint Entirely as new, perfect

condition; as used to describe vintage or collectable guitars.

mint green (snot green) Descriptive term for the color of a type of Fender pickguard material used from late 1959 to 1963 (and reproduced on some vintage-style reissues). Originally white, the celluloid nitrate material can age to a dirty pale green.

mod Abbreviation for modification. Any change or after-market customization made to a guitar, amplifier or effects pedal.

modeling amp Guitar amplifier using digital technology (though occasionally analog solid-state circuitry) to emulate, or model, the sounds of classic tube amps.

mother-of-pearl Shell of some molluscs, for example abalone, used for inlays in decoration of rosettes, fingerboards, headstocks, tuning pegs etc.

mother-of-toilet-seat Slang for plastic mother-of-pearl-like material used for inlays in place of the real thing.

mounting ring Usually plastic unit within which Gibson-style pickups are fitted to the guitar body.

mustache bridge Describes the shape of a flat-top acoustic guitar bridge plate, typically found on the Gibson J-200 model.

Nashville tuning Replacing the lowest three strings with strings tuned an octave higher in order to fill out recorded rhythm parts.

neck Part of the guitar supporting the fingerboard and strings; glued or bolted to the body, or on "though-neck" types forming a support spine on to which "wings" are usually glued to form the body.

neck block In acoustic guitars, the end of the neck inside the body where it is built up to meet the top and back of the guitar.

neck pickup Pickup placed nearest the neck. At one time known as the rhythm or bass pickup.

neck pitch Angle of a guitar's neck relative to the body face.

neckplate Single metal plate

through which screws pass to achieve a bolt-on neck fixing (Fender-style). Some bolt-on neck-to-body joints use separate washers for each screw.

neck pocket Rout, or recess, into which the neck fits on the body of a bolt-on-neck guitar.

neck relief Small amount of concave bow in a neck (dipping in the middle) that can help to create a relatively buzz-free action.

neck-tilt Device on some Fender (and other) neck-to-body joints that allows easier adjustment of the neck pitch.

nickel Major component of most metal guitar strings.

nitro-cellulose (US: lacquer) Type of finish used commonly in the '50s and '60s but now rarely seen on production guitars.

Nocaster Collector's term to describe Fender guitars made during the transition from the Broadcaster model name, contested by Gretsch, to Telecaster. These guitars had the part of the decal (transfer) bearing the model name clipped from the headstock.

nodal bar In some classical guitars by David Rubio, a strut extending from beneath the bridge on the treble side of the soundboard. Intended to modify treble response. (From "node," a stationary part of a vibrating body.)

noise Any undesirable sound, such as mains hum or interference.

noise-canceling Type of pickup with two coils wired together to cancel noise, often called humbucking. Any arrangement of pickups or pickup coils that achieves this.

nut Bone, metal or (now usually) synthetic slotted guide bar over which the strings pass to reach the tuners and which determines string height and spacing at the headstock end of neck.

nut lock See *locking nut.*

Offset Contour Body Fender trademark used to describe the distortion of a conventional solidbody shape to aid the player's

comfort and present the neck at a more comfortable angle. Fender's Jazzmaster and Jaguar models were the first with this design.

offshore Made overseas; more specifically and often used to mean outside the US.

ohm Unit of electrical resistance.

open tuning Tuning the guitar to a chord or altered chord, often for slide playing.

out of phase Audible result of the electrical linking of two coils or two pickups in either series or parallel in such a way as to provide at least partial cancellation of the signal. Usually the low frequencies are cancelled so that the resulting sound is thin, lacking in warmth, and often quite brittle. To create an audible result that is in-phase (for example of two coils within a humbucker) the coils must be linked electrically out-of-phase. Phase relationship also depends on polarity of magnets. See also *humbucker.*

oxblood Describes the color of the woven grille cloth used on Fender amps in the early '60s.

PAF Gibson pickup with Patent Applied For decal (sticker) on base – as was the first, vintage version of the Gibson humbucker.

parallel Electrical circuit that has all the positive points joined together and all the negative points joined together. If we consider that a single-coil pickup has a positive (live, hot) and negative (ground, earth) output, when two single-coil pickups on a Stratocaster (position two and four on a five-way switch), for example, are selected together, they are linked in parallel. Can also apply to the parallel linking of resistors or capacitors in a circuit, etc. See also *series.*

passive Normal, unboosted circuit.

P Bass Commonly used abbreviation for Fender's Precision Bass and similar models.

PCB Abbreviation for printed circuit board, a mass-produced fiber board with copper "tracks" making connections between components. It is now the most common circuit board in modern consumer electronics, and is employed in the majority of guitar amplifiers, other than those that use expensive hand-wired designs.

pearl See *mother-of-pearl.*

pearloid Fake pearl, made of plastic and pearl dust.

pentode Tube (valve) containing five functional elements. Most output tubes in guitar amplifiers are pentodes. Also see *triode.*

phase Relationship of two waveforms with respect to time. See also *out of phase.*

Phillips screwdriver See *cross-head screwdriver.*

pick (plectrum, flat pick) Small piece of (usually) plastic or metal – and in olden times tortoiseshell – that is used to pluck or strum a guitar's strings.

pickguard (UK: scratchplate) Protective panel raised above body or fitted flush on to guitar body.

pickup Any unit mounted on a guitar (or other stringed instrument) which transforms string vibration to an electrical signal to be passed along to an amplifier. See *magnetic pickup, piezo pickup, transducer.*

pickup switch Selector switch

that specifically selects pickups individually or in combination.

piezo pickup (piezo-electric pickup) Transducer with piezo-electric crystals that generate electricity under mechanical strain. In a guitar, it senses string and body movement. "Piezo-loaded saddles" are bridge saddles with an integral piezo element.

pin bridge Acoustic guitar bridge that secures the strings by pins rather than by tying.

pitch Frequency of a note: the perceived "lowness" or "highness" of a sound. See also *neck pitch.*

P-J Bass Describes a Fender Precision Bass with an additional Jazz Bass pickup added at the bridge position. A popular mod with bass players, and subsequently adopted by Fender on a number of its basses.

plain strings Plain steel guitar strings with no outer windings. See *wound strings.*

plantilla In classical terminology, the outline of a guitar body.

plate Scientific term for the vibrating soundboard (also known as top plate, where back plate is used for the back of the guitar). See *soundboard, top;* and also *anode.*

plectrum See *pick.*

plexi Nickname for Marshall amplifiers of the mid to late-'60s that used gold-painted "plexiglas" plastic control panels. Also used to refer to the sound produced by Marshall amps of this era, or the reproduction of such a tone.

P-90 Model name for early Gibson single-coil pickup.

point-to-point Method of constructing hand-wired amplifier circuits where individual components are connected directly to each other, without the use of a circuit board.

pointed headstock See *dropped headstock*.

pointy Type of body design generally used by rock players – prevalent in the 1980s and since – with a jagged, pointed, angular outline. Also used of headstock: see *dropped headstock*.

polarity Relationship of positive and negative electrical currents (or north and south magnetic poles) to each other. The magnetic polarity of a pickup refers to the north or south orientation of the magnetic field as presented to the strings.

pole Simultaneously-switched circuit within an electrical switch; thus "two-pole."

polepieces Non-magnetic (but magnetically conductive) polepieces are used to control, concentrate and/or shape a pickup's magnetic field. Can be either adjustable (screw) or non-adjustable (slug) as in an original Gibson humbucker. Magnetic polepieces are those where the magnet itself is aimed directly at the strings, as in an original Stratocaster single-coil.

polyester Type of modern plastic finish used on some guitars.

polyphonic Music made up of several independent lines, each of which is known as a voice.

polyurethane (urethane) Type of modern plastic finish that is used on some guitars.

position markers Fingerboard inlays of various designs; visual clues to the player of fret positions.

pot (potentiometer) Variable electrical resistor that alters voltage by a spindle turning on an electrically resistive track. Used for volume and tone controls, etc.

power amp Output stage of a guitar amplifier that converts the preamp signal to the signal capable of driving a speaker. In a tube (valve) amp, this is where the big tubes live.

preamp (pre-amplifier) Circuit designed to boost low-level signals to a standard level and EQ them before they're sent toward the power amp (hence "pre-amplifier") for full amplification. Guitar circuit usually powered by battery that converts the pickup's output from high to low impedance (preamp/buffer) and can increase the output signal and boost or cut specific frequencies for tonal effect. Also, the first gain stage in a guitar amp, which generally also includes the EQ circuitry and any overdrive-generating stages.

pre-CBS Fender guitars and amps made before CBS takeover in 1965.

prelude Originally the opening piece of a set. But since the 19th century, preludes no longer have to precede. Put it where you want it.

pressed top Arched top (usually laminated) of hollowbody guitar made by machine-pressing rather than hand-carving.

pull/push pot Combination component offering the functions of both a volume/tone potentiometer and a mini-toggle (usually of DPDT type) switch. See also *push-pull*.

purfling Usually synonymous with binding, but more accurately refers to the decorative inlays around the perimeter of a guitar alongside the binding.

push-pull Power amplifier in which output tubes (valves) operate

on alternate cycles of the signal. (This is the most common power amp format in guitar amps that contain more than one output tube.) See also *pull/push pot*.

pyramid bridge Flat-top acoustic guitar bridge having pyramid shaped "bumps" at each side. Common to early Martins.

quarter-sawn Wood cut on radius of tree so that "rings" are perpendicular to the surface of the plank. Structurally preferable to flat-sawn wood for guitar building.

quilted Undulating figure seen on surface of wood, usually maple.

radius Slight curve, or camber, of a fingerboard surface, of the strings, or of the bridge saddles. The term comes from the way that this curve is measured, where the fingerboard, for example, is considered as the top part of a wedge cut from a cylinder of a certain radius. Conical (or compound) radius is where the fingerboard radius increases from the nut to the top fret.

rectifier Component within a guitar amplifier which converts electrical current from AC to DC; can comprise solid-state diodes or a tube (valve) rectifier.

refinish (refin) New finish on a guitar, replacing or added to the original. Usually considered detrimental to a collectable guitar.

reissue Instrument or amp based on an earlier and usually classic model, reintroduced at a later date.

relief See *neck relief*.

resistor Electrical component which introduces a known value of resistance (measured in ohms) to the electrical flow in a circuit.

resonant frequency Frequency at which any object vibrates most

with the least stimulation.

resonator Generic term for guitar with metal resonator(s) in its body to increase volume.

retro Past style reintroduced, often with some changes, as a "new" design, usually with deliberate references. Thus retro guitars use flavors of mainly '50s and '60s designs to inform new concoctions.

retrofit Any component added to a guitar after it leaves the place where it was made (retrofit pickup, vibrato, tuner etc) and one that fits directly onto the intended guitar with no alteration to the instrument.

reverb (reverberation) Ambience effect combining many short echoes; can be imitated electronically, generally by the installation of a spring unit in guitar amps, or digitally in pedals and studio effects units.

rhythm pickup See *neck pickup*.

ribs Classical term for the sides of a guitar.

Ricky Common abbreviation of Rickenbacker; do not allow it ever to lose that number.

rosette Intricate decoration around soundhole, usually in marquetry, abalone inlay or wooden mosaic, often on classical guitars.

rosewood Variegated hardwood traditionally used for acoustic guitar backs, sides and fingerboards. Brazilian or Rio is the most highly prized; Indian is more common.

rout Hole or cavity cut into a guitar, usually into the body. Cavities of this kind are thus said to be routed (rhymes with "shouted") into the body.

saddle(s) Part(s) of a bridge

where the strings make contact; the start of the speaking length of the string; effectively the opposite of the (top) nut.

sag Slight drop in power supply of a guitar amplifier (particularly noticeable in designs comprising tube rectifiers) when a powerful note or chord is played, producing a compression-like softening and squeezing of the signal.

salmon pink Popular (unofficial) name for Fiesta Red, an early Fender Custom Color. Paint is likely to fade depending on its exposure to ultra-violet light, and faded Fiesta Red can look pink. Often confused with Shell Pink, a rare Fender color introduced in the '50s.

samba Portuguese word for a Brazilian dance with African origins.

scale length (string length) Theoretical length of the vibrating string from nut to saddle; actually twice the distance from nut to 12th fret. The actual scale length (the distance from the nut to saddle after intonation adjustment) is slightly longer. See *intonation*, *compensation*.

scallop Gentle sloping of sides of bracing for lightness and tonal modification. Also describes mid-'80s fad for scooping out the fingerboard between frets, allegedly to assist speedy playing.

scratchplate See *pickguard*.

scratch test To verify if a pickup on a guitar plugged into an amp is working by gently rubbing ("scratching") the tip of a screwdriver on the pickup's polepieces and listening for sound.

selector Control that selects from options, usually of pickups.

semi See *semi-acoustic*.

semi-acoustic (semi-solid, semi) Electric guitar with wholly or partly hollow thin body. Originally referred specifically to an electric guitar with a solid wooden block running down the center of thinline body, such as Gibson's ES-335.

semi-solid See *semi-acoustic*.

serial number Added by maker for own purposes; sometimes useful for determining the period of the instrument's construction.

series Electrical linkage of positive and negative points within an electrical circuit with additive effect – for example, the two pickup coils within a series-wired humbucker. In this instance, the total resistance of a series-wired humbucker is the sum of the resistance of each coil. Parallel linkage of the same two coils results in the resistance being one quarter of the sum total. Generally, the higher the resistance the "darker" the resulting tone. Also applies to method of linkage of capacitors or resistors within an amplifier or other electrical circuit. See *parallel*.

set neck (glued neck, glued-in neck, fixed neck) Type of neck/body joint popularized by Gibson which permanently "sets" the two main components together, usually by gluing.

set-up General term including but not restricted to a broad and complex combination of factors (string height, saddle height, intonation adjustments, fret condition, neck relief, etc) required to get the guitar playing to its optimum level.

shellac Natural thermoplastic resin made from secretions of lac insect, which lives on trees in India and Thailand. Dissolved in alcohol, it creates a finish that is applied to guitars by French polishing.

shielding (screening) Barrier to any outside electrical interference. Special paint or conductive foil in the control or pickup cavity to reduce electrical interference. See also *ground*.

signal Transmitted electrical information – for example between control circuits, or guitar and amplifier, etc – usually by means of a connecting wire or cord (lead).

silverface Fender guitar amps with silver control panels, generally produced between 1968 and the late '70s and considered somewhat

inferior tonally to earlier "blackface" versions, though often still very good amps by today's standards. See also *blackface*, *brownface*.

single-coil Original pickup type with a single coil of wire wrapped around (a) magnet(s).

single-ended Amplifier in which the power tube (valve) – usually just one – operates through the entire cycle of the signal. Such amps are necessarily, therefore, class A. Classic examples include the Fender Champ and Vox AC-4.

sitka spruce (picea sitchensis) Large conifer, originally from North America. Popularly used for soundboards on acoustic guitars, especially by US makers.

skunk-stripe Walnut strip inserted in back of one-piece Fender maple necks after truss-rod is inserted.

slab board (slab fingerboard) Fender type (circa 1959-62) in which the joint between the top of the neck and the base of the fingerboard is flat. Later this joint was curved.

slash soundhole Scimitar-shaped soundhole, used primarily by Rickenbacker, but seen on some Gretsch Electromatics and other guitars.

slide Metal or glass tube worn over a guitarist's finger to produce glissando effects. Also, the style of playing using these effects; thus "Did Lowell like to play slide?" See also *bottleneck*.

slot-head screw Type with a single slot in its head.

slot-head screwdriver Type with a flat, single blade, also known as a flat-blade screwdriver.

slot-head tuner Tuner with a slot cut into the top of its string-post with a hole running down the center of its string post.

slotted headstock One with cut-outs that allow access to the tuning-peg posts.

slush lever See *vibrato*.

snakehead Headstock shape that is narrower at the top than the bottom. Usually refers to early Gibson type.

snot green See *mint green*.

soapbar Nickname for P-90 pickup with a cover that has no mounting "ears". See *dog-ear*.

solid General term for any solidbody guitar.

solid-state Circuitry using transistorized components rather than tubes (valves).

soundboard Vibrating top of a guitar body. See *top*, *plate*.

soundhole Aperture in the top of an acoustic guitar's body that increases sound projection. Similar function to f-holes on hollowbody and semi-acoustic guitars.

spaghetti logo Early Fender logo with thin, stringy letters resembling spaghetti, prominent in the '50s and early '60s and on reissues of those designs.

SPDT switch Single-pole double-throw miniature switch.

speaker (loudspeaker, driver) Component consisting of a ceramic or alnico magnet, voice coil, and paper cone, driven by an amplified signal to reproduce sound waves in moving air.

speaking length Sounding length of a guitar's string: the part running from the nut down to the bridge saddle.

splice-joint One method of fixing a guitar head to its neck when each has been carved from a different section of wood.

splined Grooved surface of potentiometer shaft that assists tight fitting of a control knob.

spring claw Anchor point for vibrato springs in body-rear vibrato cavity. Adjusting the spring claw's two screws will affect the position and potential travel of the vibrato.

spruce Soft, light hardwood used for the soundboard on many acoustic guitars.

stock State of a guitar, irrespective of condition, where everything is exactly as supplied when new. Individual items on a guitar exactly as supplied when new (thus "stock pickup," for example).

stop-tail Slang for the style of wrapover bridge fitted to low and mid-priced Gibson solidbodies. See *wrapover bridge*.

stop tailpiece See *stud tailpiece*.

strap button Fixing point on body to attach a guitar-strap; usually two, on sides (or side and back) of guitar body.

straplock Safety device for preventing a guitar from falling off the guitar strap during wild and uninhibited performance. Most common are those made by Jim Dunlop and Schaller.

Strat Abbreviation of Fender Stratocaster, so universally used that Fender have trademarked it and use it themselves.

string block In classical-guitar terminology, this is the drilled section of a bridge through which the strings are threaded.

string length Sounding length of string, measured from nut to bridge saddle (see also *scale length*).

string post Metal shaft on tuner with a hole or slot to receive the string and around which the string is wound.

string-retainer bar Metal bar typically placed behind locking nut to seat strings over curved surface of locking nut prior to locking. Also occasionally used like a string tree to increase behind-the-nut string angle on guitars without nut locks.

string tree Small unit fitted to headstock that maintains downward string-tension at nut.

string winder Device to assist in the speedy winding of a string onto the tuner's string-post.

struts (strutting) Classical-guitar term for braces. See *braces*.

stud tailpiece (stop tailpiece) Type of tailpiece fixed to solid or semi-acoustic guitar top, either as a single combined bridge/tailpiece unit, or else as a unit separate from the bridge.

sunburst Decorative paint finish in which (usually) pale-colored center graduates to darker edges.

superstrat Updated, hot-rodded Fender Stratocaster-inspired design popularized in the '80s with more frets, deeper cutaways, more powerful pickups in a revised layout, and a high-performance (locking) vibrato system.

sustain Length of time a string vibrates. Purposeful elongation of a musical sound, either by playing technique or electronic processing.

sustain block (inertia block) Metal block under the bridgeplate of a floating vibrato (vintage-style Fender, for example) which, because the vibrato is not permanently fixed to the body,

replaces the body mass necessary for sufficient string sustain.

sympathetic resonances Sounds produced by open strings that are not struck.

syncopation Displacement of the normal beat.

synth access Guitar type with a built-in pickup to enable connection to an external synthesizer unit.

synthesizer Electronic instrument for sound creation, using analog techniques (oscillators, filters, amplifiers) or digital techniques (FM or harmonic synthesis, sample-plus-synthesis etc). Preset synthesizers offer a selection of pre-programmed sounds which cannot be varied; programmable types allow the user to vary and store new sounds. Guitar synthesizers at first attempted to build much of the required circuitry into the guitar itself, but the trend now is to synth-access systems. See *synth access*.

system vibrato See *vibrato system*.

tab (tablature) System of musical notation indicating the position of the fingers on frets and strings.

table See *plate, soundboard, top*.

tag See *lug*.

tags See *hang-tags*.

tailpiece Unit on body separate from bridge that anchors strings. See also *trapeze tailpiece, stud tailpiece*.

taper Of a potentiometer: determines how smoothly the resistance is applied as the control is turned down. Most modern pots use a logarithmic taper as opposed to a linear taper.

tapped pickup See *coil-tap*.

Tele Abbreviation of Fender Telecaster, so universally used that Fender have trademarked the name and use it themselves.

thinline Hollowbody electric guitar with especially narrow body depth; term coined originally by Gibson for its Byrdland model introduced in 1955.

three-position switch See *three-way switch*.

three-way switch (three-position switch) Selector switch that offers three options.

through-neck (thru-neck) Neck that travels the complete length of a guitar, "through" the body, and usually with "wings" added to complete the body shape.

tigerstripe Dramatic figure, usually on maple. See *flame*.

timbre Tone quality or "color" or "flavor" of a sound.

tin To apply solder to a wire before making the soldered joint.

tobacco burst Dark red-to-brown sunburst finish originally popularized by Gibson.

toggle switch Type of selector switch that "toggles" between a small number of options. It is sometimes called a leaf switch.

Tolex Trade name of vinyl covering manufactured by DuPont corporation and commonly used by Fender (and some others) on guitar amps and hardshell cases. (Often generically – if incorrectly – used to refer to any vinyl amp covering.)

tone wood Fancy name for wood used in making musical instruments; wood purported to have superior tonal qualities.

top Vibrating face of the guitar. See *soundboard, plate*.

top nut See *nut*.

tranny Short for "transistorized."

Nickname given to solid-state circuitry or equipment.

transcription Adaptation of music originally written/intended for instruments other than guitar; the piece of music that emerges from such an adaptation.

transducer Unit that converts one form of energy to another; the term is sometimes used generically for piezo-electric pickups, but technically applies to any type of pickup or loudspeaker, etc. See *magnetic pickup*, *piezo pickup*.

transverse bar Bar glued across back of guitar, especially in classical guitar building.

trapeze tailpiece Simple tailpiece of trapezoidal shape.

treble-bleed cap Simple circuit where capacitor (sometimes with an additional resistor) is attached to volume control potentiometer and thus retains high frequencies when the volume control is turned down.

treble pickup See *bridge pickup*.

tree-of-life inlay Very decorative inlay on guitar fingerboard depicting vine-like foliage. Interpreted by a number of manufacturers over the years on high-end models, for example the PRS Rosewood Limited.

tremolo (tremolo arm, tremolo system, trem) Erroneous but much-used term for vibrato device/system. The musical definition of tremolo is the rapid repetition of a note or notes. Perhaps this is why Fender applied the name to its amplifier effect, which is a regular variation in the sound's volume.

triode Tube (valve) containing three functional elements, and most common in the preamp circuits of guitar amplifiers in the form of "dual triodes" – tubes which contain two triodes in a single glass bottle.

truss-rod Metal rod fitted inside the neck, almost always adjustable and which can be used to control neck relief.

truss-rod cover Decorative plate covering truss-rod access hole, usually on headstock.

tube US term for the electrical component that the British call a

valve; an abbreviation of electron(ic) vacuum tube. In a guitar amp, a tube amplifies the input signal by regulating the flow of electrons.

Tune-o-matic Gibson-originated bridge adjustable for overall string height as well as for individual string intonation.

tuner Device almost always fitted to the headstock, one per string, that alters a string's tension and pitch. Also called machine head or (archaically) tuning peg. See also *electronic tuner*.

tuner button Knob that the player moves to turn the tuner mechanism in order to raise or lower a string's pitch.

TV finish Translucent off-white or "limed mahogany" finish used by Gibson on low and medium-priced solidbodys in the '50s, especially certain Les Paul models.

twang Essential element of early rock'n'roll guitar tone, achieved by using bridge pickup on Fender Strat, Gretsch 6120 or similar, and popularized by players such as Duane Eddy.

tweed Linen material used primarily by Fender – but by some other makers as well – to cover guitar cases and amplifier cabinets, originally in the '50s. The term is now generally used to define an amp from that period (such as a '59 Bassman), or the sonic characteristics produced by such amps, or the emulation of such characteristics in modern amps.

12-fret/14-fret Refers to the point at which a flat-top acoustic guitar's neck joins the body.

twin-neck See *double-neck*.

two-pole See *pole*.

'ud Arabic stringed instrument introduced into Spain by the Moors, with important consequences for lute making.

unwound string See *wound string*.

up-bend Upward shift in the strings' pitch brought about by using a vibrato.

up-market See *high-end*.

upper bout See *bout*.

upscale See *high-end*.

valve Short for "thermionic valve;" the British term for electron tube. See *tube*.

Variac Trademarked variable AC transformer. Not a safety transformer.

Varitone Six-way switch fitted to some Gibson semi-solid guitars, typically the ES-345 and ES-355. Linked to network of chokes and capacitors, makes guitar sound like it's played down a telephone line.

varnish Protective and decorative surface applied to guitar bodies. Includes shellac, applied by French polishing, to man-made urethane, applied by spray.

vibrato (slush lever, trem, tremolo, tremolo arm, vibrato bridge, vibrato system, wang bar, whammy) Bridge and/or tailpiece which alters the pitch of the strings when the attached arm is moved. Vibrato is the technically correct term because it means a regular variation in pitch. Also used to define this effect when contained within a guitar amp.

vibrato system System comprising locking vibrato bridge

unit, friction-reducing nut, and locking tuners.

virtuoso Instrumental performer with excellent technical abilities.

V-joint One method of fixing head to neck, or neck to body. More complex than normal splice-joint.

V-neck Describes shape of cross-section of neck on, typically, some older Strats, Teles, and Martins.

waist In-curved shape near the middle of the guitar body, usually its narrowest point.

wang bar See *vibrato*.

Watt Unit of electrical power, commonly used to define the output of guitar amps, the power-handling capabilities of speakers, etc. Technically, the rate that energy is transferred (or work is done) over time, equal to a certain amount of horse-power, or joules per second. Named for James Watt, British pioneer of steam power.

western red cedar Not a cedar at all, but Thuya plicata, the North American arbor vitae, a conifer. First used as a soundboard material by classical guitar maker José Ramírez III and now used by many classical (and some flat-top) builders.

whammy See *vibrato*.

wolf note (wolf tone, dead note) Note with a sound unpleasantly different from or less resonant than those around it. The phenomenon is much affected by instrument construction, and can be indicative of a minor flaw in a guitar.

wrapover bridge Unit where strings are secured by wrapping them around a curved bar.

X-brace Pattern of bracing in an "X" shape, popularized by Martin.

zero fret Extra fret placed in front of the nut. It provides the start of the string's speaking length and creates the string height at the headstock end of the fingerboard. In this instance the nut is simply used to determine string spacing. Used by some manufacturers to make the tone of the open string and the fretted string more similar.

An *italic* page number indicates an illustration. A **bold** page number indicates a main text entry in the guitar manufacturers directory. The acts with which guitarists have played are not generally noted in the main text, but more conveniently are shown in this index, in brackets after the guitarist's name. Only the principal acts with which the guitarist is or has been associated are noted.

ABC (band) 469
Abercrombie, John 281
Abreu, Sergio and Eduardo 10
Acoustic 300
 Black Widow 300
Acoustic (amps) 49
Acoustic Control Corp 300
acoustic-electric guitars 24–25
acoustic guitar amps 53
action 77
 adjustment 70, 77
Acousti-Lectric 390
Adams, Bryan 166–167
Adams, Derek 476
Ade, Sunny 261
Airline **300**, 524
 unnamed model 300
Akai 321, 499
Akkerman, Jan (Focus) 385, 386
Alamo **300**
 Titan 300
Alamo Music Products 525
Albanus 20
Alembic 33, **300-302**
 active electronics 302
 multi-laminate construction 302
 Series I 301, 302
 Series II 302
Allman, Gregg (Allman Brothers) 574
Almeida, Laurindo 255
altered tunings 123, 134–139
Alvarez **302**, 582
 Dana AE650 "Scoop" 302, 303
Ampeg 46, 49, **303**
 and Bill Lawrence 303
 and Burns 303
 and Dan Armstrong 303
 Dan Armstrong "Black" 303
 Dan Armstrong "See-through" 302, 303
 De Luxe Wild Dog 303
 and Harmony 475
 Patch 2000 synthesizer 302, 470
Anastasio, Trey (Phish guitarist) 56
Anderson, Tom 40, 41, 571
Andrews, David 465

Anthrax 226
Antoria 468, 484
Apollo 333
Arai, Shiro 305
Arbiter 362, 476
Arbor 322
archtop acoustics 20–23
Archer, Gem (Oasis) 425
Archies, The 324
Arden, Suzi 553, 557
Aria **305-307**, 337, 484
 Diamond ADSG12T 304
 Korea production 306
 Nashville/615 Custom 307
 Pro II Fullerton series 307
 Pro II Knight Warrior 305
 Pro II M-650T 307
 Pro II PE Prototype series 305
 Pro II PE-160 304
 Pro II PE-175 306
 Pro II PE-1000 305
 Pro II Rev Sound RS-850 305
 Pro II Thor Sound TS-500 305
 Pro II Titan TA-60 306
 Pro II Urchin series 306, 306
 Pro II Urchin Deluxe 306
 Pro II ZZ Bladerunner 307
 Pro II ZZ Deluxe 307
 Ventures models 307
Armadillo Enterprises 331
Armiger, Billy 533
Armstrong, Billy Joe (Green Day guitarist) 150
Armstrong, Dan 303, 328
Artzt, Alice 10
AR Musical Enterprises 505
Ash, Sam 458
Ashdown (amps) 53
Astron Engineering 441
atmospheric conditions (effect of on guitar) 115
Atkins, Chet 205, 218–219, 224, 329, 342, 377, 430, 436, 448, 449, 453, 454, 460, 461
Auerswald, Jerry 323
Award-Session 50
Avalon 510
Avnet 443, 464

Bad Cat (amps) 47
Baldwin **309**
 and Burns 309, 315
 Double Six 308
 and Gretsch 457, 460
 Marvin 308
Bar Rashi, Avraham 441
Barden, Joe (pickups) 97
Barker, Bill 20
Barnes, George 463
Barre, Martin (Jethro Tull) 574

Barrios, Agustin 11, 267
Barrueco, Manuel 278
Barth, Paul 511, 550
Bartolini **309**
 unnamed model 308
 bass guitar 300
 six-string 324, 326
Basie, Count 21
Baxter, Shaun 236
BBE Sound Inc 365, 387
B.C. Rich 306, **309-310**, 322
 Bich NJ 309
 Bich Six 309
 Eagle 309
 Emi 310
 Ignitor 310
 Jeff Cook 310
 Kerry King 310
 Mockingbird Standard 309
 Seagull 309
 Warlock 310
B.C. Rico 310
Beach Boys, The 226
Beach, Reb (Winger) 491
Bean, Travis 491
Beatles, The 45, 51, 166, 337, 338, 359, 363, 369, 386, 446, 554, 557
Beauchamp, George 550
Bebop Deluxe 167
Beck, Jeff (Yardbirds) 29, 55, 141, 216, 377, 425, 447, 496
Beck, Joe 323
Becker, Jason (David Lee Roth) 318, 319
Beckmen 579
Beecher, Frank/Frannie (Bill Haley's Comets) 395, 403
Bell, Vinnie 322, 323, 327, 328
Bellson, Julius 396
bends (string bending)
 blues 198–199
 metal 233–234
 rock-pop 168–170
Benedetto, Robert 22, 23, 25, 468
Benson, George 24, 281, 293, 396, 486, 487
Benson, Ray (Asleep At The Wheel) 572
Bensusan, Pierre 123, 129, 138
Berardi, Dennis 507, 509
Berlin, Maurice 326, 391
Bernabé, Paulino 12, 13
Berry, Chuck 25, 142, 221, 224, 226 397, 403
Berryman, David 436
Bettencourt, Nuno (Extreme) 42, 244–245, 580, 581
Betts, Dickie (Allman Brothers) 532
Bigsby **311**, 349, 426
 Billy Byrd 311
 and Fender 349
 "Grady Martin" double-neck 311
 and Magnatone 311, 511

"Merle Travis" guitar 311
 vibrato 311
Bigsby, Paul 311, 349, 511
Bigsby vibrato 30, 35, 89
Birch, John 500
Bishop, Dickie (Lonnie Donegan) 478
Bishop, Elvin 319
BKL Corp 507
Black, J.W. 380
Black Sabbath 226
Blackmore, Ritchie (Deep Purple, Rainbow) 141, 226, 242, 481, 500
Blade 332
Blair, Tony 505
Blanda, George 377
Bloomfield, Mike (Butterfield Blues Band, Electric Flag) 179, 412
Blucher, Steve 103
Boatright, Ray 517
Bogue, Rex 484, 485
Bolan, Marc (T Rex) 145, 315, 410, 574, 587
bolt-on necks
 adjustment 72–74
 construction 26-28
 guitars 26–29
Bond **312**
 Electraglide 312
Bond, Andrew 312
Booker T. and the M.G.s 27
bop (bebop) 294–295
Boss 55, 56–59
boutique amps 46–47
Bowie, David 147
bracing patterns 17
Bran, Ken 45
brass saddles 26
Bream, Julian 269
Brian Moore **313**
 Guitar synthesizer 313
 M/C1 312
bridge saddles 90
Britton, Chris (Troggs) 315
Brooks, Larry 381
Brown, Joe 462, 481
Bruno, Jimmy 23
Bryant, Jimmy 205, 351, 511, 567
Buchanan, Roy 27, 216, 466
Buck, Peter (REM) 164, 557, 559
Budda (amps) 47
Buegeleisen & Jacobson 505
Bullock, Hiram 323
Bunker, Dave 491
Burge, Chuck 431
Burnette, Billy (Fleetwood Mac) 342
Burns **313-317** (see also Burns London, Burns UK, Jim Burns)
 active pre-amp 315
 and Ampeg 303
 Artiste 314
 and Baldwin 309, 315
 Bison 28, 313, 314
 Ike Isaacs Short-

Scale 313
 Marvin 314, 315
 Split Sonic 313
 Vibra Artiste 313
Burns, Jim 313, 317, 384, 476, 483
Burns London (original) 314, (recent) 317
 Drifter 317
 Nu-Sonic 316, 316
 Club Marquee 315
 30/50 Anniversary 317
Burns UK 315, 563
 Flyte 314
Burnside 466
Burrell, Kenny 391, 396
Burton, James (Ricky Nelson, Elvis Presley) 205, 208, 371, 378, 378
Bernard Butler (Suede) 35, 413
Burke, Dick 553
Buzz Feiten tuning system 571
Byrd, Billy (Ernest Tubb) 311, 404
Byrd, Charlie 255
Byrds, The 36

capo 124
Caiola, Al 334, 335, 340
Campbell, Glen 527
Campbell, Tim 533
Cantrell, Jerry (Alice In Chains) 387
Capital 391
Carlton, Larry 413, 572
Carson, Bill (Hank Thompson) 351
Carter, Maybelle 205
Carvin amps
 Belair 45
 Legacy 47, 49
Carvin guitars 33, **317-319**
 DC-200C 318
 hex-pole pickups 318
 SGB3 317
 2-MS double-neck 318
 V220T 318
 Allan Holdsworth 319
Casady, Jack (Jefferson Airplane) 300
cases 114
Casey, Bert T. 513
Casio **319**
 PG-380 synthesizer 319
CBS 362
CBS/Arbiter 476
Celebrity By Ovation 527
Celestion speakers 45, 47, 48
Chandler **319**
 Austin Special 319
 555 model 319
Chandler, Charlie 106
channel switching 44, 46–47, 49–51
Chaquico, Craig (Jefferson Starship) 309, 318
Charney, Alan 508
Charvel **320-321**, 482, 496, 499

Contemporary Spectrum 321
 and Edward Van Halen 320, 321
 Fusion Custom 320
 Model-4 320
 Model-5 320
 Model-6 320
 San Dimas 321
 and Steve Vai 489
 and superstrats 320
 Surfcaster 321
Charvel, Wayne 320, 496
Charvette By Charvel 321
Chinery Collection 23
chord progressions
 acoustic (folk) 124–127
 blues 196–197
 jazz 282–285
Christian, Charlie (Benny Goodman) 24, 281, 283, 388, 392
Chusin Gakki 484
Cipollina, John (Quicksilver Messenger Service) 317, 415, 418
Citron, Harvey 465, 574
Clapton, Eric (John Mayall, Yardbirds, Cream) 15, 30, 35, 47, 51, 141, 179, 367, 371, 374, 377, 404, 405, 411, 412, 416, 417, 418, 421, 502, 574, 587
Clark (amps) 47
Clark, Roy 527
Clarke, Gilby (Guns N'Roses) 584
Clash, The The Clash 414
Class Axe 310
classical guitars 10–13, 68–69
cleaning
 electronics 92
 fingerboard 111
 finishes 110
 hardware 112
 strings 111
CLF Research 521
Cobain, Kurt (Nirvana) 52, 141, 381
Cochran, Eddie 141, 150, 221, 453
Codé 329
Collen, Phil (Def Leppard) 490, 499
Collings 18
Collins, Albert 179, 188
Collins, Bootsy 59
Collins, John (Nat King Cole) 396
Collins, Larry 317
Coloursound Tone Bender 54, 55
Continental 502
Cooder, Ry 253, 259, 513
Cook, Jeff (Alabama) 310, 319, 530
Coombes, Gaz (Supergrass) 315, 316
Coral **322**
 Sitar 322, 323

index

Cort **322-323**, 515
Larry Coryell Thinline *323*
and Steinberger 322
Cortez 322
Coryell, Larry *300*, 319, 323
Coxon, Graham (Blur) 379
Crate *52*
Craven, Dudley 45
Cray, Robert 179, *197*
Cream 35, 166
Crenshaw, Marshall 319
Cromwell 391
Crooks, Bob 566
Cropper, Steve (Booker T & The MGs, Otis Redding) 27, 164, 371, 531
Crow, Sheryl *146–147*
Crosby, Robin (Ratt) 498
Cry Baby Wah *56*
CSL 484
Cuccurullo, Warren (Duran Duran) 567
Cummings, Patrick 313
Curtis, Arnold B. 513
Curtis, Ian (Joy Division) 577
Custom Kraft **323**, 333, 504
Ambassador Vibramatic *323*

D'Addario 62
DADGAD tuning 138–139
Dallas/Arbiter Fuzz Face 54, *55*
Dale, Dick 361, 377
Dallas(-Arbiter) 384, 476, 578
Danelectro *29*, *32*, **324-329**, 461
amp-in-case guitar 328
Bellzouki 227, 328
Dan Armstrong models 328
and Evets 329
Guitarlin *328*
Hodad *329*
long horn 326
Long Horn Model 4623 six-string bass *326*
and MCA 328
and Sears 324, 328
short-horn 326
"short-horn" double-neck *326*
and Silvertone 324, 326, 564
Sitar *328* (see also Coral)
six-string bass 324
Standard 3021 *325*
U-1/U-2 *324*
U-3 *328*, *329*
and Vinnie Bell 328
D'Angelico *20*, *21*, *25*, **329**
unnamed model *239*
D'Angelico, John 329
Daniel, Nathan I. (Nat) 322, 324, 329, 335
Dantzig, Jol 470
D'Aquisto *20*, *23* **329**

Centura Electric *329*
D'Aquisto, Jimmy *329*, 375, 470
Darrell, Dimebag (Pantera) 51, 57, *581*
Davis, Miles 281
Davoli 510
Dawes Tom (The Cyrkle) 322
Dean **330-331**, *581*
Bel Aire *330*
Cadillac Ultima *330*
Golden Elite *330*
ML *330*
V *330*
Z *330*
Dean, Paul 509
DeArmond **331**, 468
M-75 *330*
pickups 445, 472, 512, 313
DeArmond, Harry 445, 468
Deaver, Claude 568
Deaver, Russ 567
Deep Purple *157*
Deering 573
Deftones 226
Delmonte, Syd *562*
DeLorenzo 506
Deniz, Frank 478
Denney, Dick *510*
Derakh, Amir (Orgy) *529*
Derringer, Rick 309
Deurloo, Jim 436
Devlin, Adam (Bluetones) *559*
Devo *149*
Diamond S 515
Dickerson Brothers 511
Diddley, Bo *39*, *447*, 458, 482
Go Bo Diddley *447*
Digitech 59
DiMarzio (pickups) *38*, 94–95, 103 472, 515
DiMeola, Al 236, 319, *428*, 533
Dixon, Willie 179
Dobro 512, 524
Domino **331**
Baron *331*
California Rebel *331*
Donahue, Jerry 208, 377, 378
Donegan, Lonnie 478
Dopyera, Ed 512, 523
Dopyera, John 523
Dopyera, Louis 524, 568
Dopyera, Rudy 512, 523
Douglas, Jon 368
Draper, Rusty 573
dreadnought 14, *15–19*
Dream Theater 226, 229, 231
Dronge, Alfred 463, 465
dropped D tuning 136–137
Dr. Z (amps) 47
Duffy, Billy 25, (The Cult) *450*
Duhamell, Art 511
Dumble (amps) 47
Dunlop, Jim 55
Dunnery, Frank (It Bites) 384
Dupree, Cornell 584
Dwight **331-332**
unnamed model *331*
Dyna 487
Dynacord 582

Dylan, Bob *130*

Eagles, 14, 208
Earle, Steve 19
Easton, Elliot (Cars) 509
Eco Timber 517
Eddy, Duane 141, 326, 339, 453, *461*, *462*, 463
Edge (U2) (U2 guitarist) 54, *150*, *371*
Edwards, Clyde 459
Edwards, Nokie (Ventures) 518
Eggle **332**
Berlin Pro *332*
Eggle, Patrick 332
Egmond **332**
3 model *332*
Elienberg, Charles **300**
Eko **333**
and Vox 577
700/4V *332*
Electar 324, **333**, 335
and pickup polepieces 333
Century *333*
Electra **333**
Lady XV1RD *333*
and Westone 582
Electraphone 335
Electro **333**, 551
ES-17 *333*
Electro-Harmonix *54–59*
electronics (guitar) 94–101
Elger Guitars 484
Ellis, Herb *306*, 341, 409
EMG (pickups) 94, 97
Emmett, Rik (Triumph) 330
Emperor 226
Engelhardt, Robert 504, 525, 564
Entertainment Music 531
Epiphone 324, **334-345**
brand revived 341
Caiola Custom *340*
Casino 37, 337, *338*, 339
Century 335
Coronet 331, 335, 336, *341*, *342*
Crestwood 336, *337*
Crestwood Custom *337*
Crestwood Deluxe *338*
and Dwight 331
and Electar 333, 335
Emperor 21, 25, *335*
ET-270 *341*
Flying V *343*
Genesis 338, *342*
and George Van Eps 459
Gibson "copies" *341*, 342
Jorma Kaukonen Riviera Deluxe 345
Les Paul model *343*
Les Paul ES *343*
"map" guitar 341
Masterbilt 334
move to Philadelphia 335
"New York" pickup 336
Olympic 337
Professional *340*

Riviera 37, *340*
Riviera 12-string *341*
Scroll 338, *342*
Sheraton 36–37, *336*, 344
Sorrento *337*
Spirit 340
Spotlight *342*
Supernova 343, *345*
USA Coronet *342*
Wilshire 337
Zephyr 24, 25, *334*, 335
Zephyr Deluxe
Regent *334*
Zephyr Emperor
Regent *334*
Erlewine, Dan 82
Ernie Ball/Music Man guitars
Albert Lee 27
Axis Sport *40*, *41*
Esanu, Warren 534
ESP 330, **345**
Ltd M-250 *345*
Esteso, Domingo *13*
Everly, Ike 205
Evets Corp 329
Excel 539

Faces, The 147
Fahey, John 123, *136*
fan-strut *12*
Farlow, Tal 404, 418, 420
Tal *420*
Farner, Mark (Grand Funk Railroad) 574, *575*, 576
Fass Corp 446
Feiten, Buzz 571
Fender amps
Acoustasonic 53
Bassman 45, 48, 53
Champ 45
Champion 46
Cyber-Twin 53
Deluxe *44*, 45
Deluxe-90 *51*
Princeton 46
Pro 46
Super Amp *46*
Super Reverb 45
Fender guitars **346-383**
acoustic guitars 366, 370
American Classic Stratocaster *383*
American Classic Telecaster *379*
American Standard Stratocaster 374, 376
American Standard Telecaster 374, 376
Big Apple Stratocaster *381*
and Bigsby 349
Blue Flower Stratocaster 373
Blue Flower Telecaster *361*
Broadcaster 26, *346*, 349, 350
Bronco *360*
Bullet 372
CBS acquires company 362-363
CBS sells company 375
Closet Classics 381

Contemporary Stratocaster 376
Coronado 360, 368
Custom 362, 369
custom colors 349, 356-359, 369, 370
Custom Esquire 359
Custom Shop 374, 377, 380, 381
Custom Team 377, 378
Custom Telecaster 355, 359, 366, 372
Cyclone 379, 383
Danny Gatton Telecaster *378*
D'Aquisto 329, *372*, 375
and De Armond 331
D'Aquisto Custom *23*
Deluxe Telecaster *366*, 372
Dick Dale Stratocaster 377
Duo-Sonic *350*, 355
Electric-Acoustic Telecaster *381*
Electric XII 356, *357*, 365-366
Elite Stratocaster *370*, *371*, 374
Elite Telecaster *371*, 374
Eric Clapton Stratocaster 374, 377
Esprit 375
Esquire *346*, *347*, 349, 350, *354*
Fat Strat 380
Flame 375
and G&L 387
hang-tag *351*
and Heartfield 476
Hendrix Voodoocaster 377
HLE Stratocaster 378
Jaguar *355*, *357*, 359-360, *381*
Jag-Stang *381*
Japan production 373, 374, 376, 381
Jazzmaster *351*, *353*, 355, *381*
Jazzmaster pickup *32*
James Burton Telecaster 378
Jeff Beck Stratocaster *377*
Jerry Donahue Telecaster 377, 378
Jimi Hendrix Stratocaster 382
John Jorgensen 383
Katana *373*
Lead 371, 372
LTD 361, 369
Marauder *357*, 366
"Mary Kaye" Stratocaster *349*, 357, 380, 381
Master Built 377
Master Series 375
Mexico factory 376, 379
Montego 369
Moto Stratocaster 379
Muddy Waters Telecaster 377
Musicmaster *350*, 355

Mustang 356
Paisley Red Telecaster *361*
pedal-steel guitars 359, 370
Performer 372, 376
Power Tele 379
Prodigy 376, 378
Relic 380, *380*, 381
Rhinestone Stratocaster 368
Richie Sambora Stratocaster *382*
Robben Ford 378
Rosewood Telecaster *368*
Standard Stratocaster *370*
Starcaster 368, 372
Stevie Ray Vaughan Stratocaster 377, 379
Stock Team 377, 378
Strat 369
Strat Plus 376, 377
Strat Ultra 376
Strat XII 373
Stratocaster 28–29, 31, 221, *348*, 349, 352, 353-355, *353*, 358, 359, 364, 365, 368, 369, 370, 371, 372, 373, 374, 375, 376, 377, 379, 380, 381, 382
Strat pickup 27, 92
Swinger *362*, 369
Telecaster 26, 27, 29, 52, *347*, 349, 351, *354*, 355, 361, 362, 363, 366, 371, 374, 375, 378, 379, 381
Telecaster bridge 26, 85 90, 98
Telecaster Custom 26, 27,
Telecaster pickups 26, 27, 28, 94–95, 98
Telecaster Thinline 36, 37, *362*, 366, 368
Tex-Mex Stratocaster 382
Toronado 379, *383*
Vintage reissues 373
Vintage 57
Stratocaster 370
Waylon Jennings Telecaster 377
Yngwie Malmsteen Stratocaster 375
25th Anniversary Stratocaster *369*
40th Anniversary Telecaster 375, 377
52 Telecaster *371*
Fender Japan 373, 378, 381, 476, 565, 571
Fender, Leo 26, 46
Fenton-Weill **384**
Triplemaster *384*
Fernandes **384-385**
Fernandez, Julio (Spyro Gyra) 342
Ferry, Bryan (Roxy Music) *469*
FET electronics 51
Finnerty, Barry 584
Firstman catalog *518*
Fishman, Larry 528
fingerboard radius 75–76
fingerpicking 130–133

Fischer, Paul *10*, 13
Fishman *19*, *41*
Fisk, Eliot *274*
Fitzgerald, Ella *21*
flamenco 13
Fleetwood Mac 179
Flick, Vic 141
flightcases *46*, *114*
floating vibratos 83
Floyd Rose *29*, 40, 86–87, *374*, 507, 508, 509
Focus 152
Ford, Lita 309, 319
Forsyth, Brian "Damage" (Kix) 539
Frampton, Peter 333, 440, 533
Framus **385-386**
  Jan Akkerman *385*, 386
  Melodie nine-string *385*
  Organtone 385, 386
  Strato Deluxe *385*
  and Warwick 386
Freed, Jerry 482
Frehley, Ace (Kiss) 440, 574, *579*, 580
French polish 23
frets *29*, 77
Fret-King 332
Fretted Industires 579
Frey, Glenn (Eagles) 559
Fripp, Robert (King Crimson) *399*, 425
Frisell, Bill 281, 507
Fujigen (Gakki) 374, 376, 476, 484, 562, 565
Fullerton, George 348, 365, 387
Futurama **387**, 469

G&L 365, **387**, 521
  ASAT *387*
  BBE acquires company 387
  Broadcaster *387*
  Cavalier *387*
  Comanche *386*
  F-100 *386*, 387
  Rampage *387*
Gabrels, Reeves (David Bowie) *41*, *528*, 529
Gabriel, Peter 259
Gallagher, Noel (Oasis) *142–143*, 336, 343, *344*
Gallagher, Rory (Taste) 468
Gallup, Cliff 221
Gambale, Frank 489, 491
Garcia, Jerry (Grateful Dead) 324, 572
Garland, Hank 396, 404
Gatton, Danny 216, 378
Gibbons, Billy (ZZ Top) 384
Gibson **388-440**
  Alnico pickup 395
  Alpha Q-3000 *436*
  Barney Kessel 418, *420*
  B.B. King Lucille *434*
  Byrdland *34*, 35, 36, *396*, *401*, 403, 404
  Charlie Christian

pickup 389, 391
and Chet Atkins 391, 460
Chet Atkins CEC *12*, 13,
Chet Atkins Country Gentleman 435, 437
CMI acquires company 391
CMI merger to make Norlin 426
Corvus *432*, 434
custom colors 422
Custom Shop 438, 439
and cutaway body 391
Double Electric Hawaiian lap-steel *389*
double-necks 412, 415-416, 418, 419
EDS-1275 double-neck *412*, *418*, *419*
EH-150 lap-steel *389*
EH Electric Hawaiian guitars 391
and Epiphone 335, 336, 407
ES Artist *430*, 432
ES-5 *390*, *391*, 393
ES-5 Switchmaster 393, *397*, 398
ES-135 *437*
ES-150 *24*, *388*, *389*, 391
ES-175 *24*, *25*. *391*, *392*, 393, 404
ES-225 34, 36
ES-225T *403*
ES-295 *395*, 400
ES-300 *25*, *390*
ES-330 *36*, *37*, *39*
ES-335 *412*, 413-414, *413*, *421*, 422
ES-335TN *35*
ES-345 *37*, *39*, *413*
ES-350 *24*, *36*, *221*, *390*, 393
ES-350T *397*, 403
ES-355 *37*, *39*, *413*, *414*, 434
Explorer 409-410, *411*, 431
Explorer Heritage *432*
Firebird models 420-425
Firebird I "non-reverse" *425*
Firebird I "reverse" 420, *422*
Firebird III "reverse" 420
Firebird III "non-reverse" *425*
Firebird V *32*, 33
Firebird V "non-reverse" *425*
Firebird V "reverse" 420, *422*
Firebird VII "non-reverse" *425*
Firebird VII "reverse" 420, *423*, 440
and floating pickguard *387*
Flying V 30, *31*, 409-410, *410*, 424, 423, *433*, 440
Flying V Gothic 440
"Futura" *409*

Gothic Series *438*
Historic Collection 435, 437
Historic Collection Firebird VII *440*
Historic Collection Les Paul Standard *437*
humbucking pickup *27*, *92*, 97, *398*, 400, 404, 407
J-45 14
J-200 (Super Jumbo) *9*, 14, *15*
Jimmy Page Les Paul *403*, 440
Joe Perry Les Paul *439*, 440
Johnny Smith 20
L-00 15
L-1 14
L-5 20, *21*, *25*
L-5 archtop acoustic *390*
L-5CES *393*, 395, 396, *414*
L-5S 429
L-6S *428*, 431
and Les Paul 396-401
Les Paul 25, 28, 29, *30*
Les Paul Aged 40th Anniversary 438
Les Paul Artisan *428*
Les Paul Artist *430*, 432
Les Paul Custom *395*, *398*, 401, 407, *426*
Les Paul DC Standard *440*
Les Paul Deluxe *426*, 427
Les Paul gold-top *394*, 400, *426*
Les Paul Heritage Standard 326 *431*, 432-433
Les Paul Junior double-cutaway 30, 411, *414*
Les Paul Junior single-cutaway *396*, 401
Les Paul Personal 428
Les Paul Pro Deluxe 430
Les Paul Professional 428
Les Paul Recording *427*, 428
Les Paul reissues 426, 435
Les Paul Signature *427*, 429
Les Paul Special double-cutaway 31, 411, *414*
Les Paul Special single-cutaway *396*, 403
Les Paul Spotlight Special *432*
Les Paul Standard 30, *402*, *403*, 404, *405*, 406, 407, 408, 409, 411-413, *434*
Les Paul Studio Lite 435, 437

Les Paul Studio Lite/M-III *435*, 437
Les Paul TV *403*, 411
Les Paul 25/50 431
Les Paul 30th Anniversary *431*
M-III Standard *437*
Marauder 431
Melody Maker 416
"Moderne" 410-411, 433, 435
Moderne Heritage *433*, 435
Modernistic guitars 408-410
Nighthawk Special *438*
P-90 pickup 30, *38*
PAF pickup 407
Peter Frampton Les Paul 440
RD *430*, 431-432
Reissue Outfits 435
Replicas 435
S-1 *428*
SG/Les Paul Custom *415*
SG/Les Paul Junior *415*
SG/Les Pauls 418
SG Special 416
SG Standard *416*, *417*
SG-62 *415*
SG-90D *437*
Slash Les Paul *439*, 440
Sonex-180 433
Spirit II XPL *436*
steel guitars 389
stereo 414
Super 400 *22*, *23*, *25*
Super 400CES *393*, 395, *401*
Super 400CN *24*
Super Jumbo 14,
Tak Matsumoto Les Paul *439*
Tal Farlow 418, *420*
The Les Paul *429*, 430
The SG *431*
Tony Iommi SG 438, *439*
Tune-O-Matic 30, *78*
Tune-o-matic bridge 403
US-1 *436*, 438
Varitone 414
Victory 443
V-II *431*
Wes Montgomery L-5CES *438*, 440
Zakk Wylde Les Paul 438, *439*
59 Flametop Reissue *434*
60 Corvette 438
Gibson, Orville H. 389
Gilbert, John *11*
Gilbert, Paul 239, 244, *246*
Gillis, Brad (Nightranger) 384, 508
Gilmour, David (Pink Floyd) 481, 587
Giltrap, Gordon 123, *136*
Gimpel, Dudley 522
Gipsy Kings 13
Gittler **441**

Gittler, Allan 441
Global 475
Godin 41, **441-442**
  G-1000 *441*
  LG-X 442
  LG-XT 442
  Multiac 442
  Radiator *442*
  synth-access 442
Godin, Robert 441
Godwin **442**
  Super Professional Guitar-Organ *443*
Goldentone 483
Golder, Jack 476, 563
Golub, Jeff (Billy Squier) 508
Goodrick, Mick 281
Gotoh (tuners) 67
Gordon Smith **443**
  Gypsy 60 "SS" *443*
Gordy 443
Gould, Geoff 516, 561
Goya **442**, 464, 469
  Rangemaster *442*
G&L Comanche 28, *29*
Graham, Davey 123, *136*, 138
Graph Tech 87, 89, *90*
Green Day 150
Green, Freddie *21*, 285, 287
Green, Grant *21*
Green, Peter (Fleetwood Mac) 179, *406*
Gretsch **444-461**
  Anniversary *453*, 454
  Astro-Jet *457*
  Beast BST-1000 *460*
  Bikini 456
  Black Falcon 461
  Blue Pearl Sparkle Jet *461*
  Brian Setzer 461
  Broadkaster *459*
  and Chet Atkins 448, 460
  Chet Atkins Country Gentleman *453*, 454, *455*,
  Chet Atkins Deluxe Chet 459
  Chet Atkins Hollow Body *448*, 449, 455
  Chet Atkins Solid Body 448
  Chet Atkins Super Axe *459*
  Chet Atkins Super Chet 459
  Chet Atkins Tennessean 454
  Committee *460*
  Corvette (hollowbody) *444*, 447
  Corvette (solidbody) *455*, 456
  Country Club *445*, 447, *453*, 454, 461
  Country Club stereo *454*
  Country Roc *460*
  custom colors 447
  Duo Jet *38*, *39*, 445-447, *445*, *446*, *447*, 456, 461
  Electro II *444*, 445
  Electromatic Spanish *444*, 445

and Fender 350, 445
Filter'Tron pickup *38*
"Gold Duke" *456*, 458
humbucking pickup 453
Japan production 461
Jet Fire Bird *447*, 457, 461
Melita bridge 447
Monkees 458
Princess 456
Round Up *447*, 461
Silver Jet *447*, *457*, 461
Streamliner *445*, 447
Syncromatic *21*
Grossman, Stefan 123
Grover (tuners) 22, Traveling Wilburys 461
Twist 457
Van Eps seven-string 458
Viking *458*
White Falcon *450*, *452*, *454*, *459*, 461
White Falcon stereo *450*, *454*, *459*
White Penguin *451*, 452
Grimshaw **462**
  Plectric Deluxe *462*
  SS De Luxe 462
Grimshaw, Emile 462
Grissom, David 544
Groehsl 501
Guild **463-468**
  Artist Award 463, *465*, 468
  Benedetto 468
  Benny 468
  Bert Weedon Model *463*
  Blues *39*, *468*
  Bluesbird solidbodies 465, 468
  Brian May MHM-1 *466*
  Brian May Pro 468
  Brian May Signature *467*, 468
  Brian May Special 468
  Brian May Standard 468
  and De Armond 331
  Duane Eddy *463*
  and Epiphone 463
  flat-top acoustics 463
  Flyer *466*
  Johnny Smith Award *462*, 463
  Liberator 466
  M-75 Bluesbird *463*, 465
  M-75 BCG BluesBird *465*
  Roy Buchanan T-200 466
  Nightbird 466
  S series solidbodies 465
  S-70D *466*
  S-100 *465*, 468
  S-100 Carved *465*
  Starfire series 463-464, 468
  Starfire III *464*
  Starfire IV *468*
  Stratford X-350 *462*

Stuart X-550 *24, 463*
Stuart X-700 *468*
Thunderbird *464*
X series archtops 463
X series solidbodies 465
X-79 *466*
Guitar Slim 403
Guitars 1–320
Guy, Buddy 179, *189,* 355
Guyatone **468**, 505
"Les Paul" 468
LG-160T Telstar 468, *469*
LG-350T Sharp Five 468, *469*
G.W. Lyon 581

Hagar, Sammy 330
Haggard, Merle 205
Hagstrom 387, 443, 464, **469-470**
Impala *470*
Kent PB42G *470*
P-46 Deluxe *469*
Patch 2000 synthesizer *470*
Standard *469*
Swede *470*
Viking *470*
Hagstrom, Albin 467
Haley, Bill 221, 222, 395
Hall, Francis (F.C.) 347, 351, 552
Hall, Jim *25*, 281, *290, 391,* 404
Hall, Joe 470
Hall, John 559
Hall, Nicola *11*
Hallmark **470**
Swept Wing *470, 471*
Hamer **470-472**
Chaparral Elite *472*
Duo Tone *41, 472*
multi-string basses 470
Phantom A-5 *472*
Prototype 470, *472*
Special 470
Standard 470, *471*
Steve Stevens 470
Sunburst *39*
Sustainiac system 472
Hamer, Paul 470
Hammett, Kirk (Metallica) 49, 345
Hannon, Frank (Tesla) 343
Harmony 37, *38, 39,* **470-475**
and Ampeg 475
H65 *472*
H75 *474*
H77 *474*
Meteor 472, *474*
Rebel 474
Rocket H-59 472, *473*
Silhouette 474
and Silvertone 472, 564
Stratotone series 472
Stratotone Jupiter H-49 *473*
Stratotone Newport H-42/1 *473*
Harptone 566
Harris, Emmylou 205
Harrison, George

(Beatles) 337, *358,363, 369,* 386, *387, 446,* 455, 512, *554, 557,* 587
Harvey Thomas **475**
Maltese 475
Riot King 475
Haskett, Chris (Rollins Band) 544
Haskew, Jere 466
Hasselberger, Jeff 484
Havenga, Clarence 396
Havens, Richie *134*
Haycock, Pete (Climax Blues Band) 574, *575*
Haydn, Joseph 270
Hayes, Charlie 351
Hayman 315, **476**, 563
Modular 476
White Cloud 476
1010 476
2020 476
3030 476
Head (Korn) 494
Healey, Jeff 179
Healy, Patrick J. 579
Heartfield **476**
Talon *476*
Hedges, Michael 123, *129, 507*
Helland, Dan 510
Henderson, Marlo (Minnie Ripperton) *484*
Hendrix, Jimi *28,* 56, 58, 141, 160–*161*, 184, 324, 359, 364, 365, 369, 371, 377, 382, 410, *424,* 475, 565, 587
Heritage 436, **476-477**
H-150CM 476, 477
H-535 476
Hershman 443, 464, 469
Hetfield, James (Metallica) 49, 345
Hicks, Tony (Hollies) 577
Hill, Dave (Slade) 315, 500
Hiwatt 48–49
Hoffs, Susanna (Bangles) 559
Hofner 35, **477-481**
A2-L *481*
"Beatle" bass 478, 481
Club *477, 478*
Colorama *478,* 480
Committee *478,* 480
Galaxie 478, *480, 481*
Golden Hofner 478 *479, 480*
Golden Hofner Thin *479*
President *478,* 480
and Selmer 478
Senator *478,* 480
Verithin 478, *480*
175 model *481*
459/VTZ *481*
500/1 bass 478, *481*
Höfner, Josef 477
Höfner, Karl 477
Höfner, Walter 477
Hohner 384
Holdsworth, Allan 239, 281, *292*
Holly, Buddy 221, *348,* 355, 371, 511

Holman-Woodell 510, 511, 582
Hondo (-II) **482**, 562
H-2 *482*
Honeyman-Scott, James *587*
Hooker, John Lee 179, *189,* 336, 345, 403
Hopf **482**
Saturn 63 *482*
Hopf, Dieter 482
Hornstein, Barry 505
Hoshino (Gakki Ten) 483, 566
Hoshino, Junpei 483
Hoshino, Matsujiro 483
Hoshino, Yoshitaro 483
Hotei 384
Houlder, Norman 563
Howe, Greg 246–247
Howe, Steve (Yes, Asia) *25, 322, 392,* 393, 418, 425
Hoyer **482**
35 model *482*
Höyer **482**
35 model *482*
Huff, Dan (David Bowie, Michael Jackson) 213–214, *500*
Huis, John 396, 426
Hull, Everett 303
Hunter, Ian (Mott The Hoople) 475
Hyatt, Dale 347, 365
hybrid
amps 50–51
guitars 34–34

Ibanez effects *54–57*
Ibanez guitars **483-495**
Allan Holdsworth 488
American Master 490
Artist 485, *488, 489,* 491
Artist Professional *485*
Artist 2618 *489*
Artstar 492
Artwood Nouveau 485
Artwood Twin double-neck *484, 485*
AX7 *495*
Axstar AX45 *489*
Blazer 487, 495
Bob Weir *487*
Concert 487
copies 484
Custom Agent 485
Destroyer II 487, *490*
EX series 491
Exotic Wood 490
Firebrand 2348 *485*
Frank Gambale 486
George Benson GB series *487*
Ghostrider 494
and Gibson *487*
Iceman 485, 487, *488,* 494
IMG2010 synthesizer 489, *490*
JEM 489–490, *492*
Joe Pass 487
Joe Satriani 491
John Petrucci 495
JS 10th 491, *493*
Korea production 491, 494
Lee Ritenour 487
Maxxas 489, 490

Millennium series 495
Model-882 483
Musician 487
Musician MC500 *33*
Pat Metheny 495
Paul Gilbert 495
Performer 485, *487*
Pro Line 489, *491*
Professional 485, *487*
Radius 540R *28,* 489, *493, 494*
RG series 489
RG7620 seven-string 489, *491, 494*
Roadstar II 487, 488, *491*
Roadster 487, *488*
Rocket Roll II 487, *489*
RS series 488
RX series 494
S Classic SC420 *495*
Saber 540S 489, *494*
Steve Lukather 488 and Steve Vai 489-490, *491*
Studio 487
Talman 494, *495*
Universe 491, *492, 494*
US custom shop 490-491
USA Custom Graphic 490, 491
Voyager 491
X Series 488, *490*
2347 model *484*
2351 model *484*
2364 model *484*
IMC 38, 482, 499
import/export 115
improvisation (jazz) 288–295
Ingram, John 534
International Music Corp see IMC
intonation 84–86
Iommi, Tony
Iommi, Tony (Black Sabbath) 49, 141, 226, 309, 418, 438, 439, 500
Isaacs, Ike 305, 313, 478
Isbin, Sharon 271

Jackson **496-499**
Custom Shop 499
Dinky 499
Double Rhoads 498 and IMC 499
"Instant Sex" custom *498*
JJP *499*
Kelly 498, 499
King V 498, 499 and Music Man 521
PC3 *499*
Phil Collen 499
Randy Rhoads 496, 498
Soloist *496, 498*
Stealth TH2 28, *29, 499*
Strat Body 496, 498 and superstrats 496, 498
Surfcaster *499*
US Series 499

Vintage Style *499*
Jackson, Grover 320, 496, 499, 581
Jam, The *167*
Jamboree 483
James Tyler **500**
Studio Elite *500*
jangle 166–167
Jansch, Bert *123,*
Jason 484
JBL *47*
J.B. Player 482
Jefferson Airplane 512
Jefferson, Blind Lemon 205
Jenkins 391
Jennings 362, 576, 578
Jennings, Tom 576
Jennings, Waylon 378
Jensen speakers 44, 45, *47*
Jim Burns 315
Scorpion *315*
John Birch **500**
AJS Custom *500*
Johnnie 5 (Marilyn Manson) 495
Johnson 52, *58*
Johnson, Eric 562
Johnstone, Rick 597
Johnson, Robert 14, 179, 205
Jones, Brian (Rolling Stones) 422, 512, *576,* 577
Jones, Mick (Clash, Big Audio Dynamite) 57, 313, 414
Jones, Ralph J. 514
Jones, Stacie *341*
Jordan, Stanley *319,* 572
Jorgenson, John 205
Juskiewicz, Henry 436

Kalamazoo (brand) 391, 425
Kaman 470, 526, 527
Kaneko, Atswo 569
Kapa **500**
Continental 12-string *500*
Kasuga 484
Katz, Sidney M. 503
Kauffman, Doc 347
Kaukonen, Jorma (Jefferson Airplane) 345, 464
Kawai **500-501**
Concert *501*
Moon Sault 501 and Teisco 569
Kay 24, *25, 39,* **501-505**
Barney Kessel Artist 503
Barney Kessel Pro 503
Barney Kessel Special 503
Busker 504
Double Cutaway K592 504
Jazz II K776 502
K-1 archtop 503
K-30 504
K-125 solidbody 503
Seeburg acquires company 504 and Silvertone 564

Solo King *501,* 503
Thin Twin K161 *501,* 503
Up-Beat K8995J *502*
Valco acquires company 504, 524
Kay, John (Steppenwolf) *553,* 559
KayKraft 502
Keifer, Tom (Cinderella) 343
Kelly (Heaven) 498
Kely, Tim (Slaughter) *561*
Kendrick (amps) 47
Kent (Buegeleisen & Jacobson) **505**
742 model 505
Kent (Hagstrom) 469
Kessel, Barney 404 418, *420,* 503
K&F 347
Kiesel 317
Kiesel, Lowell C. 317
Kiesel, Mark 318
Kim Sisters, The *524*
King, Albert *189,* 410
King, B.B. 179, *194,* 413, *434,* 576
King, Freddy 403
Kinks, The 141
Klein **506-507**
BF *506*
Klein, Steve 506
Klier, Johannes 507
Klier, Otto Josef 507
Klira **507**
320 Star Club *507*
Klugh, Earl 12
Kluson (tuners) *67*
Knaggs, Joe 548
Knopfler, Mark 154, 168, *170,* 173
Kohno, Masaru *12, 13*
Kooper, Al 359
Korg 59, 528, 577
Korn 226
Kornbloom, Bernard 323
Kossoff, Paul (Free) 141, 150, *407*
Kottke, Leo 19, 123, *126, 129*
Kramer 322, **507-509**
aluminum necks 507
Baretta 508, 509
DMZ-2000 Custom *508*
Duke *508*
Elliot Easton 509
Floyd Rose Signature 508
Gene Simmons Axe 508
Gorky Park 509
Japan production 508
Korea production 508
Nightswan *509*
Pacer *507,* 508, 509
Richie Sambora 509
Ripley Stereo RSG-1 508, *509*
Stagemaster 508, 509 and superstrats 508
Sustainer *509*
Voyager 508, *509*
450 *507*
650 *507*
Kramer, Duke 460
Kramer, Gary 507
Kraus, Jay 472, 474
Kravitz, Lenny 57

Krieger, Robbie (Doors) 418
Krundaal **510**
  Bikini *510*
Kuhrmeyer, Henry Kay "Hank" 501, 503
Kustom (amps) 50
Kustom 443, 460

LaBaye **510-511**
  2-By-4 *510*
Laine, Denny (Moody Blues, Wings) 558
Lalonde, Larry (Primus) *541*
Lamb, Marv 436
Landau, Michael 500
Lane, Ronnie (Faces) 587
Laney (amps) 49
Lang, Artur 20
Lang, Eddie *282*, 390
LaPlace, Peter 507
LaSiDo 441
Lasner, Rich 516, 586
Lawrence, Bill 303, 385, 386
lead guitar
  blues 188–195
  country 206–207, 216–219
  metal 231–251
  rock-pop 168–177
Leadbelly 19
Led Zeppelin 128, *130*, 138, 160, 168, *176–177*
Lee, Albert *26*, 206, 387, *520, 521, 522*
Lee, Alvin (Ten Years After) *413, 574*
Lee, Ronny 458
Leeper, Edna *15*
Leese, Howard (Heart) 533
legato 239–240
Legg, Adrian *131*
Leo & Ichiro *276*
Lennon, John (Beatles) 337, 369, *446, 477*, 478, 551, 553, *555*, 557, 559
Levin 443
Levinson, Gary 332
Liati, James 509
Lifeson, Alex (Rush) 319, *419, 539*
Lindley, David (Jackson Browne) 513
Line 6
  DL4 Delay *42, 59*
  Flextone II *52*
  POD *52*
  POD Pro *58*
  Vetta *52*
Linsk, Dave (Overkill) 498
Lipsky, Maurice 331
lipstick tube pickup *32*
Llewellyn, Jack 480
Llobet, Miguel *267*
Loar, Lloyd 21
"Log" (Les Paul's guitar) 397, 398
Lorento, Billy see Bill Lawrence
Los Lobos 324
Love, Courtney (Hole) 565
Lover, Seth 404, 407

L.R. Baggs *41*, 551
Lucia, Paco de *13*
Lukather, Steve (Toto) *40*, 488, 521, 522, 523, *572*
Lynch, George (Dokken) 496
Lynch, Steve 319
Lynne, Jeff (ELO) 574
Lynott, Phil *157*
Lyon & Healy 579
Lyon, George Washburn 579

Maccaferri *22, 23*
Macari, Larry & Joe 55
Mack, Lonnie 511
Madeira 468
Maestro
  Fuzz-Tone *54*
  Echoplex *57*
MacAlpine, Tony 226
Magnatone **511**
  Mark V *511*
  and Paul Bigsby 311, 511
  Zephyr X-5 *511*
Malmsteen, Yngwie 236, *242, 375*
Manitas de Plata *13*
Mann, John 536
Manson guitars *18*
Manzanera, Phil (Roxy Music) *423*
Maphis, Joe 317, *518*
Margolis, Carl 506
Marker, Steve (Garbage) *465*
Marker, Wilbur 396
Marr, Johnny (Smiths) 164, 559
Marriott, Steve (Small Faces, Humble Pie) *526*
Mars, Mick (Motley Crue) 410, 465
Marsden, Gerry (Gerry & The Pacemakers) 387, 557
Marshall 404
Marshall amps
  AS50R *53*
  AS100D *53*
  AVT50 *50*
  Bluesbreaker *47*
  ED-1 Compressor *54*
  JCM2000 TSL100 *48*
  JCM2000 TSL602 *47*
  JTM45 *45, 48*
  Plexi *52, 53*
Marshall, Jim 45, 48
Martin, C.F. 10, *14, 16, 17*
Martin guitars 443, **512**
  0-45 *16, 17*
  00-21 *16, 17*
  00-42 *15*
  000-18 *15*
  000-28 14, *16, 17*
  Backpacker *18*
  D-18 14, *17,*
  D-28 *15*
  Ditson Dreadnought *15*
  EM-18 *512*
  GT-75 *512*
  OM-45 *17*
Martin, Grady 311
Martino, Pat 281, *289, 429*
Marvel 531

Marvin, Hank (Shadows) 141, *314*, 315, *352*, 361, 468
Mascis, J. (Dinosaur Jr.) 381
Mason Bernard 310
Mason, Brent 205
Matchless 44, *45*, 47, 53, 58
Matsuda, Doryu 569
Matsuki, Mitsuo 468
Matsumoku 582
Maton **512**
  Wedgetail *512*
Matsumoto, Tak *439*
Maxon 55
May, Bill 512
May, Brian (Queen) *466, 467*
May, Reg 512
Mayall, John (and the Bluesbreakers) *30*, 384, 404
Mayfield, Curtis 319
Mayhem 226
MBT International 482
MCA 322, 328
McCartney, Paul (Beatles, Wings) 332, 337, 338, *339*, 369, 400, *409, 446*, 478, 522
McCarty, Ted 395, 396, 398, 426, *540*, 544, *546, 549*
McGeoch, John 57
McGuinn, Roger (Byrds) 55–56, 164, 557, 559
McGuire, Mike *572*
McHugh, Ted 390
McLaren, John 373
McLaughlin, John (Miles Davis, Mahavishnu Orchestra) 281, 484, 485
McPhee, Tony (Groundhogs) 418
Medley Music 484
Megadeth 226
Melita bridge 447
Melobar **512-513**, *513*
Merson 469
Mesa/Boogie amps
  Dual Rectifier *47*
  MkI 47
  MkIIC *53*
  MkIV 47
  Rect-O-Verb *46*, 47
  Studio 22
  Triple Rectifier *49*
Messenger **513**
  ME-11 *513*
Messina, Jim 527
Messina, Joe 154
Metallica 226
Metheny, Pat 25, 281, *292*, 393, 495
Metropolitan 525
Micro-Frets 500, **514-515**
  Calibrato vibrato *514*
  Golden Melody *514*
  Huntington *515*
  Micro-Nut *514*
  Orbiter *514*
  Signature *515*
  wireless system 515
Mighty Mite **515**
  Mercury *515*
  Motherbucker pickup 515

Miller, Steve 51, 485, *488, 507*
Mills, Crispian (Kula Shaker) 565
Ministry 226
Mitchell, Joni *134–135*, 507
Moats, J.P. 436
modeling amps 52–53
Modulus **516-517**
  carbon-graphite necks 516
Monocoque *516*
  Genesis 516
Monkees, The 324, 456, *458*
Montgomery-Ward 300, 324, 391, 501, 502
Montgomery, Wes 281, 286, *293*, 393, 396, 438, 440
Montrose, Ronnie (Edgar Winter, Montrose) 506, 574
Moore, Brian (guitars) *39*, 313
Moore, Gary (Thin Lizzy) 406, 496, 576
Moore, Oscar (Nat King Cole) 335
Moore, Scotty (Elvis Presley) 25, 221, 224, *393*, 395, *401*, 453
Moore, Thurston (Sonic Youth) *356*
Morse, Steve (Dregs, Deep Purple) 236, 521, 522
Moseley, Loretta 518
Moseley, Semie 300, 512, 517, 566
Mosrite 500, **517-518**
  Brass Rail 518
  copies 518
  custom double-neck *518*
  custom six-string 517, *518*
  custom 12-string 517
  Excellent-65 *518*
  Johnny Ramone 518
  Mark I Ventures *516*, 518
  and Melobar 512
  Model-88 *518*
  Nokie Edwards 518
  and The Ventures 518
  40th Anniversary 518
Mothersbaugh, Mark (Devo) 511
Mottola, Tony 335
Multivox 531
Munky (Korn) *494*
Murphy, Matt "Guitar" 323
Music Man guitars (see also Ernie Ball/Music Man) *27*, 387, **519-523**
  Albert Lee *520, 521*, 522, 523
  Axis *522*
  bass guitars 519, 522
  EVH *519*, 522
  Luke *519*, 523
  Sabre 521
  Silhouette *519*, 522
  Silhouette Special *522*

Steve Morse 522
  StingRay *519*
Music Man amps 49, 51
Music Trader 432
Musical Exchanges 332
Musicraft Inc 513
Musitronics Mu-Tron III *56*, 59
MXR *54*–59

National 46, **523-525**
  bridge pickups 525
  fiberglass guitars 525
  Glenwood-95 *524*
  and Kay 525
  and Metropolitan 525
  Newport-82 *525*
  Newport-84 *524*
  "map-shape" guitars 525
  ResoLectric 525
  resonator guitars 523
  and Rickenbacker 550
  Sonora 524
  Studio-66 *523*
  Val-Trol 525
  Varsity-66 *523*
  Westwood 75 *525*
  Westwood 77 *525*
Navarro, Dave (Red Hot Chili Peppers and Jane's Addiction guitarist) 41, *529*
Navigator 354
neck angle *30*–31
neck relief 70–72
neck shims *73*
Nelson, Carl 573
Nelson, Julius 573
Nelson, Ricky 205
Neoton 386, 387
Nevermore 229
Newman-Jones, Ted 319
NHF Industies 305
Nicastro, Louis J. 504
Nichol, Al (The Turtles) 322
Nielsen, Rick (Cheap Trick) 319, 470, *471*
Nine Inch Nails 226
Nirvana *141*, 166, 226
Noble 510, 578
Nobels Tremolo *56*
Norlin 426, 436, 487
Norsworthy, Phil 82
Nouveau By Gibson 342
Nugent, Ted 25, 45, *533, 539*
nut height 74

Oahu 502
O'Brien, Danny 587
Ojeda, Ed (Twisted Sister) 508
Oasis 142
Old Kraftsman 391
Olmsted, Karl 348
Orange *42*, 49
Orbison, Roy 160
Orlando Quagliardi 582
Ormston 510
Ormston Burns 313, 314
Orpheum 331, 510
Osbourne, Ozzy *231*
Osibisa 261
Ott, Ed (Neon Cross) 342

Ovation *18*, **526-527**
  active electronics 527
  Breadwinner *526*, 527
  bridge pickup 526
  Deacon *526, 527*
  Electric Storm series 526
  electro-acoustic guitars 526, 527
  Preacher *527*
  UK II *527*
  Viper III *527*
Owens, Buck *362*

Pagan, Pete (Skin & Bones) 343
Paganini *267*
Page, Jimmy (Led Zeppelin) *52, 57, 130*, 138, 141, 149, 174, *176–177*, 208, *324, 325, 329, 402, 403*, 416, 440, 513
Page, John 377
parallel bracing *20, 22*
Parkening, Christopher *274*
Parker **528-529**
  Fly Artist *40, 41, 528*
  Fly models 529
  hybrid guitars 528, 529
  and korg 528
  MIDI Fly *529*
  Nitefly *40, 528*
Parker, Ken *40, 41*, 528, 529
Parsons-White B-Bender 354, 369
Pass, Joe 25, *21, 290*, 335, 393, 487
Patton, Charlie 205
Paul, Les 55, 349, *394*, 396-401, 404, 418, 426, 428, 430, 431
PBS 491
Pearl Jam 226
Pearl Works 537
Pearson, Bob 476
Peavey **529-531**
  computer-control building 530
  Cropper Classic *531*
  EVH Wolfgang *531*
  Jeff Cook 530
  Nitro 530
  Predator 530
  Razer *530*
  T-25 Special *530*
  T-60 *529, 530*
  Vandenberg Signature 530
Peavey amps
  5150 47
  Bandit 50, *51*
  Classic 30 *44*
  Classic 50 *46*
  pickups
Pender, Mike (Searchers) 315
Perkins, Carl 355, *397, 403*, 453, 485
Perry, Joe (Aerosmith) 439, 440
Petillo, Phil 20, 507, 572
Petrucci, John (Dream Theater) *491*, 495

pickups
  acoustic *19*, 106–107
  height 91–92
  replacement 94–98

Petty, Tom 559, *561*
Peverett, Dave (Savoy Brown) 574, *575*
Phair, Liz *350*
Phantom Guitarworks 577
Phillips, Freddie 480
piezo pickups 41, *108*
Pigini, Oliviero 333
Pignose *51*
Pink Floyd 128, 160
Pioli, Wandre 510, 578
Play In A Day 479
Plummer, Roy 314, 480
Polytone 50
Ponty, Jean-Luc 259
Porter, Dean 459
potentiometers *94*
Powell, Andy (Wishbone Ash) 410
Powell, Baden *255*
power chords 149–151, 228–230
Prefix (acoustic pickups) *19*
Premier 46, **531**
  Scroll *531*
  wireless guitar 531
Presley, Elvis 14, *15*, *221, 470*
Pritchard, Eric 538
PRS 332, **532-549**
  Artist Limited *538, 544*
  Artist I *541, 535*
  Artist II *544, 538*
  Artist III 30, *31, 543, 547*
  Artist IV *543, 547*
  CE models 539
  CE-22 Maple Top *541, 539*
  CE-24 *548*
  Classic Electric *534*
  Custom *530, 534, 536*
  Custom-22 *539, 543*
  Custom 22 Soapbar *545*
  Custom-24 *549*
  Dragon I *537, 543*
  Dragon II *537, 544*
  Dragon III *540, 544*
  Dragon 2000 544, *549*
  EG models 539
  EG-3 *536*
  EG-4 *536*
  EG-II *536*
  finishes *31*
  Golden Eagle *544*
  Hollowbody II 36, *37*
  Limited Edition 535, 538
  McCarty Archtop *546, 548*
  McCarty Archtop II *546*
  McCarty Archtop Artist *547*
  McCarty Hollowbody *545, 548*
  McCarty Hollowbody II *547*
  McCarty Model *540, 541, 545*
  McCarty Soapbar *545, 548*
  McCarty Standard *540, 545*
  Metal *533, 537*

Private Stock 545, 547
PRS wrapover bridge *30*
PRS locking tuners *67*
Rosewood Limited *544, 547*
rotary pickup selector 536
Santana (custom original) *542*
Santana (production model) *543*, 545-546
Santana II *545, 548*
Signature *533*, 538
Singlecut *549*
Special 537
Standard *533, 536*
Standard-24 *549*
Studio Maple Top *534, 536*
Swamp Ash Special *544, 547*
"sweet switch" 536
and Ted McCarty 544
vibrato 536
10th Anniversary *541, 545*
Puplett, Bill 89

Quagliardi, Orlando 582
quarter sawn 21
Queen 144
Queensrÿche 226
Quelle 507

Rabin, Trevor 302
Race & Olmsted 348
Race, Lymon 348
Radio & Television Equipment Co (Radio-Tel) 347, 351, 552
Rager, Mose 205
Raitt, Bonnie 179, 513
Ramîrez II *11*, 13
Ramone, Johnny (The Ramones) 517, 518
Randall, Don 347, 351, 365, 369
Raney, Jimmy *389*, 404
Recording King 391
Reed, Jerry *205*,
Reed, Jimmy 501, 503
Reed, Lou (Velvet Underground) 377, 507, 574
Reinhardt, Django 23, 205
Reid, Michael 540
Reid, Vernon (Living Colour) 472
Renaissance 561
Renbourn, John *126*
Rendell, Stan 426
Rhoads, Randy (Ozzy Osbourne) 231, 496, 497
Rhodes, Orville "Red" 530
rhythm(s)
  African 260, 262
  blues 180–183, 201–203
  country 214–215
  jazz 287
  Latin 254
  metal 228–229

rock-pop 142–155
Ricco, John (Warrior Soul) 343
Rice, Tim 19
Richards, Keith (Rolling Stones) *129*, 137, 149, *303*, 319, *380, 404*, 513, 522, 587
Rick Turner **561**
  and Alembic 561
  Model T *561*
Rickenbacker **550-560**
  Astro kit *558*
  bass guitars 558
  Carl Wilson 559
  Combo-400 553
  Combo-450 *551*
  Combo-600 552
  Combo-800 *550*, 552
  Combo-850 *551*, 553
  double-neck guitars *558*, 560
  "horseshoe" pickup 550
  John Kay 381JK *553*, 559
  John Lennon 355/12JL 12-string *555*, 559
  "light show" 331
  model 558
  Model B 551
  Model 1000 *550*
  and National 550
  Pete Townshend 1998PT *556*, 559
  pickups *38*
  "Rickenbacher" 551
  Roger McGuinn 370/12RM 12-string *557*, 559
  and Rose-Morris 555, 558
  Spanish (Electro) 551
  stereo 555
  Susanna Hoffs 559
  through-neck 553
  Tom Petty 660/12TP 12-string 559, *561*
  V series reissues 560
  12-string guitar 553, 555-557, 558
  325 model 553, *555*, 557
  325V59 *560*
  325/1966 *555*
  330 model *552*, 553
  336/12 Convertible *558*
  360 model *32, 33*, 552, 553, *557*
  360SF *559*
  360/12 12-string *36, 554*, 558
  360/12 Tuxedo 12-string *560*
  360/12/1993 12-string *556*
  362/12 double-neck *560*
  375F model *553*
  381 model 552
  381 V69 36, *37, 553*
  460 model *32, 33*, *551*
  481 model 558, *559*
  650 series 560
  4080/12 double-neck *560*
Rickenbacker, Adolph 550

Rico, Bernardo Chavez (Bernie) 309, 310
riffs 156–159, 210–213,
Rio Grande (pickups) *94*
Rios, Carlos (Gino Vannelli) 584
Ripley, Steve 508, 527
Ritenour, Lee 487
Rivera *43, 47*
Robbs, The *510*, 511
Roberts, Howard 342
Roberts, Ken 551
Robertson, Robbie (The Band) 579
Robillard, Duke (Fabulous Thunderbirds, Roomful Of Blues) *334*
Robin 525, **561**
  Machete Custom *561*
  Ranger 561
  and Tokai 561, 571
Robinson, Richie (Black Crowes) 587
Rocco Company 54
Rodriguez, Manuel *13*
Roger **562**
  "German carve" 562
  54 model *562*
Roland **562**
  G-707 synthesizer *562*
  GR-1 synthesizer *562*
  JC-120 Jazz Chorus 50
  Space Echo 55, 57
Rolling Stones 141, 147
Rolph (pickups) 94
Romero, Pepe 13
Ro-Pat-In 550
Rosenberg, Jim 343
Rosenblum, Harry 484, 485
Rosetti 332
  Solid-7 332
Ross Compressor 54
Rossdale, Gavin (Bush) 565
Rossmeisl, Roger 368, 369, 552, 553, 555, 562
Rossmeisl, Wenzel 562
Roth, Arlen 208, 216
Roth, Uli Jon 226
Rowe Industries 445, 468
Roy, Charlie 460
Rundgren, Todd 416, *575*, 576
Rush, Otis *179*, 192–*193*, 340
Russell, David *273*
Rutherford, Mike (Genesis) 566

St. John, Mark (Kiss) 496
St. Louis Music 302, 323, 333, 582
Sambora, Richie (Bon Jovi) *382*, 509
Samick 341, 482, **562-563**
  DCV9500 *562*
  and Hondo 562
  and Valley Arts 563
Santa Cruz *19*
Santana, Carlos *33*, 47,

141, 253, 256, 431, 533-534, *542, 543*, 545, 549, 583
Satriani, Joe 28, *239, 241*, 242, 489, 491, *493*
Schaller (tuners) 22, *67*
Schecter **563**
  Hellcat-10 *563*
Schenker, Michael 226, 410
Schlacher, Rudy 579
Scholz, Floyd 544
Schon, Neal (Journey) 508
Schultz, Bill 373, 375
Schultz, Wilhelm J.F. 472
Scofield, John 281, 485
Scott, Keith (Bryan Adams) *479*
Scruggs, Randy (Nitty Gritty Dirt Band) 485
S.D. Curlee **563**
  Aspen AE-700 *563*
Sears, Roebuck 324, 472, 502, 564
Sebastian, John (Lovin' Spoonful) 574
Seeburg 504
Segovia, Andrés 10, 268
Selby, Andrew 332
Selmer 362, 387, 425, 467, 478
Selmer Tremolo *56*
Sepultura 226
set-neck guitars 30–31
Setzer, Brian (Strat Cats) *452, 461*
Seymour Duncan (pickups) *38*, 94–*95*, 97, 103
Shadows, The *314*, 317, *352*
Sharp 5, The 469
Shergold 476, **563**
  Custom Masquerader *563*
Sherman Clay 458
Shinei Siren/Hurricane *56*
shipping guitars 115
shuffle (rhythm) 182–183
Silvertone 324, 326, 328, 472, 502, 564
  G01301L *324*
  and Sears 564
  1437 model *564*
  1457 "amp-in-case" *564*
Simmons, Gene (Kiss) 508
Simon & Garfunkel 324
Simon, Paul 259
Sisme 442
Skaggs, Ricky 17
Sky (pickups) 103
Slash (Guns N'Roses) 343, 439, 440, 572
Slayer 226
Slipknot 226
slot-head acoustics 68
Smallman, Greg *11*, 13
Smeck, Roy 472, 474
Smith, Barbara 534
Smith, Dan 373, 376
Smith, John 443
Smith, Johnny *20, 462*, 463

Smith, Paul Reed 532, 536, 537, 538, 540, 546, 549
Smith, Randall 46-47
Smith, Steuart 205
Smith, Ted 513
Smiths, The 162, 164
Smith, Victor 524, 568
Smith, Walt 512
Sola Sound 55
Soldano 47
soldering techniques 104–105
solid state amps 50–51
soloing (see lead guitar)
Sorkin 531
SoundWood 517
speakers 47–49
speaker cabinets 48-49
Spector **564**
  NS-6A *564*
Spector, Stuart 508, 564
Sperzel (tuners) *64, 67*
Spiegel 391, 501
Spin Doctors 154
Squier 374, **564-565**
  Stagemaster 565
  Standard Stratocaster 44, *565*
  Venus 565
Squier, Victor Caroll 565
SSD 564
Standel **566**
  Custom Deluxe *566*
Standel (amps) 50
Stanley, Paul (Kiss) 485, 487, 494
Staples, Pops (Staple Singers) 529
Star 468, 483
Starfield **566**
  Altair SJ Custom *566*
  and Ibanez 566
Stathopoulo, Anastasios 334
Stathopoulo, Epaminondas (Epi) 334 335
Stathopoulo, Frixo 335, 336
Stathopoulo, Orphie 335
Status Quo 144
Stradivari, Antonio 10
Strait, George *212*
Straits, Dire 168, *173*
Steele, Tommy 478
Steinberger 40, **566-567**
  bass guitar 566
  composite material 566
  and Cort 322
  GL *566*
  GM4T 566
  headless design 566
  and Spector 566, 568
Steinberger, Ned 506, 564, 566
Stepanek, Frank (Black Uhuru) 496
Stern, Mike 281, *586*
Stern, Stephen 23
Stevens, Steve (Billy Idol) 384, 470, 581
Stewart, Dave (Eurythmics) 313
Stills, Stephen (Crosby Stills & Nash) 450, 461
Strad-O-Lin 531

Stratosphere **567**
Twin double-neck *567*
Strawberry Alarm Clock 517
string gauges 66–67
string height 78
string types 17, 62, 66, 69
Strings & Things 432
Stromberg 20, *21*
Stromberg (Kay electric) 502
Stromberg-Voisinet 501
Sumlin, Hubert 179
strumming patterns 128–129
Summerfield Bros 484
Summerfield, Maurice 484
Summers, Andy (Police) 152, 164, 470, *506*, 507
Sunn (amps) 49
Sunshine, Herb 324, 333, 335
Super Furry Animals 144
Supersound 314
superstrat 330, 376
Supro 46, 52, 502, 524, **568-569**
Belmont *568*
bridge pickup 569
Dual Tone *568*, 569
fiberglass guitars 569
and Kay 569
Sahara *569*
Sustainer 384
Sutton, Bryan 17
Sweet, Matthew *338*
switches (types and replacement) 100–103
SWR *53*
Synsonics 460

Tama Seisakusho 483
Takamine *18*
Tavares, Freddie 351, 353
Taylor guitars 18, *19*
Taylor, James 14
Taylor, Martin *585*
Taylor, Mick (John Mayall, Rolling Stones) 384
Tedesco, Tommy *372*
Teisco (Del Rey) 322, 505, 569
Del Rey May Queen *569*
SD-4L *569*
and Silvertone 564
Telestar catalog *501*
Terada 461
Teuffel **570**
Birdfish *570*
Teuffel, Ulrich 570
Thayil, Kim (Soundgarden) *465*, 468
THD (amps) 47
Thielemans, Toots (George Shearing) *551*
Thin Lizzy 157
Thomas 582
Thomas, Harvey 475
Thompson, Hank 395

Thompson, Richard *15*
through-neck guitars 32–33
Todd, Chip 529
Tokai 482, 561, **570-571**
copies 571
Humming Bird *570*
Talbo *571*
Toler, Dan (Gregg Allman) 343
Tom Anderson Guitarworks **571**
"drop top" 571
Grand Am Lam T *571*
Hollow Drop Top *571*
Tommy James & The Shondels 511
Tonk Bros 579
tone woods 10, 15, *16*, 20–22, 27, *29*,
tools 112–*113*
Torn, David *506*, 507
Torres, Antonio de *10-11*, 13
Toure, Ali Farke 259
Townshend, Pete (Who) 32, 49, 418, 556, 558, 559, 563
Trace Acoustic *53*
Trainwreck (amps) 47
Travers, Pat *330*
Travis Bean **572**
aluminum necks 572
TB1000 *572*
Travis, Merle 205, 216, 311, 395
Travis picking 216–217
T.Rex 144, 145
tremolo effect 56
tremolo tailpiece (see vibrato tailpiece)
Triggs, Jim 323
Triumphator 507
Tropical Music 330
Trout, Walter, 179
Trower, Robin 56
truss rod 16, 70–71
tubes *44*
Tufnel, Nigel (Spinal Tap) 522
tuners (machine heads) 64, 65 67
turnarounds 185–186
Turnbull, John (Ian Dury) 313
Turner, Rick 300, 516, 561
Turner, Steve (Mudhoney) *356*, 381
tweed 44–46
two-handed tapping 246–248
Tyler, James 500

U2 *150*
Uni-Vox Uni-Vibe 56, *57*
United Guitars 329
US Music Corp 466

Vaccaro **572**
Stingray *572*
Vaccaro, Henry 507, 509, 572
Vai, Steve 49, 103, 234, *241*, 459, 489-490, 491, *492, 498*
Valco 300, 323, 504, 524, 525, 568

Valentine, Hilton (Animals) 558
Valley Arts 563, **572**
Custom Pro *572*
valves (see tubes)
Van Eps, George 335, 458
Van Halen *227*
Van Halen, Edward (Van Halen) 29, 47, *231*, 239, 246, 320, *321*, 445, 507, *508, 519*, 522, 531, 566
Vandenberg, Adrian (Whitesnake) 530
Vaughan, Jimmie (Fabulous Thunderbirds) *382*, 561
Vaughan, Stevie Ray 12, *28*, 45, 55, 186, *326*, 377
V.C. Squier 564
Vega **573**
E-300 Duo-Tron *573*
Westerner *573*
1200 Stereo *573*
Veillette Shark Baritone *574*
Veillette-Citron **574**
Shark Baritone *574*
Veillette, Joe 574
Veleno **574-576**
"ankh" custom *575*, 576
Original *573*
Traveller 576
Veleno, John 574
Veneman, Kope 500
Ventures, The 141, 371, *516*, 518
VHT *46*, 47
vibrato effect 45, 56
vibrato tailpiece 28, *29*, *35*, *79*
Victoria (amps) 47
Vigier **576**
Arpege V6-V *576*
Nautilus memory guitar 576
Surfreter fretless guitar 576
10/90 carbon fibre necks 576
Vigier, Patrice 576
Vivi Tone 390
Voisinet 501
Von Dutch 517
Vox 384, **576-577**
Apache *576*
and Eko 577
Guitar Organ *577*
and Korg 577
Mando-Guitar 577
Mark models 577
Mk VI *576*
Phantom models 576-577
Phantom Special *577*
Phantom XII Stereo *577*
and Welson 582
Winchester *581*
Vox amps
AC15 *47*, 48
AC30 *42*, *45*, 47, 52, 58
Conqueror *51*
Super Beatle *49*
Vox Wah *56*, 58

Wagner, Dick (Alice Cooper, Lou Reed) 309
Walker, T-Bone 25
Walker, Tom 519
Walsh, Joe (James Gang, Eagles) 403, 507
Walter Hoyer (brand) 482
Wandre 510, **578**
Modele Karak *578*
Rock Oval *578*
Warmoth 515, 586
Warwick 386
Washburn **579-581**
Ace Frehley 579, 580
Bantam headless guitars 579
and Beckmen 579
Chicago 579
Dime-3 *581*
Dime Culprit CP2003 *581*
Force *579*, 580
and Fretted Industries 579
George Washburn EC-36 318, *579*
and Grover Jackson 581
KC-70 model *580*
and Lyon & Healy 579
Nuno Bettencourt 580, 581
Nuno Bettencourt N-8 double-neck *580*
Paul Stanley PS-500 *580*
Paul Stanley PS-2000 *580*
Stage *578, 579*
Stephens Extended Cutaway (EC) 579, 580
Steve Stevens 581
and Tonk Bros 579
Tour series 579, 580
US production 581
Wing series 579, 581
Waters, Muddy 179, *184*, 361, 377, 464
Watkins **581**
Circuit-4 *581*
Copicat 57
Rapier-33 *581*
Watkins, Charlie 581
Watkins, Sid 581
Watson, Doc 14
Watson, Harry 550
Wayne 320
Webster, Jimmie 414, 445, *445*, 450, 451, 454, *454*, 456
Weedon, Bert 462, 463, *477, 478, 479*, 480
Weidner, Heinrich 507
Weill, Henry 384
Weindling, Sol 505
Weir, Bob (Grateful Dead) 485, *487*
Weiss, Sid 569
Welch, Bruce (Shadows) 462
Weller, Paul (Jam, Style Council) 556
Welson 582
Jazz Vedette *582*
WEM 581
West, Leslie 582

Westheimer, Jack 332, 569
Westone 302, 333, **582**
and Electra 582
Paduak II *582*
Wexler, David 443
Wheeler, Tim (Ash) *410*
White, Clarence 205, 208
White, Forrest 353, 365, 519
Whitford, Brad (Aerosmith) *532*
Whitney, Charlie (Family) *418*
Whittam, Gordon 443
Who, The 141, *32*,
Wilaford, Russell (Gene Vincent) 347
Wilfer, Fred 385
Wilkinson 332
Wilkinson vibrato *80*
Wilkinson, Trev 307, 332
Williams, John *11*, 12
Williams, Lewis 389, 390
Wilson 581
Wilson, Carl (Beach Boys) 560
Wings 157
Winter, Johnny *32*, 179, *422*, 482
wiring modifications 101–103
Wishbone Ash 152
WMI 515, 569
Wood, Ron (Faces, Rolling Stones) *345*, 522, 587
Wood, Roy (Move, ELO, Wizzard) 481, 500
wrapover bridge *30*, *79*, *85*
Wright, Denny (Lonnie Donegan) *478*
Wurlitzer 511, **582**
Cougar 2512 *582*
Wylde, Zakk (Ozzy Osbourne) 234, 342, 433, 439

X bracing *12*, *14*, 16, 22

Yardbirds, The 141, 179
Yamaha **583-586**
AES-500 *586*
AES-800 *586*
AEX-1500 *585*
"flying samurai" *583*
Mike Stern Pacifica 511MS *584*
Pacifica *585*, 586
RGX *584*, *585*
SA-15 *583*
SA-1100 *584*
SBG-2000 *584*
SC-400 *584*
SG early models 583
SG-5A *583*
SG-60T *583*
SG-2000 *33*, *583*, 584
SGV reissues 586
Taiwan production 584
US production 584
Yamashita, Kazuhito *276*
Yandell, Paul 333
Yanovsky, Zal (Lovin' Spoonful) 464

Yes *392*
Yorke, Thom (Radiohead) *378*
Young, Angus (AC/DC) *415*, 418
Young, Malcolm (AC/DC) 461
Young, Neil (Buffalo Springfield, Crosby Stills Nash & Young) 45, *400*, 450
Young, Rusty (Poco) 512, *513*

Z, Joey (Life Of Agony) *499*
Zacuto, Randy 515
Zappa, Frank 418, 470
Zebrowski, Gary 436
Zelinsky, Dean 330
Zemaitis **587**
Budget 587
"metal-front" *587*
Zemaitis, Tony 587
Zigante, Frédéric *12*
Zoom 58, 59
Zummo, Vinnie (Joe Jackson) 342

THE PUBLISHERS would like to acknowledge all those who helped with the preparation of this book: the musicians, record companies, guitar collectors, magazine editors, teachers, picture agencies, music notators, makers and manufacturers, photographers, guitar stores, journalists, and auction houses. Thanks be to all.